Investing

ALL-IN-ONE

2nd Edition

by Eric Tyson, MBA; Brendan Bradley;
Kiana Danial; Steven R. Gormley; Robert
S. Griswold, CRE; Matt Krantz; Paul
Mladjenovic; and Russell Wild, MBA

for dummies®
A Wiley Brand

Investing All-in-One For Dummies®, 2nd Edition

Published by: **John Wiley & Sons, Inc.**, 111 River Street, Hoboken, NJ 07030-5774, www.wiley.com

Copyright © 2022 by Eric Tyson and John Wiley & Sons, Inc., Hoboken, New Jersey

Published simultaneously in Canada

For general information on our other products and services, please contact our Customer Care Department within the U.S. at 877-762-2974, outside the U.S. at 317-572-3993, or fax 317-572-4002. For technical support, please visit https://hub.wiley.com/community/support/dummies.

Wiley publishes in a variety of print and electronic formats and by print-on-demand. Some material included with standard print versions of this book may not be included in e-books or in print-on-demand. If this book refers to media such as a CD or DVD that is not included in the version you purchased, you may download this material at http://booksupport.wiley.com. For more information about Wiley products, visit www.wiley.com.

Library of Congress Control Number: 2022933655

ISBN 978-1-119-87303-7 (pbk); ISBN 978-1-119-87304-4 (ebk); ISBN 978-1-119-87305-1 (ebk)

SKY10033316_032122

Contents at a Glance

Table of Contents

BOOK 9: INVESTING IN TRENDS 527

Introduction

Successful investing takes diligent work and knowledge, like any other meaningful pursuit. *Investing All-in-One For Dummies* presents basic investing topics — such as building an emergency fund, determining your financial goals, and choosing a broker (if you're not a do-it-yourself investor) — but also introduces some slightly more advanced subjects, like fundamental analysis, that can enhance your investing strategies. In between, you find the basics of investing in stocks, bonds, mutual funds, exchange-traded funds, real estate, and trends like cryptocurrencies.

This book can help you avoid the mistakes others have made and can point you in the right direction as you build your portfolio. Explore the pages of this book and find the topics that most interest you within the world of investing.

In all the years that we've counseled and educated investors, the single difference between success and failure, between gain and loss, has boiled down to two words: applied knowledge. Take this book as your first step in a lifelong learning adventure.

About This Book

To build wealth, you don't need a fancy college or graduate-school degree, and you don't need a rich parent, biological or adopted! What you do need is a desire to read and practice the many simple yet powerful lessons and strategies in this book.

This book is designed to give you a realistic approach to making money. It provides sound, practical investing strategies and insights that have been market-tested and proven from more than 100 years of stock market history. You're not expected to read it from cover to cover. Instead, this book is designed as a reference tool. Feel free to read the chapters in whatever order you choose. You can flip to the sections and chapters that interest you or those that include topics that you need to know more about.

Investing intelligently isn't rocket science. By all means, if you're dealing with a complicated, atypical issue, get quality professional help. Hiring someone is dangerous if you're financially challenged. If you do decide to hire someone, you'll be much better prepared if you educate yourself. Doing so can also help you focus your questions and assess that person's competence.

Foolish Assumptions

No matter your skill or experience level with investing, you can get something out of *Investing All-in-One For Dummies.* We assume that some readers haven't invested in anything other than baseball cards or Pez dispensers and have no clue of where to even start. If that describes you, the first part of the book is custom-made for you and takes extra care to step through all the key points in as much plain English as possible. (When we have no choice but to use investing jargon, we tell you what it means.) But we also assume that more advanced investors may pick this book up, too, looking to discover a few things. The book takes on more advanced topics as you progress through it.

Here are some assumptions we made about you as we crafted this book:

>> You have about seven cents in your checking account and you're working to pay off credit card debt or student loans (or both), but you know you need to start saving for the future.

>> You're debt-free, and you'd like to start a portfolio.

>> You may have some investments, but you're looking to develop a full-scale investment plan.

>> You're tired of feeling overwhelmed by your investing choices and stressed out by the ever-changing economic and investing landscape, and you want to get more comfortable with your investment selections.

>> You want to evaluate your investment advisor's advice.

>> You have a company-sponsored investment plan, like a 401(k), and you're looking to make some decisions or roll it over into a new plan.

If one or more of these descriptions sound familiar, you've come to the right place.

Icons Used in This Book

Throughout this book, icons help guide you through the maze of suggestions, solutions, and cautions. We hope the following images make your journey through investment strategies smoother.

We think the name says it all, but this icon indicates something really, really important — don't you forget it!

Skip it or read it; the choice is yours. You'll fill your head with more stuff that may prove valuable as you expand your investing know-how, but you risk overdosing on stuff that you may not need right away.

This icon denotes strategies that can enable you to build wealth faster and leap over tall obstacles in a single bound. (Okay, maybe just the first one.)

This icon indicates treacherous territory that has made mincemeat out of lesser mortals who have come before you. Skip this point at your own peril.

Beyond the Book

In addition to the material in the print or e-book you're reading right now, this product comes with a free access-anywhere Cheat Sheet that can set you on the path to successful investing. To get this Cheat Sheet, simply go to www.dummies.com and enter "Investing All-in-One For Dummies Cheat Sheet" in the Search box.

Where to Go from Here

If you're a new investor, you may want to consider starting from the beginning. That way, you'll be ready for some of the more advanced topics introduced later in the book. But you don't have to read this book from cover to cover. If you have a specific question or two that you want to focus on today, or if you want to find some additional information tomorrow, that's not a problem. *Investing All-in-One For Dummies* makes it easy to find answers to specific questions. Just turn to the table of contents or index to locate the information you need. You can get in and get out, just like that.

1

Getting Started with Investing

Contents at a Glance

Chapter 1

Exploring Your Investment Choices

In many parts of the world, life's basic necessities — food, clothing, shelter, healthcare, and taxes — consume the entirety of people's meager earnings. Although some Americans do truly struggle for basic necessities, the bigger problem for other Americans is that they consider just about *everything* — eating out, driving new cars, hopping on airplanes for vacation — to be a necessity.

This book is here to help you recognize that investing — that is, putting your money to work for you — is a necessity. If you want to accomplish important personal and financial goals, such as owning a home, starting your own business, helping your kids through college (and spending more time with them when they're young), retiring comfortably, and so on, you must know how to invest well.

It's been said, and too often quoted, that the only certainties in life are death and taxes. You can add one more to these two certainties: being confused by and ignorant about investing. Because investing is a confounding activity, you may be tempted to look with envious eyes at those people in the world who appear to be savvy with money and investing. Keep in mind that everyone starts with the same level of financial knowledge: none! *No one* was born knowing this stuff! The only difference between those who know and those who don't is that those who know have either devoted their time and energy to acquiring useful knowledge about the investment world or have had their parents instill a good base of investing knowledge.

Getting Started with Investing

Before the rest of this chapter discusses the major investing alternatives, this section starts with something that's quite basic yet important. What exactly does "investing" mean? Simply stated, *investing* means you have money put away for future use.

You can choose from tens of thousands of stocks, bonds, mutual funds, exchange-traded funds, and other investments. Unfortunately for the novice, and even for the experts who are honest with you, knowing the name of the investment is just the tip of the iceberg. Underneath each of these investments lurks a veritable mountain of details.

REMEMBER

If you wanted to and had the ability to quit your day job, you could make a full-time endeavor out of analyzing economic trends and financial statements and talking to business employees, customers, suppliers, and so on. However, you shouldn't be scared away from investing just because some people do it on a full-time basis. Making wise investments need not take a lot of your time. If you know where to get high-quality information and you purchase well-managed investments, you can leave the investment management to the best experts. Then you can do the work that you're best at and have more free time for the things you really enjoy doing.

An important part of making wise investments is knowing when you have enough information to do things well on your own versus when you should hire others. For example, foreign stock markets are generally more difficult to research and understand than domestic markets. Thus, when investing overseas, hiring a good money manager, such as through a mutual or exchange-traded fund, makes more sense than going to all the time, trouble, and expense of picking individual international stocks.

This book is here to give you the information you need to make your way through the complex investment world. The rest of this chapter clears a path so you can identify the major investments, understand the strengths and weaknesses of each, and get information on seeking advice.

Building Wealth with Ownership Investments

If you want your money to grow faster than the rate of inflation over the long term and you don't mind a bit of a roller-coaster ride from time to time in your investments' values, ownership investments are for you. *Ownership investments* are those investments where you own an interest in some company or other asset (such as stock or real estate) that has the ability to generate revenue and profits.

Observing how the world's richest have built their wealth is enlightening. Not surprisingly, many of the champions of wealth around the globe gained their fortunes largely through owning a piece (or all) of a successful company that they (or others) built.

In addition to owning their own businesses, many well-to-do people have built their nest eggs by investing in real estate and the stock market. With softening housing prices in many regions in the late 2000s, some folks newer to the real estate world incorrectly believe that real estate is a loser, not a long-term winner. Likewise, the stock market goes through down periods but does well over the long term. (See Chapter 2 in Book 1 for the scoop on investment risks and returns.)

And, of course, some people come into wealth through an inheritance. Even if your parents are among the rare wealthy ones and you expect them to pass on big bucks to you, you need to know how to invest that money intelligently.

REMEMBER

If you understand and are comfortable with the risks and take sensible steps to *diversify* (you don't put all your investment eggs in the same basket), ownership investments are the key to building wealth. For most folks to accomplish typical longer-term financial goals, such as retiring, the money that they save and invest needs to grow at a healthy clip. If you dump all your money in bank accounts that pay little if any interest, you're more likely to fall short of your goals.

Not everyone needs to make their money grow, of course. Suppose that you inherit a significant sum and/or maintain a restrained standard of living and work well into your old age simply because you enjoy doing so. In this situation, you may not need to take the risks involved with a potentially faster-growth investment. You may be more comfortable with *safer* investments, such as paying off your mortgage faster than necessary.

Entering the stock market

Stocks, which are shares of ownership in a company, are an example of an ownership investment. If you want to share in the growth and profits of companies like Skechers (footwear), you can! You simply buy shares of their stock through a brokerage firm. However, even if Skechers makes money in the future, you can't guarantee that the value of its stock will increase.

Some companies today sell their stock directly to investors, allowing you to bypass brokers. You can also invest in stocks via a stock mutual fund (or an exchange-traded fund), where a fund manager decides which individual stocks to include in the fund.

REMEMBER

You don't need an MBA or a PhD to make money in the stock market. If you can practice some simple lessons, such as making regular and systematic investments and investing in proven companies and funds while minimizing your investment expenses and taxes, you should make decent returns in the long term.

However, you shouldn't expect that you can "beat the markets," and you certainly are not likely to beat the best professional money managers at their own full-time game. This book shows you time-proven, non-gimmicky methods to make your money grow in the stock market as well as in other financial markets. Books 3 and 5 explain more about stocks and mutual funds.

Owning real estate

People of varying economic means build wealth by investing in real estate. Owning and managing real estate is like running a small business. You need to satisfy customers (tenants), manage your costs, keep an eye on the competition, and so on. Some methods of real estate investing require more time than others, but many are proven ways to build wealth.

John, who works for a city government, and his wife, Linda, a computer analyst, have built several million dollars in investment real estate *equity* (the difference between the property's market value and debts owed) over the decades. "Our parents owned rental property, and we could see what it could do for you by providing income and building wealth," says John. Investing in real estate also appealed to John and Linda because they didn't know anything about the stock market, so they wanted to stay away from it. The idea of *leverage* — making money with borrowed money — on real estate also appealed to them.

John and Linda bought their first property, a duplex, when their combined income was just $35,000 per year. Every time they moved to a new home, they kept the prior one and converted it to a rental. Now in their 50s, John and Linda own seven pieces of investment real estate and are multimillionaires. "It's like a second retirement, having thousands in monthly income from the real estate," says John.

John readily admits that rental real estate has its hassles. "We haven't enjoyed getting some calls in the middle of the night, but now we have a property manager who can help with this when we're not available. It's also sometimes a pain finding new tenants," he says.

Overall, John and Linda figure that they've been well rewarded for the time they spent and the money they invested. The income from John and Linda's rental properties also allows them to live in a nicer home.

TIP

Ultimately, to make your money grow much faster than inflation and taxes, you must take some risk. Any investment that has real growth potential also has shrinkage potential! You may not want to take the risk or may not have the stomach for it. In that case, don't despair: This book discusses lower-risk investments as well. You can find out about risks and returns in Chapter 2 of Book 1. Book 8 covers investing in real estate in more detail.

WHO WANTS TO INVEST LIKE A MILLIONAIRE?

Having a million dollars isn't nearly as rare as it used to be. In fact, according to the Spectrem Group, a firm that conducts research on wealth, more than 11 million U.S. households now have at least $1 million in wealth (excluding the value of their primary home). More than 1.5 million households have $5 million or more in wealth.

Interestingly, households with wealth of at least $1 million rarely let financial advisors direct their investments. Only one of ten such households allows advisors to call the shots and make the moves, whereas 30 percent don't use any advisors at all. The remaining 60 percent consult an advisor on an as-needed basis and then make their own moves.

As in past surveys, recent wealth surveys show that affluent investors achieved and built on their wealth with ownership investments, such as their own small businesses, real estate, and stocks.

Generating Income from Lending Investments

Besides ownership investments (which are discussed earlier in this chapter), the other major types of investments include those in which you lend your money. Suppose that, like most people, you keep some money in a bank, either locally or online — most likely in a checking account but perhaps also in a savings account or certificate of deposit (CD). No matter what type of bank account you place your money in, you're lending your money to the bank.

TECHNICAL STUFF

How long and under what conditions you lend money to your bank depends on the specific bank and the account that you use. With a CD, you commit to lend your money to the bank for a specific length of time — perhaps six months or even one or more years. In return, the bank probably pays you a higher rate of interest than if you put your money in a bank account offering you immediate access to the money. (You may demand termination of the CD early; however, you'll usually be penalized.)

As Book 4 discusses in more detail, you can also invest your money in bonds, another type of lending investment. When you purchase a bond that's been issued by the government or a company, you agree to lend your money for a predetermined period of time and receive a particular rate of interest. A bond may pay you 4 percent interest over the next ten years, for example.

An investor's return from lending investments is typically limited to the original investment plus interest payments. If you lend your money to Netflix through one of its bonds that matures in, say, ten years, and Netflix triples in size over the next decade, you won't share in its growth. Netflix's stockholders and employees reap the rewards of the company's success, but as a bondholder, you don't; you simply get interest and the face value of the bond back at maturity.

REMEMBER

Many people keep too much of their money in lending investments, thus allowing others to reap the rewards of economic growth. Although lending investments appear safer because you know in advance what return you'll receive, they aren't that safe. The long-term risk of these seemingly safe money investments is that your money will grow too slowly to enable you to accomplish your personal financial goals. In the worst cases, the company or other institution to which you're lending money can go under and stiff you for your loan.

THE DOUBLE WHAMMY OF INFLATION AND TAXES

Bank accounts and bonds that pay a decent return are reassuring to many investors. Earning a small amount of interest sure beats losing some or all of your money in a risky investment.

The problem is that money in a savings account, for example, that pays 1.5 percent isn't actually yielding you 1.5 percent. It's not that the bank is lying; it's just that your investment bucket contains some not-so-obvious holes.

The first hole is taxes. When you earn interest, you must pay taxes on it (unless you invest the money in municipal bonds that are federal and state tax-free or in a retirement account, in which case you generally pay the taxes later when you withdraw the money). If you're a moderate-income earner, you may end up losing about a third of your interest to taxes. Your 1.5 percent return is now down to 1 percent.

But the second hole in your investment bucket can be even bigger than taxes: inflation. Although a few products become cheaper over time (computers, for example), most goods and services increase in price. Inflation in the United States has been running about 2 percent per year over recent years (3 percent over the much longer term). Inflation depresses the purchasing power of your investments' returns. If you subtract the 2 percent "cost" of inflation from the remaining 1 percent after payment of taxes, you've lost 1 percent on your investment.

To recap: For every dollar you invested in the bank a year ago, despite the fact that the bank paid you 1.5 pennies of interest, you're left with only 99 cents in real purchasing power for every dollar you had a year ago. In other words, thanks to the inflation and tax holes in your investment bucket, you can buy less with your money now than you could have a year ago, even though you've invested your money for a year.

Considering Cash Equivalents

Cash equivalents are any investments that you can quickly convert to cash without cost to you. With most bank checking accounts, for example, you can conduct online transactions to pay bills or do the old-fashioned writing of a check or withdraw cash through an ATM machine or from retailers like a grocery store that enable you to get cash back when making a purchase.

Money market mutual funds (more commonly known as money market funds) are another type of cash equivalent. Investors, both large and small, invest hundreds of billions of dollars in money market mutual funds because the best money market funds historically have produced higher yields than bank savings accounts. (Some online banks offer higher yields, but you must be careful to understand ancillary service fees that can wipe away any yield advantage.) The yield advantage of a money market fund over a savings account almost always widens when interest rates increase because banks move to raise savings account rates about as fast as molasses on a cold winter day.

Why shouldn't you take advantage of a higher yield? Many bank savers sacrifice this yield because they think that money market funds are risky — but they're not. Money market mutual funds generally invest in safe things such as short-term bank certificates of deposit, U.S. government–issued Treasury bills, and commercial paper (short-term bonds) that the most creditworthy corporations issue.

Another reason people keep too much money in traditional bank accounts is that the local bank branch office or online bank makes the cash seem more accessible. Money market mutual funds, however, offer many quick ways to get your cash. Most money market mutual funds can be accessed online, just like most bank accounts. You can also write a check (most funds stipulate the check must be for at least $250), or you can call the fund and request that it mail or electronically transfer your money.

TIP

Move extra money that's dozing away in your bank savings account into a higher-yielding money market mutual fund. Even if you have just a few thousand dollars, the extra yield more than pays for the cost of this book. If you're in a high tax bracket, you can also use tax-free money market funds. (See Chapter 4 in Book 2 to find out about money market funds.)

Choosing Where to Invest and Get Advice

Selecting the firm or firms through which to do your investing is a hugely important decision. So is the decision about from whom to get or pay for investing advice. The following sections address both of these topics.

Finding the best fund companies and brokers

Insurance companies, banks, investment brokerage firms, mutual funds — the list of companies that stand ready to help you invest your money is nearly endless. Most people stumble into a relationship with an investment firm. They may choose a company because their employer uses it for company retirement plans or they've read about or been referred to a particular company. Maybe one of your family members or friends recommended or got you started with a particular investment company.

When you invest in certain securities — such as stocks and bonds and exchange-traded funds (ETFs) — and when you want to hold mutual funds from different companies in a single account, you need brokerage services. Brokers execute your trades to buy or sell stocks, bonds, and other securities and enable you to centralize your holdings of mutual funds, ETFs, and other investments. Your broker can also assist you with other services that may interest you.

Deciding which investment company is best for you depends on your needs and wants. In addition to fees, consider how important having a local branch office is to you. If you want to invest in mutual funds, you'll want to choose a firm that offers access to good funds, including money market funds in which you can deposit money awaiting investment or proceeds from a sale.

TIP

For the lowest trading commissions, you generally must place your trades online. But you should be careful. A low brokerage fee of, say, $7 or $10 per trade doesn't really save you money if you trade a lot and rack up significant total commissions. (As you may know, some brokers are offering free online trading for stocks and certain other securities, but of course, they have to make this up elsewhere with fees for other needed services and by paying you little to nothing on your cash balances.) Also, you pay more in taxes when you trade more frequently and realize shorter-term (one year or less) profits.

WARNING

Trading online is an easy way to act impulsively and emotionally when making important investment decisions. If you're prone to such actions, or if you find yourself tracking and trading investments too closely, stay away from this form of trading and use the internet only to check account information and gather factual information. Increasing numbers of brokers offer account information and trading capabilities via apps, which, of course, can also promote addictive investment behaviors.

Finding an acceptable advisor

Be sure to get educated before engaging the services of any financial advisor. How can you possibly evaluate the competence of someone you may hire if you yourself are financially clueless? You've got this book, so read it before you consider hiring someone for financial advice.

By taking the themes and major concepts of this book to heart, you greatly minimize your chances of making significant investment blunders, including hiring an incompetent or unethical advisor. You may be tempted, for example, to retain the services of an advisor who claims that their firm can predict the future economic environment and position your portfolio to take advantage. But you find in reading this book that financial advisors don't have crystal balls and that you should steer clear of folks who purport to be able to jump into and out of investments based upon their forecasts.

WARNING

Finding a competent and objective financial advisor isn't easy. Historically, most financial consultants work on commission, and the promise of that commission can cloud their judgment. Among the minority of fee-based advisors, almost all manage money, which creates other conflicts of interest. The more money you give them to invest and manage, the more money these advisors make. That's why you should seek financial (and tax) advice from advisors who sell their time (on an hourly basis) and don't sell anything else.

Because investment decisions are a critical part of financial planning, take note of the fact that the most common designations of educational training among professional money managers are MBA (master of business administration) and CFA (chartered financial analyst). Financial planners often have the CFP (certified financial planner) credential, and some tax advisors who work on an hourly basis have the PFS (personal financial specialist) credential.

Advisors who provide investment advice and oversee at least $100 million must register with the U.S. Securities and Exchange Commission (SEC); otherwise, they generally register with the state that they make their principal place of business. All advisors must file Form ADV, otherwise known as the Uniform Application for Investment Adviser Registration. This lengthy document asks investment advisors to provide in a uniform format such details as a breakdown of where their income comes from, their education and employment history, the types of securities the advisory firm recommends, and the advisor's fee schedule.

TIP

You can ask the advisor to send you a copy of his Form ADV. You can also find out whether the advisor is registered and whether he has a track record of problems by calling the SEC at 800-732-0330 or by visiting its website at www.adviserinfo. sec.gov. Many states require the registration of financial advisors, so you should also contact the department that oversees advisors in your state. Visit the North American Securities Administrators Association's website (www.nasaa.org), and click the Contact Your Regulator link on the home page.

Chapter **2**

Weighing Risks and Returns

A woman passes up eating a hamburger at a picnic because she heard that she could contract a deadly *E. coli* infection from eating improperly cooked meat. The next week, that same woman hops in the passenger seat of her friend's old-model car that lacks airbags.

Risk is in the eye of the beholder. Many people base their perception of risk, in large part, on their experiences and what they've been exposed to. In doing so, they often fret about relatively small risks while overlooking much larger risks.

Sure, a risk of an *E. coli* infection from eating poorly cooked meat exists, so the woman who was leery of eating the hamburger at the picnic had a legitimate concern. However, that same woman got into her friend's car without an airbag and placed herself at far greater risk of dying in that situation than if she had eaten the hamburger. In the United States, more than 35,000 people typically die in automobile accidents each year.

In the world of investing, most folks worry about certain risks — some of which may make sense and some of which may not — but at the same time, they completely overlook or disregard other, more significant risks. This chapter discusses a range of investments and their risks and expected returns.

Evaluating Risks

Everywhere you turn, risks exist; some are just more apparent than others. Many people misunderstand risks. With increased knowledge, you may be able to reduce or conquer some of your fears and make more sensible decisions about reducing risks. For example, some people who fear flying don't understand that statistically, flying is much safer than driving a car. You're approximately 110 times more likely to die in a motor vehicle than in an airplane. But when a plane goes down, it's big news because dozens and sometimes hundreds of people, who weren't engaging in reckless behavior, perish. Meanwhile, the national media seem to pay less attention to the 100 people, on average, who die on the road every day.

Then there's the issue of control. Flying seems more dangerous to some folks because the pilots are in control of the plane, whereas in your car, you can at least be at the steering wheel. Of course, you can't control what happens around you or mechanical problems with the mode of transportation you're using.

This doesn't mean that you shouldn't drive or fly or that you shouldn't drive to the airport. However, you may consider steps you can take to reduce the significant risks you expose yourself to in a car. For example, you can get a car with more safety features, and you can choose to drive less aggressively and to minimize riding as a passenger with poor drivers.

Although some people like to live life to its fullest and take "fun" risks (how else can you explain mountain climbers, parachutists, and bungee jumpers?), most people seek to minimize risk and maximize enjoyment in their lives. The vast majority of people also understand that they'd be a lot less happy living a life in which they sought to eliminate all risks, and they likely wouldn't be able to do so anyway.

REMEMBER

Likewise, if you attempt to avoid all the risks involved in investing, you likely won't succeed, and you likely won't be happy with your investment results and lifestyle. In the investment world, some people don't go near stocks or any investment that they perceive to be volatile. As a result, such investors often end up with lousy long-term returns and expose themselves to some high risks that they overlooked, such as the risk of having inflation and taxes erode the purchasing power of their money.

You can't live without taking risks. Risk-free activities or ways of living simply don't exist. You can minimize but never eliminate all risks. Some methods of risk reduction aren't palatable because they reduce your quality of life. Risks are also composed of several factors. The sections that follow discuss the various types of investment risks and go over proven methods you can use to sensibly reduce these risks while not missing out on the upside that growth investments offer.

Market-value risk

Although the stock market can help you build wealth, most people recognize that it can also drop substantially — by 10, 20, or 30 percent (or more) in a relatively short period of time. That's an example of market-value risk — that is, the risk that the value of an investment can decline.

Check out these historic stock market drops:

>> **2020:** After hitting a new all-time high in February 2020, the U.S. stock market got clobbered by COVID-19–related concerns and containment measures that impeded people's travel and other activities and ended up leading to a sharp, short-term recession. In a little over one month, from peak to bottom, the Dow Jones Industrial Average plunged 36 percent.

>> **2008:** After a multi-year rebound, stocks peaked in 2007, and then dropped sharply during the "financial crisis" of 2008. From peak to bottom, U.S. and global stocks dropped by 50-plus percent.

>> **2002:** After peaking in 2000, U.S. stocks, as measured by the large-company S&P 500 index, dropped about 50 percent by 2002. Stocks on the Nasdaq, which is heavily weighted toward technology stocks, plunged more than 76 percent from 2000 through 2002!

>> **1998:** In a mere six weeks (from mid-July 1998 to early September 1998), large-company U.S. stocks fell about 20 percent. An index of smaller-company U.S. stocks dropped 33 percent over a slightly longer period of two and a half months.

>> **1987:** The U.S. stock market plunged 36 percent in a matter of weeks. On October 19, 1987, now known as Black Monday, the Dow Jones fell 508 points, the largest percentage drop in one day at that time.

If you think that the U.S. stock market crash that occurred in the fall of 1987 was a big one, take a look at Table 2-1, which lists major declines over the past 100-plus years that were all as bad as or *worse* than the 1987 crash.

Real estate exhibits similar unruly, annoying tendencies. Although real estate (like stocks) has been a terrific long-term investment, various real estate markets get clobbered from time to time.

TABLE 2-1 **Largest U.S. Stock Market Declines***

Period	Size of Fall
1929–1932	89% (ouch!)
2007–2009	55%
1937–1942	52%
1906–1907	49%
1890–1896	47%
1919–1921	47%
1901–1903	46%
1973–1974	45%
1916–1917	40%
2000–2002	39%
2020	36%

As measured by changes in the Dow Jones Industrial Average

U.S. housing prices took a 25 percent tumble from the late 1920s to the mid-1930s. When the oil industry collapsed in the southern United States in the early 1980s, real estate prices took a beating in that area. Later in the 1980s and early 1990s, the northeastern United States became mired in a severe recession, and real estate prices fell by 20-plus percent in many areas. After peaking near 1990, many of the West Coast housing markets, especially those in California, experienced falling prices — dropping 20 percent or more in most areas by the mid-1990s. The Japanese real estate market crash also began around the time of the California market fall. Property prices in Japan collapsed more than 60 percent.

Declining U.S. housing prices in the mid- to late 2000s garnered unprecedented attention. Some folks and pundits acted like it was the worst housing market ever. Foreclosures increased in part because of buyers who financed their home purchases with risky mortgages. Keep in mind that housing market conditions vary by area. For example, some portions of the Pacific Northwest and South actually appreciated during the mid- to late 2000s, while other markets experienced substantial declines.

After reading this section, you may want to keep all your money in the bank — after all, you know you won't lose your money, and you won't have to be a nonstop worrier. Since the FDIC came into existence in 1933, no one has lost 20, 40, 60, or 80 percent of their bank-held savings vehicle within a few years (major losses prior to then did happen, though). But just letting your money sit around would be a mistake.

REMEMBER

If you pass up the stock and real estate markets simply because of the potential market-value risk, you miss out on a historic, time-tested method of building substantial wealth. Instead of seeing declines and market corrections as horrible things, view them as potential opportunities or "sales." Try not to give in to the human emotions that often scare people away from buying something that others seem to be shunning.

Later in this chapter, you find out about the generous returns that stocks and real estate as well as other investments have historically provided. The following sections suggest some simple things you can do to lower your investing risk and help prevent your portfolio from suffering a huge fall.

Diversify for a smoother ride

If you worry about the health of the U.S. economy, the government, and the dollar, you can reduce your investment risk by investing overseas. Most large U.S. companies do business overseas, so when you invest in larger U.S. company stocks, you get some international investment exposure. You can also invest in international company stocks, ideally via mutual funds and exchange-traded funds (see Chapter 1 in Book 5).

Of course, investing overseas can't totally protect you in the event of a global economic catastrophe. If you worry about the risk of such a calamity, you should probably also worry about a huge meteor crashing into Earth. Maybe there's a way to colonize outer space. . . .

TIP

Diversifying your investments can involve more than just your stock portfolio. You can also hold some real estate investments to diversify your investment portfolio. Many real estate markets actually appreciated in the early 2000s while the U.S. stock market was in the doghouse. Conversely, when U.S. real estate entered a multi-year slump in the mid-2000s, stocks performed well during that period. In the late 2000s, stock prices fell sharply while real estate prices in most areas declined, but then stocks came roaring back.

Consider your time horizon

Investors who worry that the stock market may take a dive and take their money down with it need to consider the length of time that they plan to invest. In a one-year period in the stock and bond markets, a wide range of outcomes can occur (as shown in Figure 2-1). History shows that you lose money about once in every three years that you invest in the stock and bond markets. However, stock market investors have made money (sometimes substantial amounts) approximately two-thirds of the time over a one-year period. (Bond investors made money about two-thirds of the time, too, although they made a good deal less on average.)

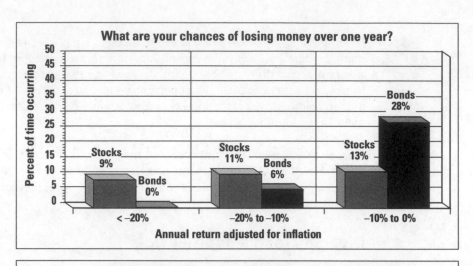

FIGURE 2-1:
What are the odds of making or losing money in the U.S. markets? In a single year, you win far more often (and bigger) with stocks than with bonds.

© John Wiley & Sons, Inc.

Although the stock market is more volatile than the bond market in the short term, stock market investors have earned far better long-term returns than bond investors have. (See the later section "Stock returns" for details.) Why? Because stock investors bear risks that bond investors don't bear, and they can reasonably expect to be compensated for those risks. Remember, however, that bonds generally outperform a boring old bank account.

REMEMBER

History has shown that the risk of a stock or bond market fall becomes less of a concern the longer that you plan to invest. Figure 2-2 shows that as the holding period for owning stocks increases from 1 year to 3 years to 5 years to 10 years and then to 20 years, there's a greater likelihood of seeing stocks increase in value. In fact, over any 20-year time span, the U.S. stock market, as measured by the S&P 500 index of larger company stocks, has *never* lost money, even after you subtract the effects of inflation.

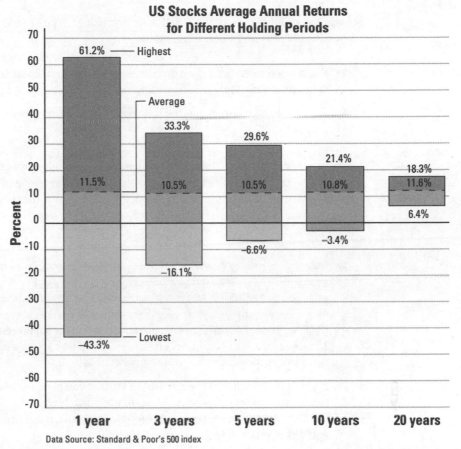

US Stocks Average Annual Returns for Different Holding Periods

61.2% —— Highest

—— Average

33.3%

29.6%

21.4%

18.3%

11.5%   10.5%   10.5%   10.8%   11.6%

6.4%

−6.6%   −3.4%

−16.1%

−43.3% —— Lowest

Percent

1 year   3 years   5 years   10 years   20 years

Data Source: Standard & Poor's 500 index

FIGURE 2-2:
The longer you hold stocks, the more likely you are to make money.

Most stock market investors are concerned about the risk of losing money. Figure 2-2 clearly shows that the key to minimizing the probability that you'll lose money in stocks is to hold them for the longer term. Don't invest in stocks unless you plan to hold them for at least five years — and preferably a decade or longer. Check out Book 3 for more on using stocks as a long-term investment.

Pare down holdings in bloated markets

Perhaps you've heard the expression "buy low, sell high." Although you can't *time the markets* (that is, predict the most profitable time to buy and sell), spotting a greatly overpriced or underpriced market isn't too difficult. There are some simple yet powerful methods you can use to measure whether a particular investment market is of fair value, of good value, or overpriced. You should avoid overpriced investments for two important reasons:

>> If and when these overpriced investments fall, they usually fall farther and faster than more fairly priced investments.

>> You should be able to find other investments that offer higher potential returns.

TIP

Ideally, you want to avoid having a lot of your money in markets that appear overpriced. Practically speaking, avoiding overpriced markets doesn't mean that you should try to sell all your holdings in such markets with the vain hope of buying them back at a much lower price. However, you may benefit from the following strategies:

>> **Invest new money elsewhere.** Focus your investment of new money somewhere other than the overpriced market; put it into investments that offer you better values. As a result, without selling any of your seemingly expensive investments, you make them a smaller portion of your total holdings. If you hold investments outside of tax-sheltered retirement accounts, focusing your money elsewhere also allows you to avoid incurring taxes from selling appreciated investments.

>> **If you have to sell, sell the expensive stuff.** If you need to raise money to live on, such as for retirement or for a major purchase, sell the pricier holdings. As long as the taxes aren't too troublesome, it's better to sell high and lock in your profits.

Individual-investment risk

A downdraft can put an entire investment market on a roller-coaster ride, but healthy markets also have their share of individual losers. For example, from the early 1980s through the late 1990s, the U.S. stock market had one of the greatest appreciating markets in history. You'd never know it, though, if you held one of the great losers of that period.

Consider a company now called Navistar, which has undergone enormous transformations in recent decades. This company used to be called International Harvester and manufactured farm equipment, trucks, and construction and other industrial equipment. Today, Navistar makes mostly trucks.

In 1979, this company's stock traded at more than $400 per share. It then plunged more than 90 percent over the ensuing decade (as shown in Figure 2-3). Even with a rally in recent years, Navistar stock still trades at less than $35 per share (after dipping below $10 per share). If a worker retired from this company in the late 1970s with $200,000 invested in the company's stock, the retiree's investment would be worth about $14,000 today! On the other hand, if the retiree had simply swapped his stock at retirement for a diversified portfolio of stocks, his $200,000 nest egg would've instead grown to more than $5 million!

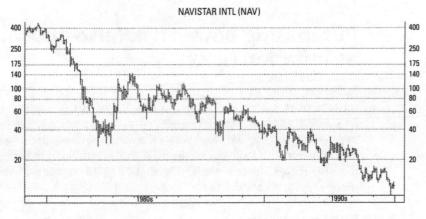

FIGURE 2-3:
Even the bull market of the 1990s wasn't kind to every company.

© John Wiley & Sons, Inc.

Just as individual stock prices can plummet, so can individual real estate property prices. In California during the 1990s, for example, earthquakes rocked the prices of properties built on landfills. These quakes highlighted the dangers of building on poor soil. In the decade prior, real estate values in the communities of Times Beach, Missouri, and Love Canal, New York, plunged because of carcinogenic toxic waste contamination. (Ultimately, many property owners in these areas received compensation for their losses from the federal government as well as from some real estate agencies that didn't disclose these known contaminants.)

TIP

Here are some simple steps you can take to lower the risk of individual investments that can upset your goals:

>> **Do your homework.** When you purchase real estate, a whole host of inspections can save you from buying a money pit. With stocks, you can examine some measures of value and the company's financial condition and business strategy to reduce your chances of buying into an overpriced company or one on the verge of major problems. Book 3 give you information on researching your stock investments.

>> **Diversify.** Investors who seek growth invest in securities such as stocks. Placing significant amounts of your capital in one or a handful of securities is risky, particularly if the stocks are in the same industry or closely related industries. To reduce this risk, purchase stocks in a variety of industries and companies within each industry.

>> **Hire someone to invest for you.** The best funds offer low-cost, professional management and oversight as well as diversification. Stock funds typically own 25 or more securities in a variety of companies in different industries.

Purchasing-power risk (also known as inflation risk)

Increases in the cost of living (that is, inflation) can erode the value of your retirement resources and what you can buy with that money — also known as its *purchasing power*. When Teri retired at the age of 60, she was pleased with her retirement income. She was receiving a $1,600-per-month pension and $2,400 per month from the money that she had invested in long-term bonds. Her monthly expenditures amounted to about $3,000, so she was able to save a little money for an occasional trip.

Fast-forward 15 years. Teri still receives $1,600 per month from her pension, but now she gets only $1,800 per month of investment income, which comes from some certificates of deposit. Teri bailed out of bonds after she lost sleep over the sometimes roller-coaster-like price movements in the bond market. Her monthly expenditures now amount to approximately $4,000, and she uses some of her investment principal (original investment). She's terrified of outliving her money.

Teri has reason to worry. She has 100 percent of her money invested without protection against increases in the cost of living. (Her Social Security does have inflation adjustments.) Although her income felt comfortable at the beginning of her retirement, it doesn't work at age 75, and Teri may easily live another 15 or more years.

The erosion of the purchasing power of your investment dollar can, over longer time periods, be as bad as or worse than the effect of a major market crash. Table 2-2 shows the effective loss in purchasing power of your money at various rates of inflation and over differing time periods.

REMEMBER

Skittish investors often try to keep their money in bonds and money market accounts, thinking they are "playing it safe." The risk in this strategy is that your money won't grow enough over the years for you to accomplish your financial goals. In other words, the lower the return you earn, the more you need to save to reach a particular financial goal.

TABLE 2-2

Inflation's Corrosive Effect on Your Money's Purchasing Power

Inflation Rate	10 Years	15 Years	25 Years	40 Years
2%	–18%	–26%	–39%	–55%
4%	–32%	–44%	–62%	–81%
6%	–44%	–58%	–77%	–90%
8%	–54%	–68%	–85%	–95%
10%	–61%	–76%	–91%	–98%

A 30-year-old wanting to accumulate $500,000 by age 65 would need to save $440 per month if she earns a 5 percent average annual return, but she needs to save only $170 per month if she earns a 9 percent average return per year. Younger investors need to pay the most attention to the risk of generating low returns, but so should younger senior citizens. At the age of 65, seniors need to recognize that a portion of their assets may not be used for a decade or more from the present.

Career risk

REMEMBER

Your ability to earn money is most likely your single biggest asset or at least one of your biggest assets. Most people achieve what they do in the working world through education and hard work. By education, we're not simply talking about what one learns in formal schooling. Education is a lifelong process. You may learn far more about business from your own front-line experiences and those of others than you learn in educational settings.

If you don't continually invest in your education, you risk losing your competitive edge. Your skills and perspectives can become dated and obsolete. Although that doesn't mean you should work 80 hours a week and never do anything fun, it does mean that part of your "work" time should involve upgrading your skills.

The best organizations are those that recognize the need for continual knowledge and invest in their workforce through training and career development. Just remember to consider your own career objectives, which may not be the same as your company's.

Analyzing Returns

When you choose investments, you have the potential to make money in a variety of ways. Each type of investment has its own mix of associated risks that you take when you part with your investment dollar and, likewise, offers a different potential rate of return. The following sections cover the returns you can expect with each of the common investing avenues. But first, you go through the components of calculating the total return on an investment.

The components of total return

To figure out exactly how much money you've made (or lost) on your investment, you need to calculate the *total return.* To come up with this figure, you need to determine how much money you originally invested and then factor in the other components, such as interest, dividends, and appreciation (or depreciation).

If you've ever had money in a bank account that pays *interest,* you know that the bank pays you a small amount of interest when you allow it to keep your money. The bank then turns around and lends your money to some other person or organization at a much higher interest rate. The rate of interest is also known as the *yield.* So if a bank tells you that its savings account pays 2 percent interest, the bank may also say that the account yields 2 percent. Banks usually quote interest rates or yields on an annual basis. The interest that you receive is one component of the return you receive on your investment.

If a bank pays monthly interest, the bank also likely quotes a *compounded effective annual yield.* After the first month's interest is credited to your account, that interest starts earning interest as well. So the bank may say that the account pays 2 percent, which compounds to an effective annual yield of 2.04 percent.

When you lend your money directly to a company — which is what you do when you invest in a bond that a corporation issues — you also receive interest. Bonds, as well as stocks (which are shares of ownership in a company), fluctuate in value after they're issued.

When you invest in a company's stock, you hope that the stock increases (*appreciates*) in value. Of course, a stock can also decline, or *depreciate,* in value. This change in market value is part of your return from a stock or bond investment:

$$\frac{\text{Current investment value} - \text{Original investment}}{\text{Original investment}} = \text{Appreciation or depreciation}$$

For example, if one year ago you invested $10,000 in a stock (you bought 1,000 shares at $10 per share) and the investment is now worth $11,000 (each share is worth $11), your investment's appreciation looks like this:

$$\frac{\$11,000 - \$10,000}{\$10,000} = 10\%$$

Stocks can also pay *dividends,* which are the company's sharing of some of its profits with you as a stockholder. Some companies, particularly those that are small or growing rapidly, choose to reinvest all their profits back into the company. (Of course, some companies don't turn a profit, so they don't have anything to pay out!) You need to factor any dividends into your return as well.

Suppose that in the previous example, in addition to your stock appreciating from $10,000 to $11,000, it paid you a dividend of $100 ($1 per share). Here's how you calculate your total return:

$$\frac{(\text{Current investment value} - \text{Original investment}) + \text{Dividends}}{\text{Original investment}} = \text{Total return}$$

You can apply this formula to the example like so:

$$\frac{(\$11,000 - \$10,000) + \$100}{\$10,000} = 11\%$$

After-tax returns

Although you may be happy that your stock has given you an 11 percent return on your invested dollars, note that unless you held your investment in a tax-sheltered retirement account, you owe income taxes on your return. Specifically, the dividends and investment appreciation that you realize upon selling are taxed, although often at relatively low rates. The tax rates on so-called long-term capital gains (for investments held more than one year) and stock dividends are lower than the tax rates on other income.

If you've invested in savings accounts, money market accounts, or bonds, you owe federal income taxes on the interest plus whatever state income taxes your state levies.

Often, people make investing decisions without considering the tax consequences of their moves. This is a big mistake. What good is making money if the federal and state governments take away a substantial portion of it?

If you're in a moderate tax bracket, taxes on your investment probably run in the neighborhood of 30 percent (federal and state). So if your investment returned 6 percent before taxes, you're left with a return of about 4.2 percent after taxes.

Psychological returns

Profits and tax avoidance can powerfully motivate your investment selections. However, as with other life decisions, you need to consider more than the bottom line. Some people want to have fun with their investments. Of course, they don't want to lose money or sacrifice a lot of potential returns. Fortunately, less expensive ways to have fun do exist!

Psychological rewards compel some investors to choose particular investment vehicles such as individual stocks, real estate, or a small business. Why? Because compared with other investments, such as managed mutual and exchange-traded funds, they see these investments as more tangible and, well, more fun.

REMEMBER

Be honest with yourself about why you choose the investments that you do. Allowing your ego to get in the way can be dangerous. Do you want to invest in individual stocks because you really believe that you can do better than the best full-time professional money managers? Chances are high that you won't. Such questions are worth considering as you contemplate which investments you want to make.

Savings and money market account returns

You need to keep your extra cash that awaits investment (or an emergency) in a safe place, preferably one that doesn't get hammered by the sea of changes in the financial markets. By default and for convenience, many people keep their extra cash in a bank savings account. Although the bank offers the U.S. government's backing via the Federal Deposit Insurance Corporation (FDIC), it comes at a price. Most banks pay a relatively low interest rate on their savings accounts. (Chapter 4 in Book 2 discusses banking options.)

Another place to keep your liquid savings is in a money market mutual fund. These are the safest types of mutual funds around and, for all intents and purposes, equal a bank savings account's safety. The best money market funds generally pay higher yields than most bank savings accounts. Unlike a bank, money market mutual funds tell you how much they deduct for the service of managing your money. If you're in a higher tax bracket, tax-free versions of money market funds exist as well. See Chapter 4 in Book 2 for more on money market funds.

TIP

If you don't need immediate access to your money, consider using Treasury bills (T-bills) or bank certificates of deposit (CDs), which are usually issued for terms such as 3, 6, or 12 months. Your money will generally earn more in one of these vehicles than in a bank savings account. (In recent years, the yields on T-bills has been so low that the best FDIC-insured bank savings accounts have higher yields.) Rates vary by institution, so it's essential to shop around. The drawback to T-bills and bank certificates of deposit is that you generally incur a penalty (with CDs) or a transaction fee (with T–bills) if you withdraw your investment before the term expires.

Bond returns

When you buy a bond, you lend your money to the issuer of that bond (borrower), which is generally a government or a corporation, for a specific period of time. When you buy a bond, you expect to earn a higher yield than you can with a money market or savings account. You're taking more risk, after all. Companies can and do go bankrupt, in which case you may lose some or all of your investment.

Generally, you can expect to earn a higher yield when you buy bonds that

>> **Are issued for a longer term:** The bond issuer is tying up your money at a fixed rate for a longer period of time.

>> **Have lower credit quality:** The bond issuer may not be able to repay the principal.

Wharton School of Business professor Jeremy Siegel has tracked the performance of bonds and stocks back to 1802. Although you may say that what happened in the 19th century has little relevance to the financial markets and economy of today, the decades since the Great Depression, which most other return data track, are a relatively small slice of time. Figure 2-4 presents the data, so if you'd like to give more emphasis to the recent numbers, you may.

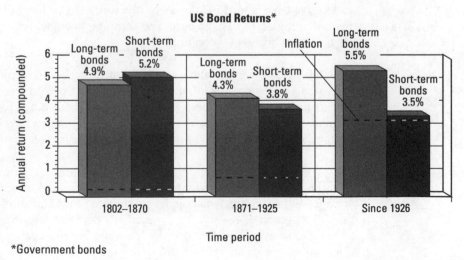

FIGURE 2-4: A historical view of bond performance: Inflation has eroded bond returns more in recent decades.

*Government bonds

© John Wiley & Sons, Inc.

Note that although the rate of inflation has increased since the Great Depression, bond returns haven't increased over the decades. Long-term bonds maintained slightly higher returns in recent years than short-term bonds. The bottom line: Bond investors typically earn about 4 to 5 percent per year.

Stock returns

Investors expect a fair return on their stock investments. If one investment doesn't offer a seemingly high enough potential rate of return, investors can choose to move their money into other investments that they believe will perform better. Instead of buying a diversified basket of stocks and holding, some investors frequently buy and sell, hoping to cash in on the latest hot investment. This tactic seldom works in the long run.

WARNING

Unfortunately, some of these investors use a rearview mirror when they purchase their stocks, chasing after investments that have recently performed strongly on the assumption (and the hope) that those investments will continue to earn good returns. But chasing after the strongest performing investments can be dangerous if you catch the stock at its peak, ready to begin a downward spiral. Chasing high-flying investments can lead you to buy high, with the prospect of having to sell low if the stock runs out of steam. Even though stocks as a whole have proved to be a good long-term investment, picking individual stocks is a risky endeavor. See Book 3 for advice on making sound stock investment decisions.

REMEMBER

A tremendous amount of data exists regarding stock market returns. In fact, in the U.S. markets, data going back more than two centuries document the fact that stocks have been a terrific long-term investment. The long-term returns from stocks that investors have enjoyed, and continue to enjoy, have been remarkably constant from one generation to the next.

Going all the way back to 1802, the U.S. stock market has produced an annual return of 8.3 percent, while inflation has grown at 1.4 percent per year. Thus, after subtracting for inflation, stocks have appreciated about 6.9 percent faster annually than the rate of inflation. The U.S. stock market returns have consistently and substantially beaten the rate of inflation over the years (see Figure 2-5).

Stocks don't exist only in the United States, of course (see Figure 2-6). More than a few U.S. investors seem to forget this fact, as they did during the sizzling performance of the U.S. stock market during the late 1990s and 2010s. As discussed in the earlier section "Diversify for a smoother ride," one advantage of buying and holding overseas stocks is that they don't always move in tandem with U.S. stocks. As a result, overseas stocks help diversify your portfolio.

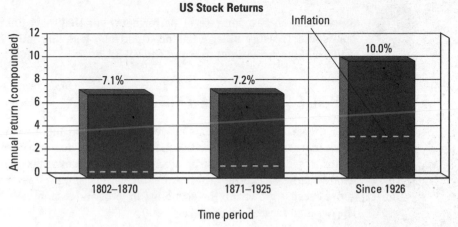

US Stock Returns

Annual return (compounded)

- 1802–1870: 7.1%
- 1871–1925: 7.2%
- Since 1926: 10.0%

Inflation

FIGURE 2-5:
History shows that stocks have been a consistent long-term winner.

© *John Wiley & Sons, Inc.*

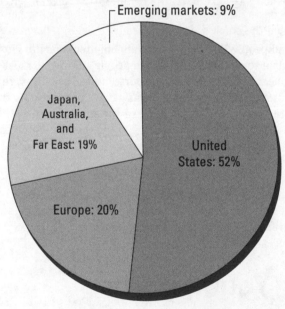

Total Value of Stocks Worldwide

- Emerging markets: 9%
- Japan, Australia, and Far East: 19%
- United States: 52%
- Europe: 20%

FIGURE 2-6:
Plenty of investing opportunities exist outside the United States.

© *John Wiley & Sons, Inc.*

In addition to enabling U.S. investors to diversify, investing overseas has proved to be profitable. The investment banking firm Morgan Stanley tracks the performance of stocks in both economically established countries and so-called emerging economies. As the name suggests, countries with *emerging economies* (for example, Brazil, China, India, Malaysia, Mexico, Russia, and Taiwan) are "behind" economically but show high growth and progress rates.

Stocks are the best long-term performers, but they have more volatility than bonds and Treasury bills. A balanced portfolio gets you most of the long-term returns of stocks without much of the volatility.

Real estate returns

Over the years, real estate has proved to be about as lucrative as investing in the stock market. Whenever the U.S. has a real estate downturn, folks question this historic fact. However, just as stock prices have down periods, so, too, do real estate markets. The fact that real estate offers solid long-term returns makes sense because growth in the economy, in jobs, and in population ultimately fuels the demand for real estate.

Consider what has happened to the U.S. population over the past two centuries. In 1800, a mere 5 million people lived within U.S. borders. In 1900, that figure grew to 76.1 million, and today, it's more than 330 million. All these people need places to live, and as long as jobs exist, the income from jobs largely fuels the demand for housing.

Businesses and people have an understandable tendency to cluster in major cities and suburban towns. Although some people commute, most people and businesses locate near major highways, airports, and so on. Thus, real estate prices in and near major metropolises and suburbs generally appreciate the most. Consider the areas of the world that have some of the most expensive real estate prices: Singapore, Hong Kong, Vancouver, San Francisco, Los Angeles, New York, and Boston. What these areas have in common are lots of businesses and people and limited land.

Contrast these areas with the many rural parts of the United States where the price of real estate is relatively low because of the abundant supply of buildable land and the relatively lower demand for housing.

Compounding Your Returns

During the past century, stocks and investment real estate returned around 9 percent per year, bonds around 5 percent, and savings accounts about 3 percent.

In case you're curious about some alternative investments like gold and currencies, here are those numbers. Gold has just kept investors up with inflation with a tiny bit to spare — returning an average of about 0.5 percent per year after inflation. Currencies like the U.S. dollar have depreciated about 1.5 percent per year adjusting for inflation.

This section illustrates how compounding seemingly modest investment returns can help you accumulate a substantial sum of money to help you accomplish your personal and financial goals.

The value of getting a few extra percent

As discussed earlier in this chapter, investing in the stock market (and real estate) can be risky, which logically raises the question of whether investing in stocks and real estate is worth the anxiety and potential losses. Why bother for a few extra percent per year?

Here's a good answer to that sensible question: Over many years, a few extra percent per year will increase your nest egg dramatically. The more years you have to invest, the greater the difference a few percent makes in your returns (see Table 2-3).

These numbers are simply amazing! Start first with the 25-year column in Table 2-3. For every $1,000 invested over 25 years, you'll have $1,282 at a 1 percent annual return. At a 9 percent return, you'll have $8,623, or nearly seven times as much!

TABLE 2-3

How Compounding Grows Your Investment Dollars

For Every $1,000 Invested at This Return	In 25 Years	In 40 Years
1%	$1,282	$1,489
2%	$1,641	$2,208
3%	$2,094	$3,262
4%	$2,666	$4,801
5%	$3,386	$7,040
6%	$4,292	$10,286
7%	$5,427	$14,974
8%	$6,848	$21,725
9%	$8,623	$31,409

Now look at what happens over 40 years. At a 9 percent investment return, you'll have more than 21 times as much money versus what you'd have with a 1 percent annual investment return.

Here's a practical example to show you what a dramatic difference earning a few extra percent can make in accomplishing your financial goals. Consider a 30-year-old investor who's saving toward financial independence/retirement on a $60,000 annual salary. Suppose that their goal is to retire by age 67 with about $45,000 per year to live on (in today's dollars), which would be about 75 percent of the investor's working salary.

If this person begins saving at age 30, they need to save about $690 per month if you assume that they earn an average return on investments of about 5 percent per year. That's a big chunk to save each year (about $8,300) — amounting to about 14 percent of gross (pretax) salary.

But what if this investor can earn an average return of just a few percent more per year — 8 percent instead of just 5 percent? In that case, the same goal could be accomplished by saving just half as much: $345 per month (or $4,150 per year)!

Considering your goals

How much do you need or want to earn on your investments?

You have to balance your goals with how you feel about risk. Some people can't handle higher-risk investments. Although investing in stocks, real estate, or small business can produce high long-term returns, investing in these vehicles comes with greater risk, especially over the short term.

Others are at a time in their lives when they can't afford to take great risk. If you're still in school, if you've lost your job, or if you're starting a family, your portfolio and nerves may not be able to wait a decade for your riskier investments to recover after a major stumble.

If you work for a living, odds are that you need and want to make your investments grow at a healthy clip. Should your investments grow slowly, you may fall short of your goals of owning a home or retiring or changing careers. All this is to say that you should take the time to contemplate and prioritize your personal and financial goals.

Chapter 3

The Workings of Stock and Bond Markets

To buy and enjoy using a computer or smartphone, you don't need to know the intricacies of how each device is put together and how it works. The same holds true for investing in stocks and bonds. However, spending some time understanding how and why the financial markets function may make you more comfortable with investing and make you a better investor.

This chapter explains the ways that companies raise capital, and you get a brief primer on financial markets and economics so you can understand and be comfortable with investing in the financial markets.

How Companies Raise Money through the Financial Markets

All businesses start small — whether they begin in a garage, a spare bedroom, or a rented office. As companies begin to grow, they often need more money (known as *capital* in the financial world) to expand and afford their growing needs, such as hiring more employees, buying computer systems, and purchasing other equipment.

Many smaller companies rely on banks to lend them money, but growing and successful firms have other options, too, in the financial markets. Companies can choose between two major money-raising options when they go into the financial markets: issuing stocks and issuing bonds.

Deciding whether to issue stocks or bonds

REMEMBER

A world of difference exists between the two major types of securities, both from the perspective of the investor and from that of the issuing company:

» **Bonds are loans that a company must pay back.** Instead of borrowing money from a bank, many companies elect to sell *bonds,* which are IOUs to investors. The primary disadvantage of issuing bonds compared with issuing stock, from a company's perspective, is that the company must repay this money with interest. On the other hand, the business founders/owners don't reduce or relinquish ownership when they borrow money. Companies are also more likely to issue bonds when interest rates are relatively low and/or if the stock market is depressed, meaning that companies can't fetch as much for their stock.

» **Stocks are shares of ownership in a company.** Some companies choose to issue stock to raise money. Unlike bonds, the money that the company raises through a stock offering isn't paid back because it's not a loan. When the investing public buys stock, these outside investors continue to hold and trade it. (Although companies occasionally buy their own stock back, usually because they think it's a good investment, they're under no obligation to do so.)

Issuing stock allows a company's founders and owners to sell some of their relatively illiquid private stock and reap the rewards of their successful company. Many growing companies also favor stock offerings because they don't want the cash drain that comes from paying loans (bonds) back.

Although many company owners like to take their companies public (issuing stock) to cash in on their stake of the company, not all owners want to go public, and not all who do go public are happy that they did. One of the numerous drawbacks of establishing your company as public is the burdensome financial reporting requirements, such as publishing quarterly earnings statements and annual reports. Not only do these documents take lots of time and money to produce, but they can also reveal competitive secrets. Some companies also harm their long-term planning ability because of the pressure and focus on short-term corporate performance that comes with being a public company.

Ultimately, companies seek to raise capital in the lowest-cost way they can, so they elect to sell stocks or bonds based on what the finance folks and investment bankers tell them is the best option. For example, if the stock market is booming and new stock can sell at a premium price, companies opt to sell more stock. Also, some companies prefer to avoid debt because they don't like carrying it.

From your perspective as a potential investor, you can usually make more money in stocks than bonds, but stocks are generally more volatile in the short term (see Chapter 2 in Book 1).

Taking a company public: Understanding IPOs

Suppose that The Capitalist Company (TCC) wants to issue stock for the first time, which is called an *initial public offering* (IPO). If TCC decides to go public, the company's management team works with *investment bankers,* who help companies decide when and at what price to sell stock and then help sell (distribute) the new shares to investors willing to purchase them.

Now suppose that based upon their analysis of the value of TCC, the investment bankers believe that TCC can raise $100 million by issuing stock that represents a particular portion of the company. When a company issues stock, the price per share that the stock is sold for is somewhat arbitrary. The amount that a prospective investor will pay for a particular portion of the company's stock should depend on the company's profits and future growth prospects. Companies that produce higher levels of profits and grow faster can generally command a higher sales price for a given portion of the company.

Consider the following ways that investment bankers can structure the IPO for TCC:

Price of Stock	Number of Shares Issued
$5	20 million shares
$10	10 million shares
$20	5 million shares

In fact, TCC can raise $100 million in an infinite number of ways, thanks to varying stock prices. If the company wants to issue the stock at a higher price, the company sells fewer shares.

REMEMBER

A stock's price per share by itself is meaningless in evaluating whether to buy a stock. Ultimately, the amount that investors will pay for a company's stock should depend greatly on the company's growth and profitability prospects. To determine the price–earnings ratio of a particular company's stock, you take the price per share of the company's stock and divide it by the company's earnings per share.

In the case of TCC, suppose that its stock is currently valued in the marketplace at $30 per share and that it earned $2 per share in the past year, which produces a price–earnings ratio of 15. Here is the formula: $30 per share divided by $2 per share equals a price–earnings ratio of 15.

Understanding Financial Markets and Economics

Tens of thousands of books, millions of articles, and enough PhD dissertations to pack a major landfill explore the topics of how the financial markets and economy will perform in the years ahead. You can spend the rest of your life reading all this stuff, and you still won't get through it. The following sections explain what you need to know about how the factors that influence the financial markets and economy work so you can make informed investing decisions.

Driving stock prices through earnings

The goal of most companies is to make money or earnings (also called *profits*). *Earnings* result from the difference between what a company takes in (*revenue*) and what it spends (*costs*). We say *most* companies because some organizations' primary purpose is not to maximize profits. Nonprofit organizations, such as colleges and universities, are a good example. But even nonprofits can't thrive without a steady money flow.

Companies that trade publicly on the stock exchanges seek to maximize their profit — that's what their shareholders want. Higher profits generally make stock prices rise. Most private companies seek to maximize their profits as well, but they retain much more latitude to pursue other goals.

REMEMBER

Among the major ways that successful companies increase profits are by doing the following:

>> **Developing new and better products and services:** Some companies develop or promote an invention or innovation that better meets customer needs. We have smartphones, 3D printers, electric cars, online investing through low-cost mutual funds, fast casual restaurants that can serve up healthy food at a decent price in just minutes — the list goes on and on.

>> **Opening new markets to their products:** Many successful U.S.-based companies, for example, have been stampeding into foreign countries to sell their products. Although some product adaptation is usually required to sell overseas, selling an already proven and developed product or service to new markets generally increases a company's chances of success.

>> **Expanding into related businesses:** Consider the hugely successful Walt Disney Company, which was started in the 1920s as a small studio that made cartoons. Over the years, it expanded into many new but related businesses, such as theme parks and resorts, movie studios, radio and television programs, toys and children's books, and video games.

>> **Building a brand name:** In blind taste tests, popular sodas and many well-known beers rate comparably to many generic colas and beers that are far cheaper. Yet some consumers fork over more of their hard-earned loot because of the name and packaging. Companies build brand names largely through advertising and other promotions. (*For Dummies* is a brand name, but *For Dummies* books cost about the same as lower-quality and smaller books on similar subjects!)

>> **Managing costs and prices:** Smart companies control costs. Lowering the cost of manufacturing their products or providing their services allows companies to offer their products and services more cheaply. Managing costs may help fatten the bottom line (profit). Sometimes, though, companies try to cut too many corners, and their cost-cutting ways come back to haunt them in the form of dissatisfied customers — or even lawsuits based on a faulty or dangerous product.

>> **Watching the competition:** Successful companies usually don't follow the herd, but they do keep an eye on what the competition is up to. If lots of competitors target one part of the market, some companies target a less-pursued segment that, if they can capture it, may produce higher profits thanks to reduced competition.

Weighing whether markets are efficient

Companies generally seek to maximize profits and maintain a healthy financial condition. Ultimately, the financial markets judge the worth of a company's stock or bond. Trying to predict what happens to the stock and bond markets and to individual securities consumes many a market prognosticator.

In the 1960s, to the chagrin of some market soothsayers, academic scholars developed a theory called the *efficient market hypothesis.* This theory basically maintains the following logic: Lots of investors collect and analyze all sorts of information about companies and their securities. If investors think that a security, such as a stock, is overpriced, they sell it or don't buy it. Conversely, if many investors believe that a security is underpriced, they buy it or hold what they already own. Because of the competition among all these investors, the price that a security trades at generally reflects what many (supposedly informed) people think it's worth.

Therefore, the efficient market theory implies that trading in and out of securities and the overall market in an attempt to be in the right stocks at the right time is a futile endeavor. Buying or selling a security because of "new" news is also fruitless because the stock price adjusts so quickly to this news that investors can't profit by acting on it. As Burton Malkiel so eloquently said in his classic book *A Random Walk Down Wall Street,* this theory, "taken to its logical extreme . . . means that a blindfolded monkey throwing darts at a newspaper's financial pages could select a portfolio that would do just as well as one carefully selected by the experts."

Some money managers have beaten the market averages. In fact, beating the market over a year or three years isn't difficult, but few can beat the market over a decade or more. Efficient market supporters argue that some of those who beat the markets, even over a ten-year period, do so because of luck. Consider that if you flip a coin five times, on some occasions, you get five consecutive heads. This coincidence actually happens, on average, once every 32 times you do five coin-flip sequences because of random luck, not skill. Consistently identifying in advance which coin flipper will get five consecutive heads isn't possible.

Strict believers in the efficient market hypothesis say that it's equally impossible to identify the best money managers in advance. Some money managers, such as those who manage mutual and exchange-traded funds, possess publicly available track records. Inspecting those track records (and understanding the level of risk taken for the achieved returns) and doing other common-sense things, such as investing in funds that have lower expenses, improve your odds of performing a bit better than the market.

REMEMBER

Various investment markets differ in how efficient they are. *Efficiency* means that the current price of an investment accurately reflects its true value. Although the stock market is reasonably efficient, many consider the bond market to be even more efficient. The real estate market is less efficient because properties are unique, and sometimes less competition and access to information exist. If you can locate a seller who really needs to sell, you may be able to buy property at a sizeable discount from what it's really worth. Small business is also less efficient. Entrepreneurs with innovative ideas and approaches can sometimes earn enormous returns.

Moving the market: Interest rates, inflation, and the Federal Reserve

For decades, economists, investment managers, and other (often self-anointed) gurus have attempted to understand the course of interest rates, inflation, and the monetary policies set forth by the Federal Reserve. Millions of investors follow these economic factors. Why? Because interest rates, inflation, and the Federal Reserve's monetary policies seem to move the financial markets and the economy.

Realizing that high interest rates are generally bad

Many businesses borrow money to expand. People, who are affectionately referred to as *consumers*, also borrow money to finance home and auto purchases and education.

Interest rate increases tend to slow the economy. Businesses scale back on expansion plans, and some debt-laden businesses can't afford high interest rates and go under. Most individuals possess limited budgets as well and have to scale back some purchases because of higher interest rates. For example, higher interest rates translate into higher mortgage payments for home buyers.

If high interest rates choke business expansion and consumer spending, economic growth slows or the economy shrinks — and possibly ends up in a recession. The most common definition of a *recession* is two consecutive quarters (six months) of contracting economic activity.

The stock market usually develops a case of the queasies as corporate profits shrink. High interest rates may depress investors' appetites for stocks as the yields increase on certificates of deposit (CDs), Treasury bills, and other bonds.

Higher interest rates actually make some people happy. If you locked in a fixed-rate mortgage on your home or on a business loan, your loan looks much better than if you had a variable-rate mortgage. Some retirees and others who live off the interest income on their investments are happy with interest rate increases as well. Consider back in the early 1980s, for example, when a retiree received $10,000 per year in interest for each $100,000 that he invested in certificates of deposit that paid 10 percent.

Fast-forward to the early 2000s: A retiree purchasing the same CDs saw interest income slashed by about 70 percent because rates on the CDs were just 3 percent. So for every $100,000 invested, only $3,000 in interest income was paid.

If you try to live off the income that your investments produce, a 70 percent drop in that income is likely to cramp your lifestyle. So higher interest rates are better if you're living off your investment income, right? Not necessarily.

Discovering the inflation and interest rate connection

Consider what happened to interest rates in the late 1970s and early 1980s. After the United States successfully emerged from a terrible recession in the mid-1970s, the economy seemed to be on the right track. But within just a few years, the economy was in turmoil again. The annual increase in the cost of living (known as the *rate of inflation*) burst through 10 percent on its way to 14 percent. Interest rates, which are what bondholders receive when they lend their money to corporations and governments, followed inflation skyward.

REMEMBER

Inflation and interest rates usually move in tandem. The primary driver of interest rates is the rate of inflation. Interest rates were much higher in the 1980s because the United States had double-digit inflation. If the cost of living increases at the rate of 10 percent per year, why would you, as an investor, lend your money (which is what you do when you purchase a bond or CD) at 5 percent? Interest rates were so much higher in the early 1980s because you would never do such a thing.

In recent years, interest rates have been very low. Therefore, the rate of interest that investors can earn lending their money has dropped accordingly. Although low interest rates reduce the interest income that comes in, the corresponding low rate of inflation doesn't devour the purchasing power of your principal balance. That's why lower interest rates aren't necessarily worse, and higher interest rates aren't necessarily better as you try to live off your investment income.

REMEMBER

So what are investors to do when they're living off the income they receive from their investments but don't receive enough because of low interest rates? Some retirees have woken up to the risk of keeping all or too much of their money in short-term CD and bond investments. A simple but psychologically difficult solution is to use some of your principal to supplement your interest and dividend income. Using your principal to supplement your income is what effectively happens anyway when inflation is higher — the purchasing power of your principal erodes more quickly. You may also find that you haven't saved enough money to meet your desired standard of living — that's why you should consider your retirement goals well before retiring.

UNDERSTANDING SUPER-LOW (AND NEGATIVE) INTEREST RATES

In the aftermath of the 2008 financial crisis, interest rates were at rock-bottom levels. And then they went even lower in some countries. In fact, in a number of European countries and Japan, interest rates have at times been negative — as in less than zero.

What the heck is a negative interest rate, and what exactly does that mean? Normally, when an investor buys a government bond for, say, $10,000, the bond issuer pays the investor interest — such as 3 percent per year. So, the investor would get paid $300 of interest annually. Suppose the governments of Germany, Japan, or Switzerland issue $10,000 bonds that have a negative interest rate — at, say, minus 1 percent per year. In that case, those bond buyers would pay the government bond issuer $100 per year for the privilege of holding their bond!

Why on earth would an investor ever willingly agree to buy a bond with a negative inter-est rate? It can happen in a country where there's low demand for borrowing money (due typically to a weak economy) and where investors are more concerned with pre-serving their money than they are with risking and attempting to grow their money. By literally paying a person or company to borrow money, negative rates may encourage people to take risks/actions that can help the economy.

One final perceived benefit of negative rates is that they are viewed as leading to deval-uing that country's currency. Foreign investors generally aren't going to be lining up to buy bonds with a negative interest rate! In theory, a devaluing currency helps a country with lowering the effective price of its exports.

Exploring the role of the Federal Reserve

When the chairman of the Federal Reserve Board speaks (currently, it's Jerome Powell; before him, it was Janet Yellen; and before her, it was Ben Bernanke), an extraordinary number of people listen. Most financial market watchers and the media want to know what the Federal Reserve has decided to do about *monetary policy.* The Federal Reserve is the central bank of the United States. The Federal Reserve Board comprises the 12 presidents from the respective Federal Reserve district banks and the 7 Federal Reserve governors, including the chairman who conducts the Federal Open Market Committee meetings behind closed doors eight times a year.

REMEMBER

What exactly is the Fed (as it's known), and what does it do? The *Federal Reserve* sets monetary policy. In other words, the Fed influences interest-rate levels and the amount of money or currency in circulation, known as the *money supply,* in an attempt to maintain a stable rate of inflation and growth in the U.S. economy.

Buying money is no different from buying lettuce, computers, or sneakers. All these products and goods cost you dollars when you buy them. The cost of money is the interest rate that you must pay to borrow it. And the cost or interest rate of money is determined by many factors that ultimately influence the supply of and demand for money.

The Fed, from time to time and in different ways, attempts to influence the supply of and demand for money and the cost of money. To this end, the Fed raises or lowers short-term interest rates, primarily by buying and selling U.S. Treasury bills on the open market. Through this trading activity, known as *open market operations,* the Fed is able to target the Federal funds rate — the rate at which banks borrow from one another overnight.

The senior officials at the Fed readily admit that the economy is quite complex and affected by many things, so it's difficult to predict where the economy is heading. If forecasting and influencing markets are such difficult undertakings, why does the Fed exist? Well, the Fed officials believe that they can have a positive influence in creating a healthy overall economic environment — one in which inflation is low and growth proceeds at a modest pace.

Over the years, the Fed has come under attack for various reasons. Various pundits accused former Fed Chairman Alan Greenspan of causing speculative bubbles, such as the boom in technology stock prices in the late 1990s or in housing in the early 2000s. Some economists have argued that the Federal Reserve has, at times, goosed the economy by loosening up on the money supply, which leads to a growth spurt in the economy and a booming stock market, just in time to make El Presidente look good prior to an election. Conveniently, the consequences of inflation take longer to show up — they're not evident until after the election. In recent years, others have questioned the Fed's ability to largely do what it wants without accountability.

Many factors influence the course of stock prices. Never, ever make a trade or investment based on what someone at the Federal Reserve says or what someone in the media or some market pundit reads into the Fed chairman's comments. You need to make your investment plans based on your needs and goals, not what the Fed does or doesn't do.

What the heck is "quantitative easing"?

During and after the 2008 financial crisis, many pundits interviewed on financial cable television programs and website pontificators used the Federal Reserve as a punching bag, blaming the Fed for various economic problems, including the 2008 financial crisis. Despite the rebounding economy and stock market, some of the critics got even more vocal in blasting the Fed's quantitative easing program begun late in 2010. (It's worth noting that this program was again used in 2020 during the COVID-19 pandemic and government-mandated economic shutdowns.)

More often than not, these critics, who typically and erroneously claim to have predicted the 2008 crisis, have an agenda to appear smarter than everyone else, including the Fed. Some of these pseudo-experts are precious metals hucksters and thus like to claim that the Fed is going to cause hyperinflation that will impoverish you unless you buy gold, silver, and the like.

In one popular video from 2010 that has millions of views on YouTube, the author claims the following using goofy cartoonish characters:

>> The Fed is printing a ton of money to implement quantitative easing (QE).

>> QE is being done to stop deflation (falling prices), but the Fed is too dumb to realize that consumer prices are rising, not falling.

>> The Fed has been wrong about everything the past 20 years.

>> Then Fed Chairman Ben Bernanke is unqualified for his job because he has no business experience, has no policy experience, and has never held an elected office. He is a fool who's been wrong about everything during his tenure in office and has already blown up the American economy and is now working on blowing up the world economy.

>> The government is stupidly buying Treasuries from Goldman Sachs at grossly inflated prices (rather than buying Treasuries from the Treasury department). Goldman Sachs is ripping off the American people.

Although it's stunning in and of itself that this video has been watched millions of times, even more amazing and disturbing is how many mainstream media and other websites and outlets have promoted and recommended the video, making little if any effort to fact-check and reality-check its contents. Here we set the record straight and advance your understanding of what quantitative easing really is and why the Fed is doing it. We go through the video's main assertions point by point:

>> The Fed is not printing a ton of money (expanding the money supply) to implement QE. Retail money market assets and bank deposits could increase, for example, if individuals decided to hold more cash. Demand for these highly liquid assets can come from folks around the world, so increased demand for the U.S. dollar during times of stress can lead to the growth of M2 (the leading measure of the money supply). Changes in money supply are complicated.

>> The Fed is well aware that there's inflation right now but has been concerned that the rate has been quite low by historical standards and that there were signs of accelerating deflation during the severe recession.

>> If the Fed had been wrong about everything the past 20-plus years, our economy would be in shambles and our stock market wouldn't have appreciated more than 1,400 percent since 1990. Before the COVID-19 pandemic and government-mandated shutdowns, the U.S. unemployment rate was at a 50-year low at 3.5 percent.

>> Bernanke was well qualified for his job.

>> The Fed is buying Treasuries from banks at competitive prices and is doing so to encourage more bank lending. Saying that the Fed is directing this buying solely to Goldman Sachs is absurd. The Fed conducts such Treasury open market operations through an approved list of 18 primary dealers, and Goldman is one of the 18 dealers operating in a highly competitive environment. Goldman bashing has been going on for a long time.

Interestingly, there hasn't been much questioning of the background and agenda of the person behind this fact-challenged YouTube video, who in some articles is referred to as a "30-year-old real estate manager." He has no discernible background or expertise in the subject matter discussed in the video, which helps explain why nearly every statement in the video is wrong.

In various speeches and selected interviews, former Fed Chairman Bernanke has explained QE. Here's one fairly plain English explanation that Bernanke gave during the height of the credit crisis (*Note:* "Central bank" means the Federal Reserve):

> Quantitative easing can be thought of as an expansion of the central bank's balance sheet with no intentional change in its composition. That is, the central bank undertakes more open market operations with the objective of expanding bank reserve balances, which the banking system should then use to make new loans and buy additional securities. However, when credit spreads are very wide, as they are at present, and the credit markets are quite dysfunctional, it becomes less likely that new loans and additional securities purchases will result from increasing bank reserve balances.

> In contrast, credit easing focuses on the mix of loans and securities that the central bank holds as assets on its balance sheet as a means to reduce credit spreads and improve the functioning of private credit markets. The ultimate objective is improvement in the credit conditions faced by households and businesses. In this respect, the Federal Reserve has focused on improving functioning in the credit markets that are severely disrupted and that are key sources of funding for financial firms, nonfinancial firms, and households.

2

Investing in Your 20s and 30s

Contents at a Glance

Chapter 1

Using Investments to Accomplish Your Goals

S aving and investing money can make you feel good and in control. Ultimately, most folks are investing money to accomplish particular goals. Saving and investing for a car purchase, expenses for higher education, a home purchase, new furniture, or a vacation are typical short-term goals. You can also invest toward longer-term goals, such as your financial independence or retirement decades in the future.

This chapter discusses how you can use investments to accomplish common shorter- and longer-term goals.

Setting and Prioritizing Your Shorter-Term Goals

Unless you earn really big bucks or expect to have a large family inheritance to tap, your personal and financial desires will probably outstrip your resources. Thus, you must prioritize your goals.

One of the biggest mistakes people make is rushing into a financial decision without considering what's really important to them. Because many people get caught up in the responsibilities of their daily lives, they don't take time for reflection often because they feel that they lack the time. Take that time, because people who identify their goals and then work toward them, which often requires changing some habits, are far more likely to accomplish something significant.

This section discusses common "shorter-term" financial goals — such as establishing an emergency reserve, making major purchases, owning a home, and starting a small business — and how to work toward them. Accomplishing such goals almost always requires saving money.

Accumulating a rainy-day fund

The future is unpredictable. Take the uncertainty simply surrounding your job: You could lose your job, or you may want to leave it.

Consider what happened in 2020 with the COVID-19 pandemic and the unexpected and lengthy government-mandated shutdowns in some parts of the country, which led to large layoffs in particular industries like restaurants, retail, and travel-related businesses. While the 2020 recession was unusual in many respects, recessions aren't unusual, and even when the overall economy is growing, some employers let employees go. Suppose an elderly relative, for example, needs some assistance for a period of time? You don't need to be negative or a pessimist, but problems happen, and sometimes financial downsides can come with them.

Because you don't know what the future holds, preparing for the unexpected is financially wise. Enter the emergency or rainy-day fund.

REMEMBER

The size of your emergency fund depends on your personal situation. Begin by considering how much you spend in a typical month. Here are some benchmarks for how many months' worth of living expenses you should have:

>> **Three months' living expenses:** When you're starting out, this minimalist approach makes sense if your only current source of emergency funds is a high-interest credit card. Longer-term, you could make do with three months' living expenses if you have other accounts, such as a 401(k), or family members and close friends whom you can tap for a short-term loan.

>> **Six months' living expenses:** If you don't have other places to turn for a loan, or if you have some instability in your employment situation or source of income, you need more of a cushion.

>> **Twelve months' living expenses:** Consider this large stash if your income fluctuates greatly or if your occupation involves a high risk of job loss, finding another job could take you a long time, or you don't have other places to turn for a loan.

Saving for large purchases

Most people want things — such as furniture, a vacation, or a car — that they don't have cash on hand to pay for. Save for your larger consumer purchases to avoid paying for them over time with high-interest consumer credit. Don't take out credit card or auto loans — otherwise known as *consumer credit* — to make large purchases.

And don't be duped by a seemingly low interest rate on, for example, a car loan. You could get the car at a lower price if you don't opt for such a loan.

TIP

Paying for high-interest consumer debt can undermine your ability to save toward your goals and your ability to make major purchases in the future. Don't deny yourself gratification if it's something you really need and want and can afford given your overall financial situation; just figure out how to delay it. When contemplating the purchase of a consumer item on credit, add up the total interest you'd end up paying on your debt, and call it the price of instant gratification.

Investing for a small business or home

In your early years of saving and investing, deciding whether to save money to buy a home or to put money into a retirement account (for the tax benefits and to work toward the goal of future financial independence) presents a dilemma. In the long run, owning your own home is usually a wise financial move. On the other hand, saving sooner for retirement makes achieving your goals easier and reduces your income tax bill.

Presuming that both goals are important to you, you can save toward both goals: buying a home and retiring. If you're eager to own a home, you can throw all your savings toward achieving that goal and temporarily put your retirement savings on hold.

TIP

You can make penalty-free withdrawals of up to $10,000 from Individual Retirement Accounts (IRAs) toward a first-time home purchase. You may also be able to have the best of both worlds if you work for an employer that allows borrowing against retirement account balances. You can save money in the retirement account and then borrow against it for the down payment on a home. Consider this option with great care, though, because retirement account loans generally must be repaid within a few years or when you quit or lose your job (ask your employer for the details).

When saving money for starting or buying a business, most people encounter the same dilemma they face when deciding to save to buy a house: If you fund your retirement accounts to the exclusion of earmarking money for your small-business dreams, your entrepreneurial aspirations may never become reality. Consider hedging your bets by saving money in your tax-sheltered retirement accounts as well as toward your business venture. An investment in your own small business can produce great rewards, so you may feel comfortable focusing your savings on your own business.

Saving for kids' higher educational costs

Do you have little ones or plan to have them in your future? You probably know that rearing a child (or two or more) costs really big bucks. But the biggest potential expense awaits when they reach young adulthood and consider heading off to college, so your instincts may be to try to save money to accomplish and afford that goal.

WARNING

The college financial-aid system effectively penalizes you for saving money outside tax-sheltered retirement accounts and penalizes you even more if the money is invested in the child's name. Wanting to provide for your children's future is perfectly natural, but doing so before you've saved adequately toward your own goals can be a major financial mistake.

This concept may sound selfish, but the reality is that you need to take care of *your* future first. Take advantage of saving through your tax-sheltered retirement accounts before you set aside money in custodial savings accounts for your kids.

TIP

There are numerous higher education options besides costly four-year colleges and universities. The traditional college path isn't right for everyone. Consider alternatives to traditional college (and whether they are right for your child). While college is a traditional path that many high-school seniors follow, there are increasing numbers of attractive, low-cost, and faster alternatives to consider. For example:

- » **Last-mile boot camps:** Last-mile programs teach students technical skills and clear the pathways to jobs in growing industries like technology, biotech, fintech, and healthcare.

- » **College minimum viable products (MVPs):** These programs combine the technical skill training and placement of traditional last-mile programs with significant cognitive and noncognitive skill development that students get from a good college.

- » **Apprenticeships:** Emerging apprenticeships provide pathways for jobs in the manufacturing, healthcare, pharmacy, information technology (IT), insurance, financial services, and software development industries.

- » **Staffing firms:** These companies hire workers and staff them out to clients. For example, Revature, an IT staffing company, hires experienced software developers. Also, Avenica places students from many colleges and offers last-mile training across many industries.

- » **Vocational and trade schools:** Also known as career and technical education (CTE), these schools provide gateways to a wide range of jobs in the automotive industry, culinary arts, emergency services, healthcare, and more.

Investing short-term money

So where should you invest money earmarked for a shorter-term goal? A money market account or short-term bond fund is a good place to store your short-term savings. See Chapter 4 in Book 2 as well as Book 4 for more information on these options. The best bank or credit union accounts may be worth considering as well.

Investing in Retirement Accounts

During your younger adult years, you may not be thinking much about retirement because it seems to be well off in the distance. But if you'd like to scale back on your work schedule someday, partly or completely, you're best off saving toward that goal as soon as you start drawing a regular paycheck.

TIP

Maybe the problem with thinking about this goal stems in part with the term *retirement.* Perhaps thinking about it in terms of saving and investing to achieve *financial independence* is better.

This section explains the benefits and possible concerns of investing through so-called retirement accounts. It also lays out the retirement account options you may access.

Understanding retirement account perks

Where possible, try to save and invest in accounts that offer you a tax advantage, which is precisely what retirement accounts offer you. These accounts — known by such enlightening acronyms and names as 401(k), 403(b), SEP-IRA, and so on — offer tax breaks to people of all economic means. Consider the following advantages to investing in retirement accounts:

>> **Contributions often provide up-front tax breaks.** By investing through a retirement account, you not only plan wisely for your future but also get an immediate financial reward: lower taxes, which mean more money available for saving and investing. Retirement account contributions generally aren't taxed at either the federal or state income tax level until withdrawal (but they're still subject to Social Security and Medicare taxes when earned). If you're paying, say, 30 percent between federal and state taxes (see Chapter 2 in Book 2 to determine your tax bracket), a $4,000 contribution to a retirement account lowers your income taxes by $1,200.

Modest income earners also may get an additional government tax credit known as the Retirement Savings Contributions Credit. A maximum credit of 50 percent applies to the first $2,000 contributed for single taxpayers with an adjusted gross income (AGI) of no more than $19,750 and married couples filing jointly with an AGI of $39,500 or less. Singles with an AGI of between $19,750 and $21,500 and married couples with an AGI between $39,500 and $43,000 are eligible for a 20 percent tax credit. Single taxpayers with an AGI of more than $21,500 but no more than $33,000, as well as married couples with an AGI between $43,000 and $66,000, can get a 10 percent tax credit.

>> **Your employer may match some of your contributions.** This cash is free money from your employer, and it's use it or lose it, so don't miss out!

>> **Investment returns compound tax-free.** After you put money into a retirement account, you get to defer taxes on all the accumulating gains and profits (including interest and dividends) until you withdraw the money down the road. Thus, more money is working for you over a longer period of time. (One exception: Roth IRAs offer no up-front tax breaks but permit tax-free withdrawal of investment earnings in retirement.)

Grappling with retirement account concerns

There are legitimate concerns about putting money into a retirement account. First and foremost is the fact that once you place such money inside a retirement account, you can't generally access it before age 59½ without paying current income taxes and a penalty — 10 percent of the withdrawn amount in federal tax, plus whatever your state charges.

WARNING

This poses some potential problems. First, money placed inside retirement accounts is typically not available for other uses, such as buying a car or starting a small business. Second, if an emergency arises and you need to tap the money, you'll get hit with paying current income taxes and penalties on amounts withdrawn.

TIP

You can use the following ways to avoid the early-withdrawal penalties that the tax authorities normally apply:

>> You can make penalty-free withdrawals of up to $10,000 from IRAs for a first-time home purchase or higher educational expenses for you, your spouse, or your children (and even grandchildren).

>> Some company retirement plans allow you to borrow against your balance. You're essentially loaning money to yourself, with the interest payments going back into your account.

>> If you have major medical expenses (exceeding 10 percent of your income) or a disability, you may be exempt from the penalties under certain conditions. (You will still owe ordinary income tax on withdrawals.)

>> You may withdraw money before age 59½ if you do so in equal, annual installments based on your life expectancy. You generally must make such distributions for at least five years or until age 59½, whichever is later.

REMEMBER

If you lose your job and withdraw retirement account money simply because you need it to live on, the penalties do apply. If you're not working, however, and you're earning so little income that you need to access your retirement account, you would likely be in a relatively low tax bracket. The lower income taxes you pay (compared with the taxes you would have paid on that money had you not sheltered it in a retirement account in the first place) should make up for most, if not all, of the penalty.

But what about simply wanting to save money for nearer-term goals and to be able to tap that money? If you're saving and investing money for a down payment on a home or to start a business, for example, you'll probably need to save that money outside a retirement account to avoid those early-withdrawal penalties.

If you're like most young adults and have limited financial resources, you need to prioritize your goals. Before funding retirement accounts and gaining those tax breaks, be sure to contemplate and prioritize your other goals (see the earlier section "Setting and Prioritizing Your Shorter-Term Goals").

Taking advantage of retirement accounts

REMEMBER

To take advantage of retirement savings plans and the tax savings that accompany them, you must spend less than you earn. Only then can you afford to contribute to these retirement savings plans, unless you already happen to have a stash of cash from previous savings or an inheritance.

WARNING

The common mistake that many younger adults make is neglecting to take advantage of retirement accounts because of their enthusiasm for spending or investing in nonretirement accounts. Not investing in tax-sheltered retirement accounts can cost you hundreds, perhaps thousands, of dollars per year in lost tax savings. Add that loss up over the many years that you work and save, and not taking advantage of these tax reduction accounts can easily cost you tens of thousands to hundreds of thousands of dollars in the long term.

The sooner you start to save, the less painful it is each year to save enough to reach your goals, because your contributions have more years to compound. Each decade you delay saving approximately doubles the percentage of your earnings that you need to save to meet your goals. If saving 5 percent per year in your early 20s gets you to your retirement goal, waiting until your 30s to start may mean socking away approximately 10 percent to reach that same goal; waiting until your 40s means saving 20 percent. Start saving and investing now!

Surveying retirement account choices

If you earn employment income (or receive alimony), you have options for putting money away in a retirement account that compounds without taxation until you withdraw the money. In most cases, your contributions to these retirement accounts are tax-deductible. This section reviews your options.

Company-based retirement plans

Larger for-profit companies generally offer their employees a *401(k)* plan, which typically allows saving up to $19,500 per year (for tax year 2021). Many nonprofit organizations offer their employees similar plans, known as *403(b)* plans. Contributions to both traditional 401(k) and 403(b) plans are deductible on both your federal and state taxes in the year that you make them. Employees of nonprofit organizations can generally contribute up to 20 percent or $19,500 of their salaries, whichever is less.

There's a benefit in addition to the up-front and ongoing tax benefits of these retirement savings plans: Some employers match your contributions. (If you're an employee in a small business, you can establish your own SEP-IRA.) Of course, the challenge for many people is to reduce their spending enough to be able to sock away these kinds of contributions.

Some employers are offering a Roth 401(k) account, which, like a Roth IRA (discussed in the next section), offers employees the ability to contribute on an after-tax basis. Withdrawals from such accounts generally aren't taxed in retirement.

If you're self-employed, you can establish your own retirement savings plans for yourself and any employees you have. *Simplified Employee Pension-Individual Retirement Accounts* (SEP-IRAs) allow you to put away up to 20 percent of your self-employment income up to an annual maximum of $58,000 (for tax year 2021).

Individual Retirement Accounts

If you work for a company that doesn't offer a retirement savings plan, or if you've exhausted contributions to your company's plan, consider an *Individual Retirement Account* (IRA). Anyone who earns employment income or receives alimony may contribute up to $6,000 annually to an IRA (or the amount of your employment income or alimony income, if it's less than $6,000 in a year). A nonworking spouse may contribute up to $6,000 annually to a spousal IRA.

Your contributions to an IRA may or may not be tax-deductible. For tax year 2021, if you're single and your adjusted gross income is $66,000 or less for the year, you can deduct your full IRA contribution. If you're married and you file your taxes jointly, you're entitled to a full IRA deduction if your AGI is $105,000 per year or less.

TIP

If you can't deduct your contribution to a standard IRA account, consider making a contribution to a nondeductible IRA account called the *Roth IRA.* Single taxpayers with an AGI less than $125,000 and joint filers with an AGI less than $198,000 can contribute up to $6,000 per year to a Roth IRA. Although the contribution isn't deductible, earnings inside the account are shielded from taxes, and unlike withdrawals from a standard IRA, qualified withdrawals from a Roth IRA account are free from income tax.

TIP

Should you be earning a high enough income that you can't fund a Roth IRA, there's an indirect "backdoor" way to fund a Roth IRA. First, you contribute to a regular IRA as a nondeductible contribution. Then, you can convert your regular IRA contribution into a Roth IRA. Please note that this so-called backdoor method generally only makes sense if you don't have other money already invested in a regular IRA because in that case, you can't simply withdraw your most recent contribution and not owe any tax.

Annuities: Maxing out your retirement savings

What if you have so much cash sitting around that after maxing out your contributions to retirement accounts, including your IRA, you still want to sock more away into a tax-advantaged account? Enter the annuity. *Annuities* are contracts that insurance companies back. If you, the investor (annuity holder), should die during the so-called accumulation phase (that is, before receiving payments from the annuity), your designated beneficiary is guaranteed reimbursement of the amount of your original investment.

Annuities, like IRAs, allow your capital to grow and compound tax-deferred. You defer taxes until you withdraw the money. Unlike an IRA, which has an annual contribution limit of a few thousand dollars, an annuity allows you to deposit as much as you want in any year — even millions of dollars, if you've got millions! As with a Roth IRA, however, you get no up-front tax deduction for your contributions.

WARNING

Because annuity contributions aren't tax-deductible, and because annuities carry higher annual operating fees to pay for the small amount of insurance that comes with them, don't consider contributing to one until you've fully exhausted your other retirement account investing options. Because of their higher annual expenses, annuities generally make sense only if you won't need the money for 15 or more years.

Selecting retirement account investments

When you establish a retirement account, you may not realize that the retirement account is simply a shell or shield that keeps the federal, state, and local governments from taxing your investment earnings each year. You choose what investments you want to hold inside your retirement account shell.

You may invest the money in your IRA or self-employed plan retirement account (SEP-IRAs and so on) in stocks, bonds, mutual funds, and some other common investments, including bank accounts. Mutual funds (offered in most employer-based plans) and exchange-traded funds (ETFs) are ideal choices because they offer diversification and professional management. See Book 5 for more on mutual funds and ETFs.

Chapter **2**

Minimizing Your Taxes When Investing

You should pay attention to tax issues when making investing decisions. Actually, let's rephrase that. Like plenty of other folks, you could ignore or pay half attention to taxes on your investments. Unless you enjoy paying more taxes, however, you should understand and consider tax ramifications when choosing and managing your investments over the years.

Tax considerations alone shouldn't dictate how and where you invest your money. You should also weigh investment choices, your desire and the necessity to take risk, personal likes and dislikes, and the number of years you plan to hold the investment.

This chapter explains how the different components of investment returns are taxed. You find proven, up-to-date strategies to minimize your investment taxes and maximize your returns. Finally, you discover tax considerations when selling an investment.

Understanding Investment Taxes

When you invest outside tax-sheltered retirement accounts, the profits and distributions on your money are subject to taxation. (Distributions are taxed in the year that they are paid out; appreciation is taxed only when you sell an investment at a profit.) So the nonretirement-account investments that make sense for you depend (at least partly) on your tax situation.

Tracking taxation of investment distributions

The distributions that various investments pay out and the profits that you may make are often taxable, but in some cases, they're not. It's important to remember that it's not what you make before taxes (pretax) on an investment that matters, but what you get to keep after taxes.

REMEMBER

Interest you receive from bank accounts and corporate bonds is generally taxable. U.S. Treasury bonds, which are issued by the U.S. federal government, pay interest that's state-tax-free but federally taxable.

Municipal bonds, which state and local governments issue, pay interest that's federally tax-free and also state-tax-free to residents in the state where the bond is issued. (For more on bonds, see Book 4.)

Taxation on your *capital gains,* which is the profit (sales price minus purchase price) on an investment, is computed under a unique federal taxation system. Investments held and then sold in less than one year at a profit generate what is called short-term capital gains, which are taxed at your normal marginal income tax rate (which is explained in the next section).

Profits from investments that you hold longer than 12 months and then sell at a profit generate what are called long-term capital gains. Under current tax law, these long-term gains are taxed at a maximum 20 percent rate, except for most folks in the two lowest income tax brackets: 10 percent and 12 percent. For these folks, the long-term capital gains tax rate is 0 percent (as in nothing). Dividends paid out on stock are also taxed at the same favorable long-term capital gains tax rates under current tax law.

The Patient Protection and Affordable Care Act (informally referred to as Obamacare) increased the tax rate on the net investment income for taxpayers with adjusted gross income above $200,000 (single return) or $250,000 (joint return). Net investment income includes interest, dividends, and capital gains. The increased tax rate is 3.8 percent.

Determining your tax bracket

Many folks don't realize it, but the federal government (like most state governments) charges you different income tax rates for different parts of your annual income. You effectively pay less tax on the first dollars of your earnings and more tax on the last dollars of your earnings. As a wage earner receiving a paycheck, you won't actually notice or see your actual tax rate rising during the year. The reason: Taxes are withheld at a constant rate from your paycheck based upon estimating your expected income for the year and your total expected tax bill for the year.

Your *federal marginal income tax rate* is the rate of tax that you pay on your last, or so-called highest, dollars of income (see Table 2-1). Your taxable income is the income that is left after taking allowed deductions on your return.

TABLE 2-1

2021 Federal Income Tax Rates for Single and Married Households Filing Jointly

Federal Income Tax Rate	Singles Taxable Income	Married Filing Jointly Taxable Income
10%	Up to $9,950	Up to $19,900
12%	$9,951 to $40,525	$19,901 to $81,050
22%	$40,526 to $86,375	$81,051 to $172,750
24%	$86,376 to $164,925	$172,751 to $329,850
32%	$164,926 to $209,425	$329,851 to $418,850
35%	$209,426 to $523,600	$418,851 to $628,300
37%	Over $523,600	Over $628,300

Your actual marginal tax rate includes state income taxes if your state levies an income tax. Though this chapter focuses on the federal income tax system and strategies to reduce those taxes, most of what is discussed also helps you reduce your state income taxes, which the vast majority of states levy. Each state income tax system is unique, so covering them all here is impossible. All but eight states — Alaska, Florida, Nevada, South Dakota, Tennessee, Texas, Washington, and Wyoming — impose a state income tax. (New Hampshire has only a state income tax on dividend and interest investment income.)

There's value in knowing your marginal tax rate. This knowledge allows you to determine the following (among other things):

>> How much you could reduce your taxes if you contribute more money to retirement accounts

>> How much you would pay in additional taxes on extra income you could earn from working more

>> How much you could reduce your taxable income if you use investments that produce tax-free income (which may make sense only if you're in a higher tax bracket — more on this later in the chapter)

Devising tax-reduction strategies

Use these strategies to reduce the taxes you pay on investments that are exposed to taxation:

>> **Make use of retirement accounts and health savings accounts.** Most contributions to retirement accounts gain you an immediate tax break, and once they're inside the account, investment returns are sheltered from taxation, generally until withdrawal. Think of these as tax reduction accounts that can help you work toward achieving financial independence. See Chapter 1 in Book 2 for details on using retirement accounts when investing.

Similar to retirement accounts are health savings accounts (HSAs). With HSAs, you get a tax break on your contributions up-front; investment earnings compound without taxation over time; and there's no tax on withdrawal so long as the money is used to pay for health-related expenses (which enjoy a fairly broad list as delineated by the IRS).

>> **Consider tax-free money market funds and tax-free bond funds.** Tax-free investments yield less than comparable investments that produce taxable earnings, but because of the tax differences, the earnings from tax-free investments can end up being greater than what taxable investments leave you with. If you're in a high-enough tax bracket, you may find that you come out ahead with tax-free investments.

For a proper comparison, subtract what you'll pay in federal and state income taxes from the taxable investment income to see which investment nets you more.

>> **Invest in tax-friendly stock funds.** Mutual funds and exchange-traded funds that tend to trade less tend to produce lower capital gains distributions. For funds held outside tax-sheltered retirement accounts, this reduced trading effectively increases an investor's total rate of return. *Index funds* invest in a relatively static portfolio of securities, such as stocks and bonds. They don't attempt to beat the market; rather, they invest in the securities to mirror or match the performance of an underlying index. Although index funds can't beat the market, the typical actively managed fund usually doesn't, either, and index funds have several advantages over actively managed funds.

>> **Invest in small business and real estate.** The growth in value of business and real estate assets isn't taxed until you sell the asset. Even then, with investment real estate (see Book 8), you often can roll over the gain into another property as long as you comply with tax laws. Increases in value in small businesses can qualify for the more favorable longer-term capital gains tax rate and potentially for other tax breaks. However, the current income that small business and real estate assets produce is taxed as ordinary income.

REMEMBER

Short-term capital gains (investments held one year or less) are taxed at your ordinary income tax rate. This fact is another reason why you shouldn't trade your investments quickly (within 12 months).

Reducing Your Taxes When Selling Investments

Do your homework so you can purchase and hold on to good investments for many years and even decades. That said, each year, folks sell and trade lots of investments. Too many investors sell for the wrong reasons (while other investors hold on to investments for far too long and should sell them).

This section highlights important tax and other issues to consider when you contemplate selling your investments, but it starts with the nontax, bigger-picture considerations.

Weighing nontax issues

Although the focus of this chapter is on tax issues to consider when making, managing, and selling your investments, it's time to raise bigger-picture considerations:

WARNING

>> **Meeting your goals and preferences:** If your life has changed (or if you've inherited investments) since the last time you took a good look at your investment portfolio, you may discover that your current holdings no longer make sense for you. To avoid wasting time and money on investments that aren't good for you, be sure to review your investments at least annually.

Don't make quick decisions about selling. Instead, take your time, and be sure you understand tax and other ramifications before you sell.

>> **Keeping the right portfolio mix:** A good reason to sell an investment is to allow yourself to better diversify your portfolio. Suppose that through your job, you've accumulated such a sizeable chunk of stock in your employer that this stock now overwhelms the rest of your investments. Or perhaps you've simply kept your extra money in a bank account or inherited stock from a dear relative. Conservative investors often keep too much of their money in bank accounts, Treasury bills, and the like. If your situation is like these, it's time for you to diversify. Sell some of the holdings of which you have too much, and invest the proceeds in some of the solid investments that I recommend in this book.

WARNING

If you think your employer's stock is going to be a superior investment, holding a big chunk is your gamble. At minimum, review Book 3 to see how to evaluate a particular stock. Be sure to consider the consequences if you're wrong about your employer's stock. Develop an overall investment strategy that fits your personal financial situation (see Chapter 3 in Book 2). A problem with holding a large amount of stock in your employer is that both the stock and your job are compromised if the company has a significant downturn.

>> **Deciding which investments are keepers:** Often, people are tempted to sell an investment for the wrong reasons. One natural tendency is to want to sell investments that have declined in value. Some people fear a further fall, and they don't want to be affiliated with a loser, especially when money is involved. Instead, step back, take some deep breaths, and examine the merits of the investment you're considering selling. If an investment is otherwise still sound per the guidelines discussed in this book, why bail out when prices are down and a sale is going on? What are you going to do with the money? If anything, you should be contemplating buying more of such an investment.

REMEMBER

Also, don't make a decision to sell based on your current emotional response, especially to recent news events. If bad news has hit recently, it's already old news. Don't base your investment holdings on such transitory events. Use the criteria in this book for finding good investments to evaluate the worthiness of your current holdings. If an investment is fundamentally sound, don't sell it.

Tuning in to tax considerations

When you sell investments that you hold outside a tax-sheltered retirement account, such as in an IRA or a 401(k), taxes should be one factor in your decision. If the investments are inside retirement accounts, taxes aren't an issue because the accounts are sheltered from taxation until you withdraw funds from them.

Just because you pay tax on a profit from selling a nonretirement-account investment doesn't mean you should avoid selling. With real estate that you buy directly, as opposed to publicly held securities like real estate investment trusts (REITs), you can often avoid paying taxes on the profit you make. (See Book 8 for an introduction to real estate investing.)

With stocks and mutual funds, you can specify which shares you want to sell. This option makes selling decisions more complicated, but you may want to consider specifying what shares you're selling because you may be able to save taxes. (Read the next section for more information on this option.) If you sell all your shares of a particular security that you own, you don't need to concern yourself with specifying which shares you're selling.

Determining the cost basis of your shares

When you sell a portion of the shares of a security (such as a stock, bond, or mutual fund) that you own, specifying which shares you're selling may benefit you taxwise. Here's an example to show you why you may want to specify selling certain shares — especially those shares that cost you more to buy — so you can save on your taxes.

Suppose you own 300 shares of a stock, and you want to sell 100 shares. You bought 100 of these shares a long, long time ago at $10 per share, 100 shares two years ago at $16 per share, and the last 100 shares one year ago at $14 per share. Today, the stock is at $20 per share. Although you didn't get rich, you're grateful that you haven't lost your shirt the way some of your stock-picking pals have.

The Internal Revenue Service allows you to choose which shares you want to sell. Electing to sell the 100 shares that you purchased at the highest price — those you bought for $16 per share two years ago — saves you in taxes now. To comply with the tax laws, you must identify the shares that you want the broker to sell by the original date of purchase and/or the cost when you sell the shares. The brokerage firm through which you sell the stock should include this information on the confirmation that you receive for the sale.

The other method of accounting for which shares are sold is the method that the IRS forces you to use if you don't specify before the sale which shares you want to sell — the *first-in-first-out (FIFO) method.* FIFO means that the first shares that you sell are simply the first shares that you bought. Not surprisingly, because most stocks appreciate over time, the FIFO method usually leads to your paying more tax sooner. The FIFO accounting procedure leads to the conclusion that the 100 shares you sell are the 100 that you bought long, long ago at $10 per share. Thus, you owe a larger amount of taxes than if you'd sold the higher-cost shares under the specification method.

REMEMBER

Although you save taxes today if you specify selling the shares that you bought more recently at a higher price, when you finally sell the other shares, you'll owe taxes on the larger profit. The longer you expect to hold these other shares, the greater the value you'll likely derive from postponing, realizing the larger gains and paying more in taxes.

When you sell shares in a mutual fund, the IRS has yet another accounting method, known as the *average cost method,* for figuring your taxable profit or loss. This method comes in handy if you bought shares in chunks over time or reinvested the fund payouts in purchasing more shares of the fund. As the name suggests, the average cost method allows you to take an average cost for all the mutual fund shares you bought over time.

Selling large-profit investments

No one likes to pay taxes, of course, but if an investment you own has appreciated in value, someday you'll have to pay taxes on it when you sell. (There is an exception: You hold the investment until your death and will it to your heirs. The IRS wipes out the capital gains tax on appreciated assets at your death.)

Capital gains tax applies when you sell an investment at a higher price than you paid for it. As explained earlier in this chapter, your capital gains tax rate is different from the tax rate that you pay on ordinary income (such as from employment earnings or interest on bank savings accounts).

Odds are that the longer you've held securities such as stocks, the greater the capital gains you'll have, because stocks tend to appreciate over time. If all your assets have appreciated significantly, you may resist selling to avoid taxes. If you need money for a major purchase, however, sell what you need and pay the tax. Even if you have to pay state as well as federal taxes totaling some 35 percent of the profit, you'll have lots left. (For "longer-term" profits from investments held more than one year, your federal and state capital gains taxes probably would total somewhat less.)

Before you sell, do some rough figuring to make sure you'll have enough money left to accomplish what you want. If you seek to sell one investment and reinvest in another, you'll owe tax on the profit unless you're selling and rebuying real estate.

TIP

If you hold several assets, to diversify and meet your other financial goals, give preference to selling your largest holdings with the smallest capital gains. If you have some securities that have profits and some with losses, you can sell some of each to offset the profits with the losses.

TIP

Handling losers in your portfolio

Perhaps you have some losers in your portfolio. If you need to raise cash for some particular reason, you may consider selling select securities at a loss. You can use losses to offset gains as long as you hold both offsetting securities for more than one year (long term) or hold both for no more than one year (short term). The IRS makes this delineation because it taxes long-term gains and losses on a different rate schedule from short-term gains and losses.

If you sell securities at a loss, you can claim up to $3,000 in net losses for the year on your federal income tax return. If you sell securities with net losses totaling more than $3,000 in a year, you must carry the losses over to future tax years.

Some tax advisors advocate doing year-end tax-loss selling with stocks, bonds, and mutual funds. The logic goes that if you hold a security at a loss, you should sell it, take the tax write-off, and then buy it (or something similar) back. When selling investments for tax-loss purposes, be careful of the so-called wash sale rules. The IRS doesn't allow the deduction of a loss for a security sale if you buy that same security back within 30 days. As long as you wait 31 or more days, you won't encounter any problems.

WARNING

If you're selling a mutual fund or exchange-traded fund, you can purchase a fund similar to the one you're selling to easily sidestep this rule.

TIP

Selling investments when you don't know their original cost

Sometimes, you may not know what an investment originally cost you, or you received some investments from another person, and you're not sure what they paid for them.

If you don't have the original statement, start by calling the firm where the investment was purchased. Whether it's a brokerage firm or mutual fund company, the company should be able to send you copies of old account statements, although you may have to pay a small fee for this service.

Also, increasing numbers of investment firms, especially mutual fund companies, can tell you upon the sale of an investment what its original cost was. The cost calculated is usually the average cost for the shares you purchased.

Chapter **3**

Laying Out Your Financial Plans

B efore you make any great, wealth-building investments, you should get your financial house in order. Understanding and implementing some simple personal financial management concepts can pay off big for you in the decades ahead. This chapter explains what financial housekeeping you should do before you invest, as well as how to translate your overall personal and financial plans into an investment plan and ways to protect yourself and your property.

First Priorities: Paying Off High-Cost Debt and Building a Safety Reserve

Plenty of younger adults have debts to pay and lack an emergency reserve of money for unexpected expenses. High-cost debts, such as on a credit card, can be a major impediment to investing, in particular, and accomplishing your future personal and financial goals, in a broader sense. A high interest rate keeps the debt growing and can cause your debt to spiral out of control, which is why the following sections discuss dealing with such consumer debt as your first priority, just before establishing an emergency reserve.

Paying off high-cost consumer debt

Paying down debts isn't nearly as exciting as investing, but it can make your investment decisions less difficult. Rather than spending your time investigating specific investments, paying off your debts with money you've saved may indeed be your best investment.

Consumer debt includes borrowing on credit cards, auto loans, and the like, which are often costly ways to borrow. Banks and other lenders charge higher interest rates for consumer debt than for debt for investments, such as real estate and business, because consumer loans are the riskiest type of loans for a lender. Risk means the chance of the borrower's defaulting and being unable to pay back all that they borrowed.

Many folks have credit card debt that costs 18 percent or more per year in interest. Some credit cards levy interest rates well above 20 percent if you make a late payment or two. Reducing and eventually eliminating this debt with your savings is like putting your money in an investment with a guaranteed tax-free return equal to the rate that you pay on your debt.

For example, if you have outstanding credit card debt at 18 percent interest, paying off that debt is the same as putting your money to work in an investment with a guaranteed 18 percent tax-free annual return. Because the interest on consumer debt isn't tax-deductible, you would need to earn more than 18 percent by investing your money elsewhere to net 18 percent after paying taxes. Earning such high investing returns is highly unlikely, and to earn those returns, you'd be forced to take great risk.

REMEMBER

Consumer debt is hazardous to your long-term financial health (not to mention damaging to your credit score and future ability to borrow for a home or general ability to save and invest) because it encourages you to borrow against your future earnings. People say such things as "I can't afford to buy a new car for cash, given how expensive new cars are." Well, okay. New cars are expensive, so you need to set your sights lower and buy a good used car that you can afford. You can then invest the money that you'd otherwise spend on your auto loan.

Establishing an emergency reserve

You never know what life will bring, so having an accessible reserve of cash to meet unexpected expenses makes good financial sense. If you have generous parents or dear relatives, you can certainly consider using them as your emergency reserve. Just be sure you ask them in advance how they feel about that before you count on receiving funding from them. If you don't have a financially flush family member, the onus is on you to establish a reserve.

TIP

You should have at least three months' worth of living expenses to as much as 12 months' worth of living expenses as an emergency reserve (see Chapter 1 in Book 2). Invest this personal-safety-net money in a money market fund (see Chapter 4 in Book 2). You may also be able to borrow against your employer-based retirement account or against your home's equity, should you find yourself in a bind, but these options are much less desirable.

If you don't have a financial safety net, you may be forced, under duress, to sell an investment (at a relatively low price) that you've worked hard for. And selling some investments, such as real estate, can take time and cost significant money (transaction costs, taxes, and so on).

WARNING

Riskier investments like stocks aren't a suitable place to keep your emergency money invested. While stocks historically have returned about 9 percent per year, about one-third of the time, stocks decline in value in a given year, sometimes substantially. Stocks can drop and have dropped 20, 30, or 50 percent or more over relatively short periods of time. Suppose that such a decline coincides with an emergency, such as the loss of your job or a health problem that creates major medical bills. During the 2020 government-mandated economic shutdowns due to the COVID-19 pandemic, remember how (U.S. and most international) stocks dropped more than 30 percent in just a few weeks while millions of people lost their jobs? Your situation may force you to sell at a loss, perhaps a substantial one. Stocks are intended to be a longer-term investment, not an investment that you expect (or need) to sell in the near future.

What about Paying Down Other Debts?

Getting out from under 18 percent interest rate credit card debt is clearly a priority and a bit of a no-brainer. But what should you do about other debts that carry a more reasonable interest rate? This section talks you through some common examples: student loans and mortgage debt.

Assessing student loans

If you're one of many young adults with lingering student loan debt, you're probably wondering whether you should focus your efforts on paying down that debt or instead invest the extra cash you have.

The best choice hinges on the interest rate on this debt (after factoring in any tax breaks) and how that compares with the expected return from investing. Of course, you must be reasonable and not pie-in-the-sky about the rate of return you expect from your investments.

Under current tax laws, with student loans, you can deduct up to $2,500 in student loan interest annually on your federal 1040 income tax return. So this deduction can lower the effective interest rate you're paying on your student loans. This deduction is available to single taxpayers with adjusted gross incomes (before subtracting the student loan interest) of $70,000 or less and married couples filing jointly with such incomes of $140,000 or less. Partial deductions are allowed for incomes up to $85,000 for singles and $170,000 for married couples filing jointly. Another requirement for taking this deduction is that you and your spouse, if filing jointly, cannot be claimed as dependents on someone else's income tax return.

If you can deduct student loan interest on your tax return, to determine the value of that deduction, see Chapter 2 in Book 2 to understand what tax bracket you're in (what your marginal tax rate is). For most moderate income earners, 25 percent is a reasonable number to work with.

Suppose you have student loans outstanding at the attractive interest rate of just 3.5 percent. Assume that you're able to deduct all this interest and that your income tax bracket is 25 percent. So, after taxes, the effective interest rate on your student loan is 3.5 percent − (0.25 × 3.5 percent) = 2.63 percent.

Now, the question to consider is this: Can you reasonably expect to earn an average annual rate of return from your investments of more than this 2.63 percent? If you invest your money in a sleepy bank account, the answer will surely be no. If you instead invest in things like stocks and bonds, over the long term, you should come out with a higher return.

If you have student loans at a higher interest rate — say, 6 percent — it may make more sense to pay those loans down faster with your extra cash than to invest that money elsewhere. To get a higher return than that from investments, you need to take a fair amount of risk, and of course there's no guarantee that you'll actually make a high enough return to make it worth your while.

When deciding whether you should pay down student loans faster, there are some factors to consider besides the cost of your student loans and comparing this cost to the expected return on your investments. Other good reasons not to pay off your student loans any quicker than necessary include the following:

>> **Paying off your student loan faster has no tax benefit.** Instead, you could contribute to your retirement (also known as tax reduction) accounts, such as a 401(k), an IRA, or a SEP-IRA plan (especially if your employer offers matching money). Putting additional money in a retirement plan can immediately reduce your federal and state income tax bills. The more years you have until retirement, the greater the benefit you receive if you invest in your retirement accounts. Thanks to the compounding of your retirement account

investments without the drain of taxes, you can actually earn a lower rate of return on your investments than you pay on your student loans and still come out ahead.

>> **You're willing to invest in growth-oriented investments, such as stocks and real estate.** To have a reasonable chance of earning more on your investments than it costs you to borrow on your student loans, you must be aggressive with your investments. Stocks and real estate have produced annual average rates of return of about 9 percent. You may be able to earn even more in your own small business or by investing in others' businesses.

REMEMBER

Keep in mind that you have no guarantee, especially in the short term, of earning high returns from growth-type investments, which can easily drop 20 percent or more in value over a year or two.

>> **Paying down your student loans depletes your emergency reserves.** Psychologically, some people feel uncomfortable paying off debt more quickly if it diminishes their savings and investments. You probably don't want to pay down your debt if doing so depletes your financial safety cushion. Make sure you have access — through a money market fund or other sources (a family member, for example) — to at least three months' worth of living expenses (see the earlier section "Establishing an emergency reserve").

Considering paying down mortgage debt

Paying off your mortgage more quickly is an "investment" for your spare cash that may make sense for your financial situation. However, the wisdom of making this financial move isn't as clear as is paying off high-interest consumer debt; mortgage interest rates are generally lower, and the interest is typically tax-deductible.

As with the decision to pay off a student loan faster (look to the previous section), when evaluating whether to pay down your mortgage quicker than necessary, compare your mortgage interest rate with your investments' rates of return. Suppose you have a fixed-rate mortgage with an interest rate of 5 percent. If you decide to make investments instead of paying down your mortgage more quickly, your investments need to produce an average annual rate of return, before taxes, of more than 5 percent for you to come out ahead financially.

TIP

Don't get hung up on mortgage tax deductions. Although it's true that mortgage interest is usually tax-deductible, you must also pay taxes on investment profits generated outside retirement accounts. You can purchase tax-free investments like municipal bonds, but over the long haul, such bonds and other types of lending investments (bank savings accounts, CDs, and other bonds) are unlikely to earn a rate of return that's higher than the cost of your mortgage.

Sorting Out Your Financial Plans

You should establish your financial goals before you begin investing. Otherwise, you won't know how much to save or how much risk you need to take or are comfortable taking. You may want to invest money for several goals, or you may have just one purpose.

Considering your investment options and desires

Numerous good investing choices exist: You can invest in real estate, the stock market, mutual funds, exchange-traded funds, or your own business or someone else's. Or you can pay down debts such as student loans, credit cards, an auto loan, or mortgage debt more quickly.

What makes the most sense for you depends on your goals as well as your personal preferences. If you detest risk-taking and volatile investments, paying down some debts, as recommended earlier in this chapter, may make better sense than investing in the stock market.

To determine your general investment desires, think about how you would deal with an investment that plunges 20 percent or 40 percent, over a short period of time. Some aggressive investments can fall fast. You shouldn't go into the stock market, real estate, or small-business investment arena if such a drop is likely to cause you to sell or make you a miserable wreck. If you haven't tried riskier investments yet, you may want to experiment a bit to see how you feel with your money invested in them.

TIP

A simple way to mask the risk of volatile investments is to diversify your portfolio — that is, put your money into different investments. Not watching prices too closely helps, too; that's one of the reasons why real estate investors are less likely to bail out when the market declines. Unfortunately, stock market investors can get minute-by-minute price updates. Add that fact to the quick click of your computer mouse or tap on your smartphone that it takes to dump a stock or fund in a flash, and you have all the ingredients for shortsighted investing — and potential financial disaster.

Making investing decisions and determining your likes and dislikes is challenging when you consider just your own concerns. When you have to also consider someone else, dealing with these issues becomes doubly hard, given the typically different money personalities and emotions that come into play. Usually one person takes primary responsibility for managing the household finances, including investments. The couples who do the best job with their investments are those who communicate well, plan ahead, and compromise.

TIP

Couples stuck in unproductive patterns of behavior should get the issue out on the table. For these couples, the biggest step is making the time to discuss their financial management, whether as a couple or working with an advisor or counselor. The key to success is taking the time for each person to explain their different point of view and then offer compromises. So be sure to make time to discuss your points of view or hire a financial advisor or psychologist/marriage counselor to help you deal with these issues and differences.

Assessing your savings rate

To accomplish your financial goals, you need to save money, and you also should know your savings rate. Your savings rate is the percentage of your past year's income that you saved and didn't spend.

Part of being a smart investor involves figuring out how much you need to save to reach your goals. Not knowing what you want to do a decade or more from now is perfectly normal; after all, your goals, wants, and needs evolve over the years. But that doesn't mean you should just throw your hands in the air and not make an effort to see where you stand today and think about where you want to be in the future.

An important benefit of knowing your savings rate is that you can better assess how much risk you need to take to accomplish your goals. Seeing the amount that you need to save to achieve your dreams may encourage you to take more risk with your investments.

REMEMBER

During your working years, if you consistently save about 10 percent of your annual income, you're probably saving enough to meet your goals (unless you want to retire at a relatively young age). On average, most people need about 75 percent of their preretirement income throughout retirement to maintain their standard of living.

If you're one of the many people who don't save enough, it's time to do some homework. To save more, you need to reduce your spending, increase your income, or both. For most people, reducing spending is the more feasible way to save.

To reduce your spending, first figure out where your money goes. You may have some general idea, but to make changes, you need to have the data and facts. Examine your bill-paying records and review your credit card bills and any other documentation that shows your spending history. Tally up how much you spend on getting food out, operating your car(s), paying your taxes, and everything else. After you have this information, you can begin to prioritize and make the necessary trade-offs to reduce your spending and increase your savings rate. Earning more income may help boost your savings rate as well. Perhaps you can get a higher-paying job or increase the number of hours you work. But if you already work a lot, reining in your spending is usually better for your emotional and economic well-being.

If you don't know how to evaluate and reduce your spending or haven't thought about your retirement goals, looked into what you can expect from Social Security, or calculated how much you should save for retirement, now's the time to do so. Pick up the latest edition of *Personal Finance in Your 20s & 30s For Dummies* by Eric Tyson, MBA (Wiley) to find out all the necessary details for retirement planning and much more.

Investing regularly with dollar cost averaging

Regularly investing money at set time intervals, such as monthly or quarterly, in volatile investments such as stocks, stock mutual funds, or exchange-traded funds is called *dollar cost averaging* (DCA). If you've ever had money regularly deducted from your paycheck and contributed to a retirement savings plan investment account, you've done DCA.

Most folks invest a portion of their employment compensation as they earn it, but if you have extra cash sitting around, you can choose to invest that money in one fell swoop or to invest it gradually via DCA. The biggest appeal of gradually feeding money into the market via DCA is that you don't dump all your money into a potentially overheated investment just before a major drop. No one has a crystal ball and can predict which direction investments will move next in the short term. DCA helps shy investors psychologically ease into riskier investments.

DCA is made to order for skittish investors with larger lump sums of money sitting in safe investments like bank accounts. It also makes sense for investors with a large chunk of their net worth in cash who want to minimize the risk of transferring that cash to riskier investments, such as stocks.

As with any risk-reducing investment strategy, DCA has its drawbacks. If growth investments appreciate (as they're supposed to over time), a DCA investor misses out on earning higher returns on his money awaiting investment. Studying U.S. stock market data over seven decades, finance professors Richard E. Williams and Peter W. Bacon found that approximately two-thirds of the time, a lump-sum stock market investor earned higher first-year returns than an investor who fed the money in monthly over the first year.

However, knowing that you'll probably be ahead most of the time if you dump a lump sum into the stock market is little consolation if you happen to invest just before a major drop in prices. For example, from late 2007 to early 2009, global stocks shed about half of their value. And how about those who invested in stocks in late 2019 and early 2020 only to see stocks slide by more than one-third in just a matter of weeks in March of 2020 due to the government-mandated economic shutdowns resulting from the COVID-19 pandemic?

If you use DCA too quickly, you may not give the market sufficient time for a correction to unfold, during and after which some of the DCA purchases may take place. If you practice DCA over too long a period of time, you may miss a major upswing in stock prices. Consider using DCA over one to two years to strike a balance. Alternatively, if you're comfortable with the risk, get your money invested and get on with your life!

TIP

When you use DCA, establish an automatic investment plan so you're less likely to wimp out of your strategy. Your money that awaits investment in DCA should have a suitable parking place. Consider a money market fund that's appropriate for your tax situation.

Knowing the Impact of Investing for College Costs

Many well-intentioned parents want to save for their children's future educational expenses. The mistake that they often make, however, is putting money in accounts in the child's name (in so-called custodial accounts) or saving outside retirement accounts in general. The more money you accumulate outside tax-sheltered retirement accounts, the more you will generally end up paying for college costs.

REMEMBER

Under the current financial needs analysis used by most colleges and universities in awarding "financial aid" (that is, how much of their very high sticker price they will charge you), the value of your retirement plan is not considered to be an asset. Money that you save outside retirement accounts, including money in the child's name, is counted as an asset and reduces eligibility for financial aid.

Also, be aware that your family's assets, for purposes of financial aid determination, generally include equity in real estate and businesses you own. Although the federal financial aid analysis no longer counts equity in your home as an asset, many private (independent) schools continue to ask parents for this information when they make their own financial aid determinations. Thus, paying down your home mortgage more quickly instead of funding retirement accounts can harm you financially. You may end up paying more for college costs and pay more in taxes.

TIP

Make it a priority to contribute to your retirement savings plan(s). If you instead save money in a nonretirement account for your children's college expenses, you will pay higher taxes both on your current income and on the interest and growth of this money. In addition to paying higher taxes, you'll be expected to pay a higher price for your child's educational expenses.

Paying for college

If the way in which the financial aid system works effectively encourages you to save in your own retirement accounts, how will you pay for your kid's education expenses? Here are some ideas and resources:

>> **Home equity:** You can borrow against your home at a relatively low interest rate, and the interest is generally tax-deductible.

>> **Company retirement plans:** Some 401(k)s allow borrowing for educational costs.

>> **Student loans:** Several financial aid programs allow you to borrow at reasonable interest rates. The Unsubsidized Stafford Loans and Parent Loans for Undergraduate Students (PLUS), for example, are available, even when your family isn't deemed financially needy.

>> **Grants and scholarships:** Grant programs are available through schools and the government, as well as through independent sources. Complete the Free Application for Federal Student Aid (FAFSA) application to apply for the federal government programs. Grants available through state government programs may require a separate application. Specific colleges and other private organizations — including employers, banks, credit unions, and community groups — also offer grants and scholarships.

>> **Work and save:** Your child can work and save money during high school and college. In fact, if your child qualifies for financial aid, they're generally expected to contribute a certain amount to education costs from employment (both during the school year and summer breaks) and from savings. Besides giving your teen a stake in their own future, this training encourages sound personal financial management down the road.

No one enjoys filling out financial aid forms. It's difficult, intimidating, invasive, and stressful. Yet it's a necessary step many families must take in order to make college more affordable. First, let's clear up a major misconception: Receiving financial aid doesn't actually mean you receive money for college. Rather it means they charge different customers widely differing prices based upon the college's assessment of your ability to pay. Your goal is to position your finances to receive more favorable pricing. And doing that is not as hard as it may seem. Here are some tips:

>> **Assume that you qualify for financial aid.** Financial aid consultants agree that you should assume you're eligible. Don't rule yourself out because of income or academics. And don't rule out a college because you think it's too expensive. The higher the cost, the more aid you may receive.

>> **Use colleges' "net price calculator" to estimate your expected costs.** No matter where you are in the planning process, there is a simple method you can use now to get a general idea as to what price you may pay at a given college or university (and therefore how much financial aid or discount you will receive from those institutions). Colleges are required to have a net price calculator (NPC) on their websites. The pricing among private colleges can differ by tens of thousands of dollars among schools driven by factors like how much equity a family has in their home.

>> **Fill out the FAFSA form online.** The Free Application for Federal Student Aid — also known as the FAFSA form — is the starting point in applying for financial aid. You can complete the FAFSA form online (studentaid.gov).

>> **Don't wait around to be accepted to a college to apply for aid.** The coffers may be empty by spring, so get application forms completed as soon as possible. You'll need the latest version of the federal FAFSA form. You may also need to complete the College Board's CSS Profile application (cssprofile.collegeboard.org), state aid forms, and/or forms provided by the colleges. The FAFSA form and Profile become available for the next academic year on October 1 of the current year (meaning the soonest you can apply for financial aid for your first year of college is October 1 of senior year of high school).

Parents, keep in mind that the questions presume that the student is applying for aid (even though parents fill out the form!). Be aware that questions like name, address, social security number, date of birth, and so on in the beginning part of the form refer to the student. Parent information is collected later in the form. Entering parent information in a student section is a common mistake, and it can cause problems for your financial aid application.

TIP

As Chapter 1 in Book 2 discusses, there are increasing numbers of faster and cheaper alternatives to traditional four-year colleges which lead to interesting and rewarding jobs and careers. For more information, pick up a copy of *Paying For College For Dummies* by Eric Tyson, MBA (Wiley).

Considering educational savings account options

You'll hear about various accounts you can use to invest money for your kid's future college costs. Tread carefully with these, especially because they can affect future financial aid.

The most popular of these accounts are qualified state tuition plans, also known as Section 529 plans. These plans offer a tax-advantaged way to save and invest more than $100,000 per child toward college costs. (Some states allow upward of $300,000 per student.) After you contribute to one of these state-based accounts, the invested funds grow without taxation. Withdrawals are also tax-free provided the funds are used to pay for qualifying higher-education costs (which include college, graduate school, and certain additional expenses of special-needs students) as well as up to $10,000 per year toward K–12 school expenses. (The schools need not be in the same state as the state administering the Section 529 plan.)

Section 529 plan balances can harm your child's financial aid chances. Thus, such accounts make the most sense for affluent families who are sure they won't qualify for any type of financial aid. If you do opt for a 529 plan and intend to apply for financial aid, you should be the owner of the accounts (not your child) to maximize qualifying for financial aid.

Investing money earmarked for college

Diversified mutual funds and exchange-traded funds — which invest in stocks in the United States and internationally, as well as bonds — are ideal vehicles to use when you invest money earmarked for college. Be sure to choose funds that fit your tax situation if you invest your funds in nonretirement accounts.

When your child is young (preschool age), consider investing up to 80 percent of your investment money in stocks (diversified worldwide) with the remainder in bonds. Doing so can maximize the money's growth potential without taking extraordinary risk. As your child makes their way through the later years of elementary school, you need to begin to make the mix more conservative. Scale back the stock percentage to 50 or 60 percent. Finally, in the years just before the child enters college, reduce the stock portion to no more than 20 percent or so.

Some 529s offer target-date-type funds that reduce the stock exposure as target college dates approach so you don't have to make the adjustments yourself.

Securing Proper Insurance

Although many people lack particular types of insurance, others possess unnecessary policies. Many people also keep very low deductibles. Remember to insure against potential losses that would be financially catastrophic for you; don't waste your money to protect against smaller losses.

REMEMBER

You may be at risk of making a catastrophic investing mistake by not protecting your assets properly. Decisions regarding what amount of insurance you need to carry are, to some extent, a matter of your desire and ability to accept financial risk. But some risks aren't worth taking. Don't overestimate your ability to predict what accidents and other bad luck may befall you.

Consider the following types of insurance to protect yourself, your loved ones, and your assets:

>> **Major medical health insurance:** You need a policy that pays for all types of major illnesses and major medical expenditures. If your financial situation allows, consider taking a health plan with a high deductible, which can minimize your premiums. Also consider channeling extra money into a health savings account (HSA), which provides tremendous tax breaks. As with a retirement account, contributions provide an up-front tax break, and money can grow over the years in an HSA without taxation. You can also tap HSA funds without penalty or taxation for a wide range of current health expenses.

>> **Adequate liability insurance on your home and car to guard your assets against lawsuits:** You should have at least enough liability insurance to protect your net worth (assets minus your liabilities/debts) or, ideally, twice your net worth. If you run your own business, get insurance for your business assets if they're substantial. Also consider professional liability insurance to protect against a lawsuit. You may also want to consider incorporating your business.

>> **Long-term disability insurance:** Even if you don't have dependents, odds are that you're dependent on your employment income. What would you (and your family) do to replace your income if a major disability prevented you from working? Most large employers offer group plans that have good benefits and are much less expensive than coverage you'd buy on your own. Also check with your professional association for a competitive group plan.

>> **Life insurance, if others are dependent on your income:** If you're single or your loved ones can live without your income, skip life insurance. If you need coverage, buy term insurance that, like your auto and home insurance, is pure insurance protection. The amount of term insurance you need to buy largely depends on how much of your income you want to replace.

>> **Estate planning:** Most folks need a simple will to delineate to whom they would like to leave all their worldly possessions. If you hold significant assets outside retirement accounts, you may also benefit from establishing a living trust, which keeps your money from filtering through the hands of probate lawyers. Living wills and medical powers of attorney are useful to have in case you're ever in a medically incapacitated situation. If you have substantial assets, doing more involved estate planning is wise to minimize estate taxes and ensure the orderly passing of your assets to your heirs.

For all the details on the best and most effective ways to buy insurance, what to look for in policies, and where to get good policies, see *Personal Finance For Dummies* by Eric Tyson, MBA (Wiley).

Chapter **4**

Starting Out with Bank and Credit Union Accounts

C ustomer visits to stand-alone bank branches with a lobby and tellers are going the way of the big-city newspaper business. Both are in decline and in industries that are being disrupted by the internet.

Who needs retail banks, with their costly-to-maintain branches, when you can do your banking online? You can conduct most transactions quicker online, and it saves the bank money, which enables it to offer you better account terms. And there's no need to rush out at lunchtime to be sure you make it to your bank during its limited open hours. Online banking is generally available 24/7.

But here are even bigger questions for you to consider: Do you even need a bank account? What are your best alternatives? That's what this chapter explores.

Everyone needs an account or two from which to conduct transactions, including paying bills and storing newly earned money. Such foundational accounts are essential to get in order before proceeding with investing that has the potential to produce higher returns.

Understanding FDIC Bank Insurance

What makes keeping your money in a U.S. bank unique is the Federal Deposit Insurance Corporation (FDIC) insurance that protects bank deposits. If your bank fails (and as history shows, some banks do fail), and if your bank participates in the FDIC system, your bank account is insured by the U.S. government up to $250,000. The stamp of FDIC backing and insurance is soothing to some folks who worry about all the risks and dangers in the investment world.

While the FDIC insurance is worth something, banks have to pay for this protection. That cost is effectively passed along to you in the form of lower interest rates on your deposits.

WARNING

Just because the federal government stands behind the banking FDIC system doesn't mean your money is 100 percent safe in the event of a bank failure. Although you're insured for $250,000 in a bank, if the bank fails, you may wait quite a while to get your money back — and you may get less interest than you thought you would. Banks fail and will likely continue to do so. During the 1980s and early 1990s, and again in the late 2000s, hundreds of insured banks and savings and loans failed. (Between the early 1990s and mid-2000s — a relatively strong economic period — only a handful of banks failed annually.)

REMEMBER

Any investment that involves lending your money to someone else or to some organization, including putting your money in a bank or buying a Treasury bond that the federal government issues, carries risk. Any student of history knows that governments and civilizations fail.

FDIC backing is hardly a unique protection. Every Treasury bond is issued and backed by the federal government, the same debt-laden organization that stands behind the FDIC. Plenty of other nearly equivalent safe lending investments yield higher returns than bank accounts. Highly rated corporate bonds are good examples (see Book 4 for more on bonds). That's not to say that you shouldn't consider keeping some of your money in a bank. But first, you should be aware of the realities and costs of FDIC insurance.

Investing in Banking Account and Savings Vehicles

While traditional banks with walk-in branch locations are shrinking in number due to closures, bank mergers, and failures, online banks are growing — and for good reason. Some of the biggest expenses of operating a traditional retail bank are the cost of the real estate and the related costs of the branch. An online bank eliminates much of those costs; thus, these banks are able, for example, to pay their customers higher interest rates on their account balances. And online banks can offer better terms on checking accounts and loans.

The internet is lowering costs for many industries, and the banking industry is one of those. This doesn't mean, however, that you should rush to become a customer of an online bank, because other financial companies, like mutual funds and brokerage firms, offer attractive investment accounts and options as well. (See the section "Exploring Alternatives to Bank Accounts" later in this chapter.)

Bank checking accounts and debit cards

Whether it's paying monthly bills or having something in your wallet to make purchases with at restaurants and retail stores, we all need the ability to conduct transactions and access our money. Credit cards aren't a good idea for most people, because the credit feature enables you to spend money you don't have and carry a debt balance month to month. Notwithstanding the lower short-term interest rates some cards charge to lure new customers, the reality is that borrowing on credit cards is expensive — usually, to the tune of more than 18 percent for most young adults.

Paying a credit card bill in full each month is the smart way to use such a card and avoid these high interest charges. But about half of all credit card holders use the high-interest-rate credit feature on their cards. And, even if you pay your bill in full each month, it's worth considering whether charging purchases on your credit card encourages you to spend more.

Debit cards are useful transaction vehicles and a better alternative for folks who are prone to borrow via their credit cards. A debit card connects to your checking account, thus eliminating the need for you to carry around excess cash. Unlike a credit card, a debit card has no credit feature, so you can't spend money you don't have. (Some checking accounts offer prearranged lines of credit for overdrafts.) And as with a credit card, you can dispute debit card transactions if the product or service isn't what the seller claimed it would be and fails to stand behind it.

TIP

During periods of relatively low interest rates like those of the last several years, the fees levied on a transaction account, like a checking account, should be of greater concern to you than the interest paid on account balances. After all, you shouldn't be keeping lots of extra cash in a checking account; you've got better options for that, which are discussed in the rest of this chapter.

One reason why bank customers have gotten worse terms on their accounts is that they gravitate toward larger banks and their extensive ATM networks so they can easily get cash when they need it. These ATM networks (and the often-associated bank branches) are costly for banks to maintain. So you generally pay higher fees and get lower yields when you're the customer of a bank with a large ATM network, especially a bank that does tons of advertising.

By using a debit card that carries a Visa or Mastercard logo, you won't need to access and carry around much cash. Debit cards are widely accepted by merchants and are connected to your checking account. These cards can be used for purchases and for obtaining cash from your checking account.

Savings accounts and certificates of deposit

Banks generally pay higher interest rates on savings account balances than they do on checking account balances. But they have often lagged behind the best money market funds, offered by mutual fund companies and brokerage firms. Online banking is changing that dynamic, however, and now the best banks offer competitive rates on savings accounts.

The virtue of most savings accounts is that you can earn some interest yet have penalty-free access to your money. The investment won't fluctuate in value the way that a bond will, and you don't have early-withdrawal penalties, as you do with a certificate of deposit (CD).

The yield on bank savings accounts is generally pretty crummy. That's why your friendly neighborhood banker will be quick to suggest a CD as a higher-yielding investment alternative to a bank savings account. They may tout the fact that unlike a bond, a CD doesn't have fluctuating principal value. CDs also give you the peace of mind afforded by the government's FDIC insurance program.

CDs pay higher interest rates than savings accounts because you commit to tie up your money for a period of time, such as six or twelve months, or three or five years. The bank pays you, say, 2 percent and then turns around and lends your money to others through credit cards, auto loans, and so on. The bank often charges those borrowers an interest rate of 10 percent or more. Not a bad business!

WARNING

Some investors (typically older ones who are worried about risk) use CDs by default without researching their pros and cons. Here are some drawbacks that your banker may neglect to mention:

>> **Early-withdrawal penalties:** When you tie up your money in a CD and later decide you want it back before the CD matures, a hefty penalty (typically, about six months' interest) is usually shaved from your return. With other lending investments, such as bonds and bond mutual funds, you can access your money without penalty and generally at little or no cost.

>> **Mediocre yields:** In addition to carrying penalties for early withdrawal, a CD yields less than a high-quality bond with a comparable maturity (such as two, five, or ten years). Often, the yield difference is 1 percent or more, especially if you don't shop around and simply buy CDs from the local bank where you keep your checking account.

>> **Only one tax flavor:** High-tax-bracket investors who purchase CDs outside their retirement accounts should be aware of a final and perhaps fatal flaw of CDs: The interest on CDs is fully taxable at the federal and state levels. Bonds, by contrast, are available in tax-free (federal and/or state) versions, if you desire.

TIP

You can earn higher returns and have better access to your money when it's in bonds and bond funds than you can when it's in CDs. Bonds make especially good sense when you're in a higher tax bracket and would benefit from tax-free income in a nonretirement account. CDs may make sense when you know, for example, that you can invest your money for, say, two years, after which time you need the money for some purchase that you expect to make. Just make sure you shop around to get the best interest rate from an FDIC-insured bank. If having that U.S. government insurance gives you peace of mind, consider investing in Treasury bonds, which tend to pay more interest than many CDs.

Negotiating with Bankers

Especially at traditional brick-and-mortar banks in your local community, you may be able to get better terms and deals if you ask. Here's a common example.

Suppose that for several years, you've had a checking account at your local bank and have not had any real issues or problems. Then one month, you end up bouncing several check payments (say, four at $30 each) because a deposit into your account didn't clear in time. You may very well be able to get some or even all of these fees waived by pleading your case to the local branch manager. Explain how long you've been a good customer and why this was a one-time case of bad luck, something beyond your control, and so on. The worst that can happen is that the manager will turn down your request, and you'll have wasted a few minutes of your day. More likely, however, is that you may save yourself $90 to $120 for a small amount of your time.

Deposit account terms and loan terms are harder to negotiate, but some folks have had some success even in those arenas. Your regular bank may offer better mortgage terms if it knows it needs to match or beat a more competitive offer from another bank you've shopped, for example.

Feeling Secure with Your Bank

Putting your money in a bank may make you feel safe for a variety of reasons. For your parents and your grandparents, the first investing experience was likely at the neighborhood bank where they established checking and savings accounts.

Part of your comfort in keeping your money in a bank may stem from the fact that the bank is where your well-intentioned mom and dad may have first steered you financially. Also, at a local branch, often within a short distance of your home or office, you find vaults and security-monitoring cameras to protect your deposits.

Bank branches cost a lot of money to operate. Guess where that money comes from? From bank depositors and the customers of the banks' various services, of course! These operating costs are one of the reasons why the interest rates that banks pay often pale in comparison to some of the similarly secure alternatives discussed later in this chapter. This also explains why an online bank may be your best choice if you want to keep some of your money in a bank.

Evaluating any bank

Most folks know to look for a bank that participates in the U.S.-government-operated FDIC program. Otherwise, if the bank fails, your money on deposit isn't protected. FDIC covers your deposits up to a cool $250,000.

WARNING

Some online banks are able to offer higher interest rates because they are based overseas and, therefore, are not participating in the FDIC program. (Banks must pay insurance premiums into the FDIC fund, which adds, of course, to a bank's costs.) Another risk for you is that noncovered banks may take excessive risks with their business to be able to pay depositors higher interest rates.

When considering doing business with an online bank or a smaller bank you've not heard of, you should be especially careful to ensure that the bank is covered under FDIC. Don't simply accept the bank's word for it or the display of the FDIC logo in its offices or on its website.

TIP

Check the FDIC's website database of FDIC-insured institutions to see whether the bank you're considering doing business with is covered. Search by going to the FDIC's Bank Find page (banks.data.fdic.gov/bankfind-suite/bankfind). You can search by the name, city, state, or zip code of the bank. For insured banks, you can see the date when it became insured, its insurance certificate number, the main office location for the bank (and branches), its primary government regulator, and other links to detailed information about the bank. In the event that your bank doesn't appear on the FDIC list, yet the bank claims FDIC coverage, contact the FDIC at (877) 275-3342.

In addition to ensuring that a bank is covered by the FDIC, investigate the following:

>> **What is the bank's reputation for its services?** This may not be easy to discern, but at a minimum, you should conduct an internet search of the bank's name along with the word "complaints" or "problems" and examine the results.

>> **How accessible are customer-service people at the bank?** Is a phone number provided on the bank's website? How hard is it to reach a live person, the local branch, and its personnel (including the manager)? Are the customer-service representatives you reach knowledgeable and service-oriented?

>> **What are the process and options for getting your money out?** This issue is a good one to discuss with the bank's customer-service people.

>> **What fees are charged for particular services?** This information should be posted on the bank's website in a section called something like Account Terms or Disclosures. Also, request and inspect the bank's Truth in Savings Disclosure, which answers relevant account questions in a standardized format. Figure 4-1 is an example of an online bank's disclosure for savings accounts.

Protecting yourself when banking online

The attractions of banking online are pretty obvious. For starters, it can be enormously convenient, as you bank when you want on your computer or smartphone. You don't have to find a local bank branch during their limited open hours. And thanks to their lower overhead, the best online banks are able to offer competitive interest rates and account terms to their customers.

You probably know from experience that conducting any type of transaction online is safe as long as you use some common sense and know who you're doing business with before you go forward. That said, others who've gone before you have gotten ripped off, and you do need to protect yourself.

Truth in Savings Disclosure: Savings Account

Minimum balance to open the account — You must deposit $50.00 to open this account.

Rate information — Your interest rate is variable, and the annual percentage yield may be changed at any time at our discretion.

Compounding and crediting frequency — Interest will be compounded every quarter. Interest will be credited to your account every quarter.

Daily balance computation method — We use the daily balance method to calculate the interest on your account. This method applies a daily periodic rate to the principal in the account each day of the statement cycle.

Accrual of interest on noncash deposits — Interest begins to accrue on the first business day after the banking day you deposit noncash items (for example, checks).

Minimum balance to obtain the annual percentage yield disclosed — You must maintain a minimum balance of $15.00 in the account each day of the quarter to obtain the disclosed annual percentage yield.

Transaction limitations — Transfers from an Advantage Savings account to another account or to third parties by preauthorized, automatic, or telephone transfer are limited to six per month, with no transfers by check, draft, debit card, or similar order to third parties.

Minimum balance to avoid imposition of fees — You must maintain a minimum balance of $200.00 each day of the month to avoid monthly maintenance fees.

Fees — A monthly maintenance fee of $3.00 will be imposed if your account balance falls below the daily minimum balance requirement on any day during the month.

May be subject to additional fees for overdrafts or items returned for nonsufficient funds (NSF returned item fee).

© John Wiley & Sons, Inc.

FIGURE 4-1:
A sample Truth in Savings Disclosure statement from an online bank.

Take the following steps to protect yourself and your identity when conducting business online:

REMEMBER

>> Never access your bank accounts from a shared computer or on a shared network, such as the free access networks offered in hotel rooms and in other public or business facilities.

» Use two-factor authentication to minimize the chances that anyone other than you can access your account(s).

» Be aware of missed statements, which could indicate that your account has been taken over.

» Report unauthorized transactions to your bank or credit card company as soon as possible; otherwise, your bank may not stand behind the loss of funds.

» Use a complicated and unique password (including letters and numbers) for your online bank account.

» Log out immediately after completing your transactions on financial websites.

Exploring Alternatives to Bank Accounts

If you've been reading since the beginning of this chapter, you know that the best banks that are focused online should have a cost advantage over their peers that have branch locations. Well, there are other financial companies that have similar, and in some cases even better, cost advantages (which translates into better deals for you): credit unions, discount and online brokerage firms, and mutual fund companies.

Credit union accounts and benefits

Credit unions are unique creatures (well, a unique species) within the financial-services-firm universe. Credit unions are similar to banks in the products and services that they offer (although private banks tend to offer a deeper array).

However, unlike banks, which are run as private businesses seeking profits, credit unions operate as nonprofit entities and are technically owned by their members (customers). If they're efficiently operated, the best credit unions offer their customers better terms on deposits, including checking and savings accounts (higher interest rates and lower fees) and some loans (lower rates and fees).

REMEMBER

Don't assume that credit unions necessarily or always offer better products and services than traditional banks, because they don't. The profit motive of private businesses isn't evil; quite to the contrary, the profit motive spurs businesses to keep getting better at and improving on what they do.

Credit unions have insurance coverage up to $250,000 per customer through the National Credit Union Administration (NCUA), similar to the FDIC protection that banks offer their customers. As when checking out a bank, be sure that any credit union you may deposit money into has NCUA insurance coverage.

The trick to getting access to a credit union is that by law, each individual credit union may offer its services only to a defined membership. Examples of the types of credit union memberships available include

>> Alumni

>> College and university

>> Community

>> Employer

>> Place of worship

There can be some overlap between these groups. To access a credit union, you also may be able to use your family ties.

TIP

To find credit unions in your local area, visit the Credit Union National Association consumer's website at www.asmarterchoice.org/.

Brokerage cash management accounts

A type of account worth checking out at brokerage firms is generally known as an asset management account. When these types of accounts first came into existence decades ago, they really were only for affluent investors. That is no longer the case, although the best deals on such accounts at some firms are available to higher-balance investors.

Brokerage firms enable you to buy and sell stocks, bonds, and other securities. Among the larger brokerage firms or investment companies with substantial brokerage operations you may have read or heard about are Charles Schwab, ETrade, Fidelity, and T.D. Ameritrade. Vanguard has a solid brokerage offering but discontinued their cash management account and is exploring whether to offer another again.

Now, some of these firms have fairly extensive branch office networks, and others don't. But those that have a reasonable number of branch offices have been able to keep a competitive position because of their extensive customer and asset base and because they aren't burdened by banking regulations (they aren't banks) and the costs associated with operating as a bank.

The best of brokerage firm asset management accounts typically enable you to

>> Invest in various investments, such as stocks, bonds, mutual funds, and exchange-traded funds, and hold those investments in a single account.

>> Write checks against a money market balance that pays competitive yields.

>> Use a Visa or Mastercard debit card for transactions.

Money market mutual funds

Because bank savings accounts historically have paid pretty crummy interest rates, you need to think long and hard about keeping your spare cash in the bank during normal times for interest rates and the economy. Instead of relying on the bank, try keeping your extra savings in a money market fund, which is a type of mutual fund. (Other funds focus on bonds or stocks.) Money market funds historically have offered a higher-yielding alternative to bank savings and bank money market deposit accounts. You can use a money market fund that offers unlimited check writing at a mutual fund company.

During recent periods of ultra-low interest rates, you may find slightly better interest rates on some of the best online bank savings accounts and at some credit unions.

A money market fund is similar to a bank savings account except that it is offered by a mutual fund company and therefore lacks FDIC coverage. Historically, this hasn't been a problem because retail money market funds have lost shareholder principal in only one case for retail investors (the Reserve Primary fund lost less than 1 percent of assets during the 2008 financial crisis).

The attraction of money market funds has been that the best ones pay higher yields than bank savings accounts and also come in tax-free versions, which is good for higher-tax-bracket investors.

3
Checking Out Stock Investing

Contents at a Glance

IN THIS CHAPTER

» **Using stock exchanges to get investment information**

» **Applying accounting and economic know-how to your investments**

» **Keeping abreast of financial news**

» **Deciphering stock tables**

» **Understanding dividend dates**

» **Recognizing good (and bad) investing advice**

Chapter **1**

Gathering Information on Stocks

Knowledge and information are two critical success factors in stock invest‐ing. (Isn't that true about most things in life?) People who plunge headlong into stocks without sufficient knowledge of the stock market in general, and current information in particular, quickly learn the lesson of the eager diver who didn't find out ahead of time that the pool was only an inch deep (ouch!). In their haste to avoid missing so‐called golden investment opportunities, investors too often end up losing money.

REMEMBER

Opportunities to *make* money in the stock market will always be there, no matter how well or how poorly the economy and the market are performing in general. There's no such thing as a single (and fleeting) magical moment, so don't feel that if you let an opportunity pass you by, you'll always regret that you missed your one big chance.

For the best approach to stock investing, build your knowledge and find quality information first so you can make your fortunes more assuredly. Before you buy, you need to know that the company you're investing in is

>> Financially sound and growing

>> Offering products and/or services that are in demand by consumers

>> In a strong and growing industry (and general economy)

Where do you start, and what kind of information do you want to acquire? Keep reading.

Looking to Stock Exchanges for Answers

Before you invest in stocks, you need to be completely familiar with the basics of stock investing. At its most fundamental, stock investing is about using your money to buy a piece of a company that will give you value in the form of appreciation or income (or both). Fortunately, many resources are available to help you find out about stock investing. Some of the best places are the stock exchanges themselves.

Stock exchanges are organized marketplaces for the buying and selling of stocks (and other securities). The New York Stock Exchange (NYSE; also referred to as the *Big Board*), the premier stock exchange, provides a framework for stock buyers and sellers to make their transactions. The NYSE makes money not only from a cut of every transaction but also from fees (such as listing fees) charged to companies and brokers that are members of its exchanges. In 2007, the NYSE merged with Euronext, a major European exchange, but no material differences exist for stock investors. In 2008, the American Stock Exchange (Amex) was taken over by (and completely merged into) the NYSE. The new name is NYSE American.

TIP

The main exchanges for most stock investors are the NYSE (www.nyse.com) and Nasdaq (www.nasdaq.com). Technically, Nasdaq isn't an exchange, but it's a formal market that effectively acts as an exchange. Because the NYSE and Nasdaq benefit from increased popularity of stock investing and continued demand for stocks, they offer a wealth of free (or low-cost) resources and information for stock investors. Go to their websites to find useful resources such as the following:

>> Tutorials on how to invest in stocks, common investment strategies, and so on

>> Glossaries and free information to help you understand the language, practice, and purpose of stock investing

>> A wealth of news, press releases, financial data, and other information about companies listed on the exchange or market, usually accessed through an on-site search engine

>> Industry analysis and news

>> Stock quotes and other market information related to the daily market movements of stocks, including data such as volume, new highs, new lows, and so on

>> Free tracking of your stock selections (you can input a sample portfolio or the stocks you're following to see how well you're doing)

Grasping the Basics of Accounting and Economics

Stocks represent ownership in companies. Before you buy individual stocks, you want to understand the companies whose stock you're considering and find out about their operations. It may sound like a daunting task, but you'll digest the point more easily when you realize that companies work very similarly to the way you work. They make decisions on a daily basis just as you do.

Think about how you grow and prosper as an individual or as a family, and you see the same issues with businesses and how they grow and prosper. Low earnings and high debt are examples of financial difficulties that affect both people and companies. You can better understand companies' finances by taking the time to pick up some information in two basic disciplines: accounting and economics. These two disciplines, which are discussed in the following sections, play a significant role in understanding the performance of a firm's stock.

Accounting for taste and a whole lot more

REMEMBER

Accounting. Ugh! But face it: Accounting is the language of business, and believe it or not, you're already familiar with the most important accounting concepts! Just look at the following three essential principles:

>> **Assets minus liabilities equals net worth.** In other words, take what you own (your *assets*), subtract what you owe (your *liabilities*), and the rest is yours (your *net worth*)! Your own personal finances work the same way as Microsoft's (except yours have fewer zeros at the end).

A company's *balance sheet* shows you its net worth at a specific point in time (such as December 31). The net worth of a company is the bottom line of its asset and liability picture, and it tells you whether the company is *solvent* (has the ability to pay its debts without going out of business). The net worth of a successful company grows regularly. To see whether your company is successful, compare its net worth with the net worth from the same point a year earlier. A firm that has a $4 million net worth on December 31, 2020, and a $5 million net worth on December 31, 2021, is doing well; its net worth has gone up 25 percent ($1 million) in one year.

>> **Income minus expenses equals net income.** In other words, take what you make (your *income*), subtract what you spend (your *expenses*), and the remainder is your *net income* (or *net profit* or *net earnings* — your gain).

A company's profitability is the whole point of investing in its stock. As it profits, the business becomes more valuable, and in turn, its stock price becomes more valuable. To discover a firm's net income, look at its income statement. Try to determine whether the company uses its gains wisely, either by reinvesting them for continued growth or by paying down debt.

>> **Do a comparative financial analysis.** That's a mouthful, but it's just a fancy way of saying how a company is doing now compared with something else (like a prior period or a similar company).

If you know that the company you're looking at had a net income of $50,000 for the year, you may ask, "Is that good or bad?" Obviously, making a net profit is good, but you also need to know whether it's good compared to something else. If the company had a net profit of $40,000 the year before, you know that the company's profitability is improving. But if a similar company had a net profit of $100,000 the year before and in the current year is making $50,000, then you may want to either avoid the company making the lesser profit or see what (if anything) went wrong with the company making less.

Accounting can be this simple. If you understand these three basic points, you're ahead of the curve (in stock investing as well as in your personal finances). For more information on how to use a company's financial statements to pick good stocks, see Chapter 4 in Book 3.

Understanding how economics affects stocks

Economics. Double ugh! No, you aren't required to understand "the inelasticity of demand aggregates" (thank heavens!) or "marginal utility" (say what?). But a working knowledge of basic economics is crucial to your success and proficiency as a stock investor. The stock market and the economy are joined at the hip. The good (or bad) things that happen to one have a direct effect on the other. The following sections give you the lowdown.

Getting the hang of the basic concepts

REMEMBER

Alas, many investors get lost on basic economic concepts (as do some so-called experts you see on TV). Understanding basic economics will help you filter the financial news to separate relevant information from the irrelevant in order to make better investment decisions. Be aware of these important economic concepts:

>> **Supply and demand:** How can anyone possibly think about economics without thinking of the ageless concept of supply and demand? *Supply and demand* can be simply stated as the relationship between what's available (the supply) and what people want and are willing to pay for (the demand). This equation is the main engine of economic activity and is extremely important for your stock investing analysis and decision-making process. Do you really want to buy stock in a company that makes elephant-foot umbrella stands if you find out that the company has an oversupply and nobody wants to buy them anyway?

>> **Cause and effect:** If you pick up a prominent news report and read, "Companies in the table industry are expecting plummeting sales," do you rush out and invest in companies that sell chairs or manufacture tablecloths? Considering cause and effect is an exercise in logical thinking, and logic is a major component of sound economic thought.

When you read business news, play it out in your mind. What good (or bad) can logically be expected given a certain event or situation? If you're looking for an effect ("I want a stock price that keeps increasing"), you also want to understand the cause. Here are some typical events that can cause a stock's price to rise:

- **Positive news reports about a company:** The news may report that the company is enjoying success with increased sales or a new product.

- **Positive news reports about a company's industry:** The media may be highlighting that the industry is poised to do well.

- **Positive news reports about a company's customers:** Maybe your company is in industry A, but its customers are in industry B. If you see good news about industry B, that may be good news for your stock.

- **Negative news reports about a company's competitors:** If the competitors are in trouble, their customers may seek alternatives to buy from, including your company.

>> **Economic effects from government actions:** Political and governmental actions have economic consequences. As a matter of fact, nothing has a greater effect on investing and economics than government. Government actions usually manifest themselves as taxes, laws, or regulations. They also can take on a more ominous appearance, such as war or the threat of war. Government can willfully (or even accidentally) cause a company to go bankrupt, disrupt an entire industry, or even cause a depression. Government controls the money supply, credit, and all public securities markets.

Gaining insight from past mistakes

Because most investors ignored some basic observations about economics in the late 1990s, they subsequently lost trillions in their stock portfolios during 2000–2002. During 2000–2008, the United States experienced the greatest expansion of total debt in history, coupled with a record expansion of the money supply. The Federal Reserve (or "the Fed"), the U.S. government's central bank, controls both. This growth of debt and money supply resulted in more consumer (and corporate) borrowing, spending, and investing. The debt and spending that hyperstimulated the stock market during the late 1990s (stocks rose 25 percent per year for five straight years during that time period) came back with a vengeance afterwards.

When the stock market bubble popped during 2000–2002, it was soon replaced with the housing bubble, which popped during 2005–2006. And February 2020 witnessed a major correction (the Dow Jones industrials, for example, fell over 11 percent during the five trading days ending February 28) over fears due to the coronavirus.

Of course, you should always be happy to earn 25 percent per year with your investments, but such a return can't be sustained and encourages speculation. In the end, spending started to slow down because consumers and businesses became too indebted. This slowdown in turn caused the sales of goods and services to taper off. Companies were left with too much overhead, capacity, and debt because they had expanded too eagerly. At this point, businesses were caught in a financial bind. Too much debt and too many expenses in a slowing economy mean one thing: Profits shrink or disappear. To stay in business, companies had to do the logical thing — cut expenses. What's usually the biggest expense for companies? People! Many companies started laying off employees. As a result, consumer spending dropped further because more people were either laid off or had second thoughts about their own job security.

As people had little in the way of savings and too much in the way of debt, they had to sell their stock to pay their bills. This trend was a major reason that stocks started to fall in 2000. Earnings started to drop because of shrinking sales from a sputtering economy. As earnings fell, stock prices also fell.

With some hiccups along the way, the stock market has solidly zigzagged upward since the early 2000s, and the Dow Jones breached the 29,000 level in early 2020, but investors should be just as wary when the market is at nosebleed levels as they are when bear markets hit because market highs tend to be followed by the next bear market or downward move. Stock markets in February 2020 did correct painfully (a fall of 10 percent or more is a correction; a bear market is 20 percent or more), and they offered a buying opportunity for value oriented investors.

REMEMBER

The lessons from the 1990s and the 2000–2020 time frame are important ones for investors today:

>> Stocks are not a replacement for savings accounts. Always have some money in the bank.

>> Stocks should never occupy 100 percent of your investment funds.

>> When anyone (including an expert) tells you that the economy will keep growing indefinitely, be skeptical and read diverse sources of information.

>> If stocks do well in your portfolio, consider protecting your stocks (both your original investment and any gains) with stop-loss orders.

>> Keep debt and expenses to a minimum.

>> If the economy is booming, a decline is sure to follow as the ebb and flow of the economy's business cycle continues.

Staying on Top of Financial News

Reading the financial news can help you decide where or where not to invest. Many newspapers, magazines, and websites offer great coverage of the financial world. Obviously, the more informed you are, the better, but you don't have to read everything that's written. The information explosion in recent years has gone beyond overload, and you can easily spend so much time reading that you have little time left for investing. The following sections describe the types of information you need to get from the financial news.

TIP

Here are some of the best publications, resources, and websites to assist you:

>> The most obvious publications of interest to stock investors are the *Wall Street Journal* (www.wsj.com) and *Investor's Business Daily* (www.investors.com). These excellent publications report the news and stock data as of the prior trading day.

>> Some of the more obvious websites are MarketWatch (www.marketwatch.com), Yahoo! Finance (finance.yahoo.com), Bloomberg (www.bloomberg.com), and Investing.com (www.investing.com). These websites can actually give you news and stock data within minutes after an event occurs.

>> Don't forget the exchanges' websites that are listed in the earlier section "Looking to Stock Exchanges for Answers."

Figuring out what a company's up to

Before you invest, you need to know what's going on with the company. When you read about the company, either from the firm's literature (its annual report, for example) or from media sources, be sure to get answers to some pertinent questions:

>> **Is the company making more net income than it did last year?** You want to invest in a company that's growing.

>> **Are the company's sales greater than they were the year before?** Keep in mind that you won't make money if the company isn't making money.

>> **Is the company issuing press releases on new products, services, inventions, or business deals?** All these achievements indicate a strong, vital company.

Knowing how the company is doing, no matter what's happening with the general economy, is obviously important. To better understand how companies tick, see Chapter 4 in Book 3.

Discovering what's new with an industry

As you consider investing in a stock, make a point of knowing what's going on in that company's industry. If the industry is doing well, your stock is likely to do well, too. But then again, the reverse is also true.

Yes, some investors have picked successful stocks in a failing industry, but those cases are exceptional. By and large, it's easier to succeed with a stock when the entire industry is doing well. As you're watching the news, reading the financial pages, or viewing financial websites, check out the industry to ensure that it's strong and dynamic.

Knowing what's happening with the economy

No matter how well or how poorly the overall economy is performing, you want to stay informed about its general progress. It's easier for the value of stock to keep going up when the economy is stable or growing. The reverse is also true: If the economy is contracting or declining, the stock has a tougher time keeping its value. Some basic items to keep tabs on include the following:

>> **Gross domestic product (GDP):** The GDP is roughly the total value of output for a particular nation, measured in the dollar amount of goods and services. It's reported quarterly, and a rising GDP bodes well for your stock. When the GDP is rising 3 percent or more on an annual basis, that's solid growth. If it rises but is less than 3 percent, that's generally considered less than stellar (or mediocre). A GDP under zero (a negative number) means that the economy is shrinking (heading into recession).

>> **The index of leading economic indicators (LEI):** The LEI is a snapshot of a set of economic statistics covering activity that precedes what's happening in the economy. Each statistic helps you understand the economy in much the same way that barometers (and windows!) help you understand what's happening with the weather. Economists don't just look at an individual statistic; they look at a set of statistics to get a more complete picture of what's happening with the economy.

Seeing what politicians and government bureaucrats are doing

Being informed about what public officials are doing is vital to your success as a stock investor. Because federal, state, and local governments pass literally thousands of laws, rules, and regulations every year, monitoring the political landscape is critical to your success. The news media report what the president and Congress are doing, so always ask yourself, "How does a new law, tax, or regulation affect my stock investment?"

TIP

You can find laws being proposed or enacted by the federal government through Congress's search page (www.congress.gov). Also, some great organizations inform the public about tax laws and their impact, such as the National Taxpayers Union (www.ntu.org) and the Tax Foundation (www.taxfoundation.org).

Checking for trends in society, culture, and entertainment

TIP

As odd as it sounds, trends in society, popular culture, and entertainment affect your investments, directly or indirectly. For example, when you see a headline such as "There are now more millennials than Baby Boomers," you should find out what their buying habits are, what products and services they favor, and so on. Understanding the basics of demographic shifts can give you some important insights that can help you make wiser long-term choices in your stock portfolio. With that particular headline, you know that companies that are well positioned to cater to that growing market's wants and needs will do well — meaning a successful stock pick for you.

Keep your eyes open to emerging trends in society at large by reading and viewing the media that cover such matters (*Time* magazine, CNN, and so on). What trends are evident now? Can you anticipate the wants and needs of tomorrow's society? Being alert, staying a step ahead of the public, and choosing stocks appropriately gives you a profitable edge over other investors. If you own stock in a solid company with growing sales and earnings, other investors eventually notice. As more investors buy up your company's stock, you're rewarded as the stock price increases.

Reading (And Understanding) Stock Tables

The stock tables in major business publications such as the *Wall Street Journal* and *Investor's Business Daily* are loaded with information that can help you become a savvy investor — *if* you know how to interpret them. You need the information in the stock tables for more than selecting promising investment opportunities. You also need to consult the tables after you invest to monitor how your stocks are doing.

Looking at the stock tables without knowing what you're looking for or why you're looking is the equivalent of reading *War and Peace* backwards through a kaleidoscope — nothing makes sense. But this section can help you make sense of it all (well, at least the stock tables!). Table 1-1 shows a sample stock table. Each item gives you some clues about the current state of affairs for that particular company. The sections that follow describe each column to help you understand what you're looking at.

TABLE 1-1 **A Sample Stock Table**

52-Wk High	52-Wk Low	Name (Symbol)	Div	Vol	Yld	P/E	Day Last	Net Chg
21.50	8.00	SkyHighCorp (SHC)		3,143		76	21.25	+.25
47.00	31.75	LowDownInc (LDI)	2.35	2,735	5.9	18	41.00	-.50
25.00	21.00	ValueNowInc (VNI)	1.00	1,894	4.5	12	22.00	+.10
83.00	33.00	DoinBadlyCorp (DBC)		7,601			33.50	-.75

REMEMBER

Every newspaper's financial tables are a little different, but they give you basically the same information. Updated daily, these tables aren't the place to start your search for a good stock; they're usually where your search ends. The stock tables are the place to look when you own a stock or know what you want to buy, and you're just checking to see the most recent price.

52-week high

The column in Table 1-1 labeled "52-Wk High" gives you the highest price that particular stock has reached in the most recent 52-week period. Knowing this price lets you gauge where the stock is now versus where it has been recently. SkyHighCorp's (SHC) stock has been as high as $21.50, whereas its last (most recent) price is $21.25, the number listed in the "Day Last" column. (Flip to the later section "Day last" for more on understanding this information.) SkyHigh-Corp's stock is trading very high right now because it's hovering right near its overall 52-week high figure.

Now, take a look at DoinBadlyCorp's (DBC) stock price. It seems to have tumbled big time. Its stock price has had a high in the past 52 weeks of $83, but it's currently trading at $33.50. Something just doesn't seem right here. During the past 52 weeks, DBC's stock price has fallen dramatically. If you're thinking about investing in DBC, find out why the stock price has fallen. If the company is strong, it may be a good opportunity to buy stock at a lower price. If the company is having tough times, avoid it. In any case, research the firm and find out why its stock has declined. (Chapter 4 in Book 3 provides the basics of researching companies.)

52-week low

The column labeled "52-Wk Low" gives you the lowest price that particular stock reached in the most recent 52-week period. Again, this information is crucial to your ability to analyze stock over a period of time. Look at DBC in Table 1-1, and you can see that its current trading price of $33.50 in the "Day Last" column is close to its 52-week low of $33.

Keep in mind that the high and low prices just give you a range of how far that particular stock's price has moved within the past 52 weeks. They can alert you that a stock has problems or tell you that a stock's price has fallen enough to make it a bargain. Simply reading the "52-Wk High" and "52-Wk Low" columns isn't enough to determine which of those two scenarios is happening. They basically tell you to get more information before you commit your money.

Name and symbol

The "Name (Symbol)" column is the simplest in Table 1-1. It tells you the company name (usually abbreviated) and the stock symbol assigned to the company.

When you have your eye on a stock for potential purchase, get familiar with its symbol. Knowing the symbol makes it easier for you to find your stock in the financial tables, which lists stocks in alphabetical order by the company's name (or symbol depending on the source). Stock symbols are the language of stock investing, and you need to use them in all stock communications, from getting a stock quote at your broker's office to buying stock over the internet.

Dividend

Dividends (shown under the "Div" column in Table 1-1) are basically payments to owners (stockholders). If a company pays a dividend, it's shown in the dividend column. The amount you see is the annual dividend quoted for one share of that stock. If you look at LowDownInc (LDI) in Table 1-1, you can see that you get $2.35 as an annual dividend for each share of stock that you own. Companies usually pay the dividend in quarterly amounts. If you own 100 shares of LDI, the company pays you a quarterly dividend of $58.75 ($235 total per year). A healthy company strives to maintain or upgrade the dividend for stockholders from year to year. (Additional dividend details are discussed later in this chapter.)

The dividend is very important to investors seeking income from their stock investments. For more about investing for income, see Chapter 3 in Book 3. Investors buy stocks in companies that don't pay dividends primarily for growth. For more information on growth stocks, see Chapter 2 in Book 3.

Volume

Normally, when you hear the word "volume" on the news, it refers to how much stock is bought and sold for the entire market: "Well, stocks were very active today. Trading volume at the New York Stock Exchange hit 2 billion shares." Volume is certainly important to watch because the stocks that you're investing in are somewhere in that activity. For the "Vol" column in Table 1-1, though, the volume refers to the individual stock.

Volume tells you how many shares of that particular stock were traded that day. If only 100 shares are traded in a day, then the trading volume is 100. SHC had 3,143 shares change hands on the trading day represented in Table 1-1. Is that good or bad? Neither, really. Usually the business news media mention volume for a particular stock only when it's unusually large. If a stock normally has volume in the 5,000 to 10,000 range and all of a sudden has a trading volume of 87,000, then it's time to sit up and take notice.

REMEMBER

Keep in mind that a low trading volume for one stock may be a high trading volume for another stock. You can't necessarily compare one stock's volume against that of any other company. The large-cap stocks like IBM or Microsoft typically have trading volumes in the millions of shares almost every day, whereas less active, smaller stocks may have average trading volumes in far, far smaller numbers.

The main point to remember is that trading volume that is far in excess of that stock's normal range is a sign that something is going on with that company. It may be negative or positive, but something newsworthy is happening with that company. If the news is positive, the increased volume is a result of more people buying the stock. If the news is negative, the increased volume is probably a result of more people selling the stock. What are typical events that cause increased trading volume? Some positive reasons include the following:

>> **Good earnings reports:** The company announces good (or better-than-expected) earnings.

>> **A new business deal:** The firm announces a favorable business deal, such as a joint venture, or lands a big client.

>> **A new product or service:** The company's research and development department creates a potentially profitable new product.

>> **Indirect benefits:** The business may benefit from a new development in the economy or from a new law passed by Congress.

WARNING

Some negative reasons for an unusually large fluctuation in trading volume for a particular stock include the following:

>> **Bad earnings reports:** Profit is the lifeblood of a company. When its profits fall or disappear, you see more volume.

>> **Governmental problems:** The stock is being targeted by government action, such as a lawsuit or a Securities and Exchange Commission (SEC) probe.

>> **Liability issues:** The media report that the company has a defective product or similar problem.

>> **Financial problems:** Independent analysts report that the company's financial health is deteriorating.

REMEMBER

Check out what's happening when you hear about heavier-than-usual volume (especially if you already own the stock).

Yield

In general, yield is a return on the money you invest. However, in the stock tables, *yield* ("Yld" in Table 1-1) is a reference to what percentage that particular dividend is of the stock price. Yield is most important to income investors. It's calculated by dividing the annual dividend by the current stock price. In Table 1-1, you can see that the yield du jour of ValueNowInc (VNI) is 4.5 percent (a dividend of $1 divided by the company's stock price of $22). Notice that many companies report no yield; because they have no dividends, their yield is zero.

REMEMBER

Keep in mind that the yield reported on the financial sites changes daily as the stock price changes. Yield is always reported as if you're buying the stock that day. If you buy VNI on the day represented in Table 1-1, your yield is 4.5 percent. But what if VNI's stock price rises to $30 the following day? Investors who buy stock at $30 per share obtain a yield of just 3.3 percent (the dividend of $1 divided by the new stock price, $30). Of course, because you bought the stock at $22, you essentially locked in the prior yield of 4.5 percent. Lucky you. Pat yourself on the back.

P/E

REMEMBER

The *P/E ratio* is the relationship between the price of a stock and the company's earnings. P/E ratios are widely followed and are important barometers of value in the world of stock investing. The P/E ratio (also called the *earnings multiple* or just *multiple*) is frequently used to determine whether a stock is expensive (a good value). Value investors find P/E ratios to be essential to analyzing a stock as a potential investment. As a general rule, the P/E should be 10 to 20 for large-cap or income stocks. For growth stocks, a P/E no greater than 30 to 40 is preferable. (See Chapter 4 in Book 3 for full details on P/E ratios.)

In the P/E ratios reported in stock tables, *price* refers to the cost of a single share of stock. *Earnings* refers to the company's reported earnings per share as of the most recent four quarters. The P/E ratio is the price divided by the earnings. In Table 1-1, VNI has a reported P/E of 12, which is considered a low P/E. Notice how SHC has a relatively high P/E (76). This stock is considered too pricey because you're paying a price equivalent to 76 times earnings. Also notice that DBC has no available P/E ratio. Usually this lack of a P/E ratio indicates that the company reported a loss in the most recent four quarters.

Day last

The "Day Last" column tells you how trading ended for a particular stock on the day represented by the table. In Table 1-1, LDI ended the most recent day of trading at $41. Some newspapers report the high and low for that day in addition to the stock's ending price for the day.

Net change

The information in the "Net Chg" column answers the question, "How did the stock price end today compared with its price at the end of the prior trading day?" Table 1-1 shows that SHC stock ended the trading day up 25 cents (at $21.25). This column tells you that SHC ended the prior day at $21. VNI ended the day at $22 (up 10 cents), so you can tell that the prior trading day it ended at $21.90.

Using News about Dividends

Reading and understanding the news about dividends is essential if you're an *income investor* (someone who invests in stocks as a means of generating regular income; see Chapter 3 in Book 3 for details). The following sections explain some basics you should know about dividends.

TIP

You can find news and information on dividends in newspapers such as the *Wall Street Journal* (www.wsj.com), *Investor's Business Daily* (www.investors.com), and *Barron's* (www.barrons.com/).

Looking at important dates

REMEMBER

To understand how buying stocks that pay dividends can benefit you as an investor, you need to know how companies report and pay dividends. Some important dates in the life of a dividend are as follows:

>> **Date of declaration:** This is the date when a company reports a quarterly dividend and the subsequent payment dates. On January 15, for example, a company may report that it "is pleased to announce a quarterly dividend of 50 cents per share to shareholders of record as of February 10." That was easy. The date of declaration is really just the announcement date. Whether you buy the stock before, on, or after the date of declaration doesn't matter in regard to receiving the stock's quarterly dividend. The date that matters is the date of record (see that bullet later in this list).

>> **Date of execution:** This is the day you actually initiate the stock transaction (buying or selling). If you call up a broker (or contact one online) today to buy (or sell) a particular stock, then today is the date of execution, or the date on which you execute the trade. You don't own the stock on the date of execution; it's just the day you put in the order. For an example, skip to the following section.

>> **Closing date (settlement date):** This is the date on which the trade is finalized, which usually happens one business day after the date of execution. The closing date for stock is similar in concept to a real estate closing. On the closing date, you're officially the proud new owner (or happy seller) of the stock.

>> **Ex-dividend date:** *Ex-dividend* means *without dividend*. Because it takes one day to process a stock purchase before you become an official owner of the stock, you have to qualify (that is, you have to own or buy the stock) *before* the one-day period. That one-day period is referred to as the "ex-dividend period." When you buy stock during this short time frame, you aren't on the books of record, because the closing (or settlement) date falls after the date of record. However, you will be able to buy the stock for a slightly lower price to offset the amount of the dividend. See the next section to see the effect that the ex-dividend date can have on an investor.

>> **Date of record:** This is used to identify which stockholders qualify to receive the declared dividend. Because stock is bought and sold every day, how does the company know which investors to pay? The company establishes a cut-off date by declaring a date of record. All investors who are official stockholders as of the declared date of record receive the dividend on the payment date, even if they plan to sell the stock any time between the date of declaration and the date of record.

>> **Payment date:** The date on which a company issues and mails its dividend checks to shareholders. Finally!

For typical dividends, the events in Table 1-2 happen four times per year.

TABLE 1-2   **The Life of the Quarterly Dividend**

Event	Sample Date	Comments
Date of declaration	January 15	The date that the company declares the quarterly dividend
Ex-dividend date	February 9	Starts the one-day period during which, if you buy the stock, you don't qualify for the dividend
Date of record	February 10	The date by which you must be on the books of record to qualify for the dividend
Payment date	February 27	The date that payment is made (a dividend check is issued and mailed to stockholders who were on the books of record as of February 10)

Understanding why certain dates matter

REMEMBER

One business day passes between the date of execution and the closing date. One business day passes between the ex-dividend date and the date of record. This information is important to know if you want to qualify to receive an upcoming dividend. Timing is important, and if you understand these dates, you know when to purchase stock and whether you qualify for a dividend.

As an example, say that you want to buy ValueNowInc (VNI) in time to qualify for the quarterly dividend of 25 cents per share. Assume that the date of record (the date by which you have to be an official owner of the stock) is February 10. You have to execute the trade (buy the stock) no later than February 8 to be assured of the dividend. If you execute the trade right on February 9 (the ex-dividend date), you will not qualify for the dividend because settlement will occur after the date of record.

But what if you execute the trade on February 10, a day later? Well, the trade's closing date is February 11, which occurs *after* the date of record. Because you aren't on the books as an official stockholder on the date of record, you aren't getting that quarterly dividend. In this example, the February 9–10 period is called the *ex-dividend period*.

TIP

Fortunately, for those people who buy the stock during this brief ex-dividend period, the stock actually trades at a slightly lower price to reflect the amount of the dividend. If you can't get the dividend, you may as well save on the stock purchase. How's that for a silver lining?

Evaluating Investment Tips

Here's a tip: Never automatically invest just because you get a hot tip from some-one. Good investment selection means looking at several sources before you decide on a stock. No shortcut exists. That said, getting opinions from others never hurts — just be sure to carefully analyze the information you get. Here are some important points to bear in mind as you evaluate tips and advice from others:

>> **Consider the source.** Frequently, people buy stock based on the views of some market strategist or market analyst. People may see an analyst being interviewed on a television financial show and take that person's opinions and advice as valid and good. The danger here is that the analyst may be biased because of some relationship that isn't disclosed on the show. Analysts are required to disclose conflicts of interest on business channels.

>> **Get multiple views.** Don't base your investment decisions on just one source unless you have the best reasons in the world for thinking that a particular, single source is outstanding and reliable. A better approach is to scour current issues of independent financial publications, such as *Barron's* or *Money* magazine, and other publications and websites.

>> **Gather data from the SEC.** When you want to get more objective information about a company, why not take a look at the reports that firms must file with the SEC? These reports are the same reports that the pundits and financial reporters read. Arguably, the most valuable report you can look at is the 10K. The 10K is a report that all publicly traded companies must file with the SEC. It provides valuable information on the company's operations and financial data for the most recent year, and it's likely to be less biased than the information a company includes in other corporate reports, such as an annual report. The next most important document from the SEC is the 10Q, which gives the investor similar detailed information but for a single quarter.

TIP

To access 10K and 10Q reports, go to the SEC's website (www.sec.gov). From there, you can find the SEC's extensive database of public filings called EDGAR (the Electronic Data Gathering, Analysis, and Retrieval system). By searching EDGAR, you can find companies' balance sheets, income statements, and other related information so that you can verify what others say and get a fuller picture of what a business is doing and what its financial condition is.

Chapter **2**

Investing for Long-Term Growth

What's the number-one reason people invest in stocks? To grow their wealth (also referred to as *capital appreciation*). Yes, some people invest for income (in the form of dividends), but that's a different matter (see Chapter 3 in Book 3). Investors seeking growth would rather see the money that could have been distributed as dividends be reinvested in the company so that (hopefully) a greater gain is achieved when the stock's price rises or appreciates. People interested in growing their wealth see stocks as one of the convenient ways to do it. Growth stocks tend to be riskier than other categories of stocks, but they offer excellent long-term prospects for making the big bucks. Just ask Warren Buffett, Peter Lynch, and other successful, long-term investors.

Although someone like Buffett is not considered a growth investor, his long-term, value-oriented approach has been a successful growth strategy. If you're the type of investor who has enough time to let somewhat risky stocks trend upward or who has enough money so that a loss won't devastate you financially, then growth stocks are definitely for you. As they say, no guts, no glory. The challenge is to figure out which stocks make you richer quicker; this chapter gives you tips on how to do so.

Short of starting your own business, stock investing is the best way to profit from a business venture. To make money in stocks consistently over the long haul, you must remember that you're investing in a *company*; buying the stock is just a means for you to participate in the company's success (or failure). Why does it matter that you think of stock investing as buying a *company* versus buying a *stock?* Invest in a stock only if you're just as excited about it as you would be if you were the CEO in charge of running the company. If you're the sole owner of the company, do you act differently than one of a legion of obscure stockholders? Of course you do. As the firm's owner, you have a greater interest in the company. You have a strong desire to know how the enterprise is doing. As you invest in stocks, make believe that you're the owner, and take an active interest in the company's products, services, sales, earnings, and so on. This attitude and discipline can enhance your goals as a stock investor. This approach is especially important if your investment goal is growth.

Becoming a Value-Oriented Growth Investor

A stock is considered a *growth stock* when it's growing faster and at a higher rate than the overall stock market. Basically, a growth stock performs better than its peers in categories such as sales and earnings. *Value stocks* are stocks that are priced lower than the value of the company and its assets — you can identify a value stock by analyzing the company's fundamentals and looking at key financial ratios, such as the price-to-earnings (P/E) ratio. (See Chapter 4 in Book 3.) Growth stocks tend to have better prospects for growth in the immediate future (from one to four years), but value stocks tend to have less risk and steadier growth over a longer term.

Over the years, a debate has quietly raged in the financial community about growth versus value investing. Some people believe that growth and value are mutually exclusive. They maintain that large numbers of people buying stock with growth as the expectation tend to drive up the stock price relative to the company's current value. Growth investors, for example, aren't put off by P/E ratios of 30, 40, or higher. Value investors, meanwhile, are too nervous to buy stocks at those P/E ratio levels.

However, you *can* have both. A value-oriented approach to growth investing serves you best. Long-term growth stock investors spend time analyzing the company's fundamentals to make sure that the company's growth prospects lie on a solid foundation. But what if you have to choose between a growth stock and a value stock? Which do you choose? Seek value when you're buying the stock and analyze the company's prospects for growth. Growth includes, but is not limited to, the health and growth of the company's specific industry, the economy at large, and the general political climate.

REMEMBER

The bottom line is that growth is much easier to achieve when you seek solid, value-oriented companies in growing industries. It's also worth emphasizing that time, patience, and discipline are key factors in your success — especially in the tumultuous and uncertain stock investing environment of the current time (2020–2021).

Choosing Growth Stocks with a Few Handy Tips

Although the information in the previous section can help you shrink your stock choices from thousands of stocks to maybe a few dozen or a few hundred (depending on how well the general stock market is doing), the purpose of this section is to help you cull the so-so growth stocks to unearth the go-go ones. It's time to dig deeper for the biggest potential winners. Keep in mind that you probably won't find a stock to satisfy all the criteria presented here. Just make sure that your selection meets as many criteria as realistically possible. But hey, if you do find a stock that meets all the criteria cited, *buy as much as you can!*

To pick a winning stock, don't just pick a stock and hope that it does well. In fact, your personal stock-picking research shouldn't even begin with stocks; you should first look at the investing environment (politics, economics, demographics, and so on) and choose which industry will benefit. After you know which industry will prosper accordingly, *then* you can start to analyze and choose stock(s).

After you choose a stock, you should wait. Patience is more than just a virtue; patience is to investing what time is to a seed that's planted in fertile soil. The legendary Jesse Livermore said that he didn't make his stock market fortunes by trading stocks; his fortunes were made "in the waiting." Why?

When you're told to have patience and a long-term perspective, you're waiting for a specific condition to occur: for the market to discover what you have! When you have a good stock in a good industry, it takes time for the market to discover it. When a stock has more buyers than sellers, it rises — it's as simple as that. As time passes, more buyers find your stock. As the stock rises, it attracts more attention and, therefore, more buyers. The more time that passes, the better your stock looks to the investing public.

REMEMBER

When you're choosing growth stocks, you should consider investing in a company only *if* it makes a profit and *if* you understand *how* it makes that profit and from *where* it generates sales. Part of your research means looking at the industry and sector and economic trends in general.

Looking for leaders in megatrends

A strong company in a growing industry is a common recipe for success. If you look at the history of stock investing, this point comes up constantly. Investors need to be on the alert for megatrends because they help ensure success.

A *megatrend* is a major development that has huge implications for much (if not all) of society for a long time to come. Good examples are the advent of the internet and the aging of America. Both of these trends offer significant challenges and opportunities for the economy. Take the internet, for example. Its potential for economic application is still being developed. Millions are flocking to it for many reasons. And census data tells us that senior citizens (over 65) will continue to be a fast-growing segment of the U.S. population during the next 20 years. (Millennials are another huge demographic that investors should be aware of.) Small companies can be the ones poised for the most potential growth.

Comparing a company's growth to an industry's growth

You have to measure the growth of a company against something to figure out whether its stock is a growth stock. Usually, you compare the growth of a company with growth from other companies in the same industry or with the stock market in general. In practical terms, when you measure the growth of a stock against the stock market, you're actually comparing it against a generally accepted benchmark, such as the Dow Jones Industrial Average (DJIA) or the Standard & Poor's 500 (S&P 500).

TIP

If a company's earnings grow 15 percent per year over three years or more, and the industry's average growth rate over the same time frame is 10 percent, then the stock qualifies as a growth stock. You can easily calculate the earnings growth rate by comparing a company's earnings in the current year to the preceding year and computing the difference as a percentage. For example, if a company's earnings (on a per-share basis) were $1 last year and $1.10 this year, then earnings grew by 10 percent. Many analysts also look at a current quarter and compare the earnings to the same quarter from the preceding year to see whether earnings are growing.

REMEMBER

A growth stock is called that not only because the company is growing but also because the company is performing well with some consistency. Having a single year where your earnings do well versus the S&P 500's average doesn't cut it. Growth must be consistently accomplished.

Considering a company with a strong niche

Companies that have established a strong niche are consistently profitable. Look for a company with one or more of the following characteristics:

>> **A strong brand:** Companies such as Coca-Cola and Microsoft come to mind. Yes, other companies out there can make soda or software, but a business needs a lot more than a similar product to topple companies that have established an almost irrevocable identity with the public.

>> **High barriers to entry:** United Parcel Service and Federal Express have set up tremendous distribution and delivery networks that competitors can't easily duplicate. High barriers to entry offer an important edge to companies that are already established. Examples of high barriers include high capital requirements (needing lots of cash to start) or special technology that's not easily produced or acquired.

>> **Research and development (R&D):** Companies such as Pfizer and Merck spend a lot of money researching and developing new pharmaceutical products. This investment becomes a new product with millions of consumers who become loyal purchasers, so the company's going to grow. You can find out what companies spend on R&D by checking their financial statements and their annual reports (see Chapter 4 in Book 3).

Checking out a company's fundamentals

When you hear the word *fundamentals* in the world of stock investing, it refers to the company's financial condition, operating performance, and related data. When investors (especially value investors) do *fundamental analysis*, they look at the company's fundamentals — its balance sheet, income statement, cash flow, and other operational data, along with external factors such as the company's market position, industry, and economic prospects. Essentially, the fundamentals indicate the company's financial condition. Chapter 4 in Book 3 goes into greater detail about analyzing a company's financial condition. However, the main numbers you want to look at include the following:

>> **Sales:** Are the company's sales this year surpassing last year's? As a decent benchmark, you want to see sales at least 10 percent higher than last year. Although it may differ depending on the industry, 10 percent is a reasonable, general yardstick.

>> **Earnings:** Are earnings at least 10 percent higher than last year? Earnings should grow at the same rate as sales (or, hopefully, better).

>> **Debt:** Is the company's total debt equal to or lower than the prior year? The death knell of many a company has been excessive debt.

TIP

A company's financial condition has more factors than the preceding list mentions, but these numbers are the most important. Using the 10-percent figure may seem like an oversimplification, but you don't need to complicate matters unnecessarily. Someone's computerized financial model may come out to 9.675 percent or maybe 11.07 percent, but keep it simple for now.

Evaluating a company's management

The management of a company is crucial to its success. Before you buy stock in a company, you want to know that the company's management is doing a great job. But how do you do that? If you call up a company and ask, it may not even return your phone call. How do you know whether management is running the company properly? The best way is to check the numbers. The following sections tell you the numbers you need to check. If the company's management is running the business well, the ultimate result is a rising stock price.

Return on equity

REMEMBER

Although you can measure how well management is doing in several ways, you can take a quick snapshot of a management team's competence by checking the company's return on equity (ROE). You calculate the ROE simply by dividing earnings by equity. The resulting percentage gives you a good idea whether the company is using its equity (or net assets) efficiently and profitably. Basically, the higher the percentage, the better, but you can consider the ROE solid if the percentage is 10 percent or higher. Keep in mind that not all industries have identical ROEs.

To find out a company's earnings, check out the company's income statement. The *income statement* is a simple financial statement that expresses this equation: sales (or revenue) minus expenses equals net earnings (or net income or net profit). You can see an example of an income statement in Table 2-1. (Chapter 4 in Book 3 gives more details on income statements.)

TABLE 2-1

Grobaby, Inc., Income Statement

	2019 Income Statement	2020 Income Statement
Sales	$82,000	$90,000
Expenses	–$75,000	–$78,000
Net earnings	$7,000	$12,000

To find out a company's equity, check out that company's balance sheet. (See Chapter 4 in Book 3 for more details on balance sheets.) The *balance sheet* is actually a simple financial statement that illustrates this equation: total assets minus total liabilities equals net equity. For public stock companies, the net assets are called *shareholders' equity* or simply *equity*. Table 2-2 shows a balance sheet for Grobaby, Inc.

TABLE 2-2

Grobaby, Inc., Balance Sheet

	Balance Sheet as of December 31, 2019	Balance Sheet as of December 31, 2020
Total assets (TA)	$55,000	$65,000
Total liabilities (TL)	–$20,000	–$25,000
Equity (TA minus TL)	$35,000	$40,000

Table 2-1 shows that Grobaby's earnings went from $7,000 to $12,000. In Table 2-2, you can see that Grobaby increased the equity from $35,000 to $40,000 in one year. The ROE for the year 2019 is 20 percent ($7,000 in earnings divided by $35,000 in equity), which is a solid number. The following year, the ROE is 30 percent ($12,000 in earnings divided by $40,000 in equity), another solid number. A good minimum ROE is 10 percent, but 15 percent or more is preferred.

Equity and earnings growth

Two additional barometers of success are a company's growth in earnings and growth of equity:

» Look at the growth in earnings in Table 2-1. The earnings grew from $7,000 (in 2019) to $12,000 (in 2020), a percentage increase of 71 percent ($12,000 minus $7,000 equals $5,000, and $5,000 divided by $7,000 is 71 percent), which is excellent. At a minimum, earnings growth should be equal to or better than the rate of inflation, but because that's not always a reliable number, I like at least 10 percent.

» In Table 2-2, Grobaby's equity grew by $5,000 (from $35,000 to $40,000), or 14.3 percent ($5,000 divided by $35,000), which is very good — management is doing good things here. You want to see equity increasing by 10 percent or more.

Insider buying

TIP

Watching management as it manages the business is important, but another indicator of how well the company is doing is to see whether management is buying stock in the company as well. If a company is poised for growth, who knows better than management? And if management is buying up the company's stock en masse, that's a great indicator of the stock's potential.

Noticing who's buying and/or recommending a company's stock

You can invest in a great company and still see its stock go nowhere. Why? Because what makes the stock go up is demand — when there's more buying than selling of the stock. If you pick a stock for all the right reasons and the market notices the stock as well, that attention causes the stock price to climb. The things to watch for include the following:

» **Institutional buying:** Are mutual funds and pension plans buying up the stock you're looking at? If so, this type of buying power can exert tremendous upward pressure on the stock's price. Some resources and publications track institutional buying and how that affects any particular stock. Frequently, when a mutual fund buys a stock, others soon follow. In spite of all the talk about independent research, a herd mentality still exists.

» **Analysts' attention:** Are analysts talking about the stock on the financial shows? As much as you should be skeptical about an analyst's recommendation (given the stock market debacle of 2000–2002 and the market problems in 2008), it offers some positive reinforcement for your stock. Don't ever buy a stock solely on the basis of an analyst's recommendation. Just know that if you buy a stock based on your own research, and analysts subsequently rave about it, your stock price is likely to go up. A single recommendation by an influential analyst can be enough to send a stock skyward.

>> **Newsletter recommendations:** Independent researchers usually publish newsletters. If influential newsletters are touting your choice, that praise is also good for your stock. Although some great newsletters are out there and they offer information that's as good as or better than that of some brokerage firms' research departments, don't base your investment decision on a single tip. However, seeing newsletters tout a stock that you've already chosen should make you feel good.

>> **Consumer publications:** No, you won't find investment advice here. This one seems to come out of left field, but it's a source that you should notice. Publications such as *Consumer Reports* regularly look at products and services and rate them for consumer satisfaction. If a company's offerings are well received by consumers, that's a strong positive for the company. This kind of attention ultimately has a positive effect on that company's stock.

Making sure a company continues to do well

A company's financial situation does change, and you, as a diligent investor, need to continue to look at the numbers for as long as the stock is in your portfolio. You may have chosen a great stock from a great company with great numbers in 2018, but chances are pretty good that the numbers have changed since then.

WARNING

Great stocks don't always stay that way. A great selection that you're drawn to today may become tomorrow's pariah. Information, both good and bad, moves like lightning. Keep an eye on your stock company's numbers! For more information on a company's financial data, check out Chapter 4 in Book 3.

Heeding investing lessons from history

A growth stock isn't a creature like the Loch Ness monster — always talked about but rarely seen. Growth stocks have been part of the financial scene for nearly a century. Examples abound that offer rich information that you can apply to today's stock market environment. Look at past market winners, especially those during the bull market of the late 1990s and the bearish markets of 2000–2010, and ask yourself, "What made them profitable stocks?" These two time frames offer a stark contrast to each other. The 1990s were booming times for stocks, whereas more recent years were very tough and bearish.

Being aware and acting logically are as vital to successful stock investing as they are to any other pursuit. Over and over again, history gives you the formula for successful stock investing:

>> Pick a company that has strong fundamentals, including signs such as rising sales and earnings and low debt. (See Chapter 4 in Book 3.)

>> Make sure that the company is in a growing industry.

>> Fully participate in stocks that are benefiting from bullish market developments in the general economy.

>> During a bear market or in bearish trends, switch more of your money out of growth stocks (such as technology) and into defensive stocks (such as utilities).

>> Monitor your stocks. Hold onto stocks that continue to have growth potential, and sell those stocks with declining prospects.

Chapter 3

Investing for Income and Cash Flow

S tocks are well known for their ability to appreciate (for capital gains potential), but not enough credit is given regarding stocks' ability to boost your income and cash flow. Given that income will be a primary concern for many in the coming months and years (especially baby boomers and others concerned with retirement, pension issues, and so on), you should consider this to be an important chapter.

The first income feature is the obvious — dividends! Dividends have excellent features that make them very attractive, such as their ability to meet or exceed the rate of inflation and the fact that they are subject to lower taxes than, say, regular taxable interest or wages. Dividend-paying stocks (also called income stocks) deserve a spot in a variety of portfolios, especially those of investors at or near retirement. Also, younger folks (such as millennials) can gain long-term financial benefits from having dividends reinvested to compound their growth (such as with dividend reinvestment plans). This chapter shows you how to analyze income stocks with a few handy formulas, and describes several typical income stocks.

Understanding the Basics of Income Stocks

Dividend-paying stocks are a great consideration for those investors seeking greater income in their portfolios. Stocks with higher-than-average dividends are known as *income stocks.* Income stocks take on a dual role in that they can not only appreciate but also provide regular income. The following sections take a closer look at dividends and income stocks.

Getting a grip on dividends and dividend rates

When people talk about gaining income from stocks, they're usually talking about dividends. Dividends are pro rata distributions that treat every stockholder the same. A *dividend* is nothing more than pro rata periodic distributions of cash (or sometimes stock) to the stock owner. You purchase dividend stocks primarily for income — not for spectacular growth potential.

Dividends are sometimes confused with interest. However, dividends are payouts to owners, whereas *interest* is a payment to a creditor. Stock investors are considered part owners of the company they invest in and are entitled to dividends when they're issued. A bank, on the other hand, considers you a creditor when you open an account. The bank borrows your money and pays you interest on it.

A dividend is quoted as an annual dollar amount (or percentage yield) but is usually paid on a quarterly basis. For example, if a stock pays a dividend of $4 per share, you're probably paid $1 every quarter. If, in this example, you have 200 shares, you're paid $800 every year (if the dividend doesn't change during that period), or $200 per quarter. Getting that regular dividend check every three months (for as long as you hold the stock) can be a nice perk. If the company continues to do well, that dividend can grow over time. A good income stock has a higher-than-average dividend (typically 4 percent or higher).

REMEMBER

Dividend rates aren't guaranteed, and they are subject to the decisions of the stock issuer's board of directors — they can go up or down, or in some extreme cases, the dividend can be suspended or even discontinued. Fortunately, most companies that issue dividends continue them indefinitely and actually increase dividend payments from time to time. Historically, dividend increases have equaled (or exceeded) the rate of inflation.

Recognizing who's well-suited for income stocks

What type of person is best suited to income stocks? Income stocks can be appropriate for many investors, but they're especially well-suited for the following individuals:

>> **Conservative and novice investors:** Conservative investors like to see a slow-but-steady approach to growing their money while getting regular dividend checks. Novice investors who want to start slowly also benefit from income stocks.

>> **Retirees:** Growth investing (which is described in Chapter 2 of Book 3) is best suited for long-term needs, whereas income investing is best suited to current needs. Retirees may want some growth in their portfolios, but they're more concerned with regular income that can keep pace with inflation.

>> **Dividend reinvestment plan (DRP) investors:** For those investors who like to compound their money with DRPs, income stocks are perfect.

TIP

Given recent economic trends and conditions for the foreseeable future, dividends should be a mandatory part of the stock investor's wealth-building approach. This is especially true for those in or approaching retirement. Investing in stocks that have a reliable track record of increasing dividends is now easier than ever. There are, in fact, exchange-traded funds (ETFs) that are focused on stocks with a long and consistent track record of raising dividends (typically on an annual basis). ETFs such as the iShares Core High Dividend ETF (symbol HDV) hold 45–50 companies that have raised their dividends every year for ten years or longer. HDV paid a dividend of 24 cents in 2011, and that dividend went to 82 cents in 2019 — a 241 percent increase in eight years. Similar ETFs are available and can be found at sites such as www.etfdb.com (use search terms such as "high dividend," "dividend growth," or "dividend yield" to find them). Discover more about ETFs in Chapter 1 of Book 5.

Assessing the advantages of income stocks

Income stocks tend to be among the least volatile of all stocks, and many investors view them as defensive stocks. *Defensive stocks* are stocks of companies that sell goods and services that are generally needed no matter what shape the economy is in. (Don't confuse defensive stocks with *defense stocks,* which specialize in goods and equipment for the military.) Food, beverage, and utility companies are great examples of defensive stocks. Even when the economy is experiencing tough times, people still need to eat, drink, and turn on the lights. Companies that offer relatively high dividends also tend to be large firms in established, stable industries.

TIP

Some industries in particular are known for high-dividend stocks. Utilities (such as electric, gas, and water), real estate investment trusts (REITs), and the energy sector (oil and gas royalty trusts) are places where you definitely find income stocks. Yes, you can find high-dividend stocks in other industries, but you find a higher concentration of them in these industries. For more details, see the sections highlighting these industries later in this chapter.

Heeding the disadvantages of income stocks

Before you say, "Income stocks are great! I'll get my checkbook and buy a batch right now," take a look at the following potential disadvantages (ugh!). Income stocks do come with some fine print.

What goes up . . .

Income stocks can go down as well as up, just as any stock can. The factors that affect stocks in general — politics, megatrends, different kinds of risk, and so on — affect income stocks, too. Fortunately, income stocks don't get hit as hard as other stocks when the market is declining because high dividends tend to act as a support to the stock price. Therefore, income stocks' prices usually fall less dramatically than other stocks' prices in a declining market.

Interest-rate sensitivity

Income stocks can be sensitive to rising interest rates. When interest rates go up, other investments (such as corporate bonds, U.S. Treasury securities, and bank certificates of deposit) are more attractive. When your income stock yields 4 percent and interest rates go up to 5 percent, 6 percent, or higher, you may think, "Hmm. Why settle for a 4 percent yield when I can get better elsewhere?" As more and more investors sell their low-yield stocks, the prices for those stocks fall.

Another point to note is that rising interest rates may hurt the company's financial strength. If the company has to pay more interest, that may affect the company's earnings, which in turn may affect the company's ability to continue paying dividends.

REMEMBER

Dividend-paying companies that experience consistently falling revenues tend to cut dividends. In this case, *consistent* means two or more years.

The effect of inflation

Although many companies raise their dividends on a regular basis, some don't. Or if they do raise their dividends, the increases may be small. If income is your primary consideration, you want to be aware of this fact. If you're getting the same dividend year after year and this income is important to you, rising inflation becomes a problem.

Say that you have XYZ stock at $10 per share with an indicated annual dividend of 30 cents (the yield is 30 cents divided by $10, or 3 percent). If you have a yield of 3 percent two years in a row, how do you feel when inflation rises 6 percent one year and 7 percent the next year? Because inflation means your costs are rising, inflation shrinks the value of the dividend income you receive.

Fortunately, studies show that in general, dividends do better in inflationary environments than bonds and other fixed-rate investments. Usually, the dividends of companies that provide consumer staples (food, energy, and so on) meet or exceed the rate of inflation. This is why some investment gurus describe companies that pay growing dividends as having stocks that are "better than bonds."

Uncle Sam's cut

The government usually taxes dividends as ordinary income. Find out from your tax person whether potentially higher tax rates on dividends are in effect for the current or subsequent tax year.

STOCK DIVIDENDS — OR COMPANY DIVIDENDS?

Hearing the phrase "stock dividend" is common in financial discussions about the stock market. However, the reality is that dividends are not paid by stocks; they are paid pro rata distributions of cash by companies. It may sound like splitting hairs, but it is a fundamental difference. Stock prices are subject to the whims of market buying and selling — one day the share prices are up nicely; the next day prices go down when that day's headlines spook the market. Since the dividend is not volatile and it is paid with regularity (quarterly usually), it is more predictable, and investors should be in the business of "collecting cash flows" versus fretting over the ebb and flow of the market.

What does that mean? If a hundred shares of a given dividend-paying stock provide, say, $100 per year in annual dividends, the income-minded stock investor should keep a running tally of annual dividend amounts. That way, they keep investing until they reach a desired income level (such as $2,000 annual dividend income) and feel confident that this dividend income can be relatively reliable and will keep growing as payouts grow from company operations. Lastly, keep in mind that technically a "stock dividend" is actually a pro rata distribution of stock (and not cash).

Analyzing Income Stocks

As the preceding section explains, even conservative income investors can be confronted with different types of risk. Fortunately, this section helps you carefully choose income stocks so that you can minimize potential disadvantages.

TIP

Look at income stocks in the same way you do growth stocks when assessing the financial strength of a company. Getting nice dividends comes to a screeching halt if the company can't afford to pay them. If your budget depends on dividend income, then monitoring the company's financial strength is that much more important. You can apply the same techniques listed in Chapters 2 and 4 of Book 3 for assessing the financial strength of growth stocks to your assessment of income stocks.

Pinpointing your needs first

You choose income stocks primarily because you want or need income now. As a secondary point, income stocks have the potential for steady, long-term appreciation. So if you're investing for retirement needs that won't occur for another 20 years, maybe income stocks aren't suitable for you — a better choice may be to invest in growth stocks because they're more likely to grow your money faster over a lengthier investment term. (Find out who's best suited to income stocks earlier in this chapter.)

If you're certain you want income stocks, do a rough calculation to figure out how big a portion of your portfolio you want income stocks to occupy. Suppose that you need $25,000 in investment income to satisfy your current financial needs. If you have bonds that give you $20,000 in interest income, and you want the rest to come from dividends from income stocks, you need to choose stocks that pay you $5,000 in annual dividends. If you have $100,000 left to invest, you need a portfolio of income stocks that yields 5 percent ($5,000 divided by $100,000 equals a yield of 5 percent; see the following section for more).

You may ask, "Why not just buy $100,000 of bonds (for instance) that may yield at least 5 percent?" Well, if you're satisfied with that $5,000, and inflation for the foreseeable future is 0 or considerably less than 5 percent, then you have a point. Unfortunately, inflation (low or otherwise) will probably be with us for a long time. Fortunately, the steady growth of the dividends that income stocks provide is a benefit to you.

TIP

If you have income stocks and don't have any immediate need for the dividends, consider reinvesting the dividends in the company's stock.

REMEMBER

Every investor is different. If you're not sure about your current or future needs, your best choice is to consult with a financial planner.

Checking out yield

Because income stocks pay out dividends — income — you need to assess which stocks can give you the highest income. How do you do that? The main thing to look for is *yield*, which is the percentage rate of return paid on a stock in the form of dividends. Looking at a stock's dividend yield is the quickest way to find out how much money you'll earn versus other dividend-paying stocks (or even other investments, such as a bank account). Table 3-1 illustrates this point. Dividend yield is calculated in the following way:

Dividend yield = Dividend income ÷ Stock investment

TABLE 3-1 **Comparing Yields**

Investment	Type	Investment Amount	Annual Investment Income (Dividend)	Yield (Annual Investment Income Divided by Investment Amount)
Smith Co.	Common stock	$20 per share	$1.00 per share	5%
Jones Co.	Common stock	$30 per share	$1.50 per share	5%
Wilson Bank	Savings account	$1,000 deposit	$10 (interest)	1%

The next two sections use the information in Table 3-1 to compare the yields from different investments and to show how evaluating yield helps you choose the stock that earns you the most money.

REMEMBER

Don't stop scrutinizing stocks after you acquire them. You may make a great choice that gives you a great dividend, but that doesn't mean the stock will continue to perform indefinitely. Monitor the company's progress for as long as the stock is in your portfolio by using resources such as www.bloomberg.com and www.marketwatch.com.

Examining changes in yield

Most people have no problem understanding yield when it comes to bank accounts. If someone tells you that their bank certificate of deposit (CD) has an annual yield of 3.5 percent, you can easily figure out that if they deposit $1,000 in that account, a year later they'll have $1,035 (slightly more if you include compounding). The

CD's market value in this example is the same as the deposit amount — $1,000. That makes it easy to calculate.

REMEMBER

How about stocks? When you see a stock listed in the financial pages, the dividend yield is provided, along with the stock's price and annual dividend. The dividend yield in the financial pages is always calculated based on the closing price of the stock on that given day. Just keep in mind that based on supply and demand, stock prices will fluctuate throughout trading hours, so the yield changes throughout trading hours, too. So keep the following two things in mind when examining yield:

>> **The yield listed in the financial pages may not represent the yield you're receiving.** What if you bought stock in Smith Co. (see Table 3-1) a month ago at $20 per share? With an annual dividend of $1, you know your yield is 5 percent. But what if today Smith Co. is selling for $40 per share? If you look in the financial pages, the yield quoted is 2.5 percent. Gasp! Did the dividend get cut in half?! No, not really. You're still getting 5 percent because you bought the stock at $20 rather than the current $40 price; the quoted yield is for investors who purchase Smith Co. today. They pay $40 and get the $1 dividend, and they're locked into the current yield of 2.5 percent. Although Smith Co. may have been a good income investment for you a month ago, it's not such a hot pick today because the price of the stock has doubled, cutting the yield in half. Even though the dividend hasn't changed, the yield has changed dramatically because of the stock price change.

>> **Stock price affects how good of an investment the stock may be.** Another way to look at yield is by looking at the investment amount. Using Smith Co. in Table 3-1 as the example, the investor who bought, say, 100 shares of Smith Co. when they were $20 per share paid only $2,000 (100 shares multiplied by $20 — leave out commissions to make the example simple). If the same stock is purchased later at $40 per share, the total investment amount is $4,000 (100 shares multiplied by $40). In either case, the investor gets a total dividend income of $100 (100 shares multiplied by $1 dividend per share). Which investment is yielding more — the $2,000 investment or the $4,000 investment? Of course, it's better to get the income ($100 in this case) with the smaller investment (a 5 percent yield is better than a 2.5 percent yield).

Comparing yield between different stocks

All things being equal, choosing Smith Co. or Jones Co. is a coin toss. It's looking at your situation and each company's fundamentals and prospects that will sway you. What if Smith Co. is an auto stock (similar to General Motors in 2008) and Jones Co. is a utility serving the Las Vegas metro area? Now what? In 2008, the automotive industry struggled tremendously, but utilities were generally in much better shape. In that scenario, Smith Co.'s dividend is in jeopardy, whereas Jones Co.'s dividend is more secure. Another issue is the payout ratio (see the next section). Therefore, companies whose dividends have the same yield may still have different risks.

Looking at a stock's payout ratio

You can use the *payout ratio* to figure out what percentage of a company's earnings is being paid out in the form of dividends (earnings = sales – expenses). Keep in mind that companies pay dividends from their net earnings. (Technically, the money comes from the company's capital accounts, but that money ultimately comes from net earnings and capital infusions.) Given that, the company's earnings should always be higher than the dividends the company pays out. An investor wants to see total earnings growth that exceeds the total amount paid for dividends. Here's how to figure a payout ratio:

Dividend (per share) ÷ Earnings (per share) = Payout ratio

Say that the company CashFlow Now, Inc. (CFN), has annual earnings (or net income) of $1 million. Total dividends are to be paid out of $500,000, and the company has 1 million outstanding shares. Using those numbers, you know that CFN's earnings per share (EPS) are $1 ($1 million in earnings divided by 1 million shares) and that it pays an annual dividend of 50 cents per share ($500,000 divided by 1 million shares). The dividend payout ratio is 50 percent (the 50-cent dividend is 50 percent of the $1 EPS). This number is a healthy dividend payout ratio because even if CFN's earnings fall by 10 percent or 20 percent, plenty of room still exists to pay dividends.

TIP

If you're concerned about your dividend income's safety, regularly watch the payout ratio. The maximum acceptable payout ratio should be 80 percent, and a good range is 50 to 70 percent. A payout ratio of 60 percent or lower is considered very safe (the lower the percentage, the safer the dividend).

REMEMBER

When a company suffers significant financial difficulties, its ability to pay dividends is compromised. Good examples of stocks that have had their dividends cut in recent years due to financial difficulties are mortgage companies in the wake of the housing bubble bursting and the fallout from the subprime debt fiasco. Mortgage companies received less and less income due to mortgage defaults, which forced the lowering of dividends as cash inflow shrunk. So if you need dividend income to help you pay your bills, you better be aware of the dividend payout ratio.

Studying a company's bond rating

Bond rating? Huh? What's that got to do with dividend-paying stocks? Actually, a company's bond rating is very important to income stock investors. The bond rating offers insight into the company's financial strength. Bonds get rated for quality for the same reasons that consumer agencies rate products like cars or toasters. Standard & Poor's (S&P) and Moody's are the major independent rating agencies that look into bond issuers. They look at the bond issuer and ask, "Does this bond issuer have the financial strength to pay back the bond and the interest as stipulated in the bond indenture?"

To understand why this rating is important, consider the following:

>> **A good bond rating means that the company is strong enough to pay its obligations.** These obligations include expenses, payments on debts, and declared dividends. If a bond rating agency gives the company a high rating (or if it raises the rating), that's a great sign for anyone holding the company's debt or receiving dividends.

WARNING

>> **If a bond rating agency lowers the rating, that means the company's financial strength is deteriorating** — a red flag for anyone who owns the company's bonds or stock. A lower bond rating today may mean trouble for the dividend later on.

>> **A poor bond rating means that the company is having difficulty paying its obligations.** If the company can't pay all its obligations, it has to choose which ones to pay. More times than not, a financially troubled company chooses to cut dividends or (in a worst-case scenario) not pay dividends at all.

REMEMBER

The highest rating issued by S&P is AAA. The grades AAA, AA, and A are considered *investment grade,* or of high quality. Bs and Cs indicate a medium grade, and anything lower than that is considered poor or very risky (the bonds are referred to as *junk bonds*). So if you see an XXX rating, then . . . gee . . . you better stay away!

Diversifying your stocks

If most of your dividend income is from stock in a single company or single industry, consider reallocating your investment to avoid having all your eggs in one basket. Concerns about diversification apply to income stocks as well as growth stocks. If all your income stocks are in the electric utility industry, then any problems in that industry are potential problems for your portfolio as well.

Exploring Some Typical Income Stocks

Although virtually every industry has stocks that pay dividends, some industries have more dividend-paying stocks than others. You won't find too many dividend-paying income stocks in the computer or biotech industries, for instance. The reason is that these types of companies need a lot of money to finance expensive research and development (R&D) projects to create new products. Without R&D, the company can't create new products to fuel sales, growth, and future earnings. Computer, biotech, and other innovative industries are better for growth investors. Keep reading for the scoop on stocks that work well for income investors.

It's electric! Utilities

Public utilities are among the stock market's most reliable dividend payers. They generate a large cash flow (if you don't believe me, look at your gas and electric bills!). Many investors have at least one utility company in their portfolio. Income-minded investors (especially retirees) should seriously consider utilities — and there are great utilities ETFs as well (see Chapter 1 in Book 5 for more on ETFs). Investing in your own local utility isn't a bad idea — at least it makes paying the utility bill less painful.

REMEMBER

Before you invest in a public utility, consider the following:

>> **The utility company's financial condition:** Is the company making money, and are its sales and earnings growing from year to year? Make sure the utility's bonds are rated A or higher (see the earlier section "Studying a company's bond rating").

>> **The company's dividend payout ratio:** Because utilities tend to have a good cash flow, don't be too concerned if the ratio reaches 70 percent. From a safety point of view, however, the lower the rate, the better. See the earlier section "Looking at a stock's payout ratio" for more on payout ratios.

>> **The company's geographic location:** If the utility covers an area that's doing well and offers an increasing population base and business expansion, that bodes well for your stock. A good resource for researching population and business data is the U.S. Census Bureau (www.census.gov).

An interesting mix: Real estate investment trusts (REITs)

Real estate investment trusts (REITs) are a special breed of stock. A *REIT* is an investment that has elements of both a stock and a *mutual fund* (a pool of money received from investors that's managed by an investment company):

>> A REIT resembles a stock in that it's a company whose stock is publicly traded on the major stock exchanges, and it has the usual features that you expect from a stock — it can be bought and sold easily through a broker, income is given to investors as dividends, and so on.

>> A REIT resembles a mutual fund in that it doesn't make its money selling goods and services; it makes its money by buying, selling, and managing an investment portfolio of real estate investments. It generates revenue from rents and property leases, as any landlord does. In addition, some REITs own mortgages, and they gain income from the interest.

TECHNICAL STUFF

REITs are called *trusts* only because they meet the requirements of the Real Estate Investment Trust Act of 1960. This act exempts REITs from corporate income tax and capital gains taxes as long as they meet certain criteria, such as dispensing 90 percent of their net income to shareholders. This provision is the reason why REITs generally issue generous dividends. Beyond this status, REITs are, in a practical sense, like any other publicly traded company.

The main advantages to investing in REITs include the following:

>> Unlike other types of real estate investing, REITs are easy to buy and sell (REITs are more liquid than other types of traditional real estate investing). You can buy a REIT by making a phone call to a broker or visiting a broker's website, just as you can to purchase any stock.

>> REITs have higher-than-average yields. Because they must distribute at least 90 percent of their income to shareholders, their dividends usually yield a return of 5 to 10 percent.

>> REITs involve a lower risk than the direct purchase of real estate because they use a portfolio approach diversified among many properties. Because you're investing in a company that buys the real estate, you don't have to worry about managing the properties — the company's management does that on a full-time basis. Usually, the REIT doesn't just manage one property; it's diversified in a portfolio of different properties.

>> Investing in a REIT is affordable for small investors. REIT shares usually trade in the $10 to $40 range, meaning that you can invest with very little money.

REITs do have disadvantages. Although they tend to be diversified with various properties, they're still susceptible to risks tied to the general real estate sector. Real estate investing reached manic, record-high levels during 2000–2007, which meant that a downturn was likely. Whenever you invest in an asset (like real estate or REITs in recent years) that has already skyrocketed due to artificial stimulants (in the case of real estate, very low interest rates and too much credit and debt), the potential losses can offset any potential (unrealized) income.

When you're looking for a REIT to invest in, analyze it the way you'd analyze a property. Look at the location and type of property. If shopping malls are booming in California and your REIT buys and sells shopping malls in California, then you'll probably do well. However, if your REIT invests in office buildings across the country and the office building market is overbuilt and having tough times, you'll have a tough time, too.

Many of the dangers of the "housing bubble" have passed, and investors can start looking at real estate investments (such as REITs) with less anxiety. However, choosing REITs with a view toward quality and strong fundamentals (location, potential rents, and so forth) is still a good idea.

Business development companies (BDCs)

For those seeking a relatively high dividend with some growth potential, consider taking a look at business development companies (BDCs). They sound a little arcane but they can be bought as easily as a stock, and their setup is not that difficult to understand. A BDC is essentially a hybrid between a venture capital company and a mutual fund, and it trades like a closed-end fund. A closed-end fund functions like a regular mutual fund, but it is listed in the same way as a stock and has a finite number of total shares. Regular mutual funds are referred to as "open-ended," which means that their shares are issued (or redeemed) and there is no finite number of shares as with closed-end funds.

Like a venture capital firm, a BDC invests in companies that are small or midsized and that need capital to grow in their early stages of development. A BDC is like a mutual fund in that it will invest in a batch of companies so there is some sense of diversification. The companies that the BDC invests in tend to be in a particular niche such as biotech, robotics, or another "sunrise" industry. As part of the financial structure, the companies receiving the funding from the BDC pay back the financing through higher fees and interest, so BDCs tend to have a high dividend.

TIP

Given that, a BDC can provide good dividend income, but keep in mind that there is higher risk since the companies are still in the early stages of development. For more details on BDCs, check out resources such as the following:

>> CEF Connect (www.cefconnect.com)

>> Closed-End Fund Advisors (www.cefdata.com)

>> Closed-End Fund Association (www.cefa.com/)

Chapter **4**

Using Basic Accounting to Choose Winning Stocks

Too often, the only number investors look at when they look at a stock is the stock's price. Yet what determines the stock price is the company behind that single number. To make a truly good choice in the world of stocks, you have to consider the company's financial information. What does it take to see these important numbers?

This chapter takes the mystery out of the numbers behind the stock. The most tried-and-true method for picking a good stock starts with picking a good company. Picking a company means looking at its products, services, industry, and financial strength. Considering the problems that the market has witnessed in recent years — such as subprime debt problems and derivative meltdowns wreaking havoc on public companies and financial firms — this chapter is more important than ever. Understanding the basics behind the numbers can save your portfolio.

Recognizing Value When You See It

If you pick a stock based on the value of the underlying company that issues it, you're a *value investor* — an investor who looks at a company's value to judge whether you can purchase the stock at a good price. Companies have value the same way many things have value, such as eggs or elephant-foot umbrella stands. And there's a fair price to buy them at, too. Take eggs, for example. You can eat them and have a tasty treat while getting nutrition as well. But would you buy an egg for $1,000 (and no, you're not a starving millionaire on a deserted island)? Of course not. But what if you could buy an egg for 5 cents? At that point, it has value *and* a good price. This kind of deal is a value investor's dream.

Value investors analyze a company's *fundamentals* (sales, earnings, assets, net worth, and so on) to see whether the information justifies purchasing the stock. They see whether the stock price is low relative to these verifiable, quantifiable factors. Therefore, value investors use *fundamental analysis,* whereas other investors may use technical analysis. *Technical analysis* looks at stock charts and statistical data, such as trading volume and historical stock prices. Some investors use a combination of both strategies.

History has shown that the most successful long-term investors have typically been value investors using fundamental analysis as their primary investing approach. The following sections describe different kinds of value and explain how to spot a company's value in several places.

Understanding different types of value

Value may seem like a murky or subjective term, but it's the essence of good stock-picking. You can measure value in different ways (as you discover in the following sections), so you need to know the differences and understand the impact that value has on your investment decisions.

Market value

REMEMBER

When you hear someone quoting a stock at $47 per share, that price reflects the stock's market value. The total market valuation of a company's stock is also referred to as its *market cap* or *market capitalization.* How do you determine a company's market cap? With the following simple formula:

Market capitalization = Share price × Number of shares outstanding

If Bolshevik Corp.'s stock is $35 per share, and it has 10 million shares outstanding (or the number of shares issued less treasury shares), its market cap is $350 million. Granted, $350 million may sound like a lot of money, but Bolshevik Corp. is considered a small-cap stock.

Who sets the market value of stock? The market, of course! Millions of investors buying and selling directly and through intermediaries such as mutual funds determine the market value of any particular stock. If the market perceives that the company is desirable, investor demand for the company's stock pushes up the share price.

WARNING

The problem with market valuation is that it's not always a good indicator of a good investment. In recent years, plenty of companies have had astronomical market values, yet they've proven to be very risky investments. For example, think about a company that was set to go public (in an initial public offering, or IPO) in 2019. WeWork was expected to have a market value (before going public) as high as $47 billion. Investors couldn't obtain complete financial information on this highly anticipated company, but everyone assumed it was a big deal due to its multibillion-dollar market value and the involvement of notable financial institutions such as JP Morgan and SoftBank. Hey, what could go wrong? After the discovery of financial difficulties and large losses, WeWork's IPO was cancelled, and the market value totally evaporated and hit zero. Yikes! Because market value is a direct result of buying and selling by stock investors, it can be a fleeting thing. This precariousness is why investors must understand the company behind the stock price and its market valuation.

Book value and intrinsic value

Book value (also referred to as *accounting value*) looks at a company from a balance sheet perspective (assets minus liabilities equals net worth, or *stockholders' equity*). It's a way of judging a firm by its net worth to see whether the stock's market value is reasonable compared to the company's intrinsic value. *Intrinsic value* is tied to what the market price of a company's assets — both *tangible* (such as equipment) and *intangible* (such as patents) — would be if they were sold.

Generally, market value tends to be higher than book value. If market value is substantially higher than book value, the value investor becomes more reluctant to buy that particular stock because it's overvalued. The closer the stock's market capitalization is to the book value, the safer the investment.

WARNING

You should be cautious with a stock whose market value is more than five times its book value. If, for example, the market value is north of $2 billion and the book value is less than $500 million, that's a good indicator that the business may be *overvalued,* or valued at a higher price than its book value and ability to generate a profit. Just understand that the farther the market value is from the company's book value, the more you'll pay for the company's real potential value. And the more you pay for the company's real value, the greater the risk that the company's market value (the stock price, that is) can decrease.

Sales value and earnings value

A company's intrinsic value is directly tied to its ability to make money. For this reason, many analysts like to value stocks from the perspective of the company's income statement. Two common barometers of value are expressed in ratios: the price to sales ratio (PSR) and the price-to-earnings (P/E) ratio. In both instances, the price is a reference to the company's market value (as reflected in its share price). Sales and earnings are references to the firm's ability to make money. These two ratios are covered more fully in the later section "Tooling around with ratios."

REMEMBER

For investors, the general approach is clear. The closer the market value is to the company's intrinsic value, the better. And, of course, if the market value is lower than the company's intrinsic value, you have a potential bargain worthy of a closer look. Part of looking closer means examining the company's income statement (which is discussed later in this chapter), also called the *profit and loss statement*, or simply the *P&L*. A low price-to-sales ratio is 1, a medium PSR is between 1 and 2, and a high PSR is 3 or higher.

Putting the pieces together

REMEMBER

When you look at a company from a value-oriented perspective, here are some of the most important items to consider (see the later section "Accounting for Value" for more information):

>> **The balance sheet, to figure out the company's net worth:** Value investors don't buy a company's stock because it's cheap; they buy it because it's *undervalued* (the company is worth more than the price its stock reflects — its market value is as close as possible to its book value).

>> **The income statement, to figure out the company's profitability:** A company may be undervalued from a simple comparison of the book value and the market value, but that doesn't mean it's a screaming buy. For example, what if you find out that a company is in trouble and losing money this year? Do you buy its stock then? No, you don't. Why invest in the stock of a losing company? (If you do, you aren't investing — you're gambling or speculating.) The heart of a firm's value, besides its net worth, is its ability to generate profit.

>> **Ratios that let you analyze just how well (or not so well) the company is doing:** Value investors basically look for a bargain. That being the case, they generally don't look at companies that everyone is talking about, because by that point, the stock of those companies ceases to be a bargain. The value investor searches for a stock that will eventually be discovered by the market and then watches as the stock price goes up. But before you bother digging into the fundamentals to find that bargain stock, first make sure that the company is making money.

The more ways that you can look at a company and see value, the better:

>> **Examine the P/E ratio.** Does the company have one? (This question may sound dumb, but if the company is losing money, it may not have one.) Does the P/E ratio look reasonable or is it in triple-digit, nosebleed territory?

>> **Check out the debt load.** Next, look at the company's *debt load* (the total amount of liabilities). Is it less than the company's equity? Are sales healthy and increasing from the prior year? Does the firm compare favorably in these categories versus other companies in the same industry?

TIP

>> **Think in terms of 10s.** Simplicity is best. If net income is rising by 10 percent or more, that's fine. If the company is in the top 10 percent of its industry, that's great. If the industry is growing by 10 percent or better (sales and so on), that's terrific. If sales are up 10 percent or more from the prior year, that's wonderful. A great company doesn't have to have all these things going for it, but it should have as many of these things happening as possible to ensure greater potential success.

Does every company/industry have to neatly fit these criteria? No, of course not. But it doesn't hurt you to be as picky as possible. You need to find only a handful of stocks from thousands of choices.

TIP

Value investors can find thousands of companies that have value, but they can probably buy only a handful at a truly good price. The number of stocks that can be bought at a good price is relative to the market. In mature *bull markets* (markets in a prolonged period of rising prices), a good price is hard to find because most stocks have probably seen significant price increases, but in *bear markets* (markets in a prolonged period of falling prices), good companies at bargain prices are easier to come by.

Accounting for Value

Profit is to a company what oxygen is to you and me. Without profit, a company can't survive, much less thrive. Without profit, it can't provide jobs, pay taxes, and invest in new products, equipment, or innovation. Without profit, the company eventually goes bankrupt, and the price of its stock plummets toward zero.

In the heady days leading up to the bear market of 2008–2009, many investors lost a lot of money simply because they invested in stocks of companies that weren't making a profit. Lots of public companies ended up like bugs that just didn't see the windshield coming their way. Companies such as Bear Stearns entered the graveyard of rather-be-forgotten stocks. Stock investors as a group lost trillions of dollars investing in glitzy companies that sounded good but weren't making money. When their brokers were saying, "buy, buy, buy," their hard-earned money was saying, "bye, bye, bye!" What were they thinking?

Stock investors need to pick up some rudimentary knowledge of accounting to round out their stock-picking prowess and to be sure that they're getting a good value for their investment dollars. Accounting is the language of business. If you don't understand basic accounting, you'll have difficulty being a successful investor. Investing without accounting knowledge is like traveling without a map. However, if you can run a household budget, using accounting analysis to evaluate stocks is easier than you think, as you find out in the following sections.

TIP

Finding the relevant financial data on a company isn't difficult in the age of information and 24-hour internet access. Websites such as www.nasdaq.com can give you the most recent balance sheets and income statements of most public companies. You can find out more about public information and company research in Chapter 1 of Book 3.

Breaking down the balance sheet

REMEMBER

A company's balance sheet gives you a financial snapshot of what the company looks like in terms of the following equation:

Assets – Liabilities = Net worth (or net equity)

The following sections list the questions that a balance sheet can answer and explain how to judge a company's strength over time from a balance sheet.

Answering a few balance sheet questions

Analyze the following items that you find on the balance sheet:

>> **Total assets:** Have they increased from the prior year? If not, was it because of the sale of an asset or a write-off (uncollectable accounts receivable, for example)?

>> **Financial assets.** In recent years, many companies (especially banks and brokerage firms) had questionable financial assets (such as subprime mortgages and specialized bonds) that went bad, and they had to write them off as unrecoverable losses. Does the company you're analyzing have a large exposure to financial assets that are low-quality (and hence, risky) debt?

>> **Inventory:** Is inventory higher or lower than last year? If sales are flat but inventory is growing, that may be a problem.

>> **Debt:** Debt is the biggest weakness on the corporate balance sheet. Make sure that debt isn't a growing item and that it's under control. In recent years, debt has become a huge problem.

>> **Derivatives:** A *derivative* is a speculative and complex financial instrument that doesn't constitute ownership of an asset (such as a stock, bond, or commodity) but is a promise to convey ownership. Some derivatives are quite acceptable because they're used as protective or hedging vehicles (this use isn't my primary concern). However, they're frequently used to generate income and can then carry risks that can increase liabilities. Standard options and futures are examples of derivatives on a regulated exchange, but the derivatives we're talking about here are a different animal and in an unregulated part of the financial world. They have a book value exceeding $600 trillion and can easily devastate a company, sector, or market (as the credit crisis of 2008 showed).

WARNING

Find out whether the company dabbles in these complicated, dicey, leveraged financial instruments. Find out (from the company's 10K report) whether it has derivatives and, if so, the total amount. Having derivatives that are valued higher than the company's net equity may cause tremendous problems. Derivatives problems sank many organizations ranging from stodgy banks (Barings Bank of England) to affluent counties (Orange County, California) to once-respected hedge funds (LTCM) to infamous corporations (Enron in 2001 and Glencore in 2015).

>> **Equity:** *Equity* is the company's net worth (what's left in the event that all the assets are used to pay off all the company debts). The stockholders' equity should be increasing steadily by at least 10 percent per year. If not, find out why.

Table 4-1 shows you a brief example of a balance sheet.

TABLE 4-1

XYZ Balance Sheet — December 31, 2021

Assets (What the Company Owns)	Amount
1. Cash and inventory	$5,000
2. Equipment and other assets	$7,000
3. TOTAL ASSETS (Item 1 plus Item 2)	$12,000
Liabilities (What the Company Owes)	Amount
4. Short-term debt	$1,500
5. Other debt	$2,500
6. TOTAL LIABILITIES (Item 4 plus Item 5)	$4,000
7. NET EQUITY (Item 3 minus Item 6)	$8,000

By looking at a company's balance sheet, you can address the following questions:

>> **What does the company own (assets)?** The company can own assets, which can be financial, tangible, and/or intangible. An *asset* is anything that has value or that can be converted to or sold for cash. Financial assets can be cash, investments (such as stocks or bonds of other companies), or accounts receivable. Assets can be tangible items such as inventory, equipment, and/or buildings. They can also be intangible things such as licenses, trademarks, or copyrights.

>> **What does the company owe (liabilities)?** A *liability* is anything of value that the company must ultimately pay someone else for. Liabilities can be invoices (accounts payable) or short-term or long-term debt.

>> **What is the company's net equity (net worth)?** After you subtract the liabilities from the assets, the remainder is called *net worth, net equity,* or *net stockholders' equity.* This number is critical when calculating a company's book value.

REMEMBER

Assessing a company's financial strength over time

The logic behind the assets/liabilities relationship of a company is the same as that of your own household. When you look at a snapshot of your own finances (your personal balance sheet), how can you tell whether you're doing well? Odds are that you start by comparing some numbers. If your net worth is $5,000, you may say, "That's great!" But a more appropriate remark is something like, "That's great compared to, say, a year ago."

TIP

Compare a company's balance sheet at a recent point in time to a past time. You should do this comparative analysis with all the key items on the balance sheet, which are listed in the preceding section, to see the company's progress (or lack thereof). Is it growing its assets and/or shrinking its debt? Most important, is the company's net worth growing? Has it grown by at least 10 percent since a year ago? All too often, investors stop doing their homework after they make an initial investment. You should continue to look at the firm's numbers regularly so that you can be ahead of the curve. If the business starts having problems, you can get out before the rest of the market starts getting out (which causes the stock price to fall).

To judge the financial strength of a company, ask yourself the following questions:

>> **Are the company's assets greater in value than they were three months ago, a year ago, or two years ago?** Compare current asset size to the most recent two years to make sure that the company is growing in size and financial strength.

>> **How do the individual items compare with prior periods?** Some particular assets that you want to take note of are cash, inventory, and accounts receivable.

>> **Are liabilities such as accounts payable and debt about the same, lower, or higher compared to prior periods? Are they growing at a similar, faster, or slower rate than the company's assets?** Debt that rises faster and higher than items on the other side of the balance sheet is a warning sign of pending financial problems.

>> **Is the company's net worth or equity greater than the preceding year? And is that year's equity greater than the year before?** In a healthy company, the net worth is constantly rising. As a general rule, in good economic times, net worth should be at least 10 percent higher than the preceding year. In tough economic times (such as a recession), 5 percent is acceptable. Seeing the net worth grow at a rate of 15 percent or higher is great.

Looking at the income statement

REMEMBER

Where do you look if you want to find out what a company's profit is? Check out the firm's income statement. It reports, in detail, a simple accounting equation that you probably already know:

Sales – Expenses = Net profit (or net earnings, or net income)

Look at the following figures found on the income statement:

>> **Sales:** Are they increasing? If not, why not? By what percentage are sales increasing? Preferably, they should be 10 percent higher than the year before. Sales are, after all, where the money comes from to pay for all the company's activities (such as expenses) and create subsequent profits.

>> **Expenses:** Do you see any unusual items? Are total expenses reported higher than the prior year, and if so, by how much? If the total is significantly higher, why? A company with large, rising expenses will see profits suffer, which isn't good for the stock price.

>> **Research and development (R&D):** How much is the company spending on R&D? Companies that rely on new product development (such as pharmaceuticals or biotech firms) should spend at least as much as they did the year before (preferably more) because new products mean future earnings and growth.

>> **Earnings:** This figure reflects the bottom line. Are total earnings higher than the year before? How about earnings from operations (leaving out expenses such as taxes and interest)? The earnings section is the heart and soul of the income statement and of the company itself. Out of all the numbers in the financial statements, earnings have the greatest single impact on the company's stock price.

Table 4-2 shows you a brief example of an income statement.

TABLE 4-2

XYZ Income Statement — December 31, 2021

Total Sales (Or Revenue)	Amount
1. Sales of products	$11,000
2. Sales of services	$3,000
3. TOTAL SALES (Item 1 plus Item 2)	$14,000
Expenses	Amount
4. Marketing and promotion	$2,000
5. Payroll costs	$9,000
6. Other costs	$1,500
7. TOTAL EXPENSES (Item 4 plus Item 5 plus Item 6)	$12,500
8. NET INCOME (Item 3 minus Item 7) (In this case, it's a net profit)	$1,500

Looking at the income statement, an investor can try to answer the following questions:

>> **What sales did the company make?** Businesses sell products and services that generate revenue (known as *sales* or *gross sales*). Sales also are referred to as the *top line.*

>> **What expenses did the company incur?** In generating sales, companies pay expenses such as payroll, utilities, advertising, administration, and so on.

>> **What is the net profit?** Also called *net earnings* or *net income,* net profit is the *bottom line.* After paying for all expenses, what profit did the company make?

The information you glean should give you a strong idea about a firm's current financial strength and whether it's successfully increasing sales, holding down expenses, and ultimately maintaining profitability. You can find out more about sales, expenses, and profits in the sections that follow.

Sales

Sales refers to the money that a company receives as customers buy its goods and/ or services. It's a simple item on the income statement and a useful number to look at. Analyzing a business by looking at its sales is called *top line analysis.*

As an investor, you should take into consideration the following points about sales:

>> **Sales should be increasing.** A healthy, growing company has growing sales. They should grow at least 10 percent from the prior year, and you should look at the most recent three years.

>> **Core sales (sales of those products or services that the company specializes in) should be increasing.** Frequently, the sales figure has a lot of stuff lumped into it. Maybe the company sells widgets (what the heck is a widget, anyway?), but the core sales shouldn't include other things, such as the sale of a building or other unusual items. Take a close look. Isolate the firm's primary offerings and ask whether these sales are growing at a reasonable rate (such as 10 percent).

>> **Does the company have odd items or odd ways of calculating sales?** In the late 1990s, many companies boosted their sales by aggressively offering affordable financing with easy repayment terms. Say you find out that Suspicious Sales Inc. (SSI) had annual sales of $50 million, reflecting a 25 percent increase from the year before. Looks great! But what if you find out that $20 million of that sales number comes from sales made on credit that the company extended to buyers? Some companies that use this approach later have to write off losses as uncollectable debt because the customers ultimately can't pay for the goods.

TIP

If you want to get a good clue as to whether a company is artificially boosting sales, check its accounts receivable (listed in the asset section of its balance sheet). *Accounts receivable* refers to money that is owed to the company for goods that customers have purchased on credit. If you find out that sales went up by $10 million (great!) but accounts receivable went up by $20 million (uh-oh), something just isn't right. That may be a sign that the financing terms were too easy, and the company may have a problem collecting payment (especially in a recession).

Expenses

How much a company spends has a direct relationship to its profitability. If spending isn't controlled or held at a sustainable level, it may spell trouble for the business.

When you look at a company's expense items, consider the following:

>> **Compare expense items to the prior period.** Are expenses higher than, lower than, or about the same as those from the prior period? If the difference is significant, you should see commensurate benefits elsewhere. In other words, if overall expenses are 10 percent higher compared to the prior period, are sales at least 10 percent more during the same period?

>> **Are some expenses too high?** Look at the individual expense items. Are they significantly higher than the year before? If so, why?

>> **Have any unusual items been expensed?** An unusual expense isn't necessarily a negative. Expenses may be higher than usual if a company writes off uncollectable accounts receivable as a bad debt expense. Doing so inflates the total expenses and subsequently results in lower earnings. Pay attention to nonrecurring charges that show up on the income statement and determine whether they make sense.

Profit

Earnings or profit is the single most important item on the income statement. It's also the one that receives the most attention in the financial media. When a company makes a profit, it's usually reported in both absolute dollars and as earnings per share (EPS). So if you hear that XYZ Corporation (yes, the infamous XYZ Corp.!) beat last quarter's earnings by a penny, here's how to translate that news. Suppose that the company made $1 per share this quarter and 99 cents per share last quarter. If that company had 100 million shares of stock outstanding, its profit this quarter is $100 million (the EPS times the number of shares outstanding), which is $1 million more than it made in the prior quarter ($1 million is 1 cent per share times 100 million shares).

TIP

Don't simply look at current earnings as an isolated figure. Always compare current earnings to earnings in past periods (usually a year). For example, if you're looking at a retailer's fourth-quarter results, don't compare them with the retailer's third-quarter outcome. Doing so is like comparing apples to oranges. What if the company usually does well during the December holidays but poorly in the fall? In that case, you don't get a fair comparison.

A strong company should show consistent earnings growth from the period before (such as the prior year or the same quarter from the prior year), and you should check the period before that, too, so that you can determine whether earnings are consistently rising over time. Earnings growth is an important barometer of the company's potential growth and bodes well for the stock price.

When you look at earnings, here are some things to consider:

>> **Total earnings:** This item is the most watched. Total earnings should grow year to year by at least 10 percent.

>> **Operational earnings:** Break down the total earnings, and look at a key subset — that portion of earnings derived from the company's core activity. Is the company continuing to make money from its primary goods and services?

>> **Nonrecurring items:** Are earnings higher (or lower) than usual or than expected, and if so, why? Frequently, the difference results from items such as the sale of an asset or a large depreciation write-off.

TIP

Try to keep percentages as simple as possible. Ten percent is a good number because it's easy to calculate, and it's a good benchmark. However, 5 percent isn't unacceptable if you're talking about tough times, such as a recession. Obviously, if sales, earnings, and/or net worth are hitting or surpassing 15 percent, that's great.

Tooling around with ratios

A *ratio* is a helpful numerical tool that you can use to find out the relationship between two or more figures found in a company's financial data. A ratio can add meaning to a number or put it in perspective. Ratios sound complicated, but they're easier to understand than you may think.

Say that you're considering a stock investment and the company you're looking at has earnings of $1 million this year. You may think that's a nice profit, but in order for this amount to be meaningful, you have to compare it to something. What if you find out that the other companies in the industry (of similar size and scope) had earnings of $500 million? Does that change your thinking? Or what if the same company had earnings of $75 million in the prior period? Does that change your mind?

Two key ratios to be aware of are

>> Price-to-earnings (P/E) ratio

>> Price to sales ratio (PSR)

TIP

Every investor wants to find stocks that have a 20 percent average growth rate over the past five years and have a low P/E ratio (sounds like a dream). Use stock screening tools available for free on the internet to do your research. A *stock screening tool* lets you plug in numbers, such as sales or earnings, and ratios, such as the P/E ratio or the debt to equity ratio, and then click! — up come stocks that fit your criteria. These tools are a good starting point for serious investors. Many brokers have them at their websites (such as Charles Schwab at www.schwab.com and E*TRADE at www.etrade.com). You can also find some excellent stock screening tools at Yahoo! Finance (finance.yahoo.com), Bloomberg (www.bloomberg.com), Nasdaq (www.nasdaq.com), and MarketWatch (www.marketwatch.com).

The P/E ratio

The *price-to-earnings (P/E) ratio* is very important in analyzing a potential stock investment because it's one of the most widely regarded barometers of a company's value, and it's usually reported along with the company's stock price in the financial page listing. The major significance of the P/E ratio is that it establishes a direct relationship between the bottom line of a company's operations — the earnings (or net profit) — and the stock price.

The *P* in P/E stands for the stock's current price. The *E* is for earnings per share (typically the most recent 12 months of earnings). The P/E ratio is also referred to as the *earnings multiple* or just *multiple*.

REMEMBER

You calculate the P/E ratio by dividing the price of the stock by the earnings per share. If the price of a single share of stock is $10 and the earnings (on a per-share basis) are $1, then the P/E is 10. If the stock price goes to $35 per share and the earnings are unchanged, then the P/E is 35. Basically, the higher the P/E, the more you pay for the company's earnings.

Why would you buy stock in one company with a relatively high P/E ratio instead of investing in another company with a lower P/E ratio? Keep in mind that investors buy stocks based on expectations. They may bid up the price of the stock (subsequently raising the stock's P/E ratio) because they feel that the company will have increased earnings in the near future. Perhaps they feel that the company has great potential (a pending new invention or lucrative business deal) that will eventually make it more profitable. More profitability in turn has a beneficial impact on the firm's stock price. The danger with a high P/E is that if the company doesn't achieve the hoped-for results, the stock price can fall.

TIP

You should look at two types of P/E ratios to get a balanced picture of the company's value:

>> **Trailing P/E:** This P/E is the most frequently quoted because it deals with existing data. The trailing P/E uses the most recent 12 months of earnings in its calculation.

>> **Forward P/E:** This P/E is based on projections or expectations of earnings in the coming 12-month period. Although this P/E may seem preferable because it looks into the near future, it's still considered an estimate that may or may not prove to be accurate.

The following example illustrates the importance of the P/E ratio. Say that you want to buy a business, and we're selling a business. You come to us and say, "What do you have to offer?" We say, "Have we got a deal for you! We operate a retail business downtown that sells spatulas. The business nets a cool $2,000 profit per year." You reluctantly say, "Uh, okay, what's the asking price for the business?" We reply, "You can have it for only $1 million! What do you say?"

If you're sane, odds are that you politely turn down that offer. Even though the business is profitable (a cool $2,000 a year), you'd be crazy to pay a million bucks for it. In other words, the business is way overvalued (too expensive for what you're getting in return for your investment dollars). The million dollars would generate a better rate of return elsewhere and probably with less risk. As for the business, the P/E ratio of 500 ($1 million divided by $2,000) is outrageous. This is definitely a case of an overvalued company — and a lousy investment.

What if we offered the business for $12,000? Does that price make more sense? Yes. The P/E ratio is a more reasonable 6 ($12,000 divided by $2,000). In other words, the business pays for itself in about 6 years (versus 500 years in the prior example).

REMEMBER

Looking at the P/E ratio offers a shortcut for investors asking the question, "Is this stock overvalued?" As a general rule, the lower the P/E, the safer (or more conservative) the stock is. The reverse is more noteworthy: The higher the P/E, the greater the risk.

When someone refers to a P/E as high or low, you have to ask the question, "Compared to what?" A P/E of 30 is considered very high for a large-cap electric utility but quite reasonable for a small-cap, high-technology firm. Keep in mind that phrases such as *large cap* and *small cap* are just a reference to the company's market value or size. *Cap* is short for *capitalization* (the total number of shares of stock outstanding multiplied by the share price).

The following basic points can help you evaluate P/E ratios:

>> **Compare a company's P/E ratio with its industry.** Electric utility industry stocks, for example, generally have a P/E that hovers in the 9–14 range. Therefore, an electric utility with a P/E of 45 indicates that something is wrong with that utility.

>> **Compare a company's P/E with the general market.** If you're looking at a small-cap stock on the Nasdaq that has a P/E of 100 and the average P/E for established companies on the Nasdaq is 40, find out why. You should also compare the stock's P/E ratio with the P/E ratio for major indexes such as the Dow Jones Industrial Average (DJIA), the Standard & Poor's 500 (S&P 500), and the Nasdaq Composite. Stock indexes are useful for getting the big picture.

>> **Compare a company's current P/E with recent periods** (such as this year versus last year). If it currently has a P/E ratio of 20 and it previously had a P/E ratio of 30, you know that either the stock price has declined or that earnings have risen. In this case, the stock is less likely to fall. That bodes well for the stock.

>> **Low P/E ratios aren't necessarily a sign of a bargain,** but if you're looking at a stock for many other reasons that seem positive (solid sales, strong industry, and so on) and it also has a low P/E, that's a good sign.

>> **High P/E ratios aren't necessarily bad,** but they do mean that you should investigate further. If a company is weak and the industry is shaky, heed the high P/E as a warning sign. Frequently, a high P/E ratio means that investors have bid up a stock price, anticipating future income. The problem is that if the anticipated income doesn't materialize, the stock price can fall.

WARNING

>> **Watch out for a stock that doesn't have a P/E ratio.** In other words, it may have a price (the *P*), but it doesn't have earnings (the *E*). No earnings means no P/E, meaning that you're better off avoiding the stock. Can you still make money buying a stock with no earnings? You can, but you aren't investing; you're speculating.

The PSR

The *price to sales ratio (PSR)* is a company's stock price divided by its sales. Because the sales number is rarely expressed as a per-share figure, it's easier to divide a company's total market value (explained earlier in this chapter) by its total sales for the last 12 months.

TIP

As a general rule, stock trading at a PSR of 1 or less is a reasonably priced stock worthy of your attention. For example, say that a company has sales of $1 billion, and the stock has a total market value of $950 million. In that case, the PSR is 0.95. In other words, you can buy $1 of the company's sales for only 95 cents. All things being equal, that stock may be a bargain.

Analysts frequently use the PSR as an evaluation tool in the following circumstances:

>> In tandem with other ratios to get a more well-rounded picture of the company and the stock.

>> When they want an alternative way to value a business that doesn't have earnings.

>> When they want a true picture of the company's financial health, because sales are tougher for companies to manipulate than earnings.

>> When they're considering a company offering products (versus services). PSR is more suitable for companies that sell items that are easily counted (such as products). Firms that make their money through loans, such as banks, aren't usually valued with a PSR because deriving a usable PSR for them is more difficult.

REMEMBER

Compare the company's PSR with other companies in the same industry, along with the industry average, so that you get a better idea of the company's relative value.

4

Looking at Bond Investing

Contents at a Glance

IN THIS CHAPTER

» Getting a handle on the nature of bonds

» Knowing why some bonds pay more than others

» Understanding the rationale behind bond investing

» Meeting the major bond issuers

» Considering individual bonds versus bond funds

Chapter **1**

Bond Fundamentals

A bond is really not much more than an IOU with a serial number. People in suits, to sound impressive, sometimes call bonds *debt securities* or *fixed-income securities.* You get the basics on bonds in this chapter.

Understanding What Makes a Bond a Bond

A bond is always issued with a specific *face amount,* also called the *principal,* or *par value.* Most often, simply because it is convention, bonds are issued with face amounts of $1,000. So to raise $50 million, a corporation or government would have to issue 50,000 bonds, each selling at $1,000 par. Of course, they would then have to go out and find investors to buy the bonds.

Every bond pays a certain rate of *interest,* and typically (but not always) that rate is fixed over the life of the bond (hence *fixed-income* securities). The life of the bond is the period of time until maturity. *Maturity,* in the lingo of financial people, is the period of time until the principal is due to be paid back. (Yes, the bond world is full of jargon.) The rate of interest is a percentage of the face amount and is typically (again, simply because of convention) paid out twice a year.

So if a corporation or government issues a $1,000 bond paying 4 percent interest, that corporation or government promises to fork over to the bondholder $40 a year — or, in most cases, $20 twice a year. Then, when the bond matures, the corporation or government repays the $1,000 to the bondholder.

In some cases, you can buy a bond directly from the issuer and sell it back directly to the issuer. But you're more likely to buy a bond through a brokerage house or a bank. You can also buy a basket of bonds through a company that sells mutual funds or exchange-traded funds (ETFs). These brokerage houses and fund companies will most certainly take a piece of the pie — sometimes a quite sizeable piece.

In short, dealing in bonds isn't really all that different from a deal worked out between classmates lending each other money. It's just a bit more formal. And the entire business is regulated by the Securities and Exchange Commission (among other regulatory authorities), and most (but not all) bondholders wind up getting paid back!

Choosing your time frame

Almost all bonds these days are issued with life spans (maturities) of up to 30 years. Few people are interested in lending their money for longer than that, and people young enough to think more than 30 years ahead rarely have enough money to lend. In bond lingo, bonds with a maturity of less than five years are typically referred to as *short-term bonds.* Bonds with maturities of 5 to 12 years are called *intermediate-term bonds.* Bonds with maturities of 12 years or longer are called *long-term bonds.*

In general (sorry, but you're going to read those words a lot in Book 4; bond investing comes with few hard-and-fast rules), the longer the maturity, the greater the interest rate paid. That's because bond buyers generally demand more compensation the longer they agree to tie up their money. At the same time, bond issuers are willing to fork over more interest in return for the privilege of holding onto your money longer.

It's exactly the same theory and practice with bank CDs (certificates of deposit): Typically, a two-year CD pays more than a one-year CD, which in turn pays more than a six-month CD.

The different rates that are paid on short, intermediate, and long bonds make up what is known as the *yield curve. Yield* simply refers to the actual return you get from the bond. Chapter 2 in Book 4 provides an in-depth discussion of interest rates, bond maturity, and the many types of yields.

Picking who you trust to hold your money

Consider again the analogy between bonds and bank CDs. Both tend to pay higher rates of interest if you're willing to tie up your money for a longer period of time. But that's where the similarity ends.

When you give your money to a savings bank to plunk into a CD, that money — your principal — is almost certainly guaranteed (up to $250,000 per account) by the Federal Deposit Insurance Corporation (FDIC). If solid economics be your guide, you should open your CD where you're going to get FDIC insurance (almost all banks carry it) and the highest rate of interest. End of story.

REMEMBER

Things aren't so simple in the world of bonds. A higher rate of interest isn't always the best deal. When you fork over your money to buy a bond, your principal, in most cases, is guaranteed only by the issuer of the bond. That "guarantee" is only as solid as the issuer itself. That's why U.S. Treasury bonds (guaranteed by the U.S. government) pay one interest rate, and Valeant Pharmaceutical bonds pay another rate. Can you guess where you'll get the highest rate of interest?

You would expect the highest rate of interest to be paid by Valeant. Why? Because lending your money to Valeant, a company that once saw its CEO resign in the face of numerous investigations for price gouging, is very risky. If the company is in disarray — facing a ton of negative publicity, loss of sales, and potentially large fines — and then it goes belly up, you may lose a good chunk of your principal. That risk requires any shaky company to pay a relatively high rate of interest. Without being paid some kind of *risk premium*, you would be unlikely to lend your money to a company that may not be able to pay you back. Conversely, the U.S. government, which has the power to levy taxes and print money, is not going bankrupt anytime soon. Therefore, U.S. Treasury bonds, which are said to carry only an infinitely small risk of *default,* tend to pay relatively modest interest rates.

Bonds that carry a relatively high risk of default are commonly called *high-yield* or *junk* bonds. Bonds issued by solid companies and governments that carry very little risk of default are commonly referred to as *investment-grade* bonds.

There are many, many shades of gray in determining the quality and nature of a bond. It's not unlike wine tasting in that regard. Chapter 2 of Book 4 gives you many specific tips for "tasting" bonds and choosing the finest vintages for your portfolio.

Differentiating among bonds, stocks, and collectibles

Aside from the maturity and the quality of a bond, other factors could weigh heavily in how well a bond purchase treats you. The rest of Book 4 introduces you to such bond characteristics as *callability*, *duration*, and *correlation*, and you find out how the winds of the economy, and even the whims of the bond-buying public, can affect the returns on your bond portfolio.

By and large, bonds' most salient characteristic — and the one thing that most, but not all, bonds share — is a certain stability and predictability, well above and beyond that of most other investments. Because you are, in most cases, receiving a steady stream of income, and because you expect to get your principal back in one piece, bonds tend to be more conservative investments than, say, stocks, commodities, or collectibles (like stamps and comic books).

Is conservative a good thing? Not necessarily. It's true that many people invest their money too aggressively, just as many people invest their money too conservatively. The appropriate portfolio formula depends on what your individual investment goals are (see Book 2, Chapter 1).

Why Hold Bonds?

In the real world, plenty of people own plenty of bonds — but often the wrong bonds in the wrong amounts and for the wrong reasons. Some people have too many bonds, making their portfolios too conservative; some have too few bonds, making their stock-heavy portfolios too volatile. Some have taxable bonds where they should have tax-free bonds, and vice versa. Others are so far out on a limb with shaky bonds that they may as well be lending their money to an irresponsible seventh grader.

The first step in building a bond portfolio is to have clear investment objectives. ("I want to make money" — something heard from clients all the time — is *not* a clear investment objective!) Here are some of the typical reasons — both good and bad — why people buy and hold bonds.

Identifying the best reason to buy bonds: Diversification

Most people buy bonds because they perceive a need for steady income, and they think of bonds as the best way to get income without risking principal. This is one of the most common mistakes investors make: compartmentalization. They think of principal and interest as two separate and distinct money pools. They are not.

Consider this explanation: Joe Typical buys a bond for $1,000. At the end of six months, he collects an interest payment (income) of, say, $25. He spends the $25, figuring that his principal (the $1,000) is left intact to continue earning money. At the same time, Joe buys a stock for $1,000. At the end of six months, the price of his stock, and therefore the value of his investment, has grown to, say, $1,025. Does he spend the $25? No way. Joe reckons that spending any part of the $1,025 is spending principal and will reduce the amount of money he has left working for him.

REMEMBER

In truth, whether Joe spends his "interest" or his "principal," whether he spends his "income" or generates "cash flow" from the sale of stock, he is left with the *very same* $1,000 in his portfolio.

Thinking of bonds, or bond funds, as the best — or only — source of cash flow or income can be a mistake.

Bonds are a better source of steady income than stocks because bonds, in theory (and usually in practice), pay regular interest; stocks may or may not pay dividends and may or may not appreciate in price. Bonds also may be a logical choice for people who may need a certain sum of money at a certain point in the future — such as college tuition or cash for a new home — and can't risk a loss.

But unless you absolutely need a steady source of income or a certain sum on a certain date, bonds may not be such a hot investment. Over the long haul, they tend to return much less than stocks.

REMEMBER

The point is that the far better reason to own bonds, for most people, is to *diversify* a portfolio. The key to truly successful investing is to have several different *asset classes* — different investment animals with different characteristics — all of which can be expected to yield positive long-term returns but do not all move up and down together.

Going for the cash

Bonds are not very popular with the get-rich-quick crowd — for good reason. The only people who get rich off bonds are generally the insiders who trade huge amounts and can clip the little guy. Nonetheless, certain categories of bonds — high-yield corporate (junk) bonds, for example — have been known to produce impressive gains.

WARNING

High-yield bonds may have a role — a limited one — in your portfolio, as discussed in Book 4, Chapter 3. But know up-front that high-yield bonds do not offer the potential long-term returns of stocks, and neither do they offer the portfolio protection of investment-grade bonds. Rather than zigging when the stock market zags, many high-yield bonds zag right along with your stock portfolio. Be careful!

Some high-yield bonds are better than others — and they are held by relatively few people.

REMEMBER

Even high-quality, investment-grade bonds are often purchased with the wrong intentions. *Note:* A U.S. Treasury bond, though generally thought to be the safest bond of all, *will not guarantee your return of principal unless you hold it to maturity.* If you buy a 20-year bond and you want to know for sure that you're going to get your principal back, you had better plan to hold it for 20 years. If you sell it before it matures, you may lose a bundle. Bond prices, especially on long-term bonds — yes, even Uncle Sam's bonds — can fluctuate greatly! Chapter 2 in Book 4 discusses the reasons for this fluctuation.

Chapter 2 in Book 4 also discusses the very complicated and often misunderstood concept of bond returns. You may buy a 20-year U.S. Treasury bond yielding 3 percent, and you may hold it for 20 years to full maturity. And yes, you'll get your principal back, but you may actually earn far more or far less than 3 percent interest on your money!

Introducing the Major Players in the Bond Market

Every year, millions — yes, literally millions — of bonds are issued by thousands of different governments, government agencies, municipalities, financial institutions, and corporations. They all pay interest. In many cases, the interest rates aren't all that much different from each other. In most cases, the risk that the issuer will *default* — fail to pay back your principal — is minute. So why, as a lender of money, would you want to choose one type of issuer over another? Glad you asked!

Following are some important considerations about each of the major kinds of bonds, categorized by who issues them. This list just scratches the surface right now. For a more in-depth discussion, see Book 4, Chapter 3. In the meantime, here are the basics:

>> **Supporting (enabling?) your Uncle Sam with Treasury bonds:** When the government issues bonds, it promises to repay the bond buyers over time. The more bonds the government issues, the greater its debt. Voters may groan about the national debt, but they generally don't see it as an immediate problem.

Chapter 3 in Book 4 explains the many, many kinds of Treasury bonds — from EE Bonds to I Bonds to TIPS — and the unique characteristics of each. All of them are backed by the "full faith and credit" of the federal government. Despite its huge debt, the United States of America is not going bankrupt anytime soon. And for that reason, Treasury bonds have traditionally been referred to as "risk-free." Careful! That does *not* mean that the prices of Treasury bonds do not fluctuate.

>> **Collecting corporate debt:** Bonds issued by for-profit companies are riskier than government bonds but tend to compensate for that added risk by paying higher rates of interest. (If they didn't, why would you or anyone else want to take the extra risk?)

>> **Demystifying those government and government-like agencies:** Federal agencies, such as the Government National Mortgage Association (Ginnie Mae), and government-sponsored enterprises (GSEs), such as the Federal Home Loan Banks, issue a good chunk of the bonds on the market. Even though these bonds can differ quite a bit, they are collectively referred to as *agency* bonds. What are called agencies are sometimes part of the actual government, and sometimes a cross between government and private industry. In the case of the Federal National Mortgage Association (Fannie Mae) and the Federal Home Loan Mortgage Corporation (Freddie Mac), they have been, following the mortgage crisis of 2008, somewhat in limbo.

To varying degrees, Congress and the Treasury should serve as protective big brothers if one of these agencies or GSEs were to take a financial beating and couldn't pay off its debt obligations.

>> **Going cosmopolitan with municipal bonds:** The bond market, unlike the stock market, is overwhelmingly institutional. In other words, most bonds are held by insurance companies, pension funds, endowment funds, and mutual funds. The only exception is the municipal bond market.

Municipal bonds *(munis)* are issued by cities, states, and counties. They are used to raise money for either the general day-to-day needs of the citizenry (schools, roads, sewer systems) or for specific projects (a new bridge, a sports stadium).

Bond Fundamentals

Buying Solo or Buying in Bulk

One of the big questions about bond investing is whether to invest in individual bonds or bond funds.

REMEMBER

We generally advocate bond funds — both bond mutual funds and exchange-traded funds. Mutual funds and exchange-traded funds represent baskets of securities (usually stocks or bonds, or sometimes both) and allow for instant and easy portfolio diversification (see Book 5). You do, however, need to be careful about which funds you choose. Not all are created equal — far, far from it.

The following sections give you a quick rundown of the pros and cons of owning individual bonds versus bond funds.

Picking and choosing individual bonds

Individual bonds offer investors the opportunity to really fine-tune a fixed-income portfolio. With individual bonds, you can choose exactly what you want in terms of bond quality, maturity, and taxability.

For larger investors — especially those who do their homework — investing in individual bonds may also be more economical than investing in a bond fund. That's especially true for investors who are up on the latest advances in bond buying and selling.

Once upon a time, any buyers or sellers of individual bonds had to take a giant leap of faith that their bond broker wasn't trimming too much meat off the bone. No more. Chapter 4 in Book 4 shows you how to find out exactly how much your bond broker is making off you — or trying to make off you. You find out how to compare comparable bonds to get the best deals. And you discover some popular bond strategies, including the most popular and potent one, *laddering* your bonds, which means staggering the maturities of the bonds that you buy.

Going with a bond fund or funds

Investors have a choice of thousands of bond mutual funds or exchange-traded funds. All have the same basic drawbacks: management expenses and a certain degree of unpredictability above and beyond individual bonds. But even so, some make for very good potential investments, particularly for people with modest portfolios.

Where to begin your fund search? The rest of Book 4 promises to help you weed out the losers and pick the very best.

The Triumphs and Failures of Fixed-Income Investing

Picture yourself in the year 1926. Calvin Coolidge occupies the White House. Ford's Model T can be bought for $200. Charles Lindbergh is gearing up to fly across the Atlantic. And you, having just arrived from your journey back in time, brush the time-travel dust off your shoulders and reach into your pocket. You figure that if you invest $100, you can then return to the present, cash in on your investment, and live like a corrupt king. So you plunk down the $100 into some long-term government bonds.

Fast-forward to the year 2015, and you discover that your original investment of $100 is now worth $11,730. It grew at an average annual compound rate of return of 5.5 percent. (In fact, that's just what happened in the real world.) Even though you aren't rich, $11,730 doesn't sound too shabby. But you need to look at the whole picture.

Beating inflation, but not by very much

REMEMBER

Yes, you enjoyed a return of 5.5 percent a year, but while your bonds were making money, inflation was eating it away at a rate of about 3 percent a year. What that means is that your $11,730 is really worth about $885 in 1926 dollars.

To put that another way, your real (after-inflation) yearly rate of return for long-term government bonds was about 2.5 percent. In about half of the 89 years between 1926 and 2015, your bond investment either didn't grow at all in real dollar terms, or actually lost money.

Compare that scenario to an investment in stocks. Had you invested the very same $100 in 1926 in the S&P 500 (500 of the largest U.S. company stocks), your investment would have grown to $567,756 in *nominal* (pre-inflation) dollars. In 1926 dollars, that would be about $42,800. The average nominal return was 10.2 percent, and the average real annual rate of return for the bundle of stocks was 7.0 percent. (Those rates ignore both income taxes and the fact that you can't invest directly in an index, but they are still valid for comparison purposes.)

So, which would you rather have invested in: stocks or bonds? Obviously, stocks were the way to go. In comparison, bonds seem to have failed to provide adequate return.

Saving the day when the day needed saving

But hold on! There's another side to the story! Yes, stocks clobbered bonds over the course of the last eight or nine decades. But who makes an investment and leaves it untouched for that long? Outside of maybe Rip Van Winkle, no one! Real people in the real world usually invest for much shorter periods. And there have been some shorter periods over the past eight or nine decades when stocks have taken some stomach-wrenching falls.

The worst of all falls, of course, was during the Great Depression that began with the stock market crash of 1929. Any money that your grandparents may have had in the stock market in 1929 was worth not even half as much four years later. Over the next decade, stock prices would go up and down, but Grandma and Grandpa wouldn't see their $100 back until about 1943. Had they planned to retire in that period, well, they may have had to sell a few apples on the street just to make ends meet.

REMEMBER

A bond portfolio, however, would have helped enormously. Had Grandma and Grandpa had a diversified portfolio of, say, 70 percent stocks and 30 percent long-term government bonds, they would have been pinched by the Great Depression but not destroyed. While $70 of stock in 1929 was worth only $33 four years later, $30 in long-term government bonds would have been worth $47. All told, instead of having a $100 all-stock portfolio fall to $46, their 70/30 diversified portfolio would have fallen only to $80. Big difference.

Closer to the present time, a $10,000 investment in the S&P 500 at the beginning of 2000 was worth only $5,800 after three years of a growly bear market. But during those same three years, long-term U.S. government bonds soared. A $10,000 70/30 (stock/bond) portfolio during those three years would have been worth $8,210 at the end. Another big difference.

In 2008, stocks took a big nosedive. The S&P 500 tumbled 37 percent in that dismal calendar year. And long-term U.S. government bonds? Once again, our fixed-income friends came to the rescue, rising nearly 26 percent. In fact, nearly every investment imaginable, including all the traditional stock-market hedges, from real estate to commodities to foreign equities, fell hard that year. Treasury bonds, however, continued to stand tall.

Clearly, long-term government bonds can, and often do, rise to the challenge during times of economic turmoil. Why are bad times often good for many bonds? Bonds have historically been a best friend to investors at those times when investors have most needed a friend. Given that bonds have saved numerous stock investors from impoverishment, bond investing in the past eight to nine decades may be seen not as a miserable failure but as a huge success.

Gleaning some important lessons

Bonds have been a bulwark of portfolios throughout much of modern history, but that's not to say that money — some serious money — hasn't been lost. The following sections offer examples of some bonds that haven't fared well so you're aware that even these relatively safe investment vehicles carry some risk.

Corporate bonds

Corporate bonds — generally considered the riskiest kind of bonds — did not become popular in the United States until after the Civil War, when many railroads, experiencing a major building boom, had a sudden need for capital. During a depression in the early to mid-1890s, a good number of those railroads went bankrupt, taking many bondholders down with them. Estimates indicate that more than one out of every three dollars invested in the U.S. bond market was lost. Thank goodness we haven't seen anything like that since (although during the Great Depression of the 1930s, plenty of companies of all sorts went under, and many corporate bondholders again took it on the chin).

In more recent years, the global bond default rate has been less than 1 percent a year. Still, that equates to several dozen companies a year. In recent years, a number of airlines (Delta, Northwest), energy companies (Enron), and one auto parts company (Delphi) defaulted on their bonds. Both General Motors and Ford experienced big downgrades (from *investment-grade* to *speculative-grade*), costing bondholders (especially those who needed to cash out holdings) many millions.

Lehman Brothers, the fourth largest investment bank in the United States, went belly-up in the financial crisis of 2008. Billions were lost by those in possession of Lehman Brothers bonds. (Many more billions were also lost in mortgage-backed securities and collateralized debt obligations. These investments are debt instruments issued by financial corporations, but they are very different animals than typical corporate bonds.) Most recently, corporations that were once very healthy, from Borders to Sharper Image to Kodak, have collapsed. Corporations sometimes go under. None are too big to fail.

Municipal bonds

Municipal bonds, although much safer overall than typical corporate bonds, have also seen a few defaults. In 1978, Cleveland became the first major U.S. city to default on its bonds since the Great Depression. Three years prior, New York City likely would have defaulted on its bonds had the federal government not come to the rescue.

The largest default in the history of the municipal bond market occurred in 2013, when Detroit declared bankruptcy, leaving holders of more than $8 billion in bonds wondering whether they would ever get their money back.

Largely because of the situation in Detroit, there has been lots of talk about municipal bankruptcies. Yet not many have occurred. In recent years, the number of municipalities defaulting on their bonds has been estimated to run about $\frac{6}{10}$ of one percent.

Several budget-challenged cities and counties have had to make the difficult choice between paying off bondholders or making good on pension obligations for retired police, firefighters, and teachers. Thus far, the retired workers have suffered more financial pain than the bondholders, perhaps because they have less political clout — and no one wants to alienate bondholders, who may provide much-needed cash in the future.

Sovereign bonds

Nations worldwide also issue government bonds. These are often called *sovereign* bonds. The largest default of all time occurred in 1917 as revolutionaries in Russia were attempting to free the people by breaking the bonds, so to speak, of imperialist oppression. Bonds were broken, for sure; with the collapse of the czarist regime, billions and billions of rubles-worth of Russian bonds were suddenly worth less than nonalcoholic vodka. Most had been sold to Western Europeans. In France, the Parisian government urged people to reject the new Bolshevik regime and show their support of the monarch in Moscow by purchasing Russian bonds. About half of all French households held at least some Russian debt.

Sometimes history can repeat itself or, at least, create echoes of the past. In 1998, one of the largest bond defaults of the modern era occurred once again in Moscow. The Russian government, facing a collapse of its currency, stopped payment on about $40 billion of bonds. And in 2002, Argentina's financial decline forced bondholders to accept 25 cents on the dollar for its outstanding debt of $90 billion.

REMEMBER

Bonds of *emerging-market* nations (such as Russia, Argentina, Mexico, and Turkmenistan) had been a hot investment sector for several years before turning downward in 2016, largely due to the drying up of commodity markets. Emerging-market bonds can be very volatile, and investing in them means risking your principal.

Indeed, global awareness of serious debt problems in several European nations has resulted in fears that even these developed nations (which presumably have already emerged) could default on their bond obligations. This fear has caused their bond prices to drop dramatically and yields to rise sharply.

Realizing How Crucial Bonds Are Today

We could talk about the importance of corporate debt to the growth of the economy, the way in which municipal bonds help to repair roads and build bridges, and how Ginnie Mae and Fannie Mae bonds help to provide housing to the masses, but we think we'll just let this one sentence suffice. This is, after all, not a book on macroeconomics and social policy but a book on personal investing. So allow us to address the crucial role that bonds play in the lives of individual investors — everyday people.

With trillions of dollars invested in bonds, U.S. households' economic welfare is closely tied to the fortunes of the bond market.

REMEMBER

With the demise of the traditional pension, bond investing is more important than ever. Back when you knew your company would take care of you in old age, you may have played footloose and fancy free with your portfolio without having to worry that a scrambled nest egg might mean you couldn't afford to buy eggs. Today, a well-tuned portfolio — that almost certainly includes a good helping of bonds — can make the difference between living on Easy Street and living *on* the street.

Keep in mind that most of the money in the U.S. bond market is institutional money. Should you have a life insurance policy, chances are that your life insurance company has most of your future payoff invested in bonds. Should you have money in your state's prepaid college tuition program, chances are that your money is similarly indirectly invested in bonds. Should you be one of the fortunate employees whose company still offers a pension, chances are that your company has your future pension payout invested in bonds.

Many economists speculate that as the boomer generation continues to move into retirement, the demand for income-generating investments like bonds will only grow. If you live and work in a developed nation, your economic well-being is much more closely tied to the bond markets than you think.

Viewing Recent Developments, Largely for the Better

As the price of everything from groceries and gas to college tuition and medical care continues to climb, it's nice to know that at least two things on this planet have gotten cheaper in the past few years: computers and bond trades. And, as any seasoned bond investor will tell you, saving money on trades isn't the only exciting development of late. Here are some others worth noting:

TIP

>> **New and better bond funds:** You have thousands of bond funds in which to invest. Of these, several hundred are bond *index funds* — funds that seek to capture the returns of an entire swatch of the bond market — which tend to be the best options for most bond investors. These funds carry an average yearly expense ratio of 28 basis points ($^{28}/_{100}$ of 1 percent), which is way, way less than most bond funds (the overall average of just about 1 percent).

The newest kid on the block, *exchange-traded funds* (ETFs) — funds similar to mutual funds — are the greatest thing to happen to bond investing in a very long time. ETFs, the vast majority of which are index funds, allow small investors to invest like the Big Boys, with extremely low expenses and no minimum investment requirements. Hundreds of bond ETFs exist. Some of them, such as several offerings from Vanguard and Schwab, carry annual expense ratios of less than $^1/_{10}$ of one percent. (See Book 5 for more on ETFs and mutual funds.)

>> **Greater access to information:** One of the advantages of all index funds, but especially exchange-traded funds over traditional actively managed mutual funds, is their relative *transparency.* That means that when you invest in an ETF, you know exactly what you're buying. Traditional mutual funds are not required to reveal their specific investments; you may think you're buying one thing and end up with another.

When it comes to buying and selling individual bonds, it's as if a muddy pond has been transformed into a glass aquarium. Not long ago, a bond broker would give you a price for a bond, and you'd have absolutely no idea how fair a deal you were getting. Nowadays, you can search online and usually get a very good idea of how fair a deal you're getting, how much the broker is making, and whether better deals can be had. Chapter 4 in Book 4 gives you a complete tour of the aquarium.

>> **The expansion of Uncle Sam's treasury chest:** If you are going to invest in individual bonds, U.S. Treasury bonds may make the most sense. The Treasury has a website, http://www.treasurydirect.gov/, where you can

buy its bonds directly and not have to deal with any brokers whatsoever, nor will you need to fork over any kind of markup. Chapter 3 in Book 4 walks you through the process.

TIP

One special kind of Treasury bond — Treasury Inflation-Protected Securities, or TIPS — has been in existence since the mid-1990s. It is a very exciting development in the world of bonds. TIPS offer only very modest interest rates, but the principal is readjusted twice annually to keep up with inflation. TIPS represent an entirely new *asset class* (kind of investment), and you should consider holding at least one-quarter of your bond allocation in TIPS. They can be important portfolio diversifiers. Read all about them in Book 4, Chapter 3.

» **Internationalization of the bond market:** The U.S. government isn't the only government to issue bonds. U.S. corporations aren't the only corporations to issue bonds, either. For added portfolio diversification, and possibly a higher yield, you may want to look abroad. Until recently, international diversification in fixed income was very difficult. Now, it's as easy as (but not as American as) apple pie. As with U.S. bonds, you have your pick of short-term or long-term bonds, safe-and-simple or risky-with-high-return potential. You can invest in the relatively calm waters of Canada, Japan, or Germany. Or you can travel to countries such as Russia and Brazil where the bond markets are choppy and exciting.

IN THIS CHAPTER

» **Calculating true return on bond investments**

» **Understanding the meaning of various yields**

» **Explaining what makes the bond markets move**

» **Discovering why tomorrow's interest rates matter today**

» **Figuring out your potential for profit**

Chapter **2**

All about the Interest

I n the city of Uruk, in the month of Ululu, on the 11th day of the 9th year of Nebuchadnezzar (that would be 595 B.C.), a man named Nabu-usabsi lent a half mina (about half a pound) of silver to Nabu-sar-ashesu. They signed an agreement witnessed by a holy priest and four countrymen. The agreement stated that within one year, Nabu-sar-ashesu would return to Nabu-usabsi his half mina of silver plus another ten shekels, each shekel equal to about 1/60 of a pound of silver. If you do the math, that equates to a yearly rate of interest of 33⅓ percent.

That story from an ancient Babylonian text was retold, nearly 2,600 years later, in *A History of Interest Rates,* a 700-page textbook by Sidney Homer and Richard Sylla, first published in 1963. (A fourth edition was published by Wiley in 2005.) The book is an amazing collection of research into credit and interest rates not only going back to the 9th year of Nebuchadnezzar but also offering some speculation that interest payments of one sort or another existed in prehistoric times.

And why, pray tell, are we bringing this up in a chapter on bond investing in the computer age? Because most of today's credit is tied up in bonds, and the most salient feature of any bond is the interest rate paid. Interestingly (pardon the pun), many of the same forces that drove interest rates 2,600 years ago are *still* driving interest rates today, as you find out in this chapter.

This chapter examines what forces affect interest rates and the demand for credit. You're introduced to the many (and often confusing, sometimes *purposely* confusing) ways in which bond returns are measured and reported. And you find the tools you need to determine whether Mr. Nabu-usabsi was getting a fair return on his investment, as well as what you, as a thoroughly modern bond investor, should expect in return for *your* bond investments.

The Tricky Business That Is Calculating Rates of Return

Bond investing can be tricky business indeed — way trickier than stock investing. To help explain why, this section is going to call upon our Babylonian friends, Nabu-usabsi and Nabu-sar-ashesu. And you're going to meet two new characters, Lila-Ir-lender and Kudur-Broker. The two Nabus are real characters from a bygone era. Lila-Ir-lender is fictional. Kudur-Broker is also fictional.

Lila-Ir-lender, like Nabu-sar-ashesu, is a moneylender. Kudur-Broker is, appropriately enough, a broker. Instead of dealing only in minas and shekels and agreements written on parchment, assume the existence of bonds. With lenders, borrowers, and a broker, you have a complete bond market!

Okay, are you ready to see why this bond business can be so tricky? Good. Time to return to ancient Babylonia!

Cutting deals

Instead of merely signing an agreement, suppose that Nabu-usabsi, in return for lending his half mina of silver to Nabu-sar-ashesu, gets a bond. Nabu-sar-ashesu's bond clearly states that Nabu-usabsi will get his investment back in one year, plus 33⅓ percent interest. In the parlance of the bond world, the bond is issued with a *face value* of a half mina of silver, a *coupon rate* (or interest rate) of 33⅓ percent, and a *maturity* (or expiration date) of one year. (You get the details about these terms later.)

For now, just know that measuring bond returns is not always an easy matter. Why not? After all, the agreement calls for 33⅓ percent interest. Simple enough, eh? Not really.

Suppose that Nabu-usabsi wants to get his 33⅓ percent interest not as a lump sum at the end of the year but in two installments (as most bonds work): 16⅔ percent after six months, and another 16⅔ percent after another six months. That is obviously a better deal for Nabu-usabsi because he gets 16⅔ percent of his investment back sooner and can, if he likes, reinvest that money for another six months. Suppose that, in fact, he is able to reinvest that money for a very high interest rate. By the end of the year, Nabu-usabsi will actually earn more than 33⅓ percent on his original investment. But how is his *real* rate of return calculated?

Changing hands

To complicate matters further, suppose that Nabu-sar-ashesu, the bond issuer, has agreed that his bond can be sold, and that he will continue to pay 33⅓ percent interest to whomever buys the bond. In walks Lila-Ir-lender, who wants to buy the bond from Nabu-usabsi but uses Kudur-Broker, the bond broker, to make the deal. Kudur-Broker pays Nabu-usabsi one-half pound of silver to obtain the bond. Eager to buy himself a new camel, Kudur-Broker turns around and sells it to Lila-Ir-lender for one pound of silver and pockets the difference for himself.

Lila-Ir-lender is now the proud owner of a bond that is paying 33⅓ percent on the *original face value* (one-half pound of silver). She, however, paid much more for the bond, thanks to the bond broker's handsome markup. So even though she is holding a bond that is paying 33⅓ percent, she isn't really getting 33⅓ percent on her money; she's getting a significant amount less.

Now how much is the true rate of return on the bond? Is it 33⅓ percent, or is it 16⅔ percent, which is the actual percentage return that Lila-Ir-lender would be getting on the money she laid out?

Embracing the complications

You see why this bond business can be so confusing? (Yes, it would be just as confusing if the names were Mike and Sue instead of Nabu-usabsi and Nabu-sar-ashesu!)

Note that this chapter is the most technical one in Book 4. You are about to read some things that confuse even many financial professionals. We do our best to present the information clearly, and we promise to give you an intermission halfway through the chapter so you can catch your breath! But you are probably right now wondering the following: Do I really need to know all this? Can I skim this chapter, or should I really know how to calculate yield-to-maturity, yield-to-call, and things like that? It depends.

REMEMBER

If you are okay investing in bond mutual funds and you're going to buy and hold your investment, then a cursory knowledge of what makes bonds tick is probably just fine. (Knowing how they fit into a well-diversified portfolio is probably more important.) If you are intent, however, on dealing in individual bonds or trying to flip bonds to make a profit (good luck!), you'd better either know this stuff or find a bond broker you can really trust. (Understanding what follows is easier than finding a bond broker you can really trust. Trust us.)

Measuring the Desirability of a Bond

Determining the true value of a bond investment, and how much you're really going to get out of it in the end, requires three levels of research:

>> **Level one:** You notice the curb appeal of the bond: What is the face value, coupon rate, and sales price?

>> **Level two:** You dig deeper into the qualities of the bond: What are its ratings and maturity, and is it callable?

>> **Level three:** You look at broader economic factors (the bond's "neighborhood"), which can greatly influence the value of your bond investment: the prevailing interest rates, inflation rate, state of the economy, and forces of supply and demand in the fixed-income market.

You may not be familiar with all the terms used here, such as *ratings* and *callable*. They are all introduced later in this chapter.

Level one: Getting the basic information

You can ascertain the first things you need to know about a bond quite readily, either by looking at the bond offer itself or by having a conversation with the broker.

Face value

Also known as *par value* or the *principal*, the *face value* is the original dollar amount of the bond. This is the amount that the bond issuer promises to pay the bond buyer at maturity. The face value of the vast majority of bonds in today's market is $1,000. But note that a $1,000 par value bond doesn't necessarily have to sell for $1,000. After the bond is on the open market, it may sell for an amount above or below par. If it sells above par, it's known as a *premium* bond. If it sells below par, it's known as a *discount* bond.

REMEMBER

Know this: Discount bonds are discounted for a reason — or, perhaps, two or three reasons. Most commonly, the discounted bond isn't paying a very high rate of interest compared to other similar bonds. Or the bond issuer is showing some signs of financial weakness that could potentially lead to a default. Don't think you're getting a bargain by paying less than face value for a bond. Chances are, you aren't.

Coupon rate

The *coupon rate* is the interest rate the bond issuer (the debtor) has agreed to pay the bondholder (the creditor), given as a percent of the face value. The term *coupon rate* refers to the fact that in the old days, bonds had actual coupons attached that you would rip off at regular intervals to redeem for cash. Bonds no longer have such coupons; in fact, they aren't printed on paper anymore. Bonds are all electronic, but the term remains.

The coupon rate never changes. That's the reason that bonds, like CDs, are called *fixed-income* investments, even though (as you see shortly) the term is a bit of a misnomer. A 5 percent bond always pays 5 percent of the face value (which is usually $50 a year, typically paid as $25 every six months). As mentioned in the preceding section, the bond doesn't have to be bought or sold at par. But the selling price of a bond doesn't affect the coupon rate.

REMEMBER

Know this: The coupon rate, set in stone, tells you how much cash you'll get from your bond each year. Simply take the coupon rate and multiply it by the face value of the bond. Divide that amount in half. That's how much cash you'll typically receive twice a year. A $1,000 bond paying 8 percent gives you $40 cash twice a year.

Sale price

In general, a bond sells at a *premium* (above face value) when prevailing interest rates have dropped since the time that bond was issued. If you think about it, that makes sense. Say your bond is paying 6 percent, and interest rates across the board have dropped to 4 percent. The bond in your hand, which is paying considerably more than new bonds being issued, becomes a valuable commodity. On the other hand, when general interest rates rise, existing bonds tend to move to *discount* status (selling below face value). Who wants them when new bonds are paying higher rates?

REMEMBER

Don't ask why, but bond people quote the price of a bond on a scale of 100. If a bond is selling at *par* (face value), it will be quoted as selling at 100. But that doesn't mean that you can buy the bond for $100. It means you can buy it at par. On a $1,000 par bond, that means you can buy the bond for $1,000. If the same bond is selling at 95, that means you're looking at a discount bond, selling for $950. And if that bond is selling for 105, it's a premium bond; you need to fork over $1,050.

REMEMBER

Know this: Most investors put too much weight on whether a bond is a discount bond or a premium bond. Although it matters somewhat, especially with regard to a bond's volatility (see the later section "Measuring the Volatility of Your Bond Holdings"), it doesn't necessarily affect a bond's total return. *Total return* refers to the sum of your principal and income, capital gains on your original investment, *plus* any income or capital gains on money you've earned on your original investment and have been able to reinvest. Total return is, very simply, the entire amount of money you end up with after a certain investment period, minus what you began with. More on that later in this chapter.

Level two: Finding out intimate details

After you know the face value, coupon rate, and sale price (discount or premium), you are ready to start a little digging. The upcoming sections show you what you want to know next about the bond.

Ratings: Separating quality from junk

Not all bonds pay the same coupon rates. In fact, some bonds pay way more than others. One of the major determinants of a bond's coupon rate is the financial standing of the issuer.

The U.S. Treasury, a major issuer of bonds, pays modest rates of return on its bonds (generally less than similar bonds issued by corporations). The reason? Uncle Sam doesn't have to pay more. People assume that the U.S. government isn't going to cheat on its debts, so they are willing to lend the government money without demanding a high return. Shakier entities, such as a new company, a city in financial trouble, or the Russian government (which has a history of default-ing) would have to offer higher rates of return to find any creditors. So they must, and so they do.

An entire industry of bond-rating companies, such as Moody's, Standard and Poor's (S&P), and Fitch Ratings, exists to help bond investors figure their odds of getting paid back from a company or municipality to which they lend money. These firms dig into a bond issuer's financial books to see how solvent the entity is. Theoretically, the higher the rating, the safer your investment; the lower the rating, the more risk you take. In addition, other resources can tell you how much extra interest you should expect for taking on the added risk of lending to a shaky company. You find much more on the ratings in Book 4, Chapter 3.

REMEMBER

Know this: Ratings are very helpful — it's hard to imagine markets working without them — but neither the ratings nor the raters are infallible. In the case of Enron, the major ratings firms — S&P and Moody's — had the company's bonds rated as *investment-grade* until four days before the company declared bankruptcy. Investment-grade means that the risk of loss is very low and the odds of getting repaid very high. Weren't Enron bondholders surprised!

Insurance

Some bonds come insured and are advertised as such. This is most common in the municipal bond market, although less common than it was years ago. Even though default rates are very low among municipalities, cities know that people buy their bonds expecting safety. So they sometimes insure. If a municipality goes to the trouble of having an insurance company back its bonds, you know that you are getting a safer investment, but you shouldn't expect an especially high rate of interest. (No, you can't decline the insurance on an insured bond. It doesn't work like auto-rental insurance.)

TIP

Know this: Some proponents of holding individual bonds say you should delve not only into the financial health of the bond issuer but also, in the case of an insured bond, the financial health of the insurance company standing behind the issuer. That's a fair amount of work, which is one reason we favor bond funds for most middle-class family portfolios.

Maturity

Generally, the longer the maturity of the bond, the higher the interest rate paid. The reason is simple enough: Borrowers generally want your money for longer periods of time and are willing to pay accordingly. Lenders generally don't want their money tied up for long periods and require extra incentive to make such a commitment. And finally, the longer you invest your money in a bond, the greater the risk you are taking — both that the issuer could default and that interest rates could pop, lessening the value of your bond.

REMEMBER

No matter who the issuer is, when you buy a 20-year bond, you are taking a risk. Anything can happen in 20 years. Who would have thought 20 (or so) years ago that General Motors could find itself on the verge of bankruptcy? Or that RadioShack would be boarding up stores, and its bonds selling for nickels to the dollar?

Callability

A bond that is *callable* is a bond that can be retired by the company or municipality on a certain date before the bond's maturity. Because bonds tend to be retired when interest rates fall, you don't want your bond to be retired; you generally aren't going to be able to replace it with anything paying as much. Because of the added risk, callable bonds tend to carry higher coupon rates to compensate bond buyers.

WARNING

Please be careful when buying any individual callable bond. Much of the real pain in the bond market has occurred over calls. There have been cases where a bond buyer will pay a broker a hefty sum to buy a bond callable in, say, six months. The bond, sure enough, gets called, and the bondholder suddenly realizes that he paid the broker a fat fee and made nothing — perhaps got a *negative* return — on his investment. Of course, the broker never bothered to point out this potentially ugly scenario.

Taxes

Back in the early days of the bond market in the United States, the federal government made a deal with cities and states: You don't tax our bonds, and we won't tax yours. And, so far, all parties have kept their word. When you invest in Treasury bonds, you pay no state or local tax on the interest. And when you invest in municipal (muni) bonds, you generally pay no federal tax on the interest. Accordingly, muni bonds typically pay a lower rate of interest than equivalent corporate bonds. But you may still wind up ahead on an after-tax basis.

Level three: Examining the neighborhood

Your home, no matter how well you maintain it or whether you renovate the kitchen, tends to rise or fall in value along with the value of all other houses in your neighborhood. Many things outside of your control — the quality of the schools, employment opportunities, crime rates, and earthquake tremors — can greatly influence the value of homes in your area, including yours. Similarly, a bond, no matter its quality or maturity, tends to rise and fall in value with the general conditions of the markets and of the economy.

Prevailing interest rates

Nothing affects the value of bonds (at least in the short to intermediate run) like prevailing interest rates. When interest rates go up, bond prices go down, usually in lockstep. When interest rates fall, bond prices climb. The relationship is straightforward and logical enough. If you're holding a bond paying yesterday's interest rate, and today's interest rate is lower, then you are holding something that is going to be in hot demand, and people will pay you dearly for it. If you're holding a bond paying yesterday's interest rate, and today's rate is higher, then you are holding mud.

Okay, that part is simple. Interest rates drive bond prices. But what drives interest rates?

Interest rates come in many different flavors. At any point in time, there are prevailing interest rates for home mortgages, credit card payments, bank loans, short-term bonds, and long-term bonds, but to a great extent they all move up and down together. The forces that drive interest rates are numerous, entwined, and largely unpredictable (even though many people claim they can predict them).

In the short run — from hour to hour, day to day — the Federal Reserve (Fed), which controls monetary policy in the United States, has great power to manipulate interest rates across the board. The Federal Reserve's job is to help smooth the economy by tinkering with interest rates to help curb inflation and boost growth. Low interest rates make borrowing easy, both for businesses and consumers. That helps to heat up the economy, but it can also result in inflation. High interest rates discourage borrowing and so tend to slow economic growth, but they also help to rein in inflation. So when inflation is running too high, in the eyes of the Fed, it moves to raise interest rates. And when the economy is growing too slowly, the Fed tends to lower interest rates. Obviously, it's a balancing act, and perfect balance is hard to achieve.

In the longer run — month to month, year to year — interest rates tend to rise and fall with inflation and with the anticipated rate of future inflation.

TIP

Rising interest rates are, in the short run, a bondholder's worst enemy. The possibility that interest rates will rise — and bond prices will therefore fall — is what makes long-term bonds somewhat risky. If you want to avoid the risk of price volatility, go with short-term bonds, but be willing to accept less cash flow from your bond holdings. Or hold your long-term bonds to maturity and ladder them (more on laddering is in Book 4, Chapter 4).

The rate of inflation

The *inflation rate* signals the degree to which you have to cough up more money to buy the same basket of goods; it indicates your loss of purchasing power. In the long run, the inflation rate has great bearing on returns enjoyed by bondholders. The ties between the inflation rate and the bond market are numerous.

In economic theory, bondholders are rational beings with rational desires and motivations. (In reality, individual investors often act irrationally, but as a group, the markets seem to work rather rationally.) A rational buyer of bonds demands a certain *inflation-risk premium.* That is, the higher the rate of inflation or the expected rate of inflation, the higher an interest rate bondholders demand. If inflation is running at 3 percent, which it has, more or less, for the past several years, bond buyers know that they need returns of at least 3 percent just to break even. If the inflation rate jumps to 6 percent, the inflation-risk premium doubles; bond buyers won't invest their money (or won't invest it happily) unless they get double what they were getting before.

Inflation is also a pretty good indicator of how hot the economy is. When prices are rising, it usually reflects full employment and companies expanding. When companies are expanding, they need capital. The need for capital raises the demand for borrowing. An increased demand for borrowing raises prevailing interest rates, which lowers bond prices.

As a bondholder, you can get stung by inflation. Badly. Ask anyone who lived through the 1970s. That's why a certain portion of your bonds (around one-quarter, or more if you are shunning stocks) should be held in inflation-adjusted bonds, such as Treasury Inflation-Protected Securities (TIPS). It's also why a 100 percent bond portfolio rarely, if ever, makes sense. Stocks have a much better track record at keeping ahead of inflation. Real estate and commodities can do a pretty good job, too.

Forces of supply and demand

The public is fickle, and that fickleness is perhaps nowhere better seen than in the stock market. Although the bond market tends to be less affected by the public's whims, it does happen. At times, the public feels pessimistic, and when the public feels pessimistic, it usually favors the stability of government bonds. When the public is feeling optimistic, it tends to favor the higher return potential of corporate bonds. When the public feels that taxes are going to rise, it tends to favor tax-free municipal bonds. As in any other market — shoes, automobiles, lettuce — high consumer demand can raise prices, and low demand tends to lower prices.

Understanding Yield

Yield is what you want in a bond. Yield is income. Yield contributes to return. Yield is confusion! People (including overly eager bond salespeople) often misuse the term or use it inappropriately to gain an advantage in the bond market.

Don't be a yield sucker! Understand what kind of yield is being promised on a bond or bond fund and know what it really means.

Coupon yield

This one is easy. The coupon yield, or the coupon rate, is part of the bond offering. A $1,000 bond with a coupon yield of 4 percent is going to pay $40 a year. A $1,000 bond with a coupon yield of 6 percent is going to pay $60 a year. Usually, the $40 or $60 or whatever is split in half and paid out twice a year on an individual bond.

REMEMBER

Bond funds don't really have coupon yields, although they have an average coupon yield for all the bonds in the pool. That average tells you something, for sure, but you need to remember that a bond fund may start the year and end the year with a completely different set of bonds — and a completely different average coupon yield.

Current yield

Current yield is the most often misused kind of yield. In short, *current yield* is derived by taking the bond's coupon yield and dividing it by the bond's price.

Suppose you had a $1,000 face value bond with a coupon rate of 5 percent, which would equate to $50 a year in your pocket. If the bond sells today for 98 (in other words, it is selling at a discount for $980), the current yield is $50 divided by $980, which equals 5.10 percent. If that same bond rises in price to a premium of 103 (selling for $1,030), the current yield is $50 divided by $1,030, which equals 4.85 percent.

TIP

The current yield is a sort of snapshot that gives you a very rough (and possibly entirely inaccurate) estimate of the return you can expect on that bond over the coming months. If you take the current yield for just one day (translated into nickels and dimes) and multiply that amount by 30, you'd think that would give you a good estimate of how much income your bond will generate in the next month, but that's not the case. The current yield changes too quickly for that kind of prediction to hold true. The equivalent would be kind of like taking a measure of today's rainfall, multiplying it by 30, and using that number to estimate rainfall for the month.

Yield-to-maturity

A much more accurate measure of return, although still far from perfect, is the *yield-to-maturity*. It's a considerably more complicated deal than figuring out current yield. Yield-to-maturity factors in not only the coupon rate and the price you paid for the bond, but also how far you have to go to get your principal back, and how much that principal will be.

Yield-to-maturity calculations make a big assumption that may or may not prove true: They assume that as you collect your interest payments every six months, you reinvest them at the same interest rate you're getting on the bond. With this (often faulty) assumption in mind, here's the formula for calculating yield-to-maturity:

> Um, we don't know.

It's a terribly long formula with all kinds of horrible Greek symbols and lots of multiplication and division and maybe a muffler and an ice tray thrown in. But (thank goodness) you don't need to know the formula!

Thanks to the miracle of modern technology, you can punch a few numbers into your financial calculator, or you can go to any number of online calculators. (Try putting "yield-to-maturity calculator" in your favorite search engine.) Check out the calculator on www.moneychimp.com (a great financial website that features all sorts of cool calculators).

After you find a yield-to-maturity calculator, you'll be asked to put in the par (face) value of the bond (almost always $1,000), the price you are considering paying for the bond, the number of years to maturity, and the coupon rate. Then you simply punch the "calculate" icon. If, for example, we were to purchase a $1,000 par bond for $980, and that bond was paying 5 percent, and it matured in ten years, the yield-to-maturity would be 5.262 percent.

A few paragraphs ago, we calculated the current yield for such a bond to be 5.10 percent. The yield-to-maturity on a discounted bond (a bond selling for below par) is always higher than the current yield. Why? Because when you eventually get your principal back at maturity, you'll be, in essence, making a profit. You paid only $980, but you'll see a check for $1,000. That extra $20 adds to your yield-to-maturity. The reverse is true of bonds purchased at a premium (a price higher than par value). In those cases, the yield-to-maturity is lower than the current yield.

Unscrupulous bond brokers have been known to tout current yield, and only current yield, when selling especially premium-priced bonds. The current yield may look great, but you take a hit when the bond matures by collecting less in principal than you paid for the bond. Your yield-to-maturity, which matters more than current yield, may, in fact, stink.

Yield-to-call

If you buy a *callable* bond, the company or municipality that issues your bond can ask for it back, at a specific price, long before the bond matures. Premium bonds, because they carry higher-than-average coupon yields, are often called. What that means is that your yield-to-maturity is pretty much a moot point. What you're likely to see in the way of yield is yield-to-call. This amount is figured out the same way that you figure out yield-to-maturity (use www.moneychimp.com if you don't have a financial calculator), but the end result — your actual return — may be considerably lower.

Keep in mind that bonds are generally called when market interest rates have fallen. In that case, not only is your yield on the bond you're holding diminished, but your opportunity to invest your money in anything paying as high an interest rate has passed. From a bondholder's perspective, calls are not pretty, which is why callable bonds must pay higher rates of interest to find any buyers. (From the issuing company's or municipality's perspective, callable bonds are just peachy; after the call, the company or municipality can, if it so desires, issue a new bond that pays a lower interest rate.)

WARNING

Certain hungry bond brokers, although required to provide you with yield-to-call figures along with yield-to-maturity figures, may downplay the risk of a call. Of course, there's never a risk to the broker! In the case of a call, you may pay the broker a big cut to get the bond, hold it for a short period, and then have to render it to the bond issuer, actually earning yourself a *negative* total return. Ouch.

Worst-case basis yield

Usually, a callable bond has not just one possible call date, but several. *Worst-case basis yield* (or *yield-to-worst-call*) looks at all possible yields and tells you what your yield would be if the company or municipality decided to call your bond at the worst possible time.

REMEMBER

Callable bonds involve considerably more risk than noncallable bonds. If interest rates drop, your bond will likely be called. Your yield on the existing bond just dropped from what you expected, and you won't be able to reinvest your money for a like rate of return. If interest rates have risen, the company probably won't call your bond, but you are stuck with an asset, if you should try to sell it, that has lost principal value. (Bond prices always drop when interest rates rise.)

The 30-day SEC yield

Because you have so many ways of measuring yield, and because bond mutual funds were once notorious for manipulating yield figures, the U.S. Securities and Exchange Commission (SEC) requires that all bond funds report yield in the same manner. The 30-day SEC yield, which attempts to consolidate the yield-to-maturity of all the bonds in the portfolio, exists so the mutual fund bond shopper can have some measure with which to comparison shop. This measure isn't perfect, in large part because the bonds in your bond fund today may not be the same bonds in your bond fund three weeks from now. Nonetheless, the 30-day SEC yield can be helpful in choosing the right funds.

Recognizing Total Return (This Is What Matters Most!)

Even though bonds are called *fixed-income* investments, and even though bond returns are easier to predict than stock returns, ultimately you can't know the exact total return of any bond investment until after the investment period has come and gone. That's true for bond funds, and it's also true for most individual bonds (although many die-hard investors in individual bonds refuse to admit it). *Total return* is the entire pot of money you wind up with after the investment period has come and gone. In the case of bonds or bond funds, that amount involves not only your original principal and your interest but also any changes in the value of your original principal. Ignoring for the moment the risk of default (and potentially losing all your principal), here are other ways in which your principal can shrink or grow.

Figuring in capital gains and losses

In the case of a bond fund, your principal is represented by a certain number of shares in the fund multiplied by the share price of the fund. As bond prices go up and down (usually due to a number of factors, but primarily in response to prevailing interest rates), so too does the share price of the bond fund go up and down. As you find out in the later section on bond volatility, the share price of a bond fund may go up and down quite a bit, especially if the bond fund is holding long-term bonds, and doubly so if those long-term bonds are of questionable quality (junk bonds).

In the case of individual bonds, unless you buy a bond selling at a premium, your principal comes back to you whole — but only if you hold the bond to maturity or if the bond is called. If, on the other hand, you choose to sell the bond before maturity, you wind up with whatever market price you can get for the bond at that point. If the market price has appreciated (the bond sells at a premium), you can count your capital gains as part of your total return. If the market price has fallen (the bond sells at a discount), the capital losses offset any interest you've made on the bond.

Factoring in reinvestment rates of return

REMEMBER

Total return of a bond can come from three sources:

>> Interest on the bond

>> Any possible capital gains (or losses)

>> Whatever rate of return you get, if you get any, when you reinvest the money coming to you every six months

Believe it or not, on a very long-term bond, the last factor — your so-called *reinvestment rate* — is probably the most important of the three! That's because of the amazing power of compound interest.

The only kind of bond where the reinvestment rate is not a factor is a bond where your only payment comes at the very end when the bond matures. These kinds of bonds are called *zero-coupon* bonds. In the case of zero-coupon bonds, no compounding occurs. According to Investor.gov, zero-coupon bonds "do not pay interest during the life of the bonds. Instead, investors buy zero-coupon bonds at a deep discount from their face value, which is the amount the investor will receive when the bond 'matures' or comes due." (Find more information at `www.investor.gov/introduction-investing/investing-basics/glossary/zero-coupon-bond`.)

Suppose you buy a 30-year, $1,000 bond that pays 6 percent on a semiannual basis. If you spend the $30 you collect twice a year, you get $1,000 back for your bond at the end of 30 years, and your total annual rate of return (ignoring taxes and inflation) is 6 percent simple interest. But now suppose that on each and every day that you collect those $30 checks, you immediately reinvest them at the same coupon rate. Over the course of 30 years, that pile of reinvested money grows at an annual rate of 6 percent *compounded*.

In this scenario, at the end of six months, your investment is worth $1,030. At the end of one year, your investment is worth $1,060.90. (The extra 90 cents represents a half year's interest on the $30.) The following six months, you earn 6 percent on the new amount, and so on, for 30 more years. Instead of winding up with $1,000 after 30 years, as you would if you spent the semiannual bond payments, you instead wind up with $5,891.60 — almost six times as much!

Allowing for inflation adjustments

Of course, that $5,891.60 due to 6 percent compound interest probably won't be worth $5,891.60 in 30 years. Your truest total rate of return needs to account for inflation. If *inflation* — the rise in the general level of prices — continues over the next 30 years at the same rate it has been over the last 30 years (about 3 percent), your $5,891.60 will be worth only $2,642.05 in today's dollars — a real compound return of 3.26 percent.

TIP

To account for inflation when determining the real rate of return on an investment, you can simply take the nominal rate of return (6 percent in our example) and subtract the annual rate of inflation (3 percent in our example). That gives you a very rough estimate of your total real return.

Pretax versus post-tax

Taxes almost always eat into your bond returns. Here are two exceptions:

>> Tax-free municipal bonds where you experience neither a capital gain nor a capital loss, nor is the bondholder subject to any alternative minimum tax

>> Bonds held in a tax-advantaged account, such as a Roth IRA or a 529 college savings plan

For most bonds, the interest payments are taxed as regular income, and any rise in the value of the principal, if the bond is sold (and sometimes even if the bond is not sold), is taxed as capital gain.

For most people these days, long-term capital gains (more than one year) on bond principal are taxed at 15 percent. Any appreciated fixed-income asset bought and sold within a year is taxed at your normal income-tax rate, whatever that is. (Most middle-income Americans today are paying somewhere around 30 percent in income tax.)

Measuring the Volatility of Your Bond Holdings

When investment pros talk of *volatility*, they are talking about risk. When they talk about risk, they are talking about volatility. Volatility in an investment means that what is worth $1,000 today may be worth $900 — or $800 — tomorrow. Bonds are typically way less risky than stocks (that's why we love bonds so much), but bonds can fall in value. Some bonds are much more volatile than others, and before you invest in any bond, you should have a good idea what kind of volatility (risk) you are looking at.

Time frame matters most

The more time until the bond matures, the greater the bond's volatility. In other words, with long-term bonds, there's a greater chance that the principal value of the bond can rise or fall dramatically. Short-term bonds sway much less. On the other hand — and here's a somewhat funny contradiction — the further off your need to tap into the bond's principal, the less that volatility should matter to you.

As explained earlier in this chapter, nothing affects the value of your bond holdings as much as prevailing interest rates. If you're holding a bond that pays 5 percent, and prevailing interest rates are 6 percent, your bond isn't worth nearly as much as it would be if prevailing interest rates were 5 percent (or, better yet, 4 percent). But just how sensitive is the price of a bond to the ups and downs of interest rates? It depends, mostly on the maturity of the bond.

Suppose you are holding a fresh 30-year bond with a coupon rate of 5 percent, and suddenly prevailing interest rates move from 5 percent to 6 percent. You are now looking at potentially 30 years of holding a bond that is paying less than the prevailing interest rate. So how attractive does that bond look to you, or anyone else? Answer: It looks like used oil dripping from the bottom of an old car.

But suppose you are holding either a very short-term bond or an old 30-year bond that matures next month. In either case, you will see your principal very soon. Does it matter much that prevailing interest rates have risen? No, not really. The price of your bond isn't going to be much affected.

Quality counts

High-quality, investment-grade bonds, issued by solid governments or corporations, tend to be less volatile than junk bonds. This has nothing to do with interest rates but with the risk of default. When the economy is looking shaky and investor optimism fades, few people want to be holding the debt of entities that may fail. In times of recession and depression, high-quality bonds may rise in value and junk bonds may fall, as people clamor for safety. Overall, the junk bonds bounce in price much more than the investment-grade bonds.

The coupon rate matters, too

Returning to the effect of interest rates on bond prices, not all bonds of like maturity have the same sensitivity to changes in prevailing rates. Aside from the maturity, you also need to consider the coupon rate. Bonds with the highest coupon rates on the market (bonds currently selling at a premium) tend to have the least volatility. Can you guess why that might be?

Imagine that you are considering the purchase of two $1,000 bonds: One matures in three years and is paying a 10 percent interest rate ($100 a year). The other also matures in three years and is paying a 5 percent rate of interest ($50 a year). Obviously, the market price of the 10 percent bond will be much higher. (It will sell at a premium vis-à-vis the 5 percent bond.) It will also be less sensitive to interest rates because you are, in effect, getting your money back sooner.

With the 5 percent bond, your investment won't pay off until the bond matures and you get your $1,000 face value (probably much more than you paid for the bond). And who knows where interest rates will be then? With the 10 percent bond, you get your investment paid back much sooner, and you are free to reinvest that money. You have much less *reinvestment* risk — the risk that you will be able to reinvest your money only at pitifully low rates.

REMEMBER

The most volatile of bonds — those most sensitive to fluxes in interest rates — are zero-coupon bonds that make a single payment at maturity.

A wickedly complex formula allows you to compare and contrast various bonds of various kinds to estimate their future volatility by measuring something called *duration.* Duration tells you how much a bond will move in price if interest rates change by 1 percent.

Figuring out the duration of a bond is pretty much impossible without either a PhD in mathematics from M.I.T. or a computer (just search "bond duration calculator"). Or you can ask the broker who wants to sell you the bond to do it for you. If you're considering purchasing a bond mutual fund, you'll find the fund's average duration (sometimes called *average effective duration*) in the prospectus or other fund literature. You'll also find it on www.morningstar.com, your brokerage firm's website, or a number of sources where bond funds are contrasted and compared.

The duration formula takes into account a bond's or bonds' par value, coupon rate, yield-to-maturity, and the number of years until the bond or bonds mature. It then spits out a single number. Here's what it means: The principal value of a bond or bond fund with a duration of, say, 6, can be expected to change 6 percent with every 1 percent change in interest rates. If prevailing interest rates go up 1 percent, the bond or bond fund should drop in value 6 percent. If interest rates fall by 1 percent, the bond or bond fund should rise 6 percent.

Of course, if you're holding an individual bond to maturity, or if you have no intention of selling off your bond fund any time in the near future, such fluctuations in price are less important than if you plan to collect your money and run any time soon.

Returning to the Bonds of Babylonia

We return for a moment to the beginning of this chapter and to ancient Babylonia. Here's the question: Was Mr. Nabu-usabsi's 33⅓ percent return a good or bad investment?

Part of the answer lies in the ability of Mr. Nabu-sar-ashesu (the guy who got the silver) to repay the loan. History doesn't tell us whether he was a good credit risk or whether, in fact, the loan was ever repaid. The other part of the answer is whether that interest rate was fair for the time. Was it in line with other similar loans? We don't quite know that, either.

What we do know is that lending money at a certain fixed interest rate (such as you do when you buy a bond) is often a good idea if prevailing interest rates are falling and a bad idea if interest rates are rising. At least that's true in the short run, such as a one-year period. Mr. Nabu-usabsi was probably gleeful if interest rates fell throughout the 9th year of Nebuchadnezzar.

REMEMBER

Historical records make it clear that interest rates have fluctuated all across the board over the millennia. But lending your money (as you do when you buy a bond), if done wisely, is a time-honored way of making your money work for you.

IN THIS CHAPTER

» Savoring U.S. debt securities

» Considering corporate bonds

» Getting a load of agency bonds

» Investing in other people's mortgages

» Mulling municipal bonds

Chapter **3**

Checking Out Types of Bonds

This chapter gives you a good picture of the major categories of bonds, including Treasuries, corporate bonds, agencies, and municipal bonds. In each section, you discover the nuances that make each bond category unique. You find out why certain kinds of bonds pay higher rates of interest than others and, at the same time, may carry more risk. You can start to zero in on the kinds of bonds that make the most sense for you — the kinds of bonds that will make your portfolio shine.

Exploring the Many Ways of Investing with Uncle Sam

Umpteen different kinds of debt securities are issued by the U.S. Treasury. *Savings bonds,* which can be purchased for small amounts and, until recently, came in certificate form (making for nice, if not slightly deceptive, bar mitzvah and birthday gifts), are but one kind. In fact, when investment people speak of *Treasuries,* they usually are not talking about savings bonds but about larger-denomination bonds known formally as *Treasury bills*, *Treasury notes*, and *Treasury bonds*. All of these are now issued only in electronic (sometimes called *book-entry*) form.

Aside from their cyber commonality, all U.S. Treasury debt securities, whether a $50 savings bond or a $1,000 Treasury note, have four other important things in common:

REMEMBER

>> Every bond, an IOU of sorts from Uncle Sam, is backed by the "full faith and credit" of the U.S. government and, therefore, is considered by many investors — all around the world — to be one of the safest bets around.

>> Because it's assumed that any principal you invest is safe from default, Treasury bonds, of whatever kind, tend to pay relatively modest rates of interest — lower than other comparable bonds, such as corporate bonds, that may put your principal at some risk.

>> True, the U.S. government is very unlikely to go bankrupt anytime soon, but Treasury bonds are nonetheless still subject to other risks inherent in the bond market. Prices on Treasury bonds, especially those with long-term maturities, can swoop up and down like hungry hawks in response to such things as prevailing interest rates and investor confidence in the economy.

>> All interest on U.S. government bonds is off-limits to state and local tax authorities (just as the interest on most municipal bonds is off-limits to the Internal Revenue Service). However, except in rare cases, you are required to pay federal tax.

Beyond these similarities, the differences among U.S. government debt securities are many and, in some cases, like night and day.

Savings bonds

Savings bonds start as low as $25. Beyond that, you don't need to pick a specific denomination. If you want to invest, say, $43.45, go for it, or if you want to invest $312.56, that's fine too. Any amount over $25 but under $10,000 (per individual, per year) is accepted.

REMEMBER

Aside from the ability to invest a small amount, savings bonds are also unique among Treasury debt securities in that they are strictly nonmarketable. When you buy a U.S. savings bond, you either put your own name and Social Security number on the bond or the name and Social Security number of the giftee. The only person entitled to receive interest is the one whose name appears on the bond. The bond itself (just like an airline ticket) cannot be sold to another buyer — in stark contrast to Treasury bills and bonds that can, and often do, pass hands more often than poker chips.

EE bonds

Series EE bonds carry a face value of twice their purchase price. They are *accrual bonds,* which means they earn interest as the years roll on even though you aren't seeing any cash. You can pay taxes on that interest as it accrues, but in most cases it makes more sense to defer paying the taxes until you decide to redeem the bond. Uncle Sam allows you to do that.

EE bonds are nonredeemable for the first year you own them, and if you hold them for fewer than five years, you surrender three months of interest. Any individual can buy up to $10,000 in EE savings bonds a year. Interest compounds twice a year for 30 years.

I bonds

These babies are built to buttress inflation. The I Series bonds offer a fixed rate of return plus an adjustment for rising prices. Both factors are mixed in to give you the real return on the bond, known as the *combined* (or sometimes called the *composite*) *rate.* Every May 1 and November 1, the Treasury announces both the fixed rate for all new I bonds and the inflation adjustment for all new and existing I bonds. At the time of writing, the combined rate is 7.12 percent.

After you buy an I bond, the fixed rate is yours for the life of the bond. The inflation rate adjusts every six months. You collect all your interest only after cashing in the bond. (That is called *accrual* interest.)

The rules and parameters for I bonds are pretty much the same as they are for EEs (see the preceding section): You have to hold them a year, and if you sell within five years, you pay a penalty. There's a limit to how many I bonds you can invest in — $10,000 a year, per person. And in certain circumstances, the proceeds may become tax-free if used for education expenses.

Treasury bills, notes, and bonds

About 99 percent of the trillions of dollars in outstanding Treasury debt is made up not of savings bonds but of *marketable* (tradable) securities known as bills, notes, and bonds. This "bills, notes, and bonds" stuff can be a little confusing because technically they are all bonds. They are all backed by the full faith and credit of the U.S. government. They are all issued electronically (you don't get a fancy piece of paper). They can all be purchased either directly from the Treasury, through a broker, or in fund form. They can all trade like hotcakes.

REMEMBER

The major difference among them is the time you need to wait to collect your principal:

>> Treasury bills have maturities of a year or less.

>> Treasury notes are issued with maturities from two to ten years.

>> Treasury bonds are long-term investments that have maturities of 10 to 30 years from their issue date.

The bills carry denominations of $100 but are sold on the open market at a discount from their face value. You get the full amount when the bill matures. The notes and bonds, on the other hand, are sold at their face value, have a fixed interest rate, and kick off interest payments once every six months. The minimum denomination for notes and bonds is $1,000.

TIP

The main difference among various Treasury offerings is the maturity. Generally, but not always, the longer the term, the higher the rate of interest. Therefore, the longer you can tie up your money, the greater your investment returns are likely to be. So one of the first questions you need to ask yourself before investing in Treasuries (or most other bonds) is the following: "When might I need to cash this baby out?"

REMEMBER

Keep in mind that you don't have to hold any of these securities (bills, notes, or bonds) until maturity. You can, in fact, cash out at any point. The more time remaining before your bond is fully matured, the more its price can fluctuate and the more you risk losing money.

Treasury Inflation-Protected Securities (TIPS)

Like the I bonds, Treasury Inflation-Protected Securities (TIPS) receive both interest and a twice-yearly kick up of principal for inflation. As with interest on other Treasury securities, interest on TIPS is free from state and local income taxes. Federal income tax, however, must be coughed up each year on both the interest payments and the growth in principal.

TIPS, unlike I bonds, are transferable. You can buy TIPS directly from the Treasury or through a broker. (More detailed purchasing instructions come later in this chapter.) They are currently being issued with terms of 5, 10, and 30 years, although plenty of 20-year term TIPS are in circulation. The minimum investment is $100.

One of the sweet things about TIPS is that if inflation goes on a rampage, your principal moves north right along with it. If *deflation*, a lowering of prices, occurs — though it hasn't since the 1930s — you won't get any inflation adjustment, but you won't get a deflation adjustment, either. You'll get back at least the face value of the bond.

REMEMBER

TIPS sound great, and in many ways they are. Be aware, though, that the coupon rate on TIPS varies with market conditions and tends to be minimal — perhaps a couple of percentage points or less. If inflation is calmer than expected moving into the future, you will almost certainly do better with traditional Treasuries. If inflation turns out to be higher than expected, your TIPS will be the stars of your fixed-income portfolio.

Also keep in mind that TIPS with longer maturities can be quite volatile, even more so than other bonds. TIPS are designed to keep you even with inflation, and they may do just that, but there is no guarantee. For example, if we experience an inflation rate of 5 percent over the course of the next year, your $1,000 invested in TIPS will get you $50 from Uncle Sam. On that score, you have your guarantee. But if investor sentiment turns away from TIPS, your principal may potentially drop by $50 or even more. So as you can see, TIPS are not manna from heaven.

Industrial Returns: Corporate Bonds

Corporate bonds can be something of a pain in the pants, especially when compared to Treasury bonds. Here's what you need to worry about when investing in corporate bonds:

>> **The solidity of the company issuing the bond:** If the company goes down, you may lose some or all of your money. Even if the company doesn't go down but merely limps, you can lose money.

>> **Callability:** There's a chance that the issuing company may call in your bond and spit your money back in your face at some terribly inopportune moment (such as when prevailing interest rates have just taken a tumble).

>> **Liquidity:** Will someone be there to offer you a fair price if and when you need to sell? Will selling the bond require paying some broker a big, fat markup?

>> **Economic upheaval:** In tough economic times, when many companies are closing their doors (and the stocks in your portfolio are plummeting), your bonds may decide to join in the unhappy nosedive, *en masse.* There go your hopes for an easy, sleep-in-late retirement.

Comparing corporate bonds to Treasuries

When it comes to adding stability to a portfolio — the number one reason that bonds belong in your portfolio — Treasuries and investment-grade (high-quality) corporate bonds are your two best choices. They may have saved your grandparents from destitution during the Great Depression. They may have spared your 401(k) when most stocks hit the skids in 2000–2002 or when your savings again took a nosedive in 2008.

REMEMBER

Generally, corporate bonds tend to outperform Treasuries when the economy is good and underperform when the economy lags.

The crucial credit ratings

Whether you decide to invest your money with corporate bond purveyors, and to what degree, will depend on your individual risk tolerance, your need for return, and your trust in the economy.

Just as risk-return trade-off exists between corporate bonds and Treasuries, there is also a big risk-return trade-off among corporate bonds. The largest determinant of the risk and return you take on a bond is the fiscal muscle of the company behind the bond. That fiscal muscle is measured in theory, and often, but not always, in practice by a company's credit ratings.

An entire industry is devoted to rating companies by their financial strength. The most common ratings come from Moody's and Standard & Poor's, but other rating services exist, such as Fitch Ratings, Dominion, and A.M. Best. Your broker assuredly subscribes to at least two of these services and will be happy to share the ratings with you.

The highest ratings — Moody's Aaa and Standard & Poor's AAA — are the safest of the safe among corporate bonds, and those ratings are given to few corporations ("few" meaning that you can count the number on your fingers). If you lend money to one of these stellar companies, you should expect in return a rate of interest only modestly higher than Treasuries (even though S&P in 2011 downgraded Treasuries to a "mere" AA rating). As you progress from these five-star companies down the ladder, you can expect higher rates of interest to compensate you for your added risk.

According to data from Standard & Poor's, the odds of a corporate bond rated AAA or AA defaulting over the past few decades have been rather minor: less than 1 percent. Of all corporate bonds, only the most solid companies are given those gloriously high ratings.

Moving down the ladder, as you would expect, the default numbers jump. Of course, these rates can vary greatly with economic conditions.

Special considerations for investing in corporate debt

Just as maturity is a major consideration when choosing a Treasury, it should also be a big consideration when choosing corporate bonds. In general (but certainly not always), the longer the bond's maturity, the higher its interest rate will be because your money will potentially be tied up longer. And the longer the maturity, the greater the volatility of the price of the bond should you want to cash out at any point.

Calculating callability

One consideration that pertains to corporate bonds but not to Treasuries is the nasty issue of callability. Treasuries aren't called. (Once upon a time they were, but no longer.) Corporate bonds (as well as municipal bonds) often are. And that can make a huge difference in the profitability of your investment.

TIP

If you're inclined to go for the extra juice that comes with a callable bond, we say fine. *But* you should always do so with the assumption that your callable bond will be called. With that in mind, ask the broker to tell you how much (after taking their markup into consideration) your yield will be between today and the call date. Consider that a worst-case yield. (It's often referred to as *yield-to-worst-call*, sometimes abbreviated YTW; see Chapter 2 in Book 4.) Assume that's the yield you'll get and compare it to the yield you'll be getting on other comparable bonds. If you choose the callable bond and it winds up not being called, hey, that's gravy.

Coveting convertibility

Another wrinkle in corporate bonds is a particular kind of issue called a *convertible* bond. Some corporate bond issuers sell bonds that can be converted into a fixed number of shares of common stock. With a convertible bond, a lender (bondholder) can become a part owner (stockholder) of the company by converting the bond into company stock. Having this option is a desirable thing (options are always desirable, no?), and so convertible bonds generally pay lower interest rates than do similar bonds that are not convertible.

If the stock performs poorly, no conversion happens; you are stuck with your bond's lower return (lower than what a nonconvertible corporate bond would get). If the stock performs well, a conversion happens, so you win — so to speak.

REMEMBER

Know this: Convertible bonds, which are fairly common among corporate bonds, introduce a certain measure of unpredictability into a portfolio. Perhaps the most important investment decision you can make is how to divide your portfolio between stocks and bonds. With convertibles, whatever careful allotment you come up with can be changed overnight. Your bonds suddenly become stocks. You are rewarded for making a good investment, but just as soon as you receive that reward, your portfolio becomes riskier. It's the old trade-off in action.

Although convertible bonds aren't horrible investments, they may not deserve a very sizeable allotment in most individuals' portfolios.

Reversing convertibility . . . imagine that

One relative newcomer to the world of corporate bonds is the *reverse convertible* security, sometimes referred to as a *revertible* or a *revertible note.*

WARNING

A reverse convertible converts to a stock automatically if a certain company stock tumbles below a certain point by a certain date. Why would anyone want such a thing? You guessed it: The bond pays a thrillingly high interest rate (perhaps 2 or 3 or more percentage points above and beyond even the high rates paid on junk bonds), but only for a year or so. That's the hook. The catch is that the company paying the high interest rate is often in dire trouble. If it goes under, you could lose a bundle. Is that really the kind of risk you want to take with a fixed-income investment?

The volatility of high-yield bonds

No definitive line exists between investment-grade and high-yield bonds, sometimes known as *junk* bonds. But generally, if a bond receives a rating less than a Baa from Moody's or a BBB from Standard & Poor's, the market considers it high-yield.

High-yield bonds offer greater excitement for the masses. The old adage that risk equals return is clear as day in the world of bonds. High-yield bonds offer greater yield than investment-grade bonds, and they are more volatile. But they are also one other thing: much more correlated to the stock market. In fact, Treasuries and investment-grade corporate bonds generally aren't correlated to the stock market at all. So if bonds are going to serve as ballast for people's portfolios, which is what they do best, why would anyone want high-yield bonds?

Many people misunderstand them, and if they understood them better, they probably wouldn't invest. They certainly would not opt to give high-yield bonds a major allocation on the fixed-income side of the portfolio.

Lots of Protection, a Touch of Confusion: Agency Bonds

Some agency bonds are, like Treasury bonds, backed by the so-called full faith and credit of the U.S. government. You're going to get your principal back even if Congress has to do the unthinkable and tax the rich.

Most agency bonds, however, are not backed by the full faith and credit, but perhaps by half the faith and credit, of the U.S. government. The language used is that the federal government has assumed a "moral obligation" or "an implied guarantee" to stand behind these bonds. No one seems to know what "an implied guarantee" really means. However, no one ever lost their principal investing in agency bonds due to a default.

Some agency bonds are traditional in the sense that they pay a steady rate of interest and usually, like most bonds, issue payments twice a year. Others are more free-floating. But the majority of agency bonds, roughly three-quarters of them, are entirely different animals — not big elephants with tusks and tails, but maybe odd ducks with oily wings. These odd ducks are called *mortgage-backed securities*; they pay interest *and* principal, usually monthly, with the amount potentially varying greatly from payment to payment.

Identifying the bond issuers

Who or what issues agency bonds? The answer to that question is more complex than you may imagine.

Some of the agencies that issue bonds really are U.S. federal agencies; they are an actual part of the government just as Congress, the jet engines on Air Force One, and the fancy silverware at the White House are. Such official agencies include the General Services Administration, the Government National Mortgage Association, and the Small Business Administration.

Most of the so-called agencies, however, aren't quite parts of the government. They are, technically speaking, *government-sponsored enterprises* (GSEs): corporations created by Congress to work for the common good but then set out more or less on their own. Many of these faux agencies are publicly held, issuing stock on the major exchanges. Such pseudo-agencies include the Federal Home Loan Mortgage Corporation (known colloquially as *Freddie Mac*), the Federal National Mortgage Association (known as *Fannie Mae*), and the Federal Home Loan Banks.

REMEMBER

What's the difference between the two groups, especially with regard to their bonds? The first group (the official-government group) issues bonds that carry the full faith and credit of the U.S. government. The second group, well, their bonds carry that mysterious implicit guarantee or moral obligation. Because this second group is much larger than the first — both in terms of the number of agencies and the value of the bonds they issue — when investment experts speak of "agency bonds," they are almost always talking about the bonds of the GSEs.

After finding themselves in hot water during the subprime mortgage crisis, the two largest of the GSEs — Freddie Mac and Fannie Mae — are currently in *receivership*. In other words, they've been more or less taken over by the federal government. So for the moment, they are, in effect, more like real federal agencies than they are GSEs. At least as far as bondholders are concerned, the bonds of these two agencies now — for the time being — no longer carry the implicit government guarantee of your investments. Instead, they now carry an explicit guarantee. The future remains uncertain.

Sizing up the government's actual commitment

No GSE yet has defaulted on its bonds — either traditional bonds or mortgage-backed securities. The closest ever seen was the Federal Farm Credit Banks (FFCB) during the 1980s when banks were foreclosing on small farms faster than a swarm of locusts can chew up a crop. No FFCB bonds were defaulted, but nervousness in the markets caused their prices to plunge. Would the Treasury have stepped in to save the day if the crisis continued? Perhaps, in theory, yes. But because the theory has never really been put to the test, investors got sweaty palms.

Those who sold their FFCB bonds before maturity lost a bundle. Of course, those intrepid investors who scooped up the bonds at bargain prices made a mint.

Because of the very small risk of default inherent in agency bonds and the greater risk of price volatility due to public sentiment, and because of lesser liquidity and less certain tax considerations, agency bonds — at least those that are not mortgage-backed — tend to pay slightly higher rates of interest than Treasury bonds. The spread between Treasuries and the agency bonds is extremely small, almost never beyond half a percentage point.

The mortgage-backed securities issued by agencies tend to yield higher returns than other agency bonds — not because of the risk of default but because of their greater volatility given the ups and downs of the mortgage market (particularly of late) to which the interest payments are tied.

Eyeing default risks, yields, markups, and more

The honest-and-true federal agencies, such as the Small Business Administration (SBA), are said to have no risk of default; therefore, their bonds pay more or less what Treasuries do. You may get a smidgen more interest (maybe 5 basis points, or $5/100$ of 1 percent) to compensate you for the lesser liquidity of such agency bonds (the lesser ability to sell them in a flash).

Other agency bonds are issued by government-sponsored enterprises (GSEs), and the risk of default, although real, is probably next to nothing. You get a higher rate of interest on these bonds than you do with Treasuries to compensate you for the fact that the risk of default does exist.

REMEMBER

With all agency bonds, you pay a markup when you buy and sell, which you don't with Treasuries if you buy them directly from the government. If you're not careful, that markup could easily eat up your first several months of earnings. It also could make the difference between agency bonds and Treasury bonds a wash.

Most agency bonds pay a fixed rate of interest twice a year. About 25 percent of them are *callable,* meaning that the agencies issuing the bonds have the right to cancel the bond and give you back your principal. The other 75 percent are non-callable bonds (sometimes referred to as *bullet* bonds). Callable bonds tend to pay somewhat higher rates of interest, but your investment takes on a certain degree of uncertainty.

TIP

When choosing among different agencies, you want to carefully compare yields-to-maturity (see Book 4, Chapter 2) and make sure you know full well whether you are buying a traditional bond or a mortgage-backed security. They are totally different animals.

Weighing taxation matters

REMEMBER

The taxes you pay on agency bonds vary. Interest from bonds issued by Freddie Mac and Fannie Mae is fully taxable. The interest on most other agency bonds — including the king of agency bonds, the Federal Home Loan Banks — is exempt from state and local tax.

Treasury bonds, which most resemble agency bonds, are always exempt from state and local tax. Municipal bonds are almost always free from federal tax. Your personal tax bracket will make some bonds look better than others.

Banking Your Money on Other People's Mortgages

Far more complicated even than floaters are the mortgage-backed securities issued by federal agencies such as Ginnie Mae and by some government-sponsored enterprises, such as Fannie Mae and Freddie Mac.

Mortgage-backed securities — the vast majority of which are issued by agencies — are very different from most other bonds. They do not offer as consistent and predictable a stream of interest income as do most bonds.

Bathing in the mortgage pool

When you purchase a mortgage-backed security from, say, Ginnie Mae (minimum investment $25,000), your money goes into a pool of mortgages. Whereas most bonds pay you a set rate of interest, usually twice a year, mortgage-backed securities pay you a certain rate of interest plus the steady or not-so-steady return of your principal. (You don't get a big lump sum when the bond matures.) Most mortgage-backed securities issue monthly payments.

The amount of principal you get back on a monthly basis is determined largely by the rate at which mortgage holders pay off their debt. If interest rates drop and thousands of the mortgage holders decide suddenly to prepay their existing mortgages (in order to refinance), you may get back your principal much faster than you had anticipated. In a sense, a mortgage-backed security has the same "back-at-ya" risk as a callable bond.

Deciding whether to invest in the housing market

You don't need to invest the $25,000 minimum required by Ginnie Mae to invest in mortgage-backed securities. You can get a Freddie Mac for as little as $1,000. But should you?

No, we don't think so.

TIP

Neither does David Lambert, a financial planning colleague who is the founding partner of Artisan Wealth Management (now Collins Lambert Integrated Wealth Management), based in Lebanon, New Jersey. Lambert was formerly the head trader at the agency-bond desk for a major Wall Street firm. This guy knows *a lot* about agency bonds. "If I were a retail investor, unless I had a really huge amount of money and felt that I really knew what I was doing, I wouldn't invest directly in mortgage-backed securities," Lambert says. "The complexity of them makes them inappropriate for the average investor."

Instead, says Lambert, if you want to invest in mortgage-backed securities, do so by investing in, say, a good mortgage-backed security fund. He suggests mutual funds and exchange-traded funds from solid companies like Vanguard, Fidelity, iShares, or PIMCO.

(Almost) Tax-Free Havens: Municipal Bonds

If not for the fact that municipal bonds are exempt from federal income tax, their popularity over the years would have rivaled a pitcher of buttermilk at a college keg party. Historically, the returns on high-quality munis have been about 80 percent of what Treasuries have paid. But a strange thing has happened lately. In the past few years, munis, as a bond category, have paid out at just about the same rate as Treasuries — at times, even more. Keep in mind, of course, that Treasuries aren't exactly world-famous for their high returns — they never were, and they especially aren't these days. However, while munis are generally safe investments, they aren't as safe as Treasuries.

But of course, most munis *are* tax-exempt.

Sizing up the muni market

The municipal bond market is now about $3.8 trillion. But unlike Treasuries, which are held by investors all over the world — by both individuals and governments — municipal bonds are purchased primarily by U.S. households. Munis, due to their tantalizing tax advantage, are generally the only major kind of bond more popular with individual investors than with institutions.

The issuers of municipal bonds include, of course, municipalities (duh), such as cities and towns. But they also include counties, public universities, certain private universities, airports, not-for-profit hospitals, public power plants, water and sewer administrations, various and sundry nonprofit organizations, bridge and tunnel authorities, housing authorities, and an occasional research foundation.

Any government, local agency, nonprofit, or what-have-you that is deemed to serve the public good, with a blessing from the IRS (and sometimes voters), may have the honor of issuing a municipal bond.

Comparing and contrasting with other bonds

The tax-exempt status of munis is unquestionably their most notable and easily recognizable characteristic. Like most bonds, munis come with differing maturities. Some mature in a year or less, others in 20 or 30 years, and a select few have even longer maturities. Unlike most bonds, they tend to be issued in minimal denominations of $5,000 and multiples of $5,000 (not a minimum of $1,000 and multiples of $1,000, like corporate bonds and most Treasuries).

Unlike Treasuries, both corporate bonds and munis are often *callable*, meaning the issuer can kick back your money and sever your relationship before the bond matures. Like other bonds, the interest rate on munis is generally fixed, but the price of the bond can go up and down; unless you hold your bond to maturity, you may or may not get your principal returned in full. (And even if you get your principal back in full, it may have been seriously eaten away by inflation after several decades in hiding.) If the maturity of the bond is many years off, the price of the bond can go up and down considerably — usually in inverse relation to interest rates.

Delighting in the diversification of municipals

The tax-exempt status of munis isn't the only reason they may belong in your portfolio. Municipal bonds also offer a fair degree of diversification, even from other bonds.

REMEMBER

Because they are the only kind of bond more popular with households than with institutions, the muni market may, at times, be swayed more by public demand than other bond markets. For example, when the stock market tanks and individual investors get butterflies in their stomachs, they tend to sell out of their stock holdings (often a mistake) and load up on what they see as less risky investments — bonds of all sorts, including munis.

But the butterflies may also flock in the other direction. At the end of 2010, CBS's *60 Minutes* aired a story titled "The Day of Reckoning" featuring the predictions of a highly reputable bank analyst, Meredith Whitney. Her forecast, backed by interviews with several state governors and comptrollers, proclaimed that a muni-market collapse was in the imminent future. Because of this widely seen segment, the muni market nearly did collapse. Investors panicked about the market for any securities issued by local governments. Prices on munis, especially those issued in financially troubled areas of the country, took a nosedive. Fortunately, the air cleared quickly, and the value of the muni market made a quick recovery.

When the demand for munis goes up, just as when the demand for, say, gold or oil goes up, it tends to drive prices higher. And when the demand for munis goes down, as it did in December 2010, the same thing happens. Popular demand or lack of demand can have a huge effect on muni pricing — more so than individual-investor caprices influence the values of corporate bonds and Treasuries. Those taxable bonds, in contrast, tend to be more interest-rate sensitive. When interest rates rise, bond prices generally fall; when interest rates drop, bond prices tend to move up.

The differences among the many kinds of bonds indicate it's likely a good idea to hold at least several varieties in your portfolio. As an example of diversification, consider that in 2010, investment-grade (high-quality) corporate bonds returned nearly 18 percent. (Interest rates were falling, which is good for bonds, and corporations were starting to look stronger after the pummeling of 2008.) But that same year, munis — partly due to the *60 Minutes* story — returned a mere 2 percent. The following year (2011), munis made a phenomenal comeback; it was their turn to shine. They earned, in the aggregate, a (tax-free) 10 percent. Meanwhile, corporate bonds began to slow, earning about 7.5 percent for the year.

Interestingly enough, when, in July 2013, Detroit became the largest municipal bankruptcy in history, it rattled the market perhaps no more than the *60 Minutes* story. Muni bonds lost only 2.6 percent in 2013 and then rallied in 2014, returning 9.1 percent. In 2015, they returned a less-than-sensational, but still respectable, 3.3 percent.

Choosing from a vast array of possibilities

TIP

You definitely want munis that are rated. Some municipal offerings are not rated, and these can be risky investments or very *illiquid* (you may not be able to sell them when you want, if at all). If you are an average investor, you should go mostly with the top-rated munis: Moody's Aa or higher. The lower-rated munis may give you a bit of extra yield but probably aren't worth the added risk, except perhaps for a limited portion of your portfolio.

Keep in mind that a lower-rated bond can be more volatile than a high-rated bond. Default isn't the only risk. If you suddenly need to cash out the muni part of your portfolio and high-yield munis are in the tank, you may not have access to much of your cash.

Of great importance in choosing munis is clearly their tax benefits, which can vary. Do you want a muni that is merely free from federal income tax, or do you want a muni that is double- or triple-tax-free?

Here's the scoop:

REMEMBER

>> *National munis* are exempt from federal tax but are not necessarily exempt from state income tax. (Some states tax bond coupon payments, and others do not.)

>> *State munis,* if purchased by residents of the same state, are typically exempt from state tax, if there is one. Some, but not all, state munis are also exempt from all local taxes.

>> Munis that are exempt from both federal and state tax are called *double-tax-free* bonds. Some locally issued bonds may be exempt from federal, state, *and* local tax; these are often referred to as *triple-tax-free* bonds.

>> Munis issued by Puerto Rico and Guam are free from federal and state taxes, regardless of where you live.

REMEMBER

You need to do a bit of math to determine which kind is better for you: national or state, double- or triple-tax-free. Consult your tax advisor before laying out any big money on munis. The tax rules are complicated and forever changing. Some states — but not all — impose taxes if you invest in states other than your own, but others may even tax you on munis issued by your own state. Bonds issued in Puerto Rico and other U.S. territories carry their own tax peculiarities. It's a jungle out there!

WARNING

Will you *never* pay federal tax on a muni? Never say never. In some very rare instances, the tax can grab you from behind and make you not want to wake up on April 15.

Chapter **4**

Investing (Carefully!) in Individual Bonds

B y the time you read these words, this very chapter may well seem anti-quated. That's how rapidly the world of individual bond trading is changing.

Nevertheless, this chapter does its best to get you up to current speed. And, should the tales told here become faded by time, fear not: You find a few online resources so that with the tap of some keys and the click of a mouse, you can access the most modern methods — the most efficient, friendly, and profitable methods — for buying and selling individual bonds.

Navigating Today's Individual Bond Market

You often don't pay commissions when you trade individual bonds (you may pay a small one, as you usually do when you trade stocks). Your broker's money comes from the spread. A broker buys a bond at one price and sells it at a higher price. The difference, known as the *bid/ask spread,* is what the broker brings home. We're sometimes talking *lots* of bacon here. The bid/ask spreads on bonds can be big enough to make the commissions and spreads on stocks look like greyhound fat.

Once upon a time, and for many decades, commissions on stocks were as fat as spreads on bonds, sometimes fatter. In 1975, the Securities and Exchange Commission (SEC) deregulated the stock markets, allowing for open competition and discount brokerage houses. The competition brought prices down somewhat. Internet trading, which allowed the brokerage houses to economize, brought prices down even more. Within fairly few years, the money that most people spent to make a stock trade was reduced to a fraction of what it had been. In the 1970s, a typical stock trade cost $100 (about $400 in today's dollars). Today, a stock trade may cost as little as $5, and rarely more than $10.

Getting some welcome transparency

Bond trading today is, in a sense, about where stock trading was in the early 1980s. You can still spend $300, $400, or way more on the cost of a single trade. But you shouldn't have to anymore. Thanks to a system called the *Trade Reporting and Compliance Engine* (TRACE), bond trading is becoming a bit more like stock trading.

TIP

TRACE is a system run by the Financial Industry Regulatory Authority (FINRA) that can be accessed through many financial websites, such as FINRA's own: `finra-markets.morningstar.com/MarketData/`.

Because of TRACE, bond trading no longer has to be a muddied affair in which individual investors are at the mercy of brokers. This system ensures that every corporate bond trade in the United States is reported, and the details appear on the web. (The Municipal Securities Rulemaking Board runs a similar system for municipal bonds.)

REMEMBER

TRACE ensures that trading costs are no longer hidden, bond yields (greatly affected by the bid/ask spreads) are easy to find, and good information is available. Among investment people, access to information is generally referred to as *transparency.* TRACE provides some pretty amazing transparency.

Unfortunately, not everyone knows about the TRACE system, so not everyone realizes that they can find out — for free — the price a broker paid for a bond. In fact, lots of people don't know. The world today is divided more or less evenly between those who know about TRACE and those who don't. Those who don't pay a heavy price.

Ushering in a new beginning

The new transparency, ushered into practice between 2002 and 2005, has removed much of the mystery from bond trading. You can now go online and quickly get a pretty good idea of how much a single bond is being bought and sold for — by brokers, institutions, and individuals. You'll also see how far a broker — *your* broker — is trying to mark a bond up, and exactly what yield you'll get after the middlemen and all their cousins have taken their cuts.

Unfortunately, the cuts taken on bond trades still tend to be too high, and you can't (except in rare circumstances) bypass the middlemen. But with some tough negotiating on your part, you won't make them terribly rich at your expense, either.

Dealing with Brokers and Other Financial Professionals

You're probably better off investing in bond funds rather than individual bonds unless you have a bond portfolio (not your total portfolio, but just the bond side of your portfolio) of, oh, $350,000 or more. Building a diversified bond portfolio — diversified by type of bond, by issuer, and by maturity — is hard unless you have at least that amount to work with. Negotiating good prices on bonds is also hard when you're dealing with amounts brokers tend to sneeze at.

REMEMBER

Investing in individual bonds also requires substantially more work than investing in bond funds. With individual bonds, you not only need to haggle, but you need to haggle again and again. After all, with individual bonds, you get interest payments on a regular basis, usually every six months. Unless you spend the money right away, you need to concern yourself with constantly reinvesting those interest payments. Doing so can be a real job.

WARNING

Then there's the risk of default. With Treasuries and agency bonds, you can presume that the risk of default is zero to negligible, and with high-quality municipal bonds (munis) and top corporations, the risk is minimal. With many corporate bonds and some munis, however, the risk of the company or municipality losing its ability to pay you back is very real. Even when issuers don't default, their bonds may be downgraded by the major rating agencies. A downgrade can mean a loss of money, too, if you decide that you can't hold a bond until maturity. Don't start dabbling in individual corporate bonds or munis unless you're willing to put in some serious time and effort doing research.

With these caveats in mind, the first thing you need in order to be an investor in individual bonds is a *dealer*: someone or some institution to place the actual trades for you — without robbing you blind or steering you astray.

Identifying the role of the middleman

Most bond dealers are traders or brokers who buy a bond from Client A at one price, sell it to Client B at another, leave the office for a few rounds of golf, and then come back to harvest more profits. Sorry to be cynical, but the money some of these Brooks Brothers cowboys make at investors' expense is truly shameful.

Some bond dealers are very knowledgeable about fixed-income investing and can help walk you through the maze, making good suggestions for your portfolio. Some are very talented at finding the best buys in bonds and using certain sophisticated strategies to juice your fixed-income returns.

WARNING

Unfortunately, the way dealers are paid creates a system where the traditional dealer's financial interests are in opposition to the clients' interests. The more the dealer makes, the less the client keeps. The more the client keeps, the less the dealer makes. The more the dealer can get you to *flip,* or trade one bond for another, the more the dealer makes. Generally, the more you flip, the less likely you are to come out ahead.

Dealers aren't bad people or greedy people; they're no more so than car salespeople are. But bond dealers are salespeople (some of them fabulously paid salespeople) and need to be seen as such.

Like the car salesperson, the bond trader who acts as *principal* (taking ownership of the bond) is not required to reveal what kind of markup they're making. And you won't find this information in *Consumer Reports.* (Fortunately, though, you can find it on TRACE; see the earlier section "Getting some welcome transparency.")

TIP

Some bond dealers today work as *agents* and charge you a flat fee, an hourly rate, a certain amount per trade, or a percentage of assets under management. A good agent, like a good broker, may know the ropes of bond trading well enough to help you make the best selections and get the best prices.

Agents, unlike brokers, *do* have to reveal exactly what they are charging you. Alas, whereas an agent is generally better to deal with than a broker (simply because the conflict of financial interest doesn't exist), a good one is very hard to find. And even if you do find one, agents often must work with dealers to get trades done.

Do you need a broker or agent at all?

You don't need a broker or agent to buy Treasury bonds. You can do so easily and without any markup on www.treasurydirect.gov.

REMEMBER

Municipal bonds and corporate bonds must be purchased through an intermediary; you can't buy these securities directly from the issuers. Sure, you can loan your neighbor or brother-in-law $1,000 and demand the money back with interest (good luck!), and that's a bond, of sorts. But if you want to buy and sell marketable fixed-income securities, you must go through a recognized agent.

Going through a financial supermarket, such as Fidelity, T Rowe Price, or Vanguard, is (generally) cheaper than going through a full-service, markup kind of broker. The supermarket's pricing, which is a *concession* or a fee (more or less), not a markup, is perhaps more clear-cut. But the supermarket agents generally hold your hand only so much, and they won't make actual bond selections for you the way a full-service broker will.

You'll note that some qualifiers are injected into the preceding paragraph, such as "generally" and "perhaps." Find out why in the upcoming section "Doing It Yourself Online," which discusses online bond trading. The financial supermarkets, alas, sometimes make their way of trading sound easier, cheaper, and more transparent than it really is.

Selecting the right broker or agent

Whether you go with a full-service, markup kind of broker or with an agent, you should do a few things:

TIP

>> **Find someone who truly specializes in bonds — preferably the kind you're looking to buy.** If you needed hand surgery, you wouldn't go to a gastroenterologist, would you? If dealing in individual bonds is going to be any more profitable than, say, investing in a bond index fund, you need a broker or agent who truly knows and tracks the markets carefully — someone who can jump on a good deal. You don't want a broker who deals in bonds, stocks, gold coins, and collector art!

Start by asking people you know and respect for referrals. Make calls. Ask lots of questions about a broker's background, including academic and professional history. Ask for client recommendations. Don't be shy.

>> **Be on guard.** Always. Whenever you find a broker and agree to buy or sell individual bonds, be certain you aren't paying an excessive markup. Although different people in the investment business have different concepts of what constitutes "excessive," if you're asked to cough up the equivalent of more than three months' interest, that's excessive.

>> **Know a dealer's limitations.** Most bond dealers are not the best people to build your entire portfolio. They often have limited knowledge of investments beyond bonds. (And that's probably a good thing; see the first bullet in this list.) If they deal in stocks at all, they may deal in pricey stock mutual funds that you don't want — the kinds that earn them a nice commission.

Checking the dealer's numbers

TIP

The later section "Doing It Yourself Online" covers online bond trading. If you deal with a full-service broker, you won't have to know every detail about trading bonds online. But at a minimum, you should become familiar with finra-markets. morningstar.com/MarketData (the website of the Financial Industry Regulatory Authority). On this website, you can plug in information on any bond, and you'll experience the type of transparency discussed earlier in this chapter.

If a bond has recently been sold, this website can provide you with lots of information: the bond's selling price; how it's been rated by Moody's, S&P, and Fitch; and its coupon rate, price, and current yield (see Book 4, Chapter 2).

Hiring a financial planner

TIP

Lots of people today, including stock and bond brokers, call themselves financial planners. If you hire a financial planner, you seriously should consider a *fee-only* planner, who takes no commissions and works only for you. To find one in your area, contact the National Association of Personal Financial Advisors (NAPFA) at 847-483-5400, or go online to www.napfa.org.

LOOKING INTO A BROKER'S RECORD

If you want to make sure the bond broker you hire isn't going to take your money and buy a one-way ticket to Rio the next morning, check their background before you hand over the check. You can get information on the disciplinary record, professional background, and registration and license status of any properly registered broker or brokerage firm by using FINRA BrokerCheck. FINRA makes BrokerCheck available at no charge to the public. Investors can access this service by linking directly to BrokerCheck at brokercheck.finra.org/ or by calling 800-289-9999. A recent industry ruling requires brokers to provide the FINRA link on their websites.

Some NAPFA-registered financial advisors work with you on an hourly basis. Others want to take your assets under management. Know that if you hire a financial planner who takes your assets under management, you typically pay a fee, usually 1 percent a year. We think 1 percent is plenty; you shouldn't pay more than that unless you're getting help from that planner that extends to insurance, estate planning, and other matters beyond investing.

If you have a sizeable bond portfolio, a fee-only financial planner who is trading bonds for you can potentially save you enough money to compensate for their fee. Even though the planner will be dealing with a broker, just as you would, planners with numerous clients can bundle their bond purchases, so the broker often settles for a substantially lesser markup.

Here's an example of this type of savings. Matthew Reznik, a NAPFA-registered financial planner with Balasa Dinverno & Foltz LLC of Itasca, Illinois, explains, "If an individual investor is buying a $25,000 bond for his or her portfolio, the markup can be as high as 2.25 percent. If that bond is yielding 5 percent, that's a pretty big haircut. If we buy bonds, we buy the same issue in a $1 million piece. In that case the spread would be reduced to 0.10 percent."

Doing It Yourself Online

A growing number of financial supermarkets and specialty bond shops now allow you to trade bonds online, and they advertise that you can do so for a fixed price. In the case of Fidelity, the price is generally $1 per bond.

WARNING

"Whoa," you may say. "That's a great deal!" Well, yes and no. If that were all that Fidelity and the other middlemen were making, it would be a great deal. But what you see and what you get are two different things. The "flat fees" quoted by Fidelity and its competitors are a bit misleading.

"The idea that there are no broker markups is not the case," says Reznik. "No matter who sells you a bond, there is always a spread built in to compensate the broker." In other words, Fidelity (or Vanguard, or whomever) may charge you "only $1 to trade a bond," but the price you get for your bond, to buy or sell, has already been marked up from the price that someone else just got to sell or buy. Either your own broker may have marked up the price, or some other broker may have previously done so. Just don't kid yourself into thinking that $1 is all you're paying to trade.

The online trading process with Fidelity is similar to that of other financial supermarkets that offer flat-fee bond shopping. The following sections explain how it works. Just know that yes, you can get good buys on bonds online, but you can also get zapped hard. Many other investment pros have had very similar experiences at other financial supermarkets, such as Vanguard and Schwab.

REMEMBER

You are most likely to get a fair deal online when you're *buying* a bond and dealing in large quantities. You are most likely to get zapped when you're *selling* a bond prior to maturity, especially if you're selling a small number of bonds and if those particular bonds are traded infrequently. In such cases, you may let go of your bonds for one price and, using TRACE, find out that they were sold seconds afterward for 3 percent (or more) higher than the price you just got. Someone is making very quick money in that situation, and it isn't you.

The following sections explain how online trading generally works.

If you're looking to buy

You first choose a bond category: Do you want a Treasury bond, an agency bond, a corporate bond, or a municipal bond? (For reminders about each category, see Book 4, Chapter 3.) What kind of rating are you looking for? What kind of maturity? What kind of yield? (Book 4, Chapter 2 contains the goods on ratings, maturity, and yield.)

Most online bond shops walk you through this process step by step; it isn't that hard. The most difficult piece of the process is making sure that after you know what kind of bond you want, you get the best deal on your purchase.

REMEMBER

You want the *highest yield.* The yield reflects whatever concession you're paying the financial supermarket, and it reflects whatever markup you're paying a broker.

Comparing yields, however, can be tricky, especially when looking at callable bonds, because you never know how long you'll have them. Keep in mind that in the past, when interest rates were falling, callable bonds were very often called because the issuers could issue newer bonds at lower interest rates. In the future, that may not be the case. So you need to look at two possible scenarios: keeping the bond to maturity, or having it called.

As David Lambert, founding partner of Artisan Wealth Management (now Collins Lambert Integrated Wealth Management) in Lebanon, New Jersey, suggests, "When considering callable bonds, be sure to examine whether the bonds are selling at a premium or a discount to the call price. If trading at a premium, consider the yield-to-call first. If trading at a discount, consider the yield-to-maturity first. Both of these will give you your most realistic picture of future performance. You can pretty much ignore just about everything else."

What he is saying is that the yield-to-call on premium bonds and yield-to-maturity on discount bonds both represent *yield-to-worst* (or *worst-case basis yield*). That yield is what you're likely going to get, so you'd darned well better factor it into your bond purchasing decisions.

If two comparable bonds — comparable in maturity, duration, ratings, callability, and every other way — are offering yields-to-worst of 4.1 percent and 4.2 percent, unless you have an inside track and therefore know more about the issuer than the ratings companies do, go with the 4.2 percent bond. Just make sure you've done your homework so you know that the two bonds are truly comparable.

REMEMBER

To reiterate: The yield reflects the middleman's cut. *Focus on the yield,* and especially on the yield-to-worst, to get the best deal. Don't overconcern yourself with the bid/ask spread on the bond.

TIP

When you go to place your order, use the "Limit Yield" option. You are telling the brokers that you'll buy this bond only if it yields, say, 4.2 percent. Anything less, and you aren't interested. Putting in a "Market" order on a bond can get you chewed up — don't do it.

If you're looking to sell

Selling bonds online can be a much trickier business. You have a particular bond you want to dump, and the market may or may not want it.

TIP

At Fidelity, you're best off calling a Fidelity fixed-income trader and asking that trader to give you a handle on what the bond is worth. You can then go online, place a "Limit Price" order to sell, and you'll very likely get what the Fidelity trader told you you'd get. But here's the catch: Fidelity itself may wind up buying your bond and selling it to someone else at a large markup.

Truth be told, you are likely to pay a high markup anywhere if you sell a bond before its maturity. Charles Schwab is similar to Fidelity in that you tend to pay through the nose when selling. An average investor should build a bond ladder and hold until maturity. See the following section for more on bond ladders.

Perfecting the Art of Laddering

Bond laddering is a fancy term for diversifying your bond portfolio by maturity. Buy one bond that matures in two years, another that matures in five, and a third that matures in ten, and — presto! — you have just constructed a bond ladder (see Figure 4-1).

FIGURE 4-1:
A typical bond ladder.

© John Wiley & Sons, Inc.

Why bother? Why not simply buy one big, fat bond that matures in 30 years and will kick out regular, predictable coupon payments between now and then? Laddering makes more sense for a few reasons, which are explained in the following sections.

Protecting you from interest rate flux

The first rationale behind laddering is to temper interest rate risk. If you buy a 30-year bond right now that pays 3 percent, and if interest rates climb over the next year to 5 percent and stay there, you're going to be eating stewed crow for 29 more years with your relatively paltry interest payments of 3 percent. Obviously, you don't want that. (You could always sell your 30-year bond paying 3 percent, but if interest rates pop and new bonds are paying significantly higher rates, the price you would get for your lousy 3 percent bond is not going to make you jump for joy.)

Of course, you don't have to buy a 30-year bond right now. You could buy a big, fat two-year bond. The problem with doing that is twofold:

>> You won't get as much interest on the two-year bond as you would on the 30-year bond.

>> You are subjecting yourself to *reinvestment risk:* If interest rates fall rather than rise over the next two years, you may not be able to reinvest your principal in two years for as much as you are getting today.

REMEMBER

If you ladder your bonds, you shield yourself to a certain degree from interest rates rising and falling. If you're going to invest in individual bonds, laddering is really the only option.

Tinkering with your time frame

Note that as each bond in your ladder matures, you would typically replace it with a bond equal to the longest maturity in your portfolio. For example, if you have a two-year bond, a five-year bond, and a ten-year bond, when the two-year bond matures, you replace it with a ten-year bond. Why? Because your five-year and ten-year bonds are now two years closer to maturity, so the average weighted maturity of the portfolio will remain the same: 5.6 years.

Of course, over the course of two years, your economic circumstances may change, so you may want to tinker with the average weighted maturity. That depends on your need for return and your tolerance for risk.

REMEMBER

A perfectly acceptable (and often preferable) alternative to bond laddering is to buy a bond mutual fund or exchange-traded fund. This option is the heart of Book 4, Chapter 5. But whether you ladder your bonds or you buy a bond fund, note that relying only on fixed income to fund your retirement is probably not the wisest path. You should have a bond ladder or bond funds *and* other investments (stocks, real estate) as well. Returns on bond funds are always poor during rising interest rates.

Chapter 5

Picking a Bond Fund That Will Serve You for Life

For the vast majority of individual investors, funds are the way to go. That was true several years ago, and it's even truer today with the advent of hundreds of bond exchange-traded funds (ETFs) that allow the small investor ready access to some darned good and ultra-low-cost bond portfolios.

There's nothing wimpy about bond funds, and provided you do your homework, they can be as intelligent and sophisticated an investment vehicle as you'll ever find. (Index funds, which include most of the fixed-income ETFs, are seen by some as the wimpiest things under the sky but turn out to be mighty tough themselves.)

This chapter introduces you to the many kinds of bond funds — index, active, mutual funds, ETFs, closed-end funds, and unit investment trusts — and reveals that although none are worth dying for, some may well be worth fighting for.

Defining the Basic Kinds of Funds

With hundreds upon hundreds of bond funds to choose from, each representing a different basket of bonds, where do you start? That part is actually easy: You start with the particular class of bonds you want to own. Treasuries? Corporate bonds? Munis? Long-term? Short-term? Investment-grade? High-yield? A blend of all of the above? And knowing what class of bonds you want in the basket isn't enough. You also need to know what kind of *basket* you want.

Bond baskets (funds) come in five varieties:

>> Open-end mutual funds, typically referred to simply as *mutual funds,* are far and away the most common.

>> Closed-end mutual funds, usually referred to only as *closed-end funds,* offer comparatively greater return for greater risk.

>> Exchange-traded funds (ETFs) are the newer kids on the block, catching on very quickly — for good reason.

>> Unit investment trusts are not well known but perhaps worth knowing.

>> Exchange-traded notes (ETNs) are sort of bonds within bonds with bells and whistles and their own unique characteristics.

Mining mutual funds

When most investors speak of funds, they're talking about mutual funds. Like all funds, a mutual fund represents a collection of securities. You, as the investor, pay the mutual fund company a yearly fee and sometimes a sales charge (called a *load,* see "Laying down the law on loads" later in this chapter) to buy the fund. In exchange for your money, the mutual fund company offers you an instant portfolio with professional management.

Most mutual funds are *open-end* funds. This means that the number of shares available is not limited. Within reason, as many people who want to buy into the fund can do so. As more people buy into the fund, more bonds are purchased. The mutual fund shares then sell at a price that directly reflects the price of all the bonds held by the mutual fund. The payment you receive from the fund is a *pro rata* portion of the total income received by all the bonds in the basket, minus whatever management fees are taken out.

Mutual fund orders can be placed at any time, but they are priced only at the end of the day (4 p.m. on Wall Street), and that's the price you get. If you place an order to buy after 4 p.m., the trade is executed at the next day's closing price.

Most mutual funds are actively managed, which means that the managers try to beat the broad bond market by picking certain issues of bonds or by trying to time the markets. Other mutual funds are passively run, or *indexed*, which means they are set up to track standard fixed-income indexes. Index funds tend to cost you a lot less in fees than actively managed funds.

TIP

Regardless of whether you go with active or passive, choose only those bond mutual funds that have solid track records over several years and are reasonably priced. Look at the average yearly operating expense of a bond mutual fund. Because total return on bond funds, over time, tends to be less than that of stock funds, the cost ratio is usually a bigger factor. You shouldn't touch anything over 1 percent without a very compelling reason to do so. You likely don't need to buy more expensive funds; you have many inexpensive alternatives to choose from, and they tend to offer better performance over time. Find more details about mutual funds in Book 5.

Considering an alternative: Closed-end funds

Most mutual funds are open-ended, and some are not. The closed-end funds are a universe unto themselves. Unlike open-end funds, closed-end funds have a finite number of shares. The price of the fund does not directly reflect the value of the securities within the fund. Nor does the yield directly reflect the yield of the bonds in the basket. In investment-speak, the *net asset value* (NAV) of the fund, or the price of the securities within the fund, may differ significantly from the price of the fund itself.

Supply and demand for a closed-end fund may have more bearing on its price than the actual securities it holds. Closed-end funds tend to have high management fees (almost always more than 1 percent a year), and they tend to be more volatile than open-end funds, in part because they are often leveraged. Closed-end funds are traded like stocks (yes, even the bond closed-end funds), and they trade throughout the day. You buy and sell them through any brokerage house — not directly from the mutual fund company, as you can do with most mutual funds.

All closed-end funds are actively managed. There are hundreds of closed-end funds, of which nearly two-thirds are bond funds. If you do buy a closed-end fund, you choose one selling at a discount to the NAV, not at a premium. Studies show that discounted closed-end funds tend to see better performance (similar to value stocks outperforming growth stocks).

Establishing a position in exchange-traded funds

Exchange-traded funds (ETFs) have caught on big in the past several years. ETFs, like closed-end funds, trade on the exchanges like individual stocks. (Yes, even the bond ETFs trade that way.) You usually pay a small brokerage fee ($10 or so) when you buy and another when you sell. But while you own the fund, your yearly fees are very low; they are, in fact, a fraction of what you'd pay for a typical bond mutual fund, closed-end fund, or any other kind of fund.

Unlike closed-end funds, ETFs usually maintain a price that closely matches the net asset value, or the value of all the securities in the portfolio. However — at least at the present time — the vast majority of ETFs are index funds, unlike both closed-end and mutual funds.

REMEMBER

There aren't as many fixed-income ETFs relative to mutual funds, but the number will surely continue to expand. Their popularity is in part due to their super-low expense ratio. The average bond ETF charges only 0.30 percent a year in operating expenses, and a good many are less than 0.20 percent.

Stock ETFs tend to be much more tax-efficient than stock mutual funds. In the bond arena, the difference isn't as great. ETFs tend to be lower cost, but you may have to deal with small trading commissions. And at times the net asset value of your ETF's securities may rise above, or fall below, the market price. This flux shouldn't be a major concern to buy-and-hold investors. Book 5 has more about ETFs.

Understanding unit investment trusts

A unit investment trust (UIT) is a bundle of securities handpicked by a manager. You buy into the UIT as you would an actively managed mutual fund. But unlike the manager of the mutual fund, the UIT manager does not actively trade the portfolio. Rather, the manager buys the bonds (or in some cases, bond funds), perhaps 10 or 20 of them, and holds them throughout the life of the bonds or for the life of the UIT.

A UIT, which may contain a mix of corporate bonds, Treasuries, and munis, has a maturity date — it could be a year, 5 years, or even 30 years down the road. Interest payments (or principal payments, should a bond mature or be called) from a

UIT may arrive monthly, quarterly, or semiannually. Management expenses for a UIT range from 0.2 to 1 percent, and you also pay a commission of about 1 to 3 percent when they're bought. (You don't pay anything when you sell them.) Contact any major brokerage house (or check out its website) if you're interested.

Bond ETFs can also give you the diversification and transparency of a UIT, but only a handful of bond ETFs offer target maturity dates, as UITs do.

Taking a flyer (or not) on an exchange-traded note

Although they sound alike, exchange-traded notes and exchange-traded funds are hugely different. ETNs, which trade just like ETFs or individual stocks, are debt instruments. The issuer, a company such as Direxion or PowerShares or Barclays (all big players in the ETN game), issues an ETN and promises shareholders a rate of return based on the performance of X. What is X? It could be the price of a commodity, or the value of a certain currency, or the return on a certain bond portfolio.

Unlike ETFs, the underlying investments (bonds, commodities, what have you) are not necessarily owned by the issuer of the ETN.

ETNs have been proliferating of late, with dozens having popped up in the past few years. Of these, only a handful are based on any simple and recognizable index of bonds. All the other bond ETNs give you exposure to bonds in a strange, distorted fashion, typically offering you either a doubling or tripling of the bonds' returns or, conversely, the inverse of the bonds' performance. For instance, if Treasuries lose 3 percent tomorrow, some ETNs will go up 3 percent in value. Others may go up 6 percent . . . or 9 percent.

WARNING

Although bond ETNs have one big advantage over ETFs (they are generally taxed more gingerly), they really are not very good vehicles for bond exposure. As noted earlier, these are debt instruments. As such, when you buy an ETN issued by, say, JP Morgan, you may be taking on double credit risk. You need to worry about the creditworthiness of those who issue the bonds in the portfolio, as well as the creditworthiness of PowerShares itself. This is not the case with ETFs.

WARNING

More troubling is the nature of the beast itself. Yes, a leveraged ETN may double or triple your money, but read the fine print! The doubling or tripling is done on a *daily* basis. The strange mathematics of daily returns means that you will lose money over the long run. Seriously: *You will lose money over the long run.* Your principal will simply be eaten away by the extreme volatility.

What Matters Most in Choosing a Bond Fund of Any Sort

For years, alchemists tried to turn common metals into gold. It can't be done. The first rule to follow when choosing a bond fund is to find one appropriate to your particular portfolio needs, which means finding a bond fund made of the right material. After all, bond fund managers can't do all that much more than alchemists.

Selecting your fund based on its components and their characteristics

If you're looking for a bond fund that's going to produce steady returns with little volatility and very limited risk to your principal, start with a bond fund that is built of low-volatility bonds issued by creditworthy institutions. A perfect example would be a short-term Treasury bond fund. If you're looking for fantastic returns in a fixed-income fund, start looking for funds built of high-yield fixed-income securities.

REMEMBER

One of the main characteristics you look for in a bond is its tax status. Most bonds are taxable, but municipal bonds are federally tax-free. If you want to laugh off taxes, choose a municipal bond fund. But just as with the individual muni bonds themselves, expect lower yield with a muni fund. Also pick and choose your muni fund based on the level of taxation you're looking to avoid. State-specific municipal bond funds filled with triple-tax-free bonds (free from federal, state, and local tax) are triple-tax-free themselves.

Pruning out the underperformers

Obviously, you want to look at any prospective bond fund's performance *vis-à-vis* its peers. If you are examining index funds, the driving force behind returns will be the fund's operating expenses. Intermediate-term Treasury bond index fund X will generally do better than intermediate-term Treasury bond index fund Y if less of the profits are eaten up by operating expenses.

With actively managed funds, guess what? Operating expenses are also a driving force. One study conducted by Morningstar, reported in the *Wall Street Journal*, looked at high-quality, taxable bond funds available to all investors with minimums of less than $10,000. More than half of those funds charge investors 1 percent or more. Not surprisingly, almost three-quarters of those pricier funds showed performance that was in the bottom half of the category for the previous year.

TIP

Don't pay more than 1 percent a year for any bond fund unless you have a great reason. And don't invest in any actively managed bond fund that hasn't outperformed its peers — and any proper and appropriate benchmarks — for at least several years. "Proper and appropriate benchmarks" refers to bond indexes that most closely match the composition of the bond fund in question. A high-yield bond fund, given that you can expect more volatility, *should* produce higher yields than, say, a Treasury index. Any comparison of a high-yield fund's return to a Treasury index is practically moot.

Laying down the law on loads

REMEMBER

An astonishing number of bond funds charge loads. A *load* is nothing more than a sales commission, sometimes paid when buying the fund (that's called a *front-end* load) and sometimes paid when selling (that's called a *back-end* or *deferred* load). The best advice? *Never pay a load.* There is absolutely no reason you should ever pay a load of 5.5 percent to buy a bond fund. The math simply doesn't work in your favor.

If you pay a 5.5 percent load to buy into a fund with $10,000, you lose $550 up-front. You start with an investment of only $9,450. Suppose that the fund manager is a veritable wizard and gets a 7 percent return over the next five years, whereas similar bond funds with similar yearly operating expenses are paying only 6 percent. Here's what you'll have in five years with the load fund, even though there's a wizard at the helm: $13,254. Here's what you'd have with the no-load fund, assuming the manager is merely average: $13,382.

WARNING

Buying a load bond fund is plain-and-simple dumb. Unless you get some kind of special deal that allows for the load to be waived, don't buy load funds. Repeat: Don't buy load funds.

Sniffing out false promises

Although morally dubious, and in some cases even illegal, some brokerage houses and financial supermarket websites have been known to promote certain bond funds over others not because those funds are any better but because a certain fund company paid to be promoted. (In the industry, this is sometimes known as "buying shelf space.") Buyer beware!

"Investors need to fully understand how their broker is being compensated, and if a firm is promoting certain bonds or bond funds, investors should ask if the firm is being compensated for that promotion," says Gerri Walsh, vice president for investor education with the Financial Industry Regulatory Authority (FINRA).

5 Moving on to Mutual Funds and Exchange-Traded Funds

Contents at a Glance

Chapter **1**

Considering Mutual Funds' Pros and Cons

Where does the *mutual* in mutual funds come from? Perhaps it's so named because the best funds allow many people of differing economic means to mutually invest their money for

» Easy diversification

» Access to professional money managers

» Low investment management costs

No matter where the word came from, mutual funds, like any other investment, have their strengths and weaknesses that you need to know about before you invest your money. This chapter discusses the advantages and disadvantages of funds.

Introducing Mutual Funds and Exchange-Traded Funds

If you already understand stocks and bonds, their risks and potential returns, and the benefits of diversification, terrific. Most people, however, don't really comprehend investment basics, which is one of the major reasons people make investment mistakes in the first place.

REMEMBER

After you understand the specific types of securities (stocks, bonds, and so on) that funds can invest in, you've mastered one of the important building blocks to understanding mutual funds. A *mutual fund* is a vehicle that holds other investments: When you invest in a mutual fund, you're contributing to a big pool of money that a mutual fund manager uses to buy other investments, such as stocks, bonds, and/or other assets that meet the fund's investment objectives.

Exchange-traded funds (ETFs) are a very close relative of mutual funds and differ from them in one particular way. ETFs trade like stocks on a stock exchange and thus can be bought or sold during the trading day when the financial markets are open. (Later in this chapter, you find one exception to this rule. A type of mutual fund, known as a closed-end fund, trades on a stock exchange during the trading day and has a fixed number of shares outstanding.) Find out more about ETFs in Chapters 4 and 5 of Book 5.

Differences in investment objectives are how funds broadly categorize themselves, like the way an automaker labels a car a *sedan* or a *sport utility vehicle.* This label helps you, the buyer, have a general picture of the product even before you see the specifics. On the dealer's lot, the salespeople take for granted that you know what *sedan* and *sport utility vehicle* mean. But what if the salesperson asks you whether you want a Pegasus or a Stegosaurus? If you don't know what those names mean, how can you decide?

Fund terms, such as *municipal bond fund* or *small-cap stock fund,* are thrown around casually. Fact is, thanks to our spending-oriented culture, the average American knows car models better than types of funds! In this chapter, you discover the investment and fund terms and concepts that many writers assume you already know (or perhaps that they don't understand well enough themselves to explain to you). But don't take the plunge into funds until you determine your overall financial needs and goals. (Check out Chapters 1 and 3 in Book 2 for help with this task.)

Getting a Grip on Funds

A *mutual fund* is a collection of investment money pooled from many investors to be invested for a specific objective. When you invest in a fund, you buy shares and become a *shareholder* of the fund. The fund manager and a team of assistants determine which specific securities (for example, stocks or bonds) they should invest the shareholders' money in to accomplish the objectives of the fund and keep shareholders happy.

A misconception some investors hold regarding mutual funds is that they invest only in stocks and, therefore, are too risky. They don't, and they're not. By using funds, you can invest in a whole array of securities, ranging from money market funds to bonds, stocks, and even real estate.

All funds aren't created equal. Some funds, such as money market funds, carry virtually zero risk that your investment will decline in value. Bond funds that invest in shorter-term bonds don't generally budge by more than several percentage points per year. And you may be surprised to find out that some conservative stock funds aren't that risky if you can plan on holding them for a decade or more.

REMEMBER

Because good funds take most of the hassle out of figuring out which securities to invest in, they're among the best investment vehicles ever created for the following reasons:

» They allow you to *diversify* your investments — that is, invest in many different industries and companies instead of in just one or two. By spreading the risk over a number of different securities representing many different industries and companies, funds lessen your portfolio's instability and the chances of a large loss.

» They enable you to give your money to the best money management firms and managers in the country.

» They are the ultimate couch potato investment! However, unlike staying home and watching television or playing video games, investing in funds can pay you big rewards.

What's really cool about funds is that when you understand them, you realize they can help you meet many different financial goals. Maybe you're building up an emergency savings stash of three to six months' living expenses (a prudent idea, by the way). Perhaps you're saving for a home purchase, retirement, or future educational costs. You may know what you need the money for, but you may not know how to protect the money you have and make it grow.

Don't feel bad if you haven't figured out a long-term financial plan or don't have a goal in mind for the money you're saving. Many people don't have their finances organized! Chapters 1 and 3 in Book 2 talk about setting goals and making plans.

Financial intermediaries

REMEMBER

A mutual fund company is a type of financial intermediary. (Now that's a mouthful!) Why should you care? Because if you understand what a financial intermediary is and how fund companies stack up to other financial intermediaries, you'll better understand when funds are appropriate for your investments and when they probably aren't. A *financial intermediary* is nothing more than an organization that takes money from people who want to invest and then directs the money to those who need investment *capital* (another term for money).

Suppose you want to borrow money to invest in your own business. You go to a bank that examines your financial records and agrees to loan you $20,000 at 8 percent interest for five years. The money that the banker is lending you has to come from somewhere, right? Well, the banker got that money from a bunch of people who deposited money with the bank at, say, 2 percent interest. Therefore, the banker acts as a financial intermediary, or middleman — one who receives money from depositors and lends it to borrowers who can use it productively.

Insurance companies do similar things with money. They sell investments such as annuities and then turn around and lend the money — by investing in bonds, for example — to businesses that need to borrow. (Keep in mind that a *bond* is nothing more than a company's promise to repay borrowed money over a specified period of time at a specified interest rate.)

The best mutual fund companies are often the best financial intermediaries for you to invest through because they skim off less (that is, they charge lower management fees) to manage your money and allow you more choice and control over how you invest your money.

Open-end versus closed-end funds

Open end and *closed end* are general terms that refer to whether a mutual fund company issues an unlimited or a set amount of shares in a particular fund:

>> **Open-end funds:** *Open end* simply means the fund issues as many (or as few) shares as investors demand. Open-end funds theoretically have no limit to the number of investors or the amount of money that they hold. You buy and sell shares in such a fund from the fund company.

>> **Closed-end funds:** *Closed-end* funds are those where the mutual fund companies decide up-front, before they take on any investors, exactly how many shares they'll issue. After they issue these shares, the only way you can purchase shares (or more shares) is to buy them from an existing investor through a broker. (This process happens with buying and selling stock and exchange-traded funds, too.)

REMEMBER

The vast majority of funds in the marketplace are open-end funds, and they're also the funds that are the focus of this book because the better open-end funds are superior to their closed-end counterparts.

Open-end funds are usually preferable to closed-end funds for the following reasons:

>> **Management talent:** The better open-end funds attract more investors over time. Therefore, they can afford to pay the necessary money to hire leading managers. We're not saying that closed-end funds don't have good managers, too, but generally open-end funds attract better talent.

>> **Expenses:** Because they can attract more investors, and therefore more money to manage, the better open-end funds charge lower annual operating expenses. Closed-end funds tend to be much smaller and, therefore, more costly to operate. Note that operating expenses are deducted out of shareholder returns before a fund pays its investors their returns; therefore, relatively higher annual expenses depress the returns for closed-end funds.

WARNING

Brokers who receive a hefty commission generally handle the initial sale of a closed-end fund. Brokers' commissions usually siphon anywhere from 5 to 8 percent out of your investment dollars, which they generally don't disclose to you. (Even if you wait until after the initial offering to buy closed-end fund shares on the stock exchange, you still pay a brokerage commission, although it's generally a lot less than the initial sale commission.) You can avoid these high commissions by purchasing a *no-load* (commission-free), open-end mutual fund. (See the later section "Funds save you money and time" for details on no-load funds.)

>> **Fee-free selling:** With an open-end fund, the value of a share (known as the *net asset value*) always equals 100 percent of what the fund's investments (less liabilities) are currently worth. And you don't have the cost and troubles of selling your shares to another investor as you do with a closed-end fund. Because closed-end funds trade like securities on the stock exchange and because you must sell your shares to someone who wants to buy, closed-end funds sometimes sell at a discount. Even though the securities in a closed-end fund may be worth, say, $20 per share, the fund may sell at only $19 per share if sellers outnumber buyers.

You could buy shares in a closed-end fund at a discount and hold on to them in hopes that the discount disappears or — even better — turns into a *premium* (which means that the share price of the fund exceeds the value of the investments it holds). You should *never* pay a premium to buy a closed-end fund, and you shouldn't generally buy one without getting at least a 5 percent discount (to make up for its deficiencies, versus its open-ended peers, especially higher expenses).

REMEMBER

Sorry to complicate things, but two clarifications are necessary:

>> First, open-end funds can, and sometimes do, decide at a later date to "close" their funds to new investors. This doesn't make it a closed-end fund, however, because investors with existing shares can generally buy more shares from the fund company. Instead, the fund becomes an open-end fund that's closed to new investors!

>> Second, exchange-traded funds, which are covered in Chapters 4 and 5 of Book 5 and which have similarities to closed-end funds, may have low costs if they are modeled after an index fund.

Opting for Mutual Funds

To understand why funds are so sensible is to understand how and why funds can work for you. Keep reading in this section to discover their many benefits. (Funds also have their drawbacks, which are covered in the later section "Addressing the Drawbacks.")

Fund managers offer expertise

Mutual funds are investment companies that pool your money with the money of hundreds, thousands, or even millions of other investors. The company hires a portfolio manager and a team of researchers whose full-time job is to analyze and purchase investments that best meet the fund's stated objectives.

Typically, fund managers are Chartered Financial Analysts (CFAs) and/or graduates of the top business and finance schools in the country, where they study the principles of portfolio management and securities valuation and selection. In addition to their educational training, the best fund managers typically have a decade or more of experience in analyzing and selecting investments.

A mutual fund management team does more research and due diligence than you could ever have the energy or expertise to do in what little free time you have. Investing in mutual funds can help your friendships, and maybe even your love life, because you'll have more free time and energy!

Consider the following activities that a fund manager does before investing in stocks and bonds:

>> **Analyze company financial statements.** Companies whose securities trade in the financial markets are required to issue reports every three months detailing their revenue, expenses, profits and losses, and assets and liabilities. Unless you're a numbers geek, own a financial calculator, and enjoy dissecting tedious corporate financial statements, this first task alone is reason enough to invest through a mutual fund and leave the driving to the mutual fund management team.

>> **Talk with the muckety-mucks.** Most fund managers log thousands of frequent-flier miles and hundreds of hours talking to the folks running the companies they're invested in or are thinking about investing in. Because of the huge amounts of money they manage, large fund companies even get visits from company executives, who fly in to grovel at the fund managers' feet.

>> **Analyze company and competitor strategies.** Corporate managers have an irritating tendency to talk up what a great job they're doing. Some companies may look as if they're making the right moves, but what if their products are soon to lag behind the competition's? The best fund managers and their researchers take a skeptical view of what a company's execs say — they read the fine print and check under the rugs. They also keep on top of what competitors are doing. Sometimes they discover investment ideas better than their original ones this way.

>> **Talk with company customers, suppliers, competitors, and industry consultants.** Another way fund managers find out whether a company's public relations story is full of holes instead of reality is by speaking with the company's customers, suppliers, competitors, and other industry experts. These people often have more balanced viewpoints and can be a great deal more open about the negatives. These folks are harder to find but can provide valuable information.

>> **Attend trade shows and review industry literature.** It's truly amazing how specialized the world's becoming. Do you really want to subscribe to business newsletters that track the latest happenings with ball bearing or catalytic converter technology? They'll put you to sleep in a couple of pages. Unlike popular mass-market publications, they'll also charge you an arm and a leg to subscribe.

REMEMBER

Are you, as the investor, going to do all these tasks and do them well? Probably not. Even in the unlikely event that you could perform investment research as well as the best fund managers, don't you value your time? A good fund management team happily performs all the required research for you, does it well, and does it for a fraction of what it costs you to do it haphazardly on your own.

A (BRIEF) HISTORY OF MUTUAL FUNDS

Mutual funds date back to the 1800s, when English and Scottish investment trusts sold shares to investors. Funds arrived in the United States in 1924. They were growing in assets until the late 1920s, when the Great Depression derailed the financial markets and the economy. Stock prices plunged and so did mutual funds that held stocks.

As was common in the stock market at that time, mutual funds were *leveraging* their investments — leveraging is a fancy way of saying that they put up only, for example, 25 cents on the dollar for investments they actually owned. The other 75 cents was borrowed. That's why, when the stock market sank in 1929, some investors and fund shareholders got clobbered. They were losing money on their investments *and* on all the borrowed money. But, like the rest of the country, mutual funds, although bruised, pulled through this economic calamity.

The Securities Act of 1933 and the Investment Company Act of 1940 established ground rules and oversight of the fund industry by the Securities and Exchange Commission (SEC). Among other benefits, this landmark federal legislation required funds to register and have their materials be reviewed by the SEC *before* issuing or selling any fund shares to the public. Funds were required to disclose cost, risk, and other information in a uniform format through a legal document called a *prospectus*.

During the 1940s, '50s, and '60s, funds grew at a fairly high and constant rate. From less than $1 billion in assets in 1940, fund assets grew to more than $50 billion by the late 1960s — more than a fifty-fold increase. Before the early 1970s, funds focused largely on investing in stocks. Since then, however, money market mutual funds and bond mutual funds have mushroomed. They now account for about 50 percent of all mutual fund assets.

Today, at the time of writing, thousands of mutual funds manage about $16 trillion with exchange-traded funds holding another $2 trillion.

Funds save you money and time

Chances are the last thing you want to do with your free time is research where to invest your savings. If you're like many busy people, you've kept your money in a bank just to avoid the hassles. Or maybe you turned your money over to some smooth-talking broker who sold you a high-commission investment that you still don't understand but are convinced will make you rich.

REMEMBER

Mutual funds and exchange-traded funds are cheaper, more communal ways to get the investing job done. A fund spreads out the cost of extensive — and expensive — research over thousands of investors. How does a fund save you time and money? Count the ways:

>> **Funds can produce a much better rate of return over the long haul than a dreary, boring bank or insurance company account.** You can purchase them by writing a check or calling a toll-free number. What does it cost to hire such high-powered talent to do all the dreadful research and analysis? A mere pittance if you pick the right funds. In fact, when you invest your money in an efficiently managed mutual fund, the cost should be less than it would be to trade individual securities on your own.

>> **Funds manage money efficiently through effective use of technology.** Innovations in information-management tools enable funds to monitor and manage billions of dollars from millions of investors at a very low cost. In general, moving around $5 billion in securities doesn't cost them much more than moving $500 million. Larger investments just mean a few more zeros in the computer database.

The most efficiently managed funds cost less than 1 percent per year in expenses. (Bond funds and money market funds cost much less — good ones charge just 0.5 percent per year or less.) Some of the larger and more established funds, including index funds and exchange-traded funds (see Chapters 4 and 5 in Book 5), charge annual expenses of less than 0.2 percent per year.

>> **Many funds don't charge a commission (load) to purchase or redeem shares.** Commission-free funds are called *no-load funds*. Such opportunities used to be rare. Fidelity and Vanguard, the two largest distributors of no-load funds today, exacted sales charges as high as 8.5 percent during the early 1970s. Even today, some mutual funds known as *load funds* charge you a commission for buying or selling shares in their funds. (See Chapter 2 in Book 5 for the complete story on fund fees.)

Fund diversification minimizes your risk

Diversification is a big attraction for many investors who choose mutual funds and exchange-traded funds. Here's an example of why, which should also explain what diversification is all about: Suppose you heard that Phenomenal Pharmaceuticals developed a drug that stops cancer cells in their tracks. You run to the phone, call your broker, and invest all your savings in shares of Phenomenal stock. Years later, the Food and Drug Administration (FDA) denies the company approval for the drug, and the company goes belly up, taking your entire nest egg with it.

Your money would've been much safer in a fund. A fund may buy some shares of a promising but risky company like Phenomenal without exposing investors like you to financial ruin. A fund owns stocks or bonds from dozens of companies, diversifying against the risk of bad news from any single company or sector. So when Phenomenal goes belly up, the fund may barely feel a ripple.

Diversifying like that on your own would be difficult — and expensive — unless you have a few hundred thousand dollars and a great deal of time to invest. You'd need to invest money in at least 8 to 12 different companies in various industries to ensure that your portfolio could withstand a downturn in one or more of the investments.

Funds typically invest in 25 to 100 securities, or more. Proper diversification increases the probability that the fund receives the highest possible return at the lowest possible risk, given the objectives of the fund.

We're not suggesting that funds escape without share-price declines during major market downturns. For example, during the early 2000s bear market, many funds declined in value. But again, the investors who were most harmed were those who held individual stocks that, in the worst cases, ended up plummeting to zero as companies went bankrupt, or those investors who loaded up on technology and internet stocks that dropped 80 to 90 percent or more. The same fate befell investors who were overloaded with stock in financial firms like AIG, Bear Stearns, Lehman, and so on that plunged far more than the broad market averages in the late 2000s bear market.

WARNING

Although most funds are diversified, some aren't. For example, some stock funds, known as *sector funds,* invest exclusively in stocks of a single industry (for instance, healthcare). Others focus on a single country (such as India). Beware of such funds because of the lack of diversification and because such funds typically charge higher operating fees. It's also worth noting that investors who bought sector funds investing exclusively in internet stocks got hammered in the technology stock crash of the early 2000s. Many of those funds dropped 80 percent or more, whereas broadly diversified funds fared far better. (The same thing happened in the late 2000s to investors in financial sector funds.)

Funds undergo regulatory scrutiny

Before a fund can take in money from investors, the fund must go through a tedious review process by the Securities and Exchange Commission (SEC). After it offers shares, a fund is required to publish in its prospectus historical data on the fund's returns, its operating expenses and other fees, and its rate of trading (turnover) of the fund's investments.

But know that government regulators aren't perfect. Conceivably, a fund operator could try to slip through some bogus numbers, but we haven't heard of this happening and certainly not with the reputable fund companies recommended in this book.

You choose your risk level

Choosing from a huge variety of funds, you can select those that meet your financial goals and take on the kinds of risks that you're comfortable with. Funds to choose from include

>> **Stock funds:** If you want your money to grow over a long period of time (and you can put up with some bad years thrown in with the good), select funds that invest primarily in stocks.

>> **Bond funds:** If you need current income and don't want investments that fluctuate as widely in value as stocks do, consider bond funds.

>> **Money market funds:** If you want to be sure your invested principal doesn't drop in value because you may need to use your money in the short term, you can choose a money market fund.

Most investors choose a combination of these three types of funds to diversify and help meet different financial goals.

Fund risk of bankruptcy is nil

Fund companies don't work like banks and insurance companies, hundreds of which have failed in recent decades. (The number going under spiked during the late 2000s recession.) Banks and insurers can fail because their *liabilities* (the money customers have given them to invest) can exceed their *assets* (the money they've invested or lent). When a big chunk of a bank's loans goes sour at the same time that its depositors want their money back, the bank fails. That happens because banks have less than 20 cents on deposit for every dollar that people place with them. Likewise, if an insurance company makes several poor investments or underestimates the number of claims that insurance policyholders will make, it too can fail.

Such failures can't happen with a fund company. The situation in which the investors' demand for withdrawals of their investment exceeds the value of a fund's assets simply can't occur because for every dollar of assets that a fund holds for its customers, that fund has a dollar's worth of redeemable securities.

REMEMBER

That's not to say that you can't lose money in a mutual fund or exchange-traded fund. The share price of a fund is tied to the value of its underlying securities: If the underlying securities, such as stocks, decrease in value, so, too, does the net asset value (share price) of the fund. If you sell your shares when their price is less than what you paid for them, you get back less cash than you originally put into the fund. But that's the worst that can happen; you can't lose all your investment in a fund unless every single security owned by that fund simultaneously becomes worthless — an extraordinarily unlikely event.

You may be interested to know that the specific stocks and/or bonds that a mutual fund buys are held by a *custodian* — a separate organization or affiliate of the fund company. The employment of a custodian ensures that the fund management company can't embezzle your money (like the crook Bernie Madoff did) or use assets from a better-performing fund to subsidize a poor performer.

Funds save you from sales sharks

WARNING

Stockbrokers (also known as financial consultants) and commission-based financial planners make more money by encouraging trading activity and by selling you investments that provide them with high commissions — limited partnerships and mutual funds with high-load fees, for example. Brokers and planners also get an occasional message from the top brass asking them to sell some newfangled investment product. All this creates inherent conflicts of interest that can prevent brokers from providing objective investment and financial advice and recommendations.

The better no-load (commission-free) fund companies discussed in this book generally don't push specific products. Their toll-free telephone lines are staffed with knowledgeable people who earn salaries, not commissions. Sure, they want you to invest with their company, but the size of their next paycheck doesn't depend on how much they persuade you to buy or trade.

You have convenient access to your money

What's really terrific about dealing with the best fund companies is that they're set up for people who don't like to waste time going to a local branch office and waiting in line. With mutual funds, you can make your initial investment from the comfort of your living room by filling out and mailing a simple form and writing a check. Later, you can add to your investment by mailing in a check or by authorizing money transfers by phone or online from one mutual fund account to another.

Selling shares of your mutual fund for cash is usually easy. Generally, all you need to do is call the fund company's toll-free number or click your computer mouse at your investment firm's website 24/7. Some companies even have representatives available by phone 24 hours a day, 365 days a year. (Signature guarantees, although much less common, are still sometimes required by fund companies.)

Many fund companies also allow you to wire money back and forth from your local bank account, allowing you to access your money almost as quickly through a money market fund as through your local bank. (You probably need to keep a local bank checking account to write smaller checks and for immediate ATM access to cash.)

DON'T FRET ABOUT THE CROOKS

Folks who grew up dealing only with local banks often worry about others having easy access to the money you've invested in funds. Even if someone were able to convince a fund company through the toll-free phone line or on its website that they were you (say, by knowing your account number and Social Security number), the impostor, at worst, could only request a transaction to occur between accounts registered in your name. You'd find out about the shenanigans when the confirmation arrived in the mail, at which time you could call the fund company and undo the whole mess. (Just by listening to a tape of the phone call, which the fund company records, or a record of the online transaction, the company could confirm that you didn't place the trade.)

No one can actually take money out of your account, either. Suppose that someone does know your personal and account information and calls a fund company to ask that a check be sent from a redemption on the account. Even in such a scenario, the check would be sent to the address on the account and be made payable to you.

The only way that someone can actually take money out of your account is with your authorization. And there's only one way to do that: by completing a full trading authorization or power-of-attorney form. Generally you should not grant this authority to anyone. If you do, make sure that the investment firm makes checks payable only to you, not to the person requesting the money from the account.

TIP

When dealing with a money market fund, in particular, the ease of access is even greater. Most money market funds also offer check-writing privileges. These accounts often carry a restriction, however, that your bank checking account doesn't have: Money market checks must be greater than a specified minimum amount — typically $250.

If you like to conduct some transactions in person, some of the larger fund companies, such as Fidelity, and certain discount brokers, such as Charles Schwab and TD Ameritrade, have branch offices in convenient locations.

Addressing the Drawbacks

After all, no investment vehicle is perfect, and you need to understand fund negatives before you take the plunge. Still, the fund drawbacks in the following sections are different from the ones that some critics like to harp on. Here's a take on which fund drawbacks you shouldn't worry about — and which ones you should stop and think about a little more.

Don't worry about these . . .

If you've read some articles or heard some news stories about the downsides of funds, you may have heard of some of the following concerns. However, you shouldn't let them trouble you.

>> **The investment Goliath:** One of the concerns you may still hear about is the one that, because the fund industry is growing, if stock fund investors head for the exits at the same time, they may get stuck or trampled at the door. You could make this argument about any group of investors, including institutions. Little evidence suggests that most individual investors are prone to rash moves. Funds have grown in importance simply because they're a superior alternative for a whole lot of people.

>> **Doing business long distance:** Some people, particularly older folks who grew up doing all their saving through a local bank, feel uncomfortable doing business with a company that they can reach only via a toll-free number, the mail, or a website. But please recognize the enormous benefits of fund companies *not* having branch offices all over the country. Branch offices cost a lot of money to operate, which is one of the reasons bank account interest rates are so scrawny.

TIP

If you feel better dropping your money off in person to an organization that has local branch offices, invest in funds through one of the firms recommended in Chapter 3 of Book 5. Or do business with a fund company that's headquartered near your abode.

» **Fund company scandals:** A number of funds earned negative publicity due to their involvement in problematic trading practices. In the worst cases, some fund managers placed their own selfish agendas (or that of certain favored investors) ahead of their shareholders' best interests. Rightfully, these fund companies have been hammered for such behavior and forced to reimburse shareholders and pay penalties to the government. However, the amount of such damage and reimbursement has been less than 1 percent of the affected funds' assets, which pales in comparison to the ongoing drag of high expenses discussed in the next section. The parent company responsible for an individual fund should be an important consideration when deciding which funds to entrust with your money. Avoid fund companies that don't place their shareholders' interests first.

Worry about these (but not too much) . . .

No doubt you hear critics in the investment world state their case for why you should shun funds. Not surprisingly, the most vocal critics are those who compete with fund companies.

You can easily overcome the common criticisms raised about fund investing if you do your homework and buy the better available mutual funds and exchange-traded funds. Make sure that you consider and accommodate these factors before you invest in any fund:

» **Volatility of your investment balance:** When you invest in funds that hold stocks and/or bonds, the value of your funds fluctuates with the general fluctuations in those securities markets. These fluctuations don't happen if you invest in a bank certificate of deposit (CD) or a fixed insurance annuity that pays a set rate of interest yearly. With CDs or annuities, you get a statement every so often that shows steady — but slow — growth in your account value. You never get any great news, but you never get any bad news either (unless your insurer or bank fails, which could happen).

Over the long haul, if you invest in solid funds — ones that are efficiently and competently managed — you should earn a better rate of return than you would with bank and insurance accounts. And if you invest in stock funds, you'll be more likely to keep well ahead of the double bite of inflation and taxes.

If you panic and rush to sell when the market value of your fund shares drops (instead of holding on and possibly taking advantage of the buying opportunity), then maybe you're not cut out for funds. Stock fund investors who joined the panic taking place in late 2008 and early 2009 and sold got out at fire-sale prices and missed out on an enormous rebound that took place beginning in early 2009.

>> **Mystery (risky) investments:** Some funds have betrayed their investors' trust by taking unnecessary risks by investing in volatile financial instruments such as futures and options (also known as *derivatives*). Because these instruments are basically short-term bets on the direction of specific security prices, they're very risky when not properly used by a fund. If a fund discloses in its prospectus that it uses derivatives, look to see whether the derivatives are used only for hedging purposes to reduce risk instead of as speculation on stock and bond price movements, which would increase risk.

>> **Investments that cost an arm and a leg:** Not all funds are created equal. Some charge extremely high annual operating expenses that put a real drag on returns. Find out more about expense ratios and how to find great funds with low expenses in Chapter 2 of Book 5.

>> **Taxable distributions:** The taxable distributions that funds produce can also be a negative. When fund managers sell a security at a profit, the fund must distribute that profit to shareholders in the fund (dividends are also passed through). For funds held outside tax-sheltered retirement accounts, these distributions are taxable.

Chapter 2

Finding the Best Mutual Funds

When you go camping in the wilderness, you can do a number of things to maximize your odds of happiness and success. You can take maps and a GPS navigator to stay on course, good food to keep you nourished, proper clothing to stay dry and warm, and some first-aid stuff in case something awful happens, such as an outbreak of mosquitoes. But no matter how much preparation you do, you still may not have the best of times. You may get sick, trip over a rock and break your leg, or face inclement weather.

And so it is with mutual funds and exchange-traded funds. Although funds can help you reach your financial goals, they come with no guarantees. You can, however, use a number of simple, common-sense criteria to greatly increase your chances of investment success. The issues in this chapter are the main ones you should consider when trying to separate the funds most likely to succeed from those most likely to perform poorly.

Evaluating Gain-Eating Costs

A survey conducted by the Investment Company Institute asked mutual fund buyers what information they reviewed about a fund *before* purchasing it. Fifth on the list, mentioned by only 43 percent of the respondents, was fees and expenses. Therefore, the majority of fund buyers surveyed — a whopping 57 percent — did *not* examine the fees and expenses for the funds they bought.

Additionally, only 27 percent of fund buyers surveyed bothered to look at how much of a load or sales charge was levied by the fund. At the other end of the spectrum, past fund performance was the most cited information reviewed by fund buyers (with 75 percent considering).

Such survey results aren't surprising. Some investors look first — and sometimes only — at the prior performance of a fund while completely ignoring fees. Doing so is generally a major mistake.

REMEMBER

The charges you pay to buy or sell a fund and the ongoing fund-operating expenses have a big impact on the rate of return you ultimately earn on your investments because fees are deducted from your investment returns. All other things being equal, high fees and other expenses reduce your returns. You can and should examine a fund's expenses and fees *before* you buy into it. In contrast, past performance is actually a relatively poor indicator of a fund's likely future returns. (Later in this chapter, you find out how many of yesterday's star funds turn into tomorrow's losers or mediocre performers.) You just can't know what tomorrow will bring.

Although you have no idea how much of a return you'll make, you *can* find out, before buying a fund, how much the fund has been charging in fees — both up-front (in the form of sales commissions) and ongoing (in the form of fund operating expenses). Factor these known reductions in returns into your fund-buying decisions.

Losing the load: Say no to commissions

When the Securities and Exchange Commission (SEC) deregulated brokers' commissions in 1975, the vast majority — more than 85 percent — of all mutual funds were sold through brokers. The funds they sold are known as *load funds. Load* simply means *commission.* When you purchase a load fund through a broker (who often calls himself something other than a broker), the broker is paid a commission (typically ranging from 4 percent to 8.5 percent) out of the amount that you invest.

Thanks in part to the deregulation of brokerage commissions and to the technological revolution that's taken place over subsequent decades, the growth of the *no-load* (commission-free) mutual fund industry took off. Technology provided fund companies with a cost-effective way to handle thousands of accounts for folks like you who don't have millions of dollars to invest. This fact also enabled fund companies to sell no-load funds directly to investors. Today, no-load funds account for the majority of investors' mutual fund holdings.

Loads deducted from your investment money are an additional and unnecessary cost when you're in the market for the best mutual funds. The best no-load funds are every bit as good as, if not better than, the best load funds. Today, you can stick with the no-load funds and keep more of your investment dollars working for you.

WARNING

Not surprisingly, those who have a vested interest in sales loads argue in favor of funds that carry sales loads. Be wary of brokers or planners pitching house brands — for example, a Prudential broker recommending Prudential mutual funds. The fund industry scandal in the early 2000s further shined the light on this problematic practice. Salespeople often get higher commissions by pushing house brands.

Refuting myths about loads

WARNING

Brokers have much to say about paying loads, and you should be aware of the arguments they use. Here are a few examples:

>> **"Don't concern yourself with commissions — I get paid by the mutual fund company."** It's true that the mutual fund company pays the broker's commission. But where do you think this money comes from? From your investment dollars — that's where. Brokers like to imply that you're not effectively paying for the commission because it comes from the mutual fund company.

>> **"You get what you pay for — load funds have better fund managers."** Bunk! Objective studies show that paying a load doesn't get you a better fund manager. Remember, loads wind up in the pockets of the selling brokers and don't go toward the management of the fund.

Studies have shown that, on average, load funds underperform no-loads. Why? It's simple: Those commissions paid to the brokers come out of the fund's returns, although you may not know that from a fund's published rankings. Some published mutual fund rankings and ratings services completely ignore sales commissions in their calculations of funds' returns.

>> **"No-loads have higher ongoing fees."** Investment salespeople imply or state that no-loads have to make it up somewhere if they aren't charging you a sales commission. Although this may sound logical, remember that sales commissions go to the broker, not toward the expenses of managing the fund. Fact is, the reverse is true: Load funds, on average, have higher, not lower, annual operating expenses than no-load funds.

All funds have to spend money to market themselves. Load funds spend money to market themselves both to brokers and to the investing public like you and me. And the better no-load companies, such as those recommended in Chapter 3 of Book 5, benefit from the thousands of investors who call, based on word-of-mouth or other recommendations (such as through this book!), seeking to invest.

>> **"No-loads have hidden costs."** In this case, a half-truth doesn't make a whole. Both no-load *and* load funds incur brokerage transaction costs when securities are bought and sold in the fund. These costs aren't really "hidden." They're disclosed in a fund's Statement of Additional Information, which is part of the fund's prospectus; however, they're not included in the calculated annual operating costs for any type of mutual fund, either load or no-load.

>> **"No-loads are for do-it-yourself types. People who need help buy load funds."** This either/or mentality is trumpeted not only by investment brokers but also by some financial writers and others in the media who sometimes parrot what brokers say to them. If you need advice, you have options. One alternative is to hire a financial advisor and pay a fee for that person's time to recommend specific no-load mutual funds. No-loads are hardly just for do-it-yourself types (see Chapter 3 in Book 5 for the different types of advisors you may hire), although you can see from this book that you have what it takes to just do it yourself.

>> **"I'll do a financial plan for you to determine your needs."** Try as they may, investment salespeople can't perform objective, conflict-free financial planning. (You should *never* pay for a "financial plan" from an investment salesperson.) The problem with sales loads is the power of self-interest (discussed in Chapter 3 of Book 5). This issue is rarely talked about, but brokers' self-interest is even more important than the extra costs you pay. When you buy a load fund through a salesperson, you miss out on the chance to objectively assess whether you should buy a mutual fund at all. Maybe you'd be better off paying debts or investing in something entirely different. But salespeople almost never advise you to pay off your credit cards or your mortgage — or to invest through your company's retirement plan — instead of buying an investment through them.

Too many people get into investments without understanding what they're buying and what the risks are. People who sell mutual funds usually sell other investments, too. And some of those other products — vehicles such as limited partnerships, cash-value life insurance, annuities, futures, and options — hold the allure (for the salespeople) of high commissions. Salespeople tend to exaggerate the potential rewards and obscure the risks and drawbacks of what they sell and often don't take the time to educate investors.

>> **"I can get you those funds that you're interested in from the same no-load companies, such as Fidelity."** Brokers like to imply that they can sell you basically the same funds that you could buy on your own through no-load companies. However, top no-load companies, such as Vanguard, for example, don't sell any load funds through brokers. Fidelity sells a series of load funds, called Fidelity Advisor funds, through commission-based brokers. These funds carry hefty up-front sales charges and/or much higher ongoing fees — up to a full 1 percent more per year — than their no-load counterparts.

In recent years, increasing numbers of brokerage firms are offering their customers access to some no-load mutual funds through a service known as a *wrap* (or *managed*) *account.* To get into these funds, you must agree to pay the brokerage firm an annual investment management fee on top of the fees the underlying mutual funds charge. High-fee wrap accounts aren't in your best interest.

>> **"The no-loads won't call you to tell you when to get out of the market or switch funds."** True. But far from being a disadvantage, not getting a call to switch funds is actually a plus. Although mutual funds offer daily liquidity, funds are meant to be a longer-term investment.

A broker who stands to gain financially when you trade is hard-pressed to be a source of objective advice for when to trade funds.

>> **"No-loads are impersonal organizations."** When you call a no-load fund's toll-free number, you'll surely get a different representative every time. Visiting a fund's website is even less personal. If it's important for you to have a relationship with someone at these firms, however, some representatives give you their names and extensions (just ask) so you can reach them in the future. (Higher-balance customers at some fund companies can be assigned a dedicated representative, so inquire.)

A broker can be a personal contact who asks you about your golf game, how your family is doing, and . . . by the way . . . "What's the phone number of your rich Uncle Johnny?" Independent financial counselors who charge a fee for their time can serve the same role. Likewise, discount brokerage firms such as Charles Schwab, TD Ameritrade, and Fidelity maintain branch offices that offer a personal, local touch if you need and want it.

HIDDEN LOADS IN ALPHABET SOUP: ABCD SHARES

Over the years, investors have learned about the sales loads that are deducted from their investments in load mutual funds. Perhaps you just discovered this yourself. Well, the companies that specialize in selling load funds have, with the unwitting assistance of government regulators, developed various types of funds that make finding the load much harder.

Just as some jewelers flog fake diamonds on late-night TV commercials, some brokers are selling funds that they *call* no-loads, when they're really *not* no-loads. By any other name, these funds are load funds: The only difference is that, with these funds, someone has taken the time to hide the sales commission.

For a given load fund, some fund companies have introduced different classes of shares, usually labeled by the letters A, B, C, or D. No matter what letter they slap onto it, remember that you're getting the same fund manager and the same fund. The only difference is how much the company's charging you to own it.

Shares with the traditional front-end load are usually sold as Class A shares. Class B, C, and D shares are the classes for which the mutual fund marketers deploy tricky techniques, such as *back-end loads* or ongoing commissions known as *12b-1 fees.* These commissions often end up being more expensive than the old up-front loads.

Take the back-end sales load, for example, which is the typical technique of Class B shares. Instead of assessing a load when you purchase these shares, you're charged a load when you sell them. But wait, the broker tells you, the more years you hold on to the shares, the lower the sales charge when you sell. In fact, if you hold on to the shares long enough — usually five to seven years — the load disappears altogether. This deal sounds a lot better than the Class A shares, which charge you an up-front load no matter what. Not so fast. The broker selling the Class B shares still gets a commission. The company simply raises the fund's operating expenses (much higher than on Class A shares) and pays the broker commissions out of that. One way or another, the broker gets his pound of flesh from your investment dollars.

You can easily avoid these hidden loads. Don't buy funds through salespeople. Buy no-loads, such as those recommended in this book.

Exposing loads

TIP

The only way to be sure that a fund is truly no-load is to look at the prospectus for the fund. Only there, in black and white and absent of all marketing hype, must the organization tell the truth about its sales charges and other fund fees.

Figure 2-1 is a sample of a typical fee table from a fund prospectus for a load fund. Note that the Class A shares have an up-front 6.5 percent sales commission that's deducted when you invest your money.

WARNING

The Class B shares don't have an up-front commission but instead have a deferred sales charge, which decreases over time. *However,* note that this class can charge you up to an extra 1 percent per year (12b-1 marketing expense fees). Class B shares in this example (as in most real cases) cost you more in the long run because you pay this cost each year as long as you own the fund. Check out the nearby sidebar "Hidden loads in alphabet soup: ABCD shares" for even more details on this game of "hide the load."

Considering a fund's operating expenses

One cost of fund ownership that you simply can't avoid is *operating expenses.* Every fund — load and no-load — has operational costs: paying the fund manager and research assistants, employing people to answer the phone lines and operate a website, printing and mailing prospectuses, buying technology equipment to track all those investments and customer-account balances, and so on.

Running a fund business costs money! Fund fees also include a profit for the fund company. (The brokerage costs that a fund pays to buy and sell securities aren't included in a fund's operating expenses. You can find this information in a fund's Statement of Additional Information.)

A fund's operating expenses are quoted as a percentage of the fund's assets or value. The percentage represents an annual fee or charge. In the case of load funds, this fee is in addition to the stated load. You can find this number in the expenses section of a fund's prospectus, usually denoted by a line, such as *Total Fund Operating Expenses.* Or you can call the fund's toll-free number and ask a representative or dig for the information on most fund companies' websites.

Some people ask how the expenses are charged and whether they're itemized on your fund statement. The answer is that a fund's operating expenses are essentially invisible to you because they're deducted before you're paid any return. Because these expenses are charged on a daily basis, you don't need to worry about trying to get out of a fund before these fees are deducted.

FEE TABLE

Shareholder Transaction Expenses:	Class A Shares	Class B Shares
Maximum Sales Charge Imposed on Purchase (as a percentage of offering price)	6.50%	None
Sales Charge Imposed on Dividend Reinvestments	None	None
Deferred Sales Charge	None	4.0% during the first year, decreasing 1.0% annually to 0.0% after the fourth year
Exchange Fee	None	None

Annual Fund Operating Expenses (as a percentage of average net assets):

	Class A Shares	Class B Shares
Management Fee	1.00%	1.00%
12b-1 Fees	None	1.00%
Other Expenses	0.25%	0.35%
Total Fund Operating Expenses	1.25%	2.35%

Example:

Cumulative Expenses Paid for the Period of:

	1 Year	3 Years	5 Years	10 Years

You would pay the following expenses on a $1,000 investment, assuming a 5% annual return, and redemption at the end of the period:

	1 Year	3 Years	5 Years	10 Years
Class A	$78	$106	$137	$229
Class B	$64	$93	$124	$265

You would pay the following expenses on the same $1,000 investment, assuming no redemption at the end of the period:

	1 Year	3 Years	5 Years	10 Years
Class A	$78	$106	$137	$229
Class B	$24	$73	$124	$265

FIGURE 2-1: How to spot load funds.

REMEMBER

Although all funds must charge operating expenses, some funds charge much more than others. By picking the right funds, you can minimize the operating expenses you pay. And minimize them you should: Operating expenses come right out of your returns. Higher expenses translate into a lower return to you.

Expenses matter on all types of funds but more on some and less on others:

>> **Expenses are critical on money market mutual funds and are very important on bond funds.** These funds are buying securities that are so similar and so efficiently priced in the financial markets. In other words, your expected returns from similar bond and money funds are largely driven by the size of a fund's operating expenses. This fact has been especially true in recent years with such low interest rates.

>> **With stock funds, expenses are a less important (but still important) factor in picking a fund.** Don't forget that, over time, stocks have averaged returns of about 10 percent per year. So if one stock fund charges 1.5 percent *more* in operating expenses than another, you're giving up an extra 15 percent of your expected annual returns.

Some people argue that stock funds that charge high expenses may be justified in doing so — *if* they're able to generate higher rates of return. *But there's no evidence that high-expense stock funds do generate higher returns.* In fact, funds with higher operating expenses, on average, tend to produce *lower* rates of return, which makes sense because operating expenses are deducted from the returns that a fund generates.

WARNING

If a given fund's expenses are much higher than its peers, one of two things is usually happening: Either the fund has little money under management — and therefore has a smaller group of investors to bear the management costs — or the fund owners are raking in huge profits. Another possibility could be that the fund company is inefficiently managed. (Maybe the company rents high-cost, big-city office space, and its telephone reps spend half the day talking with friends!) In any case, you don't want to be a shareholder of such a fund. Steel yourself against clever marketing brochures and charming salespeople. Read the fine print and walk the other way to a better fund if costs are too high.

These high-expense funds have another insidious danger built in: To produce returns comparable to those of similar funds with lower costs, the manager of such a high-cost fund may take extra risks to overcome the performance drag of high expenses. So on top of reducing a fund's returns, higher expenses may expose you to greater risk than you desire.

In some cases, a fund (particularly a newer one that's trying to attract assets) will "reimburse" a portion of its expense ratio to show a lower cost. But if (or when) the fund terminates this reimbursement, you're stuck owning shares in a fund that has higher costs than you intended to pay.

REMEMBER

All fund fees — both loads and operating expenses — are disclosed in a fund's prospectus, which is why getting a fund's prospectus *before* you buy it is so important. Reviewing the prospectus is especially critical for funds pitched to you by brokers or by brokers who masquerade as "financial planners" and "consultants."

Weighing Performance and Risk

Although a fund's *performance*, or its historic rate of return, is certainly an important factor to weigh when selecting a fund, investors tend to overemphasize its importance. Choosing funds on simplistic comparisons of performance numbers is dangerous.

As all mutual fund materials are required to state, past performance is no guarantee of future results. Analysis of historic fund performance proves that some of yesterday's stars may turn into tomorrow's skid row bums.

WARNING

Realize that funds with relatively high returns may achieve their results by taking on a lot of risk. Those same funds often take the hardest fall during major market declines. Remember that risk and return go hand in hand; you can't afford to look at return independent of the risk it took to get there. Before you invest in a fund, make sure you're comfortable with the level of risk the fund is taking on.

Star today, also-ran tomorrow

Some fund managers may have a fabulous quarter or year or two. Suddenly, their face is plastered across the financial magazines; they're hailed as the next investing genius, and then hundreds of millions and perhaps billions of new investor dollars come pouring into their fund.

REMEMBER

Short-term (one year is a short time period) fund performance numbers don't mean much — luck can be just as big a factor as skill. Also remember that earning much higher returns than other similar funds often means that the manager took a lot of risk. The greater the short-term returns for that fund and manager, the greater the odds of a sharp slump.

The history of short-term mutual fund star funds confirms this: Of the number-one top-performing stock and bond funds in each of the last 20 years, a whopping 80 percent of them subsequently performed worse than the average fund in their peer group over the next five to ten years! Some of these former number-one funds actually went on to become the worst-performing funds in their particular category.

The following sections provide a historic sampling of the many examples of short-term stars becoming tomorrow's also-rans (and in some cases, downright losers).

CGM Focus

The CGM Focus fund is part of a small family of funds managed by Ken Heebner. His Focus fund more than doubled in value from early 2007 to mid-2008, which capped off a very good first decade for the fund that had begun operations in late 1997.

Money flooded into the Focus fund after its eye-popping returns in 2007, thanks in part to all the gushing media accolades the fund was accumulating around that time. For example, the *New York Times* published an article, "Three Strategies That Kept Sizzling," that said, "Ken Heebner, manager of CGM Focus, achieved a double distinction with his fund. He placed among the top performers for the most recent quarter and the five-year period. For the quarter, CGM Focus, which invests mainly in large-capitalization domestic stocks, returned 30.3 percent, while for the five years ended Sept. 30, it returned 32.9 percent, annualized. . . . Mr. Heebner sniffs out trends — economic, social or demographic — and then tries to find well-run companies poised to benefit from them."

Kiplinger also published a glowing article referring to Heebner's "brilliance at picking investment themes and the stocks that go best with them." And Heebner even graced the cover of *Fortune* magazine in June 2008. The article was titled "America's Hottest Investor," and the intro read, "Never mind the rocky market. After a string of supersmart calls, mutual fund manager Ken Heebner is putting up the best numbers of his sterling career."

During the severe stock market downturn that occurred primarily late in 2008, CGM Focus got crushed much worse than the overall market. It plunged about 65 percent in just eight months after June 2008. And in the years since, it has continued to dramatically underperform the market averages. While the S&P 500 has soared 325 percent since early 2009, at the time of writing, CGM Focus is up only 86 percent. So since its peak in June 2008, CGM Focus is down 34 percent while the S&P 500 is up 90 percent.

Fidelity Growth Strategies

Launched in 1991, Fidelity Growth Strategies invests in medium-size growth companies. The fund performed a little better than the market averages in the early to mid-1990s, and then it dramatically outperformed its peer group in the late 1990s.

So Fidelity promoted the heck out of the fund, and investors piled into it to the tune of nearly $10 billion in 1999. And Fidelity had some help from articles like the one that ran in the July 18, 1999, issue of the *New York Times*.

In a positively glowing profile of the fund, and its manager, Erin Sullivan, the *Times* called Sullivan "the quintessential portfolio manager." And it added in the following material, which caused investors to send Ms. Sullivan's fund their investment dollars:

> Ms. Sullivan, 29, has been in charge of the $5.96 billion Fidelity Aggressive Growth fund since April 1997. In that time, the fund has posted total returns of 51.83 percent, annualized, versus 33.16 percent for the Standard & Poor's 500-stock index. . . . This year through July 15, the fund was up 44.34 percent, nearly tripling the 15.4 percent gain of the S & P 500.
>
> Ms. Sullivan goes about her business with the self-assurance of a Harvard graduate, the analytical rigor of a math theoretician, and the vigor of a marathon runner, all of which she is. But she has not entered a marathon race roughly since she took the reins of Aggressive Growth. "It's hard to find time for anything else," she said.

Within months of the *Times* article, the fund's fortunes changed. Overloaded with overpriced technology stocks, the fund plunged 84 percent in value from early 2000 to late 2002. It was one of the worst performing funds over the next decade with its −9.9 percent per year annualized return. (Sullivan departed the fund during this time and went off to run her own hedge fund.) Although the fund has performed better in recent years, over a recent 15-year period, it was in the bottom 1 percent of funds in its category.

Van Wagoner Emerging Growth fund

With a mere three years of stellar returns under his belt, Garrett Van Wagoner, manager of the Govett Smaller Companies Fund, decided to cash in on his exploding popularity and start his own money management firm — Van Wagoner Capital Management. Calling Van Wagoner the hottest small company stock picker around, several of the nation's largest financial magazines recommended investing in his new Emerging Growth fund. Investor cash came flooding in — more than a billion dollars in the fund's first six months of existence.

The Van Wagoner Emerging Growth fund (since renamed the Embarcadero Small Cap Growth fund) invests in high-flying smaller company growth stocks. In its first full year of operations (1996), the fund posted a respectable total return of nearly 27 percent, placing it within the top 20 percent of funds within its peer group.

In the next year, 1997, the fund dropped by 20 percent, dramatically under-performed its peer group, and was among the worst of its peers. Money flowed out, and the fund was largely ignored until 1999 when Van Wagoner piled into technology stocks, which were zooming to the moon. In 1999, this fund produced a total return of a whopping 291 percent (making it the year's number-one stock fund) while assets under management swelled from less than $200 million to nearly $1.5 billion!

Investors who came to Van Wagoner's party in 1999 were subsequently treated to one of the greatest collapses in the history of the fund industry. Following a drop of 20.9 percent in 2000, the fund posted horrendous losses in the next two years as well — losing 59.7 percent in 2001 and then 64.5 percent in 2002. In fact, the poor investors who bought in at or near the top during late 1999 through early 2000 experienced a stomach-wrenching plunge of more than 90 percent through September 2002. The fund also had many horrendous years in the 2000s. (See Table 2-1 for how this fund performed versus its relevant index — the Russell 2000 Growth Index.)

TABLE 2-1

Comparing the Van Wagoner Emerging Growth Fund's Performance

Year	Van Wagoner Emerging Growth Fund Total Return	Russell 2000 Growth Index Total Return
2000	–20.9%	–22.4%
2001	–59.7%	–9.2%
2002	–64.6%	–30.3%
2003	47.2%	48.5%
2004	–16.0%	14.3%
2005	–22.3%	4.1%
2006	10.8%	13.3%
2007	–7.8%	7.1%
2008	–56.8%	-38.5%
2009	12.6%	34.5%

Over the decade after the tech stock peak, this fund plunged in value by more than 94 percent! If you'd invested $10,000 in this fund at its inception in 1996, your investment would've shrunk to $1,841, whereas the same investment in its aver-age peer would've grown to $22,383!

Apples to apples: Comparing performance numbers

Remember back in school when the teacher returned exams and you were delighted to get a 92 (unless you're from an overachieving family)? But then you found out that the average on the exam was a 95. You still may have been pleased, but a lot of air was let out of your balloon.

Fund performance numbers are the same: They don't mean much until they're compared to the averages. A 15 percent return sounds great until you find out that the return from the relevant index market average (that invests in similar securities) was 25 percent during the same period.

The trick is picking the correct benchmark for comparison. Dozens of market indexes and fund category averages measure various components of the market. You always want to compare a fund's returns to its most appropriate benchmark. Comparing the performance of an international stock fund to that of a U.S. stock market index isn't fair, just as comparing a sixth-grader's test results on a given test to those of a tenth-grader taking the same test is unfair.

WARNING

Context matters, and fund companies realize this. So in their marketing literature, fund companies usually compare their funds' returns to selected benchmarks. Keep a wary eye on these comparisons. In the great American advertising tradition, fund companies often pick benchmarks that make it easy for their funds to look good. And in like manner, more than a few investment advisors who manage money do the same.

Here's an example of how a fund can make itself look a lot better than it really is.

A number of years ago, the Strong Short-Term Bond Fund (subsequently acquired by Wells Fargo) ran ads claiming to be the number-one, short-term bond fund. The ads featured a 12-month comparison graph that compared the Strong fund's yield to the average yield on other short-term bond funds. The Strong Short-Term Bond Fund, according to the graph, consistently outperformed the competition by 2 to 2.5 percent!

A bond fund must take a *lot* more risk to generate a dividend yield this much higher than the competition's. You should also be suspicious of any bond fund claiming to be this good with an annual operating expense ratio of 0.8 percent. With a yield and expenses that high, a fund has to take higher risks than supposedly comparable funds to make up for the drag of its expenses. And if the fund's taking that much more risk, then it needs to be compared to its true competition — which, in Strong's case, are other funds whose investments take similarly high risks. This fund isn't a bad fund, but it isn't nearly as good as the ad would've had you think.

This fund was on steroids! The Strong Short-Term Bond Fund wasn't comparable to most other short-term bond funds because

>> **A high percentage of its bonds weren't high quality.** About 40 percent of its bonds were rated BBB or below.

>> **Many of its bonds weren't short-term bonds.** The Strong Fund invested in mortgage bonds that are more like intermediate-term bonds.

Strong's ad also claimed that its bond fund was ranked number one for the year. If a fund takes more risk than the funds it compares itself to, then sure, during particular, brief periods, it can easily end up at the top of the performance charts. But how strong of a long-term performer is this "number-one" fund? Over the five years before this ad ran, even including the year the ad was so proud of, Strong's fund had *underperformed* most short-term bond funds.

Recognizing Manager Expertise

Much is made of who manages a specific mutual fund. Although the expertise of the individual fund manager is important, managers aren't islands unto themselves. And if the fund manager leaves or retires from the company, you're left holding the fund. The earlier section "Star today, also-ran tomorrow" explains how a star fund can flare for its moment of investor glory and then easily twinkle down to become just another average or worse-than-average fund. Too many people want to believe that, in every field of endeavor — sports, entertainment, business — there are superhumans who can walk on water.

It's true that in the investment world some people shine at what they do. But compared to other fields, the gap between the star investment manager and the average one, over long time periods, typically is small.

If the stocks of large U.S. companies, for example, have increased an average of 13 percent per year over a decade, the money manager focusing on such securities may vault to star status if their fund earns 15 percent over the same time period. An extra 2 percent per year ain't nothin' to sneeze at — especially if you have millions invested. But a 2 percent higher return is a lot smaller than what most people think they can achieve with the best investment managers.

REMEMBER

Therefore, the resources and capabilities of the parent company should be equally important in your selection of which funds to invest in. Different companies have different capabilities and levels of expertise with different types of funds.

WARNING

Avoid fund companies with little fund management experience and success. If you need surgery, you place your trust with a surgeon who's successfully performed the operation hundreds of times, not with a rookie who's only seen it on the local cable station. Avoid novelty funds as well. Mutual funds have been around for many decades. Yet not a week goes by without some newfangled fund coming out with a new concept. Most of these ideas come from the fund company's marketing department, which in some companies has too much clout. Instead of coming up with investments that meet investors' needs, they come up with gimmicky funds that involve extra risk and that almost always cost extra in their high annual operating expenses.

Chapter 3

Buying Mutual Funds from the Best Firms

H undreds of investment companies offer thousands of fund options. However, only a handful of these fund companies offer many top-notch funds, so this chapter tells you which companies are the best places for your fund investing.

In addition to recommending the best parent fund companies, this chapter also recommends the best discount brokers. Although these guys are slightly more expensive, discount brokers make buying the best funds from different fund companies and holding all the funds in a single account a lot easier.

Finding the Best Buys

When studying the different mutual fund companies, you may see a lot of different funds. Some are better than others. Using the criteria in Chapter 2 of Book 5, this chapter presents the best buys. The following sections discuss the best companies through which to invest in funds directly.

The Vanguard Group

The Vanguard Group (investor.vanguard.com/home) is now the largest mutual fund company in America, having surpassed Fidelity. Vanguard's significant growth since the early 1990s has been somewhat of a vindication for a company that was underrated for many years.

One of the reasons for Vanguard's underrating is the fact that its funds are almost never at the very tiptop of the performance charts for their respective categories. As Chapter 2 in Book 5 discusses, this sign is actually good, because many number-one-performing funds are rarely even above average over the long haul. Although Vanguard offers a broad spectrum of funds in terms of risk, it doesn't take excessive risks with the funds it offers; thus, its funds rarely are ranked number one over short time periods.

Because of Vanguard's unique shareholder-owned structure (see the nearby sidebar "Vanguard's roots: The Bogle difference"), the average operating-expense ratio of its funds — 0.19 percent per year for U.S. stock funds, 0.23 percent for international stock funds, and 0.14 percent for bond funds at the time of writing — is lower than that of any other fund family in the industry. In fact, the average fund family's expense ratio is a whopping four times higher than Vanguard's. Vanguard also offers its Admiral series of funds with lower expense ratios for higher-balance customers and low-cost exchange-traded funds (ETFs; see Chapters 4 and 5 in Book 5).

A pioneer in the field, Vanguard was the first to offer to the public *index funds*, which are unmanaged portfolios of the securities that comprise a given market index. Some other fund companies have since added index funds to their lists of offerings. But Vanguard is still the indexing leader with the broadest selection of index funds and the lowest operating expenses in the business.

Vanguard's low expenses translate into superior performance. Especially with money market and bond funds (markets in which even the best fund managers add relatively little value), Vanguard's funds are consistently near the head of the class.

REMEMBER

Vanguard is best at funds appealing to safety-minded investors — those who want to invest in money market, bond, and conservative stock funds. However, Vanguard also offers aggressive stock funds with solid performance and low-expense ratios. In managing stock funds, where performance is supposed to be more closely tied to the genius of the fund manager, Vanguard's thriftiness enhances performance.

VANGUARD'S ROOTS: THE BOGLE DIFFERENCE

In the early 1970s when Vanguard was formed, John Bogle, its founder and former CEO, made the big decision that to this day clearly differentiates Vanguard from its competition: Vanguard distributes funds and provides shareholder administration on an *at-cost basis* — that is, with no markup

Bogle insisted that the management of most of the stock funds be contracted out to private money management firms, from whom Vanguard would negotiate the best deals. Thus, Vanguard's fund investors would own the management company. Contrast this arrangement to that of traditional fund companies, in which the parent management company receives the profits from managing the funds.

Bogle felt that this unique corporate structure ensured that fund shareholders would obtain the best deals possible on money managers. "Funds ought to be run for the benefit of shareholders, not for the fund managers," Bogle reasoned. History has proven Bogle not only to be right but also to be a fund investor's best advocate.

Fidelity Investments

Fidelity Investments (www.fidelity.com/) is the second-largest mutual fund company in America. A mutual fund Goliath, Fidelity offers hundreds of funds. As evidence of Fidelity's enormous buying power, representatives from dozens of companies visit its Boston offices every day. Most fund managers have to travel to the companies they're interested in researching; if you're a Fidelity fund manager, however, many companies come to you.

If you're venturing to do business with Fidelity on your own, you have your work cut out for you. One of the biggest problems novice investors have at Fidelity is discerning the good funds from the not-so-good ones.

WARNING

You should shun the following types of funds at Fidelity:

>> **Bond funds:** Relative to the best of the competition, Fidelity's bond funds charge higher operating expenses that depress an investor's returns. (**Note:** For larger balance customers, Fidelity offers a decent series of bond funds known as Spartan funds that have lower operating expense ratios.)

>> **Adviser funds:** Fidelity sells this family of load funds through investment salespeople; these funds carry high sales loads or high ongoing fees.

>> **Sector funds:** You should also avoid Fidelity's sector funds (Select), which invest in just one industry — such as air transportation, insurance, or retailing. These funds have rapid changeover of managers. Being industry focused, these funds are poorly diversified (highly concentrated) and quite risky. Fidelity, unfortunately, encourages a trader mentality with these funds.

TIP

One of Fidelity's strengths is its local presence — it operates more than 100 branch offices throughout the United States and staffs its phones 24 hours a day, 365 days a year.

FUNDS WITH BRANCH OFFICES: EVEN BETTER?

Many fund companies have their offices in one location. If you happen to live in the town or city where they're located and want to do business with them, you can visit them in person. However, odds are that, unless you maintain several homes, you won't be living near the fund companies with which you want to do your fund-investing business.

Some fund companies, such as Fidelity, have greater numbers of branch offices, which are located primarily in densely populated and more affluent areas. You may feel more comfortable dropping a check off or speaking to an investment representative face to face instead of being navigated through an automated voice message system or mouse-clicking through a website. However, there's no sound *financial* reason that you need to go in person to a fund company — you can do everything you need to do by phone, mail, and/or computer.

In most cases, you pay a cost for doing your fund investing through firms with branch offices. Operating all those branch offices in areas where rent and employees don't come cheaply costs a good chunk of money. Ultimately, firms that maintain a large branch network need to build these extra costs into their funds' fees. Higher fees lower your investment returns.

A counterargument that fund companies with many branch offices make is that if the branch offices succeed in enticing more investors to use the funds offered by the company, more total money is brought in. Having more money under management helps to lower the average cost of managing each dollar invested.

Dodge & Cox

Dodge & Cox (www.dodgeandcox.com/) is a San Francisco–based firm that has been in the fund business since the Great Depression. It's best known for its conservatively managed funds with solid track records and modest fees.

Unfortunately for new investors, from time to time, Dodge & Cox has closed some of its funds. The company does so to keep funds from becoming too bloated with assets to manage, which could undermine the performance of those funds. So if any of its funds appeal to you, you should establish an account in case it shuts any of its funds again to new investors.

Oakmark

Harris Associates, which has managed money since 1976, is the investment management company that oversees the management of Oakmark (oakmark.com/), a value–oriented Chicago–based family of funds.

As with the Dodge & Cox funds (see the preceding section), a number of the best Oakmark funds have closed from time to time to new investors. Be aware that when some of its funds have closed in the past, investors who establish accounts directly with Oakmark can still buy some of the closed funds.

T. Rowe Price

Founded in 1937, T. Rowe Price (www.troweprice.com/personal-investing/home.html) is one of the oldest mutual fund companies — named after its founder, T. (Thomas) Rowe Price, who's generally credited with popularizing investing in growth-oriented companies. The fund company has also been a fund pioneer in international investing.

T. Rowe Price remained a small company for many years, focusing on its specialties of U.S. growth stocks and international funds. That stance changed in recent decades as the company offered a comprehensive menu of different fund types. It offers 401(k) retirement plans specifically for smaller companies. The fund company also offers a series of lower-cost money market and bond funds called Summit funds with a minimum initial investment of $25,000.

TIAA

This nonprofit organization (www.tiaa.org/public/) provides an array of investment services to education, hospitals, and other nonprofit organizations and offers a solid family of funds to the general public. Its funds have low operating expense ratios and are conservatively managed.

Headquartered in New York City, the company has major operations in Charlotte, North Carolina; Dallas, Texas; and Denver, Colorado; as well as about 70 local offices. The organization got its start in 1918 when Andrew Carnegie and his Carnegie Foundation established a pension system for professors. Funding initially came from grants from the foundation and Carnegie Corporation of New York, and regular contributions from participating institutions and individuals. Today, TIAA invests more than $800 billion on behalf of investors.

The funds' low minimums make them a good choice for investors with smaller sums to invest. They have no-minimum-investment IRAs with no annual administrative fees.

USAA

Headquartered in San Antonio, Texas, USAA (www.usaa.com) is a conservative family of efficiently managed funds (and generally low-cost, high-quality insurance). Although you (or a family member) need to be a military officer, enlistee, or military retiree to gain access to its homeowner's and auto insurance, anyone can buy its mutual funds.

USAA also offers investors, with small amounts to invest (minimum of $50 monthly) and without several thousand dollars required to meet fund minimum requirements, the ability to invest via electronic monthly transfers.

Other fund companies

Hundreds of mutual fund companies offer thousands of funds. Many aren't worth your consideration because they don't meet the commonsense selection criteria outlined in Chapter 2 of Book 5. So if you're wondering why this chapter doesn't mention a particular fund family, it's probably because the record shows that its funds are high cost, low performance, managed in a schizophrenic fashion, or all the above. Check them out against the criteria in Chapter 2 of Book 5 to see for yourself.

Discount Brokers: Mutual Fund Supermarkets

For many years, you could purchase no-load mutual funds only directly from mutual fund companies. If you wanted to buy some funds at, say, Vanguard, Oakmark, T. Rowe Price, and Dodge & Cox, you needed to call these four different companies and request each firm's application. So you ended up filling out four different sets of forms and mailing them in with a separate check to each of the companies.

Soon, you received separate statements from each of the four fund companies reporting how your investments were doing. (Some fund companies make this even more of a paperwork nightmare by sending you a separate statement for each individual mutual fund that you buy through them.)

Now suppose that you wanted to sell one of your T. Rowe Price funds and invest the proceeds at Oakmark. Doing so was also a time-consuming pain in the posterior, because you had to contact T. Rowe Price to sell, wait days for it to send you a check for the sale's proceeds, and then send the money with instructions to Oakmark. Shopping this way can be tedious. Imagine wanting to make a salad and having to go to a lettuce farm, a tomato farm, and an onion farm to get the ingredients. That's why we have supermarkets!

In 1984, Charles Schwab came up with the idea to create a supermarket for mutual funds. Charles Schwab is the discount broker pioneer who created the first mutual fund supermarket (which other discount brokers have since copied) where you can purchase hundreds of individual funds from dozens of fund companies — one-stop mutual fund shopping.

The major benefit of such a service is that it greatly simplifies the paperwork involved in buying and selling different companies' mutual funds. No matter how many mutual fund companies you want to invest in, you need to complete just one application for the discount broker. And instead of getting a separate statement from each company, you get one statement from the discount broker that summarizes all your mutual fund holdings. (*Note:* You still must maintain separate nonretirement and IRA accounts.)

Moving from one company's fund into another's is generally a snap. The discount broker can usually take care of all this with one phone call from you. Come tax time, you receive just one 1099 statement summarizing your fund's taxable distributions to record on your tax return.

REMEMBER

You weren't born yesterday, so you know that all this convenience must have a catch. Here's a hint: Because discount brokers serve as intermediaries for the buying and selling of funds and the time and money spent sending you statements, they expect to make some money in return. So guess what? It costs you more to use a discount broker. Discount brokers charge you a small transaction fee whenever you buy or sell most of the better funds that they offer.

Buying direct versus discount brokers

Buying funds directly from fund companies versus buying funds through a discounter's mutual fund supermarket isn't inherently better. For the most part, it's a trade-off that boils down to personal preference and individual circumstances.

Why to buy funds direct

Many reasons exist to buy funds directly from fund companies. Here are a few:

>> **You're thrifty.** And you can take that as a compliment. Being vigilant about your investing costs boosts your returns. By buying direct from no-load fund companies, you avoid the discount brokerage transaction costs.

>> **You don't have much money to invest.** If you're investing less than $5,000 per fund, the minimum transaction fees of a discount broker will gobble up a large percentage of your investment. You don't have to hassle with transaction fees when you buy direct from a no-load fund company.

>> **You're content investing through one of the bigger fund companies with a broad array of good funds.** For example, if you deal directly with one fund company that excels in all types of funds, you can minimize your fees and maximize your investment returns. Given the breadth and depth of the bigger company's fund selections, you should feel content centralizing your fund investments through one of the better companies. However, if you sleep better at night investing through multiple fund companies' funds, this book won't try to change your mind.

TIP

Given the fact that most of the major fund companies, such as Vanguard, Fidelity, and T. Rowe Price, have discount brokerage divisions offering mutual funds from companies other than their own, you could use one of these companies as your base and have the best of both worlds. Suppose, for example, that you want to invest a large portion but not all your money in Fidelity funds. By establishing a discount brokerage account at Fidelity, all your Fidelity fund purchases would be free of transaction fees; then through that same account, you could also buy other fund companies' funds.

Why to buy through a discount broker

Here are the main reasons to go with a discount broker:

>> **You want to invest in funds from many fund companies.** In general, different fund companies excel in different types of investments: You may want to build a portfolio that draws on the specific talents of various fund companies. Although you can buy directly through each individual fund company, the point eventually comes where the hassle and clutter just aren't worth it. The one-stop shopping of a discount broker may well be worth the occasional transaction fee.

>> **You hate paperwork.** For those of you out there whose disdain of paperwork is so intense that it keeps you from doing things that you're supposed to do, a discount broker is for you.

>> **You want easy access to your money.** Some discount brokerage accounts offer such bells and whistles as debit cards and unlimited check-writing privileges, making it simple for you to tap in to your money. (That can be a bad thing if this tempts you to spend your money!)

>> **You want to buy into a high-minimum fund.** One unique feature available through some discount broker's fund services is the ability to purchase some funds that aren't normally available to smaller investors.

TECHNICAL STUFF

>> **You want to buy funds on margin.** Another interesting but rarely used feature that comes with a brokerage account is that you can borrow *on margin* (take out a loan from the brokerage firm) against mutual funds and other securities (which are used as collateral) held in a nonretirement account. Borrowing against your funds generally costs less than your other loan options, and it's potentially tax-deductible. That said, buying and holding funds on margin can be costly and risky, and you may be forced to sell some funds or add cash to your account if the value of your investments declines too much.

TIP

You have a way (that involves hassle) to buy and sell your funds and use a discounter but reduce the total transaction fees: Purchase your funds initially from the mutual fund company and then transfer the shares at no charge into a discount brokerage account. Conversely, when you're ready to sell shares, you can transfer shares from the discounter to the mutual fund company before you're ready to sell.

Debunking "No Transaction Fee" funds

After several years of distributing funds for all these different fund companies, discount brokers came up with another innovation. Discount brokers were doing a lot for mutual fund companies (for instance, handling the purchase and sale of funds as well as the ongoing account recordkeeping and reporting), but they weren't being paid for all their work.

In 1992, Charles Schwab & Company negotiated to be paid an ongoing fee to service and handle customer accounts by some mutual fund companies. Today, through Schwab and other discount brokers who replicated this service, you can purchase hundreds of funds without paying any transaction fees (that is, you pay the same cost as if you'd bought the funds through the mutual fund company itself). These are called *No Transaction Fee (NTF) funds.*

On the surface, this idea certainly sounds like a great deal for you — the mutual fund investor wanting to buy funds from various companies through a discount brokerage account. You get access to many funds and one account statement without paying transaction fees.

WARNING

The no-transaction fee fund is a case of something sounding much better than it really is. Although some discount brokers say or imply that NTF funds are free, they're hardly free. Discount brokers are able to waive the transaction costs to you only because the participating fund companies have agreed to foot the bill. In a typical arrangement, the participating fund company shares a portion of its operating expense ratio with the discount broker handling the account. But as you know if you read Chapter 2 in Book 5, annual operating expenses are drawn from the shareholders' investment dollars. So in the end, you're still the one paying the transaction costs.

As a group, NTF funds are inferior to the best no-load funds that you pay the discounters a transaction fee to purchase because NTF funds tend to

>> Have higher operating expenses than non-NTF funds

>> Be offered by smaller, less experienced fund companies who may be struggling to compete in the saturated mutual fund market

>> Exclude big, well-established fund companies (including the ones discussed earlier in this chapter, such as Vanguard, Fidelity, and T. Rowe Price). These companies don't participate in NTF programs because they don't have to; the demand for their funds is high even with transaction costs.

WARNING

In their rush to sign up more NTF funds, some discounters have ignored the quality of the NTF funds they offer. Some financial publications encourage and effectively endorse this lack of quality control by giving higher ratings (in articles purporting to review and rate various discount brokers) to those discounters offering more "free" funds to customers. As with a restaurant meal, more isn't always better — quality counts as well!

REMEMBER

Whenever you make a mutual fund investment decision through a discount broker, try not to be influenced by the prospect, or lack thereof, of a transaction fee. In your efforts to avoid paying a small transaction fee today, you can end up buying a fund with high ongoing fees and subpar performance. If you're so concerned about paying additional fees, deal directly with fund companies and bypass the discount brokers and their transaction fees.

Using the best discount brokers

Although this chapter speaks of fund companies and discount brokers as separate entities, the line between them has greatly blurred in recent years. For example, Schwab started as a discount broker but later began offering its own funds. Other companies started selling mutual funds but have now moved into the discount brokerage business. The most obvious example is Fidelity, which offers brokerage services through which you can trade individual securities or buy many non-Fidelity mutual funds.

TIP

Vanguard and T. Rowe Price have excellent discount brokerage divisions that offer an extensive array of funds from other leading fund companies and charge competitive transaction fees. Vanguard charges $20 per online trade (and offers many funds including their own without any transaction fee); T. Rowe Price charges $35 per trade.

REMEMBER

The discount brokerage services of Fidelity, Vanguard, and T. Rowe Price make a lot of sense if you plan on doing the bulk of your fund investing through their respective funds. Note that you only have to pay brokerage transaction fees on funds offered by other fund companies. You won't pay for buying a Fidelity fund from Fidelity or a Vanguard fund from Vanguard or a T. Rowe Price fund from T. Rowe Price.

Places to Pass By

WARNING

Don't base your investment decisions on your gut: Some fund companies have plush offices, and they charge relatively high fees for their funds (to pay for all their overhead costs) or sell poorly performing funds — or both. What types of places are likely to make you feel comfortable but lead you astray? Many people do their fund investing through a list of wrong places:

>> **The First Faithful Community Bank:** Many people feel comfortable turning their money over to the friendly neighborhood banker. You've done it for years with your checking and savings accounts. The bank has an

impressive-looking branch close to your home, complete with parking, security cameras, and a vault. And then there's that FDIC insurance that guarantees your deposits. So now that your bank offers mutual funds, you may feel comfortable taking advice from the "investment specialist" or "consultant" in the branch (and may erroneously believe that the funds it sells carry FDIC coverage).

Well, the branch representative at your local bank is probably a broker who's earning commissions from the funds they're selling you. Bank funds generally charge sales commissions and higher operating expenses and generally have less-than-stellar performance relative to the best no-load funds. And because banks are relatively new to the mutual fund game, the broker at your bank may have spent last year helping customers establish new checking accounts and may have little knowledge and experience with investments and mutual funds. Remember, brokers who work on commission are salespeople, not advisors. And the funds they're selling are load funds. You can do better.

>> **Plunder and Pillage Brokerage Firm:** Brokers work on commission, so they can and will sell load funds. They may even try to hoodwink you into believing that they can do financial planning for you. Don't believe it. As Chapter 2 in Book 5 discusses, purchasing a load fund has no real benefit; you have better alternatives.

>> **Fred, the Friendly Financial Planner:** You may have met Fred through a free seminar, adult education class, or a cold call that he made to you. Fred may not really be a financial planner at all; instead, he could be a salesperson/broker who sells load funds.

>> **Igor, Your Insurance Broker:** Igor isn't just selling insurance anymore. He now may sell mutual funds as well and may even call himself a financial consultant. (See the preceding remarks for brokers.)

>> **The Lutheran-Turkish-Irish-Americans-Graduated-from-Cornell-and-Now-Working-in-the-Music-Business Fund:** Hoping to capitalize on the booming fund business, special interest groups everywhere have been jumping into the fray with funds of their own. Don't be surprised if your church, your alma mater, or your ethnic group makes a passionate pitch to pool your money with that of like-minded individuals in the hands of a manager who truly understands your background.

Although something can possibly be said for group solidarity, leave your nest egg alone. Such special-interest funds carry loads and high operating fees and, because they have relatively little money to manage, are usually managed by money managers with little experience.

IN THIS CHAPTER

» Distinguishing what makes ETFs unique

» Appreciating ETFs' special attributes

» Understanding that ETFs aren't perfect

» Taking a look at who is making the most use of ETFs, and how

» Asking whether ETFs are for you

Chapter **4**

What the Heck Is an ETF, Anyway?

anking your retirement on stocks is risky enough; banking your retirement on any individual stock, or even a handful of stocks, is about as risky as wrestling crocodiles. Banking on individual bonds is less risky (maybe wrestling an adolescent crocodile), but the same general principle holds. There is safety in numbers. That's why gnus graze in groups. That's why smart stock and bond investors grab onto exchange-traded funds (ETFs).

This chapter explains not only the safety features of ETFs but also the ways in which they differ from their cousins, mutual funds (introduced in Chapter 1 of Book 5). By the time you're done with this chapter, you should have a pretty good idea of what ETFs can do for your portfolio.

The Nature of the Beast

Just as a deed shows that you have ownership of a house, and a share of common stock certifies ownership in a company, a share of an ETF represents ownership (most typically) in a basket of company stocks. To buy or sell an ETF, you place an order with a broker, generally (and preferably, for cost reasons) online, although you can also place an order by phone. The price of an ETF changes throughout the trading day (which is to say from 9:30 a.m. to 4:00 p.m., New York City time), going up or down with the market value of the securities it holds. Sometimes there can be a little sway — times when the price of an ETF doesn't exactly track the value of the securities it holds — but that situation is rarely serious, at least not with ETFs from the better purveyors.

Originally, ETFs were developed to mirror various indexes:

» The SPDR S&P 500 (ticker SPY) represents stocks from the S&P (Standard & Poor's) 500, an index of the 500 largest companies in the United States.

» The DIAMONDS Trust Series 1 (ticker DIA) represents the 30 or so underlying stocks of the Dow Jones Industrial Average index.

» The Invesco QQQ Trust Series 1 (ticker QQQ; formerly known as the NASDAQ-100 Trust Series 1) represents the 100 stocks of the NASDAQ-100 index.

Since ETFs were first introduced, many others, tracking all kinds of things, including some rather strange things that you shouldn't even call investments, have emerged.

The component companies in an ETF's portfolio usually represent a certain index or segment of the market, such as large U.S. value stocks, small growth stocks, or micro-cap stocks. Sometimes, the stock market is broken up into industry sectors, such as technology, industrials, and consumer discretionary. ETFs exist that mirror each sector.

REMEMBER

Regardless of what securities an ETF represents, and regardless of what index those securities are a part of, your fortunes as an ETF holder are tied, either directly or in some leveraged fashion, to the value of the underlying securities. If the price of Microsoft stock, U.S. Treasury bonds, gold bullion, or British Pound futures goes up, so does the value of your ETF. If the price of gold tumbles, your portfolio (if you hold a gold ETF) may lose some glitter. If Microsoft stock pays a dividend, you are due a certain amount of that dividend — *unless* you happen to have bought into a leveraged or inverse ETF.

Some ETFs allow for leveraging, so that if the underlying security rises in value, your ETF shares rise doubly or triply. If the security falls in value, well, you lose according to the same multiple. Other ETFs allow you not only to leverage but also to *reverse* leverage, so that you stand to make money if the underlying security falls in value (and, of course, lose if the underlying security increases in value). Beware of leveraged and inverse ETFs.

Choosing between the Classic and the New Indexes

Some of the ETF providers (Vanguard, iShares, Charles Schwab) tend to use traditional indexes, such as those mentioned in the previous section. Others (Dimensional, WisdomTree) tend to develop their own indexes.

For example, if you were to buy 100 shares of an ETF called the iShares S&P 500 Growth Index Fund (IVW), you'd be buying into a traditional index (large U.S. growth companies). At about $70 a share (at this writing), you'd plunk down $7,000 for a portfolio of stocks that would include shares of Apple, Microsoft, Amazon, Facebook, Alphabet (Google), and Tesla. If you wanted to know the exact breakdown, the iShares prospectus found on the iShares website (or any number of financial websites, such as finance.yahoo.com) would tell you specific percentages: Apple, 11.3 percent; Microsoft, 10.3 percent, Amazon, 7.8 percent; and so on.

Many ETFs represent shares in companies that form foreign indexes. If, for example, you were to own 100 shares of the iShares MSCI Japan Index Fund (EWJ), with a market value of about $69 per share as of this writing, your $6,900 would buy you a stake in large Japanese companies such as Toyota Motor, SoftBank Group, Sony Group, Keyence, and Mitsubishi UFJ Financial Group.

Both IVW and EWJ mirror standard indexes: IVW mirrors the S&P 500 Growth Index, and EWJ mirrors the MSCI Japan Index. If, however, you purchase 100 shares of the Invesco Dynamic Large Cap Growth ETF (PWB), you'll buy roughly $7,100 worth of a portfolio of stocks that mirror a very unconventional index — one created by the Invesco family of exchange-traded funds. The large U.S. growth companies in the PowerShares index that have the heaviest weightings include Facebook and Alphabet, but also NVIDIA and Texas Instruments. Invesco PowerShares refers to its custom indexes as *Intellidex* indexes.

A big controversy in the world of ETFs is whether the newfangled, customized indexes offered by companies like Invesco make any sense. Most financial professionals are skeptical of anything that's new. They are a conservative lot. Those who have been around for a while have seen too many "exciting" new investment ideas crash and burn.

Another big controversy is whether you may be better off with an even newer style of ETFs — those that follow no indexes at all but rather are "actively" managed. We prefer index investing to active investing, but that's not to say that active investing, carefully pursued, has no role to play. More on that topic appears later in this chapter.

Other ETFs — a distinct but growing minority — represent holdings in assets other than stocks, most notably bonds and commodities (gold, silver, oil, and such). And then there are exchange-traded notes (ETNs), which allow you to venture even further into the world of alternative investments — or speculations — such as currency futures.

Preferring ETFs over Individual Stocks

Okay, why buy a basket of stocks rather than an individual stock? Quick answer: You'll sleep better.

You may recall that in 2018, supermodel Kate Upton accused the executive and cofounder of GUESS of harassment. The company's shares fell 18 percent overnight. A few months later, Tesla's CEO Elon Musk smoked marijuana and sipped whiskey during a bizarre podcast. Tesla's stock fell 9 percent the next day.

Those sorts of things — sometimes much worse — happen every day in the world of stocks.

A company you can call ABC Pharmaceutical sees its stock shoot up by 68 percent because the firm just earned an important patent for a new diet pill; a month later, the stock falls by 84 percent because a study in the *New England Journal of Medicine* found that the new diet pill causes people to hallucinate and think they are Genghis Khan — or Elon Musk.

Compared to the world of individual stocks, the stock market as a whole is as smooth as a morning lake. Heck, a daily rise or fall in the Dow of more than a percent or two (well, maybe 2 or 3 percent these days) is generally considered a pretty big deal.

REMEMBER

If you, like many people, are not especially keen on roller coasters, then you are advised to put your nest egg into not one stock, not two, but many. If you have a few million sitting around, hey, you'll have no problem diversifying — maybe individual stocks are for you. But for most of us commoners, the only way to effectively diversify is with ETFs or mutual funds.

Distinguishing ETFs from Mutual Funds

REMEMBER

So what is the difference between an ETF and a mutual fund? After all, mutual funds also represent baskets of stocks or bonds. The two, however, are not twins. They're not even siblings. Cousins are more like it. Here are some of the big differences between ETFs and mutual funds:

>> ETFs are bought and sold just like stocks (through a brokerage house, either by phone or online), and their prices change throughout the trading day. Mutual fund orders can be made during the day, but the actual trading doesn't occur until after the markets close.

>> ETFs tend to represent indexes — market segments — and the managers of the ETFs tend to do very little trading of securities in the ETF. (The ETFs are *passively* managed.) Most mutual funds are actively managed.

>> Although they may require you to pay small trading fees, ETFs usually wind up costing you much less than mutual funds because the ongoing management fees are typically much lower, and there is never a *load* (an entrance and/or exit fee, sometimes an exorbitant one), as you find with many mutual funds.

>> Because of low portfolio turnover and also the way ETFs are structured, ETFs generally declare much less in taxable capital gains than mutual funds.

Table 4-1 provides a quick look at some ways that investing in ETFs differs from investing in mutual funds and individual stocks. Find out more about mutual funds in Chapters 1, 2, and 3 of Book 5.

TABLE 4-1   ETFs versus Mutual Funds versus Individual Stocks

	ETFs	Mutual Funds	Individual Stocks
Are they priced, bought, and sold throughout the day?	Yes	No	Yes
Do they offer some investment diversification?	Yes	Yes	No
Is there a minimum investment?	No	Yes	No
Are they purchased through a broker or online brokerage?	Yes	Yes	Yes
Do you pay a fee or commission to make a trade?	Rarely	Sometimes	Rarely
Can that fee or commission be more than a few dollars?	No	Yes	No
Can you buy/sell options?	Sometimes	No	Sometimes
Are they indexed (passively managed)?	Typically	Atypically	No
Can you make money or lose money?	Yes	Yes	You bet

Why the Big Boys Prefer ETFs

When ETFs were first introduced, they were primarily of interest to institutional traders — insurance companies, hedge fund people, banks — whose investment needs are often considerably more complicated than yours and other people's. The following sections explain why ETFs appeal to the largest investors.

Trading in large lots

Prior to the introduction of ETFs, a trader had no easy way to buy or sell instantaneously, in one fell swoop, hundreds of stocks or bonds. Because they trade both during market hours and, in some cases, after market hours, ETFs made that possible.

Institutional investors also found other things to like about ETFs. For example, ETFs are often used to put cash to productive use quickly or to fill gaps in a portfolio by allowing immediate exposure to an industry sector or geographic region.

Savoring the versatility

Unlike mutual funds, ETFs can also be purchased with limit, market, or stop-loss orders, taking away the uncertainty involved with placing a buy order for a mutual fund and not knowing what price you're going to get until several hours after the market closes. See the nearby sidebar "Your basic trading choices (for ETFs or stocks)" if you're not certain what limit, market, and stop-loss orders are.

And because many ETFs can be sold short, they provide an important means of risk management. If, for example, the stock market takes a dive, then *shorting* ETFs — selling them now at a locked-in price with an agreement to purchase them back (cheaper, you hope) later on — may help keep a portfolio afloat. For that reason, ETFs have become a darling of hedge fund managers who offer the promise of investments that won't tank should the stock market tank.

YOUR BASIC TRADING CHOICES (FOR ETFs OR STOCKS)

Buying and selling an ETF is just like buying and selling a stock; there really is no difference. Although you can trade in all sorts of ways, the vast majority of trades fall into the following categories:

- **Market order:** This is as simple as it gets. You place an order with your broker or online to buy, say, 100 shares of a certain ETF. Your order goes to the stock exchange, and you get the best available price.

- **Limit order:** More exact than a market order, you place an order to buy, say, 100 shares of an ETF at $23 a share. That is the maximum price you will pay. If no sellers are willing to sell at $23 a share, your order will not go through. If you place a limit order to sell at $23, you'll get your sale if someone is willing to pay that price. If not, there will be no sale. You can specify whether an order is good for the day or until canceled (if you don't mind waiting to see if the market moves in your favor).

- **Stop-loss (or stop) order:** Designed to protect you should the price of your ETF or stock take a tumble, a stop-loss order automatically becomes a market order if and when the price falls below a certain point (say, 10 percent below the current price). Stop-loss orders are used to limit investors' exposure to a falling market, but they can (and often do) backfire, especially in very turbulent markets. Proceed with caution.

- **Short sale:** You sell shares of an ETF that you have borrowed from the broker. If the price of the ETF then falls, you can buy replacement shares at a lower price and pocket the difference. If, however, the price rises, you are stuck holding a security that is worth less than its market price, so you pay the difference, which can sometimes be huge.

For more information on different kinds of trading options, see the U.S. Securities and Exchange Commission discussion at www.sec.gov/investor/alerts/trading101basics.pdf.

Why Individual Investors Are Learning to Love ETFs

People are often amazed that they can get a financial product that will cost them a fraction in expenses compared to what they are currently paying. People also love their low costs, tax efficiency, transparency (you know what you're buying), and — now in their third decade of existence — good track record of success.

The cost advantage: How low can you go?

In the world of actively managed mutual funds (which is to say most mutual funds), the average annual management fee, according to the Investment Company Institute and Morningstar, is 0.63 percent of the account balance. That may not sound like a lot, but don't be misled. A well-balanced portfolio with both stocks and bonds may return, say, 5 percent over time. In that case, paying 0.63 percent to a third party means that you've just lowered your total investment returns by one-eighth. In a bad year, when your investments earn, say, 0.63 percent, you've just lowered your investment returns to *zero*. And in a *very* bad year . . . you don't need anyone else to do the math.

Active ETFs, although cheaper than active mutual funds, aren't all that much cheaper, averaging 0.51 percent a year, although a few are considerably higher than that.

WARNING

What some funds charge is astounding. Whereas the average active fund charges between 0.51 (for ETFs) and 0.63 percent (for mutual funds), there have been charges five times that amount. Crazy. Investing in such a fund is tossing money to the wind. Yet people do it. The chances of your winding up ahead after paying such high fees are next to nil. Paying a *load* (an entrance and/or exit fee) that can total as much as 6 percent is just as nutty. Yet people do it.

In the world of index funds, the expenses are much lower, with index mutual funds averaging 0.06 percent and ETFs averaging 0.17 percent, although many of the more traditional indexed ETFs cost no more than 0.06 percent a year in management fees, and as more competition has entered the market, even that price now seems high. A handful are now under 0.03 percent. And one purveyor, BNY Mellon, has actually introduced two ETFs with *no* fees.

No fees?

How can no fees make sense?

The multibillion-dollar BNY Mellon Bank didn't enter the ETF game until 2020, and they took the price-cutting war to a new level. The bank issued two ETFs with an expense ratio of *zero*. How can the company do that and expect to make money? They don't. "It's a courtesy to investors, and we're hoping that they'll look at our other ETFs," says a BNY Mellon official. Indeed, all of their ETF offerings are very reasonably priced. However, there may be no more freebies in the pipeline, and to date, no other ETF purveyors have dropped their price to zero, although a number of index mutual fund purveyors have.

REMEMBER

Do keep in mind that price is just one of the characteristics — albeit a very important one — that you'll be looking at in deciding how to pick "best-in-class" when choosing an ETF.

Some fees, as you can see in Table 4-2, are so low as to be negligible (or even less than negligible). Each ETF in this table has a yearly management expense of 0.05 percent or less.

TABLE 4-2 **Rock-Bottom-Priced ETFs**

ETF	Ticker	Total Annual Management Expense
BNY Mellon Core Bond ETF	BKAG	0.00%
JPMorgan BetaBuilders U.S. Equity ETF	BBUS	0.02%
Charles Schwab U.S. Broad Market	SCHB	0.03%
Vanguard S&P 500	VOO	0.03%
Vanguard Total Stock Market	VTI	0.03%
Charles Schwab U.S. Large-Cap	SCHX	0.03%
SPDR Portfolio S&P 500 Index	SPLG	0.03%
iShares Core U.S. Aggregate Bond ETF	AGG	0.04%
Invesco PureBeta SM US Aggregate Bond ETF	PBND	0.05%
Charles Schwab 1000 Index ETF	SCHK	0.05%

REMEMBER

Numerous studies have shown that low-cost funds have a huge advantage over higher-cost funds. One study by Morningstar looked at stock returns over a five-year period. In almost every category of stock mutual fund, low-cost funds beat the pants off high-cost funds. Do you think that by paying high fees you're getting better fund management? Hardly. The Morningstar study found, for example, that among mutual funds that hold large blend stocks (*blend* meaning a combination of value and growth — an S&P 500 fund would be a blend fund, for example), the annualized gain was 8.75 percent for those funds in the costliest quartile (or quarter) of funds; the gain for the least costly quartile was 9.89 percent.

Why ETFs are cheaper

The management companies that bring us ETFs, such as BlackRock and Invesco, are presumably not doing so for their health. No, they're making a good profit. One reason they can offer ETFs so cheaply compared to mutual funds is that their expenses are much less. When you buy an ETF, you go through a brokerage house, not BlackRock or Invesco. That brokerage house (Merrill Lynch, Fidelity, TIAA CREF) does all the necessary paperwork and bookkeeping on the purchase. If you have any questions about your money, you'll likely call Fidelity, not BlackRock. So, unlike a mutual fund company, which must maintain telephone operators, bookkeepers, and a mailroom, the providers of ETFs can operate almost entirely in cyberspace.

ETFs that are linked to indexes do have to pay some kind of fee to S&P Dow Jones Indices or MSCI or whoever created the index. But that fee is *nothing* compared to the exorbitant salaries that mutual funds pay their dart throwers, er, stock pickers, er, market analysts.

An unfair race

Active mutual funds (and the vast majority of mutual funds are active mutual funds) really don't have much chance of beating passive index funds — whether mutual funds or ETFs — over the long run, at least not as a group. (There are individual exceptions, but it's virtually impossible to identify them before the fact.) Someone once described the contest as a race in which the active mutual funds are "running with lead boots." Why? In addition to the management fees that eat up a substantial part of any gains, there are also the trading costs. Yes, when mutual funds trade stocks or bonds, they pay a spread and a small cut to the stock exchange, just like you do. That cost is passed on to you, and it's on top of the annual management fees previously discussed.

An actively managed fund's annual turnover costs will vary, but one study several years ago found that they were typically running at about 0.8 percent. And active mutual fund managers must constantly keep some cash on hand for all those trades. Having cash on hand costs money, too: The opportunity cost, like the turnover costs, can vary greatly from fund to fund, but a fund that keeps 20 percent of its assets in cash — and there are many that do — is going to see significant cash drag. After all, only 80 percent of its assets are really working for you.

So you take the 0.63 percent average management fee, and the perhaps 0.8 percent hidden trading costs, and the cash-drag or opportunity cost, and you can see where running with lead boots comes in. Add taxes to the equation, and while some actively managed mutual funds may do better than ETFs for a few years, over the long haul, don't bank on many of them coming out ahead.

Uncle Sam's loss, your gain

Alas, unless your money is in a tax-advantaged retirement account, making money in the markets means that you have to fork something over to Uncle Sam at year's end. That's true, of course, whether you invest in individual securities or funds. But before there were ETFs, individual securities had a big advantage over funds in that you were required to pay capital gains taxes only when you actually enjoyed a capital gain. With mutual funds, that isn't so. The fund itself may realize a capital gain by selling off an appreciated stock. You pay the capital gains tax regardless of whether you sell anything and regardless of whether the share price of the mutual fund increased or decreased since the time you bought it.

WARNING

There have been times (pick a bad year for the market — 2000, 2008, . . .) when many mutual fund investors lost a considerable amount in the market, yet had to pay capital gains taxes at the end of the year. Talk about adding insult to injury! One study found that over the course of time, taxes have wiped out approximately 2 full percentage points in returns for investors in the highest tax brackets.

In the world of ETFs, such losses are very unlikely to happen. Because most ETFs are index-based, they generally have little turnover to create capital gains. Perhaps even more importantly, ETFs are structured in a way that largely insulates shareholders from capital gains that result when mutual funds are forced to sell in order to free up cash to pay off shareholders who cash in their chips.

TECHNICAL STUFF

If you hold a mutual fund, and that fund sells shares for more than their purchase price, you, as an existing shareholder, will likely get slapped with a capital gains tax. Capital gains tax rates are always subject to change, but at the time of this writing, you're most likely going to have to cough up between 15 percent and 20 percent of the appreciation.

No tax calories

The structure of ETFs makes them different than mutual funds. Actually, ETFs are legally structured in three different ways: as exchange-traded open-end mutual funds, exchange-traded unit investment trusts, and exchange-traded grantor trusts. The differences are subtle. For now, this chapter focuses on one seminal difference between ETFs and mutual funds, which boils down to an extremely clever setup whereby ETF shares, which represent stock holdings, can be traded without any actual trading of stocks.

Think of the poker player who plays hand after hand, but thanks to the miracle of little plastic chips, doesn't have to touch any cash.

Market makers

Market makers are people who work at the stock exchanges and create (like magic!) ETF shares. Each ETF share represents a portion of a portfolio of stocks, sort of like poker chips represent a pile of cash. As an ETF grows, so does the number of shares. Concurrently (once a day), new stocks are added to a portfolio that mirrors the ETF. See Figure 4-1, which may help you envision the structure of ETFs and what makes them such tax wonders.

Traditional Mutual Fund

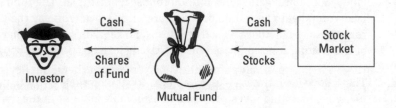

Exchange-Traded Fund

FIGURE 4-1: The secret to ETFs' tax friendliness lies in their very structure.

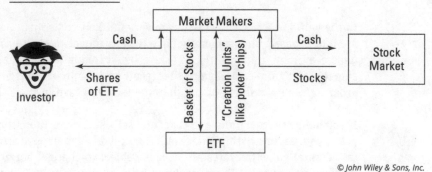

© *John Wiley & Sons, Inc.*

When an ETF investor sells shares, those shares are bought by a market maker who turns around and sells them to another ETF investor. By contrast, with mutual funds, if one person sells, the mutual fund must sell off shares of the underlying stock to pay off the shareholder. If stocks sold in the mutual fund are being sold for more than the original purchase price, the shareholders left behind are stuck paying a capital gains tax. In some years, that amount can be substantial.

In the world of ETFs, no such thing has happened or is likely to happen, at least not with the vast majority of ETFs, which are index funds. Because index funds trade infrequently, and because of ETFs' poker-chip structure, ETF investors rarely see a bill from Uncle Sam for any capital gains tax. That's not a guarantee that there will never be capital gains on any index ETF, but if there ever are, they are sure to be minor.

The actively managed ETFs — currently a small fraction of the ETF market, but almost certain to grow — may present a somewhat different story. They are going to be, no doubt, less tax friendly than index ETFs but more tax friendly than actively managed mutual funds. Exactly where will they fall on the spectrum? It may take another few years before we really know.

REMEMBER

Tax efficient does not mean tax-free. Although you won't pay capital gains taxes, you will pay taxes on any dividends issued by your stock ETFs, and stock ETFs are just as likely to issue dividends as are mutual funds. In addition, if you sell your ETFs and they are in a taxable account, you have to pay capital gains tax (15 percent for most folks; 20 percent for those who make big bucks) if the ETFs have appreciated in value since the time you bought them. But hey, at least you get to decide when to take a gain, and when you do, it's an actual gain.

ETFs that invest in taxable bonds and throw off taxable-bond interest are not likely to be very much more tax friendly than taxable-bond mutual funds.

ETFs that invest in actual commodities, holding real silver or gold, tax you at the "collectible" rate of 28 percent. And ETFs that tap into derivatives (such as commodity futures) and currencies sometimes bring with them very complex (and costly) tax issues.

Taxes on earnings — be they dividends or interest or money made on currency swaps — aren't an issue if your money is held in a tax-advantaged account, such as a Roth IRA.

What you see is what you get

A key to building a successful portfolio, right up there with low costs and tax efficiency, is diversification, a subject discussed more in Chapter 5 of Book 5. You cannot diversify optimally unless you know exactly what's in your portfolio. In a rather infamous example, when tech stocks (some more than others) started to go belly up in 2000, holders of Janus mutual funds got clobbered. That's because they discovered after the fact that their three or four Janus mutual funds, which gave the illusion of diversification, were actually holding many of the same stocks.

Style drift: An epidemic

REMEMBER

With a mutual fund, you often have little idea of what stocks the fund manager is holding. In fact, you may not even know what *kinds* of stocks they are holding — or even if they are holding stocks! We're talking here about *style drift,* which occurs when a mutual fund manager advertises their fund as aggressive, but over time it becomes conservative, and vice versa. Think about mutual fund managers who say they love large value but invest in large growth or small value.

One classic case of style drift cost investors in the popular Fidelity Magellan Fund a bundle. The year was 1996, and then fund manager Jeffrey Vinik reduced the stock holdings in his "stock" mutual fund to 70 percent. He had 30 percent of the fund's assets in either bonds or short-term securities. He was betting that the market was going to sour, and he was planning to fully invest in stocks after that happened. He was dead wrong. Instead, the market continued to soar, bonds took a dive, Fidelity Magellan seriously underperformed, and Vinik was out.

One study by the Association of Investment Management concluded that a full 40 percent of actively managed mutual funds are not what they say they are. Some funds bounce around in style so much that you, as an investor, have scant idea of where your money is actually invested.

ETFs are the cure

When you buy an indexed ETF, you get complete transparency. You know exactly what you are buying. No matter what the ETF, you can see in the prospectus or on the ETF provider's website (or on any number of independent financial websites) a complete picture of the ETF's holdings. See, for example, either www.etfdb.com or finance.yahoo.com. If you go to either website and type the letters *IYE* (the ticker symbol for the iShares Dow Jones U.S. Energy Sector ETF) in the box in the upper-right corner of the screen, you can see in an instant what your holdings are. Check out Table 4-3.

You simply can't get that information on most actively managed mutual funds. Or, if you can, the information is both stale and subject to change without notice.

Transparency also discourages dishonesty

REMEMBER

The scandals that have rocked the mutual fund world over the years have left the world of ETFs untouched. There's not a whole lot of manipulation that a fund manager can do when their picks are tied to an index. And because ETFs trade throughout the day, with the price flashing across thousands of computer screens worldwide, there is no room to take advantage of the "stale" pricing that occurs after the markets close and mutual fund orders are settled. All in all, ETF investors are much less likely ever to get bamboozled than are investors in active mutual funds.

TABLE 4-3

Holdings of the iShares Dow Jones U.S. Energy Sector ETF as of Mid-August 2021

Name	% Net Assets
ExxonMobil Corporation	23.9
Chevron Corporation	19.6
ConocoPhillips	4.8
EOG Resources, Inc.	4.3
Schlumberger Ltd.	3.8
Marathon Petroleum Corporation	3.6
Phillips 66	3.5
Kinder Morgan, Inc.	3.3
Pioneer Natural Resources Company	3.2
Valero Energy Corporation	3.0

Getting the Professional Edge

The difference between investment amateurs and investment professionals can be huge. But you can close much of that gap with ETFs.

By investment professionals, we're not talking about stockbrokers or variable-annuity salesmen, or maybe your barber, who always has a stock recommendation. We're talking about the managers of foundations, endowments, and pension funds with $1 billion or more in invested assets. By amateurs, we're talking about the average U.S. investor with a few assorted and sundry mutual funds in their 401(k).

Here's a comparison of the two: During the 30-year period from 1990 to the end of 2020, the U.S. stock market, as measured by the S&P 500 Index, provided an annual rate of return of 10.7 percent. Yet the average stock fund investor, according to a study by the Massachusetts-based research firm Dalbar, earned an annual rate of 6.24 percent over that same period. The Bloomberg–Barclays U.S. Aggregate Bond Index earned 5.86 percent a year over that same period, while the average bond fund investor earned but 0.45 percent.

Why the pitiful returns? Although there are several reasons, here are three main ones:

>> Mutual fund investors pay too much for their investments.

>> These investors jump into hot funds in hot sectors when they're hot and jump out when those funds or sectors turn cold. (In other words, they are constantly buying high and selling low.)

>> Small investors panic easily, and all too often cash out when the going gets rough.

Professionals tend not to do those things. To give you an idea of the difference between amateurs and professionals, consider this: For the 10-year period ended December 31, 2020, the average small investor, per Dalbar, earned a 4.9 percent annual return on their investments. Compare that to, say, the endowments of MIT (11.4 percent), Yale (10.9 percent), or Dartmouth (10.4 percent).

REMEMBER

Professional managers, you see, don't pay high expenses. They don't jump in and out of funds. They know that they need to diversify. They tend to buy indexes. They know exactly what they own. And they know that asset allocation, not stock picking, is what drives long-term investment results. In short, they do all the things that an ETF portfolio can do for you. So do it. Well, maybe . . . but first, read the rest of this chapter!

Passive versus Active Investing: Your Choice

Fun fact: For the first years of their existence, all ETFs were index funds.

On March 25, 2008, Bear Stearns introduced an actively managed ETF: the Current Yield ETF (YYY). As fate would have it, Bear Stearns was just about to go under, and when it did, the first actively managed ETF went with it. Prophetic? Perhaps. In the years since, hundreds of actively managed ETFs have hit the street. Many have died. At the time of this writing, there are 586, but they are not enjoying enormous commercial success. At the time of this writing, active ETFs, per Morningstar Direct, accounted for a very measly 2.8 percent of the nearly $7 trillion invested in ETFs.

According to Cerulli Associates, however, the majority (79 percent) of U.S. ETF issuers, as of end-of-year 2020, were either developing or planning to develop active ETFs.

The following sections look at a few of the pros and cons of index investing versus investing in actively managed funds, and then they look at how the ETF wrapper throws a wrinkle into the equation.

The index advantage

The superior returns of indexed mutual funds and ETFs over actively managed funds have had much to do with the popularity of ETFs to date. As discussed, the vast majority of ETFs — 77 percent in terms of actual numbers, and nearly 98 percent in terms of assets — are index funds (which buy and hold a fixed collection of stocks or bonds). And, as index funds, they can be expected to outperform actively managed funds rather consistently. According to Standard & Poor's SPIVA Scorecard, 88 percent of large-cap core stock funds underperformed their benchmark index in the past five years. High-yield bond funds? Ninety-five percent underperformed. Flipping that around, only 5 to 12 percent of actively managed funds succeeded at beating the index funds.

REMEMBER

Here are some reasons why index funds (both mutual funds and ETFs) are hard to beat:

>> They typically carry much lower management fees, sales loads, or redemption charges.

>> Hidden costs — trading costs and spread costs — are much lower when turnover is low.

>> They don't have cash sitting around idle (as the manager waits for what they think is the right time to enter the market).

>> They are more — sometimes much more — tax efficient.

>> They are more "transparent" — you know exactly what securities you are investing in.

WARNING

Perhaps the greatest testament to the success of index funds is how many allegedly actively managed funds are actually index funds in (a very expensive) disguise. We're talking about closet index funds. According to a report in *Investment News*, a newspaper for financial advisors, the number of actively managed stock funds that are closet index funds has tripled over the past several years. As a result, many investors are paying high (active) management fees for investment results that could be achieved with low-cost ETFs.

R squared is a measurement of how much of a fund's performance can be attributed to the performance of an index. It can range from 0.00 to 1.00. An R squared of 1.00 indicates *a perfect match:* When a fund goes up, it's because the index was up — every time; when the fund falls, it's because the index fell — every time. An R squared of 0.00 indicates no such correlation. This measurement is used to assess tracking errors and to identify closet index funds.

According to a study done by Credit Suisse, of all the funds in America — both mutual funds and ETFs — 27 percent are true index funds, 58 percent are actively managed funds, and a full 15 percent are closet index funds, meaning they invest as an index fund would, but charge what an active fund would.

The allure of active management

Speaking in broad generalities, actively managed mutual funds have been no friend to the small investor. Their persistence remains a testament to people's ignorance of the facts and the enormous amount of money spent on (often deceptive) advertising and PR that give investors the false impression that buying this fund or that fund will lead to instant wealth. The media often plays into this nonsense with splashy headlines, designed to sell magazine copies or attract viewers, that promise to reveal which funds or managers are currently the best.

Still, active management can make sense — and that may be especially true when some of the best aspects of active management are brought to the ETF market and some of the best aspects of ETF investing are brought to active management.

Some managers actually do have the ability to "beat the markets," but they are few and far between, and the increased costs of active management often nullify any and all advantages these market-beaters have. If those costs can be minimized, and if you can find such a manager, you may wind up ahead of the game. Actively managed ETFs cost more than indexed ETFs, but they are cheaper than actively managed mutual funds.

Active management in ETF form may also be both more tax efficient and more transparent than it is in mutual fund form. "Transparent" means you get to see the manager's secret sauce. Active managers like to keep their secret sauce, well, secret. To date, this has been easier when the wrapper has been a mutual fund, rather than an ETF. However, this may not continue to be the case, as the active managers have already gotten the okay from the SEC for partial intransparency and are busy petitioning the SEC to allow yet more smoke.

And finally, with some kinds of investments, such as commodities and micro-cap stocks, active management may simply make more sense in certain cases.

Why the race is getting harder to measure . . . and what to do about it

Unfortunately, the old-style "active versus passive" studies that consistently gave passive (index) investing two thumbs up are getting harder and harder to do. What exactly qualifies as an "index" fund anymore, now that many ETFs are set up to track indexes that, in and of themselves, were created to outperform "the market" (traditional indexes)? And whereas index investing once promised a very solid cost saving, some of the newer ETFs, with their newfangled indexes, are charging more than some actively managed funds. Future studies are only likely to become muddier.

REMEMBER

Here's some advice: Give a big benefit of the doubt to index funds as the ones that will serve you the best in the long run. If you want to go with an actively managed fund, follow these guidelines:

>> Keep your costs low.

>> Don't believe that a manager can beat the market unless that manager has done so consistently for years, and for reasons that you can understand. (That is, avoid "Madoff" risk!)

>> Pick a fund company that you trust.

>> Don't go overboard! Mix an index fund or two in with your active fund(s).

>> All things being equal, you may want to choose an ETF over a mutual fund. But the last section of this chapter can help you to determine that. Ready?

Do ETFs Belong in Your Life?

Okay, so on the plus side of ETFs, you have ultra-low management expenses, super tax efficiency, transparency, and a lot of fancy trading opportunities, such as shorting, if you are so inclined. What about the negatives? The following sections walk you through some other facts about ETFs that you should consider before parting with your precious dollars.

Calculating commissions

You may have to pay a commission every time you buy and sell an ETF. But, at the time of this writing, another brokerage house may have eliminated commissions altogether.

Trading commissions for stocks and ETFs (it's the same commission for either) have been dropping faster than the price of desktop computers. What once would have cost you a bundle, now — if you trade online, which you definitely should — is really pin money, perhaps a few dollars a trade, and increasingly, nothing at all. So, unless you are investing a very small amount of money, you needn't worry about commissions anymore. They are the smallpox of Wall Street.

Moving money in a flash

The fact that ETFs can be traded throughout the day like stocks makes them, unlike mutual funds, fair game for day-traders and institutional wheeler-dealers. For the rest of us common folk, there isn't much about the way that ETFs are bought and sold that makes them especially valuable. Indeed, the ability to trade throughout the day may make you more apt to do so, perhaps selling or buying on impulse. Impulsive investing, although it can get your endorphins pumping, is generally not a profitable way to proceed.

Understanding tracking error

At times, the return of an ETF may be greater or less than the index it follows. This situation is called *tracking error.* At times, an ETF may also sell at a price that is a tad higher or lower than what that price should be, given the prices of all the securities held by the ETF. This situation is called selling at a *premium* (when the price of the ETF rides above the value of the securities) or selling at a *discount* (when the price of the ETF drops below the value of the securities). Both foreign-stock funds and bond funds are more likely to run off track, either experiencing tracking errors or selling at a premium or discount. But the better funds do not run off track to any alarming degree.

"Off track" ETF investing is not something to worry about if you are a buy-and-hold ETF investor.

Making a sometimes tricky choice

Say you have a choice between investing in an index mutual fund that charges 0.06 percent a year and an ETF that tracks the same index and charges the same amount. Or, say you are trying to choose between an actively managed mutual fund and an ETF with the very same manager managing the very same kind of investment, with the same costs. What should you invest in?

THE INFAMOUS "FLASH CRASH" OF 2010

On the afternoon of May 6, 2010, the stock market, if you'll allow for the use of a highly technical term, went kablooey. No terrorist attacks occurred that day — no earthquakes or tsunamis or heart attacks in the White House, either. With no real reason to explain it, the stock market suddenly plunged by nearly 10 percent. Some ETFs fell in value to mere pennies on the dollar. It seemed like the start of another Great Depression.

Oops.

The "flash crash" of 2010 was just a big mistake — a few computer glitches, essentially — and within 10 minutes, the market nearly recovered. Trades made in those 10 minutes were corrected, and life went on as normal. Sort of. In the months that followed, market authorities scratched their collective chins, trying to figure out what exactly went wrong and how to make sure that it didn't happen again. They've since, they assure us, instituted circuit breakers so that the same kind of swift movement again will result in the temporary shutting down of the market, allowing troublesome computer glitches to be addressed.

So now you're safe. Probably. Very probably.

Still, if you feel nervous about another "flash crash," perhaps one in which trades won't be corrected, exercise caution when trading your ETF holdings. A "stop order" tells your broker to sell your ETF if it drops below a certain price — say, for example, below $10 a share. In theory, that protects you from a market crash. But in reality, it may actually subject you to a crash. If, say, the price of your ETF shares drops precipitously enough, as prices did on May 2, 2010, your order to sell if the price dips below $10 may kick in at 10 *cents* a share. Solution: Instead of a "stop order" use a "stop-limit" order, which tells the broker to sell your ETF if the price drops below, say, $10 a share, but not to sell if you can't get, say, at least $9 a share.

Or — perhaps a better solution — don't use stop orders at all. Rather, be prepared for some bumps in the road, and only invest money in the stock market that you or your family won't need for a good time to come. More on risk control appears in Chapter 5 of Book 5.

TIP

If your money is in a taxable account, and you're looking at stock index funds, go with the ETF, provided there are no commissions to pay; it may wind up being more tax efficient. If you're looking at bond index funds, this decision is a flip of the coin. Managed funds? Same.

But say you have, oh, $5,000 to invest in your Traditional IRA. (All Traditional IRA money is taxed as income when you withdraw it in retirement, and therefore the tax efficiency of securities held within an IRA isn't an issue.) In this case, the choice between the ETF and the mutual fund is nothing to sweat over. If all else is the same, we would have a very slight preference for the ETF, if for no other reason than its portability. (See the nearby sidebar "The index mutual fund trap.")

And what if your brokerage still charges a commission? Avoid it by going with the mutual fund (provided the mutual fund doesn't cost you a commission). What if there's a difference in management fees between the two funds? Say, an ETF charges you a management fee of 0.10 percent a year, and a comparable index mutual fund charges 0.15 percent, but buying and selling the ETF will cost you $5 at either end. Now what should you do?

The math isn't difficult. The difference between 0.10 and 0.15 (0.05 percent) of $5,000 is $2.50. It will take you two years to recoup your trading fee of $5. If you factor in the cost of selling (another $5), it will take you four years to recoup your trading costs. At that point, the ETF will be your lower-cost tortoise, and the mutual fund your higher-cost hare.

REMEMBER

If you have a trigger finger, and you are the kind of person who is likely to jump to trade every time there's a blip in the market, you would be well advised to go with mutual funds (that don't impose short-term redemption fees). You're less likely to shoot yourself in the foot!

THE INDEX MUTUAL FUND TRAP

Some brokerage houses, such as Vanguard and Fidelity, offer wonderful low-cost index mutual funds. Fidelity even offers a small handful of no-cost indexed mutual funds. But a problem with them is that you either can't buy them at other financial "supermarkets" (such as Charles Schwab or T. Rowe Price), or you have to pay a substantial fee to get into them. So building an entire portfolio of index mutual funds can be tough. If you want both Fidelity and Vanguard funds, you may be forced to pay high fees or to open up separate accounts at different supermarkets, which means extra paperwork and hassle. With ETFs, you can buy them anywhere, sell them anywhere, and keep them — even if they are ETFs from several different providers — all parked in the same brokerage house. There is no major brokerage house that now charges more than a few dollars to make an online ETF trade.

Chapter 5

Risk Control, Diversification, and Other Things to Know about ETFs

A peculiarly good writer, but also a peculiarly bad money manager, Mark Twain sent his entire fortune down the river on a few bad investments. A century and a half later, investing, especially in stocks, can still be a peculiarly dangerous game. But today you have low-cost indexed exchange-traded funds (ETFs) and a lot more knowledge about the power of diversification. Together, these two things can help lessen the dangers and heighten the rewards of the stock market. This chapter hopes to make you a better stock investor — at least better than Mark Twain.

Risk Is Not Just a Board Game

Well, okay, actually Risk *is* a board game, but we're not talking here about *that* Risk. Rather, we're talking about investment risk. And in the world of investments, risk means but one thing: volatility. Volatility is what takes people's nest eggs, scrambles them, and serves them up with humble pie. Volatility is what causes investors insomnia and heartburn. Volatility is the potential for financially crippling losses.

Ask people who had most of their money invested in stocks in 2008. For five years prior, the stock market had done pretty darned well. Investors were just starting to feel good again. The last market downfall of 2000–2002 was thankfully fading into memory. And then . . . *pow* . . . the U.S. stock market tanked by nearly 40 percent over the course of the year. Foreign markets fell just as much. Billions and billions were lost. Some portfolios (which may have dipped more than 40 percent, depending on what kind of stocks they held) were crushed. Many who had planned for retirement had to readjust their plans.

There was nothing pretty about 2008.

In early 2020, when the COVID-19 pandemic hit, investors got another taste of how quickly the markets can turn. It wasn't quite as bad as 2008 or 2000–2002 (between February and March, the Dow lost "only" 37 percent), and it lasted for just a short time, but it was still a shocker.

REMEMBER

Is risk to be avoided at all costs? Well, no. Not at all. Risk is to be mitigated, for sure, but risk within reason can actually be *a good thing.* That is because risk and return, much like Romeo and Juliet or Coronas and lime, go hand in hand. Volatility means that an investment can go way down or way up. You hope it goes way up. Without some volatility, you resign yourself to a portfolio that isn't poised for any great growth. And in the process, you open yourself up to another kind of risk: the risk that your money will slowly be eaten away by inflation.

WARNING

If you are ever offered the opportunity to partake in any investment scheme that promises you oodles and oodles of money with "absolutely no risk," run! You are in the presence of a con artist or a fool. Such investments do not exist.

The trade-off of all trade-offs (safety versus return)

To get to the Holy Grail — a big, fat payoff from your investments — you need to take on the fire-breathing dragon of risk. There simply is no way that you are going to make any sizeable amount of money off your investments without a willingness to get hurt. The Holy Grail is not handed out to people who stuff money in their mattresses or carry their pennies to the local savings bank.

If you look at different investments over the course of time, you find an uncanny correlation between risk (volatility risk, not inflation risk) and return. Safe investments — those that really do carry genuine guarantees, such as U.S. Treasury bills, FDIC-insured savings accounts, and CDs — tend to offer very modest returns (often — especially these days — negative returns after accounting for inflation). Volatile investments — like stocks and "junk" bonds, the kinds of investments that cause people to lose sleep — tend to offer handsome returns if you give them enough time.

REMEMBER

Time, then, is an essential ingredient in determining appropriate levels of risk. You would be wise to keep any cash you are going to need within the next six months to a year in a savings bank, or possibly in an ETF such as the iShares Barclays 1–3 Year Treasury Bond Fund (SHY), a short-term bond fund that yields a modest return but is very unlikely to lose value. You should *not* invest that portion of your money in any ETF that is made up of company stocks, such as the popular SPY or QQQ. True, SPY or QQQ can (and should), over time, yield much more than SHY, but they are also much more susceptible to sharp price swings. Unless you are not going to need your cash for at least a couple of years (and preferably not for six or seven or more years), you are best off avoiding any investment in the stock market, whether it be through ETFs or otherwise.

So just how risky are ETFs?

REMEMBER

Asking how risky, or how lucrative, ETFs are is like trying to judge a soup knowing nothing about the soup's ingredients, only that it is served in a blue china bowl. The bowl — or the ETF — doesn't create the risk; what's inside it does. Thus stock and real estate ETFs tend to be more volatile than bond ETFs. Short-term bond ETFs are less volatile than long-term bond ETFs. Small-stock ETFs are more volatile than large-stock ETFs. International ETFs often see more volatility than U.S. ETFs. And international "emerging-market" ETFs see more volatility than international developed-nation ETFs.

Figure 5-1 shows some examples of various ETFs and where they fit on the risk-return continuum. Note that it starts with bond ETFs at the bottom (maximum safety, minimum volatility), and nearer the top, it features the EAFE (Europe, Australia, Far East) Index and the South Korea Index Fund. (An investment in South Korean stocks involves not only all the normal risks of business but also includes currency risk, as well as the risk that some deranged North Korean dictator may decide he wants to pick a fight. Buyer beware.)

High Risk (and highest return potential)

iShares MSCI South Korea Index Fund (EWY)

iShares MSCI EAFE Index Fund (EFA)

Vanguard Mid Cap ETF (VO)

SPDR S&P 500 (SPY)

iShares Barclays 7-10 Year Treasury Bond Fund (IEF)

FIGURE 5-1:
The risk levels
of a sampling
of ETFs.

iShares Barclays 1-3 Year Treasury Bond Fund (SHY)

Low Risk (with more modest return potential)

Keep in mind when looking at Figure 5-1 that these ETFs are treated as stand-alone assets for illustration purposes. Stand-alone risk measurements are of limited value. The true risk of adding any particular ETF to your portfolio depends on what is already in the portfolio. (That statement will make sense by the end of this chapter.)

Smart Risk, Foolish Risk

There is safety in numbers, which is why teenage boys and girls huddle together in corners at school dances. In the case of the teenagers, the safety is afforded by anonymity and distance. In the case of indexed ETFs and mutual funds, safety is provided (to a limited degree only!) by diversification in that they represent ownership in many different securities. Owning many stocks, rather than a few, provides some safety by eliminating something that investment professionals, when they're trying to impress, call *nonsystemic risk.*

Nonsystemic risk is involved when you invest in any individual security. It is the risk that the CEO of the company will be strangled by their pet python, that the national headquarters will be destroyed by a falling asteroid, or that the company's stock will take a sudden nosedive simply because of some internet rumor started by a high school junior in the suburbs of Des Moines. Those kinds of risks (and more serious ones) can be effectively eliminated by investing not in individual securities but in ETFs or mutual funds.

REMEMBER

Nonsystemic risk contrasts with *systemic risk*, which, unfortunately, ETFs and mutual funds cannot eliminate. Systemic risks, as a group, simply can't be avoided, not even by keeping your portfolio in cash. Examples of systemic risk include the following:

>> **Market risk:** The market goes up, the market goes down, and whatever stocks or stock ETFs you own will generally (though not always) move in the same direction.

>> **Interest rate risk:** If interest rates go up, the value of your bonds or bond ETFs (especially long-term bond ETFs such as TLT, the iShares 20-year Treasury ETF) will fall.

>> **Inflation risk:** When inflation picks up, any fixed-income investments that you own (such as any of the conventional bond ETFs) will suffer. And any cash you hold will start to dwindle in value, buying less and less than it used to.

>> **Political risk:** If you invest your money in Canada, France, or Japan, there's little chance that revolutionaries will overthrow the government anytime soon. When you invest in the stock or bond ETFs of certain other countries (or when you hold currencies from those countries), you'd better keep a sharp eye on the nightly news.

>> **Grand scale risks:** The government of Japan wasn't overthrown, but that didn't stop an earthquake and ensuing tsunami and nuclear disaster from sending the Tokyo stock market reeling in early 2011. Similarly, in 2020 COVID-19 hit most of the world's stock markets hard — some harder than others.

Although ETFs cannot eliminate systemic risks, don't despair. For while nonsystemic risks are a bad thing, systemic risks are a decidedly mixed bag. Nonsystemic risks, you see, offer no compensation. A company is not bound to pay higher dividends, nor is its stock price bound to rise simply because the CEO has taken up mountain climbing or hang gliding.

REMEMBER

Systemic risks, on the other hand, do offer compensation. Invest in small stocks (which are more volatile and therefore incorporate more market risk), and you can expect (over the very long term) higher returns. Invest in a country with a history of political instability, and (especially if that instability doesn't occur) you'll probably be rewarded with high returns in compensation for taking added risk. Invest in long-term bonds (or long-term bond ETFs) rather than short-term bonds (or ETFs), and you are taking on more interest rate risk. That's why the yield on long-term bonds is almost always greater.

In other words,

Higher systemic risk = higher historical returns

Higher nonsystemic risk = zilch

That's the way markets tend to work. Segments of the market with higher risks *must* offer higher returns or else they wouldn't be able to attract capital. If the potential returns on emerging-market stocks (or ETFs) were no higher than the potential returns on short-term bond ETFs or FDIC-insured savings accounts, would anyone but a complete nutcase invest in emerging-market stocks?

How Risk Is Measured

In the world of investments, risk means volatility, and volatility (unlike angels or love) can be seen, measured, and plotted. People in the investment world use different tools to measure volatility, such as standard deviation and beta. Most of these tools are not very hard to get a handle on, and they can help you better follow discussions on portfolio building. Ready to dig in?

Standard deviation: The king of all risk measurement tools

So, you want to know how much an investment is likely to bounce? The first thing you do is look to see how much it has bounced in the past. Standard deviation measures the degree of past bounce and, from that measurement, gives you some notion of future bounce. To put it another way, standard deviation shows the degree to which a stock/bond/mutual fund/ETF's actual returns vary from its average returns over a certain time period.

Table 5-1 presents two hypothetical ETFs and their returns over the last six years. Note that both portfolios start with $1,000 and end with $1,101. But note, too, the great difference in how much they bounce. ETF A's yearly returns range from −3 percent to 5 percent while ETF B's range from −15 percent to 15 percent. The standard deviation of the six years for ETF A is 3.09; the standard deviation for ETF B is 10.38.

TABLE 5-1   ## Standard Deviation of Two Hypothetical ETFs

Balance, Beginning of Year	Return (% Increase or Decrease)	Balance, End of Year
ETF A		
1,000	5	1,050
1,050	–2	1,029
1,029	4	1,070
1,070	–3	1,038
1,038	2	1,059
1,059	4	1,101
ETF B		
1,000	10	1,100
1,100	6	1,166
1,166	–15	991
991	-8	912
912	15	1,048
1,048	5	1,101

Predicting a range of returns

What does the standard deviation number tell you? Take ETF A as an example. The standard deviation of 3.09 tells you that in about two-thirds of the months to come, you should expect the return of ETF A to fall within 3.09 percentage points of the mean return, which was 1.66. In other words, about 68 percent of the time, returns should fall somewhere between 4.75 percent (1.66 + 3.09) and –1.43 percent (1.66 – 3.09). As for the other one-third of the time, anything can happen.

It also tells you that in about 95 percent of the months to come, the returns should fall within two standard deviations of the mean. In other words, 95 percent of the time, you should see a return of between 7.84 percent [1.66 + (3.09 × 2)] and –4.52 percent [1.66 – (3.09 × 2)]. The other 5 percent of the time is anybody's guess.

Making side-by-side comparisons

The ultimate purpose of standard deviation is that it gives you a way to judge the relative risks of two ETFs. If one ETF has a 3-year standard deviation of 12, you know that it is roughly twice as volatile as another ETF with a standard deviation of 6 and half as risky as an ETF with a standard deviation of 24. A real-world example: The standard deviation for most short-term bond funds falls somewhere around 0.7. The standard deviation for most precious-metals funds is somewhere around 26.0.

REMEMBER

Important caveat: Don't assume that combining one ETF with a standard deviation of 10 with another that has a standard deviation of 20 will give you a portfolio with an average standard deviation of 15. It doesn't work that way at all. The combined standard deviation will not be any greater than 15, but it could (if you do your homework and put together two of the right ETFs) be much less.

Beta: Assessing price swings in relation to the market

Unlike standard deviation, which gives you a stand-alone picture of volatility, beta is a relative measure. It is used to measure the volatility of something in relation to something else. Most commonly that "something else" is the S&P 500. Very simply, beta tells you that if the S&P rises or falls by x percent, then your investment, whatever that investment is, will likely rise or fall by y percent.

The S&P is considered your baseline, and it is assigned a beta of 1. So if you know that Humongous Software Corporation has a beta of 2, and the S&P shoots up 10 percent, Jimmy the Greek (if he were still with us) would bet that shares of Humongous are going to rise 20 percent. If you know that the Sedate Utility Company has a beta of 0.5, and the S&P shoots up 10 percent, Jimmy would bet that shares of Sedate are going to rise by 5 percent. Conversely, shares of Humongous would likely fall four times harder than shares of Sedate in response to a fall in the S&P.

WARNING

In a way, beta is easier to understand than standard deviation; it's also easier to misinterpret. Beta's usefulness is greater for individual stocks than it is for ETFs, but nonetheless it can be helpful, especially when gauging the volatility of U.S. industry-sector ETFs. It is much less useful for any ETF that has international holdings. For example, an ETF that holds stocks of emerging-market nations is going to be volatile, yet it may have a low beta. How so? Because its movements, no matter how swooping, may happen independently of movement in the U.S. market. (Emerging-market stocks tend to be more tied to currency flux, commodity prices, interest rates, and political climate.)

Mixing and Matching Your Stock ETFs

Finding the perfect mix of stocks and bonds, as well as other investments with low correlation, is known among financial pros as looking for the *Efficient Frontier*. The Frontier represents the mix of investments that offers the greatest promise of return for the least amount of risk.

Reaching for the elusive Efficient Frontier means holding both stocks and bonds — domestic and international — in your portfolio. That part is fairly straightforward and not likely to stir much controversy (although, for sure, experts differ on what they consider optimal percentages). But experts definitely don't agree on how best to diversify the domestic-stock portion of a portfolio. Two competing methods predominate:

>> One method calls for the division of a stock portfolio into domestic and foreign, and then into different styles: large-cap, small-cap, mid-cap, value, and growth.

>> The other method calls for allocating percentages of a portfolio to various industry sectors: healthcare, utilities, energy, financials, and so on.

Some experts prefer that the small to mid-sized investor, especially the ETF investor, go primarily with the styles. But there's nothing wrong with dividing a portfolio by industry sector. And for those of you with good-sized portfolios, a mixture of both, without going crazy, may be optimal.

Filling in your style box

Most savvy investors make certain to have some equity in each of the nine boxes of the grid in Figure 5-2, which is known as the *style box* or *grid* (sometimes called the *Morningstar Style Box*).

The reason for the style box is simple enough: History shows that companies of differing cap (capitalization) size (in other words, large companies and small companies), and value and growth companies, tend to rise and fall under different economic conditions.

Table 5-2 shows how well various investment styles, as measured by four Vanguard index ETFs that track each style, have fared in the past several years. Note that a number of ETFs are available to match each style.

Large-cap value	Large-cap blend	Large-cap growth
Mid-cap value	Mid-cap blend	Mid-cap growth
Small-cap value	Small-cap blend	Small-cap growth

FIGURE 5-2: The style box or grid.

© John Wiley & Sons, Inc.

TABLE 5-2

Recent Performance of Various Investment Styles

	2016	2017	2018	2019	2020
Large-Cap Growth	6.17	27.75	–3.32	37.26	40.27
Large-Cap Value	16.95	17.14	–5.45	25.83	2.29
Small-Cap Growth	10.79	21.93	–5.78	32.86	35.4
Small-Cap Value	24.8	11.84	–12.28	22.77	5.91

Buying by industry sector

The advent of ETFs has largely brought forth the use of sector investing as an alternative to the grid. Examining the two models toe-to-toe yields some interesting comparisons — and much food for thought.

One study on industry-sector investing, by Chicago-based Ibbotson Associates, came to the very favorable conclusion that sector investing is a potentially superior diversifier to grid investing because times have changed since the 1960s when style investing first became popular. As Ibbotson concluded,

> Globalization has led to a rise in correlation between domestic and international stocks; large-, mid-, and small-cap stocks have high correlation to each other. A company's performance is tied more to its industry than to the country where it's based, or the size of its market cap.

The jury is still out, but for now, you're invited to do a little comparison of your own by looking at Tables 5-2 and 5-3. Note that by using either method of diversification, some of your investments should smell like roses in years when others stink. Also, all stocks crashed in 2008 but recovered at significantly different paces; this is true of various styles and sectors. And it is certainly true for various geographic regions.

Table 5-3 shows how well various industry sectors (as measured by the returns of Vanguard indexed ETFs that match the index of each of the respective sectors) fared in recent years. Yes, there are ETFs that track each of these industry sectors — and many more.

TABLE 5-3

Recent Performance of Various Market Sectors

	2016	2017	2018	2019	2020
Healthcare	–3.32	23.35	5.49	22.0	18.34
Real Estate	8.53	4.90	–5.97	28.89	-4.64
Information Technology	13.75	37.04	2.43	48.75	46.09
Energy	28.93	–2.35	–20.01	9.37	-33.03

Don't slice and dice your portfolio to death

TIP

One reason some experts tend to prefer the traditional style grid to industry-sector investing, at least for the non-wealthy investor, is that there are simply fewer styles to contend with. You can build yourself, at least on the domestic side of your stock holdings, a pretty well-diversified portfolio with but four ETFs: one small value, one small growth, one large value, and one large growth. With industry-sector investing, you would need a dozen or so ETFs to have a well-balanced portfolio, and that may be too many.

And then there's global investing. Yes, you can, thanks largely to the iShares lineup of ETFs, invest in about 50 individual countries. (And in many of these countries, you can furthermore choose between large-cap and small-cap stocks, and in some cases, value and growth.) Too much! Many experts prefer to see most investors go with larger geographic regions: U.S., developed markets, emerging markets, and so on.

You don't want to chop up your portfolio into too many holdings, or the transaction costs (even if trading ETFs commission-free, there are still small, frictional costs when you trade) can start to bite into your returns. Rebalancing gets to be a headache. Tax filing can become a nightmare. And, as many investors learned in 2008, having a very small position in your portfolio — say, less than 2 percent of your assets — in any one kind of investment isn't going to have much effect on your overall returns anyway.

TIP

As a rough rule, if you have $50,000 to invest, consider something in the ballpark of a 5- to 10-ETF portfolio, and if you have $250,000 or more, perhaps look at a 15- to 25-ETF portfolio. Many more ETFs than this won't enhance the benefits of diversification but will entail additional trading costs every time you rebalance your holdings.

6

Investing Online

Contents at a Glance

Chapter **1**

Getting Ready for Online Investing

Before doing something risky, you probably think good and hard about what you stand to gain and what you might lose. Surprisingly, many online investors, especially those just starting out, lose that innate sense of risk and reward. They chase after the biggest possible returns without considering the sleepless nights they'll suffer through as those investments swing up and down. Some start buying investments they've heard that others made money on without thinking about whether those investments are appropriate for them. Worst of all, some fall prey to fraudsters who promise huge returns in get-rich-quick schemes.

So, it's time to start from the top and make sure that the basics are covered. In this chapter, you discover what you can expect to gain from investing online — and at what risk — so that you can decide whether this is for you. You also find out what kind of investor you are by using online tools that measure your taste for risk. After you've become familiar with your inner investor, you can start thinking about forming an online investment plan that won't give you an ulcer.

It's only natural if you're feeling skittish when it comes to investing, especially if you're just starting out. After all, it's been a brutal couple of decades even for veteran investors. First came the dot-com crash in 2000, and then the vicious credit crunch that nearly drop-kicked the economy and led to a nasty bear market in 2008. The stock market then proceeded to soar starting in March 2009, roughly quadrupling in value through mid-2019. But even that rally wasn't painless, because the stock market short-circuited in May 2010, due in part to computerized trading, causing its value to plunge and largely rally back in just 20 minutes. Don't forget the 2015 Greek debt crisis and fears of a major economic slowdown in China that rattled investors. Confused yet? Get this. Even good news can hurt the market. Stocks dropped roughly 20 percent in late 2018. Why? The economy was doing so well that investors worried that the nation's central bank, the Federal Reserve, would slow it down.

Some think all this chaos is just too much to bear and choose to avoid stocks altogether. That decision is a mistake, though. Prudent investing can be a great way for you to reach your financial goals. You just need an approach that will maximize your returns while cutting your risks. And that's where this chapter (and the rest of Book 6) comes in.

Why Investing Online Is Worth Your While

Investing used to be easy. Your friend would recommend a broker. You'd give your money to the broker and hope for the best. But today, thanks to the explosion of web-based investment information and low-cost online trading, you get to work a lot harder by taking charge of your investments. Lucky you! So, is the additional work worth it? Taking the time to figure out how to invest online *is* worthwhile because

>> **Investing online saves you money.** Online trading is much less expensive than dealing with a broker. You'll save tons on commissions and fees. (Say, why not invest that money you saved?)

>> **Investing online gives you more control.** Instead of entrusting someone else to reach your financial goals, you'll be personally involved. It's up to you to find out about all the investments at your disposal, but you'll also be free to make decisions.

>> **Investing online eliminates conflicts of interest.** By figuring out how to invest and doing it yourself, you won't have to worry about being given advice that may be in your advisor's best interest and not yours.

REMEMBER

You may still decide to hire a financial advisor. For some people, the extra guidance or peace of mind you get from a person whose job it is to watch your portfolio makes a ton of sense. Even so, it's a good idea to know how investing and markets work so you can understand what your advisor is doing with your money.

Advisors, too, appreciate it when clients comprehend the plan. It's like when you travel to different parts of Europe — the locals like to see you at least try to speak their language.

Getting Started

Many investors just starting out ask the same question. Maybe it's the same question that's running through your head right now: "I want to invest, but where do I start?"

Getting started in investing seems so overwhelming that some people get confused and wind up giving up and doing nothing. Others get taken in by promises of gigantic returns and enroll in seminars, subscribe to stock-picking newsletters with dubious track records, or invest in speculative investments hoping to make money overnight, only to be disappointed. Others assume that all they need to do is open a brokerage account and start madly buying stocks. But as you'll notice if you flip ahead in this book, you don't find out about choosing a broker and opening an account until Chapter 3 in Book 6. You have many tasks to do before then.

However, don't let that fact intimidate you. Check out the easy-to-follow list of things you need to do to get started. Follow these directions, and you'll be ready to open an online brokerage account and start trading:

1. **Decide how much you can save and invest.**

   You can't invest if you don't have any money, and you won't have any money if you don't save. No matter how much you earn, you need to set aside some cash to start investing. (Think saving is impossible? You find digital tools later in this chapter that can help you build up savings that you can invest.)

2. **Master the terms.**

   The world of investing has its own language. You get tips to understand investing terminology now so that you don't get confused in the middle of a trade when you're asked to make a decision about something you've never heard of. (Chapter 2 in Book 6 has more on the language of online investing.)

3. **Familiarize yourself with the risks and returns of investing.**

   You wouldn't jump out of an airplane without knowing the risks, right? Don't jump into investing without knowing what to expect, either. Luckily, online resources later in this chapter can help you get a feel for how markets have performed over the past 100 years. By understanding how stocks, bonds, and other investments have done, you'll know what a reasonable return is and set your goals appropriately.

Investors who know how investments typically behave don't panic — they keep their cool even during times of volatility. Panic is your worst enemy because it has a way of talking you into doing things you'll regret later.

4. **Get a feel for how much risk you can take.**

   People have different goals for their money. You may already have a home and a car, in which case you're probably most interested in saving for retirement or building an estate for your heirs. Or perhaps you're starting a family and hope to buy a house within a year. These two scenarios call for different tastes for risks and *time horizons* — how long you'd be comfortable investing money before you need it. You need to know what your taste for risk is before you can invest. You find out how to measure your *risk tolerance* later in this chapter.

5. **Understand the difference between being an active and a passive investor.**

   Some investors want to outsmart the market by owning stocks at just the right times or by choosing the "best" stocks. Others think doing that is impossible and don't want the hassle of trying. At the end of this chapter, you find out how to distinguish between these two types of investors, active and passive, so that you're in a better position to choose which one you are or want to be.

6. **Find out how to turn your computer, tablet, or smartphone into a trading station.**

   If you have a computer, tablet, or smartphone and a connection to the internet, you have all you need to turn it into a source of constant market information. You just need to know where to look, which you find out in Chapter 2 of Book 6.

7. **Take a dry run.**

   Don't laugh. Many professional money managers have told me they got their start by pretending to pick stocks and tracking how they would have performed. It's a great way to see whether your strategy might work, before potentially losing your shirt. You can even do this online, which is covered in Chapter 2 of Book 6.

8. **Choose the type of account you'll use.**

   You can hold your investments inside all sorts of accounts, which have different advantages and disadvantages. They are introduced later in this chapter.

9. **Set up an online brokerage account.**

At last, the moment you've been waiting for: opening an online account. After you've tackled the preceding steps, you're ready to get going. This important step is covered in Chapter 3 of Book 6.

10. **Understand the different ways to place trades and enter orders.**

Chapter 4 in Book 6 explains the many different ways to buy and sell stocks, each with very different results. (You also need to understand the tax ramifications of selling stocks.)

11. **Boost your knowledge.**

After you have the basics down, you're ready to tackle advanced topics like choosing an asset allocation, researching stocks to buy and knowing when to sell, and evaluating more exotic investments.

THE DANGER OF DOING NOTHING

After reading through the 11 steps for getting started, you may be wondering whether you've taken on more than you bargained for. Stick with it. The worst thing you can do now is put this book down, tell yourself you'll worry about investing later, and do nothing.

Doing nothing is extremely costly because you lose money if you don't invest. Seriously. Even if you stuffed your cash under a mattress and didn't spend a dime, each year that money would become worth, on average, 3 percent less due to inflation. Suppose you won $1 million in the lottery and stuffed it in a hole in your backyard with the plan of taking it out in 30 years to pay for your retirement. In 30 years, all 1 million greenbacks would still be there, but they'd buy only $400,000 worth of goods.

Even if you put your extra cash in a savings account, you're not doing much better. Because savings accounts usually give you access to your money anytime, they pay low levels of interest, usually around 1 or 2 percent. Even high-yield savings accounts and certificates of deposit (CDs) typically pay only slightly higher interest than the level of inflation or sometimes below, meaning that you're barely keeping up — or falling behind. If you want your money to grow, you need to move money you don't need for a while out of savings and into investments, which have the potential to generate much higher returns.

Note: The Federal Reserve Bank of Minneapolis offers a free calculator that tells you how much something you bought in the past would cost today (www.minneapolisfed.org). You'll need to scroll down a bit to see the calculator.

Gut-Check Time: How Much Risk Can You Take?

It's time to get a grip — a grip on how much you can invest, that is. Most beginning investors are so interested in finding stocks that make them rich overnight that they lose sight of risk. But academic studies show that risk and return go hand in hand. That's why you need to know how much risk you can stomach before you start looking for investments and buying them online.

TIP

Several excellent online tools can help you get a handle on how much of a financial thrill seeker you are. Most are structured like interviews that ask you a number of questions and help you decide how much volatility you can comfortably stomach. These interviews are kind of like personality tests for your investment taste. Answering these questionnaires right away is worthwhile so that you can understand what kind of investor you are:

>> **Vanguard's Investor Questionnaire** (personal.vanguard.com/us/FundsInvQuestionnaire) asks ten salient questions to determine how much of a risk taker you are with your money. It determines your ideal asset allocation. Take note of the breakdown. The closer to 100 percent that Vanguard recommends you put in stocks, the more risk-tolerant you are, and the closer to 100 percent in bonds, the less risk-tolerant you are.

>> **Index Fund Advisors Risk Capacity Survey** (www.ifa.com/SurveyNET/index.aspx) offers a quick risk survey that can tell you what kind of investor you are after answering just five questions. You can also find a complete risk capacity survey that hits you with a few dozen questions. Whichever you choose, the survey can characterize what kind of investor you are and even display a painting that portrays your risk tolerance.

>> **Charles Schwab Investor Profile Questionnaire** (www.schwab.com/resource/investment-questionnaire) gets you to think about the factors that greatly determine how you should be investing, such as your investment time horizon and tolerance for risk. The Schwab questionnaire can be printed so you don't have to be in front of a computer to take it. At the bottom of the questionnaire is a chart that helps you see how aggressive or conservative you should be with your portfolio.

Passive or Active? Deciding What Kind of Investor You Plan to Be

Investing may not seem controversial, but it shouldn't surprise you that anytime you're talking about money, people have some strong opinions about the right way to do things. The first way investors categorize themselves is by whether they are passive or active. Because these two approaches are so different, the following sections help you think about what they are and which camp you see yourself in. Where you stand not only affects which broker is best for you, as discussed in Chapter 3 of Book 6, but also affects which chapters in this book appeal to you most.

How to know if you're a passive investor

Passive investors don't try to beat the stock market. They merely try to keep up with it by owning all the stocks in an index. An *index* is a basket of stocks or bonds that track a market by measuring movement by all the investments in it. For instance, the S&P 500 index tracks a selection of the largest and most valuable 500 U.S. stocks. Passive investors are happy matching the market's performance.

You know you're a passive investor if you

>> **Aren't interested in choosing individual stocks:** These investors buy large baskets of stocks that mirror the performance of popular stock indexes such as the Dow Jones Industrial Average or the Standard & Poor's 500 index. Passive investors don't worry if a small upstart company they invested in will release its new product on time and whether it will be well received. They typically own small pieces of hundreds of stocks instead.

>> **Want to own mutual and exchange-traded funds:** Because passive investors aren't looking for the next Microsoft, Facebook, or Apple, they buy mutual and exchange-traded funds that buy hundreds of stocks. (Book 5 covers mutual and exchange-traded funds in more detail.)

>> **Want to reduce taxes:** Passive investors tend to buy investments and forget about them until many years later when they need the money. This approach can be lucrative because by holding onto diversified investments for a long time and not selling them, passive investors can postpone when they have to pay capital gains taxes.

>> **Do not want to stress about stocks' daily, monthly, or even annual movements:** Passive investors tend to buy index or mutual funds and forget about them. They don't need to sit in front of financial TV shows, surf countless financial websites, read magazines, or worry about where stocks are moving. They're invested for the long term, and everything else is just noise to them.

Sites for passive investors to start with

One of the toughest things about being a passive investor is sitting still during a bull market when everyone else seems to be making more than you. Yes, you might be able to turn off the TV, but inevitably you'll bump into someone who brags about their giant gains and laughs at you for being satisfied with 10 percent average annual market returns.

TIP

When that happens, it's even more important to stick with your philosophy. Following the crowd at this moment undermines the value of your strategy. That's why even passive investors are well served going to websites where other passive investors congregate:

>> **Bogleheads** (www.bogleheads.org) is an electronic water cooler for fans of Vanguard index funds and passive investors to meet, encourage, and advise each other. They call themselves Bogleheads in honor of the founder of Vanguard, John Bogle.

>> **The Arithmetic of Active Management** (www.stanford.edu/~wfsharpe/art/active/active.htm) is a reprint of an article by an early proponent of passive investing, William Sharpe, who explains why active investing can never win.

>> **Vanguard** (www.vanguard.com) contains many helpful stories about the power of index investing and offers them for free, even if you don't have an account.

How to know whether you're an active investor

Active investors almost feel sorry for passive investors. Why would anyone be satisfied just matching the stock market and not even try to do better? Active investors feel that if you're smart enough and willing to spend time doing homework, you can exceed 10 percent annual returns. Likewise, active investors question the logic of holding stocks even as markets plunge. Active investors also find investing to be thrilling, almost like a hobby. Some active investors try to find undervalued stocks and hold them until they're discovered by other investors. Another class of active investors are short-term traders, who bounce in and out of stocks trying to get quick gains.

You're an active investor if you

>> **Think long-term averages of stocks are meaningless:** Active investors believe they can spot winning companies that no one knows about yet or are underappreciated, buy their shares at just the right time, and sell them for a profit.

>> **Are willing to spend large amounts of time searching for stocks:** These are the investors who sit in front of financial TV shows, analyze stocks that look undervalued, and do all sorts of prospecting trying to find gems.

>> **Believe they can hire mutual fund managers who can beat the market:** Some active investors think that certain talented mutual fund managers are out there and that if they just give their money to those managers, they'll win.

>> **Suspect certain types of stocks aren't priced correctly and many investors make bad decisions:** Active investors believe they can outsmart the masses and routinely capitalize on the mistakes of the great unwashed.

>> **Understand the risks:** Most active traders underperform index funds, some without even realizing it. Before deciding to be an active trader, be sure to test out your skills with online simulations, as Chapter 2 in Book 6 describes, or make sure that you're measuring your performance correctly. If you're losing money picking stocks, stop doing it. Be sure to know how dangerous online investing can be when trying to be an active investor by reading a warning from the Securities and Exchange Commission here: sec.gov/investor/pubs/onlinetips.htm.

WARNING

Many investors try, but few are able to consistently beat the market. Consider Bill Miller, portfolio manager for the Legg Mason Capital Management Value Trust mutual fund. Miller had beaten the market for 15 years and turned into a poster child for active investors and proof that beating the market was possible if you were smart enough. But even Miller's streak came to an end in 2006. That's when his Legg Mason Value Trust fund didn't just trail the market, it lagged by a mile, returning just 5.9 percent while the market gained 15.8 percent. The fund lagged the market by 12.2 percent in 2007 and again in 2008 by 18.1 percent. While the fund beat the market in 2009, active investors had already lost their hero. Even now, more than a decade later, there's yet to be a mutual fund with an equivalent record.

Sites for the active investor to start with

Ever hear of someone trying to learn a foreign language by moving to the country and picking it up through immersion? The idea is that by just being around the language, and through the necessity of buying food or finding the restroom, the person eventually gets proficient.

TIP

If you're interested in active investing, you can do the same thing by hitting websites that are common hangouts for active investors, picking up how these types of investors find stocks that interest them and trade on them. These sites can show you the great pains active investors go through in their attempt to beat the market. A few to start looking at follow:

» **TheStreet.com** (www.thestreet.com) collects trading ideas and tips from writers mainly looking for quick-moving stocks and other investments.

» **Investor's Business Daily** (www.investors.com) provides tools and research for investors looking for promising stocks. The site highlights stocks that have moved up or down by a large amount, which usually catches the attention of traders.

» **Seeking Alpha** (seekingalpha.com) provides news and commentary for investors of all skill levels who are trying to beat the market.

Chapter **2**

Getting Your Device Ready for Online Investing

pps and online services have reinvented convenience. Admit it — you've probably shopped online from the couch in your PJs. But with the ease of online transactions comes the assumption that you will do more tasks yourself. You compare routes and times and prices before booking your own airline tickets, and you research and compare medical plans before enrolling in a health insurance plan. The process is convenient, but you also need to know what you're doing.

The story is the same with investing. If you want to reach your financial goals and retire comfortably, it's up to you to make it happen. The age of employers looking after their workers' futures with pensions is vanishing and being replaced with do-it-yourself retirement plans such as 401(k)s.

If you ask for help, you're almost always directed to search online or do your own research. That sounds reasonable, except that the internet contains billions of web pages, and you can find dozens if not hundreds of sources for investing advice, much of which is conflicting or, worse, wrong. No wonder many investors throw their hands up in utter frustration.

That's where this chapter comes in. Chapter 1 in Book 6 fills you in on what it takes to prepare yourself to be an online investor. Here in Chapter 2 of Book 6, it's time to prepare your computer, smartphone, or tablet for online investing and make it a tool that quickly provides you with the answers you need. This chapter helps you tweak your device until it's like your personal investing workstation. By the time you're finished, your trading device will feel as comfortable to you as an old leather chair. And by using mostly free online resources, you'll save yourself some money in the process.

This chapter escorts you through the morass of financial websites and apps and shows you which ones you need to know. You find out what types of investing information are available online and how to access what you need from your computer or other device. You also find out how to use online simulation sites that let you take a dry run investing with fake money to make sure that you know what you're doing before using real cash.

REMEMBER

With all this talk about researching and analyzing, don't forget job number 1: buying or selling investments. You need to either log on to the website of your broker or download a smartphone app or special software from your broker that can handle the trades. Chapter 3 in Book 6 goes over the dizzying number of choices you have for online brokers.

Turning Your Device into a Trading Station

When you think of a stock trading floor, you probably picture a room full of traders wearing brightly colored jackets, throwing papers around, and yelling out market orders. Some of that drama still exists on the New York Stock Exchange floor, but it's largely a throwback from the old days.

Today, trading floors look more like insurance offices. They have rows of desks with computers not unlike the ones you see, well, in insurance offices. Professional traders do have an advantage: Many have high-end trading systems and software that costs thousands of dollars a month. That may be beyond your price range, but you may be amazed at how much market information you can get, for free or for little money, if you know where to go.

REMEMBER

Mobile devices have become go-to devices for checking mail — and yes — playing Fortnite. When you're looking for a quick update on your portfolio or want to see how your stocks are doing, your smartphone is your trusty mobile companion. Because of the increased popularity of mobile devices, they are included in this section. But the emphasis, still, is on good ol' fashioned computers. Why? Online brokers say that most trading still happens on PCs. The bigger screen, dedicated keyboard, and better tools still make the PC the tool of choice when it comes to investing.

Using favorites to put data at your fingertips

The easiest way to turn your computer into a market-monitoring station is by bookmarking or creating favorites to key sites with data you need. *Favorites* (also sometimes called *bookmarks*) are links in your internet browser that let you quickly reach a web page when you need it, without typing a long website address. Most internet browsers have this capability, and they all work slightly differently. The following steps show you how to create favorites by using Microsoft's Edge browser in Windows 10:

1. **Navigate to the website you're interested in saving.**

2. **Click the Favorites icon (star) in the upper-right corner of the screen, labeled in Figure 2-1.**

   A menu opens.

3. **Make sure the Favorites tab is selected and give the favorite a name.**

   Choose a name that will quickly identify the site for you.

4. **In the Save In space, choose the Favorite folder into which you want to put the favorite.**

   If you want to put this favorite in a separate folder, you can create a folder by clicking the Create New Folder option. If you're not sure, just use the default Favorite folder.

5. **Click the Add button.**

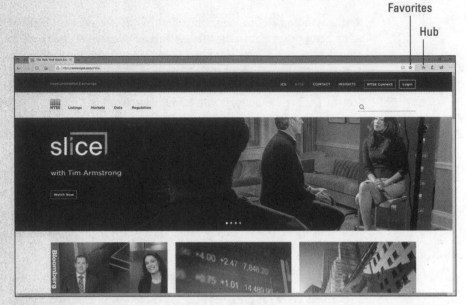

Favorites

Hub

FIGURE 2-1:
Setting financial
websites as
favorites is a
matter of just
clicking a few
buttons.

Source: NYE.com

When you want to access that address again, click the Hub icon (labeled in Figure 2-1) and scroll down until you see the title of the page you're interested in. Again, make sure the Favorites tab is selected.

TIP

Don't worry — your favorites are still available when you're away from your office PC. There's an app for that! You can download and install a free version of Edge for your smartphone, too, if you're using iOS or Android. Just download the Edge browser from your phone's app store, start the mobile browser, and log in using your Microsoft account (the same username and password you use on your computer). All the favorites and folders you created on your computer will be pulled over and accessible if you tap the Hub icon.

Putting key mobile apps a touch away

Investors are increasingly looking to their smartphones and tablets as a way to keep up with the markets, especially when they're away from the office. The computer is still the ideal place to do most of your work — given the spacious size of the screen, increased processing power, and greater storage. But some investors like the simplicity of a mobile device or use it to keep an eye on their money at all times.

Both of the major mobile platforms (Apple's iOS and Google's Android) provide an app store. That's where you go to download the apps you'll want to track your money.

TIP

To make it easier to find the apps you're looking for on your phone, consider creating an app folder called Investing or Money and putting all your finance-related apps there. You'll save yourself lots of wasted time scrolling through menus. If you're using a phone running Android or iOS, you create a folder by dragging one app's icon on top of another icon of a related app. A folder will be created automatically.

Compiling a list of must-watch sites

So you know how to create favorites and organize your mobile apps. But what sites are worth creating as favorites? Take a page from the professionals and try to replicate the data they're most interested in. Most professional trading workstations are set up so that they can take on five distinct tasks:

>> Track the market's every move.

>> Monitor news that has the potential to affect stock prices.

>> Check in on Wall Street chatter.

>> Access company financial statements and regulatory filings.

>> Execute trades.

TECHNICAL STUFF

The world between PCs and mobile devices continues to blur. Microsoft's Surface Pro is basically a tablet that's also a computer. And Windows 10 is designed to give you the power of a desktop computer but with the ease and apps that smartphone users have become used to. Apple followed with the iPad Pro — which still runs a mobile operating system — but touts a larger screen and the capability to connect and use a keyboard. Expect the distinction between computer and mobile devices to dissolve over time.

Tracking the Market's Every Move

You're probably hoping to study the market and find ways to score big and fast. Hey, everyone wants to get rich quick. Just remember that making money by darting in and out of stocks is extremely tough to do, and most investors, online or not, will be better off forming and sticking with a long-term investment strategy.

No matter what kind of investor you plan to be, watching real-time stock movements is fascinating. Seeing rapid price moves with stock prices dancing around and flashing on the computer screen is a guilty pleasure and a source of entertainment (or profit) for some investors.

TIP

You can find a great deal of overlap among online investing resources. Many of the following sites and apps do more than what is highlighted here. Explore the different sites and see whether certain ones suit you best.

You can get stock quotes and see the value of popular market indexes such as the Dow Jones Industrial Average, Standard & Poor's 500 index, and Nasdaq composite index in many places. Therefore, a website must excel to earn a position as one of your favorites. The next section in this chapter has a quick list that can help you get started creating general-purpose online investing favorites or decide which apps are worthy of occupying space on your phone. The sites listed here make the cut because they not only provide stock quotes but also go a step further by being the best at a certain aspect of tracking the market.

REMEMBER

When you look up a stock quote on many sites or in an app, you'll usually see three quotes: the last sale, the bid, and the ask. The *last sale* is what you probably think of as the stock quote and is featured on most websites. That's the price at which a buyer and seller agreed to a transaction. The *bid* is the highest price other investors are willing to pay for the stock. The *ask* is the lowest price that investors who own the stock are willing to sell it for.

Getting price quotes on markets and stocks

Nearly any site or finance app can give you stock quotes for the day, including the financial news websites discussed later in this chapter. But a few sites deserve special mention because they make it easy to get stock quotes for days in the past and even download them to your computer for further analysis. And because they deserve special mention, they're getting it right here:

>> **MSN Money** (money.msn.com) is handy for looking up prices of stocks and market indexes because it's fast and gives you everything you need, ranging from the stock's closing price to the amount of trading activity to when dividends (cash payments) were paid to investors. One nifty trick of MSN Money is that it has companion apps for Windows 10, iOS, and Android that remember which stocks you're most interested in. You can create this list by clicking the My Watchlist link on the website or on the Watchlist menu in the app.

>> **Yahoo! Finance** (`finance.yahoo.com`) lets you download historical data, a feature that's getting surprisingly scarce in nonprofessional tools. Enter a stock symbol and click the magnifying glass. Then, at the top of the page, click the Historical Data link. You'll see a page with a table of dates and the stock's prices on those dates. In the Time Period area near the top, you can choose a range of dates for which you'd like stock prices. On the right side is a link to Download. Yahoo! Finance also offers an app for several types of smartphones, making it a convenient choice.

>> **Google Finance** (`www.google.com/finance`) does a solid job of summarizing in one page many of the basics you need to know about a stock. You'll find not only the stock price but also a list of competitors, a summary of the company, market news, and basic financial information. Google Finance also offers free real-time stock prices.

Slicing and dicing the markets

Although quite a few market indexes exist, *all* online investors need to be familiar with some major market benchmarks. These benchmarks are so commonly discussed that they need to be part of your investor vocabulary. Table 2-1 presents them in all their market-dominating glory.

TABLE 2-1   **Key Market Indexes**

Index Name	What It Measures
Dow Jones Industrial Average	Thirty big, industrial companies. When investors hear about "the market," more often than not they think of the Dow.
Standard & Poor's 500 index	Large U.S. companies, including 500 of the nation's most well-known stocks. Moves similarly to the Dow, even though it includes more stocks.
Nasdaq Composite index	Stocks that trade on the Nasdaq stock market. Tends to closely track technology stocks.
Wilshire 5000 Total Market Index	The entire U.S. stock market. Contains all significant stocks from the largest to the smallest.
Russell 2000 Index	Small-company U.S. stocks. Tends to be more volatile than indexes that track large companies — the S&P 500, for example.
MSCI ACWI (All Country World Index)	Stocks around the world. Includes shares of big companies in developed parts of the world and small companies in less-developed nations.

Nearly all financial websites let you track all the indexes listed in the table. Yahoo! Finance (finance.yahoo.com), though, makes it easy to monitor different slices of the markets, such as foreign stocks, specific industry sectors, and bonds. The Yahoo! Finance website offers several ways for you to dig beyond the market indexes, as the following list makes clear:

>> **A quick read on all U.S. market indexes:** To see how most of the key U.S. market indexes are doing, start at Yahoo! Finance's main page at finance. yahoo.com. Hover your cursor over the Markets option at the top of the page, and click the World Indices link that appears. The top of the next page displays key U.S. market indexes, such as S&P 500, Dow Jones, and Nasdaq.

>> **A rundown of the performance of foreign stocks:** Scroll down the list that appears under World Indices and you can monitor just about any foreign market you'd care to track.

>> **A summary of the performance of industries:** The Yahoo! Finance page enables you to track the performance of different industries, if you know where to look. To find a list of industry group results, click the Industries link at the top of the Yahoo! Finance page (it's in the menu that looks like an ellipsis, after the Personal Finance menu). Set it as a favorite.

TIP

Don't confuse stocks with indexes. *Stocks* are shares in individual companies, such as Microsoft or Exxon Mobil. The prices of stocks reflect how much you would have to pay for a share of the stock. *Indexes* are mathematical formulas that tell you how much a collection of stocks has changed in value. For example, when the Dow Jones Industrial Average, which contains 30 stocks, hits 35,000, that doesn't mean you can buy it for $35,000. The 35,000 is just a number that represents relative value.

Your crystal ball: Predicting how the day will begin

Some investors like to get a jump-start on the trading day by watching the futures market. The *futures market* is an auction for future contracts, which are financial obligations that allow buyers and sellers to lock in prices for commodities and other assets in the future. The futures market allows investors to bet how much certain assets will be worth minutes, days, weeks, or years from today. Futures are commonly used with commodities, such as energy and food.

You can see what the futures market is saying about stocks, too. Bloomberg, a major financial news and data company, gives investors a sneak peek on how stocks could open the next trading day. On its Futures page (`www.bloomberg.com/markets/stocks/futures`), you can see how traders who apparently don't have anything better to do are betting after the stock market is closed and how major market indexes around the world will open. If you're the kind of person who doesn't like surprises, the Futures page is an easy way to see how investors are behaving even when the market centers are closed.

Getting company descriptions

Professional investors like to bone up on what a company does, who's in charge, and how profitable it is without poring through dozens of industry reports. You can get this type of quick snapshot information by reading online company descriptions. All the main investing sites discussed in this chapter have company description sections. Here is one more site worth checking out, plus another way to use Yahoo! Finance:

>> **Reuters** (`www.reuters.com/finance/markets`) offers in-depth profiles on companies. Just click the magnifying glass, enter the name of the company, click the magnifying glass again, and then click the name of the company. The page that opens shows you all the vital information about the company, ranging from a company description to the names of members of its management team (if you click the People tab). To see a comprehensive rundown of the company's financial results, click the Financials tab.

>> **Yahoo! Finance** (`finance.yahoo.com`) offers a comprehensive summary of a company's vitals. From the site's main page, enter the stock's symbol in the search box located on the top of the screen and then click the magnifying glass. On the top of the next page, click the Profile link. On the screen that appears, you can also find particulars on the company's financial performance by clicking the Statistics and Financials links.

Keeping tabs on commodities

The exciting world of commodities includes the oil, lumber, and coal that companies use to make their products. For details, check out the following websites:

>> **Bloomberg** (`www.bloomberg.com/markets/commodities`) has a professional-grade site that lets you watch movements in just about any commodity that you can imagine, including gold, silver, and platinum. Interested in live cattle? Yes, you can see the price. This data is necessary if you want to invest in

commodities directly. And even if you don't buy or sell commodities, they're good to watch. For instance, if you own shares of Starbucks, wouldn't you want to know what the price of coffee is doing?

>> **CME Group** (www.cmegroup.com) lists prices on many major commodities, such as corn, soybeans, wheat, and ethanol.

Tracking bonds and U.S. Treasuries

A *bond* is an IOU issued by a government, a company, or another borrower. An owner of a bond is entitled to receive the borrowed funds when they're paid back by a certain time in the future at a predetermined interest rate. Even if you have no interest in investing in bonds, you still should know what rates are doing. After all, if you could invest in *Treasury bonds* — bonds issued by the federal government that come due in 30 years — and get a 3 percent annual return guaranteed, wouldn't you be a bit less enthusiastic about a risky stock that you think will return only 4 percent? That extra return is not enough for the extra risk you're taking.

The U.S. government sells other Treasuries, including *Treasury bills* (T-bills), which generally come due in a year or less, and *Treasury notes* (T-notes), which come due in more than a year but no more than ten years. For an introduction, check out the following sites:

>> **Bloomberg** (www.bloomberg.com/markets/rates-bonds) makes tracking bonds easy. At a glance, you can see the yields on just about any major bond or Treasury you can imagine.

REMEMBER

>> **The Federal Reserve Bank** (www.federalreserve.gov/monetarypolicy/openmarket.htm) is the online presence for the *Fed,* as it's affectionately called. The Fed is in charge of strongly influencing short-term interest rates, including the *federal funds rate,* which is typically the rate at which banks lend money stored at the Fed to other banks overnight. No, you can't borrow at that rate, but it's important to watch this interest rate because it affects long-term interest rates, which you *can* borrow at. You can see past federal funds rates at the Fed's site, as shown in Figure 2-2. Traders buy and sell long-term Treasuries and set interest rates based in large part on where short-term rates are or where they're expected to be.

TIP

Would you like to find out more about how the Fed affects the nation's money supply? The Federal Reserve Bank of Kansas City maintains a useful and simple site on the topic — designed for teens and college students, but useful for any investor — at www.federalreserveeducation.org/.

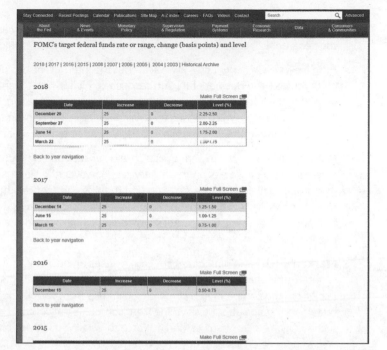

FIGURE 2-2:
The Fed's website makes it easy to track important interest rates.

Source: federalreserve.gov

Monitoring Market-Moving News

Ever see a biotech stock skyrocket after the company announces a breakthrough treatment? Tech stocks routinely jump in price on the debut of popular new gadgets or software. That's the power of news — often called *market-moving news.* Markets are constantly taking in and digesting all sorts of developments and changes, both good and bad. To stay on top of these developments, you'll want to set as favorites a few leading financial news sites. The following sections explore the different kinds of financial news sites in greater detail.

Financial websites

Many of the financial sites mentioned previously in the chapter are also great places to get market-moving news. Yahoo! Finance and MSN Money pick up wire service stories on the markets and individual stocks, making them helpful resources. Bloomberg covers just about every type of traditional investment you can imagine, thanks to its network of reporters. Others include the following:

>> **Google News** (news.google.com) has a business section that pulls in important financial stories. Its best feature is the capability to search for news

based on precise criteria, including keywords, the date the story appeared, or the geographic location of the news.

>> **Bing News** (www.bing.com/news) searches the internet for business stories after you click the Business tab. You can also scroll down to the Interests section in the left-hand menu to set markets, personal finance, or individual stocks as interests, which means they will be covered more prominently online and also in the Bing mobile app (downloaded to your smartphone).

>> **Briefing.com** (www.briefing.com) is a data service used by professional investors, who pay for its premium services. However, the site makes some of its content available for free. You can find running commentary on market-moving news and events. Briefing.com's stock market update is a great way to find out what's behind the market's day-to-day swings — and see how a random event can have a big effect on stocks.

>> **MarketWatch** (www.marketwatch.com) focuses on business stories that are so interesting that you can hardly resist clicking. The site attempts to separate itself from the competition by providing columns from various financial writers who opine about everything from companies' accounting practices to technology. You can instruct MarketWatch to email you articles of interest as well as note when a stock moves by a certain amount.

>> **BigCharts.com** (www.bigcharts.com) is a service of MarketWatch that provides graphical information about the markets. The best aspect of the site is the set of BigReports lists that show you, at a glance, the biggest movers on Wall Street that day in terms of price or percentage price change.

>> **Motley Fool** (www.fool.com) has a little something for everyone. You find content for the active trader, including stock tips galore, as well as tricks and techniques on how to deeply analyze companies' financial statements. Passive investors will appreciate the more general personal finance stories.

>> **Reuters** (www.reuters.com/markets) makes high-end systems used by many professional traders, but many of these tools are available to you as well. If you click the magnifying glass in the search box at the upper-right corner of the page, enter a company's name, and then click the company's name, you can see advanced statistics about the stock, including dividend yields and key ratios.

TIP

Many financial websites and news stories use the terms *bullish* and *bearish*. When investors are *bullish*, they think the stock market is going to go up. And when investors are *bearish*, they think stocks will go down.

Traditional financial news sites

Many financial news providers that you may already be familiar with from websites, apps, newspapers, magazines, or TV also provide data that's useful to investors online, including the following:

>> **Wall Street Journal Online** (www.wsj.com) is a source of breaking financial news. You may be familiar with the print edition of the *Wall Street Journal;* this is the online version. This site charges for much of its content.

>> **Financial Times** (www.ft.com) is a London-based business publication, so it provides a unique spin on business events here. It's a good source of merger announcements.

>> **CNBC** (www.cnbc.com) routinely updates its website, and the financial TV channel's online presence has many of the same features as other financial news sites. What makes the site unique is that it lets you stream to your browser segments that aired on CNBC.

DO YOU SPEAK TICKER SYMBOL?

Nearly every financial website is centered on the ticker symbol. These are the one-, two-, three-, or four-letter abbreviations used to symbolize stocks or investments. Originally, ticker symbols were used so that brokers could quickly read a *ticker tape,* a scrolling printout of stocks and prices. The symbol has taken on a new use in the online era, so much so that most sites enable you to search for a stock by its symbol.

Ticker symbols have become so popular that investors sometimes use them instead of a company's name. And sometimes companies have fun with their symbols to make them more memorable. In 2006, for instance, motorcycle maker Harley-Davidson changed its symbol from the boring HDI to the more exciting HOG, the nickname for its rumbling bikes. Other fun ticker symbols (and the company) include the following:

- BUD: Anheuser-Busch InBev
- CAKE: Cheesecake Factory
- EAT: Brinker (a restaurant company)
- FIZZ: National Beverage
- LUV: Southwest Airlines
- SAM: Boston Beer
- ZEUS: Olympic Steel (Get it? The Greek god)

Keep one other thing in mind regarding stock symbols. You used to be able to tell whether a stock traded on the Nasdaq or the New York Stock Exchange just by looking at the symbol. For many years, Nasdaq stocks traded with symbols with four letters, such as INTC for Intel and MSFT for Microsoft. But that changed in 2007 when Nasdaq began issuing symbols of one, two, and three letters to its member companies.

» **CNN Business** (www.cnn.com/business) has a good mix of breaking financial news and general personal financial help. It contains specialized information on markets, technology, jobs, personal finance, and real estate.

» **Investor's Business Daily** (www.investors.com) is largely geared to sophisticated investors; subscribers have access to all articles. You'll find articles for short-term active traders as well as for passive or mutual fund investors more focused on the longer term. The site also has tools to help you find stocks that are outperforming the rest of the stock market.

» **Barron's** (www.barrons.com) is a weekly publication written mainly for advanced investors and is updated online during the day. Most of the features are available only to subscribers. Subscribers to the *Wall Street Journal*'s website get access to Barron's online site because both are owned by Dow Jones.

Checking In on Wall Street Chatter

Rumor and innuendo are key parts of traders' lives. Because stock prices are highly sensitive in the short run to what other traders and investors are saying about a stock, traders make it their business to follow every murmur. As an individual investor, you're at a disadvantage in this department because you don't have portfolio managers of giant mutual funds calling you and telling you what they're hearing. But you can use social networking and social investing, online tools that allow investors to swap information.

Chat rooms were an early form of social investing, but the area has evolved to include online blogs and podcasts. Twitter has also become an important tool for investors. In addition, several online brokers' sites let users communicate with each other.

If you're a passive investor, you probably couldn't care less about rumors. Even so, you can take advantage of blogs and chat rooms that are dedicated to index investing.

Everyone is an expert: Finding blogs

Thanks to low-cost computers, mobile devices, and internet connections, just about anyone with an opinion and a keyboard or smartphone can profess to the world their view of investments. Some of these opinions are worth listening to, but many are not.

BEWARE OF RUMORS

Investors can't help themselves when it comes to rumors. And sometimes certain blogs and podcasts only feed your innate desire to get the inside scoop on an investment that's about to explode in value. Investment rumors are kind of like celebrity gossip: You're probably better off ignoring them, but sometimes it's impossible to resist. Just remember that making investment decisions based on rumors is usually a bad idea.

Even giant stocks can get swept up in rumors and result in pain for gullible investors. Here's an example: On May 17, 2012, Facebook, the world's largest social networking company, sold its stock to public investors for the first time for $38 a share. The website was (and is) so popular with consumers that the rumor mill went into overdrive. Many people with little to no experience with investing thought they had to jump into the initial public offering of Facebook since they thought it was bound to soar on its first day. But these rumors proved to be wrong. Shares of Facebook barely moved on their first day of trading, and by the end of May the stock lost 22 percent of its value from the offering price. Shares have performed very well since then, but investors who bought when the stock debuted had to endure a long period of pain.

Guess what? You may think investors would have learned their lesson from Facebook. But the same hype-fueled fever revved up again in May 2019. Unprofitable ride-sharing service Uber Technologies offered its shares at $45 each. Given how popular the service is, many expected fireworks. But the stock fizzled, falling nearly 8 percent on the first day. Even months later, shares of Uber traded below the $45 a share offer price.

One popular vehicle for sharing opinions is a *blog* (short for web log), which is a sort of online journal. Blogs can vary greatly in quality. Some are the modern-day equivalent of a crazy person on the street corner yelling at anyone who walks by, whereas other blogs are thoughtful and well-informed. It's *buyer beware* with blogs — you have to decide whether the person is worth listening to. Ask yourself what the blogger's track record is and how the blogger makes money.

With so many blogs out there, sometimes the toughest part can be finding the worthwhile ones. Here are several ways that you can locate them:

>> **General search engines:** All the leading search engines, including Google, Yahoo!, and Bing, let you search much of the blogging world. You're likely to find major general-interest finance blogs just by typing **investing blog.** You can also look for articles such as "The 7 best investing blogs" written by reputable publications like the ones described previously to get suggestions.

>> **Community sites:** Facebook (www.facebook.com) is best known as an online place for friends to keep tabs on each other and for families to share photos

with each other. But some financial blogs are also lurking there. To find them, just log on to the site and search for the words *financial, money, investing,* and *stocks.* You can also find Facebook communities focused on investing for retirement or other goals.

>> **Mainstream media:** Almost all the news sites have some of their writers penning blogs as well. Many blogs are available from the mainstream media outlet's website.

Getting in tune with podcasts

Next time you see someone listening to a smartphone with Bluetooth buds jammed into their ears, don't assume they're rocking out. They may be researching stocks or learning about investing. A *podcast* is an audio broadcast that's transferred electronically over the internet to your computer or smartphone — they're like radio shows for the internet age. Some podcasts are created by major media, but others, like some blogs, are done by amateurs, so the same need for caution applies.

It's easy to find a radio or TV station: Just turn on the radio and start flipping. But finding podcasts takes a little more doing. It's not difficult, though, if you try these different methods:

>> **Podcast smartphone apps:** You'll probably be listening to podcasts on your smartphone in the car or on a train, so it makes sense to use your phone to find them, too. With Android, you can find podcasts in two ways. The easiest method is to launch the built-in Play Music app. Press the three lines in the upper-left corner, choose Podcasts, and search for podcasts. The other method is to download the Google Podcasts app, which gives you a little more control in finding a podcast you'll love. With iOS, fire up the Podcasts app, and search for and download podcasts from there. You can also use third-party podcast apps, such as Spotify (primarily a music streaming app) and Stitcher.

>> **Podcast search engines:** Search engines dedicated to podcasts, such as Podcasts.com (www.podcasts.com), provide a giant list of podcasts that meet your requirements. Stitcher Radio (www.stitcher.com) is another popular podcast search site. You can stream from these sites, too, but more likely you'll fire up a podcast app and listen from there.

>> **Desktop audio software:** The Apple Podcasts app is included on all Apple devices, or you can listen on iTunes on a PC. (Find more info at www.apple.com/apple-podcasts/.) You can scroll through hundreds of available podcasts, including some from mainstream outlets such as *Bloomberg Businessweek,* CNBC, and National Public Radio.

Not an Apple kind of person? No problem. Spotify for the desktop, download-able from the Windows 10 app store, also has a podcast feature. To get there, click Browse in the menu on the left side of the screen and then choose Podcasts from the option at the top. You can also stream podcasts to your computer using Stitcher.com if you click the Listen option.

Taming Twitter

Social media such as Facebook and Twitter are increasingly the go-to places to keep on top of real-time business news from major outlets. Here's the quick-and-dirty of what you need to get set up: Download Twitter from your device's app store. The app, which is available for computer and mobile devices, allows you to search for news outlets, bloggers, and other sources of market news and then follow them. After you follow these outlets, Twitter will present you with all the news being tweeted so you won't miss a thing. The app is free; you just need to sign up for Twitter.

Keeping Tabs on the Regulators

Professional traders' computers also keep close tabs on regulatory filings from companies. Regulatory filings are often the best, if not the only, data that inves-tors get directly from a company. If companies make any significant announce-ments, they're required to notify the appropriate government watchdogs, which in most cases is the Securities and Exchange Commission (SEC).

It's important for you to know how to monitor these documents and quickly find them online. You can get regulatory filings online through

>> **The company's website:** Most provide a section with their complete reports.

>> **Financial sites and portals:** Most of the sites listed previously in this chapter provide links to the documents.

>> **Aggregation sites:** These sites parse the filings from companies and make them easy to find and download for free. SEC Info (www.secinfo.com) sorts all the regulatory filings into easy-to-understand categories. Last10K.com (www.last10k.com) allows you to quickly find companies' financial reports.

>> **The Securities and Exchange Commission (www.sec.gov):** For most investors, the free SEC site has as much info as any sane person would ever want, and it isn't too difficult to navigate to boot.

In fact, the Securities and Exchange Commission site is so easy to navigate that you can do it right now. To find company regulatory filings, follow these steps:

1. **Point your web browser to www.sec.gov.**

   The SEC site makes an appearance.

2. **Click the Filings link in the upper-right corner and go to Company Filings Search.**

   The EDGAR (Electronic Data Gathering Analysis and Retrieval) Company Filings page appears.

3. **Enter the company's name or ticker symbol in the appropriate box, and then click the Search button.**

   You see a giant list of company filings in the order in which they were filed.

The list is not entirely user-friendly because the filings are distinguished only by their *form*, which is regulatory code for the types of information the documents contain. Table 2-2 gives you the skinny on the most common form codes.

TABLE 2-2   SEC Forms You Can Use

Form Code	What It Contains
8-K	A news flash from the company. 8-Ks can contain just about anything that's considered "material" or important to investors, ranging from the resignation of a top official to news of the win of a new customer.
10-Q	The company's quarterly report. This form displays all the information a company is required to provide to investors each quarter. Here you can find the key financial statements, such as the income statement and balance sheet.
10-K	The company's annual report. This is one of the most important documents that a company creates. It provides a summary of everything that happened during the year, including comments from management and financial statements that have been checked, or *audited*, by the company's accounting firm.
DEF 14 and DEF 14A	The company's *proxy statement* — a document that describes company matters to be discussed and voted on by shareholders at the annual meeting. Contains all the important company information that's subject to shareholder approval and scrutiny. Most proxies contain everything that's up for a vote at the shareholder meeting, ranging from board members up for election, pay packages and other perks, and pending lawsuits. If you're going to read any document, make it this one.

TIP

Companies don't make their regulatory filings easy to read. You have to be part lawyer, part investor, and part investment banker to read between the lines in these often-cryptic statements. *Investment Banking For Dummies*, by Matt Krantz and Robert R. Johnson (Wiley), goes into the nitty-gritty.

Searching the Internet High and Low

At the risk of sounding obvious, search engines hold some gems of information for investors. Some of the most popular search engines include the following:

» **Google** (www.google.com)**:** Definitely the biggest and most popular web search engine, so much so that investors often say they'll *google* a stock. Because the site is so clean and Zen-like, it has the benefit of being easy to use. Type **stock:** and a ticker symbol, and you'll get basic price information. Click the News, Compare, and Financials links for more details.

» **Bing** (www.bing.com)**:** Microsoft's attempt to come up with a Google killer, Bing.com has a few handy features for online investors, including the capability to quickly pull up stock quotes and charts by entering **stock** and the company's name or ticker symbol. For example, to get a quick datasheet on General Electric, type **stock GE**. Clicking the information box takes you to MSN Money for more analysis.

» **Wolfram Alpha** (www.wolframalpha.com)**:** This lesser-known search engine has some valuable features. If you enter the ticker symbol of a stock, Wolfram Alpha generates an impressive page filled with all sorts of company information. Wolfram Alpha will calculate some advanced statistical information, for instance, that shows you how well the stock has done over different time periods.

» **Yahoo!** (www.yahoo.com)**:** Yahoo! remains the go-to search place for many consumers. Yahoo! Finance has excellent resources for investors, as described previously in this chapter, so it's logical to try the site for searching, too.

Keeping the Bad Guys Out: Securing Your PC

If you're going to use your computer to process your investing and banking tasks, you'd better lock it down. Cyber-criminals are sophisticated and have targeted online investors in hopes of gaining control of a person's account and stealing money.

Please, don't let such concerns scare you off from investing online. After all, cars get broken into but you still drive. Just take the following precautions to make it harder for the bad guys to get into your PC:

TIP

>> **Turn on antivirus software.** A *virus*, which is sinister code designed to wreak havoc on your computer, can corrupt system files and make your computer unreliable or unusable. Antivirus software is the easy solution. It runs in the background, looks at any program that tries to run on your computer, and stops the program if it tries to do something improper.

You can go to great lengths to lock down your aging computer, but the best defense is upgraded equipment running a modern operating system. Windows Security, which is built into Windows 10, runs efficiently and is pretty much all you need. To make sure that it's turned on, choose Start ⇨ Settings ⇨ Update & Security ⇨ Windows Security. From here, make sure that Virus and Threat Protection is turned on. Also, check the Virus & Threat Protection Updates section for updates to install.

Many third-party antivirus software programs are available for purchase, but ignore all emails and ads pitching software to clean your computer or phone. You don't need them, and many will actually harm your device.

>> **Install antispyware software.** *Spyware* is software that attaches itself to your computer without your permission and runs behind the scenes. It's especially sinister because it may forward personal information to a third party, usually for marketing. Windows Security automatically scans your computer and makes sure that no spyware has hitched a ride. You can also find dedicated software programs designed to sniff out spyware. Malwarebytes (`www.malwarebytes.org`) works well (and has the greatest name).

>> **Use a firewall.** A *firewall* is an electronic barrier that (selectively) separates you from the internet at large. A proper firewall is like a moat around a castle — only traffic that you lower the drawbridge for can get in. You can use the following types of firewalls:

- **Built-in:** If you have Microsoft's Windows 10, a firewall is turned on by default.

- **Router:** A *router* is a small box that sits between your computer and the wall jack that connects you to the internet. Many routers work like a software firewall and can even make your computer invisible to other computers. Depending on your router, you may need to enable the firewall. Check the router's instructions to find out how.

>> **Protect your passwords.** Mobile devices are often locked down with fingerprint scans. But typed-in passwords are still surprisingly important online. Most online brokers require complex passwords, which include letters, numbers, and special characters. That requirement makes life harder for

hackers but annoying for you because complex passwords are hard to remember.

TIP

You can keep track of all your passwords by using a digital vault such as LastPass (www.lastpass.com) or Dashlane (www.dashlane.com). These services encrypt all your passwords in one place, and allow you to access them by entering one master password.

>> **Be cautious when using Wi-Fi.** Jumping on a free Wi-Fi network to look up your investment portfolio may be tempting but dangerous. Hackers can take control of free Wi-Fi networks and commandeer your log-in credentials. It's always safer to skip the free Wi-Fi and use your smartphone's cellular connection instead. If you must use public Wi-Fi, make sure you also use a *virtual private network,* or *VPN*. The VPN puts your internet traffic in a digital private lane that others can't look into. If your employer doesn't offer a VPN for you to use on your personal computer or device, subscribe to a VPN service. Search the Windows app store for VPNs. They aren't free — and it's best to stick with cellular anyway.

Mastering the Basics with Online Tutorials and Simulations

Online investing is like Vegas in that you get no do-overs. If you invest all your money in a speculative company that goes belly up, you lose your money. Period. Don't expect the government to bail you out, and don't think that you can sue the company to get your money back because it's most likely gone. If you're new to investing, you may want to try the tutorials and simulations in the following sections before using real money.

Online tutorials

Before you jump into any activity with risk, it's worthwhile to take a deep breath, relax, and make absolutely sure that you understand how the process works. Several excellent online tutorials can step you through the process to make sure that you know what to expect. If you're just starting out, run through one of the following:

>> **Help For Investors.org** (helpforinvestors.org/) has links to online resources on all sorts of investing topics, from ways to report investment fraud to finding investing help.

- **American Association of Individual Investors** (www.aaii.com) provides free resources to investors, including a virtual Investor Classroom that teaches the basics (www.aaii.com/classroom).

  The AAII site provides portfolios that mirror the strategies of famous investors at www.aaii.com/journal/category/stockideas. Be sure to check out the portfolio similar to that of famed investor Warren Buffett (www.aaii.com/journal/article/hagstroms-essential-buffett-stocks).

WARNING

Be careful about which online tutorials you read and pay attention to. Many so-called tutorials are thinly guised pitches for investment professionals trying to get you to hire them. Some also promote specialized trading techniques with the purpose of getting you to buy books and other materials.

Simulations

Online games, or *simulations*, let you buy and sell real stocks using funny money. Online simulations are a good idea for investors because they let you get a taste for investing before you commit to a strategy.

Following is a list of a few simulators you can try:

- **How the Market Works** (www.howthemarketworks.com) sets you up with $100,000 in virtual cash so you can try your hand at investing. There are games and lessons for those who want to find out more about investing online.

- **Wall Street Survivor** (www.wallstreetsurvivor.com) enables you to buy and sell fake shares in real companies. You compete with others in the game, because it's more fun to be rich with fake money if you can brag about it. If you don't do well, watch the educational videos to improve your skill.

- **MarketWatch Virtual Stock Exchange** (www.marketwatch.com/game) lets you try your hand at investing in a simulated environment. You can compete in existing games or recruit your own opponents.

IN THIS CHAPTER

» **Understanding your choices of brokers**

» **Deciding what you need from a broker**

» **Knowing the differences between a self-service and full-service brokerage**

» **Making sure that your money is safe with your broker**

» **Scoping out how to access your account with your broker**

» **Setting up your account and getting started**

Chapter **3**

Connecting with an Online Broker

This chapter dives into the offerings from all the major online brokerages to pinpoint which ones could fit your needs. Why can't we save you the trouble and just tell you which broker is the best? It's not that easy. Choosing "the best" brokerage is like choosing the most beautiful painting in an art museum. Everyone has an opinion based on what is most important to them. If you're most interested in dirt–cheap commissions and don't care much for service, you have one set of brokers to pick from. If you're looking for access to physical branches staffed with live people who can help you choose stocks or navigate the website, you have a different set of candidates. If you're all about the smartphone, you have other choices.

You may think you don't need this chapter because you like a certain broker's ads on TV or have a cousin who swears by their online broker. But don't underestimate the benefits that will accrue to you if you thoroughly research your broker options. Face it: Your broker is the gatekeeper to your money, and picking the right one will partly determine how successful you are as an investor.

Finding the Best Broker for You

People are constantly looking for the "best" of everything. Music buffs pore through online reviews and websites looking for the best earphones, commuters seek the best car, and new parents search for the best stroller. Similarly, investors are on a constant quest for the best online broker. But just as different headphones, cars, and strollers fit different people's needs, the same is true with brokerages. Investors have different goals, taste for risk, and resources. And that's why one person's broker can be perfect for them but completely wrong for you.

Not thoroughly researching your broker is a mistake. Your online broker is the most important member of your investing team, handling everything from tracking your portfolio to helping you buy and sell investments and tracking your taxable gains and losses. It's a relationship you need to be happy with to be a happy online investor. Above all, you want to make sure that your broker will be there for you if you run into any problems or have questions.

The nine main factors to consider

Brokers differ from one another in nine main ways. If you're aware of these things and understand what you're looking for, you can quickly eliminate brokers that don't fit your needs. The factors to consider are as follows:

>> **Commissions:** Perhaps the most important consideration for many investors when evaluating brokers is the price charged for executing trades, known as the *commission*. (Fees are discussed at length later in this chapter.) There's good news here. Commissions charged by online brokers have been steadily falling since the 1990s, with most taking even lower dives during yet another price war that erupted in 2017. Also, most brokers now offer flat-rate commissions, meaning that all people pay the same commission no matter how many times they buy and sell or how many shares they trade. Some brokers have even started offering free commissions on certain trades. Roughly a third of self-directed investors said they're paying less than $5 a trade, according to a 2018 analysis by rating service J.D. Power.

>> **Availability of advice:** One way brokers separate themselves is by whether or not they give you any help picking investments. On one end of the spectrum are the *full-service traditional brokers* that are all about giving you personalized attention. Not only can they pick stocks for you, but they'll also pour you coffee and serve you donuts when you visit them in their fancy offices. If you're not interested in paying for such perks, the *self-service brokers* are happy to oblige. Self-service brokers give you the tools you need, and then you're pretty much on your own. A few brokers fit somewhere between full service and self-service. J.D. Power found investor satisfaction was higher when brokers proactively reached out to offer help or guidance at least once a year.

>> **Access to an office:** Some brokers exist only online. It's up to you to have your own computer and internet connection. But others have branch offices in certain cities and allow customers to stop in, do some trading, and sometimes take classes and fraternize with other investors or meet with advisors. You may not think that having access to a branch office will be important to you; after all, you're an online investor. But some find comfort in a bricks-and-mortar location.

>> **Other banking services:** A brokerage account doesn't have to be a financial island. Some brokerage firms let you move money from your trading account into other types of accounts, such as checking accounts. Some also provide ATM cards or credit cards.

>> **Speed of execution:** When you click the Buy or Sell button on the website, the trade isn't done. Your order snakes its way from your computer to other traders' computers on Wall Street, where it is filled. Some brokerages have spent a great deal of effort giving you the fastest path to other traders. That's generally beneficial because it means that you get a price that reflects the true value of the stock you're buying or selling. Depending on your strategy, you may not want your orders piling up in a bin, waiting to get filled. Speed of execution is tracked by broker-rating services, discussed later in this chapter, in the section "Finding Out What Reviewers Think."

>> **Customer service:** Do you have a question about your account or about making a trade? When you do, you'll need to reach the broker to ask it. The levels of service vary wildly. Some brokers have customer service reps available at your beck and call either in offices or on the phone. Others let you email a question and wait for an answer.

>> **Site reliability:** No one wants to be in the position of finding a promising investment only to discover that their online brokerage is down for repair. Some brokerages have focused on limiting system downtime, which may be important to you if you trade many times a day. Again, this is something brokerage-rating services measure.

» **Access to advanced stock-buying tools:** Some brokerage sites are pretty bare-bones because they assume that the investors already have the software and tools they need. This is dramatically changing, however, as many third-party investing websites are vanishing, scaling back, or starting to charge for their services. Now, investors are increasingly looking to their brokerages to provide comprehensive tools that can track tax liabilities, help them go prospecting for stocks, or monitor market movements or breaking news.

» **Ease of use:** Online brokers geared for people new to online investing or who plan to trade infrequently are minimalists and have as few buttons as possible. They're the Zen of trading. But those aimed for hyperactive traders who click Buy and Sell so many times they have calluses on their fingers tend to give investors dozens of options allowing them to do some advanced stuff. Some sites targeting advanced traders provide trading tools aimed at helping investors flip stocks or other options quickly and at set prices. But that may be overwhelming if you just want to buy 100 shares of Apple stock every couple of months.

Gotchas to watch out for

WARNING

Brokerage firms often have confusing commission structures to fool you into thinking you'll pay less than you ultimately do. Make sure that you check to see whether the firm charges extra for certain types of orders, such as limit orders (see Chapter 4 in Book 6), large orders, or mutual funds. Some brokers zing you with fees or inflate commissions if you don't keep a balance of a certain size. Some brokers also charge you for switching to another broker. Always check for covert fees before signing up. The later section "Avoiding Hidden Fees" can help you spot things to watch out for.

Separating the Types of Brokerages

Choosing a brokerage firm may seem intimidating, but it's no different than picking a restaurant. You can find fast-food restaurants, where you have to walk up to the counter, place your order, put on your own ketchup and mustard, and find a place to sit. Then there are full-service restaurants, where you're seated and pampered by dressed-up servers who bring everything at your command and even clean the bread crumbs away when you're done.

The same goes for brokerages. Self-service brokers give you everything you need to get the job done and let you have at it. Because you're doing much of the work yourself, unless you ask for help, self-service brokers tend to have the lowest commissions. Following price wars, self-service brokers are commonly grouped into two baskets: deep discounters and discounters. Then you have the full-service traditional brokerages, which hold your hand through the whole process, down to suggesting investments, analyzing your portfolio, and offering estate-planning services. Keep in mind that these are general brokerage categories, and sometimes the lines blur a bit because some self-service brokers let you buy advice from them if you ask.

TIP

If you can't find a page on the broker's site that lists all its fees, commissions, and other charges in less than three mouse clicks from the home page, look elsewhere. Brokers that bury fees do so for a reason.

How do you decide what you need? Determine how often you intend to trade, what types of investments you plan to buy, and how long you'll hold them. It's difficult to know this in advance, but there are ways to figure it out. For instance, did you perform the trading simulations mentioned in Chapter 2 of Book 6? If so, how often did you trade? Next, familiarize yourself with the three types of online brokers: deep discount, discount, and full-service traditional. Read the following descriptions and see what you can expect to get at each level. Decide whether the extra whistles and bells are worth the extra cost. To make things easy, the key stats are summarized in charts after each section. The standard commissions are included to give you the most realistic scenario for each broker.

Here's another caveat. Some brokers will greatly reduce or eliminate their commissions if you buy certain investments. Consider Schwab. The company's standard online commission is $4.95. But if you buy one of the firm's exchange-traded funds, or ETFs, there's no commission. *ETFs* are baskets of investments that you can buy or sell just like a stock. ETFs are enormously popular and a great choices for investors. You owe it to yourself to find out more about these unique investments in Book 5.

REMEMBER

Double-check brokers' fees before signing up because they change frequently. Also remember that some brokers may charge lower commissions if you pay a monthly subscription fee, meet certain balance thresholds, or hold other types of accounts in addition to the brokerage account.

Paying the minimum with a deep discounter

The deep discounters are the Walmarts and Home Depots of the brokerage world. When you sign up for a deep discounter, you are on your own. But if you know what you're doing, that's a good thing because you don't have to worry about getting pestered by a salesperson trying to pitch stocks you have no interest in.

And you'll get all the basics that you truly need, such as year-end tax statements, access to stock quotes and research, and the ability to buy and sell stocks and other investments. But the real beauty of these brokers is their sweet, low price: Because they don't offer niceties, they can have the lowest commissions, usually $5 a trade or less. Leaders include the following:

>> **Robinhood** offers the ultimate lure: Free commissions. It's different than other brokerages in that it is entirely focused on mobile devices. Instead of providing a website for investors to log into and place trades, Robinhood focuses on apps for smartphones and tablets. You won't find the rich data services available on the websites of other brokers — but you won't pay for them, either.

>> **SogoTrade**'s $4.88-a-trade is appealing not just for the low price. If you plan to be a serious trader, SogoTrade lets you download software to your computer — software similar to that provided by more expensive online brokers — which helps you track the market's daily movements. You must open an account with at least $500, but you do not need to maintain a minimum balance going forward. And the commission drops to $3 if you trade 150 times or more a quarter.

>> **Ally Invest** aims to give investors a few more bank-like niceties than other deep discounters, such as the ability to store cash balances in a high-yield savings account. Ally Invest also offers access to some company news and research reports, and a straightforward flat-fee commission of $4.95. The brokerage is a capable complement to what was primarily an online bank but is most appealing to existing bank customers. This broker isn't for the advanced trader.

No minimum account balance is required, but you'll be charged a $50-a-year fee if you have less than $2,500 in your account and don't trade at least once a year.

Table 3-1 sums up the main differences among the deep discounters.

TABLE 3-1   ## Deep Discounters

Broker	Web Address	Commission	Minimum to Open an Account
Robinhood	www.robinhood.com/	$0	None
SogoTrade	www.sogotrade.com/	$5.00	$500
Ally Invest	www.ally.com/invest/	$4.95	None

TIP

Beginning investors always ask how much money they need to begin and where they can get started investing online. You can start with next to nothing with brokers that have no minimum deposit requirements, which includes most of the deep discounters. If you're the kind of person who can't seem to save money until you've sent your cash off to a bank or brokerage, these are great places to start.

Getting more with a discounter

If the thought of being completely on your own makes you nervous but you're not willing to give up low-cost commissions, the discount brokers sit in the sweet spot for you. These brokers suit most investors ranging from beginners to the more advanced because they generally offer some advice (if you ask for it), and many have offices in most major cities.

Even if you're not looking for advice, the discounters are still appealing because they load their websites with advanced tools to help do-it-yourself investors of all levels. Some provide access to advanced trading tools, real-time stock quotes, or special computer programs that let you enter trades just as fast as the traders on Wall Street. Top-notch apps that let you check your portfolio and place trades on the go are also part of the deal. These extras sometimes come with slightly higher commissions, but the difference isn't all that significant anymore compared with the deep discounters, and it may not be a deal-breaker for you. Price wars have yanked commissions from the discounters down to between $4 and $10. Most discounters also offer price breaks if you're a hyperactive trader. Most of these brokers also offer services where you can invest in a premade mix of diversified investments, rather than picking your own stocks or funds. The names to know here are

>> **Bank of America** may not be what you think of as a stockbroker, but it's one of the large banks aggressively boosting its brokerage services. Traditionally, banks have targeted the well-heeled with personal bankers who pick out investments like personal shoppers pick out ties for rich executives. But Bank of America's Merrill Edge unit has added self-service brokerage fees with commissions starting at $6.95. And you can get 30 free trades a month if you keep at least $20,000 with the bank in a deposit account, such as a Bank of America savings account. As your account grows, you have access to the wealth management services offered by the bank. Bank of America makes its connection with Merrill Lynch clear on its website.

>> **Charles Schwab** tries to be the Toyota Camry of brokers: not flashy or exotic in any one area but practical and pleasing to the bulk of investors. Schwab lowered commission to $4.95 in 2017, keeping it competitive among the other discounters. Schwab's commissions are still among the cheapest, and for that price, the broker adds services that may be valuable, whether you're looking

for help or want to be left to your own devices. For instance, you can buy hundreds of exchange-traded funds for no commission. Do-it-yourselfers may like Schwab's Equity Ratings, a computerized system that evaluates stocks and assigns them letter-grade scores from A to F. It also provides access to Wall Street research and a full suite of banking services, including high interest rates paid on cash sitting in your account. But if you decide later you need more help, Schwab offers mutual funds designed to fit specific needs in addition to making consultants available to give you personalized advice. If you're not going to use all these extra services, though, the higher commission may not be worth it.

>> **E*Trade** has a reputation as being an innovator in the industry and seems to be always looking for ways to separate itself from others. E*Trade has long targeted active traders with computer software such as Power E*Trade, which is software that lets you find stocks and other investments that meet your criteria or test how trading strategies would have worked in the past. But E*Trade has things for beginners, too, such as access to stock research from several providers and the capability to shift cash to a checking or high-yield savings account. There's an advanced smartphone app and a more basic one, too. The commission is typically $6.95 but can be lower based on your account balance and how often you trade.

>> **Fidelity** consistently gets good marks for making its website easy to navigate and getting trades through quickly. Fidelity has also been a leader in adding functions outside of just plain-old U.S. stock trading, including an advanced online system to buy bonds, invest in initial public offerings, and trade stocks outside the United States. It's also well designed and a good value. For years, Fidelity was a premium-priced online brokerage, but after slashing its commissions to $4.95, it's competitive if not on the low end. In addition, Fidelity is offering commission-free purchases on select ETFs from Fidelity and also iShares, which is one of the largest providers of these investments.

>> **Interactive Brokers** is looking for the pros — or people who want to be. This isn't the brokerage for casual investors. You'll find advanced trading tools and software designed for sophisticated and rapid-fire trading strategies. The company maintains two pricing structures, both designed to reward frequent traders or those with relatively large balances of $100,000. If you're serious about trading, this is a broker worth considering.

>> **TD Ameritrade's** earliest customers were active traders looking for low commissions. But the brokerage's low-cost roots are eroding, as its $6.95-per-trade commission is now more than what most of its major rivals charge. But TD Ameritrade tries to make up for its higher commission by offering a variety of high-tech digital tools and services that may save you money. Investors who trade frequently during the day also like TD Ameritrade's bonus PC software trading tools, such as thinkorswim,

which let you see second-by-second stock price movements or test trading strategies and analyze how they would have done. The broker also offers solid mobile apps to keep tabs on your portfolio and to make trades.

TD Ameritrade is also a leader in offering consumers free trading in ETFs. Customers can choose from hundreds of ETFs from several leading providers, including iShares and State Street, and pay no commission as long as they are held more than 30 days. Keep in mind that Vanguard's uber-popular ETFs are not included. If you want to buy those, you may want to look elsewhere, including at Vanguard.

>> **Vanguard** wins fans for its speed, quality of customer service, and availability to help in navigating the site and making investment decisions. The company, best known as a mutual fund provider, is taking brokerage more seriously. Vanguard's commission structure, though, is a little more complex than at other brokers. For stocks, the first 25 trades you make in a year are a competitive $7 if you have less than $50,000 in your account. After you trade 25 times, trades jump to $20. If you keep more than $50,000 in your account but less than $500,000, you can get unlimited $7 trades. If you have more than $500,000 in your account, trades are discounted to $2, and trades are free if you have more than a million bucks in your account.

Here's one key selling point for Vanguard: It provides free unlimited trading to all investors in its own family of well-regarded ETFs. Remember, Vanguard's stock brokerage offering is separate from the account that lets you buy and sell Vanguard mutual funds, which is covered later. Vanguard is also top-notch in putting any uninvested cash in your brokerage account automatically in a safe, interest-bearing investment. This is a huge advantage, as you read about later in this chapter. Some investors may be charged a $20 annual account service fee unless they sign up to get account statements only online.

>> **Wells Fargo** is another bank that follows the model of using brokerage services to tempt customers to put more money in its hands. Wells Fargo's self-service stock commissions start at $8.95. But if you keep at least $25,000 in your deposit accounts, you can cut that to $2.95 without paying the monthly service charge of $30. Wells Fargo also gives you 100 trades a year with no monthly service fee if you keep $50,000 with the bank and its brokerage. But falling short of the $25,000 deposit balance or $50,000 total can be costly, resulting in a $30 a month fee. If you're a Wells Fargo customer with a decent-sized portfolio, it's worth considering. The company's mobile app is capable but not fancy. And its website provides helpful planning information, especially pertaining to taxes and dividends.

Check out Table 3-2 for an overview of what the different discounters have to offer.

TABLE 3-2　**Discounters**

Broker	Web Address	Commission	Minimum to Open an Account
Bank of America (Merrill Edge)	www.merrilledge.com/	$0 if requirements are met; otherwise, $6.95	None
Charles Schwab	www.schwab.com/	$4.95	None
E*Trade	www.etrade.com/	$6.95	$500
Fidelity	www.fidelity.com/	$4.95	None
Interactive Brokers	www.interactivebrokers.com	Varies	None
TD Ameritrade	www.tdameritrade.com/	$6.95	None
Vanguard	www.vanguard.com/	$7.00	$3,000
Wells Fargo	www.wellsfargo.com/	$2.95 if requirements are met; otherwise, $8.95	$1,000

ARE FREE TRADES REALLY FREE?

When anything claims to be "free" in online investing, your defenses should go up instantly. Robinhood and Bank of America's Merrill Edge promise free trades to investors. Several brokers offer free commissions on ETFs, too. Be on guard and evaluate all the stipulations, though, before assuming that these free offers are best for you. (See the section on hidden fees later in this chapter.) Keep three things in mind:

- **"Deal flow" is a hidden money maker.**
- **Consider cash.**
- **Commission-free ETF deals have a big catch.**

First, some firms, including those that offer free trades, such as Robinhood, do it in part by selling your orders to market makers. *Market makers* (firms such as Two Sigma, Citadel, and Virtu), compete with the exchanges (such as the New York Stock Exchange) to process orders. These market makers then pay the broker for the business with a rebate. You want to make sure your broker is getting you the best price on your trade, not looking for the best rebates for itself. Robinhood's founder Vlad Tenev says the firm doesn't consider rebates when choosing which market maker to give the order to.

Second, the interest rate you get from uninvested cash left in the account is an important factor. This is especially true if you're required to have a certain amount of cash on deposit to get the free trades, or if you tend to leave lots of cash in the account. Not paying attention to interest rates could wipe out any savings you think you're getting from free trades.

Suppose you trade ten times a year and normally leave about $10,000 of uninvested cash in your account. If trades are free, it's true that your commission costs would be zero. But you still could be overpaying if you're not getting a rate of return on your uninvested cash. In fact, you'd be $150 better off paying $9.99 a trade if you get 2.5 percent interest on cash sitting in your account. If interest rates rise, the real cost of free commissions could be higher still.

Here's a formula that takes the guesswork out of "free" trades:

1. Multiply the number of trades you do each year by the commission. Write down this number.

2. Multiply the amount of uninvested cash you expect to keep in your account by the interest rate you will collect. Divide this number by 100 and write down the result.

3. Subtract the answer in Step 2 from the answer in Step 1.

This formula helps you calculate the true cost of the broker's offering. You'll see how much the commissions are costing you after adjusting for the rate of return you'll get on your cash: The lower the number, the better. If you're choosing between a couple of brokers, crunch this formula and choose the broker with the lowest (or negative) number. When rates rise, savvy investors should pay close attention to this hidden cost of free trades.

Finally, free-commission ETF offerings from many brokers are compelling, popular, and something most investors should consider. ETFs are a fast and easy way to build a diversified portfolio. And free commissions can save you money. Just remember that the broker you choose is important. You'll have to stick to the menu of ETFs your broker has selected, which may or may not be best for you. TD Ameritrade, for instance, removed all Vanguard ETFs from its lineup of free ETFs. If you want to buy Vanguard ETFs, you have to pay TD Ameritrade's regular commission. ETF investors might decide which ETFs they want and then see which brokers offer those with no commission.

Full-service traditional

Because you're reading this book, chances are good that you're a do-it-yourself kind of investor or one looking for minimal handholding. But maybe after reading the preceding descriptions, you're looking for even more help. That's when you might consider a full-service traditional broker.

Full-service *broker-dealers* pride themselves on being part of your team of people whom you call on routinely for advice, such as your real estate agent, housekeeper, and mechanic. The top full-service traditional brokerages are the Wall Street firms you've probably heard of, such as J.P. Morgan Securities (www. jpmorgansecurities.com), Bank of America's Merrill Lynch, Morgan Stanley (www.morganstanley.com/), Edward Jones (www.edwardjones.com/), Goldman Sachs (www.goldmansachs.com/), and UBS (www.ubs.com/us/en.html). Merrill Lynch, through Bank of America, competes with the discounters. But Merrill Lynch (www.ml.com/) also provides full-service brokerage services as part of its wealth management offering, geared for wealthy investors.

And by now, most full-service traditional brokers can legitimately call themselves online brokerages because they have websites that let you view your accounts. Services that these firms provide include

>> **Constant stock recommendations:** Most big Wall Street firms have well-known strategists and analysts who think big thoughts and come up with stock tips. The brokers then spread those tips to you.

>> **Access to initial public offerings:** When companies go public, they first sell their shares to large Wall Street investment banks. Those shares, especially if the initial public offering (IPO) is expected to be popular, are often a sought-after commodity because they have the chance to rise in value the first day. If you're an active customer with these firms' brokerage divisions, you might get a shot at buying these shares at the IPO price.

>> **Availability of other financial services:** If you're a customer with a full-service traditional brokerage, you might get extra financial services, such as help with your taxes or estate planning.

WARNING

But before you get too excited about the extra services that traditional full-service brokers may provide, you also have downsides to consider, such as

>> **Relatively high cost:** Wall Street firms have to pay somehow for those fancy offices you're enjoying. The fees tend to be higher, and you might pay a lofty commission for each trade or pay a percentage of your assets.

>> **Uneven treatment:** Remember that it's unlikely you'll end up being Goldman Sachs's best customer, so don't expect to get the real goods. For instance, when shares of the next truly promising IPO are doled out, if you're not a top customer or famous, you probably won't get shares anyway. (Fees and rates can vary, too, which is why this chapter doesn't have a table comparing fee structures for the full-service traditional brokerage crowd.)

>> **Potential for conflicts:** Because brokers are often paid by commission, they may have an incentive to urge you to trade more frequently than you might like.

There are broker-dealers and then there are investment advisors. They both offer financial advice and call themselves advisors, but they are registered with regulators differently and have unique standards of conduct.

>> *Broker-dealers* must sell you investments that are suitable. They are regulated by the Securities and Exchange Commission (SEC) and the Financial Industry Regulatory Authority (FINRA).

>> *Investment advisors,* which are typically independent and not associated with giant Wall Street firms, are regulated by the SEC. They must act as *fiduciaries*, putting client's interests first. Typically investment advisors offer their own websites or use specially gated areas for clients at Schwab, Fidelity, or TD Ameritrade.

Be skeptical if a friend or family member recommends a broker to you. Many brokerage firms give customers bounties of $50 or more or dozens of free trades if someone they refer signs up. This isn't to say that you can't trust your friends. Just know that people who recommend their broker might have a motive other than telling you which broker is best for you.

Avoiding Hidden Fees

The stock trade commission is likely the fee you'll pay the most often, so it's wise to pay the most attention to it. But don't think it's the only fee. Brokers often charge a host of other fees, which, depending on your circumstance, can add up fast. These extra fees are increasingly important for online investors to monitor as brokers' trading commissions get more comparable. You should look for a page that discloses these fees.

Here are some common hidden fees you should be aware of:

>> **Maintenance fees** are monthly, quarterly, or annual fees that some brokers charge you just to have an account with them. Don't pay maintenance fees. Period. If you're paying them, you're probably at the wrong broker. Most brokers exempt you from paying maintenance fees if you meet certain requirements. If you can't meet them, switch to a different broker.

>> **Inactivity fees** are the ugly cousins of maintenance fees. A brokerage may charge these fees if you don't gin up enough commissions for the brokerage by trading. Don't allow these fees to push you to buy and sell stock more than you're comfortable with. Most brokerages that charge such fees offer exemptions for customers who meet other criteria. SogoTrade, for instance,

charges $50 a year for investors whose balance drops below $100. But SogoTrade won't charge this fee if you trade at least once in a 12-month period.

>> **Transfer fees** are charged when you want to part ways with your broker. Expect to get nicked with a $50 or higher fee, which brokers charge supposedly to cover their cost of shipping all your stock holdings and transferring cash to your new broker. One way to avoid this charge is to transfer only some of your holdings. Some brokers will do this for free. You could also sell all the stocks in the old account and then transfer the cash to the new broker drawn on your old account. But this might not work. Keep in mind that you'll incur commissions for every stock you sell, and tax considerations might cost you well over $50. Some brokers will pick up the transfer fee tab if you move the account to them.

>> **IRA fees** are sometimes assessed when opening a new retirement account. Fortunately, most brokers have done away with this fee.

>> **Certificate fees** are charged if you want your broker to mail you the physical stock certificates you own. It's usually a $500 or higher charge. Some online brokers won't help you get paper certificates at all.

>> **Check-writing or debit card fees** range dramatically from broker to broker. Some charge you an annual fee to have the privilege to make payments against your account. Others give you a certain number of free checks and charge only if you write checks that bounce.

>> **Special orders** are added fees if you trade more than a set number of shares. Most brokers also charge extra for placing *limit orders* — trades in which you set the price you're willing to accept. Limit orders are covered in more detail in the next chapter.

>> **Margin fees** are interest charges that result from borrowing money from the broker to buy investments with. Buying on margin is only for the most risk-ready investors.

Finding Out What Reviewers Think

It can be overwhelming to parse through all the brokers' commissions because there appear to be more moving parts than in a Swiss watch. Minimum requirements and fees vary, and it's hard to know how fast a broker's website will be until you actually sign up and try it. Luckily, some professional reviewers have kicked the tires for you. Different rating services and publications that evaluate brokers each year include

>> **StockBrokers.com:** This site puts all the major brokers through the paces. You'll find "best of" lists that name the top brokers based on a number of factors such as the quality of their online tools and apps plus service and commissions. You can also look up specific brokers for summaries of their capabilities and requirements. The site also has a comprehensive section that ranks the reviews of online brokers and summarizes their findings. You can find out more at — you guessed it! — www.stockbrokers.com.

>> **J.D. Power:** Although it's best known for rating cars, J.D. Power also evaluates both online and full-service traditional brokers every year. It rates brokers based on several criteria, including cost, customer service, how quickly trades are completed, website design, data that's provided, and overall satisfaction. Read the latest reviews at www.jdpower.com/business/press-releases/2021-us-self-directed-investor-satisfaction-study.

>> **Barron's:** A Wall Street fixture since the 1920s, Barron's keeps an eye out for online brokers that serve sophisticated investors best. You'll have to subscribe, though, to read the stories online. An online subscription costs $120 a year and includes access to its entire site, which contains more than just broker ratings. Barron's Online is available at www.barrons.com/.

INNOVATION IS BLURRING ONLINE BROKERAGE LINES

Classifying brokers is getting increasingly difficult. Big cuts to commissions by discounters such as Schwab and Fidelity put them into closer price competition with the deep discounters (and each other). Meanwhile, new commission-free ETF offers are putting online brokers in competition with mutual fund companies. Meanwhile, a number of online brokers are also offering advice and even helping investors find live financial advisors, putting them head-to-head with full-service brokerages.

New technology is also disrupting the online brokerage scene. New brokerage business models defy categorization. Consider brokerage firm Acorns (www.acorns.com/). Rather than paying a per-trade commission, you pay a monthly fee starting at $1. In exchange, the brokerage firm will round-up purchases or allow you to make small contributions and invest the money in ETFs. It's a novel spin on investing, in which a computer essentially builds a portfolio for you using ETFs and handles all the buying and selling. Because the process is so automated, these types of brokers are called *robo-advisors*.

Is Your Money Safe? Checking Out Your Broker

When you're about to hand over your life's savings to a broker, especially one with no offices, you want to make sure that it's a reputable outfit. As investors in the epic Bernie Madoff investment scam in 2008 learned the hard way, it's up to you to make sure that you're dealing with a legitimate broker. Unlike bank savings accounts, brokerages have no government guarantee. But you still have some safeguards.

Your first layer of protection comes from the Securities Investor Protection Corporation (SIPC). SIPC was formed by Congress in 1970 to protect investors by promising to help recover and return cash to investors if their brokerage closes due to bankruptcy. If cash or stock mysteriously goes missing in your account, the SIPC might help you recover the funds. The SIPC has provided $2.8 billion in funds and helped in the recovery of $139 billion in assets for 773,000 investors since it was formed in 1970 through 2017. If a brokerage fails and doesn't have enough money to repay customers, the SIPC covers up to $500,000 (including up to $250,000 in cash) per customer. You should always check whether a broker is an SIPC member by logging on to www.sipc.org/. In addition, some brokers carry additional insurance to protect customer assets beyond $500,000. All the brokers mentioned in this chapter are SIPC members.

Next, make sure that your broker has the appropriate approval from regulatory bodies to buy and sell investments. You wouldn't let someone who isn't a doctor remove your appendix, right? You should also make sure that your broker is registered to be a broker. You can do this using the Financial Industry Regulatory Authority (FINRA) BrokerCheck at brokercheck.finra.org/. BrokerCheck tells you whether the brokerage is registered with this important regulatory body and whether the registration is current. If you're dealing with an investment advisor, BrokerCheck will point you to their information at the SEC. Each state also keeps tabs on brokerages serving customers in its region. State regulators are coordinated by the North American Securities Administrators Association, which provides access to the public at www.nasaa.org/.

Lastly, you want to know whether the broker you're considering has been disciplined recently. You can access this info from FINRA's BrokerCheck by downloading the broker's regulatory report and checking the section that spells out disciplinary action. Information is also available from a system maintained by the New York Stock Exchange's Disciplinary Action database at `www.nyse.com/regulation/disciplinary-actions`. And the ultimate watchdog on Wall Street is the U.S. Securities and Exchange Commission, which maintains records on brokers at `www.sec.gov` and provides tips to investors looking to check out their brokers at `sec.gov/investor/brokers.htm`. The SEC leaves tracking routine disciplinary actions to FINRA, but does provide information when it pursues legal action against brokers. You can track SEC's legal actions by using the search function at `www.sec.gov`. For an in-depth look at how to make sure your advisor is on the up-and-up, see this article at The Motley Fool: `www.fool.com/investing/2019/02/17/3-ways-to-avoid-financial-advisors-who-have-scamme.aspx`.

Cutting the Cord: Mobile Trading

If the idea of checking up on your portfolio and placing trades while sipping margaritas by the pool appeals to you, get a life. Well, okay, sometimes you *do* need to check up on your account even when you're not sitting behind a computer at your desk. To help, plenty of brokers are providing wireless access to account information so that customers can access their portfolios at any time, be it from a device running Google's Android operating system, Apple's iOS, Microsoft's latest version of Windows, or other wireless devices. You have several ways to accomplish this:

>> **From a laptop:** If your laptop is set up for wireless access, you can get online at thousands of locations that offer wireless internet connections, called Wi-Fi hotspots. Go to a Starbucks and you can get online. Keep in mind, though, that Wi-Fi connections are risky because they're not private. Read the nearby sidebar "A Word about Wireless Security" for tips on keeping yourself safe when you're checking stocks and sipping a latte.

>> **From a smartphone or tablet (or computer) using an app:** Nearly all major online brokers offer one or more apps that you can download to your smartphone or tablet and use to check stock quotes or trade stocks. After you download and install these apps, you can enjoy a decent online trading experience. If mobile trading apps are important, you will want to check with the online broker before signing up to make sure the app meets your needs.

A WORD ABOUT WIRELESS SECURITY

Security is a serious concern when dealing with your money. But when you access your stock data wirelessly, especially from a public Wi-Fi network, you need to pay special attention to security. Here are four ways to do just that:

- **Avoid using public Wi-Fi for financial matters.** Free Wi-Fi is great but is not secure. Your brokerage username or password could be hijacked, so don't use public Wi-Fi connections when checking your financial accounts. When at the coffeehouse, hotel, or airport, fire up your smartphone instead and make sure you're connected to the cellular network. Use the brokerage's app on your phone if you can.

- **Make sure that your data is encrypted.** If you must use your laptop, be aware of the risks. Most internet browsers let you know whether the data is being *encrypted* — scrambled, in other words. If you're using Microsoft's Edge browser, the padlock icon is a signal to you that the data is being scrambled to make it harder for the guy sitting next to you at the coffee shop to read your information. The data is then decrypted, or unscrambled, by the website. You can click the padlock icon to get more information about the website's security. Be sure to look at the text in the pop-up window to confirm that the site's certificate, or identification, lists the name of your brokerage firm. If the padlock doesn't appear, the site might use a different method of securing data, which is something you should ask your broker about.

- **Consider virtual private network (VPN) software.** A *VPN* is technology used to protect your data from snoops over the internet. Some internet service providers (ISPs) offer this service to customers; if you're using your work laptop, a VPN might be installed already. You might also consider installing VPN software on your computer. Some VPN software is free, such as Hotspot Shield (www.hotspotshield.com), which you can download from the Windows app store. Most other VPNs charge annual fees.

- **Consider tethering with your smartphone.** You're on the hotel's Wi-Fi and need to look at your portfolio on your laptop. You don't have a VPN installed. Please, resist the urge to log on to your brokerage account. Instead, connect your laptop to your smartphone with the USB cable or a similar cable and enable tethering. Back on your laptop, your smartphone appears as a wired network connection. Connect to it just as you would any other wired network.

Be sure to ask your broker what kind of protection it gives you if a hacker gets into your account. E*Trade and TD Ameritrade, for instance, will cover the entire loss. Also, TD Ameritrade (www.tdameritrade.com/security/index.html) provides a detailed guide to all the things you can do to protect your computer when investing online. You don't need to be a TD Ameritrade customer to use the site.

Pay Attention to Where Your Cash Is Parked: Money Market Funds

You're an online investor, right? So why would you care about money that you haven't invested? It turns out that one of the biggest secrets in the brokerage world is what happens to cash sitting in your account that's not invested. Brokers often collect interest on your money for themselves and you get nothing.

REMEMBER

Don't underestimate how important this is. If you have $10,000 in cash in your account waiting to be invested, that's worth $200 a year at a 2 percent interest rate. And while rates have been historically low, if they rise to more normal levels, the interest rates earned by uninvested cash will be even more important.

Before choosing an online broker, you want to be sure what rate of interest your uninvested cash will get and how it's handled. Ideally, you want a sweep account. With a *sweep account,* idle cash is automatically scooped up and put into a savings or money market account. You don't have to do anything, and you're certain that your money is working for you. Just make sure that your money is being swept into a savings account or money market that pays an interest rate that is competitive with the going market rate. Some brokers won't automatically sweep your uninvested cash into a money market fund, so it's up to you to ask about having it done.

Since interest rates have been at historical lows since around 2009, don't expect to get rich off your savings held at a brokerage site. Still, there's usually no additional charge for sweeping cash to a money market fund, so it doesn't hurt.

WARNING

A dirty little secret in the brokerage industry is that uninvested cash gets about 0 percent interest at nearly all brokers. Even many brokerage firms' sweep accounts pay next to nothing on uninvested cash. Don't leave cash sitting in a brokerage account for a long time. Most brokerages allow you to transfer cash in and out of your account from an outside bank by using automated clearing house (ACH) technology. You can create an ACH link between your brokerage account and savings account so money earns interest when it's not invested. Be sure to set up a savings account outside the brokerage that pays a decent amount of interest. Check bankrate.com/ to find banks offering decent interest rates.

Buying Stocks and Mutual Funds without a Broker

Can you be an online investor without an online broker? Sure. Some investors want to buy stocks but don't want to bother with opening an account with an online brokerage firm. There's nothing that says you need to have a broker to buy and sell stocks or mutual funds.

Stocks: Direct investments

Direct investments are where you buy the stock straight from the company. Many large companies, such as Coca-Cola, Procter & Gamble (P&G), and Walt Disney, allow you to buy and sell your stock with them and avoid a broker. Many direct investment programs are connected with dividend reinvestment plans (DRIPs), where the companies let you use dividend payments to buy, or reinvest, additional shares.

If you're interested in going with a direct investment program, you can visit the investor-relations section of the company's website to see whether it offers one. Many companies allow you to participate in direct investment programs through their *transfer agent* — a company with the responsibility of tracking ownership of shares.

Coca-Cola, for instance, has an elaborate shareholder investment program that lets you buy as little as $500 in stock — they'll even reinvest the dividends. You can read about this program, offered through the transfer agent Computershare, at www-us.computershare.com/Investor/#DirectStock/Index. EQ by Equiniti, at www.shareowneronline.com/UserManagement/WFIndex.aspx, is another provider of direct stock purchase plans for many companies.

The other way to find direct investment programs is through directory services, such as The Moneypaper's Directinvesting.com (www.directinvesting.com/). The site provides a search function so that you can see whether a company you're interested in sells shares directly to investors. Just enter the symbol of the company you're interested in, and you can see whether the company offers a direct investment plan.

Here are the upsides to direct investing:

>> **Potential commission savings:** The fees charged by direct investment programs can be lower than what some brokers charge. Coca-Cola, for instance, charges $3 if you pay for it using an electronic transfer from your bank, and $2 if you set up a recurring order to buy the stock.

>> **Dividend reinvestments:** Dividends can often be reinvested for free. If you're with a broker, you would often incur a commission to reinvest a dividend into the company stock.

WARNING

As you may suspect, direct investing has some downsides:

>> **Not free for all transactions:** Some companies even charge commissions that exceed what deep discount brokerages charge for certain services. For instance, Coca-Cola charges $25 if you want to sell the shares immediately. There may be loads of additional fees, including quarterly maintenance fees. Be sure to check the company's website, usually in a document called a direct stock plan *prospectus,* and understand all the fees that are charged.

>> **Setup fees:** Although opening an online brokerage account is usually free, some direct investment plans charge a fee to get started. Some plans also have minimum initial deposits. Coca-Cola, for instance, requires a $500 investment for a new account. Some charge setup fees.

>> **Limited universe:** By using direct investment plans, you're narrowing your universe of possible investments to the hundreds of the largely older, blue-chip companies that offer these programs. That means you miss out on younger or smaller companies.

>> **Administrative hassles:** With direct investment plans, you need to manage all your separate accounts, which could be a pain if you have ten or more investments. You also won't get access to any of the tax assistance or research the brokers provide.

Mutual funds: Straight from the mutual fund company

Mutual funds gather money from many investors and use the cash to invest in a basket of assets. When you buy a mutual fund, you're joining a pool with other investors that own assets, rather than owning the assets yourself. You can read more about mutual funds in Book 5.

Nearly all brokers let you buy and sell mutual funds in addition to stocks and other investments. And sometimes trading in mutual funds can make sense, especially if it's free. Most brokers have a list of transaction-free mutual funds you can buy and sell for no charge. Schwab, for instance, lets you buy and sell thousands of mutual funds that are part of its OneSource Select program at no cost (www. schwab.com/research/mutual-funds/tools/select-lists/onesource).

However, if you're not going to buy from the transaction-free lists, you're wasting your money buying mutual funds this way. Schwab, for instance, charges $50 to buy a mutual fund not on its list (selling is free). Don't let your broker's commission schedule determine which mutual funds you buy.

One of the best things about mutual funds is that you can buy them with no transaction fee if you deal directly with the mutual fund company. This feature can be a tremendous advantage, especially if you're making frequent and regular investments into a fund. After you figure out what fund you want to buy, log on to the mutual fund company's website, open an account, and buy it. You'll save yourself some cash.

When opening an account with a mutual fund company to buy a mutual fund, be sure to open a *mutual fund* account, not a brokerage account. Several mutual fund companies, including Vanguard and Fidelity, offer brokerage accounts in addition to mutual fund accounts, and the fees are completely different.

Opening and Setting Up Your Account

After you've made the decision about which broker to go with, the hard work is done. All you need to do to get started is open an account and get your cash to the broker. You can do this online or through the mail. If you're comfortable doing this online, which you probably are because you're reading this book, the online route is definitely the way to go because the cash can be transferred from your bank account and you can be up and running in a few hours or days. Signing up by mailing in a check and application, on the other hand, could take weeks.

Don't be shocked by the seemingly endless number of questions you'll be asked when setting up a new account. It's common for the broker to ask for your Social Security number and other personal information. Given the sensitivity of the information you'll be sharing, that's all the more reason to make sure that you understand online security by reading the previous sections. Please don't use the Wi-Fi connection at your local park when setting up your account.

The checklist of what you need to know

The biggest button on most brokers' website is the Open an Account or Start Now button, so you won't have trouble finding it. Typically, that's all you need to click to launch the area of the website that can set up your account. (If you want to sign up through the mail, click a link to download the necessary forms.)

Typically, you need to know three things to complete the application:

>> **The kind of account you want to create:** This is usually a cash account or margin account.

>> **The number of people associated with this account:** Is this just for you or for you and a spouse? This determines whether you create an individual or joint account.

>> **The tax status of the account:** Is this a taxable account or a tax-deferred account, such as an IRA or a fund for college?

If you're opening a retirement account, make sure the broker you're considering doesn't charge a monthly, quarterly, or annual maintenance fee. Most brokers waive maintenance fees if you're opening an IRA account because they figure you'll keep your money with them for quite some time. Many also waive the minimum deposits. For these reasons, if you're just starting out with online investing, you might consider opening a retirement account first.

The checklist of what you need to have

You need these bits of info if you want to set up an account:

>> **Identification:** You need ID such as a driver's license or a government-issued ID card.

>> **Social Security number:** If you're creating a joint account, you'll also need the Social Security number of the person you're setting up the account with. This information is used for tax reporting.

>> **Bank statement of the financial institution from which you'll transfer money:** The statement contains the account and bank routing numbers you'll need to instruct the broker to get your cash. Keep in mind that some brokers won't let you open an account with electronically transferred money if you're depositing less than $500. In those cases, you need to mail a check.

>> **Address of your employer:** This information is necessary if you're an officer, director, or large shareholder of a publicly traded company.

See, that wasn't hard. And here's the best part: Now that you've entered all your information and funded your account, you're all set to start investing.

Chapter 4

Entering and Executing Trades

All the theory in the world about online investing won't do you a bit of good if you can't seal the deal and execute your trades. *Trade execution* is the process of logging on to your online broker and buying or selling invest-ments. You may be wondering what's so hard about buying a stock: Just log on to the online broker's website and click the Buy button. And in some cases, you're right. But sometimes you want to be more exacting. You have ways to tailor your buys and sells so that your broker carries out the transaction precisely how you want it to be handled. For instance, you might want to buy a stock only if it falls below $25 a share, or you might want your broker to automatically sell shares if they fall below a certain price.

This chapter starts at the beginning and goes over all the ways you can hold your stock and how that decision affects the way your trades are executed. Then you discover the main ways to enter orders — ranging from market orders to limit orders — and find out about the advantages and costs of each.

Understanding How Stock Trades and Shares Are Handled

When you buy or sell a share of stock online, you click a few buttons and everything is done. In a few seconds, if even that long, you'll often have a confirmation sitting in the messages section of your online broker's website or in your email box. The *confirmation* is a memo that shows you what stock you bought or sold, the number of shares involved, and the price at which the trade was executed.

But perhaps unbeknownst to you, after you clicked the Buy button, your trade wiggled its way through countless computer networks where buyers and sellers competed for your order to buy stock until it was ultimately *executed,* or filled. You may never need to know how the process works, much like you may never need to know what's going on under the hood of your car. However, the process is an important part of investing online, so the following sections describe a day in the life of a trade that's on its way from being an order on your computer screen to a done deal.

Ways you can hold your investments

The biggest factor that influences how your investments make their way to Wall Street depends on how you hold your shares. The three main types are as follows:

>> **Street name ownership** is the most common with most online brokers. It's so common that unless you tell your online broker to do otherwise, your broker will assume that you want your shares owned in street name. More on this is coming up in the section "Street name ownership."

>> **Holding paper stock certificates** is the old-school way of owning stocks. This form of stock ownership was glamorized in the 2019 film *Mary Poppins Returns.* Even so, it's generally not a good idea for the reasons outlined in the section "Paper certificate ownership," later in this chapter. If you insist on paper certificates, let your online broker know so that they can be mailed to you.

>> **Direct registration** is when the company that issues the stock holds your stock for you but lists you, not your broker, as the owner. This form of ownership is common if you buy stock through a direct stock purchase plan, as Chapter 3 in Book 6 discusses.

Street name ownership

If you're not sure how to hold your shares, street name ownership is probably your best bet. For most investors, the advantages of this form of ownership outweigh the few negatives.

REMEMBER

Shares kept in street name are listed on the books of the company in your broker's name, not yours. The broker then lists you as the owner of the shares on its books. That might seem scary, but you do have safeguards against broker fraud, as Chapter 3 in Book 6 describes.

Street name ownership has several advantages:

>> **Easy handling of dividends:** Dividends paid by companies you own stock in are sent directly to your online broker, which then deposits them to your account. For online investors used to doing almost everything on a website, this feature is a huge advantage and saves you from having to deposit dividend checks with your bank or broker.

>> **Central source of company documents:** If you're like most online investors, you probably own shares of several companies. When you own the stock in street name, all the paper correspondence sent out by the companies first goes to your broker. The broker then forwards it to you. This situation has a giant advantage, especially if you move often: You can just let your broker know where you live and not worry about missing important documents. If you've asked to only hear from companies electronically, rather than on paper, your brokerage will email you links so you can read the materials.

Your broker can also help make sure that you get everything that's due to you. Periodically, a company you invested in years ago is sued or forced by regulators to make payments to past investors. If you own the stock in street name, you can be certain to receive these old payments, even if you're living somewhere else, because your broker knows where to find you.

>> **Security:** It's up to the brokerage to safeguard your stock. And that's a good thing because getting paper stock certificates replaced, if you lose them, can be a hassle and an expense.

>> **Easy to sell:** If your online broker has your shares on hand, you can sell them anytime you want without having to mail in a paper certificate first. That saves you time and postage, as well as the worry about sending an important document through the mail.

WARNING

Sounds great, right? But street name ownership does come with a few disadvantages:

>> **Potential delays in dividend payments:** Some brokers are quicker about crediting dividends to your account than others. You may have to wait a few days to receive a dividend after it was paid by the company. Delays, however, are pretty rare now that many of these accounting matters are handled electronically.

>> **Hassle if your broker fails:** Getting stock certificates transferred back to your name may be harder if your brokerage becomes insolvent. Some victims of the Bernie Madoff financial scam have found this out the hard way.

Paper certificate ownership

Maybe the cons of street ownership are enough to make you consider Route No. 2 — the paper certificate option. The advantages to paper certificate ownership include the following:

>> **Cutting out the middleman:** Company materials come straight to you, which can reduce the time it takes to get some documents.

>> **Using certificates as loan collateral:** When you have the actual certificates, you may have a little easier time using the stock value to secure a loan.

>> **Having actual certificates makes it easier to give them as gifts or for display:** A paper certificate can be framed and given to young investors as a present. There's something nice about having an item to wrap.

>> **Being in control:** With the certificates in your possession, you know where they are and can decide who can have them.

WARNING

In all honesty, though, the main disadvantages to paper certificate ownership far outweigh the advantages. The disadvantages of paper certificate ownership include the following:

>> **Difficulty in selling:** You may not be able to sell the stock as quickly as you'd like. Paper certificates must be mailed to your broker or to the company or a firm it hires to handle such matters so the stock can be sold. Nearly all online brokers charge significantly more to process paper certificates and strongly discourage investors from using them.

>> **Burden of keeping your contact information current with the company:** It's up to you to make sure that the company has your current address.

>> **Responsibility for safekeeping the certificates:** It's up to you to keep the paper certificates safe. You'll probably have to spend money to get a safe deposit box or at least lock the paper stock certificates in your home somewhere. And when you send them through the mail, you will need to insure them in case they get lost. Some financial institutions recommend insuring mailed certificates for 2 percent of the market value.

If you decide to hold paper certificates rather than list them in street name, don't lose them. Getting lost paper certificates replaced can be a hassle and somewhat costly. If the unfortunate event does occur, though, here's what to do to try to make it right:

1. **Call or email your broker or the company's transfer agent and explain what happened.**

   Transfer agents are firms that companies hire to handle the processing of shares. The transfer agent will likely ask you to say how you lost the shares in a written report.

2. **Buy an indemnity bond with the help of your transfer agent.**

   An indemnity bond protects the company that issued the lost stock in case someone tries to cash it in later. Indemnity bonds usually cost up to 2 percent of the market value of the stock you lost.

TIP

For more details on what to do if you lose a stock certificate, the Securities and Exchange Commission maintains advice at www.sec.gov/answers/lostcert.htm.

BUYING PAPER STOCK CERTIFICATES ONLINE

Because of the disadvantages listed elsewhere in this chapter, it doesn't make much sense to hold paper stock certificates for the shares in your portfolio. Paper stock certificates, as a result, are quickly becoming extinct (some companies don't even offer them). But the scarcity makes paper certificates even more attractive to some. A few investors still like to buy paper stock certificates for gifts. Yet other folks collect old stock certificates much like you'd collect stamps or coins. There's even a word for the practice of collecting stock certificates: *scripophily*. If this interests you, check out these online services that let you buy paper stock certificates:

- **GiveAShare** (www.giveashare.com/) and **Frame A Stock** (uniquestockgift. com/) are single-share sales sites that understand the lost art and beauty of many stock certificates. Both let you buy a share of stock in companies that have certificates that are popular with individual investors. Both of these services even frame the certificates for you. The sites make it easy to find the perfect stock for the need. You can sort through the available certificates based on the occasion, recipient, or interest. For men, GiveAShare recommends Harley-Davidson and Boston Beer, and for women it suggests Tiffany and Starbucks. Some certificates are also popular because of the artwork on them, with Disney being the best example.

(continued)

(continued)

Just be forewarned that you'll pay much more to acquire stock this way than through an online broker. In addition to the share price and framing fees, you also pay up to a $25 transfer agent fee to acquire the stock. A $38-a-share stock can easily cost more than $100 by the time all the fees are added.

- **eBay** (www.ebay.com/), not surprisingly, is a source for paper certificates. But because eBay isn't licensed to sell securities like stocks, it has to be careful about what kinds of certificates its members sell; otherwise, eBay risks running afoul of securities law. Only two types of stock certificates may be sold on eBay. The first type concerns old or collectible certificates of defunct companies, such as old railroads or internet companies. The other type that may be sold on eBay are single-share stock certificates packaged as gifts and marked as being nontransferable. eBay requires that these certificates sell for at least twice the current market value of the stock as evidence that they're priced based on their keepsake value.

- **Scripophily.com** (www.scripophily.net) and other certificate collection sites provide prices on some hard-to-find certificates. Even if you're not a collector, it's interesting to see what some of the certificates go for when they're popular with collectors. Some Standard Oil stock certificates, personally signed by John D. Rockefeller, for instance, sell for $1,500 or more. Pixar stock certificates, decorated with characters from *Toy Story* like Buzz Lightyear, were a hot commodity when the company was bought by Disney. Old shares of *Playboy* were popular for their, um, artwork, because the company's certificates used to display some, let's say, assets. The old certificates have become even more sought after since *Playboy*'s new certificates were changed to be more PG. The old shares sell for $400 or more. And some infamous companies, like Enron, also have collectible value even though the companies themselves have largely vanished.

Direct registration

If all the earlier talk about the hassles of losing paper certificates makes you long for another way of owning stock, you can always go for direct registration. You get several advantages from having direct registration, including

>> Company correspondence coming straight to you

>> Being able to sell shares without mailing certificates to your broker

>> Not having to worry about keeping the certificates safe

WARNING

Direct registration has two main downsides:

>> **Inability to sell shares immediately:** Selling shares you hold in direct registration almost always takes longer than you might think. You may

instruct the company to sell the shares, but your request is generally put into a pool and executed at set times in the future, such as later in the day, week, or month. You may also sell your shares by instructing the company's transfer agent to electronically send the stock to your online broker. (A *transfer agent* is a firm hired by a company to track its shareholders and record transactions.) The transfer process can take a few days, so the price may change by the time you're able to sell the stock.

>> **Pool of stock choices is somewhat reduced:** Most companies offer direct registration, but not all. Many of the stocks you want to buy may not offer direct registration.

A second in the life of a trade

When you buy or sell a stock on your online broker's site, your order is usually filled in a fraction of a second. But before that transaction is completed, in milliseconds your order snakes its way through an advanced security trading system that has taken decades to build. Just a few years ago, it could take about 12 seconds for a trade to go from your desk to the floor of the New York Stock Exchange and back. Now that most of the steps have been computerized, the process takes less than a second. Using Nasdaq as an example, here's what happens in the one second it takes to execute an online trade:

1. You enter your order with your online broker.

2. The order is placed in a database.

3. The database checks all the different markets that trade the stock and looks for the best price. The different markets might include the Nasdaq and New York Stock Exchange in addition to electronic communications networks (ECNs). ECNs are computerized networks that connect buyers and sellers of stocks.

4. The market that successfully matched the buyer and seller sends a confirmation to both parties' brokers.

5. The order and the price are reported to the regulatory bodies that oversee trading activity so that they can be displayed to all investors.

6. Nasdaq stores a record of the trade in case regulators want to study past transactions.

7. Nasdaq sends a contract to the broker who sold the shares and the broker who bought them.

After all that is completed, the brokers have two business days, called T+2, to exchange the cash and shares in a process called *settlement.* Then the money or shares are officially in your account.

When you buy or sell, most online brokerages will check the prices everywhere to see where they can get the best price. If you can get a better price through an electronic network than through a traditional exchange, that's where your trade will occur. Some brokers let you choose where you want your order filled through something called *direct routing.* If your account is set up for direct routing, you can instruct the broker to execute at the exchange or electronic trading venue of your choice.

WARNING

Direct routing is a bad idea for most online investors. Online brokers have computers that shop your order to all the top markets automatically. They're required by regulators to get you the best available price. If you direct-route your order, you lose this advantage and could wind up paying more.

Getting It Done: Executing Your Trades

If you're buying something, such as a new computer, from a regular store, you can either buy it or not. End of discussion. But in more casual marketplaces, such as flea markets or garage sales, where prices are fluid and changing, there's a strategy to buying and selling things. It may surprise you that buying stock is more like a flea market than shopping at your local Walmart, where prices are set. Because investments are priced in real time through active bidding between buyers and sellers, there are techniques to buying and selling.

Surveying types of orders

When dealing with investments, you have five main ways to buy or sell them online:

>> **Market orders** are the most common types of orders and the ones you will probably use the most. This is where you tell your broker to sell your shares at the best price someone is willing to pay right now or buy shares at the price currently being offered. Because these orders are executed almost immediately and are straightforward, they typically have the lowest commissions. (Chapter 3 in Book 6, which discusses different online brokers' commissions, concentrates on market orders because they're the most common.)

» **Limit orders** let you be pickier about the price you're willing to take for a stock you're selling or the price you're willing to pay if you're buying. With a limit order, you tell your online broker the price you're willing to take if you're selling stocks and the price you're willing to pay if you're buying. The order will execute only if your price, or something better, is reached.

For example, imagine you own 100 shares of ABC Company, which are trading for $50 a share. The stock has been on a tear, but you're convinced it will fall dramatically soon, by your estimate to $30. You could just sell the stock outright with a market order, but you don't want to because you're a bit opportunistic and don't want to miss out on any gains in case you're wrong. A limit order could be the answer. Here, you'd instruct your broker to sell the stock if it fell to $45 a share. If you're right, and the stock falls to $45 a share, your online broker will sell as many shares as possible at that price. You can also set a time limit on limit orders and tell your broker to let them expire after a few days or weeks.

WARNING

The precision of limit orders can be a shortcoming. Limit orders are filled only at the price you set. If the stock falls further than the price you set, the broker might be able to sell only some of the shares, or none, at that price. If that happens, you're stuck with the stock. In the preceding example, if ABC Company opened for trading and plunged straight to $25, never stopping at $45, you would still be holding the stock. This is a serious limitation that can give you a false sense of security.

» **Stop market orders** are similar to limit orders in that they let you set a price you want to buy or sell shares at. They have an important difference, though, that addresses some of the shortcomings of limit orders. When a stock hits the price you designated, the order converts into a market order and executes immediately.

Imagine again that you have 100 shares of ABC Company, which are trading for $50 a share. But this time, you enter a stop market order for $45. And again, you wake up to find the stock plunged instantly to $25. This time, though, all your stock would have been sold. But, maybe not at $45. Your online broker will sell the shares at whatever the price was the moment your order converted to a market order, which in this case could have been $25.

» **Stop limit orders** are like stop market orders, but they're designed to cure the danger that your shares will be blindly unloaded when a stock is moving. Stop limit orders are customizable. First, you can set the *activation price.* When the activation price is hit, the order turns into a limit order with the limit price you've set.

Okay, say ABC Company is trading for $50 a share when you enter a stop limit order with an activation price of $45 and a limit price of $35. It would work like this: Again, you wake up to find that the stock plunged instantly to $25. This time, your broker would turn your order into a limit order after it fell below $45. When the stock fell to $35, the broker would try to fill orders at that price if possible. Most likely, though, you'd still be stuck with shares. But unlike with the stop market order, you would not dump the shares when they fell as low as $25.

>> **Trailing stops** are a way to keep up with the times. With regular limit orders, they're either executed or they expire. Trailing stop orders get around this problem by letting you tell your broker to sell a stock if it falls by a certain number of points or a percentage.

TIP

If you're buying and selling individual stocks, trailing stops can be a good idea. Even before you buy a stock, you should have an idea of how far you'll let it fall before you cut your losses. Some investment professionals suggest never letting a stock fall more than 10 percent below the price you paid. If this sounds like a good idea to you, a trailing stop could work for you.

Checking out costs of different orders

Market orders are the most straightforward orders, so it shouldn't be that surprising that they're also usually the least expensive. Limit orders, though, can help save investors from volatile markets. During the Flash Crash of 2010, prices of several stocks, including giants such as Procter & Gamble, plummeted for about 15 minutes for no reason other than a system malfunction. Had you entered a market order to sell P&G during those 15 minutes, you would have sold at the current market price, which was 20 percent below where it was supposed to be. However, if you'd used a limit order that was close to the accurate market price, your order would not have been executed. An increasing chorus of market experts are urging investors to use limit orders to protect themselves from such market malfunctions. Luckily, such events are rare.

WARNING

A few brokers charge extra for limit orders, so check the commission fees before you start trading.

Tailoring your trades even more

When you enter an order for a stock, you have a few other levers you can pull, including

>> **Designating lots:** Many people buy the same stock many times. Each time you buy, that bundle of stock is called a *lot*. When you sell, your broker will assume you'd like to sell the lot that you've held for the longest time for

recordkeeping purposes. This method, called *first-in-first-out,* or FIFO, is the standard and what the Internal Revenue Service expects. If, for tax reasons, you'd like to sell a specific lot that's not the oldest, you can tell your broker which lot you'd like to sell.

>> **Setting time frames:** You can enter an order for a stock that is active only for the day you place the trade. If it's not filled — perhaps a limit order for the price you ask for isn't reached — the order expires. That time frame is called *day only.* You can also enter orders and let them stay active until you cancel them. That time frame is called *good till canceled.* Good-till-canceled orders are generally active for up to six months after you enter the order, but that limit varies for each broker.

>> **Placing rules:** When you issue an "all or none" restriction on your trade, your broker must completely fill the order or not fill it at all. Say you want to sell 100 shares of stock at a limit price of $45, but the broker can find buyers for only 10 shares at that price. If you stipulated all or none, none of your 100 shares would be sold.

7

Introducing Fundamental Analysis

Contents at a Glance

IN THIS CHAPTER

» Getting an overview of why
fundamental analysis is worth
your time

» Stepping through some of the critical
concepts of fundamental analysis

» Seeing how fundamental analysis can
fit into many investment strategies

Chapter **1**

Understanding Fundamental Analysis

B efore you gulp down that neon-colored energy drink or pour yourself a bowl of super-sweetened cereal that looks like it was made by Willy Wonka himself, you probably do something first. It's probably not a bad idea to take a glance at the nutrition label that spells out what ingredients are in the box.

You may not know what guar gum, guarana, or other ingredients that often show up on the labels of such processed foods are, but you can get a pretty good idea of what's good for you and what's not. If a bottle of apple juice, for instance, has a list of ingredients longer than your arm and is filled with stuff you can't pronounce, you know you're not drinking squeezed apples. Being aware of what's in a food may or may not sway your decision to eat it, but at least you know what you're putting into your body.

Companies and stocks, too, come with similar labels. All companies that are *publicly traded,* or that take investment money from the public, are required to disclose what they're all about. Just as food processors must list all the ingredients that go into their products, companies must tell investors what they're composed of.

Unfortunately, all the information investors need to know about a company doesn't fit inside a tiny rectangle — like it does on a food label. Instead, the key elements that make up a company are broken down at length in a series of *financial statements* and other sources of fundamental data.

Reading these critical financial statements and gleaning insights from them are the most basic goals of fundamental analysis. Fundamental analysis is the skill of reading through all the information companies provide about themselves to make intelligent decisions. Just as you'd want to know what's in that Frankenfood you're about to bite into, you want to know what's in an investment you're thinking about adding to your portfolio.

Why Bother with Fundamental Analysis?

You might wonder why you need to hassle with fundamental analysis. After all, at every family picnic there's undoubtedly the loudmouthed relative who's filled with all sorts of can't-go-wrong stock tips. Why bother with technical things like net income or discounted cash flow analysis when you can just turn on the TV, write down a couple of stock symbols, buy the stocks, and hope for the best?

You might also figure finding out how companies operate is just needless information. After all, you don't need to know about fuel injection systems, suspensions, and car battery technology to drive a car. And you don't need to know what's going on behind the curtain to enjoy a play. Some investors figure they can just pick a couple of hot stocks, buy them, and drive off to riches.

REMEMBER

If vicious bear markets of the past have taught investors anything, it's that blindly buying stocks just because you "like" a company or its products is hardly a sound way to tune up a portfolio. Chasing hunches and personal opinion about stocks is often not a great way to invest. The financial crisis is now becoming a distant memory for many investors who may again think fundamental analysis doesn't matter. Investors have taken to chasing stories and hype again in the bull market that kicked off in 2011 — and most or certainly many of those "can't-go-wrong" investments will meet a poor fate as the fundamentals catch up to reality.

Some of the real values of fundamental analysis

Ever notice how there's always a new wonder diet promising to make you skinny, and a new pill to make you healthier? More times than not, though, it seems these things never work. Getting healthy comes back to the basics — a balanced diet and exercise.

The same goes with investing. Believe it or not, investing can be somewhat full of fads. There's always a new investment pundit or economist with a novel way to pick winning stocks. And just as an hour on the treadmill will do you more good than a bottle full of miracle pills, successfully choosing stocks often comes back to fundamental analysis.

Fundamental analysis is the classic way to examine companies and investments for a variety of reasons, including the fact that it is

>> **Based on fact, not opinion:** It's easy to get caught up in general enthusiasm about what a company is doing or the products it's selling. Fundamental analysis blinds you to this investment hype and gets you focused on cold, hard business realities. It doesn't matter if all the kids in your neighborhood are buying a company's products if the company isn't making any money at selling them.

>> **Good at pinpointing shifts in the business's health:** If a company's success is starting to fade, you'll see it show up in the fundamentals. No, there won't be a giant sign saying "Sell this stock." But there are clues if you know how to look. Companies are required to disclose key aspects of their business, so if there's a problem, a fundamental analyst will often be early to spot some trouble.

>> **All about execution:** Companies' CEOs are usually good at getting investors focused on the future and how things are going to get better next quarter. But fundamentals are based in reality — right now. Just think of children who say how hard they're working at school. The report card is still the tangible evidence of how things are actually going. The numbers don't lie — if you know where to look.

>> **A way to put price tags on companies:** What's a painting worth? What's a used car worth? The price of an asset with a subjective value is generally what someone else is willing to pay for it. The stock market, an auction of buyers and sellers, does a good job putting price tags on companies. But fundamental analysis gives you another way to see just how much investors, by buying or selling stock, are paying for a stock.

Driving home an example

One of the best recent examples of how fundamental analysis can help you and your portfolio is General Motors. For decades, GM represented the might of U.S. industriousness, know-how, and creativity. GM commanded a massive market value of $3.5 billion in 1928, says Standard & Poor's. GM was the most valuable company by far in 1928.

For decades, investors figured a dollar invested in GM was money in the bank. The company slugged through upturns and downturns and was a lasting power that helped drive the U.S. economy. The company kept paying fat dividends and kept powering profits higher. There was even an expression: "As GM goes, so goes the nation."

But investors who blindly bet GM would remain a lasting force and ignored the fundamental signs of trouble suffered a brutal blow on June 1, 2009. On that day, which will forever remain one of the lowlights of capitalism, GM became the fourth-largest public company to seek bankruptcy protection, according to BankruptcyData.com. Shares of GM stock collapsed to just 75 cents a share, down 97 percent from their level just three years before.

Fundamental analysis may not have helped you predict just how shocking GM's fate would be. But concrete elements from the company's financial statements could have tipped you off to just how challenged GM was well before it became a penny stock and was liquidated. GM was ultimately reborn when a new company was created and bought many of the old company's assets, including the GM name. You can be sure that investors in the new GM paid much closer attention to the fundamentals.

Putting fundamental analysis to work

It's easy to get consumed with the fast-money trading aspects of stocks. Exciting TV reports about stocks on the move and companies that have new products practically turn investing into a sporting event. If you listen to some traders talk, they rattle off companies' ticker symbols in rapid-fire delivery just as sports fans talk about teams. Flashing arrows and rapid trading can become an addiction for people who get into it.

Fundamental analysis is trying to help you avoid these headaches and insanity. Stocks rise and fall each minute, day, and week based on a random flow of news. That's mostly noise to a fundamental analyst. The constant ups and downs of stocks can sometimes confound logic and reason. Many people are baffled when a stock falls even after the company reports what appears to be good news. Trying to profit from these short-term swings is a game for gamblers and speculators. It's futile on a long-term basis.

But that's not to say investing is gambling. Remember that those stock symbols you see flashing red and green aren't dice, horses, or cards. They're more than just the two, three, or four letters of their ticker symbol.

When you buy a stock, you're buying a piece of ownership in companies that make and sell products and services. You're buying a claim to the companies' future profits. Owning a piece of a real business over time isn't gambling, it's capitalism.

REMEMBER

Fundamental analysis forces you to focus on investing in businesses, not stocks. You're not buying a lottery ticket, but a piece of ownership in an actual company. Sometimes this gets lost by investors who pay more attention to stock charts than to financial statements.

If jumping in and out of stocks at the right time isn't the way to riches, then what is the trick to successful investing? The answer is to stop thinking of stocks as just symbols that gyrate each day. The goal of fundamental analysis is to help you step away from the short-term trading and gambling of stocks. Instead, you approach investing as if you're buying a business, not rolling the dice.

Fundamental analysis ideally helps you identify businesses that sell goods and services for more than what they paid to produce them. Fundamental analysis is your tool to evaluate how good a company is at turning raw materials into profits. If there's an investor who best personifies fundamental analysis over speculation, it's famed investor Warren Buffett of Berkshire Hathaway. Buffett is one of the best-known users of fundamental analysis — in fact, he's so confident in his analysis of a business he'll often buy very large stakes and hold on for decades. You read more about how Buffett applies fundamental analysis to investing in Chapter 3 of Book 7.

TIP

No matter how you choose investments currently, you can likely apply fundamental analysis. Even if you're the kind of investor who likes to buy diversified mutual funds and hold onto them forever, called a *passive investor*, it can be helpful to understand basic financial characteristics of the companies.

Knowing what fundamentals to look for

Knowing what makes a company tick isn't as convoluted as it may sound. Companies are so regulated and scrutinized, all the things you need to pay attention to are usually listed and published for all to see. Generally, when you hear about a company's fundamentals, the key elements to be concerned about will fall into several categories, including

>> **Financial performance:** Here you're looking at how much a company collects from customers who buy its products or services, and how much it keeps in profit. Terms you probably hear quite a bit about, such as *earnings* and *revenue,* are examples of ways fundamental analysts evaluate a company's financial performance.

- » **Financial resources:** It's not enough for a company to sell goods and services. It's not even enough to turn a profit. Companies must also have the financial firepower to invest in themselves and keep their businesses going and growing. Aspects of a business, such as its assets and liabilities, are ways to measure a company's resources.

- » **Management team:** When you invest in a company, you're entrusting your money to the CEO and other managers to put your cash to work. Fundamental analysis helps you separate the good managers from the bad.

- » **Valuation:** It's not enough to identify which companies are the best. What's a "good" company anyway? Definitions of "good" can run the gamut. You also need to consider how much you're paying to own a piece of a company. If you overpay for the best company on the planet, it's still likely you'll end up losing money on the investment.

- » **Macro trends:** No company operates in a vacuum. A company's performance is highly influenced by actions of competitors or the condition of the economy. These broad factors need to be incorporated into fundamental analysis.

Knowing what you need

One of the great things about running as a hobby is all you need is a pair of decent shoes. And basketball? Just grab a ball and find a hoop. No fancy equipment is required. The same goes with fundamental analysis. Much of the data you need is provided free by companies and can be accessed in seconds from any computer connected to the internet.

Fundamental analysis can get pretty involved. But in its most basic form, fundamental analysis has just a few basic ideas behind it, including

- » **Awareness of the benefits:** Because fundamental analysis takes some know-how and time spent gaining that knowledge, you'll want to know ahead of time why you're going to the trouble. Chapters 2 and 3 in Book 7 highlight the payoff of fundamental analysis. Even if you're a passive investor, or one who simply buys a basket of stocks and holds on, there are reasons why fundamental analysis may be worth your while.

- » **Retrieval of financial data:** Getting all the key data you need to apply fundamental analysis is easy if you know where to look. Chapter 4 in Book 7 gives you quick tips on how to round up all the company financial data you'll need.

>> **Basic math:** There it is: The M word. There's no way around the fact that some number crunching is involved in some aspects of fundamental analysis. Don't worry, this book guides you to help keep the math as painless as possible.

Knowing the Tools of the Fundamental Analysis Trade

You can read all sorts of books on home repair and even take a trip to your hardware store and buy lots of screws, nails, and glue. But none of that effort will benefit you unless you have a tool belt and the knowledge of how to get started and put your plan into reality.

The same importance of execution is part of fundamental analysis. You may appreciate the importance of fundamental analysis and may even be able to download fundamental data from websites or from a company's annual report. But you need to have the tools to analyze the fundamentals to get any real value from them.

Staying focused on the bottom line

REMEMBER

If there's one thing investors may agree is of upmost importance, it's the company's profitability. When it comes down to it, when you invest in a stock, you're buying a piece of the company's earnings. Knowing how to read and understand how much profit a company is making is very important when it comes to knowing whether or not to invest.

The income statement will be your guide when you're trying to determine how profitable a company is. What may also surprise you is that the income statement can tell you a great deal about a company, in addition to just how much income it brings in.

Sizing up what a company has to its name

During times of intense financial stress, investors often make a very important mental shift. They're not so concerned about making money as they are about just getting their money back. Similarly, when things get tough in the economy, investors are less interested in how profitable a company is and are more mindful of whether a company will survive the economic downturn.

When you're trying to understand the lasting power of a company, fundamental analysis is of great value. By reading the company's *balance sheet*, you can get a rundown of what a company has — its *assets* — and what is owes — its *liabilities*. Monitoring these items gives you a very good picture of how much financial dry powder a company has to endure a tough period.

Burn, baby, burn: Cash burn

One of the biggest killers of companies, especially smaller firms just starting out, is poor cash flow. While a company may have a great product concept, excellent management, and even dedicated financial backers, timing is everything. If a company is using up cash to pay its bills and employees but not bringing in enough cold, hard cash from customers, it can run into a giant financial headache very quickly and not have enough cash to reach its potential.

REMEMBER

Fundamental analysis helps you keep a close eye on how much cash is coming into and going out of a company. Monitoring cash flow is critical to know whether a company is running perilously empty on cash. Tracking a company's cash flow is also a very important way fundamental analysis helps you put a price tag on that company.

Financial ratios: Your friend in making sense of a company

As you flip through this book and jump around to different topics that interest you, you may be a bit bewildered by just how many pieces of financial data fundamental analysts must deal with. You've got the financial statements that measure just about every aspect of the company. It can be intimidating to decide what numbers matter most and which ones can be ignored.

Financial ratios will be a great help here. These ratios draw all sorts of fundamental data from different sources and put them into perspective. Financial ratios are also important because they form the vocabulary of fundamental analysts. If you're ever at a cocktail party where analysts are talking about gross margins and accounts receivable turnover, you can be prepared. By the way, that sounds like a pretty boring party.

With financial ratios, you can use seemingly unrelated pieces of financial data about a company to glean some very important conclusions about the company.

Making Fundamental Analysis Work For You

Imagine a young child who memorized an entire dictionary but can't use a single word in a sentence. That's a basic analogy of some investors' fundamental analysis knowledge. You, too, may know some things about the income statement and balance sheet and have a great knowledge of what's contained in the statements. But when it comes to applying your know-how, that can be a bit trickier.

Putting fundamental analysis in action requires taking everything you know about a company and mixing in some estimates and best guesses about the future to arrive at a decent expectation of whether or not to invest in a company.

Using fundamentals as signals to buy or sell

Buying a stock at the right time is very difficult. But knowing when to sell it is even tougher. And while fundamental analysis won't tell you the exact best time and day to buy or sell a stock, it can at least give you a better understanding of things to look out for when it comes to making decisions.

REMEMBER

If you're a passive investor and buy large baskets of stocks, such as those in the Standard & Poor's 500 Index, you can afford to buy and hold the stocks as a group. Even if one company runs into big-time trouble, it's just one holding in a large basket of stocks and not all that catastrophic. However, if you choose to invest in individual stocks, trying to pick companies you think will beat the market, monitoring the fundamentals is critical. If you start noticing a company's trend deteriorating, you don't want to be the last investor to get out.

The perils of ignoring the fundamentals

Blindly following a company and investing in the stock can be very dangerous — if you pick the wrong one. The dot-com bubble and subsequent financial crisis of 2008 and 2009 are still the best recent examples of how ugly things can get for investors who buy what's popular and ignore the fundamentals. Table 1-1 shows a list of a few major U.S. stocks that were worth $100 a share or more at the beginning of 2000, but saw their share prices fall to below $10 a share by the start of 2009. Ouch!

REMEMBER

Avoiding stock disasters like those in Table 1-1 is one thing that makes fundamental analysis so powerful. Losses that large are nearly impossible to recover from in a single person's lifetime.

TABLE 1-1

Watch Out! A Falling Knife!

Stock	Stock price 12/31/1999	Stock price 1/1/2009
JDS Uniphase	$645.25	$3.65
InfoSpace	$535.00	$7.55
Blue Coat Systems	$326.72	$8.40
Ciena	$201.25	$6.70
Sun Microsystems	$154.88	$3.82

Source: S&P Capital IQ

Using fundamental analysis as your guide

As Table 1-1 shows, investing in individual stocks is very risky. Losses can be sizeable. That's why if you're going to buy individual stocks, you want to invest with your eyes wide open. Just as you probably wouldn't dare fire a loaded weapon or jump out of an airplane without proper training, the same goes with investing in individual stocks.

Luckily, fundamental analysis provides investors with a host of very specific tools to help them protect themselves. And while the tools of fundamental analysts aren't foolproof, they give investors guidance as to when a stock may be getting a little dangerous or the underlying trends may be changing.

Hopefully, by reading this chapter you'll see why fundamental analysis is so important and be eager to see how the rest of the book can help you. You'll find complete explanations of some of the most powerful tools used by fundamental analysts throughout the rest of Book 7.

Chapter **2**

Getting Up to Speed with Fundamental Analysis

ry to remember what it was like being a beginner at something you're good at now. Whether it was karate, ballet, or basketball, as a beginner, you may have been tempted to bypass all the basics and go straight for the advanced techniques. It's natural to want to try breaking boards with your bare hands or doing pirouettes or slam-dunks on your first day of trying something new.

Good coaches, though, encourage you to slow down and start from the very beginning. It's almost always best to start working on the basic karate stances, ballet poses, and basketball dribbling before even thinking about moving to the showy and advanced aspects of each sport.

Beginning investors often experience a similar overconfidence at first. Many hope they can skip mundane things — like reading accounting statements, understanding basic financial ratios, and calculating discounted cash-flow models — and get right to the exotic rapid-fire trading. It's tempting to think you can trade complex securities, dabble in highly volatile stocks, and dart in and out of investments with ease right away. Realistically, though, investors usually lose money when they try to get too advanced too soon. And unfortunately, there's no coach to cool off investors who are just starting out.

So, consider Book 7 to be your coach as you get started with fundamental analysis. The basics explained in this chapter will set you up for taking fundamental analysis to the next level in later chapters.

What Is Fundamental Analysis?

Ask 20 people how they choose their investments, and you'll probably hear 20 different methods. Some like to buy stocks recommended by a friend or broker. Others think it's wise to invest in companies making products they personally enjoy and use. A few even consult with astrologers (seriously). What most people, though, have in common is that they feel they're always paying too much for stocks and selling them when they're too cheap.

Perhaps you swing between different investment strategies like some folks switch diets to lose weight. Experimenting with different ways of picking stocks may have worked fine as stocks made breathtaking advances in the 1990s. But the financial crisis of 2008 and 2009 changed everything, serving up a harsh reminder to many investors today that it's possible to overpay for stocks. Not realizing that ahead of time can be hazardous to your portfolio, and perhaps after losing money a few too many times, you're looking for a method with a little more science behind it.

That's where fundamental analysis comes in. Fundamental analysis is one of the most sound and primary ways to evaluate investments. As a fundamental analyst, you carefully and thoroughly study every aspect of a company's operations. Much of your analysis will be focused on financial statements companies provide, as described briefly in this chapter.

Going beyond betting

If you're like most investors, even the words *fundamental analysis* may turn you off a bit. Fundamental analysis sounds somewhat stuffy and academic. And it's true that fundamental analysis finds much of its roots in academia. But you may be surprised to find you're probably using some basic forms of fundamental analysis in your life, perhaps even in places you wouldn't expect.

One example of where a type of fundamental analysis is used is at the horse races. Before a race, you'll notice groups of bettors doing some serious work trying to pick the day's winning horses. Some may pore over the life histories of horses in the race, getting to know the jockeys and their techniques, and even studying how wet or dry the track is.

Although investing isn't exactly like horse racing, the analogy is a helpful way to understand fundamental analysis. For instance, some fundamental analysts will study a company like a bettor will study a horse. How successful has the company been recently, and is it healthy and well-cared for? Next, in fundamental analysis you might study a company's management like a bettor would consider the jockey. Is the management experienced, and has it competed against rivals before like the ones it's facing now? Lastly, you must evaluate the broad economic climate, just like a bettor considers the weather and condition of the track.

But here's where things get even trickier. It's not good enough to find the best company, or horse, to take the metaphor a little further. After all, if all the other bettors at the track did the same work and picked the same horse that you selected, you have a problem. The odds would be adjusted so that the payout on the favorite horse would fall. Bettors know that picking a favorite horse to win doesn't pay off much. And you're also taking a chance that the favorite will surprise almost everyone by losing and cost you money. Similarly, if you invest in a company that's widely considered to be a darling with other investors, your payoff is reduced for reasons you can discover in Chapter 3 of Book 7.

REMEMBER

After you see what fundamental analysis is, broadly speaking, consider how it can be applied to investing. Fundamental analysis is used to size up investments in several key ways:

>> **Analyzing the financial statements:** Fundamental analysts pore over public documents companies provide to understand how the business is performing. Many fundamental analysts' starting point is digging into a company's financial statements to see how profitable a company is, how rapidly it is growing, what kind of financial health it's in, and whether it has the ability to withstand tough economic times.

>> **Getting an idea of how solid a company is:** Many fundamental analysts are *fixed-income investors.* These investors have loaned money to companies, usually by buying bonds. Bond investors give money to a company in exchange for an agreed-upon payment each month, quarter, or year. Because bond investors get a fixed amount of pay, they don't care if a company is wildly successful. Bond investors, unlike stock investors, don't get a share of future earnings and growth. Bond investors just want to know the company is healthy enough so it can keep paying interest and return the money it borrowed.

>> **Understanding the value of a company:** Stock investors use fundamental analysis to gauge whether a company's stock is a good deal or not. By studying financial statements, financial analysts determine whether a stock's price undervalues or overvalues the company.

>> **Going beyond the financials:** Fundamental analysis goes beyond where accounting stops. Accountants' goal is to precisely measure business activity. Fundamental analysts are looking for much more: They want to understand how a business actually works and what it's worth. Using fundamental analysis, you evaluate other factors that affect a company's prospects that go beyond what an accountant would care about. Common factors you may consider include sizing up a company against its rivals, determining how skilled a company's management team is in navigating through boom and bust times, and understanding the broad economic climate.

>> **Comparing a company's performance with its industry and competitors:** A company's value, financial resources, or performance is measured relative to its peers. Fundamental analysis shows you how to not just size up the company you're interested in, but see how it measures up with the companies it is competing with.

REMEMBER

Fundamental analysts take all the intelligence they gather to arrive at an investment decision and to take action. The most common question fundamental analysts ask themselves is whether a stock, at its current price, is cheap or expensive. The answer to that question will determine whether you choose to invest or not.

Understanding how fundamental analysis works

Fundamental analysts often dig well beyond a company's financial statements and try to unearth things. Sometimes fundamental analysts may spot a trend forming before a company's management acknowledges it. A fundamental analyst, for instance, might visit a retailer's stores and see how crowded they are to get an idea of what earnings might be in the future. Similarly, the fundamental analyst may try to get an idea of future demand by considering how busy a company's suppliers are. The goal of fundamental analysis is to measure how much a company is worth by using any shred of information possible.

The way you use fundamental analysis to understand what a company is worth gets down to the core essence of what a business is. With fundamental analysis, your goal is to monitor a company to see how it brings in money by selling goods and services to generate revenue. Next, you'll determine how much revenue a company manages to keep after paying its expenses. What's left after paying all the bills is profit, or *earnings.*

ACCOUNTANTS AREN'T SUPPOSED TO BE STOCK PICKERS

Accountants who step over the line — and try to profit from fundamental analysis — can get themselves into trouble. Most accounting firms have strict rules that prohibit employees from owning shares of companies the firm keeps the books for. Knowing the fundamentals of a company is so powerful that the knowledge can give accountants *material and non-public information* that would amount to inside information that would be illegal to profit from.

Just ask former KPMG accountant Scott London. London was charged with tipping a friend with fundamental details of five KPMG clients in 2013 — which his friend used to make more than $1.2 million in profits trading ahead of profit reports and merger deals, according to the Securities and Exchange Commission (SEC). In exchange, London's friend gave him bags of cash and a pricey Rolex watch. It's a great example that shows how fundamental analysts and accountants have very different needs from financial statements.

REMEMBER

The fact that fundamental analysts take action on their research is what separates them from accountants. Fundamental analysts compare what they think a company is worth with what other investors think. If the stock is undervalued, the fundamental analyst will buy the stock. Accountants, on the other hand, have the job of recording sales and revenue, but not trying to profit off their findings.

Fundamental analysis isn't perfect. But as you discover in this chapter, fundamental analysis is rigorous and rooted in understanding the most basic elements of business. Even if you have no plans to be a fundamental analyst, knowing how fundamental analysis works can only boost your investment success.

Knowing who can perform fundamental analysis

You don't have to be a high-powered investor to use fundamental analysis. If you have an interest in finding out more deeply about how companies work, you're a candidate for finding out about fundamental analysis. In fact, knowing how to read, analyze, and take action from information you glean about a company can be helpful for many users, including

>> **Stock investors:** Those looking to take an ownership stake in a company have a great financial incentive to master fundamental analysis. What they

find out about companies may help them decide when a good time to buy or sell may be. (Book 3 covers stock investing in more detail.)

>> **Lenders:** When you give someone a loan, you want to make sure they have the ability to pay you back. If you lend money to a company, perhaps by buying bonds it issues, you're more concerned about getting your money back than about making a killing on the investment.

>> **Mutual fund investors:** Even if you don't pick individual stocks or bonds to invest in, you probably own mutual funds that do. Mutual funds are investments that invest in a basket of individual securities. Using fundamental analysis, you can investigate some of the stocks your mutual funds may own. You might take a look at the top holdings of your mutual fund and question why your mutual fund owns them. (Flip to Book 5 for more about mutual funds.)

>> **Employees:** Workers may be anxious about the health of their company for several reasons. Using the same techniques an investor would use, you can study your company's financial resources and roughly estimate how likely it might be to pursue aggressive cost-cutting, like layoffs. Employees who depend on a pension paid by a former employer may also want to study the health of the company and make sure it will stick around.

>> **Board members:** Whether you're a board member of a large company, your local museum, or your condominium association, understanding the flow of money in and out can make you more valuable. Understanding fundamental analysis will help you be a solid watchdog of the organization's management by looking at facts, not promises.

>> **Donors:** Even some nonprofit charities disclose their financial standing. Fundamental analysis will help you see where donations are being spent and whether or not money is getting to those in need or being soaked up by the bureaucracy.

>> **Consumers:** When you buy a product or service, you may not think of yourself as investing in a company. Most of the time, you're not. But sometimes by buying a product you are forming a long-term relationship with a company. Take a car or an insurance product. These types of long-lived assets can attach you to the hip of a company for years. It's a good idea to know how to analyze a company if you plan on relying on its products for a long time.

Above all, fundamental analysts are good at not getting hoodwinked by companies. That's not a bad skill to have. You can't always take the financial statements at face value. Fundamental analysis gives you the tools you need to get to the truth beyond the numbers.

REMEMBER

Fundamental analysts spend quite a bit of time looking at companies' financial statements. But skilled fundamental analysts do more than just pick apart financial statements. After all, if that's all it was, fundamental analysis would be synonymous with accounting. Fundamental analysts use their findings to make investment decisions.

Following the money using fundamentals

One of the basic rules of investigative journalism is following the money. Tracing the movement of dollars through an organization will quickly show you the motives of the leaders, availability of resources, and vulnerabilities. Regulators will often follow the movement of money to pinpoint illegal cartels, Ponzi schemes, and other frauds.

All this may sound very cloak-and-dagger. But there's something to be learned from approaching fundamental analysis with the mind of an investigator. Your job is to take available information and dig up data yourself to get a complete picture of a company and whether or not it's a suitable place for you to entrust your money. Following the way money moves through a company tells you more about it than just about anything else.

REMEMBER

While no two companies are the same, the basics of business are universal. That's why fundamental analysis is such a powerful tool you can apply to high-tech companies, low-tech companies, and everything in between.

Companies are merely in the business of selling things they acquire for more than what they paid. Sounds simple. But that can be easy to forget after you get mired in details like profit margins, earnings per share, and P-E ratios.

Following the money at a company, so to speak, traces a predictable cycle. Just like the cycle of life repeats and refreshes, companies follow a pretty predictable pattern, too. Fundamental analysts call this the *trade cycle* — and understanding the cycle is pretty important if you want the financial statements to make sense.

The trade cycle begins with a business idea, but more specifically it starts when a company raises money so it can buy the equipment it needs to get started. Money may be raised by borrowing it, called *debt*, or by lining up investors willing to bet their money for a piece of future profits, called *equity*. The money raised is then used to acquire raw materials, office space, or whatever the company needs.

Next, the company tries to add value to the raw materials in some way and sell the product to customers. Typically, companies will also incur *indirect costs*, or overhead, to make all this happen. Overhead costs include everything from advertising, to research and development, to hiring skilled managers. The products are created and (hopefully) sold to the consumers. The cash collected from customers is then used to repay debt. The cycle then repeats all over again. Isn't this fun?

Now here's where fundamental analysis comes in. Here are a few questions a fundamental analyst might ask when taking a look at a company:

>> After factoring in all the costs, did the company make money?

>> How much money did the company raise to get started?

>> Is the company able to maintain itself without borrowing more or getting more investors?

>> Can the company create new products to keep buyers coming back?

>> Are competitors catching onto the idea and selling a similar product for less?

Comparing Fundamental Analysis with Other Ways of Picking Investments

Fundamental analysis is a well-known way of choosing investments. It's often the preferred method taught in business schools, largely because of its roots in things that can be measured and understood. But it's not, by any means, the only method of choosing stocks.

TIP

If you're still a little foggy on what fundamental analysis is, comparing it with other ways of evaluating investments may clear things up for you.

How fundamental analysis stacks up against index investing

If fundamental analysis seems like a lot of work, you can probably identify with *index investors.* Index investors think taking the time to pore over companies' financial statements is a whole lot of trouble for nothing. Index investors figure any information to be gleaned from company reports has already been extracted by other investors and acted upon.

For instance, if a company's stock were truly undervalued, other investors would have already recognized it and bought the stock. If enough investors buy a stock, they push the price up, and the shares are no longer undervalued. And thanks to the proliferation of electronic investing, analysts and investment firms with access to instantaneous information feeds can make such trading moves very quickly.

For that reason, index investors think trying to buy and sell stocks at just the right time, or use market timing, is impossible. In addition, index investors say that if there is an edge to fundamental analysis, it's wiped out by the cost and time consumed digging out the information. For that reason, index investors skip the fundamental analysis, and instead they do the following:

>> **Diversify:** Rather than trying to pick the companies and stocks that will do best, fundamental analysts buy small stakes in as many stocks as possible. Generally, index investors will buy mutual funds that own hundreds, if not thousands, of stocks. That way, if any one company stumbles badly, the loss is a very small percentage of the portfolio.

>> **Buy index funds:** Because index investors don't think fundamental analysis gives investors an edge, they don't see any reason to pay a mutual fund manager to pick stocks for them. Instead, they buy mutual funds that own all the stocks in popular stock indexes, such as the Dow Jones Industrial Average or Standard & Poor's 500. The Dow mirrors the ups and downs of 30 large, well-known companies, and the S&P 500 measures the market's performance using 500 of the largest companies' shares.

>> **Focus on costs:** Index investors assume the best way to make money in the stock market is by keeping costs low. Index funds generally have low expenses. And rather than spend personal time researching stocks, index investors generally buy a diversified basket of stocks and then forget about the holdings.

Comparing fundamental analysis with technical analysis

Like index investors, investors who use technical analysis shake their heads in disapproval when they see fundamental analysts carefully examining spreadsheets and financial statements. They, like index investors, see all the effort that goes into fundamental analysis as a waste of time and calculator batteries. That's because technical analysts assume any information worth knowing is reflected in a stock's price.

But technical analysts agree with fundamental analysts in one important way: They, too, think it's possible to beat the stock market. Unlike index investors, who think that timing the market is futile, technical analysts think stock prices move up and down in observable patterns. Knowing how to recognize patterns in stock price movements can signal a technical analyst the best times to get in, and out, of stocks. Technical analysts may not even care what a company does, because they're just looking at the price chart. To a technical analyst, buying and selling at the right time is more important than buying and selling the right stock. Technical analysts pay close attention to

>> **Stock price charts:** Technical analysts focus on stock price charts, which are graphs that plot a stock's movement over a period of time. These charts show instantly whether a stock is rising or falling in addition to how many trades, or *volume,* are occurring.

>> **Trading patterns:** Much as an astronomer sees patterns of stars in the sky, technical analysts look for stock price movements that follow a pattern. For instance, if a stock price falls to a low level, rises a bit, and sinks back down to near that same low level, technical analysts call that a *support level.* A support level is considered a point where demand for a stock is strong enough to stop it from sinking much further.

>> **Moving averages:** Technical analysts often pay close attention to a stock's average price over a period of time, say 200 days. When a stock falls below its 200-day moving average, or its average price over the past 200 days, that means the stock is vulnerable to fall further, technicians say. The idea is that when stocks fall below their 200-day-moving average, many investors who bought within the past year are losing money and may be nervous and quick to sell.

TIP

Here's an easy way to keep fundamental analysis and technical analysis clear in your mind. Fundamental analysts are looking for the *what,* or the companies that are attractively priced. Fundamental analysts often hold their investments for a long time. Technical analysis is more useful for the *when.* Technical analysts are usually just looking for opportune times to try to profit from short-term moves.

Putting Fundamental Analysis to Work For You

If you ever see the library of a fundamental analyst, it can be a pretty intimidating sight. Inevitably, there will be a copy of *Security Analysis* by Benjamin Graham and David Dodd (McGraw-Hill), a 766-page tome stuffed with gnarly formulas and arcane wording that makes your high-school algebra book look like a comic book. There will also be dog-eared copies of books with words like "value," "financial statements," and "ratios."

Fundamental analysis has the rap of being for people who wouldn't be caught dead without a pen, mechanical pencil, and calculator in their shirt pocket. But even if you don't walk around carrying such instruments, you too, can benefit from fundamental analysis. With an understanding of a few terms and basic techniques, fundamental analysis is within reach if you're interested and willing to put in a bit of time.

How difficult is fundamental analysis? Do you need to be a math wizard?

Contrary to popular belief, you don't need to be a math wizard to use fundamental analysis. Most of the math you'll use is pretty basic arithmetic. And there's no need to memorize formulas. You need to know how to build some *financial models,* which try to forecast how much profit a company will make in the future. But to help you out, there are some online tools and calculators to crunch some of the more tricky stuff for you.

TIP

Some of the more advanced techniques of fundamental analysis may require you to fire up a spreadsheet. If you want to get up to speed, Microsoft provides free help and tutorials for its Excel spreadsheet program at support.office.com/ en-us/excel. You might also take a look at the latest version of *Excel Formulas and Functions For Dummies* by Ken Bluttman (Wiley).

Is fundamental analysis for you?

If you're tired of trusting other people to tell you how a company is doing financially, you're a prime candidate for fundamental analysis. The whole premise of fundamental analysis is to reduce, if not eliminate, speculation and wild guesswork from investing. Fundamental analysis is rooted in the idea that you want to look at cold, hard data to make informed decisions on why an investment may be worth buying. If someone tells you a company is "doing well," fundamental analysis gives you the background to know whether that claim is really true.

Above all, fundamental analysis is ideal for people who want to approach an investment fully informed of the risks and with their eyes wide open. An in-depth fundamental analysis on a stock will not only alert you to potentially troubling trends at a company, but also give you clues to whether a stock may be overvalued by investors who aren't paying attention. An overvalued company is one that commands a stock price that well exceeds any possible profit it could generate for investors.

REMEMBER

In many ways, fundamental analysis is as much about helping you avoid poor investments as much as it is about helping you find good ones.

The risks of fundamental analysis

WARNING

Fundamental analysis, while it's rooted in math and objective information, isn't without its flaws. After all, if fundamental analysis were perfect, everyone would quit their day jobs, analyze stocks, and make bundles of money. That's why it's important to understand the shortcomings of fundamental analysis, which include

>> **Vulnerability to wrong data, including your assumptions:** Fundamental analysis is heavily based in fact. But if a company incorrectly reports data or you misinterpret them, you're going to have a false conclusion. Miscalculations are especially likely when making assumptions about things like a company's future growth rate, future interest rates, or profits. Even fundamental analysts are human, you know.

>> **Overreliance on past data:** Perhaps the biggest knock against fundamental analysis is how much weight it puts in a company's past performance. There is some truth to that, because numbers companies report can be a month or more old. However, true fundamental analysis uses historical numbers to make an educated guess about the future.

>> **Bad timing:** Suppose you do all the homework in researching a stock. You find a stock that appears to be a screaming buy, so you buy it. Guess what? A stock can remain a screaming buy for many years or even decades until investors come to the same conclusion. Fundamental analysts often have to be wrong for a long time before making money.

>> **Betting against the market:** If you buy a stock because you think it's a steal, you're in effect betting against thousands of the most sophisticated trading desks around the world with access to the same data. If you think a stock is too cheap, you're making the gamble that other investors are missing something you can see.

>> **Concentrated positions:** If you're going to the trouble to meticulously study a company, you're going to want to make sure you're positioned to profit if you're right. Unless you have a team of analysts working for you, when you find a stock that fits your fundamental criteria, you're going to want to own a large chunk of it. As a result, investors who use fundamental analysis may have large exposure to individual companies.

This concept contradicts the idea of *diversification,* which is owning hundreds and hundreds of small pieces of many companies. With diversification, you're spreading your risk over many companies so if one has a problem, it doesn't hurt so badly. Fundamental analysts, though, think that owning just a few investments that you know inside and out is actually safer than owning everything.

Making Money with Fundamental Analysis

Face it. You're probably not reading this book because you have a deep yearning to understand how to read and analyze company information. You're looking to dig into company reports for a reason, which is most likely to make money.

REMEMBER

Fundamental analysis can be profitable. If you're able to find hidden value in a company or its stock and buy in before other investors discover what you know, you'll cash in once the rest of Wall Street catches up to you.

Putting a price tag on a stock or bond

If you've ever wondered whether a stock is "cheap" or "pricey," fundamental analysis can be a big help. Fundamental analysis helps you understand exactly what you're getting when you buy an investment.

Here's an example to help you understand. Suppose you have the opportunity to buy a tree that literally grows dollar bills. Sounds great, right? How much should you pay for the tree? You might be tempted to pay millions of dollars, especially if others have their wallets out and start bidding.

But fundamental analysis can help you intelligently put a price tag on this amazing plant. By asking some questions and doing some due diligence, you can actually arrive at a correct price. The farmer tells you the tree grows 20 one-dollar bills every month. He also says the tree will likely die in a year and then stop growing money. Lastly, the farmer promises to pay you $20 a month if, for any reason, the tree stops growing money in less than a year. Suddenly this tree that grows money doesn't sound so wonderful.

Knowing these fundamental details, the tree can be priced. You now know the tree is expected to generate about $240 over the next 12 months until it shrivels up and dies. So, is the tree worth $240? Not so fast. Remember, the tree won't grow the $240 right away. You have to wait a year to get the entire wad of cash — as you'll only harvest $20 a month. Because you have to wait a year to get the $240, the tree is worth less than $240. That's because of the *time value of money* — a key principle to fundamental analysis — which essentially means a dollar received now is worth more than one received tomorrow. So if there's a bidding war for the tree that drives the price over $240, you know to walk away based on your fundamental research.

Being profitable by being a "contrarian"

Being a successful fundamental analyst can be pretty lonely. If you're trying to make money from studying a company and determining the company is worth more than its stock price, you're betting that other investors bidding for the stock are wrong.

Fundamental analysis, therefore, is somewhat at odds with the *efficient market theory*. Efficient market theory says that trying to beat the market by picking winning stocks is futile. The *strong form* of the efficient market theory says that all information that's knowable about a company is reflected in a company's stock price. So, suppose that after reading this book you dig through a company's financial statements and find that a company has great prospects. Efficient market theory would suggest that you're not the first person to discover this, and that other investors have already bid the stock up with the same information.

But before you throw your hands up and give up on fundamental analysis, there are some caveats to the efficient market theory worth noting. Most importantly, while stocks may reflect all information over the long term, there can be short-term periods when prices may excessively rise or fall due to extreme and fleeting optimism or pessimism. For instance, many high-technology stocks skyrocketed during the late 1990s, as investors bid up share prices on the idea that they'd be worth a fortune in the future. Fundamental analysts, looking at the fact that many of the companies didn't make money and never would, avoided the dot-com bubble. Eventually, the fundamentals caught up to them and many of the stocks collapsed 90 percent or more. In some cases, the companies completely failed.

REMEMBER

To profit from fundamental analysis, you have to be comfortable going against the crowd — or in Wall Street parlance — being a *contrarian*. When other investors are overly enthusiastic about a stock, they bid the price so high that it's practically impossible for anyone to make money. A contrarian would not be buying those stocks.

The Fundamental Analysis Toolbox

One of the great things about fundamental analysis is that you don't really need much to get started. If you have a computer and calculator, you're pretty much set.

Unlike technical analysis, which may require sophisticated and costly stock chart services, most of the data you need for fundamental analysis is provided free from nearly every company. Plus, many free online services offer increasingly detailed access to company financial data, making it easy for you to download and analyze.

There are three key financial documents that are the cornerstone of financial analysis: the income statement, balance sheet, and statement of cash flows.

Introducing the income statement

Want to know how much a company made or lost during a year or a quarter? The income statement is for you. This financial statement steps you through all the money a company brought in and how much it spent to make that money. If you've ever read news stories about how much a company earned during a quarter, for instance, the information was taken off the company's income statement.

TIP

The income statement is the financial statement containing data you probably hear the most about, including revenue, net income, and earnings per share.

Balance-sheet basics

Want to know how much money a company has or how much it owes to others? That's where the balance sheet comes in. This financial statement spells out all the cash a company has in addition to its debt. The difference between what a company owns (its *assets*) and what it owes (its *liabilities*) is its *equity*. The basic formula is as follows:

Assets = Liabilities + Equity

TIP

Sometimes it's helpful to understand corporate-finance jargon by putting it in personal-finance terms. If you've ever calculated your personal net worth by subtracting all your loans from all your savings, you've essentially created a balance sheet.

Figure 2-1 shows a favorite way to look at the relationship between assets, liabilities, and equity. Think of the company's financial position as a square. Next, cut the square in half. The left-hand side of the square, which we'll call assets, is worth the same as the right-hand side of the square, which we'll call liabilities and equity. The left-hand side of the square must always equal the right-hand side of the square. Remember that liabilities and equity don't have to equal each other, but together they must equal the assets.

Getting the mojo of cash flows

One of the first things fundamental analysts need to understand is that earnings aren't necessarily cash. Accounting rules, for instance, allow companies to include in their income statement revenue from products they may have sold to consumers but for which they haven't actually collected dollars from customers yet. Yes, you read that right. A company can say it earned $100 million, even though it hasn't collected a dime from customers. This method of accounting, called *accrual accounting*, is done for a good reason. Accrual accounting lets analysts see more accurately how much it cost a company to generate sales.

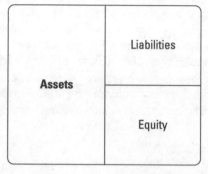

Assets | Liabilities | Equity

But accrual accounting makes it critical for investors to monitor not just a company's earnings, but how much cash it brings in. The statement of cash flows holds a company's feet to the fire and requires it to disclose how much cold, hard cash is coming into the company. The statement of cash flows lets you see how much cash a company generated from its primary business operations. The statement, though, also lets you see how much cash a company brought in from lenders and investors.

Familiarizing yourself with financial ratios (including the P-E)

While the financial statements are enormously valuable to financial analysts, they only go so far. Not only do companies tend to only give the information they're required to, the data can only tell you so much. You didn't expect companies to do everything for you, right? That's how financial ratios can be very important.

Financial ratios take different numbers from the income statement, balance sheet, and statement of cash flows, and compare them with each other. You'll be amazed at what you can find out about a company by mixing numbers from different statements. Financial ratios can provide great insight when applied to analysis.

There are dozens of helpful financial ratios. Here are the basic flavors and ratios and what they tell you:

>> **Valuation:** If you've ever heard of the price-to-earnings ratio, or P-E, you've used a financial ratio. The P-E is one of many *valuation ratios*. Valuation ratios help fundamental analysts find out if a stock is cheap or expensive by comparing the stock price to a basic piece of data about a company. For instance, the P-E ratio compares a stock's price to its earnings. The higher the P-E, the more richly valued a stock is.

>> **Financial health:** If a company is no longer a going concern and isn't functioning, it's not a great idea to invest in it. Some ratios, called *liquidity ratios,* measure how easily a company is able to keep up with its bills. Fundamental analysts look for red flags that a company might be about to face some tough times.

>> **Return on investment:** If you're going to give your money to a company, either as a loan or investment, you want to make sure you're getting enough in return. Return on investment ratios help you determine how well the company is putting your money to work.

>> **Operating performance:** The more a company can increase its sales, while at the same time lowering costs, the more profitable it is. This balancing act is the essence of business. And the stakes for investors are huge, because the more profit a company generates, the bigger the piece of pie that's left for investors. Operating performance ratios let you quickly see how well a company is managing its costs and increasing sales.

TIP

All the types of ratios and financial measures mentioned here are best understood when put into context. Fundamental analysts typically compare financial metrics to those of a company's rivals. It can be useful to have financial data not just on the company you're interested in, but on the industry for comparison.

Chapter **3**

Gaining an Edge with Fundamental Analysis

Fundamental analysis isn't the easiest way to invest. There's a bit of math involved. You'll need to learn some terms. And to perform fundamental analysis, you need to ferret out and analyze somewhat arcane pieces of financial information.

Why go to all this trouble? That's the question you find the answer to in this chapter. You discover why the rigors of fundamental analysis, and the ultimate goal of not overpaying for stocks and finding cheap stocks to buy, can help you obtain better long-term success in investing. Meanwhile, you see how some basic fundamental analysis can help you avoid making mistakes that can be difficult to recover from.

Of course, no discussion of fundamental analysis is complete without exploring its best-known master: Warren Buffett. Buffett is a hero in investing, thanks to his discipline and long-term ability to find and hold companies with attractive fundamental characteristics.

Finally, in this chapter, you get a general taste of how fundamental analysis can give you cues on when you might consider buying or selling stocks. No method will work 100 percent all the time, but fundamental analysis can at least provide a guide and keep you from getting caught up in stock manias and bubbles.

Better Investing with Fundamentals

One of the biggest strengths of fundamental analysis is the fact that it attempts to help you keep the emotion out of investing. While *momentum investors* chase after the hottest stocks hoping they'll go higher, and *day-traders* buy and sell every few minutes looking for a quick buck, fundamental analysis is more of a data-driven discipline.

Fundamental analysts analyze investments by examining the business that's behind a stock or bond. Even if you're just looking to buy a few shares of a company, you approach the analysis with the same level of research, or *due diligence*, as if you're thinking about buying the whole company. Fundamental analysis lets you approach a stock as an investor, not a speculator.

REMEMBER

Investors look to buy a stock because they believe the underlying company will generate profits in the future that exceed the price they're paying. Speculators look to make money on an investment by simply finding someone else to sell it to for a higher price.

The careful consideration of a company's fundamentals, such as revenue and earnings, is a key distinction of this approach from other methods of choosing investments. The name *fundamental analysis* really says it all, as the approach gets down to the most basic aspects of a business, including the trade cycle, which is discussed in Chapter 2 of Book 7.

Picking stocks for fundamental reasons

Fundamental analysis is generally connected with *value investors.* Value investors tend to buy stocks they think are *undervalued,* or have stock prices below what they think the company is actually worth. But fundamental analysis can help you no matter how you invest. Perhaps you're a *technical analyst,* who studies stock charts to find stocks to buy. Maybe you're an *index investor,* who buys all the stocks in a broad stock market index, such as the Standard & Poor's 500. No matter what kind of investing you prefer, fundamental analysis can help you find suitable stocks and investments.

Helping value investors

Value investors are often drawn to the idea that they can get an edge on other investors by doing their homework and studying a company's financial statements. These investors believe if they put in the time to understand a company's business, accurately forecast its future, and pay the right price, they can achieve greater upside and less downside than the market as a whole.

There's some truth to this. Academic studies have shown that stocks that are cheap, or value priced, tend to have strong long-term performance. Need proof? Table 3-1 shows how so-called *value-priced* stocks have performed compared with so-called *growth* stocks. Value-priced stocks are those that are cheaper than the market based on fundamental metrics. Growth stocks are those that are more expensive than the market. The numbers speak for themselves. Cheap stocks win over the long term. And it gets better: The edge of value stocks carries over to a company of any size — large or small.

TABLE 3-1

Fundamentals Matter: Value Beats Growth

Type of stock based on index	Average annual % growth
Large value	10.6
Large growth	8.2
Small value	12.6
Small growth	9.6

Source: Index Fund Advisors based on IFA indexes and data starting from 1928

Fundamental analysis can also help you protect yourself from your own speculative juices. By studying the cold, hard numbers of a company's business, you can get a strong dose of reality while other investors get caught up in the hype surrounding a particular stock. Because fundamental analysis is based in the laws of business, it can give you a greater perspective on how much an investment is worth.

Fundamental analysis allows you to have a pretty good idea of what a company or stock is worth, even before you buy it. That's critical in investing where the prices of stocks aren't always the same as the value of the company. How can that be?

REMEMBER

Value and price are determined by two very different things.

>> A stock's price is determined by an auction, very similar to how the price on a Pez dispenser is set on eBay. Investors frenetically buy and sell stocks every

trading day, pushing the price up and down based on how optimistic or pessimistic they are about a company's future potential that second or even nanosecond. Just as you can see a bidding war erupt over a Pez dispenser and push its value to extreme highs, the same can occur for a stock if many investors are willing to buy it.

>> A company's value is very different — and quite disconnected from the noise on Wall Street. A company's value is a mathematical measurement of what the company is worth based on how much profit it generates and how much growth it's expected to generate. The value of a company doesn't change second to second. Quite the opposite.

John Bogle, founder of the Vanguard investment company, separates the true value of companies from the market value determined by Wall Street noise. Bogle says the value of companies is determined by the slow creep upward of their dividends and earnings, which he calls the *investment return*. Then there's the *speculative return*, which is the price that traders are willing to pay for shares of that company at the moment. Speculative returns aren't rooted in anything other than how much traders are willing to pay. When you start paying more attention to the speculative gains, you're setting yourself up for trouble. "In the short run, speculative returns are only tenuously linked with investment returns," Bogle says. "But in the long run, both returns must be — and will be — identical." In other words, the company's market value will eventually match the fundamental value.

A great example of how fundamental analysis can help you spot a frenzy over a stock, causing its price to get out of line, occurred in March 2000. (Incidentally, the dot-com boom was one of the best eras in recent memory for showing the danger of speculation.) Shares of Palm Computing, a maker of the Palm electronic organizer (remember those?), soared 150 percent in their first day of trading to more than $95 a share. At that price, investors put a total price tag of $54.3 billion on the company and its 23 million shares.

Just a little bit of fundamental sleuthing could have protected investors from the coming brutal collapse in the stock. Here's how. Palm Computing was 95 percent owned by its parent company, 3Com, at the time. And the entire value of 3Com, including its 95 percent stock in Palm Computing, was just $28 billion. So why would investors be willing to pay nearly twice as much for a 5 percent piece of Palm than they would the entire parent company, 3Com? This kind of madness shows investors lose sight of fundamentals. It's kind of like paying $20 for a slice of pie when you can buy the whole pie for $10. Fundamental analysts knew something was a little off. And they were right. The stock lost more than 70 percent of its value in just seven months. Ouch!

Finding uses for the index investor

Index investors don't try to pick individual stocks or time the market. Index investors buy a broad basket of investments and hold it for a long period of time (see Chapter 2 in Book 7 for more on index investors). Many index investors think trying to choose stocks that will outperform the broad market is extremely difficult, if not impossible. As a result, index investors buy small stakes of hundreds of companies so that any difficulties that arise at one firm won't hurt much.

Index investors often say fundamental analysis is a waste of time. Even so, many index investors apply some aspects of fundamental analysis. Index investors routinely choose to invest in baskets of either *value* stocks or *growth* stocks. Value stocks are those that are largely ignored by investors and command low stock prices relative to their fundamentals, such as profits or asset values. Growth stocks, on the other hand, are the darlings of Wall Street and demand huge stock prices compared to their fundamentals.

It's not just value versus growth that index investors pay attention to, but also the size of the company. Index investors often divvy up money between shares of large companies and small companies — as companies' sizes often have a bearing on how what kinds of returns to expect. Large companies tend to generate lower returns than smaller companies — but they also tend to be less risky. These measures of size, again, are rooted in fundamental analysis.

Market value, also known as *market capitalization*, is the total price tag placed on a company and a good proxy for its size. Market value bears mentioning now because it's so important to index investors. Market value is rooted in fundamental analysis. For a company's market value, you'll need to calculate its number of shares outstanding, which comes from the balance sheet.

REMEMBER

You calculate a company's market value like this:

Stock price × Company's number of shares outstanding

So what? Does this mean the company is large or small? Table 3-2 does the work for you and shows you how to know if a company is small, mid-sized, or large.

TABLE 3-2

Measuring the Size of Companies

Stock Size Classification	Market Value More Than	Market Value Less Than
Large	$10 billion	No limit
Medium	$2 billion	$10 billion
Small	$300 million	$2 billion

Assisting technical analysts

Like fundamental analysts, technical analysts think they can beat the stock market by picking the right stocks at the right time. But unlike fundamental analysis, technical analysis calls for a close study of stock price movements over time.

Still, technical analysts can benefit from fundamental analysis, too. For instance, some technical analysts may look for companies that are increasing their revenue or earnings growth each quarter. This information is found on a company's income statement. Similarly, technical analysts may look for the best company in an industry by looking for companies with the most attractive financial ratios.

Dooming your portfolio by paying too much

REMEMBER

No matter what type of investor you are, there are several absolutes. Here's one of them: If you overpay for a stock, you're accepting a sentence of poor returns in the future. Your return on a stock is a function of how much you pay for it. By definition, the more you pay for an investment, the lower your return will be.

WHY THE "THREE FACTORS" MATTER

It's rare that academic research can make you money. But one of the most influential pieces of academic research ever written about investing is certainly worth your time.

Professors Eugene Fama and Kenneth French found that nearly 95 percent of stock price movements are explained by just three things, two of which are determined by a company's fundamentals:

- **Size:** Shares of smaller companies measured by *market value* tend to beat the stock market, in part, because they are riskier and less established. Market value, also called market capitalization or market cap, measures the total price the market assigns to a company by multiplying a stock price by the total number of its shares outstanding. You find out more about market capitalization later in this chapter.

- **Price or value:** The lower a stock's price, relative to its *book value*, the better it tends to do relative to the rest of the stock market. Book value is a key aspect of fundamental analysis. For now, know that book value is much like the net worth of a company. It's the company's total assets minus liabilities. This is the fundamental value, or equity, in the stock.

- **Market risk:** Movements of the broad economy have a large sway on how individual stocks perform. This is the part of stock values not determined by fundamental measures. Market risk can be very important in the short run, but eventually the fundamentals win out.

Imagine you have the opportunity to buy a Laundromat. The Laundromat has been open for 30 years, and in each of those years, it generates a profit of $100,000. Because the Laundromat is in a strip mall that will close in five years, you figure the business will generate $500,000 in profit over the years and then will be shut down.

TECHNICAL STUFF

To keep this example simple, forget about the role of *inflation,* or the decreasing value of money each year, at this point. Also assume that your estimate was correct, and the Laundromat generated $100,000 a year in profit.

Just imagine what would happen if you offered to buy this Laundromat for $200,000. Your gain would be 150 percent. You know this because your profit is $300,000, which is the difference between the Laundromat's earnings ($500,000) and what you paid ($200,000). Your return is your profit of $300,000 divided by the price you paid, $200,000.

Now, what if you got into a bidding war with another person interested in buying the Laundromat? In the heat of the moment, you offered to buy the business for $400,000 instead of $200,000. Your return will take a big hit, now equaling 25 percent. Nothing changed with the Laundromat. It will function the same whether you paid $400,000 or $200,000. But your return is now the profit of $100,000 divided by your purchase price of $400,000.

The same goes for investments, including stocks and bonds. If you increase the amount you pay for a share of stock, for instance, you eat into your return.

WARNING

Overpaying for a stock is even more dangerous than increasing your offer for the Laundromat. If a company you invest in suffers a slowdown and its earnings are smaller than expected, you'll find your return to be very small, or you may not get back what you invested.

Sitting through short-term volatility

Sometimes the excitement of daily market activity can get intoxicating. Ticker symbols scrolling at the bottom of the TV screen during financial programs can make you feel as if the markets are constantly moving and changing. And that's true; markets are constantly moving as investors trade shares back and forth and push stock prices up and down. This is how the speculative return, as described previously, gets generated.

But a fundamental analysis can help you block out a great deal of this noise and be a better investor as a result. An example is perhaps with your house. Suppose you're living in a home you know is worth $200,000. You know that because you hired an appraiser to look at the condition of the roof, remodeled kitchen, and bath, as well as look at the prices of identical homes in the area. You have a pretty good idea of what the house is worth.

With this in mind, would you panic if you were sitting on the patio while a person walking by randomly offered you $100,000 for the home? Probably not. After all, you know the home is worth more than $100,000. Besides, you're not in the market to sell anyway.

Still, that's what stock investors commonly do when they pay too much attention to day-to-day movements in stock prices. They may have felt great about buying a stock for $10 a share, but if the stock falls to $8 a month later, they panic and wonder if they should sell. It doesn't have to be that way.

One of the mantras of fundamental analysis comes from Benjamin Graham, the pioneer of the methods and mentor to Warren Buffett. Fundamental analysts will often say the market is a voting machine in the short term, but a weighing machine in the long run. In other words, stock prices can be kicked dramatically higher or lower in the short term. But over the longer term, the underlying value of a company will prevail, and its true heft will be recognized.

REMEMBER

Fundamental analysis helps you focus on an investment's true value, or weight, using Benjamin Graham's analogy. If you know you correctly analyzed a company and assigned the correct value to it, then you don't need to be as concerned about whether or not a company is popular in any given day, month, or year. Having a fundamental grasp of a company gives you the peace of mind to hold an investment for a long period of time and resist the urge to sell at the wrong time.

Relying on the Basic Info the Pros Use

It's natural to think successful fundamental analysts have some kind of secret that's beyond the reach of regular investors. Looking at the long-term success of Warren Buffett, for instance, makes you think perhaps he has a supercomputer that's able to forecast the future. Similarly, many analysts who study companies have deep insights about their businesses, which may lead you to think they have access to data you don't.

But here's the truth. Fundamental analysts, with a few exceptions, are using all the same financial statements you have access to. Even the professionals are looking at all the same things, such as

>> **The financial statements:** The income statement, balance sheet, and statement of cash flows are the cornerstone of the analysis done by most fundamental analysts.

>> **The financial ratios:** These seemingly simple calculations put the numbers in the financial statements into perspective. That perspective helps you determine if stocks are cheap or expensive.

>> **Industry analysis:** Understanding the dynamics of the industry a company is in can help you do a better job investing.

>> **Economic analysis:** Investments can swing in value based largely on how the broad economy is doing. The influence of the economy became clear in 2008, when shares of companies having nothing to do with sub-prime loans were dragged down with the financial debacle. But fundamental analysis also helped investors pinpoint companies that would benefit most when the economy recovered. Stocks more than doubled from the lows of 2009 through 2015.

REMEMBER

Clearly, the pros do have distinct advantages. Large investment firms can afford to deploy armies of research experts to pore over the financial statements, allowing them to trade while you're still downloading the results. Some systems used by professionals make fundamental analysis easier by automatically calculating growth trends and the financial ratios. Experience can also be a big factor in helping a fundamental analyst spot things that a beginner might miss. But that doesn't mean you can't use fundamental analysis to help boost your success.

What is "the Warren Buffett Way"?

For many fundamental analysts, Warren Buffett is the ultimate role model. There's no denying his success. Shares of Buffett's Berkshire Hathaway rose from $87,800 a share to $204,624 in the ten years ending November 2014 — an impressive 133 percent gain. That works out to about 8.8 percent a year on average. During that same time period, the Russell 3000 index, which measures the performance of the stock market in general, gained 7.5 percent in value including dividends, according to Russell Investments. Buffett's longer-term record is strong, too. No wonder he's called the Oracle of Omaha.

Trying to figure out Buffett's secret is the investment world's equivalent of the search for the Holy Grail. Scores of investors make the pilgrimage to Berkshire Hathaway shareholder meetings in Omaha each year, trying to figure out how Buffett does it. Hour-long lunches with Buffett auction off on eBay for hundreds of thousands of dollars. And there are countless books on Buffett, most notably *The Warren Buffett Way* by Robert G. Hagstrom (Wiley).

REMEMBER

Interestingly, though, Buffett doesn't make much of a secret of his techniques. Every year, in his letter to shareholders and also in Berkshire Hathaway's "Owner's Manual" he paints a picture of his approach. If you're looking to up your fundamental analysis game, you're wise to learn from the master. Much of Buffett's approach is based in key elements of fundamental analysis, including the following:

>> **Invest as an owner, not a trader.** Buffett is very clear that he looks at an investment not as a short-term trade, but a long-term relationship. Berkshire Hathaway will often invest in a company and hold it for a very long time, perhaps never selling the position. "Regardless of price, we have no interest at all in selling any good businesses that Berkshire owns," according to Berkshire's Owner's Manual.

>> **Consider carefully a company's intrinsic value.** Buffett repeatedly discusses *intrinsic value,* which is a measure of what a company is truly worth. Intrinsic value is how much cash a company is expected to generate over its lifetime, which is a good measure of what it's worth. Buying a stock for less than its intrinsic value gives you a bit of a margin of safety.

>> **Analyze management.** Buffett routinely says even a seemingly ho-hum company can generate dazzling returns with a good management team at the helm. For that reason, Buffett will often leave the top officers and directors of a company in place, even after buying a company.

>> **Stick with businesses you understand.** The better you grasp how a company makes its money and operates, the more informed you'll be after reviewing its financial statements. You'll also know better what to look for, because every industry and company has unique financial traits.

>> **Find businesses that have a real advantage.** In capitalism, if a company has a good idea, other firms will try to copy it and steal away market share. Buffett combats that by investing in businesses with a strong brand or unique product, such as Coca-Cola.

Many an investor hopes to profit like Buffett without actually learning fundamental analysis. There are plenty of ways to do that. Investors who want to ride Buffett's coattails could just invest in Berkshire Hathaway's shares. Others try to mimic what Buffett does. Some investors try to figure out what Buffett is investing in by reading Berkshire Hathaway's *annual report,* a document that discloses all the firm's large holdings.

TIP

It's never a good idea to blindly buy stocks just because another investor did. Still, reviewing the stocks that pass Buffett's fundamental analysis may be a good place to start. The list of Berkshire Hathaway's holdings in publicly traded companies can be found in the company's annual reports, available here: `www.berkshirehathaway.com/reports.html`. Table 3-3 shows you what some of Berkshire's biggest positions were at the end of 2020.

TABLE 3-3

Big Buffett Bets

Company	% of company owned by Berkshire	Market value of holding end of 2020 ($ Billions)
Apple	5.4	$120.4
Coca-Cola	9.3	$21.9
American Express	18.8	$18.3
Bank of America	11.9	$31.3
Verizon	3.5	$8.6

Source: Data from Berkshire Hathaway 2020 Annual Report

WARNING

Blindly following moves of top investors isn't an instant route to riches. That's especially the case when trying to take cues from Buffett. Buffett constantly reminds his shareholders that he plans to hold investments for a long time. And his holdings can also suffer large losses in the short term. For instance, had you bought Tesco at the beginning of 2008 after seeing it was a top holding at the end of 2007, you would have suffered a 75 percent loss. Shares in American Express — a big holding going into 2014 — lost a quarter of its value in 2015. Sometimes even Buffett's speculative plays don't pay off right away.

Checking in on Graham and Dodd

As much as Buffett is revered and admired, he, too was a student of fundamental analysis. Buffett has utilized and perfected the tools of professors Benjamin Graham and David Dodd, who are discussed at more length in this section. Graham and Dodd, whose names are synonymous with a method of investing called *value investing*, trace their roots to Columbia University, which Buffett attended.

The origins of value investing

Value investing, along with the work of Graham and Dodd, is usually central to the work of fundamental analysis. Graham and Dodd explained a stock is really a claim on the cash a company is expected to generate in the future, or its intrinsic value, as referred to earlier. Just know if a stock is trading for

>> Less than the cash it will generate, it's *undervalued* and may be bought.

>> More than the value of cash a company is expected to churn out, it's *overvalued*.

Using fundamentals to see when a stock is priced right

Graham and Dodd took things a bit further than just weighing whether stocks were over- or undervalued. Other lessons from Graham and Dodd worth noting include the following:

>> **Protect yourself.** Buy stocks well below what they are worth, or their intrinsic value. This extra cushion gives you a *margin of safety* in case the business runs into trouble and the stock price falls further.

>> **Investing isn't necessarily speculating.** While it's tempting to think of Wall Street as a giant casino, Graham and Dodd explained that wasn't necessarily the case. If you're buying stocks with little information about the companies' business, then yes, you're betting or speculating. When you speculate, you bet you can sell the stock to someone else for more. But with fundamental analysis, you can become more of an investor by understanding what you paid and what you can expect to receive in exchange.

>> **Be cautious of companies with excessive debt.** Companies that borrow heavily to finance their operations may face onerous debt payments during difficult economies.

Figuring Out When to Buy or Sell a Stock

Most investors are frustrated by the difficulty of getting the timing just right when buying or selling stocks. Even professional investors complain that while it's hard enough trying to find the right investment and buy it at a good price, it's even harder to know when to sell. Fundamental analysis can help you with this because you'll find out how to estimate what a company is worth. As discussed earlier, knowing what a company is worth is very helpful because then you know whether the current stock price is higher or lower than what you think the company's value is.

On the flip side, the discipline of fundamental analysis can help you evaluate when you may want to sell a stock. If a stock price is well below what you think the stock is worth, why would you sell at that price unless you had to?

Looking beyond the per-share price

Look at just about any financial website, and the screen will be covered with stock prices, probably flashing green or red as they move up or down. Many investors get obsessed with the per-share price of a stock. It's easy to understand why. When you buy a slice of pizza, for instance, you may not think to calculate how much, based on the per-slice price, you're paying for the entire pie.

But one of the basic premises of fundamental investing is just that. You want to know how much you're paying for your slice of a company, and how that compares to what it's really worth. And if there's one aspect of fundamental analysis you can use immediately from this chapter, it's that the per-share price of a stock, by itself, doesn't tell you much.

Just looking at a company's per-share price can lead you to make incorrect judgments. Some investors, for instance, have puzzled over how shares of Visa could trade for less than $80 a share while rival MasterCard commands a price of upwards of $100 a share, because Visa processes more credit card transactions than MasterCard does. You might assume Visa is a better value than MasterCard because the per-share stock price is lower. But that's not necessarily the case, and you need to take the analysis beyond the stock price.

Fundamental analysis, though, will show you that Visa's lower per-share price doesn't mean it's a screaming buy. Remember market value mentioned earlier? Well, it's back again. Market value tells you how much investors are paying for an entire company based on the price of the single share of stock. Using the pizza metaphor, market value tells you what the price of the whole pizza is, based on the price of one slice. You can apply this information immediately to stocks by using this formula:

Market value = share price × number of shares outstanding

The key parts of market value are

>> **Share price:** How much investors are willing to pay for a slice of ownership in a company. You can get a company's share price from many sources, ranging

from your online brokerage firm, investing websites, or in the business section of your newspaper.

>> **Number of shares outstanding:** The number of slices, or shares, a company's value is cut into. The number of shares outstanding is available in a company's balance sheet.

Here you find the stock prices of both Visa and MasterCard, as well as each company's total number of shares outstanding. Applying market value to Visa and MasterCard reveals much more than simply looking at their share prices does. The analysis shows that despite its lower per-share price, Visa is actually the company with the bigger total value. You figure this out by doing the following:

Calculating market value of Visa:

$80 share price × 2,429.5 million shares = $194.4 billion

Calculating market value of MasterCard:

$100 share price × 1,131.4 million shares = $113.1 billion

You can see that investors are in fact paying 70 percent more for Visa than MasterCard. Whether or not they're paying too much is another question. But at this point, it's important to understand how fundamental analysis goes well beyond just taking a look at a company's share price.

Seeing how a company's fundamentals and its price may get out of alignment

You don't need a long memory to remember how fundamental analysis could have helped your investing. During the tech-stock boom of the late 1990s, investors were so enamored with dot-coms they were willing to pay boundless amounts for them. Just a few years later, in the mid-2000s, investors repeated their mistakes by creating a housing boom that drove up shares of homebuilders' stocks. What's remarkable is there were at least two massive stock market bubbles in just one decade. Fundamental analysis could have helped you sidestep the intense pain after both these bubbles inevitably burst.

We can put one of these bubbles into context using our new tool: market value. KB Home, a southern California homebuilder, was at the epicenter of the housing bubble. Back in early 2006, investors awarded the company with a total market value of $6.8 billion. Fast-forward to the end of 2014 — long after the housing bubble burst. KB Home's market value was priced to $1.5 billion. Where did the missing $5.3 billion in market value go? Out of the pockets of speculators.

KB Home's market value collapsed a remarkable 78 percent, erasing $5.3 billion in market value.

Academics argue over why bubbles and manias occur with investing. And you can leave that heady discussion to them. Just know that sometimes, overenthusiasm for stocks can drive prices, albeit temporarily, to levels that aren't justified by their underlying businesses. Fundamental analysis is one way to try to see when a bubble is forming and try to profit from it.

WARNING

Even masters of fundamental analysis have difficulty timing bubbles just right. Many analysts had warned that tech stocks were overvalued in 1998, for instance. And they were right . . . eventually. These investors had to bear being wrong and missing out on huge gains as tech stocks continued to soar in 1999 and early 2000, even though they proved to be wildly overvalued.

Investors who pay attention to company fundamentals are often able to at least recognize when a bubble is forming. Weak fundamentals, for instance, were the tip-off for the dot-com bubble. More than a third of the 109 internet companies that failed had business models that didn't bring in enough revenue or had costs too high to ever make a profit, according to Boston Consulting.

Avoiding overhyped "story stocks"

Fundamental analysis can help you recognize when stocks are rising too much, well beyond what's justified by their businesses. It's a great way to resist the *story stocks* trance, or overinfatuation with companies that seem to have boundless potential and grab the attention of the masses. Like clockwork, investors go gung-ho over a type of company — usually in a seemingly promising industry. Investors have had temporary insanity over biotech firms, 3-D printing companies, social media stocks, for-profit colleges, satellite radio operators, and even retailers. Most of these spells eventually end badly.

Alternative energy stocks, including solar companies, are a recent example of stocks that lured investors with an irresistible premise but have struggled to deliver the fundamentals to support the optimism. Take the example of SolarCity. The company, which built and leased back residential solar installations, seemed like a total winner in 2014. The company was also linked to the famed CEO of Tesla, Elon Musk, as chairman. What's not to like?

SolarCity saw its stock soar 634 percent in early 2014, racing to the point where it had a market value of $7 billion in February 2014. While the company was losing money in 2012, 2013, and 2014, it told investors that customers were signing up at a rapid clip and profits would eventually roll in. Investors continued to buy in.

It took some time, but investors who made the effort to actually read the company's financial statements with horror were proven right. Fundamental analysts spotted two signs they routinely look for, including

>> **Lack of profit:** Even as SolarCity grew, the losses continued to mount. SolarCity lost money in five of the six years between 2009 and 2014. Just in 2014 alone, the company posted a net loss of $66.5 million.

>> **Large debt burden:** The company continued to pile on more and more debt as it grew. In September 2015, SolarCity was carrying $2.1 billion in *long-term debt*, or debt that's due in more than a year. That debt load was up 50 percent from 2013.

Despite the glowing promises of the company, investors ended up suffering. The company's stock price had fallen by 65 percent from the high in February 2014 to November 2015. Once again, fundamental analysis proved correct. Investors paying attention to fundamental analysis clearly knew the hype wasn't justified at the high — avoiding a massive loss.

Pairing buy-and-hold strategies with fundamental analysis

Buying and holding stocks over the long term can be a great way to make money. Just ask Warren Buffett. Fundamental analysis can help give you the insights in companies to have the faith to hold on.

Fundamental analysis doesn't require you to constantly buy and sell stocks. In fact, many investors tend to do their homework, buy a stock, and hold on. They realize that constantly buying and selling stocks can be hazardous for your portfolio because it may hurt you with

>> **Mounting trading costs:** Every time you buy or sell a stock, it costs you something. Certainly, you can reduce commissions by opening an account with a deep-discount online brokerage. But the costs are still a factor, including ones you might not notice.

REMEMBER

There are two prices for stocks, the *bid price* and the *ask price.* The ask is the price you must pay when you buy a stock. The bid is the price you get when you sell. The ask is always higher than the bid, just like the price you get for trading in a car to a dealer, the bid, is less than the price the dealer will resell the car for, or the ask. When you buy a stock, you're paying a hidden fee, which is the difference between the bid and ask, or the *spread.*

>> **Unnecessary taxes:** Flipping in and out of stocks can end up making Uncle Sam rich. If you sell a stock for a profit before you've owned it at least a year, it's a *short-term capital gain.* Short-term capital gains are taxed at your ordinary income-tax rates, which can be up to 39.6 percent. On the other hand, if you hold onto a stock for more than a year and sell it, the highest tax rate you'll likely pay is 15 percent. By just holding on a little longer, you can save a bundle on taxes.

>> **Mistakes:** It's tempting to think that you're never wrong. And after reading Book 7 and applying fundamental analysis, you'll be more informed than many other investors. Still, it's easy to make a mistake if you sell too early.

Looking to the long term

While it's not always the case, investors who rely on fundamental analysis are often resigned to being patient and waiting for the rest of the world to see how great the company you own is. After all, when you're counting on the fact that the stock market and its scores of traders, portfolio managers, and other investors are wrong, you can't expect them to arrive at your way of thinking overnight.

REMEMBER

Fundamental analysis often works best when paired with a *passive investing* strategy. With passive investing, you do all your homework, pick your stock, and then wait. The stock might fall further. But it's up to you to have the courage to trust your research and wait until other investors see what attracted you to the stock.

And because making money with fundamental analysis requires you to go against the crowd, you'll often need to buy the stock when you think others are wrong. A few of the times where stock prices may, temporarily, undervalue a company include the following:

>> **The wake of an accounting scandal:** When investors can no longer trust a management team because the financial statements have been falsified, they might sell the stock indiscriminately. If the stock is adequately beaten down to a point where you feel the company's not being properly appreciated, there could be opportunity.

WARNING

Trying to buy a stock after it's been "cooking the books" is extremely difficult. Because fundamental analysis is based on accurate financial accounting, making a decision based on false information is complicated and beyond the scope of this book.

>> **Amid pending litigation or liability claims:** Stocks will often trade at discounts, or below their true value, when investors are worried a company

might face massive claims. This has happened with companies involved in tobacco and asbestos.

>> **Slowing growth:** When a company or its industry matures, it may see the rate of increase in revenue and earnings slow. When that happens, *growth investors,* who buy growth stocks, may dump the stock so they can move on to the new darling.

>> **Industry shifts:** When there's a major disruption to an industry, the stocks in the group might get seriously punished. Following the credit crunch, for instance, stocks in the financial sector lost 58 percent of their value as a group in 2008. Certainly, not all banks and financial firms deserved to be punished that badly. Fundamentals analysts who bought the surviving bank stocks at the end of 2012 enjoyed a 56 percent rally through late 2015 — which beat the market's gain.

TIP

Being willing to step up and invest in a company others want nothing to do with can be lucrative. Beaten-down stocks that get rediscovered by investors can rally strongly.

Knowing that patience isn't always a virtue

According to classic value investing, if you've done your fundamental analysis, you can buy stocks, forget about them, and wait a few years to count your riches. Unless there's a major change that warrants changing your opinion, value investors hang on and wait for the market to wake up.

WARNING

Don't let the fact you've done your fundamental research blind you to the fact that sometimes a cheap stock can get cheaper, and stay that way. Overconfidence in fundamental analysis can turn a bad decision into a devastating one. The brutal decline suffered by Lucent shareholders is a classic example. Lucent was born out of the technology arm of AT&T, which was known for innovative patents for telecommunication and computing. Lucent, considered a blue chip by many investors, routinely showed up on lists of the most popular stocks with individual investors.

The stock's downfall remains an example of the dangers of hanging on too long. The stock hit its all-time high of $85 a share in 1999 amid the technology boom. Many investors looking at the stock's falling market value figured the company would come back. They kept thinking that as the stock fell to $75, $65, and $55. But it didn't come back. The stock collapsed to $2.34, the price at which rival Alcatel offered to buy it in 2006. Note that even when you're using fundamental analysis, you're making a bet that the market is mispricing a company. If you're wrong, you need to be prepared to either be very patient or protect yourself against an extreme downside by selling before losses become devastating.

Chapter **4**

Getting Your Hands on Fundamental Data

B y now, your financial calculator or spreadsheet is probably fired up and ready to start crunching down fundamental data. There's just one little problem: You need to get the data first.

Here's the good news. Getting your hands on financial data has never been easier, so there's never been a better time to be a fundamental analyst. You're able to get data faster, at less cost, and with less technical expertise than ever before. The ability to obtain financial data almost immediately from companies — and for free — allows fundamental analysts to closely monitor how a company is doing.

This chapter shows you what types of fundamental data companies provide to investors, what form they come in, and when you can expect to get them. You'll also get a quick refresher on accounting basics you'll need in order to understand what's contained in the reports when they land. Finally, this chapter shows you how to obtain financial data, including a detailed look at the treasure trove of fundamental data provided by the nation's top financial cop, the Securities and Exchange Commission, or SEC.

Getting in Sync with the Fundamental Calendar

Companies you can invest in don't get to decide whether or not to give you their financial information. It's not a choice — it's an obligation. Honestly, that's a good thing. Just imagine how haphazard it would be if companies could choose what and when they'd tell their investors how they're doing. What if companies just weren't in the mood to report their revenue or earnings in a quarter? If a retailer had a bad holiday selling season, for instance, it could tell investors, "Sorry, we're not going to tell you how we did." Such *selective disclosure* would be the corporate version of letting your kids only bring report cards home if they got all A's.

In reality, publicly traded companies agree to be somewhat *transparent.* Transparency is a popular buzzword in business, and it's a noble goal. To be transparent, companies must adhere to strict rules about what financial information they disclose, and they must even meet strict deadlines in getting fundamental data to investors. This goes for nearly all *publicly traded companies,* or those that sell ownership stakes of themselves to the general public. Similarly, when companies borrow money from the public, they too, must disclose their financial results to the public.

REMEMBER

By taking the public's money, companies agree to give investors quarterly updates on their financial condition and progress. Access to current and accurate fundamental data is one of your most basic rights when you either invest in or lend money to a company.

Which companies must report their financials to the public?

Just about any company you can invest in must follow financial reporting rules. That includes companies that are publicly traded, as explained earlier. But even some private companies, which haven't sold stock, must provide some financial information if they have $10 million or more in assets and have 500 or more owners.

Most major stock market exchanges, including the New York Stock Exchange (NYSE) and Nasdaq, require their listed companies to provide quarterly and annual financial reports to investors. That includes foreign companies with shares of stock that trade on either exchange.

NO DATA IS BAD DATA

If a company claims to be publicly traded but doesn't provide financial information, be highly skeptical. The lack of financial information is especially critical when dealing with stocks that trade on the lightly regulated markets known as the *OTC Pink* or *OTC Bulletin Board*. The OTC Pink market is often nicknamed the Pink Sheets.

Unlike regulated exchanges, like the New York Stock Exchange and Nasdaq, stocks that trade on the OTC Pink are not required to provide any financial information to investors. You read that right. These companies may even have ticker symbols but never disclose how much they made or even how much revenue they generated. Most of the stocks on these markets are lightly regulated, if at all. Companies that trade on the OTC Bulletin Board must disclose current financial statements but are exempt from other investor protections such as market value minimums.

The lack of financial Information is a huge reason why investors, especially those who rely on fundamental analysis, are often best served by avoiding stocks that trade on the OTC Bulletin Board or OTC Pink. These markets are infamous hangouts for so-called *penny stocks*. These stocks, which generally trade for a few pennies, are often just a name and little else. Sometimes penny-stock companies claim to have products and a management team, but don't actually generate any money to speak of. Penny stocks are popular with speculators, who like to talk up a shell company's prospects, get investors excited enough to buy in, and then dump the shares for a quick profit.

TECHNICAL STUFF

Some private companies offering generous stock option programs to employees often find themselves eventually having to start filing financial reports. Internet search company Google, for instance, was private for roughly six years after it was founded in 1998. The company quickly hit the $10 million threshold for total assets, meaning it was required to provide financial statements. At that time, Google decided it might as well become publicly traded and sell shares to investors in an IPO (initial public offering) because it was going to have to report its financial statements. Google launched its IPO in August 2004.

Kicking it all off: Earnings season

Sports fans wait all year for the beginning of football, basketball, or baseball season. Children can't help but anticipate the holiday season. But it's *earnings season* that fundamental analysts look forward to.

Four times a year, shortly after the end of the quarter, companies will begin to report their financial results to investors. Because most companies report on a calendar year, the results generally start trickling out in the second week after the quarter ends. Four times a year, usually in January, April, July, and October, thousands of companies report their financial results en masse. These times of year are called *earnings season.*

Aluminum maker Alcoa earned the unofficial designation as the company to kick off earnings season. (Alcoa's ticker symbol is AA, which is the symbolic reason for its place as first to report.) The company's advanced accounting system allows it to close its books very rapidly following the end of the quarter. Alcoa for years was the first stock in the storied Dow Jones Industrial Average to report its earnings each quarter. Alcoa was kicked out of the Dow by sports apparel giant Nike in 2013, but even to this day many investors see Alcoa's report as the start of earnings season.

Not all companies report on a calendar year. For instance, retailers generally bring in a large percentage of their sales each year during December. For that reason, many retailers close their books at the end of January, to give them time to tally up their performance in December and give a full report for the year. When a company ends its year in a month other than December for accounting purposes, it's called a *fiscal year.*

Getting the earnings press release

You don't have to be a journalist to appreciate the *earnings press release.* Contrary to its name, the earnings press release is for all investors, not just the media. When it's time for a company to tell the world how it did after the quarter ends, the first move is to issue an earnings press release. The press release is usually, but not always, accompanied by a conference call for investors and analysts. During the call, the management team goes over the quarter or year, describes the information in the earnings press release, and answers questions from the analysts who cover the company's stock for research and investment firms.

When you read or hear a company reported its financial results, the information almost always comes from the company's earnings press release. While earnings press releases are technically unofficial and preliminary, they're usually accurate enough for investors, analysts, and the news media to use the numbers immediately. It's important to remember, though, that the earnings press release is not reviewed by an accountant or auditor.

When companies issue an earnings press release, they often notify the regulators by filing a form *8-K.* The 8-K filing is the official way to signal to the world that the company has released critical information.

REMEMBER

Regulators do not directly stipulate what companies must say in earnings press releases. But generally, earnings press releases contain several key parts:

» **Summary of the results:** Most earnings press releases give the numbers investors want most right at the top, maybe even in the headline. That includes the revenue and earnings the company generated during the quarter and how much it grew (or shrunk) from the same quarter last year.

Be leery when a company brags about a quarter being a "record" quarter. Even if a company's revenue rose to a record amount, its costs may have also run out of control and eaten into its earnings.

» **Management comment:** A member of the management team usually opines on how the quarter went. As you might imagine, these statements are generally very carefully crafted, overly optimistic, and not particularly useful.

» **Description of major business events during the year:** Companies may break down — and even provide succinct bullet points — of the major accomplishments during the period.

» **Guidance for the future:** Most companies often provide *earnings guidance,* or an estimate on how much the company might earn in the upcoming year or quarter. This guidance is important because it lets you know what the company expects in the near future.

» **Financial statements:** The earnings press release is the first glimpse investors get of the company's income statement and balance sheet. These statements are among the most critical documents for fundamental data you'll get.

TIP

It's a good idea, when reading an earnings press release, to bypass most everything except the financial statements. While earnings press releases are intended to be honest representations of a company's performance, companies use the first parts of the earnings press release to put their performance in the best light. In contrast, the financial statements are the purest and least-biased parts of the press release.

Bracing for the 10-Q

Following the earnings press release, the next document to trickle out from the company is the *10-Q*. The 10-Q is the official financial report submitted by a company to summarize its performance during the quarter.

Most companies have 40 days from the end of each fiscal quarter to produce and provide the 10-Q to investors. Generally, companies file the 10-Q a week or two after they provide the earnings press release. You can see the deadlines for the key financial documents in Table 4-1. Details about the 10-K are in the next section, "Running through the 10-K." (Find more information at `www.investor.gov/introduction-investing/investing-basics/glossary/form-10-q.`)

TABLE 4-1

Filing Deadlines for Key Documents

Type of Company	10-K Deadline	10-Q Deadline
Most large firms	75 days after quarter	40 days
Small firms (less than $75 million in market value traded)	90 days	45 days

Source: Securities and Exchange Commission

TIP

Both the earnings press release and 10-Q serve the same basic purpose: They tell investors how the company did, financially, during the quarter. But because the 10-Q is written primarily to satisfy regulatory requirements, it's usually much more straightforward and contains less spin.

The 10-Q must be filed with the chief regulator of the financial markets, the SEC. As a result, companies are careful to include the following key components:

>> **Financial statements:** Companies don't waste any time getting straight to the point with the 10-Q. The key financial statements are presented right at the top, whereas they're usually at the bottom of earnings press releases.

REMEMBER

Don't make the mistake of assuming because you read the earnings press release, you don't need to bother with the 10-Q. The 10-Q goes into greater detail than the press release, not because companies feel like spilling the beans, but because these documents are filed with regulators. For instance, a vast majority of companies don't include a statement of cash flows in the earnings press release. The statement of cash flows, however, must be included in the 10-Q. The statement of cash flows is an extremely important document used in financial analysis.

>> **Footnotes:** Just as some books just don't fit correctly in your bookshelf, some financial information doesn't slip nicely into the financial statements. Unusual or noteworthy financial events may require more description than will fit into the financial statements, and those are available in the footnotes in the 10-Q.

REMEMBER

Never skip the footnotes. Companies will often throw items in the footnotes, hoping you'll miss them as an investor. Remember Enron, the energy company that failed in 2001, that was one of the biggest corporate frauds in U.S. history? The company stuffed much of the information about its cryptic partnerships in the footnotes.

>> **Management's discussion and analysis of financial condition:** This section of the 10-Q is usually called the MD&A. In the MD&A, management steps investors through its financial results for the quarter. The narrative is usually stripped down and, well, straightforward because executives know the SEC will review it. So they don't want to say anything that may haunt them later.

>> **Controls and procedures:** The company will let investors know if they found any problems in the way they monitor their accounting and present the information to investors. Following the accounting scandal at Enron, new rules from the Sarbanes-Oxley Act of 2002 forced companies to make sure they had adequate controls in place over their accounting. Many companies fought tooth-and-nail to avoid these rules. You might as well read them.

>> **Other information:** Here, companies can throw in other material that may be of note to investors. This may include any pending litigation, whether the company sold additional stock, or if it's having trouble paying interest on its debt.

Many investors don't realize a company's 10-Q is not officially audited by a third-party accounting firm. That doesn't mean you can't necessarily trust the numbers; just know a little more skepticism isn't a bad idea.

Running through the 10-K

If you've ever run a 10-K race, you know that it can be pretty grueling if you haven't trained properly. The same goes for companies looking to report their annual financial performance in the form called the 10-K. This document is a monster, and producing it is one of the biggest financial chores a company faces. It's also the most comprehensive piece of fundamental data you can get as an investor. Most companies are required to release their 10-K filings within 75 days from the end of their fiscal year. Some smaller companies, though, have 90 days to comply with the rules.

Due to the complexity of producing a 10-K, there can be a significant delay between the end of the calendar year and the time the report gets released.

The 10-K is kind of like a company's annual review. The level of detail of the 10-K is exhaustive, and unless you know what you're looking for, it's easy to get lost in the hundreds of pages of tables and text. That's why fundamental analysts rarely curl up with a 10-K and read it from start to finish like a novel. They just know how to skip around in a 10-K and look for these key elements:

>> **Everything in the 10-Q, but for the whole year:** All the data you get in the 10-Q for the quarter, you get for the year in the 10-K. That includes not only the financial statements and legal proceedings, but also, a more expanded

MD&A where the management team explains more fully how the year progressed. The controls and procedures section may also be more fleshed out, because the 10-K has been checked over by the auditors.

>> **Changes in accounting and disagreements with accountants:** You may not expect to see conflict and intrigue in a company's financial report, but sometimes you can find it here. Companies and their accountants will state in this section whether or not they saw eye to eye on financial reporting matters.

>> **Long-term financial data:** Companies give you the financial results for the year that just ended. But you'll also find data for the past three, five, or even ten years. These data are very useful when looking for *trends,* or changes in fundamentals like revenue and earnings.

>> **Business summary:** Here, the company lays out the nitty-gritty of what it does for a living. The company may break down its major business units and even, in some cases, tell you which parts of the business are the most profitable.

>> **Risk factors:** Imagine showing up to pick up a date, but before you leave for the movies, they sit you down with a huge list of everything that's wrong with themselves. That would save quite a bit of time. Yet that's precisely what companies must do in their 10-Ks. If there's a known factor that could impair a company's fundamentals, the company is required to tell you about it here.

>> **Auditor's opinion:** Close to the bottom of the 10-K, the accountants need to sign off on the books to indicate they reasonably reflect the financial condition of the firm.

TIP

When reviewing a 10-K, always read the auditor's opinion. The statement from the auditor can be telling. While an auditor may not wave a red flag and tell you not to buy stock, you can read between the lines. For instance, if you see language like "except for" or "subject to," watch out. That means the auditor has some issues with the way the books are kept, so you should too. (This statement is called a *qualified opinion.*) Also, be careful when an auditor issues a *going concern* qualification. That's accounting talk for "This company might not make it."

Flipping through the annual report

If you visit a CEO's office, you might see the annual report sitting on the coffee table. Some companies' annual reports are gorgeous, well, as much as financial documents can be. The annual report is essentially the 10-K, but formatted like a magazine. There might be lovely photos of smiling executives, employees, and customers. Even the financial statements are given a facelift, usually printed on luxurious paper using an elegant font or in a fancy website. The annual report is usually released several months after the 10-K is published, often landing around the time companies have their shareholders' meetings.

ANNUAL REPORTS: A CORPORATE BEAUTY CONTEST

Some companies go to great expense creating visually stunning annual reports. Some truly are wonders of publishing, putting some magazines to shame. Surfwear maker Quiksilver, for instance, for years produced annual reports containing full-color photos of surfers, exotic beaches, and colorful surfboards. By contrast, Warren Buffett's Berkshire Hathaway's annual report is a boring-looking document with no photos, but packed with wisdom and worth a read even if you don't own the stock. There doesn't appear to be any connection with the beauty of an annual report and company performance. Quiksilver actually filed for bankruptcy protection in 2015.

Beautiful annual reports, however, seem to be as much of an anachronism as beauty pageants. Increasingly, companies are taking the cheap way out by producing *10-K wraps* instead of full-fledged annual reports. 10-K wraps are usually a short six-page brochure with some words from the CEO and a few photos. The boring old annual report is then stapled inside. Thinning annual reports is a growing trend as companies look to cut costs — and as more companies put this information online.

TIP

Unlike the 10-Q and 10-K, which you can download directly from the SEC's website, the annual report is obtained directly from the company either through the mail in paper form or on the company's website. If you call a company, it will usually be happy to mail you a copy. You can also usually view an electronic form of the paper annual report by downloading it from the company's website.

Companies produce the annual report mainly to hand out to employees and customers while courting them.

The annual report is the management team's opportunity to put its spin on how the year went. Most annual reports, for instance, begin with a letter to shareholders that is generally very hopeful, even after a dismal year.

There's no proxy like the proxy statement

If you're looking for the most salacious statement released by companies, that must be the *proxy statement*. The proxy statement is a document the SEC requires companies to distribute to shareholders ahead of the annual shareholder meeting. It's kind of like the absentee ballot you might get prior to a presidential election.

Shareholder meetings happen every year as companies gather shareholders, usually in the spring, to go over their initiatives and goals. The proxy is sometimes known by its regulatory name, *14A*, named after the portion of the SEC rules that stipulate what it must contain.

The proxy statement is fascinating reading because it lays out all the most sensitive information most companies have to offer, including

>> **Executive compensation:** Want to find out how much a CEO gets paid? The proxy is your document. Not only are the annual salaries of the top executives spelled out, but the amounts of their bonuses, too.

>> **Corporate matters subject to a vote:** Companies' proxies contain a section that looks almost like a ballot. There will be a number of measures that require shareholder approval. Usually, the items up for a vote include the selection of the auditing firm and the board members standing for reelection on the board.

>> **Shareholder proposals:** If a company has any ill will with shareholders, it will become very clear in the proxy. Dissident shareholders may offer proposals to replace the management team. Other investors might lobby for the company to adopt more socially responsible business practices.

>> **Related-party transactions:** This part shows whether any of the company's officers or directors have business relationships with it. Individuals that have business relationships with the company, in theory, may have trouble being impartial because there's a potential conflict of interest.

Getting Up to Speed with Basic Accounting and Math

Even if you hated math in high school and avoided accounting in college, you can still put fundamental analysis to use. The more you dig into the financials of companies and see how math and accounting can help you, who knows, maybe you'll get curious to learn more. And if that's the case, you might look into *Business Math For Dummies* by Mary Jane Sterling or *Accounting For Dummies* by John A. Tracy and Tage C. Tracy (both published by Wiley).

But here, this section gives you the basics of what you need to know about the concept of accounting. You'll see that accounting is really just a way to condense millions of individual business transactions down to a form that makes it possible for you to analyze.

REMEMBER

When you're studying financial statements, just remember there are three primary functions of business you're trying to analyze: *operating activities, investing activities,* and *financing activities.*

Operating activities: Finding smooth operators

A company's operations get the most attention. Typically, when you hear a company is or isn't "doing well," that is a reference to the firm's operating activities.

Simply stated, a company's operations are the process of converting raw materials into products that are, hopefully, sold to customers for a profit. Many elements go into operations, including effective new product development, which generates revenue, in addition to cost control, marketing, and manufacturing. The income statement lets you see how well a company is operating.

Investing activities: You have to spend money to make money

Unless they've found a goose that lays platinum eggs, all companies, at some point, must put money back into their business. Equipment used to make products wears out and needs to be replaced. Companies outgrow their headquarters and must acquire a bigger building. It's common for companies to overhaul their computer systems to keep up with tracking their business.

REMEMBER

When companies spend money to make more money, they're *investing* in their future. And while investing is a necessary part of doing business, it can also be done poorly. Companies might spend too much for equipment they didn't need. Or worse, they might overexpand, resulting in a glut of their product, which hurts their profits. There are two key things for a fundamental analyst to monitor when it comes to investment:

>> **Is the return on the investment adequate?** If a company is spending money to expand, and revenue and profit aren't growing too, you may be throwing your money down the drain as an investor.

>> **Is the company using the equipment it has bought?** In business, having too much capacity is not a good idea. You don't want to spend money renting a warehouse, for instance, if it's usually empty.

Financing activities: Getting in tune with high finance

So, you can understand how a company operates and how much it's investing in itself. But who's going to pay for all this stuff? That's the final and critical element that accounting helps you with.

Generally speaking, companies can *finance,* or fund their operations, in two ways. They can either rustle up investors, or they can borrow money. Investors provide money, called *equity capital,* to companies in exchange for a piece of the company. If all goes well, the company operates extremely well, profits soar, and investors are very happy because their share of the company will be worth more. When you buy stock in a company, you are an investor.

Selling stock is a great way for companies to raise money. The company sells the stock and the investors hand over cash. But selling stock can be costly in the long run, especially if the company does well. When the profits come pouring in — the original owners must share the profits with the shareholders.

To avoid having to share ownership of the company, some companies may look to borrow money instead. Companies may borrow money from a local bank or sell IOUs, called *bonds* or *notes,* to the public. Investors who lend money to a company simply want to get their money back, plus an amount of interest agreed upon ahead of time. If the company winds up doing fabulously well, the lenders only get the pre-agreed-upon interest payments and not a penny more. The drawbacks, though, are that borrowers demand market interest rates, and companies must pay on time or the company could go into *default*. Default is when a company can no longer afford to pay the interest on its debt and can lead to a company's filing for bankruptcy protection or even *liquidating,* or selling off all its assets.

REMEMBER

If a company defaults, investors and lenders are treated very differently. The difference has a big influence on whether or not you decide to buy a company's stock or bonds. If a company is unable to keep paying interest to its lenders, the company goes into default. Typically, at that point, the bondholders take control of the company. In the worst-case scenario, when a company cannot be saved, bondholders get repaid first. So, say a company defaulted and had a giant garage sale to sell its desks and chairs. The money would be used to pay back debt holders before stock investors see a penny. That means, as a stock investor, you're accepting the possibility that you can lose your entire investment.

Undestanding a key fundamental math skill: Percentage changes

There's one math skill that you'll encounter so frequently in fundamental analysis, you might as well tackle it now. That's the concept of *percentage change.* Because fundamental analysis is infatuated with looking at increases and decreases in business factors, such as *sales* and *revenues,* the percentage change is a way to put gains and declines into context. For instance, If we told you that the price of a sweater rose $40 this year, that wouldn't tell you much. But if we told you the price was $60 before, then you'd know that the price jumped 66.7 percent to $100.

REMEMBER

You calculate a percentage change this way:

([New number – old number] ÷ old number) × 100

Going back to the sweater example, the new price is $100 and the old price was $60, so the math is as follows:

([100 – 60] ÷ 60) × 100 = 66.7%

TIP

For those of you who don't think parentheses and math belong together, here's a mantra to help you remember it: "New minus old divided by old." If you like the mantra better, follow these steps:

1. **"New minus old": Subtract the new number by the old one.**

   That's 100 minus 60, or 40.

2. **"Divide by old": Take the answer from step 1 and divide by the old number.**

   Divide the 40 you got from step 1 by the old number, 60. That's 0.667.

3. **Convert to a percentage.**

   Take the answer from step 2 and multiply by 100. That gives you a 66.7 percent increase in this example.

REMEMBER

If a value rises by 100 percent, then it has doubled. Similarly, if a number rises by 200 percent, it has tripled, and 300 percent, quadrupled. Some make the mistake, for instance, of seeing the 2 in the 200 percent and saying it has doubled when it has in fact, tripled.

Knowing How to Get the Fundamental Data You Need

You might have the fastest car in the neighborhood, but if you don't have any gas, you're not going to get far. So goes fundamental analysis. You might build the fanciest financial spreadsheet, but it's not going to do you any good if you don't have the raw financial numbers to put in it.

Until the dawn of the internet, getting fundamental data could be a real hassle. You would have to call or write a company and ask it to mail — yes, mail — its 10-K, 10-Q, and annual report to you.

Thankfully, the days of having to deal strictly with paper financial statements are over. But the skills of the fundamental analyst must keep up with the electronic age. In this section, you find out how to quickly, and at no cost, get your hands on the fundamental data you need to complete your analysis.

Getting acquainted with the SEC's database

You can spend thousands of dollars for access to websites that provide fundamental data. But really, to get started, you don't have to spend a dime.

TIP

The SEC's website at www.sec.gov is a treasure trove for fundamental analysis. You'll find all the financial forms discussed in this chapter, and then some. All the fundamental data are stored in the SEC's *Electronic Data Gathering, Analysis and Retrieval,* or EDGAR, database. You can use EDGAR to look up any public company's filings and even download the financial statements to your computer so you can do further analysis.

Accessing company fundamentals using EDGAR

When you know how powerful EDGAR is, it's time to dive in and discover how to get what you need from it. The following example shows you how to get the 10-Q, 10-K, and proxy statement for General Electric. Just follow these steps:

1. Log into the SEC's website at www.sec.gov.

2. Click the Filings tab on the upper right-hand corner of the page. Then click the Company Filings link from the drop-down menu.

3. **Enter the name of the company in the Company and Person Lookup blank.**

   It's the first blank in the top page. Type in "general electric" for this example. If you know the company's symbol, GE in this example, you can enter that in the blank.

4. **Click the Search button.**

5. **Choose the company name.**

   Because General Electric has separate business units, you'll see companies like General Electric Capital Assurance Co. But you want the main company, so click on the red numbers to the left of where it says General Electric Co.

6. **Click on the form you want.**

   If you want GE's 10-Q, scroll down until you see the form 10-Q listed and click on the Documents button. If you want the 10-K, choose 10-K, and the proxy is marked as 14-A. You'll be taken to a page outlining everything contained in that filing. (You may need to click the Next 40 button to find the forms you want.)

7. **Click on the red code under the document column in the first line.**

   This line should have the form under the Type head, which in this case is the 10-Q. When you're downloading the 10-K, the line should read 10-K.

TECHNICAL STUFF

When you're scrolling down through the list of forms, you might notice that some have a blue button that says Interactive Data. These forms are presented in a special format that computers can read, called *eXtensive Business Reporting Language* or XBRL. Financial statements available in XBRL can be easily processed and downloaded. XBRL also lets you easily download the financial statements to a spreadsheet. Because it's not required to file using XBRL, only a few companies do. But that's changing.

TIP

Most of the major web portals, such as Yahoo!, at finance.yahoo.com, and MSN, at money.msn.com, provide summaries of companies' primary financial statements. Most companies, too, put their financial data on their websites. But as a fundamental analyst, it's important to know how to get the data direct from the source: the SEC's EDGAR database.

Finding stocks' dividend histories

Dividends are periodic cash payments some companies make to their shareholders. The dividends are paid out of the company's cash as a way of returning profits to the shareholders. Dividends are a very important piece of your total return on an investment.

REMEMBER

Don't ignore dividends. These cash payments, over time, account for about one-third of the total return investors make on the market, according to Standard & Poor's. The remaining two-thirds of total return come from the stock price rising. During difficult times for the stock market, when stock prices fall, the dividends may be the only gains you get. Dividends are also important ways to help value a company. Companies that pay dividends generally pay them quarterly.

The best way to look up a dividend history is on the company's website. Nearly all companies provide an area of their websites where dividend payment histories can be looked up. You can navigate to the dividend history by finding the *investor relations* section of a company's website. Going back to the GE example, go to www.ge.com and click on the "Investors" link at the top of the page. Next, scroll down to click on the Stock link. Scroll down again and you'll find GE's Historical Dividends, which lists GE's dividend payments.

Getting stock-split information

Money for nothing is hard to find on Wall Street. But sometimes investors get additional shares — well, sort of. When a company's stock price rises dramatically and begins to approach $50 a share or more, the executives may decide to split the shares. In a stock split, the company cuts its share price, say in half, by cutting the shares into multiple shares. For instance, say you own 100 shares in a stock trading for $60 a share. If the company has a 2-for-1 split, you will suddenly have 200 shares, but they'll be worth $30 apiece. Management feels some investors are more likely to buy stock in a company for $30 a share than $60.

The theory goes that some naïve investors, who read too much into a stock's per-share price, may assume a stock trading for $50 or more is too expensive.

WARNING

Some investors assume that a stock split is a major boon because they suddenly have more shares. But, as discussed in Chapter 3 of Book 7, the per-share price of a stock doesn't tell you much. The value of your shares is still $6,000, whether you own 100 shares at $60 or 200 shares at $30 a share. The company's market value also stays the same.

Understanding when stock splits occur is important for fundamental analysis, though, because it affects the number of shares outstanding, which is described in Chapter 3 of Book 7. You'll need an accurate count of shares outstanding to do some of the fundamental analysis later in the book.

Fortunately, many companies provide stock-split histories on their websites. But not all do — and you may want to look up stock splits at multiple companies without navigating to several investor relations websites. That's where other online tools can help you find when splits happened and how many shares were affected.

TIP

Yahoo! Finance helps you look up if, and when, a company split its shares. Here's how:

1. Visit `finance.yahoo.com`.

2. Enter the name of the company or symbol in the blank at the top of the page and click on the name of the company.

For GE, for instance, enter GE and click the General Electric link.

3. Click on the Historical Data link near the top of the page.

4. In the Show: menu, choose Stock Splits and click the Apply button.

5. You get a list of recent stock splits.

In this example, the list tells you that GE last split its stock, by 1:8, on August 2, 2021.

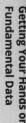

Investing in Real Estate

Contents at a Glance

Chapter **1**

Evaluating Real Estate as an Investment

I t's never too early or too late to formulate your own plan for a comprehensive wealth-building strategy. For many, such a strategy can help with the goals of funding future education for children and ensuring a comfortable retirement.

The challenge involved with real estate is that it takes some real planning to get started. Contacting an investment company and purchasing some shares of your favorite mutual fund or stock is a lot easier than acquiring your first rental property. Buying property need not be too difficult, though. With a financial and real estate investment plan, a lot of patience, and the willingness to do some hard work, you can be on your way to building your own real estate empire!

This chapter gives you information that can help you decide whether you have what it takes to make money *and* be comfortable with investing in real estate. It compares real estate investments to other investments. It provides some questions you should ask yourself before making any decisions. And finally, this chapter offers guidance on how real estate investments can fit into your overall personal financial plans. Along the way, you get insights and thoughts on a long-term strategy for building wealth through real estate that virtually everyone can understand and actually achieve.

Understanding Real Estate's Income- and Wealth-Producing Potential

Compared with most other investments, good real estate can excel at producing periodic or monthly cash flow for property owners. So in addition to the longer-term appreciation potential, you can also earn investment income year in and year out. Real estate is a true growth *and* income investment.

The following list highlights the major benefits of investing in real estate:

>> **Tax-deferred compounding of value:** In real estate investing, the appreciation of your properties compounds *tax-deferred* during your years of ownership. You don't pay tax on this profit until you sell your property — and even then, you can roll over your gain into another investment property and avoid paying taxes. (See the later section "Being aware of the tax advantages.")

>> **Regular cash flow:** If you have property that you rent out, you have money coming in every month in the form of rents. Some properties, particularly larger multi-unit complexes, may have some additional sources, such as from parking, storage, or washers and dryers.

REMEMBER

When you own investment real estate, you should also expect to incur expenses that include your mortgage payment, property taxes, insurance, and maintenance. The interaction of the revenues coming in and the expenses going out is what tells you whether you realize a positive operating profit each month.

>> **Reduced income tax bills:** For income tax purposes, you also get to claim an expense that isn't really an out-of-pocket cost — depreciation. Depreciation enables you to reduce your current income tax bill and hence increase your cash flow from a property. (The later section "Being aware of the tax advantages" explains this tax advantage and others.)

>> **Rate of increase of rental income versus overall expenses:** Over time, your operating profit, which is subject to ordinary income tax, should rise as you increase your rental prices faster than the rate of increase for your property's overall expenses. What follows is a simple example to show why even modest rental increases are magnified into larger operating profits and healthy returns on investment over time.

Suppose that you're in the market to purchase a single-family home that you want to rent out and that such properties are selling for about $200,000 in the area you've deemed to be a good investment. (*Note:* Housing prices vary widely across different areas, but the following example should give you a relative sense of how a rental property's expenses and revenue change over time.) You expect to make a 20 percent down payment and take out a 30-year fixed rate mortgage at 6 percent for the remainder of the purchase price — $160,000. Here are the details:

Monthly mortgage payment	$960
Monthly property tax	$200
Other monthly expenses (maintenance, insurance)	$200
Monthly rent	$1,400

Table 1-1 shows you what happens with your investment over time. You can assume that your rent and expenses (except for your mortgage payment, which is fixed) increase 3 percent annually and that your property appreciates a conservative 4 percent per year. (For simplification purposes, this example ignores depreciation. If the benefit of depreciation had been included, it would further enhance the calculated investment returns.)

TABLE 1-1　　**How a Rental Property's Income and Wealth Build Over Time**

Year	Monthly Rent	Monthly Expenses	Property Value	Mortgage Balance
0	$1,400	$1,360	$200,000	$160,000
5	$1,623	$1,424	$243,330	$148,960
10	$1,881	$1,498	$296,050	$133,920
20	$2,529	$1,682	$438,225	$86,400
30	$3,398	$1,931	$648,680	$0
31	$3,500	$1,000	$674,625	$0

Now, notice what happens over time. When you first buy the property, the monthly rent and the monthly expenses are about equal. By year five, the monthly income exceeds the expenses by about $200 per month. Consider why this happens — your largest monthly expense, the mortgage payment, doesn't increase. So, even though the rent increases just 3 percent per year, which is the same rate of increase assumed for your nonmortgage expenses, the compounding of rental inflation begins to produce larger and larger cash flows to you, the property owner. Cash flow of $200 per month may not sound like much, but consider that this $2,400 annual income is from an original $40,000 investment. Thus, by year five, your rental property is producing a 6 percent return on your down payment investment. (And if you factor in the tax deduction for depreciation, your cash flow and return are even higher.)

In addition to the monthly cash flow from the amount that the rent exceeds the property's expenses, also look at the last two columns in Table 1-1 to see what has happened by year five to your *equity* (the difference between market value and mortgage balance owed) in the property. With just a 4 percent annual increase in market value, your $40,000 in equity (the down payment) has more than doubled to $94,370 ($243,330 − $148,960).

By years 10 and 20, you can see the further increases in your monthly cash flow and significant expansion in your property's equity. By year 30, the property is producing more than $1,400 per month cash flow and you're now the proud owner of a mortgage-free property worth more than triple what you paid for it!

After you get the mortgage paid off in year 30, take a look at what happens in year 31 and beyond to your monthly expenses (big drop as your monthly mortgage payment disappears!) and therefore your cash flow (big increase).

Recognizing the Caveats of Real Estate Investing

Despite all its potential, real estate investing isn't lucrative at all times and for all people — here's a quick outline of the biggest caveats that accompany investing in real estate:

>> **Few home runs:** Your likely returns from real estate won't approach the biggest home runs that the most accomplished entrepreneurs achieve in the business world. That said, by doing your homework, improving properties, and practicing good management (and sometimes enjoying a bit of luck), you can do extremely well!

WARNING

>> **Up-front operating profit challenges:** Unless you make a large down payment, your monthly operating profit may be small, nonexistent, or negative in the early years of rental property ownership. During soft periods in the local economy, rents may rise more slowly than your expenses or they may even fall. That's why you must ensure that you can weather financially

tough times. In the worst cases, rental property owners lose both their investment property and their homes. See the later section "Fitting Real Estate into Your Plans."

» **Ups and downs:** You're not going to earn an 8 to 10 percent return every year. Although you have the potential for significant profits, owning real estate isn't like owning a printing press at the U.S. Treasury. Like stocks (see Book 3) and other types of ownership investments, real estate goes through down periods as well as up periods. Most people who make money investing in real estate do so because they invest and hold property over many years.

» **Relatively high transaction costs:** If you buy a property and then want out a year or two later, you may find that even though it has appreciated in value, much (if not all) of your profit has been wiped away by the high transaction costs. Typically, the costs of buying and selling — which include real estate agent commissions, loan fees, title insurance, and other closing costs — amount to about 8 to 12 percent of the purchase price of a property. So, although you may be elated if your property appreciates 10 percent in value in short order, you may not be so thrilled to realize that if you sell the property, you may not have any greater return than if you had stashed your money in a lowly bank account.

» **Tax implications:** Last, but not least, when you make a positive net return or profit on your real estate investment, the federal and state governments are waiting with open hands for their share. The profit you have left after government entities take their bites (not your pretax income) is what really matters.

REMEMBER

These drawbacks shouldn't keep you from exploring real estate investing as an option; rather, they simply reinforce the need to really know what you're getting into with this type of investing and whether it's a good match for you. The vast majority of people who don't make money in real estate make easily avoidable mistakes. The rest of this chapter takes you deeper into an assessment of real estate as an investment as well as introspection about your goals, interests, and abilities.

Comparing Real Estate to Other Investments

Surely, you've considered or heard about many different investments over the years. To help you grasp and understand the unique characteristics of real estate, the following sections compare and contrast real estate's attributes with those of other wealth-building investments like stocks and small business.

Returns

Clearly, a major reason that many people invest in real estate is for the healthy total *returns* (which include ongoing cash flow and the appreciation of the property). Real estate often generates robust long-term returns because, like stocks and small business, it's an *ownership investment.* This means that real estate is an asset that has the ability to produce periodic income *and* gains or profits upon refinancing or sale.

Total real estate investment returns are comparable to those from stocks — about 8 to 9 percent on average, annually. Over recent decades, the average annual return on real estate investment trusts (REITs), publicly traded companies that invest in income-producing real estate such as apartment buildings, office complexes, and shopping centers, has appreciated at about this pace as well.

And you can earn long-term returns that average much better than 10 percent per year if you select excellent properties in the best areas, hold them for several years, and manage them well.

Risk

Real estate doesn't always rise in value — witness the decline occurring in most parts of the U.S. during the late 2000s and early 2010s. That said, market values for real estate generally don't suffer from as much volatility as stock prices do. You may recall how the excitement surrounding the rapid sustained increase of technology and internet stock prices in the late 1990s turned into the dismay and agony of those same sectors' stock prices crashing in the early 2000s. Many stocks in this industry, including those of leaders in their niches, saw their stock prices plummet by 80 percent, 90 percent, or more. Generally, you don't see those kinds of dramatic roller-coaster shifts in values over the short run with the residential income property real estate market.

However, keep in mind (especially if you tend to be concerned about shorter-term risks) that real estate can suffer from declines of 10 percent, 20 percent, or more. If you make a down payment of, say, 20 percent and want to sell your property after a 10 to 15 percent price decline, you may find that all (as in 100 percent) of your invested dollars (down payment) are wiped out after you factor in transaction costs. So you can lose everything.

REMEMBER

You can greatly reduce and minimize your risk investing in real estate through buying and holding property for many years (seven to ten or more). Remember that many of these fantastic success stories about amazing profits on "flipping" single-family homes and small rental properties are just like gamblers who only tell you about their biggest winnings or forget to tell you that they turned around and lost much of what they won. While there is a lot of hype on cable television and the internet about "flipping properties" for crazy short-term profits, always think of real estate as a long-term investment.

Liquidity

Liquidity — the ease and cost with which you can sell and get your money out of an investment — is one of real estate's shortcomings. Real estate is relatively *illiquid:* You can't sell a piece of property with the same speed with which you can whip out your ATM card and withdraw money from your bank account or sell a stock or an exchange-traded fund with a click of your computer's mouse or by tapping on your smartphone.

REMEMBER

You may actually view real estate's relative illiquidity as a strength, certainly compared with stocks that people often trade in and out of because doing so is so easy and seemingly cheap. As a result, some stock market investors tend to lose sight of the long term and miss out on the bigger gains that accrue to patient buy-and-stick-with-it investors. Because you can't track the value of investment real estate daily on your computer, and because real estate takes considerable time, energy, and money to sell, you're far more likely to buy and hold onto your properties for the longer term.

Although real estate investments are generally less liquid than stocks, they're generally more liquid than investments made in your own or someone else's small business. People need a place to live and businesses need a place to operate, so there's always demand for real estate (although the supply of such available properties can greatly exceed the demand in some areas during certain time periods).

Capital requirements

Although you can easily get started with traditional investments such as stocks and mutual funds with a few hundred or thousand dollars, the vast majority of quality real estate investments require far greater investments — usually on the order of tens of thousands of dollars.

TIP

If you're one of the many people who don't have that kind of money, don't despair. Lower-cost real estate investment options do exist. Among the simplest low-cost real estate investment options are real estate investment trusts (REITs). You can buy these as exchange-traded stocks or invest in a portfolio of REITs through a REIT mutual fund.

Diversification value

An advantage of holding investment real estate is that its value doesn't necessarily move in tandem with other investments, such as stocks or small-business investments that you hold. You may recall, for example, the massive stock market decline in the early 2000s. In most communities around the United States, real estate values were either steady or actually rising during this horrendous period for stock prices.

However, real estate prices and stock prices, for example, *can* move down together in value (witness the severe recession and stock market drop that took hold in 2008). Sluggish business conditions and lower corporate profits can depress stock *and* real estate prices.

Opportunities to add value

Although you may not know much about investing in the stock market, you may have some good ideas about how to improve a property and make it more valuable. You can fix up a property or develop it further and raise the rental income accordingly. Perhaps through legwork, persistence, and good negotiating skills, you can purchase a property below its fair market value.

Relative to investing in the stock market, tenacious and savvy real estate investors can more easily buy property in the private real estate market at below fair market value because the real estate market is somewhat less efficient and some owners don't realize the value of their income property or they need to sell quickly. Theoretically, you can do the same in the stock market, but the scores of professional, full-time money managers who analyze the public market for stocks make finding bargains more difficult.

Being aware of the tax advantages

Real estate investment offers numerous tax advantages. This section compares and contrasts investment property tax issues with those of other investments.

Deductible expenses (including depreciation)

Owning a property has much in common with owning your own small business. Every year, you account for your income and expenses on a tax return. Be sure to keep good records of your expenses in purchasing and operating rental real estate. One expense that you get to deduct for rental real estate on your tax return — depreciation — doesn't actually involve spending or outlaying money. *Depreciation* is an allowable tax deduction for buildings because structures wear out over time. Under current tax laws, residential real estate is depreciated over 27½ years (commercial buildings are less favored in the tax code and can be depreciated over 39 years). Residential real estate is depreciated over shorter time periods because it has traditionally been a favored investment in our nation's tax laws.

Tax-free rollovers of rental property profits

When you sell a stock, mutual fund, or exchange-traded investment that you hold outside a retirement account, you must pay tax on your profits. By contrast, you can avoid paying tax on your profit when you sell a rental property if you roll over your gain into another like-kind investment real estate property.

REMEMBER

The rules for properly making one of these rollovers — called a 1031 exchange — are complex and involve third parties. Make sure that you find an attorney and/or tax advisor who is an expert at these transactions to ensure that you meet the technical and strict timing requirements so everything goes smoothly (and legally).

If you don't roll over your gain, you may owe significant taxes because of how the IRS defines your gain. For example, if you buy a property for $200,000 and sell it for $550,000, you not only owe tax on the gain from the increased property value, but you also owe tax on an additional amount, the property's depreciation you used during your ownership. The amount of depreciation that you deduct on your tax returns reduces the original $200,000 purchase price, making the taxable difference that much larger. For example, if you deducted $125,000 for depreciation over the years that you owned the property, you owe tax on the difference between the sale price of $550,000 and $75,000 ($200,000 purchase price – $125,000 depreciation).

Deferred taxes with installment sales

Installment sales are a complex method that can be used to defer your tax bill when you sell an investment property at a profit and you don't buy another rental property. With such a sale, you play the role of banker and provide financing to the buyer. In addition to often collecting a competitive interest rate from the buyer, you only have to pay capital gains tax as you receive proceeds over time from the sale that are applied toward the principal or price the buyer agreed to pay for the property.

Special tax credits for low-income housing and old buildings

If you invest in and upgrade low-income housing or certified historic buildings, you can gain special tax credits. The credits represent a direct reduction in your tax bill from expenditures to rehabilitate and improve such properties. These tax credits exist to encourage investors to invest in and fix up old or run-down buildings that likely would continue to deteriorate otherwise. The IRS has strict rules governing what types of properties qualify. See IRS Form 3468 to discover more about these credits (www.irs.gov/pub/irs-pdf/f3468.pdf).

The 2017 Tax Cuts and Jobs Act bill created "qualified opportunity zones" to provide tax incentives to invest in "low-income communities," which are defined by each state's governor and may comprise up to 25 percent of designated "low-income communities" in each state. (States can also designate census tracts contiguous with "low-income communities" so long as the median family income in those tracts doesn't exceed 125 percent of the qualifying contiguous "low-income community.")

The new qualified opportunity zone tax incentive allows real estate investors the following potential benefits:

>> The capital gains tax due upon a sale of the property is deferred if the capital gain from the sale is reinvested within 180 days in a qualified opportunity fund.

>> For investments in the qualified opportunity fund of at least five years, investors will receive a step-up in tax basis of 10 percent of the original gain.

>> For investments in the qualified opportunity fund of at least seven years, investors will receive an additional 5 percent step-up in tax basis.

>> For investments of ten or more years or earlier than December 31, 2026, investors can exclude all capital gains of the investment.

20 percent Qualified Business Income (QBI) deduction for "pass-through entities"

The 2017 Tax Cuts and Jobs Act includes lower across-the-board federal income tax rates, which benefit all wage earners and investors, including real estate investors. If you spend at least 250 hours per year on certain activities (defined in a moment) related to your real estate investments, you may also be able to utilize an additional tax break targeted to certain small business entities.

REMEMBER

In redesigning the tax code, Congress realized that the many small businesses that operate as so-called pass-through entities would be subjected to higher federal income tax rates compared with the 21 percent corporate income tax rate (reduced from 35 percent). Pass-through entities are small businesses such as sole proprietorships, LLCs, partnerships, and S corporations and are so named because the profits of the business *pass through* to the owners and their personal income tax returns.

To address the concern that individual business owners who operated their business as a pass-through entity could end up paying a higher tax rate than the 21 percent rate levied on C corporations, Congress provided a 20 percent Qualified Business Income (QBI) deduction for those businesses. So, for example, if your sole proprietorship netted you $60,000 in 2019 as a single taxpayer, that would push you into the 22 percent federal income tax bracket. But you get to deduct

20 percent of that $60,000 of income (or $12,000) so you would only owe federal income tax on the remaining $48,000 ($60,000 – $12,000).

Another way to look at this is that the business would only pay taxes on 80 percent of its profits and would be in the 22 percent federal income tax bracket. This deduction effectively reduces the 22 percent tax bracket to 17.6 percent.

This 20 percent pass-through QBI deduction gets phased out for service business owners (for example, lawyers, doctors, real estate agents, consultants, and so on) at single taxpayer incomes above $157,500 (up to $207,500) and for married couples filing jointly incomes over $315,000 (up to $415,000). For other types of businesses above these income thresholds, this deduction may be limited, so consult with your tax advisor.

The Internal Revenue Service has clarified that certain rental real estate investor entities are eligible for the QBI 20 percent pass-through deduction in a given tax year if the following conditions are met:

>> Separate books and records are maintained to reflect income and expenses for each rental real estate enterprise.

>> For tax years 2022 and earlier, 250 or more hours of rental services are performed (as described in this revenue procedure) per year with respect to the rental enterprise. For tax 2023 and beyond, in any three of the five consecutive taxable years that end with the taxable year (or in each year for an enterprise held for less than five years), 250 or more hours of rental services are performed (as described in this revenue procedure) per year with respect to the rental real estate enterprise.

>> The taxpayer maintains contemporaneous records, including time reports, logs, or similar documents, regarding the following:

- Hours of all services performed

- Description of all services performed

- Dates on which such services were performed

- Who performed the services

>> Such records are to be made available for inspection at the request of the IRS. The contemporaneous records requirement will not apply to taxable years prior to 2019.

Per the Internal Revenue Service, rental services include the following:

>> Advertising to rent or lease the real estate

>> Negotiating and executing leases

>> Verifying information contained in prospective tenant applications; collection of rent

>> Daily operation, maintenance, and repair of the property

>> Management of the real estate

>> Purchase of materials

>> Supervision of employees and independent contractors

Rental services may be performed by owners or by employees, agents, and/or independent contractors of the owners. The term *rental services* does not include financial or investment management activities, such as arranging financing; procuring property; studying and reviewing financial statements or reports on operations; planning, managing, or constructing long-term capital improvements; or time spent traveling to and from the real estate.

Real estate used by the taxpayer (including an owner or beneficiary of a relevant pass-through entity) as a residence for any part of the year is not eligible for this tax break. Real estate rented or leased under a triple-net lease is also not eligible for the QBI deduction.

TIP

Tax advisor Vern Hoven suggests that you can easily avoid the triple-net lease exclusion by changing the terms of the lease to a "net lease" in which the landlord makes the payments for both the real estate property taxes and insurance. So that the financial terms of the original lease remain the same, the landlord then increases the amount of the rent paid by the tenant to offset that full amount of taxes and insurance now paid by the landlord. Thus, your "triple-net lease" becomes a "net lease" with the same net effective financial terms, but qualifies for the 20 percent QBI deduction.

Determining Whether You Should Invest in Real Estate

Most people can succeed at investing in real estate if they're willing to do their homework, which includes selecting top real estate professionals. The following sections ask several important questions to help you decide whether you have what it takes to succeed and be happy with real estate investments that involve managing property. Income-producing real estate isn't a passive investment.

Do you have sufficient time?

Purchasing and owning investment real estate and being a landlord are time consuming. The same way an uninformed owner can sell their property for less than it's worth, if you fail to do your homework before purchasing property, you can end up overpaying or buying real estate with a slew of problems. Finding competent and ethical real estate professionals takes time. Investigating communities, neighborhoods, and zoning also soaks up plenty of hours (information on performing this research is located in Chapter 4 of Book 8), as does examining tenant issues with potential properties.

As for managing a property, you can hire a property manager to interview tenants, collect the rent, and solve problems such as leaky faucets and broken appliances, but doing so costs money and still requires some of your time. Of course, if you hire a competent and experienced property manager, you will be rewarded with less time required for oversight.

TIP

If you're stretched too thin due to work and family responsibilities, real estate investing may not be for you. So, unless you want to locate, interview, hire, and pay for a qualified property manager, then you may want to look into less time-intensive real estate investments.

Can you deal with problems?

Challenges and problems inevitably occur when you try to buy a property. Purchase negotiations can be stressful and frustrating. You can also count on some problems coming up when you own and manage investment real estate. Most tenants won't care for a property the way property owners do.

WARNING

If every little problem (especially those that you think may have been caused by your tenants — think "bed bugs"!) causes you distress, at a minimum, you should only own rental property with the assistance of a property manager. You should also question whether you're really going to be satisfied owning investment property. The financial rewards come well down the road, but you live the day-to-day ownership headaches (including the risk of litigation) immediately.

Does real estate interest you?

Some of the best real estate investors have a curiosity and interest in real estate. If you don't already possess it, such an interest and curiosity *can* be cultivated — and this chapter (along with the rest of Book 8) may just do the trick.

On the other hand, some people simply aren't comfortable investing in rental property. For example, if you've had experience and success with stock market investing (see Book 3), you may be uncomfortable venturing into real estate investments. Some people are on a mission to start their own business and may prefer to channel the time and money into that outlet.

Can you handle market downturns?

Real estate investing isn't for the faint of heart. Buying and holding real estate is a whole lot of fun when prices and rents are rising. But market downturns happen, and they test you emotionally as well as financially.

HOW LEVERAGE AFFECTS YOUR REAL ESTATE RETURNS

Real estate is different from most other investments in that you can typically borrow (finance) up to 70 to 80 percent or more of the value of the property. Thus, you can use your small down payment of 20 to 30 percent of the purchase price to buy, own, and control a much larger investment. (During market downturns, lenders tighten requirements and may require larger down payments than they do during good times.) So when your real estate increases in value (which is what you hope and expect), you make money on your investment as well as on the money that you borrowed. That's what we mean when we say that the investment returns from real estate are enhanced due to *leverage.*

Take a look at this simple example. Suppose you purchase a property for $150,000 and make a $30,000 down payment. Over the next three years, imagine that the property appreciates 10 percent to $165,000. Thus, you have a profit (on paper) of $15,000 ($165,000 – $150,000) on an investment of just $30,000. In other words, you've made a 50 percent return on your investment. (**Note:** This example ignores *cash flow* — whether your rental income that you collect from the property exceeds the expenses that you pay or vice versa, and the tax benefits associated with rental real estate.)

Remember, leverage magnifies all of your returns, and those returns aren't always positive! If your $150,000 property decreases in value to $135,000, even though it has only dropped 10 percent in value, you actually lose (on paper) 50 percent of your original $30,000 investment. (In case you care, and it's okay if you don't, some wonks apply the terms *positive leverage* and *negative leverage*.) Please see the earlier section "Understanding Real Estate's Income- and Wealth-Producing Potential" for a more detailed example of investment property profit and return.

Consider the real estate market price declines that happened in most communities and types of property surrounding the 2008 financial crisis. In many parts of the country, the impact was still a reality several years later. Such drops can present attractive buying opportunities for those with courage, a good credit score, and cash for the down payment.

No one has a crystal ball, though, so don't expect to be able to buy at the precise bottom of prices and sell at an exact peak of your local market. Even if you make a smart buy now, you'll inevitably end up holding some of your investment property during a difficult market (recessions where you have trouble finding and retaining quality tenants, where rents and property values may fall rather than rise). Do you have the financial (and emotional) wherewithal to handle such a downturn? How have you handled other investments when their values have fallen?

Fitting Real Estate into Your Plans

For most non-wealthy people, purchasing investment real estate has a major impact on their overall personal financial situation. So, before you go out to buy property, you should inventory your money life and be sure your fiscal house is in order. This section explains how you can do just that.

Ensuring your best personal financial health

If you're trying to improve your physical fitness by exercising, you may find that eating lots of junk food and smoking are barriers to your goal. Likewise, investing in real estate or other growth investments such as stocks while you're carrying high-cost consumer debt (credit cards, auto loans, and so on) and spending more than you earn impedes your financial goals.

TIP

Before you set out to invest in real estate, pay off all your consumer debt. Not only will you be financially healthier for doing so, but you'll also enhance your future mortgage applications.

Eliminate wasteful and unnecessary spending; analyze your monthly spending to identify target areas for reduction. This practice enables you to save more and better afford making investments, including real estate. Living below your means is also important. However, this takes a lot of discipline and self-control in the face of our consumer-driven "must have" world in which having the latest technology or keeping up with the "influencers" is how some people define their success. As Charles Dickens said, "Annual income twenty pounds; annual expenditures nineteen pounds; result, happiness. Annual income twenty pounds; annual expenditure twenty pounds; result, misery."

Protecting yourself with insurance

REMEMBER

Regardless of your real estate investment desires and decisions, you absolutely must have comprehensive insurance for yourself and your major assets, including

>> **Health insurance:** Major medical coverage protects you from financial ruin if you have a major accident or illness that requires significant hospital and other medical care.

>> **Disability insurance:** For most working people, their biggest asset is their future income-earning ability. Disability insurance replaces a portion of your employment earnings if you're unable to work for an extended period of time due to an incapacitating illness or injury.

>> **Life insurance:** If loved ones are financially dependent upon you, term life insurance, which provides a lump sum death benefit, can help to replace your employment earnings if you pass away.

>> **Homeowner's insurance:** Not only do you want homeowner's insurance to protect you against the financial cost due to a fire or other home-damaging catastrophe, but such coverage also provides you with liability protection. (After you buy and operate a rental property with tenants, you should obtain rental owner's insurance.)

>> **Auto insurance:** This coverage is similar to homeowner's coverage in that it insures a valuable asset and also provides liability insurance should you be involved in an accident.

>> **Excess liability (umbrella) insurance:** This relatively inexpensive coverage, available in million-dollar increments, adds on to the modest liability protection offered on your basic home and auto policies, which is inadequate for more-affluent people.

Nobody enjoys spending hard-earned money on insurance. However, having proper protection gives you peace of mind and financial security, so don't put off reviewing and securing needed policies. For assistance, see the latest edition of *Personal Finance For Dummies* by Eric Tyson, MBA (Wiley).

Considering retirement account funding

If you're not taking advantage of your retirement accounts (such as 401(k)s, 403(b)s, SEP-IRAs, and so on), you may be missing out on some terrific tax benefits. Funding retirement accounts gives you an immediate tax deduction when you contribute to them. And some employer accounts offer "free" matching money — but you've got to contribute to earn the matching money.

In comparison, you derive no tax benefits while you accumulate your down payment for an investment real estate purchase (or other investments such as for a small business). Furthermore, the operating positive cash flow or income from your real estate investment is subject to ordinary income taxes as you earn it. However, investment real estate offers numerous tax benefits, which are detailed in the earlier section "Being aware of the tax advantages."

Thinking about asset allocation

With money that you invest for the longer term, you should have an overall game plan in mind. Fancy-talking financial advisors like to use buzzwords such as *asset allocation*, a term that indicates what portion of your money you have invested in different types of investment vehicles, such as stocks and real estate (for appreciation or growth), versus lending vehicles, such as bonds and certificates of deposit, also known as CDs (which produce current income).

Here's a simple way to calculate asset allocation for long-term investments: Subtract your age from 110. The result is the percentage of your long-term money that you should invest in ownership investments for appreciation. So, for example, a 40-year-old would take 110 minus 40 equals 70 percent in growth investments such as stocks and real estate. If you want to be more aggressive, subtract your age from 120; a 40-year-old would then have 80 percent in growth investments.

As you gain more knowledge, assets, and diversification of growth assets, you're in a better position to take on more risk. Just be sure you're properly covered with insurance as discussed earlier in the section "Protecting yourself with insurance."

These are simply guidelines, not hard-and-fast rules or mandates. If you want to be more aggressive and are comfortable taking on greater risk, you can invest higher portions in ownership investments.

As you consider asset allocation, when classifying your investments, determine and use your *equity* in your real estate holdings, which is the market value of property less outstanding mortgages. For example, suppose that prior to buying an investment property, your long-term investments consist of the following:

Stocks	$150,000
Bonds	$50,000
CDs	$50,000
Total	$250,000

BECOME YOUR OWN LANDLORD

Many real estate investors are actually involved in other activities as their primary source of income. Ironically, many of these business owners come to realize the benefits of real estate investing but miss the single greatest opportunity that is right before their eyes — the prospect of being their own landlord. Business owners can purchase the buildings occupied by their own businesses and essentially pay the rent to themselves. If you own a business that rents, do yourself a favor — consider becoming your own landlord!

So, you have 60 percent in ownership investments ($150,000) and 40 percent in lending investments ($50,000 + $50,000). Now, suppose you plan to purchase a $300,000 income property, making a $75,000 down payment. Because you've decided to bump up your ownership investment portion to make your money grow more over the years, you plan to use your maturing CD balance and sell some of your bonds for the down payment. After your real estate purchase, here's how your investment portfolio looks:

Stocks	$150,000
Real estate	$75,000 ($300,000 property – $225,000 mortgage)
Bonds	$25,000
Total	$250,000

Thus, after the real estate purchase, you've got 90 percent in ownership investments ($150,000 + $75,000) and just 10 percent in lending investments ($25,000). Such a mix may be appropriate for someone under the age of 50 who desires an aggressive investment portfolio positioned for long-term growth potential.

Chapter **2**

Covering Common Real Estate Investments

I f you lack substantial experience investing in real estate, you should avoid more esoteric and complicated properties and strategies. This chapter discusses the more accessible and easy-to-master income-producing property options. In particular, *residential income property* can be an attractive real estate investment for many people.

Residential housing is easier to understand, purchase, and manage than most other types of income property, such as office, industrial, and retail property. If you're a homeowner, you already have experience locating, purchasing, and maintaining residential property.

In addition to discussing the pros and cons of investing in residential income property, this chapter adds insights as to which may be the most appropriate and profitable for you and touches on the topics of investing in commercial property as well as undeveloped land.

Identifying the Various Ways to Invest in Residential Income Property

The first (and one of the best) real estate investments for many people is a home in which to live. This section covers the investment possibilities inherent in buying a home for your own use, including potential profit to be had from converting your home to a rental or fixing it up and selling it. You also get some pointers on how to profit from owning your own vacation home.

Buying a place of your own

During your adult life, you're going to need a roof over your head for many decades. And real estate is the only investment that you can live in or rent out to produce income. A stock, bond, or mutual fund doesn't work too well as a roof over your head!

REMEMBER

Unless you expect to move within the next few years, buying a place may make good long-term financial sense. (Even if you need to relocate, you may decide to continue owning the property and use it as a rental property.) In most real estate markets, owning usually costs less than renting over the long haul and allows you to build *equity* (the dollar difference between market value and the current balance of the mortgage loans against the property) in an asset.

Under current tax law, you can also pocket substantial tax-free profits when you sell your home for more than you originally paid plus the money you sunk into improvements during your ownership. Specifically, single taxpayers can realize up to a $250,000 tax-free capital gain; married couples filing jointly get up to $500,000. In order to qualify for this homeowner's *gains tax exemption*, you (or your spouse if you're married) must have owned the home and used it as your primary residence for a minimum of 24 months out of the past 60 months. The 24 months don't have to be continuous. Additionally, this tax break allows for pro-rata (proportionate) credit based on hardship or change of employment. Also note that the full exemption amounts are reduced proportionately for the length of time you rented out your home over the five-year period referenced here.

Some commentators have stated that your home isn't an investment because you're not renting it out. But consider the fact that some people move to a less costly home when they retire (because it's smaller and/or because it's in a lower-cost area). Trading down to a lower-priced property in retirement frees up equity that has built up over many years of homeownership. This money can be used to supplement your retirement income and for any other purpose your heart desires. Your home is an investment because it can appreciate in value over the years, and you can use that money toward your financial or personal goals. The most recent version of *Home Buying Kit For Dummies* by Eric Tyson, MBA, and Ray Brown (Wiley) can help you make terrific home buying decisions.

Converting your home to a rental

Turning your current home into a rental property when you move is a simple way to buy and own more properties. You can do this multiple times (as you move out of homes you own over the years), and you can implement this strategy of acquiring rental properties not only with a house, but also with a duplex or other small multi-unit rental property where you reside in one of the units. This approach is an option if you're already considering investing in real estate (either now or in the future), and you can afford to own two or more properties. Holding onto your current home when you're buying a new one is more advisable if you're moving within the same area so that you're close by to manage the property. This approach presents a number of positives:

>> You save the time and cost of finding a separate rental property, not to mention the associated transaction costs.

>> You know the property and have probably taken good care of it and perhaps made some improvements.

>> You know the target market because the home appealed to you.

WARNING

Some people unfortunately make the mistake of holding onto their current home for the wrong reasons when they buy another. This situation typically occurs when a homeowner must sell their home in a depressed market. Nobody likes to lose money and sell their home for less than they paid for it or sell for a good deal less than it was worth several years ago. Thus, some owners hold onto their homes until prices recover. If you plan to move and want to keep your current home as a long-term investment (rental) property, you can. If you fully convert your home to rental property and use it that way for years before selling it, after you do sell you can either take advantage of the lower long-term capital gains rates or do a tax-deferred exchange. For tax purposes, you get to deduct depreciation and all the write-offs during the ownership and you can shelter up to $25,000 in income from active sources subject to income eligibility requirements. (Or even more if you or your spouse happen to qualify as a real estate professional.)

WARNING

Turning your home into a *short-term* rental, however, is usually a bad move because

>> You may not want the responsibilities of being a landlord, yet you force yourself into the landlord business when you convert your home into a rental.

>> You owe tax on the sale's profit (and recaptured depreciation) if your property is classified for tax purposes as a rental when you sell it and you don't buy another rental property. (You can purchase another rental property through a 1031 exchange to defer paying taxes on your profit. See Chapter 1 in Book 8.)

REMEMBER

You lose some of the capital gains tax exclusion if you sell your home and you had rented it out for a portion of the five-year period prior to selling it. For example, if you rented your home for two of the last five years, you may only exclude 60 percent of your gain (up to the maximums of $250,000 for single taxpayers and $500,000 for married couples filing jointly), whereas the other 40 percent is taxed as a long-term capital gain. Also be aware that when you sell a home previously rented and are accounting for the sale on your tax return, you must recapture the depreciation taken during the rental period.

Investing and living in well-situated fixer-uppers

Serial home selling is a variation on the tried-and-true real estate investment strategy of investing in well-located fixer-upper homes where you can invest your time, sweat equity, and materials to make improvements that add more value than they cost. The only catch is that you must actually move into the fixer-upper for at least 24 months to earn the full homeowner's capital gains exemption of up to $250,000 for single taxpayers and $500,000 for married couples filing jointly (as covered in the earlier section "Buying a place of your own").

REMEMBER

Be sure to buy a home in need of that special TLC in a great neighborhood where you're willing to live for 24 months or more! But if you're a savvy investor, you would've invested in a great neighborhood anyway.

Here's a simple example to illustrate the potentially significant benefits of this strategy. You purchase a fixer-upper for $275,000 that becomes your principal residence, and then over the next 24 months you invest $25,000 in improvements (paint, repairs, landscaping, appliances, decorator items, and so on), and you also invest the amount of sweat equity that suits your skills and wallet. You now have one of the nicer homes in the neighborhood, and you can sell this home for a net price of $400,000 after your transaction costs. With your total investment of $300,000 ($275,000 plus $25,000), your efforts have earned you a $100,000 profit completely tax-free. Thus, you've earned an average of $50,000 per year, which isn't bad for a tax-exempt second income without strict office hours. (Note that many states also allow you to avoid state income taxes on the sale of your personal residence, using many of the same requirements as the federal tax laws.)

WARNING

Now, some cautions are in order here. This strategy is clearly not for everyone interested in making money from real estate investments. This strategy is not likely to work well for you if any of the following apply:

>> You're unwilling or reluctant to live through redecorating, minor remodeling, or major construction.

>> You dislike having to move every few years.

>> You're not experienced or comfortable with identifying undervalued property and improving it.

>> You lack a financial cushion to withstand a significant downturn in your local real estate market as happened in numerous parts of the country during the late 2000s and early 2010s.

>> You don't have the budget to hire a professional licensed and insured contractor to do the work, and you don't have the free time or the home improvement skills needed to enhance the value of a home.

WARNING

One final caution: Beware of transaction costs. The expenses involved with buying and selling property — such as real estate agent commissions, loan fees, title insurance, escrow or closing costs, and so forth — can gobble up a large portion of your profits. With most properties, the long-term appreciation is what drives your returns. Consider keeping homes you buy and improve as long-term investment properties.

Purchasing a vacation home

Many people of means expand their real estate holdings by purchasing a *vacation home* — a home in an area where they enjoy taking pleasure trips. For most people, buying a vacation home is more of a consumption decision than it is an investment decision. That's not to say that you can't make a profit from owning a second home. However, potential investment returns shouldn't be the main reason you buy a second home.

For example, one family lived in Pennsylvania and didn't particularly like the hot and humid summer weather. They enjoyed taking trips and staying in various spots in northern New England and eventually bought a small home in New Hampshire. Their situation highlights the pros and cons that many people face with vacation or second homes. The obvious advantage this family enjoyed in having a vacation home is that they no longer had the hassle of securing accommodations when they wanted to enjoy some downtime. Also, after they arrived at their home away from home, they were, well, home! Things were just as they expected — with no surprises, unless squirrels had taken up residence on their porch.

WARNING

The downsides to vacation homes can be numerous, as the Pennsylvania family found, including

>> **Expenses:** With a second home, you have the range of nearly all the costs of a primary home — mortgage interest, property taxes, insurance, repairs and maintenance, utilities, and so on.

>> **Property management:** When you're not at your vacation home, things can go wrong. A pipe can burst, for example, and the mess may not be found for days or weeks. Unless the property is close to a good neighbor or other kind person willing to keep an eye on it for you, you may incur the additional expense of paying a property manager to watch the property for you.

>> **Lack of rental income:** Most people don't rent out their vacation homes, thus negating the investment property income stream that contributes to the returns real estate investors enjoy (see Chapter 1 of Book 8). If your second home is in a vacation area where you have access to plenty of short-term renters, you or your designated property manager can rent out the property (note that using a service like Airbnb assists with finding people to rent your property but doesn't help with the arrival/departure and security deposit issues nor applicant screening and keeping your property maintained, plus many other similar services a property manager performs). However, this entails all the headaches and hassles of having many short-term renters. (But you do gain the tax advantages of depreciation and all expenses as with other rental properties.)

>> **Obligation to use:** Some second homeowners complain about feeling obliged to use their vacation homes. Oftentimes in marriages, one spouse likes the vacation home much more than the other spouse (or one spouse enjoys working on the second home rather than enjoying the home itself).

Here are a few tax tips related to vacation homes, as found in the current tax code:

>> If you retain your vacation home or secondary home as personal property, forgoing the large income streams and tax write-offs for depreciation and operating expenses associated with rental properties, you can still make a nice little chunk of tax-free cash on the side. The current tax code permits you to rent the property for up to 14 days a year — and that income is *tax-free!* You don't have to claim it. Yes, you read that right. And you can still deduct the costs of ownership, including mortgage interest and property taxes, as you do for all other personal properties.

>> If you decide to maintain the property as a rental (you rent it out for more than 14 days a year), you, as the property owner, can still use the rental property as a vacation home for up to 14 days a year, or a maximum of

10 percent of the days gainfully rented, whichever is greater, and the property still qualifies as a rental. Also, all days spent cleaning or repairing the rental home don't count as personal use days — so that's why you paint for a couple of hours every afternoon and spend the morning fishing!

REMEMBER

Before you buy a second home, weigh all the pros and cons. If you have a partner with whom you're buying the property, have a candid discussion. Also consult with your tax advisor for other tax-saving strategies for your second home or vacation home.

Paying for timeshares and condo hotels

Timeshares, a concept created in the 1960s, are a form of ownership or right to use a property. A more recent trend in real estate investing is condo hotels, which in many ways are simply a new angle on the old concept of timeshares. A condo hotel looks and operates just like any other first-class hotel, with the difference that each room is separately owned. The hotel guests (renters) have no idea who owns their room.

Both timeshares and condo hotels typically involve luxury resort locations with amenities such as golf or spas. The difference between the traditional timeshare and condo hotel is the interval that the unit is available — condo hotels are operated on a day-to-day availability, and timeshares typically rent in fixed intervals such as weeks.

Some of the most popular projects have been the branded condo hotels such as Ritz Carlton, Four Seasons, W, Westin, and Hilton located in high-profile vacation destinations like Hawaii, Las Vegas, New York, Chicago, and Miami. You can also find many foreign condo hotel properties in the Caribbean and Mexico, and the concept is expanding to Europe, the Middle East, and Asia.

Two types of individuals are attracted to investing in condo hotels and timeshares. One group is investors who believe that the property will appreciate like any other investment. The other group is people who use the condo hotel or timeshare for personal use and offset some of their costs.

WARNING

We don't see timeshares or condo hotels as worthy real estate investments as they don't appreciate and they don't generate income. But they are often presented as a viable alternative real estate investment and millions have been purchased. You will likely be solicited to consider this opportunity during an upcoming vacation, so the following sections discuss some concerns.

Taming timeshares

Timeshares are offered as deeded and non-deeded timeshares. With deeded time-shares you own a permanent or *fee simple* interest. (Fee simple means there are no limitations as to transferability of ownership — these are the most complete ownership rights one can have.) With non-deeded timeshares you have a right to use the property, but there is an expiration date. The most popular timeshares are deeded, and they can be sold or transferred just like any other interest in real estate, assuming there is demand.

Many investors' first experiences with timeshares are tempting offers of a free meal, a great discount offer to a theme park, or even a free one- or two-night stay at the resort, with the catch that they have to spend some time listening to an informational presentation. These offers usually come from individuals contacting you in known tourist locations or when you check into a hotel that just happens to offer condos as well.

From an investment standpoint, the fundamental problem with timeshares is that they're overpriced, and like a condominium, you own no land (which is what generally appreciates well over time). For example, suppose that a particular unit would cost $150,000 to buy. When this unit is carved up into weekly ownership units, the total cost of all those units can easily approach four to five times that amount! (Now you understand why timeshare developers and promoters can give you "free stuff" if you will listen to their sales pitch — their profit margins are very high on every sale!)

To add insult to injury, investors find that another problem with timeshares is the high management fees or service fees and almost guaranteed rising annual maintenance fees over time. As the property gets older, the annual maintenance costs, which you are required to pay to retain ownership of your timeshare interval, continue to increase and can even exceed what you would pay for a comparable stay at a nearby non-timeshare. Is it worth buying a slice of real estate at a 400 to 500 percent premium to its fair market value and paying high ongoing maintenance fees on top of that? Nope.

Many owners of timeshares find that they want to vacation at a different location or time of year than what they originally purchased. To meet this need, several companies offer to broker or sell or "trade" timeshare slots for a fee. However, timeshare availability and desirability have so many variables — including location, time of year, amenities, and quality of the particular resort — that it has been difficult to fairly value and trade timeshares. For a given resort, it can be difficult online to determine which of two identical floorplan units has the prime location versus a less desirable one. As a result, resort rating systems have been developed (Resorts Condominiums International [RCI] and Interval International are two of the most well known) to compare resort location, amenities, and quality.

CASHING IN ON CANCELING

A cottage industry for timeshare cancellations has sprouted up, and undoubtedly you have seen or will soon see or hear an ad for a company that is offering to assist you in canceling or getting rid of your timeshare. The demand for these services is increasing as many timeshare properties are aging and the maintenance fees are rising, often to the point that it is more expensive to stay at your own timeshare than to simply pay for a comparable rental, possibly at a much newer and more luxurious resort property in the same area.

WARNING

However, timeshares may make sense for you if you like to vacation at the same resort around the same time every year and if the annual service or maintenance fees compare favorably to the cost of simply staying in a comparable resort. Keep in mind, though, that if the deal seems too good to be true, it *is* too good to be true. The only folks who generally make money with timeshares and condo hotels are the developers, not the folks who buy specific days of ownership.

The timeshare cancellation strategies often involve either selling your timeshare (almost always at a significant or even a complete loss), attempting to rescind the timeshare (virtually impossible unless you just bought it while on vacation early this week and are still within the "cooling off" or rescission period!), asking the developer to just take it back (most won't, but rarely one actually will), renting out or gifting your interval, or hiring an attorney who may be able to find a legitimate way to challenge the disclosures or the validity of the timeshare contract.

Timeshare laws vary greatly from state to state, so you want to find a timeshare cancellation company or attorney that specializes in canceling timeshares in the state where your timeshare is located. While you will take a large financial hit when you sell or cancel your timeshare, you need to consider that the benefits of cutting your future losses (maintenance fees) may make such a tough decision the right one.

Coping with condo hotels

The developers and operators of condo hotels love the concept because one of the most consistently successful principles of real estate is increasing value by fractionalizing interests in real estate. As with timeshares (see the previous section), the developers are able to sell each individual hotel room for much more than they could get for the entire project.

Condo hotel operators are able to generate additional revenue from service and maintenance fees to cover their costs of operations. Often the owners' use of their own rooms doesn't negatively impact the overall revenues of the property because the rooms would have sometimes been vacant anyway. Condo hotels allow their owners to stay in their units but often impose limits on the amount of personal usage. There may also be resort fees, parking fees, or other amenity costs as well.

The purchaser of the condo hotel unit sees this type of investment as an option to direct ownership of a second home and likes the ability to generate income. The professional management is another one of the attractions to investors. The owners don't pay a management fee to the hotel operator unless their room is rented, and then the collected revenue is split, typically in the 50-50 range, and the operator has complete control over the rental rate as well as which units are rented each day.

These properties are often hyped, and the expectations of the condo hotel investor are often much greater than the reality. Investors are lured to condo hotels by the potential for appreciation and cash flow as well as professional management. Many investors find themselves being pressured into pre-sale offering presentations even before the units are built. These events can be tempting, but savvy investors need to do their own due diligence. So when you hear a sales pitch indicating that your proposed investment in a condo hotel unit will provide significant income from hotel rentals and cover most or all of your mortgage and carrying costs, that's the time to grab your wallet and find the nearest exit.

Surveying the Types of Residential Properties You Can Buy

If you've been in the market for a home, you know that in addition to single-family homes, you can choose from numerous types of attached or shared housing including duplexes, triplexes, apartment buildings, condominiums, townhomes, and co-operatives. This section provides an overview of each of these properties and shows how they may make an attractive real estate investment for you.

TIP

From an investment perspective, the top recommendations are apartment buildings and single-family homes. Attached-housing units aren't generally recommended; they have associations and shared common areas. If you can afford a smaller single-family home or apartment building rather than a shared-housing unit, buy the single-family home or apartments.

WARNING

Unless you can afford a large down payment (25 percent or more), the early years of rental property ownership may financially challenge you: With all properties, as time goes on, generating a positive cash flow gets easier because your mortgage expense stays fixed (if you use fixed rate financing), while your rents increase faster than your expenses (unless you are in a rent controlled area). Regardless of what you choose to buy, make sure that you run the numbers on your rental income and expenses to see if you can afford the negative cash flow that often occurs in the early years of ownership, and always allow for unexpected vacancy or capital improvements like flooring and window coverings, appliances, and/or the water heater.

Single-family homes

As an investment, single-family, detached homes generally perform better in the long run than attached or shared housing. In a good real estate market, most housing appreciates, but single-family homes tend to outperform other housing types for the following reasons:

>> Single-family homes tend to attract more potential buyers — most people, when they can afford it, prefer a detached or stand-alone home, especially for the increased privacy and less noise from neighbors.

>> Attached or shared housing is less expensive and easier to build *and to overbuild;* because of this surplus potential, such property tends to appreciate more moderately in price.

TIP

Because so many people prefer to live in detached, single-family homes, market prices for such dwellings can often become inflated beyond what's justified by the rental income these homes can produce. That's exactly what happened in some parts of the United States in the mid-2000s and led in part to a significant price correction in the subsequent years. To discover whether you're buying in such a market, compare the monthly cost (after tax) of owning a home to the monthly rent for that same property. Focus on markets where the rent exceeds or comes close to equaling the cost of owning and shun areas where the ownership costs exceed rents.

Single-family homes that require just one tenant are simpler to deal with than a multi-unit apartment building that requires the management and maintenance of multiple renters and units. The downside, though, is that a vacancy means you have no income coming in. Look at the effect of 0 percent occupancy for a couple of months on your projected income and expense statement! By contrast, one vacancy in a four-unit apartment building (each with the same rents) means that you're still taking in 75 percent of the gross potential (maximum total) rent.

With a single-family home, you're responsible for all repairs and maintenance. You can hire someone to do the work, but you still have to find the contractors and coordinate and oversee the work. Also recognize that if you purchase a single-family home with many fine features and amenities, you may find it more stressful and difficult to have tenants living in your property who don't treat it with the same tender loving care that you may yourself.

The first rule of being a successful landlord is to let go of any emotional attachment to a home. But that sort of attachment on the tenant's part is favorable: The more they make your rental property their home, the more likely they are to stay and return it to you in good condition — except for the expected normal wear and tear of day-to-day living.

Making a profit in the early years of ownership from the monthly cash flow with a single-family home is generally the hardest stage. The reason: Such properties usually sell at a premium price relative to the rent that they can command (you pay extra for the land, which you can't rent). Also remember that with just one tenant, you have no rental income when you have a vacancy.

Attached housing

As the cost of land has climbed over the decades in many areas, packing more housing units that are attached into a given plot of land keeps housing somewhat more affordable. Shared housing makes more sense for investors who don't want to deal with building maintenance and security issues.

The following sections discuss the investment merits of three forms of attached housing: condominiums, townhomes, and co-ops.

Condos

Condominiums are typically apartment-style units stacked on top of and/or beside one another and sold to individual owners. When you purchase a condominium, you're actually purchasing the interior of a specific unit as well as a proportionate, undivided (meaning, you don't directly own a portion) interest in the common areas — the pool, tennis courts, grounds, hallways, laundry room, and so on. Although you (and your tenants) have full use and enjoyment of the common areas, the homeowners' association actually owns and maintains the common areas as well as the building structures themselves (which typically include the foundation, exterior walls, roof, plumbing, electrical, and other major building systems).

One advantage to a condo as an investment property is that of all the attached housing options, condos are generally the lowest-maintenance properties (from the perspective of unit owners) because most condominium or homeowners' associations deal with issues such as roofing, landscaping, and so on for the entire building and receive the benefits of quantity purchasing. Note that you're still responsible for necessary maintenance inside your unit, such as servicing appliances, floor and window coverings, interior painting, and so on.

Although condos may be somewhat easier to keep up, they tend to appreciate less than single-family homes or apartment buildings unless the condo is located in a desirable urban area.

Condominium buildings may start out in life as condos or as apartment complexes that are then converted into condominiums.

WARNING

Be wary of apartments that have been converted to condominiums. Although they're often the most affordable housing options in many areas of the country and may also be blessed with an excellent urban location that can't easily be re-created, you may be buying into some not-so-obvious problems. These converted apartments are typically older properties with a cosmetic makeover (new floors, new appliances, solid surface countertops, new landscaping, and a fresh coat of paint). However, be forewarned: The cosmetic makeover may look good at first glance, but the property probably still boasts 40-year-old plumbing, heating/cooling, and electrical systems; poor soundproofing; and a host of economic and functional obsolescence.

Within a few years, most of the owner-occupants move on to the traditional single-family home and rent out their condos. You may then find the property is predominantly renter-occupied and has a volunteer board of directors unwilling to levy the monthly assessments necessary to properly maintain the aging structure. Within 10 to 15 years of the conversion, these properties may well be the worst in the neighborhood.

Townhomes

Townhomes are essentially attached or row homes — a hybrid between a typical airspace-only condominium and a single-family house. Like condominiums, townhomes are generally attached, typically sharing walls and a continuous roof. But townhomes are often two-story buildings that come with a small yard and offer more privacy than a condominium because you don't have someone living on top of your unit.

REMEMBER

As with condominiums, you absolutely must review the governing documents before you purchase the property to see exactly what you legally own. Generally, townhomes are organized as *planned unit developments* (PUDs) in which each owner has a fee simple ownership of the individual lot that encompasses their dwelling unit and often a small area of immediately adjacent land for a patio or balcony. The common areas are all part of a larger single lot, and each owner holds title to an undivided, proportionate share of the common area.

Co-ops

Co-operatives are a type of shared housing that has elements in common with apartments and condos. When you buy a cooperative, you own a stock certificate that represents your share of the entire building, including usage rights to a specific living space per a separate written occupancy agreement. Unlike a condo, you generally need to get approval from the co-operative association if you want to remodel or rent your unit to a tenant. In some co-ops, you must even gain approval from the association for the sale of your unit to a proposed buyer.

WARNING

Turning a co-op into a rental unit is often severely restricted or even forbidden and, if allowed, is usually a major headache because you must satisfy not only your tenant but also the other owners in the building. Co-ops are also generally much harder to finance, and a sale requires the approval of the typically finicky association board. Therefore, it's highly recommended that you avoid co-ops for investment purposes.

Apartments

Not only do apartment buildings generally enjoy healthy long-term appreciation potential, but they also often produce positive *cash flow* (rental income – expenses) in the early years of ownership. But as with a single-family home, the buck stops with you for maintenance of an apartment building. You may hire a property manager to assist you, but you still have oversight responsibilities (and additional expenses).

In the real estate financing world, apartment buildings are divided into two groups based on the number of units:

>> **Four or fewer units:** You can obtain more favorable financing options and terms for apartment buildings that have four or fewer units because they're treated as residential property.

>> **Five or more units:** Complexes with five or more units are treated as commercial property and don't enjoy the extremely favorable loan terms of the one- to four-unit properties.

Apartment buildings, particularly those with more units, generally produce a small positive cash flow, even in the early years of rental ownership (unless you're in an overpriced market where it may take two to four years before you break even on a before-tax basis).

WARNING

One way to add value, if zoning allows, is to convert an apartment building into condominiums. Keep in mind, however, that this metamorphosis requires significant research on the zoning front and with estimating remodeling and construction costs. You also may be exposed to litigation brought by your individual unit buyers who within a few years become disenchanted with their investments and find an experienced attorney and a team of experts to make claims of construction defects or allege that you failed to have adequate reserves at the time of the conversion.

EASY FIXES CAN YIELD BIG BUCKS

Avoid shared housing units in suburban areas with substantial undeveloped land that enables building many more units. Attached housing prices tend to perform best in fully developed or built-out urban environments.

For higher returns, look for property where relatively simple cosmetic and other fixes may allow you to increase rents and, therefore, the market value of the property. Examples of such improvements may include but not be limited to

- Adding fresh paint and flooring
- Improving the landscaping, including trees and seasonal color
- Upgrading the kitchen with solid surface (also known as "granite") countertops, new designer-colored appliances, and new cabinet/drawer hardware that can totally change the look
- Converting five-unit apartment buildings into four-unit buildings (for example, by converting two one-bedroom units into a two-bedroom, two-bath unit) to qualify for more favorable mortgage terms

Look for property with a great location and good physical condition but some minor deferred maintenance. Then you can develop the punch list of items with maximum results for minimum dollars — for example, a property with a large yard but dead grass or completely overgrown and dated landscaping, or a two- or three-car garage but peeling paint or a broken garage door. You can also add a garage door opener to jazz up the property for minimum cost. You can also really add value to a property with a burnt-out, absentee, or totally disinterested owner who is tired of the property, or a property that is simply poorly managed.

Considering Commercial Real Estate

Commercial real estate is a generic term that includes properties used for office, retail, and industrial purposes. You can also include self-storage and hospitality (hotels and motels) properties in this category as well as special-purpose properties (for example, mobile home parks, amusement parks, and so on). If you're a knowledgeable real estate investor and you like a challenge, you need to know two good reasons to invest in commercial real estate:

>> You can use some of the space if you own your own small business. Just as it's generally more cost-effective to own your home rather than rent over the years, so it is with commercial real estate if — and this is a big *if* — you buy at a reasonably good time and hold the property for many years.

>> You're a more sophisticated investor who understands the more complicated aspects of commercial leases and has a higher tolerance for risk because these properties can have longer intervals of vacancy or increased tenant improvement costs plus rent concessions. Of course, just like with residential income property, only invest when your analysis of your local market suggests that it's a good time to buy.

WARNING

Commercial real estate isn't our first recommendation, especially for inexperienced investors. Residential real estate is generally easier to understand and also usually carries lower investment and tenant risks.

With commercial real estate, when tenants move out, new tenants nearly always require extensive and costly improvements to customize the space to meet their particular planned usage of the property. And you usually have to pay for the majority of the associated costs in order to compete with other building owners. Fortunes can quickly change — small companies can go under, get too big for a space, and so on. Change is the order of the day in commercial real estate, and especially in the small business world where you're most likely to find your tenants.

So how do you evaluate the state of your local commercial real estate market? You must check out the supply and demand statistics for recent years. How much total space (sublease and vacant space) is available for rent, and how has that changed in recent months or years? What's the vacancy rate for comparable space, and how has that changed over time? Also, examine the rental rates, usually quoted as a price per square foot.

WARNING

One danger sign that purchasing a commercial property in an area is likely to produce disappointing investment returns is a market where the supply of available space has increased faster than demand, leading to higher vacancies and falling rental rates. (This is called *negative absorption.* What you want instead is a track record and projections showing *positive absorption* — when the supply of space isn't keeping up with the demand.) A slowing local economy and a higher unemployment rate also spell trouble for commercial real estate prices. You not only have to consider vacant space, but also space available for subleasing (the current tenant isn't using the space and will rent it to someone else, often at favorable terms) when evaluating the overall supply and demand for commercial income properties. Each market is different, so make sure you check out the details of your area.

Buying Undeveloped or Raw Land

For prospective real estate investors who feel tenants and building maintenance are ongoing headaches, buying undeveloped land may appear attractive. If you buy land in an area that's expected to experience expanding demand in the years ahead, you should be able to make a tidy return on your investment. This is called *buying in the path of progress,* but of course the trick is to buy before everybody realizes that new development is moving in your direction. (Check out Chapter 4 in Book 8 for a full discussion on the path of progress.)

You may even hit a home run if you can identify land that others don't currently see the future value in holding. However, identifying many years in advance which communities will experience rapid population and job growth isn't easy. Land prices in areas that people believe will be the next hot spot likely already sell at a premium price. That's what happened in most major cities with new sports facilities or transportation corridors (especially because these decisions often are disclosed well in advance of the municipality leadership vote or the ballot initiative). You don't have much opportunity to get ahead of the curve — or if you guess wrong, you may own land that falls in value!

WARNING

Investing in land certainly has other drawbacks and risks:

>> **Care and feeding:** Land requires ongoing cash to pay the property taxes and liability insurance, and to keep the land clear and free of debris while it most likely produces little or no income. Although land doesn't require much upkeep compared with tenant-occupied property, it almost always does require financial feeding.

>> **Opportunity costs:** Investing in land is a cash drain, and of course, purchasing the land in the first place costs money. If you buy the land with cash, you have the opportunity cost of tying up your valuable capital (which could be invested elsewhere), but most likely you will put down 30 to 40 percent in cash and finance the balance of the purchase price instead. Although you can often

buy residential income property with much lower down payments, the fact that there is typically no periodic rental income with vacant undeveloped land means down payments are higher. Many times you can only acquire these properties with cash.

>> **Costly mortgages:** Mortgage lenders require much higher down payments and charge higher loan fees and interest rates on loans to purchase land because they see it as a more speculative investment. Obtaining a loan for buying and holding raw land, or for buying land that you will develop and for which you'll receive entitlements for future building, is challenging and more expensive than obtaining a loan for a developed property.

>> **Lack of depreciation:** You don't get depreciation tax write-offs because undeveloped or raw land isn't depreciable.

On the income side, some properties may be able to be used for parking, storage income, or maybe even growing Christmas trees in the Northwest or grain in the Midwest! (After you make sure you've complied with local zoning restrictions and have the proper insurance in place, that is.)

REMEMBER

Although large-scale land investment isn't for the entry-level real estate investor, savvy real estate investors have made fortunes taking raw land and getting the proper entitlements and then selling (or better yet, subdividing and then selling) the parcels to developers of commercial and residential properties (primarily home builders). If you decide to invest in land, be sure that you do the following:

>> **Do your homework.** Ideally, you want to buy land in an area that's attracting rapidly expanding companies with increased employment demand and that has a shortage of housing and developable land. Take your time to really know the area. This isn't a situation in which you should take a hot tip from someone to invest in faraway property in another state. Nor should you buy raw land just because you heard that irresistible opening bid price advertised on the radio for the government excess land auction down at the convention center this Saturday (lately, these are online auctions).

>> **Know all the costs.** Tally up your annual *carrying costs* (ongoing ownership expenses such as property taxes, insurance, and keeping the land clear of debris) so that you can see what your annual cash drain may be. What are the financial consequences of this cash outflow — for example, will you be able to fully fund your tax-advantaged retirement accounts? If you can't, count the lost tax benefits as another cost of owning land.

>> **Determine what improvements the land may need.** Engineering fees; subdivision map and permit costs; environmental studies; stormwater control; running utility, water, and sewer lines; building roads; curbs and gutters;

landscaping; and so on all cost money. If you plan to develop and build on the land that you purchase, research these costs. Make sure you don't make these estimates with your rose-tinted sunglasses on — improvements almost always cost more than you expect them to. (You need to check with the planning or building department for their list of requirements.)

Also make sure that you have access to the land or the right to enter and leave through a public right-of-way or another's property (known as *ingress* and *egress*). Some people foolishly invest in landlocked properties. When they discover the fact later, they think that they can easily get an *easement* (legal permission to use someone else's property). Wrong!

>> **Understand the zoning and environmental issues.** The value of land is heavily dependent on what you can develop on it. Never purchase land without thoroughly understanding its zoning status and what you can and can't build on it. This advice also applies to environmental limitations that may be in place or that may come into effect without warning, diminishing the potential of your property (with no compensation).

This potential for surprise is why you must research the disposition of the planning department and nearby communities. Attend the meetings of local planning groups, if any, because some areas that are antigrowth and antidevelopment are less likely to be good places for you to buy land, especially if you need permission to do the type of project that you have in mind. Through the empowerment of local residents who sit on community boards and can influence local government officials, zoning can suddenly change for the worse — sometimes you may find that your property has been *downzoned* — a zoning alteration that can significantly reduce what you can develop on a property and therefore the property's value.

Chapter **3**

Identifying Sources of Capital

For many people, the trouble with real estate investing is that they lack the access to cash for the down payment. The old adage that "it takes money to make money" is generally true. Most real estate investing books make one of two assumptions. Some assume that you have plenty of money and just need to figure out how to buy a property, add value to it, and then sell it. Of course, it would be great if that were true, but most people aren't flush with cash. The other common assumption is that you have no money and must resort to scouring the real estate market in search of sellers so desperate to sell that they or their lenders don't require any down payment. This chapter makes neither assumption.

So how do you get started in real estate if you don't want to own distressed properties in the worst neighborhoods and you don't have a six-figure balance in your bank account to enable you to buy in the best neighborhoods? You muster all the patience you can and embrace a long-term vision. You don't have to be wealthy or have great savings to begin making attractive real estate investments.

Calculating the Costs of Admission

At some point in your life, you've surely had the experience of wanting to do something and then realizing that you don't have sufficient money to accomplish your goal. Perhaps it was as simple as lacking the pocket change to buy a chocolate bar as a child. Or maybe it happened on a vacation when you ran low on funds and tried to do business with a merchant who only took cash, which you lacked at the time. No matter — the world of real estate investing is no different. You can't play if you can't pay.

The following sections discuss the realities of the cash requirements to be a successful real estate investor.

Forgetting the myth of no money down

The title of this chapter says it all: To invest in real estate, you need capital, and likewise you need a source from which to gather said capital. On late-night infomercials, on blogs and websites, at seminars, on podcasts, and in some books, you may hear many self-appointed real estate experts tell you that you can invest in real estate with literally no money. And if that's not enticing enough, you may hear that you can buy properties where the seller will put cash in your hands.

WARNING

Have such no-money-down situations ever existed among the billions of completed real estate transactions in the history of the modern world? Why, yes, they have. Realistically, can you find such opportunities among the best real estate investing options available to you? Why, no, you can't.

Think of the people you know who still haven't found the perfect mate after decades of searching. Mr. and Ms. Perfect don't exist. Ditto the ideal real estate investment. If you use sensible criteria when seeking out properties that'll be good real estate investments and then add the requirement that you can only make such investments with no money down, you'll probably waste years searching to no avail.

REMEMBER

No-money-down properties aren't properties you want to own. And if you receive cash out of escrow upon closing on a property, you're either buying a severely distressed property that will soon require major cash infusions or you've overleveraged the property with a loan that you will eventually have to pay in full, plus interest. If it sounds too good to be true, it *is* too good to be true!

Determining what you need to get started

Most of the time, real estate investors make a down payment and borrow the majority of the money needed to complete a purchase. That is the conventional way to purchase real estate investment properties and will be the most successful method for you in the long run.

REMEMBER

In order to qualify for the most attractive financing, lenders typically require that your down payment be at least 20 percent of the property's purchase price. The best investment property loans may require 25 to 30 percent down for the most favorable terms. Lenders tend to be more conservative and require larger down payments during periods of falling real estate prices such as most areas experienced in the late 2000s and early 2010s.

For most residential investment properties, such as single-family homes, attached housing such as condos and townhomes, and small apartment buildings of up to four units, you can get access to the best financing terms by making at least a 20 to 25 percent down payment. (Mortgages on non-owner-occupied property tend to be ¼ to ½ percent higher). You may be able to make smaller down payments (as low as 10 percent or less), but you'll pay much higher interest rates and loan fees, including private mortgage insurance.

You won't find such wonderful financing options for larger apartment buildings (five or more units), commercial real estate, and raw land. Compared with residential properties of up to four units, such investment property generally requires more money down and/or higher interest rates and loan fees.

Determining how much cash you need to close on a purchase is largely a function of the negotiated purchase price, including all closing costs and fees. Suppose you're looking to buy some modest residential housing for $100,000. For a 25 percent down payment you need $25,000, and adding in another 5 percent for closing costs brings you to $30,000. If you have your heart set on buying a property that costs three times as much ($300,000 sticker price), you need to triple these amounts to a total of about $90,000 for the best financing options.

Rounding Up the Required Cash by Saving

Most successful real estate investors got started building their real estate investment portfolio the old-fashioned way — through saving money and then gradually buying properties over the years. Many people have difficulty saving money because they don't know how to or are simply unwilling to limit their spending.

Easy access to consumer debt (through credit cards and auto loans) creates huge obstacles to saving more and spending less.

Investing in real estate requires self-control, sacrifice, and discipline. Like most good things in life, you must be patient and plan ahead to be able to invest in real estate.

As young adults, some (but not most) people are good savers out of the gate. Those who save regularly are often folks who acquired sound financial habits from their parents. Other good savers have a high level of motivation to accomplish goals such as starting a business, buying a home, having the flexibility to spend time with their kids, saving for retirement, and so on. Achieving such goals is much harder (if not impossible) when you're living paycheck-to-paycheck and worried about next month's bills.

REMEMBER

If you're not satisfied with how much of your monthly earnings you're able to save, you have two options (and you can take advantage of both):

>> **Boost your income:** To increase your take-home pay, working more may be a possibility, or you may be able to take a more lucrative career path. Keep your priorities in order. You shouldn't put your personal health and relationships on the back burner for a workaholic schedule. You should also invest in your education. A solid education, via college or a technical trade or advanced skill, is the path to greater financial rewards and leads to all the great goals discussed here. Education is key not only for your chosen profession or career but also for real estate investing. Consider getting a real estate license or learn to be an appraiser or property manager — skills that not only help you with your property investing but also may allow you to take on part-time work to supplement your income.

>> **Reduce your spending:** For most people, this is the path to increased savings. You can generate cash flow for investments by living well beneath your means. Start by analyzing how much you expend on different areas (for instance, food, clothing, transportation, insurance, and entertainment) each month. After you've got the data, decide where and how you want to cut back. Would you rather eat out less or have a housekeeper come less often? How about driving a less expensive (but not less safe) car versus taking lower cost vacations? Although the possibilities to reduce your spending are many, you and only you can decide which options you're willing and able to implement. If you need more help with this vital financial topic, consult the latest edition of *Personal Finance For Dummies* by Eric Tyson (Wiley).

Overcoming Down Payment Limitations

Most people, especially when they make their first real estate purchase, are strapped for cash. If you don't have 20–plus percent of the purchase price, don't panic and don't get depressed — you can still own real estate. The following sections have some solutions — you can either change your approach, allowing you more time to save or lowering your entry fees, or you can seek other sources of funding.

Changing your approach

Some ways you can alter your approach without having to find money elsewhere are as follows:

>> **Seek low-money-down loans with private mortgage insurance:** Some lenders may offer you a mortgage even though you may be able to put down only 10 percent of the purchase price. These lenders will likely require you to purchase *private mortgage insurance* (PMI) for your loan. This insurance generally costs several hundred dollars per year and protects the lender if you default on your loan. (When you do have at least 20 percent or higher equity in the property, you can generally eliminate the PMI.)

>> **Delay your gratification:** If you don't want the cost and strain of extra fees and bad mortgage terms, postpone your purchase. Boost your savings rate. Examine your current spending habits and plan to build up a nest egg to use to invest in your first rental. Often real estate investors get started by actually buying a new home and simply keeping their old home as a rental.

>> **Think smaller:** Consider lower-priced properties. Smaller properties and ones that need some major work can help keep down the purchase price and the required down payment. For example, a duplex where you live in one unit and rent out the other is also a cost-effective way to get started. Numerous folks have used this entry strategy into rental property ownerships to achieve two goals: an owner-occupied place to live and a rental property that is convenient to manage.

>> **Turn to low entry cost options:** For the ultimate in low entry costs while adding real estate to your investment allocation strategy, *real estate investment trusts* (REITs) are best. These stock exchange–traded securities (which can also be bought through REIT-focused mutual funds and ETFs [exchange-traded funds]) can be bought into for several thousand dollars or less (you can invest even less in ETFs). REIT mutual funds can often be purchased for $1,000 or less inside retirement accounts.

Lease options represent another low-cost (although more complicated) opportunity. With these, you begin by renting a property you may be interested in purchasing down the road. In the interim, a portion of your monthly rental payment goes toward the future purchase price. If you can find a seller willing to provide financing, you can keep your down payment to a minimum.

Tapping into other common cash sources

Saving money from your monthly earnings will probably be the foundation for your real estate investing program. However, you may have access to other financial resources for down payments. Monitor how much of your overall investment portfolio you place into real estate and how diversified and appropriate your holdings are given your overall goals. (Refer to Chapter 1 in Book 8.)

Dipping into your retirement savings

Some employer plans allow you to borrow against your retirement account balance, under the condition that you repay the loan within a set number of years. Subject to eligibility requirements, first-time homebuyers can make penalty-free withdrawals of up to $10,000 from IRA accounts. (*Note:* You still must pay regular income tax on the withdrawal, which can significantly reduce the cash available.)

Borrowing against home equity

Most real estate investors began building their real estate portfolio after they bought their own home. Conservatively tapping into your home's equity may be a good down payment source for your property investments.

REMEMBER

You can generally obtain mortgage money at a lower interest rate on your home than you can on investment property. The smaller the risk to the lender, the lower its required return, and thus, the better rates for you as the borrower. Lenders view rental property as a higher risk proposition and for good reason: They know that when finances go downhill and the going gets really tough, people pay their home mortgage to avoid losing the roof over their heads before they pay debts on a rental property.

TIP

Unless your current mortgage was locked in at lower rates than are available today, it's generally recommend to refinance the first trust deed loan and free up equity that way versus taking out a home equity loan or line of credit.

A variation on the borrowing-against-home-equity idea uses the keep-your-original-home-as-a-rental strategy. You build up significant equity in your owner-occupied home and then need or want a new home. Refinance the existing home (while you still live there, for the best owner-occupied rates) and then convert it into a rental. Take the tax-free proceeds from the refinance and use that as the down payment on your new owner-occupied home.

Before you go running out to borrow to the maximum against your home, be sure that you

WARNING

» **Can handle the larger payments:** Don't borrow more than the value of your home, as you may be enticed to do with some of the loan programs that pitch borrowing upwards of 125 percent of the value of your home. These programs are routinely touted as a way to free up equity and pay down consumer debt, and they also encourage people to borrow in excess of the current value of their home so they can invest in more real estate. This excessive leveraging is dangerous and could come back to haunt you! Please see Chapter 1 in Book 8 for the big picture on personal financial considerations.

» **Understand the tax ramifications of all your alternatives:** Borrowing more against your home at what appears to be a slightly lower rate may end up costing you more after taxes if some of the borrowing isn't tax-deductible. Under current tax laws, interest paid on home mortgages (first and second homes) of up to $750,000 is tax-deductible ($1 million for mortgage debt acquired on or before December 15, 2017).

Be careful to understand the tax-deductibility issue when you refinance a home mortgage and borrow more than you originally had outstanding on the prior loan. If any of the extra amount borrowed isn't used to buy, build, or improve your primary or secondary residence, the deductibility of the interest on the excess amount borrowed is limited.

» **Fully comprehend the risks of losing your home to foreclosure:** The more you borrow against your home, the greater the risk that you may lose the roof over your head to foreclosure should you not be able to make your mortgage payments. That's exactly what happened to too many folks during the late 2000s and early 2010s real estate market decline. Although you need to use your cash for investing in and improving real estate, you should always keep some cash in a checking or money market rainy day account (for example, for a new roof, painting, and so on) and not cut things so close that you could lose it all.

Moving financial investments into property investments

As you gain more comfort and confidence as a real estate investor, you may want to redirect some of your dollars from other investments like stocks, bonds, mutual funds, and ETFs into property. If you do, be mindful of the following:

>> **Diversification:** Real estate is one of the prime investments (the others being stocks and small business) for long-term appreciation potential. Be sure that you understand your portfolio's overall asset allocation and risk when making changes. Please see Chapter 1 in Book 8 for more details.

>> **Tax issues:** If you've held other investments for more than one year, you can take advantage of the low long-term capital gains tax rates if you now want to sell. The maximum federal tax rate for so-called long-term capital gains (investments sold for more than they were purchased for after more than 12 months) is now 20 percent. If your modified adjusted gross income exceeds $200,000 for single taxpayers or $250,000 for married taxpayers filing jointly, you have to pony up an extra 3.8 percent to help pay for the Affordable Care Act (also known as Obamacare). Investors in the two lowest federal income tax brackets of 10 and 15 percent enjoy a 0 percent long-term capital gains tax rate. Try to avoid selling appreciated investments within the first year of ownership. Be sure to check on the latest tax laws because there's no guarantee these rates will continue in the future.

Separating investments from cash-value life insurance

You may own a *cash-value* life insurance policy — one that combines a life insurance death benefit with a savings type account in which some money accumulates and on which interest is paid. In addition to being a costly cash drain with its relatively high premiums, cash-value life insurance investment returns tend to be mediocre to dismal.

REMEMBER

You're best off separating your life insurance purchases from your investing. If you need life insurance (because others are dependent on your income), buy a *term life* policy, which is pure, unadulterated life insurance. But don't cancel your current cash-value policies before replacing them with term if you do indeed need life insurance protection.

IN THIS CHAPTER

» **Choosing your investment area**

» **Looking at what makes a good investment location**

» **Discovering what's in your own backyard**

» **Comparing neighborhoods**

» **Getting to know seller's markets and buyer's markets**

Chapter **4**

Location, Location, Value

As the well-known real estate saying goes, "The three most important factors to success in real estate are location, location, and location!" There *is* a strong correlation between the location of your real estate investments and your financial success. And the location of your real estate investment is critical in determining your success as a real estate investor. But this phrase is preferable: "Location, location, value." This revised adage clearly emphasizes location but also stresses the importance of finding good value for your investment dollar.

Merely owning real estate isn't the key to success in real estate investing; acquiring and owning the right real estate at the right price is the way to build wealth! As you gain experience in real estate, you'll develop your own strategy, but to make any strategy succeed, you need to do your homework and diligently and fairly evaluate both the positive and negative aspects of your proposed real estate investment.

This chapter covers important aspects of regional and local demographics, how to analyze the economy, and which factors are most important to real estate investing. It also discusses barriers to entry and the supply/demand equation. Then you discover where to find this information and how to interpret the numbers to determine your local areas with the most potential. Finally, this chapter discusses real estate cycles and timing.

Deciding Where to Invest

If you're going to invest in real estate, you need to decide on a location. Most real estate investors initially — and wisely — look in their local communities.

REMEMBER

This chapter gives you the tools to evaluate properties anywhere, but you have an inherent advantage if you begin your search close to home. Unless you really know another real estate market and regularly find yourself there for other reasons anyway, stay close to home with your real estate investments — no more than one to two hours away by your preferred mode of transportation.

Although you should cut your teeth on an income property or two in your local market, establish parameters that meet your specific needs. For example, maybe you have family responsibilities that limit the amount of time you can devote to overseeing and managing your real estate investments.

Although virtually everyone lives in an area with opportunities for real estate investing, not everyone lives in an area where the prospects are good for real estate in general. That's why it's important to broaden your geographic investment horizon as long as you don't compromise your ability to effectively manage and control your property.

Even if you decide to invest in real estate in your own locale, you still need to do tons of research to decide where and what to buy — extremely important decisions with long-term consequences. This chapter explains what to look for in a region, a community, and even a neighborhood before you make that investment decision. Keep in mind, though, that you can spend the rest of your life looking for the *perfect* real estate investment, never find it, never invest, and miss out on lots of opportunities, profit, and even fun.

Finding Properties to Add Value

So you're looking for properties that allow you to make physical and/or fiscal improvements that will ultimately lower the expected cap rate to a future investor, which is essentially lowering the required rate of return because you have taken out much of the risk. You want to buy when you determine that the property has a strong likelihood of producing future increases in net operating income (NOI) and cash flow. So, you should look for properties where your analysis shows that the revenue for the property can be increased or the expenses reduced.

TECHNICAL STUFF

Cap rate, short for capitalization rate, is a way to determine a property's value — the NOI is divided by the cost of the property to figure the rate of return.

As you look for your next rental property, many sellers, and especially their real estate brokers, will assure you that the current rents are really too low and that there is a tremendous upside in the property to be tapped simply by buying the property and raising the rents. If it were truly that easy, then why wouldn't the current owner raise the rent and sell the property for a higher price?

However, if you thoroughly research the market, you'll know how to identify certain clues that indicate whether a property really has rents that are below market. Properties with no vacancies and a waiting list are prime candidates. Other telltale signs are properties that have low turnover and then have multiple applicants for those rare vacancies. Economics 101 says that if demand exceeds supply, the price is too low.

Some owners actually market their real estate investment properties at a below-market price. These are motivated sellers, probably with a variety of personal reasons for their need to sell more quickly and cheaply than they would if they had more time and patience. Health reasons, family dissolutions, financial issues, and so on are all likely reasons that a seller will agree to a quick sale at a below-market price.

However, some sellers don't achieve the top value in the market for other reasons. For example, some owners despise the whole process of selling their rental properties so much that they knowingly underprice the property to ensure a quick and clean transaction and retain the ability to reject any and all contingencies that a buyer would typically require in a *market deal*. The elimination of hassling and haggling is paramount to these sellers; they just want to get the sale done, so they're willing to give the buyer such a good deal that the buyer takes the property essentially as-is.

Some sellers are truly ignorant of the actual market value of the property they're selling. There really is no excuse (save laziness) for a seller in a major metropolitan area to not know the true value of the property they own, because there are many real estate professionals who can inexpensively assist sellers in determining the estimated value of their property. Simply ask a real estate broker for a comparative market analysis (CMA) or hire an appraiser, and you'll get a detailed report determining the current as-is value of the investment property based on research of the prices at which similar properties in the same area have recently sold. Of course, a seller should always keep in mind that some real estate brokers may be overly optimistic on pricing with the hope that they can get a listing and then still close the sale at a price that is really the market value.

TIP

One common question from real estate investors is "How do I find underpriced properties?" Underpriced investment properties typically have older owners with no mortgage who have exhausted the possibility of taking depreciation deductions on their tax returns.

Look for properties where you can increase value. These *value-added properties* are properties that allow you to either increase the NOI or decrease the cap rate and thus create value. The value of a property is increased with an increase in NOI or a decrease in the capitalization rate. The capitalization rate is directly correlated to the anticipated risk of the investment, so stabilizing properties through long-term leases and more financially viable tenants can reduce risk and lead to a lower cap rate and hence a higher value.

A simple example of how to increase the value of a building is to find a residential rental property in a high demand area where the current owner has set all rental rates the same for similar floor plans. In reality, the rents should reflect the fact that, say, not all two-bedroom units have the same location benefits. For example, a unit overlooking the pool is often more desirable than a unit on the main street, or units on the upper floors are in greater demand, so raising the rents for the more desirable units increases rental income. You want to create a range of unit pricing based on the more desirable and high demand locations.

Evaluating a Region: The Big Picture

Though you're advised to think local, any decision about where to invest should start with an evaluation of the overall economic viability and trends of the surrounding region. If the region isn't economically sound, the likelihood for successful real estate investments within that area is diminished. Understand how to evaluate important economic data so that you can invest in the areas that are poised for growth.

In this context, a *region* is a concentrated population base (rather than an entire state or section of the country). Data for any larger geographic area would be difficult to use for the types of real estate investments you'll be making. For example, data for the entire state of Texas isn't as important as vital economic trends for your proposed investment in the Austin area.

Gathering and analyzing the relevant economic data has never been easier, thanks to the internet. The most important data for population growth, job growth, and economic trends is available online, and there are numerous entities tracking this information. From the federal government, to state and local governments, to universities and business groups, information on regional economic trends is readily available.

TIP

In addition to the academic and governmental agencies that provide broader economic indicators, several private firms specialize in providing specific data on occupancy, availability, and rental rates for different types of real estate for many of the major cities throughout the country. These services offer limited information to non-subscribers. For example, two favorites with a national perspective are the CoStar Group (www.costar.com) and SitusAMC (www.situsamc.com). There are many smaller firms that specialize in specific geographic areas, like MarketPointe Realty Advisors, which focuses on Southern California (www.marketpointe.com), or Yardi Matrix (www.yardimatrix.com), which focuses on larger apartment communities of 50 or more units throughout most major metropolitan areas of the country. Check with real estate investment professionals that hold the Certified Commercial Investment Member (CCIM) designation in your area, because they have access to the excellent CCIM Institute's Site to Do Business (STDB) (www.stdb.com).

TIP

You can find the vital economic data you need for your evaluation through your local economic development department, chamber of commerce, or public library and their associated websites. Real estate lenders often have in-house economists who collect information concerning areas where they lend money, and these folks are often the first to detect weaknesses in the market. So if your lender isn't particularly enamored about the location for your proposed real estate investment, it probably knows something that you should heed. Also, contact a professional appraiser in your area, because they routinely collect this information for their appraisals.

These sources collect, record, analyze, and report information according to specific geographic boundaries as established by the federal government. The U.S. government divides urbanized areas of the country into *Standardized Metropolitan Statistical Areas* (SMSAs). SMSAs are large areas that consist of one or more major cities. For example, the entire San Francisco Bay Area, the combined areas of Dallas and Fort Worth, Greater Los Angeles, and Greater New York City are each a single SMSA.

If your proposed investment isn't in an area tracked as part of an SMSA, much of the same information is available, but you have to do a little more digging.

REMEMBER

You're looking for more than just numbers. Attitude and leadership are important as well. Many neighboring cities are working together with regional planning boards and economic development agencies. Their goal is job creation, and they possess great powers to make important economic decisions regarding regional airports, mass transportation, and the reuse of surplus military installations.

Clearly, such regional governance can have a major impact for better or worse on your real estate investments.

You're looking for a region or area that is growing and has a diverse economic base with strong employment prospects. The following sections cover some of the more significant factors that can impact real estate demand and values.

Population growth

Population growth is one of the cornerstones upon which demand for real estate is based. More people means more demand for housing, retail shopping, and offices and service providers. In other words, people use real estate, so the demand for real estate is enhanced as the population increases.

Increases or decreases in population are the result of three activities: births, mortality, and people moving into or out of the area. In most areas, births exceed deaths, and thus most areas experience moderate growth. So the real impact comes from a dynamic and mobile society. There have been tremendous shifts in population from northern states to the more temperate climates of the Sunbelt. Immigration has also been and will continue to be a major factor in many parts of the country.

REMEMBER

How does population growth affect your real estate decisions? Simply put, economists find that a new dwelling unit (single-family home, condo, apartment) is needed for every increase in population of approximately three persons. Household formation growth (and hence demand for more housing) is an estimate of the number of new households that are formed based on the expected population growth and the rates at which different age, income, and other groups form households. Of course, these numbers can vary, especially in urban areas with population increases from immigration. So, if you're considering investments in rental homes or small apartment buildings in a certain area, the overall net population growth can be a factor in determining current and future demand for rental housing.

But knowing the increase in population for the entire SMSA or region isn't enough because population growth isn't evenly spread and can vary. As you get down to the next level in your research (see the later section "Investigating Your Local Market"), you need to determine the communities and even neighborhoods where the increased population will want to live, work, and shop. Real estate developers, and their lenders, look closely at net population growth in specific submarkets to forecast the demand for their proposed developments.

Job growth and income levels

Job growth is another fundamental element in determining demand for real estate. Economists generally predict that a new household is needed for every 1.5 jobs created. So if a new employer moves into the area and brings 150 new jobs, the local real estate housing market will need approximately 100 new dwelling units. Of course, these new jobs also positively impact the demand for commercial, industrial, and retail properties.

TIP

The U.S. Bureau of Labor Statistics compiles job growth and other economic data by SMSA as well as by county. This info is available at the Bureau's website (www.bls.gov). Other great sources for economic data are local colleges and universities, Chamber of Commerce and similar pro-business groups, and good local libraries.

But you need more information about the types of jobs before you can estimate their effect on the demand for each type of real estate. Although job growth is critical, so are the following factors:

WARNING

>> **Income levels:** Without stable, *well-paying* jobs, an area can stagnate. Even with positive growth in population and jobs, a lack of income can stifle the demand for additional residential and commercial properties.

>> **Level of employment diversification:** If the local economy is heavily reliant on jobs in a small number of industries, that dependence increases the risk of your real estate investments. Some areas of the country have plenty of jobs, but they're lower- rather than higher-paying jobs. Ideally, look to invest in real estate in communities that maintain diverse job bases.

>> **Industries represented:** Consider which industries are more heavily represented in the local economy. If most of the jobs come from slow-growing or shrinking employment sectors, such as small retail and government, real estate prices are unlikely to rise quickly in the years ahead. On the other hand, areas with a greater preponderance of high-growth industries, such as technology and biotech, generally stand a greater chance of faster price appreciation.

>> **Types of jobs:** The specific types of jobs available can be important depending on the target market for your income property. If you're buying a class A office building in an urban area, look for statistics on current and future employment levels for professional employment. For example, owning an office building across the street from the new regional courthouse gives you a real advantage in attracting law firms and legal support firms. Of course, you also want to make sure that the area boasts a good mix of nearby retail and food services to complement and support the tenants in your building.

TIP

In addition to job growth, other good signs to look for include the following:

>> **Stable-to-increasing wages:** The demand for real estate clearly correlates to income levels, so local jobs with strong underlying demand are key. With many jobs being outsourced to other parts of the country and world, it's important that the local jobs aren't only secure but also unlikely to see an erosion in purchasing power.

>> **A recession-resistant employment base:** Traditionally, jobs that enjoy stability are in the fields of education, government, and healthcare. Even areas renowned for strong demand and a limited supply of real estate can slow down if the economy is hit hard, as shown by the collapse of some technology firms in the early 2000s and outsourcing or consolidations and mergers in the mid-2000s.

>> **Employment that's highly unlikely to be outsourced:** Jobs can flow to another area of the country or overseas to the latest low-cost manufacturing base.

>> **Declining unemployment:** Examine how the jobless rate has changed in recent years.

REMEMBER

No one can precisely predict the future. And with due respect to economists, forecasts of population and job growth can go awry. Also, human nature can defy what seem like logical trends. The record number of aging baby boomers led to the development of significant housing for seniors, yet many people prefer to stay in their own homes and the demand for senior housing has been mixed.

Investigating Your Local Market

Although everything starts at the regional level, you need to fine-tune your perspective and look at your local real estate market, too. All of the same types of economic data that you collect on a regional basis are important in evaluating your local real estate market.

REMEMBER

With real estate investing, deciding where to invest is frequently more important than choosing the specific rental property. You can have a rental property that has positive attributes, but if it's located in a declining area where the demand is weak or an area with overbuilding and an excess of available properties, your investment won't perform financially. (These properties perform the worst over time, but are typically the types of properties highly touted by the infomercial gurus who love to brag about the "value" of how much real estate they control but rarely tell you about their long-term investment returns.)

Likewise, you need to determine the areas that may be too richly priced, because your cash flow and future appreciation will be hurt if you overpay for a property. Often properties in the best neighborhoods in town are so overpriced that there is little appreciation potential, and thus you should seek other properties unless you're content with low returns similar to investing in safe and low-yielding bonds.

In many local real estate markets, the demand for real estate is impacted more by the regional economy than by the local economy as long as there are efficient and accessible transportation options. For example, bedroom communities have high demand for rental homes and apartments even though they may only have service sector jobs in the immediate area, because the higher income professional and manufacturing jobs are concentrated in other areas of the region.

REMEMBER

The following sections help you research quantitative issues to consider when deciding where to invest in real estate. But you also must consider other factors, such as the weather or recreation and entertainment options — all key factors in the livability or quality of life for citizens. All of these criteria contribute to the overall desirability of a local market area and should be important considerations for the real estate investor. And don't underestimate the image or reputation of an area.

Supply and demand

The supply and demand for real estate in a given market has a direct impact on the financial performance of your income property. And although the overall economic prospects for a region or community are vital, you must also find supply and demand information about the specific type of real estate that you plan to purchase.

Obviously, the best environment for investing in real estate is one with strong demand and limited supply. When the demand exceeds supply, shortages of available real estate push up prices.

Both sides of the equation — supply and demand — have indicators that you should evaluate in forming your consensus about the strength of the local real estate market. The following sections take a close look at each indicator in detail. Supply-side indicators include building permits, the rate at which new properties have been rented or absorbed into the market, and the availability of alternatives for similar real estate. Demand indicators include occupancy and rent levels.

The overall relationship between supply and demand determines the market conditions for real estate. For example, a large number of pending or recently issued building permits, weak absorption or rental of new properties, and an excess of income property listings that have been on the market for an extended time are all indicators that the supply of a specific product type is greater than the demand.

Such market conditions soon result in lower occupancy, lower rents, and often rental concessions like free rent or lower rental rates early in the lease, which mean lower cash flow and smaller appreciation potential. These aren't the markets you should be seeking.

When the demand for real estate is high, there are few vacancies, and property owners raise rents and eliminate or minimize any concessions. In commercial properties, landlords cut back on the tenant improvement (TI) allowance and require the tenants to take the space as-is and make any upgrades or changes to the space at their own expense.

Building permits and absorption

Building permits are often the first tangible step outlining the intent of a developer to build new real estate projects. Therefore, knowing about the issuance of building permits is an essential leading indicator to the future supply of real estate.

TIP

The trend in the number of building permits tells you how the supply of real estate properties may soon change. A long and sustained rise in permits over several years can indicate that the supply of new property may dampen future price appreciation. In the late 1990s, despite the low-interest-rate environment, most parts of the country weren't overbuilding, but by the mid-to-late 2000s, there was nevertheless an excess of supply. The problem was that the demand was artificially inflated, which was the result of governmental pressure to increase home ownership by offering creative financing to individuals who were unqualified to borrow such large amounts, as well as speculation by some real estate investors. The crazy and irresponsible speculation was particularly pronounced in certain Sunbelt areas like Las Vegas, Phoenix, and many parts of Florida.

Absorption, the rate at which new buildings are rented and occupied, can be useful to determine the potential for the market to become *saturated,* or oversupplied with certain types of real estate. A healthy real estate market is one in which the available new properties are rented in a relatively short period of time — typically measured in months. Absorption is measured in housing units for residential properties and in square footage for all commercial types of properties.

Absorption can be either a positive or negative number and is usually tracked on a quarterly and annual basis:

>> **Positive absorption:** More space is rented or occupied by owners/users during the measured time period than was built or taken out of the overall supply by demolition or even conversion to owner-occupied residential or commercial use.

>> **Negative absorption:** The new supply of a given type of real estate is being built faster than users can or want to use it.

TIP

You can obtain information on building permits from your local planning or building department. Absorption statistics aren't as easy to find, but local real estate appraisers and real estate brokers track absorption. For example, professional real estate brokers holding the CCIM (Certified Commercial Investment Member) designation specialize in the sale of income properties and often have that information.

REMEMBER

Building permits and absorption are property-type specific, and an oversupply in industrial properties generally has no bearing on other types of commercial income properties such as retail or office. The only exception is when the use of a property can be changed. For example, many industrial properties have been upgraded to add office space for manufacturing firms so they can have their administrative functions and operations in the same facility. This is called "flex space" and is a type of hybrid usage that is more difficult to track, as it can be changed easily to meet the specific needs of the occupant — but it's extremely important to note if it's occurring in your proposed investment market.

Another noteworthy trend for residential real estate investors is that new construction favors single-family homes rather than multifamily apartments. This discrepancy can have a significant impact on your decision whether to invest in single-family rental properties or multifamily properties, because existing multifamily properties benefit from the reduced competition. There are several reasons for this phenomenon, and some of them are discussed in the later section "Considering barriers to entry."

Availability of housing alternatives — renting versus buying

When the cost of buying is relatively low compared with the cost of renting, more renters can afford to purchase, thus increasing the number of home sales and lowering demand for rentals. A key indicator you can use to gauge the market is the number of property listings:

>> **Increase in property listings:** Increasing numbers of property listings or a significant increase in the time the average property is unsold is an indication of future trouble for real estate price appreciation. However, as property prices reach high levels, some investors decide that they can make more money cashing in and investing elsewhere. When the market is flooded with listings, prospective buyers can be choosier, exerting downward pressure on prices.

>> **Decrease in property listings:** A sign of a healthy real estate market is a decreasing and low level of property listings, which indicates that the demand from buyers meets or exceeds the supply of property for sale from sellers. At high prices (relative to the cost of renting), more prospective buyers elect to rent, and the number of sales relative to listings drops.

Occupancy levels

Before you invest your hard-earned money, determine the current occupancy levels for your proposed type of income property.

The market occupancy rate is another way to gauge the supply and demand for a given property type in the local market. The *market occupancy* rate for a particular type of property is the percentage of that type of property available for occupancy that's currently rented. For example, you may find data telling you that there are 2,312 total residential rental units in apartment buildings in a local market, and the occupancy rate is 97 percent (or 2,242 are occupied), which would mean that 3 percent (or approximately 70) of the units are vacant. For commercial, industrial, and retail properties, the occupancy level is calculated based on square footage.

With commercial, industrial, and retail properties, determining the occupancy levels is relatively easy. A quick look at the directory or a walkthrough of the property can give you a lot of information.

TIP

The true occupancy rate is actually much more difficult to determine with apartment buildings, and even more difficult for rental single-family homes and condos. With apartments, the vacancies aren't usually obvious, and obtaining accurate information can be challenging — most professionally managed properties don't advertise their occupancy levels or volunteer this info (nor do they post tenant directories anymore due to safety and privacy concerns). With the single-family homes and rental condos (private owners renting out their individual units within a mostly owner-occupied community), it can be virtually impossible to gather useful information on the true occupancy rate. But fear not, we have some suggestions:

>> **Trade organizations and industry service providers:** Some of these groups track this data. For example, the local affiliates of the National Apartment Association (www.naahq.org) and the Building Owners and Managers Association (www.boma.org) often publish vacancy and rent surveys for apartments and office buildings, respectively.

>> **The do-it-yourself approach:** You can contact owners of comparable properties and offer to collect this data and give them a copy of the results. You also can drive through areas you are considering for investment, and

note signs, as well as ads on rental listing services, such as Apartments.com, Craig's List, Hotpads, Oodle, Peoplewithpets.com, Realtor.com, Rent.com, Rentals.com, Sublet.com, Trulia, and Zillow.

After you acquire the info, here's how to use it:

>> **Low vacancy rates:** When combined with a low number of building permits, low vacancy rates generally foretell future real estate price appreciation. If you find minimal vacancy in your market, it's a landlord's market with higher demand from tenants for existing units, which is a good sign for real estate owners. And it's good for real estate investors, if the market prices remain reasonable.

>> **High vacancy rates:** High rates indicate an excess supply of real estate, which may put downward pressure on rental rates, or the need for rental concessions or free rent, as many landlords compete to attract tenants.

TIP

Concessions, which typically include free rent, often indicate weakness in the rental market. However, some types of real estate and rental markets almost always have concessions, no matter how strong the rental market. This practice is very common in larger professionally managed apartment communities where a prospective tenant's first question when calling to inquire about a potential rental unit is inevitably "What's your special?" Apartments in Atlanta, Dallas, Houston, Las Vegas, Orlando, Phoenix, and many other areas of the Sunbelt may be able to raise their rents and maintain occupancies at or above 95 percent, but they can't eliminate the rental concessions or their rental traffic will diminish. In commercial properties, the tenant improvement (TI) allowance is similar, with many markets requiring certain levels of dollars per square foot in custom build-outs or upgrades when the rental rate is actually less negotiable.

Rental levels

The trend in *rent levels,* or *rental rates,* that renters are willing and able to pay over the years also gives a good indication as to the supply/demand relationship for income properties. When the demand for real estate just keeps up with the supply of housing and the local economy continues to grow, rents generally increase. This increase is a positive sign for continued real estate price appreciation.

Of course, you need to be careful to make sure that you're getting the true and complete story on rents. Owners and their property managers are very smooth and savvy and don't allow their quoted rental rates to fall when the market shows some signs of softening. This strategy is logical because other tenants may have recently leased at a higher rate and would be upset to see the new tenants getting a better deal. So, owners and property managers offer concessions or other perks to make sure that they're competitive in the current market while maintaining the perception of stable rents.

TIP

As a prospective rental property owner competing against these other property owners, you need to evaluate the current rent levels on a level playing field, so you want to calculate the *effective rental rate.* For example, if you see a comparable rental property available at $1,200 per month, but the owner is offering a concession of one month's free rent on a 12-month lease, the effective rent is really $1,100 per month (the $1,200 loss of one month's rent spread out over the rest of the year).

WARNING

An advantage of investing in commercial real estate is that there are few governmental regulations and controls, and the relationship between tenants and landlords is essentially a free market. However, residential *rent control* or *rent stabilization* (local laws regulating how much rents may increase) is an issue in some cities and towns, and is a growing trend in many areas of the country. Investing in markets with rent control, or even with a pro-tenant environment where a landlord has difficulty terminating a lease, may not provide adequate returns on investment, and appreciation will be more limited. Although occupancy levels are usually strong in such areas, your overall cash flow may be threatened because the property's expenses may rise faster than you can legally raise the rents. In these communities, landlords who invest in major upgrades or capital improvements to a rental unit may not be able to raise rents or recover their costs because any rent increases must be approved by the local rent control board. Then, even if allowed at all, the approved capital improvements are amortized or spread over many years. Don't put your real estate future in the hands of others! If you're considering property in a rent-controlled area, you may find the most recent edition of *Property Management Kit For Dummies* by Robert S. Griswold (Wiley) helpful.

Focusing on the path of progress

Buying real estate in up-and-coming areas with new development or renovated properties not only greatly enhances the ease of finding and keeping good tenants but also leads to higher occupancy, lower turnover, and higher rates of appreciation.

In virtually all major cities, some neighborhoods are experiencing new construction and growth — and have the reputation of being *the* area to live in. But by the time most folks feel this way, you've lost an opportunity to get in when prices have more appreciation potential. So, here are a few indicators to use to stay ahead of the game:

>> **Follow the retailers:** You can often take a clue about where you should invest by looking for major retailers who do extensive research before making a decision to open in a given neighborhood. For instance, maybe a new Costco, Sam's Club, Target, or Walmart is anchoring the new shopping center.

>> **Follow the highways:** One of the best and most obvious indicators of where new development is headed is transportation. But make sure that the roads or mass transit projects actually get built. After they're built, you're sure to find real estate investment opportunities. With so many funding and environmental challenges today, it can be extremely risky to invest in real estate based on proposed transportation projects.

WARNING

Consider the recent controversial and now "derailed" High-Speed Rail Authority (CAHSR) project that sought and promised to connect San Diego and Los Angeles to San Francisco and Sacramento with a high-speed rail line. Originally, this concept started as a ballot initiative first proposed in 2004, then delayed to 2006, and ultimately approved by voters in 2008. The voters approved $9 billion construction bonds toward the total estimated cost of the $33.6 billion project set to open in 2028, with service between San Francisco and Los Angeles. After numerous delays and cost overruns, the now $77 billion project with a revised 2033 completion year may never be completed, and even the only segment under construction in California's limited-population Central Valley between Merced and Bakersfield may never see actual service.

But the path of progress isn't limited to new development. Many cities have areas that have seen better days and local leaders are doing their best to revitalize these tired and even blighted sections of town. A key component can be redevelopment districts that are formed with the property tax revenues being diverted to a special redevelopment agency that promotes new projects through a streamlined approval process and financial assistance. Often, the traditional downtown areas are being redeveloped with many incentives for developers and owners willing to be among the first ones in.

WARNING

Although redevelopment areas can be great opportunities, significant risk is associated with investing in areas that are dynamic and changing. Like transportation projects, sometimes the best intentions of local leaders and redevelopment agencies can hit a snag.

Considering barriers to entry

Investing in real estate in an area that has strong demand and limited supply is likely to enhance your profits. One of the trends to follow is the creation of more roadblocks to new development and thus severe limitations on the construction of additional buildings to meet even the increasing demands for real estate from natural population growth.

For example, maybe your chosen area has inhabitants with strong anti-apartment sentiments or concerns about the environment. If you currently own or quickly invest in existing apartments in such areas, these factors can actually work to your benefit because they make the addition of more housing units (competition) difficult.

TIP

Look for markets where natural and even man-made barriers to entry exist.

The popular board game Monopoly taught most people from an early age about the importance of location and barriers to entry. When you control the playing field and prime properties, you dramatically improve your odds of successfully building wealth. (*Note:* The real world of real estate isn't like Monopoly where you're getting money at the other players' expense.) The following sections cover some of the more prominent factors that limit the supply of real estate and enhance cash flow and future appreciation for those who already own existing properties.

REMEMBER

But, in the long term, the lack of buildable land in an area can prove a problem. Real estate prices that are too high may cause employers and employees to relocate to less expensive areas. If you want to invest in real estate in an area with little buildable land and sky-high prices, run the numbers to see whether the deal makes economic sense.

Environmental issues

Individuals and organizations concerned about the environment aren't a new trend. Environmental issues are a key factor in the potential development of real estate projects in just about every area of the country.

Those concerned about the environment are expressing their disapproval of new and proposed projects with more authority and success because federal and state laws require excruciating investigative reports on all aspects of proposed land development. It's extremely difficult in most urban areas to find land suitable for development that doesn't have some limitations or require remediation, such as the relocation or preservation of endangered species or plants. (Remediation can also include the cleanup and removal of contaminants.)

Many of these laws or guidelines find universal support — no one wants to live in a concrete world or destroy our beautiful countryside. And nearly everyone wants clean air, clean water, and the highest quality of living possible.

But preserving and protecting our environment comes at a cost: A significant portion of potential developable land is being taken out of production or even consideration for use. The land that isn't available for development is being broadened and now includes much of the government-owned land and virtually all land that can be classified as a hillside, wetland, or *vernal pool* (seasonal or temporary wetland). In many areas, additional swaths of public and private land are being designated and set aside by governmental agencies to protect endangered plants and wildlife.

These man-made decisions to preserve land, combined with other factors, can lead to a shortage of buildable land.

Shortage of buildable land

Economics 101 teaches that strong demand and a limited supply lead to rationing through higher pricing. Well, that is exactly what's been happening over the decades in many of America's major metropolitan areas as people exhaust the supply of buildable land (notwithstanding the general decline in real estate prices in the late 2000s and early 2010s).

Upward pressure on real estate prices tends to be greatest in areas with little buildable land. This characteristic was one of the things that attracted coauthor Eric to invest in real estate in the San Francisco Bay Area when he moved there in the mid-1980s. If you look at a map of this area, you can see that the city of San Francisco and the communities to the south are on a peninsula. The ocean, bay inlets, and mountains bound the rest of the Bay Area. More than 80 percent of the land in the greater Bay Area isn't available for development because state and federal government parks, preserves, and other areas protect the land from development, or the land is impossible to develop. Of the land available for development in San Francisco and the vast majority of it in nearby counties, virtually all of it had already been developed.

CANES: Citizens Against Nearly Everything

Many cities are now putting more authority into the hands of local and even neighborhood planning boards that exercise their influence and control over proposed new developments. Although many of the representatives on these local planning boards are just interested in maintaining the aesthetics or compatibility of proposed developments with the existing land uses, some are motivated by another agenda.

The term CANES — *Citizens Against Nearly Everything* — was coined by then-San Diego Padres President Larry Lucchino while the baseball team proposed and fought for the development of a new ballpark. Various groups claiming to represent taxpayers, citizens, and environmentalists objected at every opportunity. Ultimately, after years of delays and dozens of lawsuits, the ballpark finally opened in downtown San Diego and has been a tremendous catalyst for redevelopment just as new sports venues have been in many other cities.

This trend isn't unique to San Diego. Across the country, those opposed to growth seek to avoid increased traffic, congestion, and overcrowding of their schools and parks. In many communities and neighborhoods, homeowners are expressing their disapproval of new multifamily development. (If you want a big turnout at city hall, just announce that 300 new low-income apartments are being built across the street from the new for-sale housing tract.)

REMEMBER

Such resistance to new development or even redevelopment isn't new. But it does seem to be a trend that should be considered by even a real estate investor with a duplex or a couple of rental homes. Unbridled growth isn't the answer (nor are stagnation and decline), but the point is that you need to evaluate the impact of such attitudes on your income properties. Barriers to entry are a reality that you shouldn't overlook.

For example, increased demand in a community opposed to growth results in higher prices, so investing in these areas certainly enhances your prospects for appreciation. However, well-planned or *smart* growth can also lead to a higher quality of living and greater long-term returns on your investment.

Condo conversion and construction defect lawsuits

The real estate boom and bust cycles are often most pronounced in those cities that experience large numbers of apartment buildings being converted to condominiums. When the prices for new construction homes become too high, developers have a lucrative market to buy apartments, cosmetically upgrade the units, and sell them to entry-level buyers who want to own rather than rent. The early projects often do well, but the developers who are late entries after the initial demand has been met and when the market becomes oversaturated aren't so fortunate.

Carefully evaluate the impact of the condominium market in your area because it can have a material effect on the overall supply of rental housing. Apartments converted to condos often result in fewer rental units because condo conversion units are typically purchased by owner-occupants who find such housing to be a financially viable entry-level opportunity.

But the reverse trend is also a concern because many areas have a significant number of failed condo conversion projects where only a portion of the units are sold; the remaining units are in foreclosure or bankruptcy and are being sold in bulk to owners who rent them until the market improves. Investors often purchase new condominiums to use as rentals that will compete for tenants. Some of these projects were financially unsuccessful and are in the hands of court-appointed receivers or lenders. These are supply and demand factors that can affect your real estate market and should be part of your real estate strategy.

Many apartment buildings in urban areas were originally built as condominiums, but market weakness or the threat of construction defect legislation (discussed later in this section) led to a business decision by the developers to operate these condos as rental units. There isn't much controversy about the ultimate conversion of these rental condos to owner-occupied units; it's just a function of market timing, with most remaining as rentals in the current market environment.

However, a dilemma faced by many cities is the excessive number of conversion projects of apartment rental communities into condominiums. On one hand, the severe shortage of affordable entry-level housing in many cities made the conversion of apartments to condominiums an excellent opportunity for first-time home buyers. The concern was that conversion of apartments to owner-occupied condos reduced the supply of rentals.

How are condo conversions typically handled? The most common game plan for a conversion of an existing apartment community to a condominium project almost always consists of extensive exterior renovation, including painting, landscaping, and other cosmetic items. Occasionally, local ordinances require some structural repairs or upgrades, but the exterior work is primarily limited to the cosmetic issues. In other words, rarely do developers spend a lot of money on a new roof!

The unit interiors also receive a complete overhaul and upgrade — new flooring, window treatments, new and often upgraded appliances, and solid countertops and other decorative touches to really make the unit shine. These converted condos can be quite attractive as reasonably priced investments that look great and are well located, many times in areas where new development is difficult because the area is completely built-out and the cost to acquire the land would be prohibitive. But you need to look deeper than the smoke and mirrors that create the attractive façade of quality construction.

WARNING

The problem is that in most cases, the existing building systems, such as the roof, plumbing, electrical, and HVAC, haven't been upgraded or replaced. So you may have a brand-new interior that looks sharp, but the major structural systems are quite old. Also, properties built under the code requirements in effect at the time of original construction usually have lower standards for weatherproofing, insulation, and noise reduction. If you buy one of these converted apartments as a rental property, you may not know that your tenants can hear everything that goes on in the adjacent unit. That is, until they call to complain!

This conversion of apartments to condominiums can impact the rental market in one of two ways:

TIP

>> Some of the condos are purchased by individuals who intend to live there personally. These cases reduce the rental housing stock, which means less competition for apartments.

Further, a good balance of owner-occupied housing units (with their inherent increased pride of ownership) can be healthy for the overall rental market. Real estate investors should purchase rental homes in areas that are predominantly owner-occupied.

>> Other converted condos aren't owner-occupied, with many investors snapping up the reasonably priced units, speculating that they'll enjoy good returns. These units will be rented out, so there is no reduction in the rental housing stock.

TIP

In the long run, investing in condominiums that began life as apartments isn't wise. In the early years, when the appliances and surface interior and exterior cosmetic finishes are relatively new, not much can go wrong. But after the true age of the building begins to show through increased repairs and maintenance, the volunteer association board of directors will face challenges. Will it be willing and able to dramatically increase the monthly assessments to cover the increased costs and to accrue the funds necessary to handle major capital items? The assessments stay artificially low and the property condition declines over time. You don't want to own a unit in an association with major physical problems and no reserves.

The construction of new, attached, for-sale housing (or condominiums) has been severely restricted for decades in many parts of the country due to *construction defect lawsuits.* The building industry claims that such lawsuits are unnecessary and extremely wasteful, and the attorneys representing homeowners insist that litigation would be unwarranted if the builders simply didn't build such shoddy and poorly constructed housing units. Construction defect lawsuits are reducing the number of attached housing projects that are being built because insurance is virtually nonexistent for developers and subcontractors.

Government's effect on real estate

The United States offers many examples of the importance of state and local government on prospects for prosperity. The following are key governmental and quasi-governmental factors to consider when researching a prospective community in which to invest:

>> **Tax considerations:** Real estate investors and others with means who currently live in California, Hawaii, Oregon, Minnesota, Iowa, New Jersey, Vermont, and other states with high income taxes are establishing legal residency in increasing numbers of states without state income taxes — Alaska, Florida, Nevada, New Hampshire, South Dakota, Tennessee, Texas, Washington, and Wyoming. Many states (such as Colorado, Illinois, Indiana, Massachusetts, Michigan, Pennsylvania, and North Carolina) have established flat rate taxes, and some states (like Arkansas, Georgia, Idaho, Indiana, Missouri, North Carolina, and Utah) recently lowered their state income taxes. Of course, local taxes can be a factor for real estate investors as well.

So, relocating your place of legal residence can make a significant improvement in your overall income tax liability, and it may not even be that much of a sacrifice. For example, a California real estate syndicator found that living on the east side of beautiful Lake Tahoe (in the state of Nevada) was just as nice as the west (or California) side, where the top income-tax rate can add up to another 13.3 percent in addition to the federal income tax.

You should also have a detailed understanding of the property taxation system and appeals process. Be sure to determine whether a proposed income property acquisition is in a special assessment district where additional taxes are assessed against properties. Such special assessment districts may offer some advantages like better schools, parks, and fire and police services and may be well worth the additional annual investment. But you should know in advance how much the additional costs will be, how long you'll be required to participate, and exactly what you're getting in return so that you can properly evaluate whether you'll be able to generate a commensurate increase in your rental income.

>> **Economic development incentives:** The economic development groups for many states are advertising in business publications and major newspapers and aggressively encouraging employers to relocate with incredible real estate incentives, such as virtually free land or lower property and/or income taxation. Besides lucrative offers of real estate and tax incentives, as the global economy becomes ever more competitive, businesses are being lured to locations that can reduce their costs of labor, energy, and transportation. As mentioned in the previous point, states with competitive tax systems and welcoming environments for businesses start such state competitions with an advantage. States that are less generally inviting to businesses try to sometimes offer tax breaks and other incentives, but since these breaks are generally temporary and subject to political whims, they can unravel, as happened with Amazon in Queens, New York.

>> **Community's reputation:** Your local chamber of commerce, tourism bureau, and city hall all work very hard to establish the right reputation and attract the top employers. These organizations can have a real impact on the market

environment for businesses and thus create more jobs in the long run, which leads to increased population and higher demand for all types of real estate.

>> **Business-friendly environment:** You can't underestimate the importance of a pro-business attitude among state, regional, and local governments to help create a vibrant economy where your real estate investments can prosper.

Evaluating Neighborhoods

The reputation of particular neighborhoods can be based on many factors. Certain key or essential elements, which are discussed in the following sections, differentiate the neighborhoods with good reputations and positive trends from the areas that are stagnant or trending in the wrong direction.

Schools

If you don't have school-age children, you may not be concerned about the reputation and test scores of the local schools. But, whether you're investing in residential or commercial income properties, schools matter. The demand for residential and commercial property (and the subsequent value of the property) is highly correlated to the quality of local schools.

Ask any real estate agent about the impact of schools on the demand and sales price for a home in a great school district. Likewise, employers use the quality of local schools in recruiting their key personnel — and sometimes even relocate company facilities to be near areas known for their schools.

TIP

The internet can be a very useful tool in determining the quality of local schools. Most school districts have websites that include information on the test scores of their students for mandatory state and federal testing. Unfortunately, many people make snap judgments about school quality without doing their homework. Visit the schools and don't blindly rely on test scores. Talk to parents and teachers, and discover what goes on at the school.

Crime rates

Crime can have a significant and sobering effect on the demand and desirability of all types of income properties. No one wants to live in a high crime area, and commercial tenants and their customers neither work at nor patronize unsafe businesses. No areas are going to be crime-free, but you don't want to find out after the close of escrow that you have purchased a rental property that is claimed by rival gangs. Before you make your investment decision, consult these sources:

>> **Local law enforcement:** Contact local law enforcement and obtain the latest and historical crime statistics.

>> **Local newspapers:** Newspapers (and their websites) often have a police-blotter section that provides information on major and even petty crimes in the community.

>> **Sexual-offender databases:** Laws require certain convicted sexual offenders to register with local law enforcement. These databases allow you to identify the general locations of convicted sex offenders who have committed sexual offenses against minors and violent sexual offenses against anyone.

These databases aren't foolproof. A few states haven't been consistent in their efforts to maintain and make them available. Also, persons required to register don't always follow the requirements, but at least you can find out about the known ones.

REMEMBER

Even if not legally required in your area, be sure to advise your tenants to check the database; this information is dynamic, and people need to make their own decision about the safety of their family.

Pride of ownership

Pride of ownership is an intangible attitude that has tangible results. Pride of ownership also has no economic boundaries — even modest-income areas can really look sharp. Look for rental properties in neighborhoods that reflect pride of ownership — well-kept and litter-free grounds, trimmed plants, beautiful flowers, fresh paint, and so on. This curb appeal helps you attract and retain your tenants.

Although everyone may have a different perception of exactly what constitutes a well-maintained property, pride of ownership is readily apparent, and the effort made by business owners and homeowners to keep their properties looking sharp is important to real estate values.

You may find that some of the more aesthetically pleasing areas look that way for a reason. Homeowners' associations and business parks typically have a board of directors and architectural review committees that routinely inspect the properties under their jurisdiction, as well as review and restrict improvements to meet certain standards.

Other areas may have informal committees of neighbors who band together to keep their properties in tiptop condition. This tendency is also true of multifamily residential and commercial properties, and these properties usually must also submit to local laws and regulations enforced by the building or code enforcement departments.

You can control the appearance, condition, and maintenance of your own property, but your options are limited if the properties surrounding it fall into disrepair. Your purchase of a fixer-upper and the investment of time, money, and sweat equity won't be rewarded financially if the surrounding properties are in a state of disrepair and have owners who don't really care.

WARNING

Property values, occupancy, and rental rates all sag when property owners no longer take pride in their property. Avoid declining neighborhoods that display the red flags of dispirited owners — poorly kept properties, junk-filled vacant lots, inoperative cars in the parking lot or street, graffiti, vandalism, and deferred maintenance. Neighborhood deterioration is a blight that spreads from one property to another.

Role play: What attracts you to the property?

One of the best ways to evaluate the prospects for a particular neighborhood is to play the role of a residential tenant looking for the best place to call home. Go back in time to when you made the decision to live in your neighborhood. What were the primary criteria you used to make that determination? You're probably typical of many of your potential tenants. They prefer rental properties in close proximity to various amenities, all of which can be captured in a property knowledge sheet.

Property knowledge sheets

One of the best ways to have the answers to the questions that may be raised by your rental prospect is to prepare a property knowledge sheet for each of your rental property locations. A *property knowledge sheet* contains all the basic information about your rental property, such as the size and type of the rental unit and the unit number (for multiple-unit properties), plus the age, type of construction, and other important details about the unit.

TIP

A thorough property knowledge sheet also contains important information about the local neighborhood and general area. Like the chamber of commerce or visitor's information bureau, you want to be able to answer questions accurately about the area. Rental prospects are generally interested in knowing about employment centers, transportation, local schools, childcare, places of worship, shopping, and medical facilities. You can really make a positive impression on your rental prospect if you can tell them where the nearest dry cleaners or Thai restaurants are located.

With all this vital information from your property knowledge sheet at your fingertips, you can be ready to answer your rental prospect's questions. The more you know about your property, the easier it is for you to offer important reasons for a prospect to select your rental over the competition.

Property knowledge sheets can definitely give you the edge over your competition. Because you're often competing with large multifamily rental properties, you need to be prepared to answer important questions about the area. Often, immediately knowing a detail such as whether a certain childcare center is in your area can make the difference between success and failure.

While, if you buy the property you are considering, property knowledge sheets will become an important tool in your marketing and promotion of your rental property, the point here is that by placing yourself in the role of the prospective resident, you will see exactly what the unique selling benefits for this property are. Prepare a property knowledge sheet for each property you consider, and you will soon see that the location of certain properties is superior to that of other properties in the eyes of your prospective resident. These are the properties you want to buy.

Check out Figure 4-1 for an example of a property knowledge sheet.

Commercial property considerations

Looking at a property from a tenant's perspective is also useful if you're investing in commercial properties. Remember that your commercial tenants are in business to make money — and their location is often a key factor. Have you ever seen a small retail center that includes several vacant suites with butcher paper in the windows? That is the universal sign that a property is in financial trouble and in need of proactive ownership, management, and leasing — or the spiral toward foreclosure will continue.

Right down the street from a failing property, you may find another retail property with long-term leases and a waiting list, because successful retailers almost always flock together. That explains the success of many regional shopping malls that command high rents. Sometimes, just getting the right anchor or primary tenant in a commercial, industrial, or retail income property is all it takes to start the chain reaction toward the dream for any landlord — high occupancy, high rents, and low turnover!

Finding well-situated properties is easier when you're considering investing in an area where you've lived your entire life but not as easy for investing in other locales. Nonetheless, every area has potential if you know what you're looking for and are willing to take the time to do the research.

Property Knowledge Sheet

Property Information

Rental address _____ Unit # _____ City _____ Zip code _____

Office hours (if any) _____ Square footage of unit(s) _____

Unit mix—Studios _____ 1 Bedroom _____ 2 Bedroom/1 Bath _____ 2 Bedroom/2 Bath _____ Other _____

Rent—Studios _____ 1 Bedroom _____ 2 Bedroom/1 Bath _____ 2 Bedroom/2 Bath _____ Other _____

Application fee _____ Security deposit _____ Concessions _____

Age of rental _____ Type of construction _____ Parking _____

Recreational facilities _____ Laundry _____ Pets _____

Storage _____ Utilities (who pays?) _____ AC/Heat _____

Appliances _____ Floor coverings _____

Special features/comments _____

_____

_____

Community Information

School district _____ Grade school _____ Jr. high _____

High school _____ Jr. college _____ College _____

Trade school _____ Pre-school (s) _____

Childcare _____ Places of worship _____

Police station _____ Fire station _____ Ambulance _____

Electric _____ Natural gas _____ Telephone _____ Cable _____

Water _____ Sewer _____ Library _____ Post office _____

Hospital _____ Pharmacy _____ Vet _____

Other medical facilities _____

Nearby employment centers _____

Transportation _____

Groceries _____ Other shopping _____

Local services _____

Restaurants _____

Comments _____

_____

Rental Market Information

Rental competitors/rental rates/concessions _____

_____

Our competitive advantages _____

_____

Our disadvantages _____

_____

FIGURE 4-1:
Property
knowledge sheet.

Mastering Seller's and Buyer's Markets

Some real estate investors make the mistake of not continuing to research the economics of their real estate markets after they've made their investments. Even if you plan to buy and hold, you need to pay attention to the market conditions. The criteria you should consider in making decisions about which markets are the best for investing are dynamic and can fluctuate.

Savvy real estate investors monitor their markets and look for the telltale signs of real estate cycles. These cycles present opportunities for expanding your real estate portfolio or repositioning from weakening markets to strengthening markets because not all areas experience peaks and troughs at the same time. That is why you need to know and track the timing of seller's and buyer's markets.

Understanding real estate cycles

Real estate markets are cyclical, and successful real estate investors remain aware of the real estate cycles in their areas. First, here are the definitions of a seller's market and a buyer's market:

>> **A buyer's market** occurs when current property owners are unable to sell their properties quickly and must be more flexible on the price and terms. This is a great opportunity to seek seller financing.

>> **A seller's market** is almost like the classic definition of inflation — "too much money chasing too few goods." In this case, the goods are real estate properties, which are in high demand. When sellers are receiving multiple offers within 24 to 48 hours of a listing or you see properties selling for more than the asking price, you're in a strong seller's market.

Real estate traditionally experiences cycles as the demand for real estate leads to a shortage of supply and higher rents and appreciation. That, in turn, leads to the building of additional properties, which, along with changes in demand due to economic cycles, usually results in overbuilding and a decline in rents and property valuation.

However, not everyone agrees that real estate cycles are relevant to residential real estate investors. Some of the real estate infomercial gurus claim that real estate investing in homes and apartments is recession-proof because people always need a place to live. Although that is partly true, the economic base of the community where you invest does have a direct impact on all aspects of your operations — occupancy, turnover, rental rates, and even quality of tenant.

For example, when times are tough, residential tenants are the first to improvise, with some finding that "doubling up" or even taking in roommates is palatable if it results in lower costs for housing. Some younger renters are even willing to move back in with Mom and Dad or another relative when their personal budgets don't allow them to have their own rental unit.

Real estate cycles may be similar in a particular region but often vary from region to region. For example, when some areas of the country were setting records for rents in the mid-'80s, landlords couldn't give away their apartments in Texas.

Even venerable California was a miserable place to own real estate in the early '90s. In the late 2000s and early 2010s, areas where real estate speculation and condo converters went crazy suffered.

Can real estate investors who track these real estate cycles make investment decisions based on this information? Absolutely. That is where most successful and knowledgeable real estate investors see potential for increasing their real estate investment returns by timing the real estate market.

Timing the real estate market

Although the length and depth of the real estate cycles vary, there are clear highs and lows that real estate investors need to consider.

In some real estate markets, the double-digit appreciation over the first half of the 2000s brought record prices for homes and income properties. In the mid-2000s, the most common question for coauthor Robert on his live Southern California NBC call-in feature was "Should I buy income properties in Southern California at these seemingly high price levels, or should I invest elsewhere?" These callers didn't want to miss out on what they thought was almost guaranteed price appreciation. But what goes up must come down, so when the market corrected in the late 2000s and early 2010s with significant price declines in most areas of the country, the question Robert most heard was, "When will we reach the bottom of the market?"

No one-size-fits-all answer solves this critical question. A key factor is the *investment horizon* or planned holding period for a particular investor and that specific investment. If the holding period is long enough, even purchasing income properties in today's seemingly high-priced markets should probably look good 15 to 20 years from now.

The alternative is to identify those markets with excellent economic fundamentals where prices have remained low and invest there. The concept is similar to the "buy low, sell high" truism for stocks, except you sell in overpriced markets and reinvest in the lower-priced markets. Such markets do exist, but the question is whether the properties in the lower-priced markets are going to provide the same or better investment returns in the long run versus alternative markets.

WARNING

Unlike the stock market, real estate transactions entail significant transaction costs (as a percentage of the market value of the property). That's why selling and buying property too frequently undermines your returns.

Even in the few markets where such "bargains" exist, they aren't really great opportunities. Consider the business concept that in the long run, you usually get what you pay for! There is so much more than just the projected rent and the selling price. Without going into a detailed analysis of property condition, expenses, and other invaluable criteria, you should simply consider whether these areas pass muster after performing the economic analysis described earlier. Probably not.

Carleton Sheets, plus many other well-known infomercial gurus, have traditionally advised their followers that you should seek income properties where the projected gross monthly income is at least 1 percent of the purchase price. This strategy would mean that if you acquire a rental property with a projected monthly income of $2,000, your acquisition costs should not exceed $200,000. The advice is sound, but there are few markets these days where such properties exist. You may remember from your reading on investments that risk and return are generally related. That is, the lower the risk you take, the lower your expected return. (That is why short-term government-backed bonds and federally insured money market accounts offer nominal rates of interest or return on investment, and investments with higher risk, such as real estate, demand higher rates of return.)

So, the real question is, what are the risk-adjusted returns like for investing in these areas of the country with record high prices versus the risk-adjusted returns available in other, lower-priced real estate markets? You may find a rural property where the monthly rent exceeds 1 percent of the purchase price, but what about rent growth and appreciation? At the end of the day, you may find that your lower-priced market with all of those "bargains" provided you with minimal cash flow and marginal appreciation.

Knowing when to sell and when to buy real estate is easier said than done. But if you follow the fundamentals of economic analysis and remember that "location, location, value" is the key to successful real estate investing, you can do well.

Investing
in Trends

Contents at a Glance

Chapter **1**

Taking the Nickel Tour of Cannabis Investing

Whenever you're getting started on a new topic or trying to develop a new skill, you can benefit from having a general understanding of what's involved. It's sort of like reading the plot or synopsis of a movie or book before starting to watch or read it, or seeing the finished product before you start following the instructions to assemble it. You get the gist of what you're about to encounter, which serves as both a framework on which you can hang the details, and the context for more quickly and easily understanding those details. The purpose of this chapter is to bring you quickly up to speed on the topic of investing in cannabis.

Weighing the Pros and Cons of Investing in Cannabis

The following sections present some of the most important pros and cons you should consider and leave the decision up to you.

Pros

The biggest motive people have for investing their money in any venture is profit. Chances are good that you, too, are curious about investing in cannabis because you want to profit from it. The industry is growing in leaps and bounds, and you want in on the action. Nothing wrong with that, but consider other benefits. Here's a list:

>> Profit (which is already mentioned) is the biggie.

>> Getting in at or near the bottom of a new and exciting industry is always a thrill. By investing in cannabis, you become a participant, not merely an observer, in the green rush.

>> Being able to tell people you know that your investment portfolio or retirement account includes cannabis stock. This may sound silly, but being invested in cannabis says something about who you are and may help you engage in conversations you would otherwise be excluded from.

>> If you consume marijuana, you get to invest in a product you enjoy and help to make it more available to others.

>> If you invest in medical marijuana, you're investing in medical research and helping to bring those new medicines to market, potentially alleviating some of the world's physical and perhaps even mental suffering.

REMEMBER

Life offers few choices to invest in a new industry in its infancy. You can think of investing in cannabis as what it would have been like to invest in alcohol three to five years before prohibition was repealed. How often do you get to participate in an industry at the dawn of legalization? Investing in cannabis also may remind you what investing in the dot-com era was like. Cannabis is a new industry. It presents an opportunity for an investor to be a pioneer.

Cons

There are actually more reasons *not* to invest in cannabis than *to* invest in it. Here's a list of reasons not to invest in cannabis that you should seriously consider before investing in this industry:

WARNING

>> Cannabis attracts money, and money attracts thieves. In addition, many novices eager to invest in cannabis are easy marks because they're eager, naïve, and have money — just the combination of traits a con artist is looking for.

Many of the successful entrepreneurs in cannabis got their start in the black market, which attracts a very particular personality type. Leopards don't change their spots. Some savvy former black marketers have simply chosen a different crime — instead of dealing in illegal marijuana, they're now on the prowl for unsuspecting investors they can fleece. And they're not the only thieves that pose a threat to cannabis investors, as illustrated in the sidebar "Crooks in law enforcement."

>> With lots of money flowing into the industry from eager investors, even legitimate cannabis stocks are overvalued. The more overvalued a stock is, the further the potential fall. Short sellers often target overvalued stocks just for this reason; then, when the stock price drops, they cash in and everyone else loses. (See Book 3 for an introduction to stock investing.)

>> Cannabis businesses struggle to be profitable due to numerous factors, including the high costs of complying with federal, state, and local marijuana laws; increased security costs; increased bank fees; and the cost of specialized software.

>> Cannabis stocks have an increased susceptibility to *dilution* because cannabis companies have a tougher time getting bank loans in the United States (due to federal laws that discourage banks from doing business with cannabis companies). Companies issue and sell more shares to raise money, but that dilutes the value of existing shares.

>> Companies that grow cannabis are at risk of cannabis becoming a commodity, and if (when) that happens, prices and profits drop.

>> Laws, and enforcement of those laws, are susceptible to change, and if they change in a direction that hurts cannabis businesses, their investors suffer as well.

>> Supply-and-demand imbalances are common in the cannabis industry. These imbalances not only disrupt the supply chain but also negatively impact profits by creating market gluts (which drive down prices) or shortages (which increase costs and reduce demand); either way, profits suffer.

>> Cannabis still has a healthy black market, even in states where it's legal, and black-market growers and dealers don't pay taxes, so they can afford to sell their product for less. If state and local authorities don't crack down on illegal production and sales, legal businesses have a tough time competing.

REMEMBER

Don't rule out investing in cannabis just because of this long list of potential drawbacks. You can considerably reduce your exposure to risk by doing your homework and investing in well-run companies.

Investing in Businesses That Touch the Plant or Those That Don't

One of the first decisions to make before investing in cannabis is whether to invest in businesses that have contact with the plant or those that don't (often referred to as *ancillary* companies):

>> **Plant-touching:** These businesses come into contact with the plant at some point during the growth, manufacturing, distribution, or sale. They include grow operations, manufacturers of infused products (MIPs), shipping firms, dispensaries, and licensed delivery services. Plant-touching businesses stand to profit most from cannabis, and they're also at the greatest risk of suffering losses when the industry takes a hit.

TIP

If you decide to invest in a plant-touching business, consider a *vertically integrated company,* which means the business does its own cultivation, manufacturing, distribution, and sales. Vertically integrated companies are less susceptible to supply chain disruptions because they control their entire supply chain.

>> **Ancillary:** These businesses serve the plant-touching businesses in some way. Perhaps the best-known ancillary business is The Scotts Company, which provides fertilizer, pesticides, and disease control products, primarily for lawn care but also for agricultural operations, including cannabis cultivation companies. Other ancillary companies include manufacturers and dealers of equipment for cultivation operations; legal and accounting services that specialize in cannabis; software companies that develop point-of-sale and supply-chain managements systems; security equipment and service providers; and real estate groups that buy, sell, and rent land and buildings for cannabis businesses.

While plant-touching businesses carry the most potential for profit and risk, ancillary companies still stand to profit from the industry, but they have less exposure to risk. For example, if the U.S. federal government decided to crack down on cannabis businesses across the country, that revenue stream would be negatively impacted for The Scotts Company, but the company would still have value as a business selling lawn care products.

REMEMBER

According to a study published by Deloitte in 2016, ancillary businesses are estimated to be 2.5 times the size of the cannabis industry itself, so ancillary businesses stand to profit handsomely from the success of the cannabis industry.

Exploring Your Investment Options

You can profit from legal cannabis businesses in several ways, depending on how directly you want to be involved. The most direct approach is to start your own cannabis business. The least direct approach is to trade cannabis-related securities, such as stocks, bonds, or exchange-traded funds (ETFs).

The following sections present different ways to invest in the cannabis industry to make you aware of the wide variety of options.

Starting your own business

One approach to investing in the cannabis industry is to start your own business — either a plant-touching or an ancillary business. Here are some of the more popular opportunities cannabis entrepreneurs pursue.

>> **Cultivator:** Cultivators start and grow plants from seeds; harvest the plants; separate the usable portion of the plants and properly dispose of the green waste; dry, cure, and trim the harvested bud; arrange for third-party lab tests

to ensure the safety and quality of the product; pack and ship product to manufacturers and dispensaries; and track and report all processes as required by law to government regulatory agencies. Note that cultivation operations are the lowest profit-margin segment of the industry.

TIP

Cultivation is a great choice if you have a passion for the plant and a green thumb.

>> **Manufacturer of infused products:** MIP is an industry term used to describe a company that makes marijuana-infused products, including concentrates such as wax and shatter; oils and tinctures; and lotions and edibles. This segment of the industry acts as a laboratory as well as a processing plant. It may be even more tightly regulated than other segments of the industry, with additional rules and regulations that extend to manufacturing and commercial kitchens.

TIP

MIP is a great choice for those who want to get more into the science of extracting active ingredients from the plant and using those extracts to create a wide variety of consumer products.

>> **Processed product brand:** A processed product brand could be an MIP or a combined grow/MIP business that makes products and sells them to numerous retail outlets. For example, you could set up your own grow/MIP business to produce a line of infused chocolates that you sell to a variety of medical and recreational dispensaries in Oregon. Another option is to create your own brand and develop unique products and then farm out the growing, manufacturing, and distribution operations to other businesses that specialize in those areas.

>> **Retailer/dispensary owner:** Cannabis retailers run the dispensaries and other retail outlets that sell products directly to consumers. Depending on the rules and regulations in your area, you may be permitted to run a medical dispensary, an adult recreational dispensary, or a dispensary that serves both medical and adult recreational clients. This is like owning a liquor store but with more rules and regulations to follow.

>> **Ancillary business:** Ancillary businesses you may want to consider include the following:

- Nursery owner

- Manufacturer or seller of grow lights

- Heating, ventilation, and air conditioning (HVAC) service provider specializing in ventilation and circulation for grow operations

- Packaging and labeling manufacturer/supplier

- Security service, or manufacturer or supplier of security systems and equipment

- Marketing, public relations, or advertising specialist

- Real estate sales, rentals, or management (for more details, see the next section)

- Legal, accounting, or consulting service provider

- Banking and cash management services

WARNING

If you're interested in starting a business that comes in contact with the cannabis plant in any way, don't go it alone, and do be prepared for a high cost of doing business. Especially be sure to consult with a lawyer who has knowledge and expertise in helping businesses comply with state cannabis laws.

Investing in cannabis real estate

An often overlooked way to invest in cannabis is to buy land zoned for cannabis businesses or to buy land and have it zoned for such businesses and then sell or lease the land to cannabis businesses. You can even erect buildings on the land (or buy land with buildings suitable for certain types of businesses) and sell or lease the commercially improved land to businesses.

If you've seen the movie *The Founder*, about Ray Kroc, the founder of McDonald's, you probably remember his lawyer/advisor telling him, "You don't seem to realize what business you're in. You're not in the burger business; you're in the real estate business. You build an empire by owning the land." Kroc followed that advice and made a fortune buying the land on which McDonald's franchises were built and then leasing that land to the franchise owners.

REMEMBER

You can take a similar approach to profit off the cannabis industry. However, you really need to know not only the cannabis industry and the real estate market, but also the rules and regulations in place that govern where (and what type of) cannabis businesses can be conducted on differently zoned plots of land.

Buying and selling stocks

The most common way people invest in cannabis is to buy and sell stock in privately or publicly owned cannabis companies. Stocks provide you with a share of the company without your having to get your hands dirty or deal with the complex legal and regulatory issues (and other matters) of starting and running your own cannabis business. Of course, buying shares in an existing business leaves you with less control over the business, leaving the value of your shares in the hands of others. If they're innovative, intelligent, and manage the company effectively, your shares are likely to increase in value, but if they drop the ball, you're likely to lose money on your investment.

REMEMBER

Investing in publicly traded companies has a couple of advantages:

>> **Data availability:** To list their stocks on public stock exchanges, companies must be a certain size and comply with stringent financial reporting standards, which provides a greater level of transparency for investors. In other words, you have more data on which you can base your investment decisions.

>> **Liquidity:** Stock in publicly traded companies is a very liquid investment. You can convert your shares to cash almost immediately by listing them for sale on the exchange, assuming, of course, that someone's willing to buy the shares at a price you're willing to sell them for.

For an introduction to stock investing, see Book 3.

REMEMBER

This book assumes you're investing in cannabis by buying and selling securities (stocks or bonds) in public or private companies and not by starting your own cannabis business or investing in real estate, which may be the focus of other books on investing in real estate. The goal here is to provide the information and guidance you need to research businesses and their management teams to determine whether they're likely to be profitable and good investments for you. You can then decide whether to invest in the company.

Diversifying with exchange-traded funds and mutual funds

Most financial advisors recommend *diversification* as a way to reduce an investor's exposure to risk. A diversified investment portfolio contains both *stocks* (shares of ownership in a company) and *bonds* (like IOUs, short for "I owe you"); investments in numerous companies in a particular industry; and investments in various industries, such as cannabis, automobiles, pharmaceuticals, and energy.

One quick and easy way to diversify is to purchase shares of an exchange-traded fund (ETF) or mutual fund, both of which contain investments in a variety of businesses. The basic difference between the two is that shares of an ETF can be traded throughout the day like shares of stock, whereas shares of a mutual fund can be traded only after the markets close or before they open, because the share value is calculated a couple of hours after the markets close. You can find several cannabis-specific ETFs to invest in. Cannabis mutual funds are a rarer species. Check out Book 5 for a primer on mutual funds and ETFs.

WARNING

The main drawback of cannabis ETFs and mutual funds is that a fund manager chooses the businesses to invest in, and fund managers may not be experts in the cannabis industry, so they may not make the best choices. You're generally better off doing your own research and making your own choices.

Considering private investment opportunities

Investing in private companies (in contrast to publicly traded companies) carries significantly more risk but has more potential for a higher return on investment (ROI). You basically have four options for investing in private companies depending on the business's stage of development.

>> **Angel investing:** If you know someone who wants to start a cannabis business, you can bankroll the operation as an *angel investor*, usually in exchange for *ownership equity* (shares of stock) in the company or *convertible debt* (a loan that can later be converted to ownership equity). You can also join a group of angel investors, pooling your money to finance startup businesses.

>> **Venture capital investing:** One step up from angel investing is venture capital investing, which involves providing capital and expertise to take a promising startup to the next level. As with angel investing, you can join venture capital groups to pool money and expertise.

>> **Mezzanine investing:** One step up from venture capital investing is mezzanine investing, which involves private financing in the form of debt or preferred stock. (*Preferred stock* is a higher class of ownership than that provided by common stock. With preferred stock, you have first claim on any assets and earnings if the company struggles or folds.)

>> **Private equity:** Private equity is financing that doesn't appear on public exchanges. It usually comes from funds and investors that invest directly in companies or that engage in buyouts of public companies, which results in those companies being delisted.

REMEMBER

Private investing is usually the realm of high-net-worth individuals — and a perfect example of how the rich get richer.

Finding Investment Opportunities

Before you can invest in a cannabis business, you need to find a business to invest in. Sure, you can Google "cannabis companies to invest in" or head to an online discount brokerage such as Firstrade, Ally Invest, or E*TRADE, and use their tools to track down cannabis companies and ETFs, but those searches are likely to turn up only the biggest, publicly traded cannabis companies. (And a Google search would be likely to turn up some of the biggest scams.) To get quality leads on cannabis businesses, you have a few options, including the following:

WARNING

» **Word of mouth:** People talk, especially when they're planning something big like starting their own cannabis business. You may hear something from a friend, relative, or casual acquaintance about someone who's interested in starting a cannabis business and is looking for investors.

Be especially careful in your research of word-of-mouth leads, especially if someone approaches you out of the blue about a great investment opportunity.

» **Online resources:** Dozens of general and cannabis-specific investment websites are available to keep investors informed of opportunities. General sites include Yahoo! Finance (`finance.yahoo.com`) and Morningstar (`www.morningstar.com`). Cannabis-specific resources include The Marijuana Index (`marijuanaindex.com`), Marijuana Stocks (`marijuanastocks.com`), and Cannabis Stock Trades (`www.cannabisstocktrades.com`).

» **Apps:** Several smartphone apps are available, including Investing in Weed Stocks, Marijuana Handbook, and Scutify. Search your smartphone's app store for cannabis or marijuana investment apps.

» **Cannabis industry news:** You can find more sources for cannabis industry news than you have time to read. If you have time for only one, check out Marijuana Business Daily (`mjbizdaily.com`). Even if you don't use these sources to find leads on investment opportunities, they're valuable for getting up to speed on the industry and gaining the knowledge you need to make better-informed investment decisions.

» **ETF sites:** If you're interested specifically in cannabis ETFs, check out ETFdb.com.

» **Private investment groups:** If you're a high-net-worth individual, consider joining a group of private investors who focus on the cannabis industry. When choosing a group, decide where you want to enter the picture with new businesses — as an angel investor, venture capitalist, mezzanine investor, or member of a private equity firm. Then, look for a reputable group that fits with your investment strategy.

» **A broker:** Many investors are drawn to online discount brokers because of the cheap (or free) trades, but paying extra for a broker who knows the cannabis industry may be the best long-term investment you'll ever make.

Researching Investment Opportunities

You just got a lead on a new cannabis company looking for investors. Now what? First things first — watch your wallet. Don't invest any money until you thoroughly research the "opportunity." Your research should include the following:

>> A background check of all owners, managers, and operators. Hire a reputable private investigator to conduct the background checks, and make sure everyone on the team has experience in the industry.

>> An online search for the business and its owners, managers, and operators. Conduct a general Google search and check out some cannabis industry-specific news sites, such as mjbizdaily.com and www.cannabisbusinesstimes.com to find out more about the people starting and running the business.

>> An evaluation of the company's financial health, to ensure that it has the capital required to operate until it begins to turn a profit.

>> Verification of the business's license to operate in the state or states in which it plans to operate.

>> A careful evaluation of the business plan or business strategy to ensure that the owners and managers have a solid plan in place to turn a profit.

>> An evaluation of the company's competitive position relative to other companies in its space.

>> An evaluation of the company's existing *warrants* and *convertible securities* — essentially contracts with existing investors regarding their current or future equity ownership in the company. You want to know how ownership in the company by current investors could impact your equity ownership in the company and the share price.

>> A check with other investors and reputable analysts with expertise in the cannabis industry to find out whether they know anything about the company or its owners/managers/operators.

>> A conversation with the CEO or other leaders in the business to hear directly from them about their vision and plan for success.

>> A check with a reputable broker in Canada or the United States to verify that the prospect is real, compliant, and listed on a credible exchange. This is necessary only for publicly traded companies.

>> A conversation with your lawyer and your financial advisor to get their opinions about investing in the company. (In other words, get a second and third opinion.)

Additionally, if the business you're thinking of investing in is involved in cultivating cannabis, research the grow master (the person in charge of setting up and managing the operation), the grower's *cost per gram* (average cost to grow one gram of product) compared to competitors' cost per gram, and the cultivator's clientele (to be sure the cultivation operation has reliable customers).

REMEMBER

Bet with your head, not with your heart. Three big market movers are greed, fear of loss (FOL), and fear of missing out (FOMO). Regardless of what you choose to invest in, make rational, data-based decisions.

Planning Your Investment Strategy

Prior to investing, give some thought to your investment strategy. Common investment strategies for any industry you choose to invest in include the following:

>> **Value investing:** This strategy involves buying stocks in *undervalued companies* — companies that appear, based on their fundamentals, to be worth more than their share price indicates. Value investors believe that the markets are driven, to a large part, by emotion, and that by investing in profitable companies, they'll do better in the long run.

>> **Growth investing:** This strategy involves investing in small companies you think have the potential to increase their earnings faster than their competitors or other companies in the industry. Unlike value investors, growth investors may be willing to pay more than "book value" for shares in the company. (*Book value* is the total amount a company would be worth if it sold all its assets and paid back all its liabilities.)

>> **Momentum investing:** This strategy involves following trends in the prices of securities to capitalize on a company as its share price is rising or to short-sell shares as the share price drops. (To sell short, you borrow a stock and sell it. When the price drops, you buy back the stock and return it to the lender. The difference between the sell price and the buy price is your profit.)

>> **Income investing:** This strategy focuses on earning a steady income from investments. It usually involves buying shares in companies that pay dividends, and buying bonds, which pay out interest on a consistent basis. Income investing is generally safer than value, growth, and momentum investment strategies, but the potential return may be lower.

>> **Investing in what you know:** Many investors buy shares in only the companies they know or the companies that provide the products and services they like, believing that those products and services will likely become increasingly popular among consumers, thereby driving the company's success.

For example, if you're an Amazon Prime member, you may think to yourself, "Wow, Amazon is great. This company really has the potential to make it big," and, based solely on your personal experience, you decide to invest in Amazon.

>> **Dollar cost averaging:** With dollar cost averaging, you buy shares regularly (for example, the same day each month) whether the share price is high or low, so you're not overpaying for a large quantity of shares at any one time. Of course, with this strategy, you're not getting a large quantity of shares at a low price, either.

>> **Diversification:** This strategy involves spreading your investment dollars across a number of industries or a number of companies in the same industry to reduce your exposure to risk if one particular industry or company you invest in goes south.

In the context of cannabis investing, other strategies may include the following:

>> Investing in ancillary businesses that serve the cannabis industry but don't touch the plant. Regardless of which cannabis businesses win or lose, ancillary businesses increase their earnings as the industry as a whole grows.

>> Investing only in vertically integrated companies, which control their entire supply line. These companies also tend to be larger than those that are not vertically integrated.

>> Investing exclusively in medical cannabis or exclusively in adult recreational cannabis, or investing a specific percentage in each.

>> Investing in strong brands that have a presence in multiple states and perhaps even multiple countries.

>> Investing in foreign markets such as Canada, Uruguay, and the European Union.

Investing in a Cannabis Business

Businesses have two options for raising capital to get started or to grow.

>> **Debt:** They may borrow money from a bank or issue bonds, which are sort of like IOUs, promising to pay back the debt with interest.

>> **Equity:** They may issue stock — selling shares in the business.

As a result, you have two ways to invest in a cannabis business: by lending the business money or purchasing shares in the business. Regardless of which approach you take, the process is pretty easy. For example, if you're lending someone you know money to start a cannabis business, you have your attorney draw up a loan contract, and you and an authorized representative of the business sign the loan contract, after which you provide the agreed-upon capital. If the business issues bonds, you can buy bonds instead of using a loan contract. And if the business issues shares of stock, you simply buy shares at an agreed-upon price.

You can also buy stocks and bonds by purchasing shares of an ETF or mutual fund. These funds have a collection of investment securities (stocks and bonds) from different businesses and often different industries, which facilitates diversification; you're not putting all your eggs in one basket. (See the earlier section "Diversifying with exchange-traded funds and mutual funds" for details.)

The actual process of buying stocks, bonds, ETFs, or mutual funds is easy. You set up an account with a *broker* — a person who's licensed to buy and sell stocks and bonds, or a company that enables you to place your own orders online. You can then contact your broker to place your order or log into your online brokerage account and place the order yourself.

Regardless of whether you place orders through a broker or an online system, you need to specify several details, including the following:

>> The company name or ticker symbol

>> Whether you want to buy or sell

>> The number of shares you want to buy or sell (when selling, you usually have an option to sell all shares or a specified number of shares)

>> The order type:

- **Market:** Buy or sell the security immediately at the going price.

- **Limit:** Buy or sell the security only at the specified price or better.

- **Stop loss:** Buy or sell the security as soon as its price reaches the price specified.

- **Stop limit:** Buy or sell the security as soon as its price reaches the price specified but only within the specified price range.

- **Trailing stop:** Buy or sell the security as soon as its price reaches a specified percentage or dollar amount above or below the current market price. With a trailing stop, as the price of the security moves in a favorable direction, the trailing stop price adjusts automatically, but as soon as the price turns in an unfavorable direction by the dollar amount or percentage specified, the trade is triggered. (Trailing stop orders can be trailing stop loss or trailing stop limit orders.)

>> The timeframe:

- **Good till cancelled:** Keep the order open until you choose to cancel it.

- **Fill or kill:** Execute the transaction immediately and completely or cancel it.

- **Immediate or cancel:** Fill as much of the order as possible in the next few seconds and then cancel anything that couldn't be filled.

- **On open:** Execute the order as soon as the market opens.

- **On close:** Execute the order after the market closes.

Because many cannabis companies are not profitable (especially early on), be aware of the difference between investing and speculating:

>> *Investing* involves generating a reasonable return from a profitable company.

>> *Speculating* involves betting on a company's ability to become profitable or betting that other people will buy shares speculatively, driving up the share price. Buying shares of unprofitable companies is more about speculating than investing.

Chapter **2**

The Political, Cultural, and Regulatory Landscape of Cannabis Investing

As a cannabis investor, you can expect to experience more uncertainty in the cannabis market than in other more stable markets, largely due to changes in the political, cultural, and regulatory landscape and to the high costs and complexities of doing business. These factors place additional pressures on the industry as a whole as well as on individual companies, which can often drive companies out of business or influence decisions regarding restructuring, acquisitions, and mergers. Cannabis investors should be prepared for a wild ride until acceptance and legalization of cannabis become more widespread and the industry becomes more established. This could take several years or even decades, and may possibly never happen.

Before investing in cannabis, you would be wise to familiarize yourself with the politics, culture, and regulations that may impact cannabis demand, availability, and costs. Information and insight into these factors enable you to make well-informed decisions about whether to invest in cannabis and where to put your money if you do invest.

This chapter brings you up to speed on the political, cultural, and regulatory landscape in which cannabis businesses operate. You're encouraged to conduct your own research to access current information.

Recognizing the Impact of Laws on the Industry

When discussions arise about the legality of cannabis, they usually revolve around growing it, selling it, or possessing it. However, cannabis laws and the enforcement of those laws also impact the industry, influencing everything from where different cannabis businesses can operate and under what conditions, to the taxes and fees they pay and ultimately the cost and availability of the product.

Complications and confusion often arise over differences in laws and regulations at the federal, state, and local levels. For example, in the United States, cannabis is illegal at the federal level, legal for medical use in many states, legal for both medical and adult (recreational) use in several states, and prohibited for sale and possession in many municipalities within states where it's legal.

TECHNICAL STUFF

In 2013, Uruguay became the first country to officially legalize cannabis for both medical and adult use. In 2018, Canada became the second country and the first G7 member to legalize cannabis. In the provinces of Quebec and Alberta, the legal age is 18; in the remainder of the country, it's 19. In New Jersey, before voters even had a chance to vote on a proposition to legalize adult-use marijuana, more than 50 local governments had already passed laws banning its sale or possession.

The following sections bring you up to speed on federal, state, local, and international marijuana laws in the hopes that by knowing the laws, you'll be better prepared to ride the waves that are sure to rock the cannabis industry as its future unfolds.

Getting up to speed on U.S. federal law and enforcement

In the United States, during the 1800s marijuana was used as an ingredient in many medicinal products sold in pharmacies across the country, but by 1931,

29 states had outlawed it, citing research at the time that linked the use of marijuana with violence, criminal activity, and other deviant social behaviors.

Federal regulation didn't occur until President Franklin D. Roosevelt signed the Marihuana Tax Act of 1937, which required every person who sold, acquired, dispensed, or possessed marijuana to register with the Internal Revenue Service (IRS), pay taxes on their transactions, and complete an order form that required the name and address of both buyer and seller and the amount of marijuana being sold or bought. Although the act did not specifically criminalize marijuana, it came to be used in that way.

In 1970, the Supreme Court overturned the law, and Congress repealed it but simultaneously passed the Controlled Substances Act, designating marijuana a Schedule 1 controlled substance based on the belief that it had a high potential for abuse, no currently accepted medical use, and a lack of accepted safety regarding the use of the drug. Adding marijuana to the list of Schedule 1 controlled substances (along with heroin, LSD, ecstasy, and magic mushrooms) effectively made it illegal for anything other than very limited research.

WARNING

In particular, the following activities are federal crimes:

>> Transporting cannabis across any state line, even if it's transported from one state in which it's legal directly to another.

>> Flying with cannabis, because it enters into federal airspace.

>> Possessing or using marijuana on federal land, including national parks and forests.

Federal laws and their enforcement impact cannabis businesses and investors in the following ways:

>> Because transporting cannabis across state lines is illegal, cannabis businesses that want to expand sales into other states must duplicate their operations in those states. They can't take advantage of economies of scale simply by shipping their products across state lines.

>> The Bank Secrecy Act (BSA) and federal money-laundering statutes discourage banks from offering services to cannabis businesses. (Passed in 1970, the BSA is a U.S. law that requires financial institutions in the United States to assist federal agencies in detecting and preventing money laundering.) Violations can result in steep fines and imprisonment of bank officials. Inaccessibility to basic banking services increases the costs and complexities of operating cannabis businesses.

REMEMBER

Some banks are starting to serve cannabis businesses, and the Financial Crimes Enforcement Network (FinCEN), the financial intelligence unit of the U.S. Department of Treasury, offers guidance to banks on how to comply with regulations when serving marijuana and ancillary businesses. However, compliance places an added burden on banks to police the marijuana businesses they serve. In addition, the Department of Justice reserves the right to prosecute banks for working with these businesses.

» Without basic banking services, cannabis businesses have no access to the capital markets, which are useful for raising money for development and growth. They need to rely on private investors, which provides private investment opportunities but at a very high risk.

» According to the principles of contract law, any contract in breach of public policy is void and unenforceable, which is a major concern for investors or funds regarding any investment contract's legitimacy. This concern serves as another obstacle to cannabis businesses seeking to raise investment capital for development or expansion.

» Cannabis businesses are required to pay income taxes, but filing tax returns (federal and state) constitutes self-incrimination. In addition, without banking services, cannabis businesses must pay their taxes in cash, which is inconvenient, costly, and risky.

» Due to the 280E provision in the IRS tax code, cannabis businesses are prohibited from deducting ordinary business expenses from their gross income, thereby significantly increasing their tax burden and negatively impacting their profitability.

» Bankruptcy protections are unavailable for cannabis businesses in the United States. Without the option to restructure, cannabis businesses are often forced to shut down when they encounter credit issues. As a result, creditors may have difficulty collecting their debts, which discourages them from loaning money to cannabis businesses in the first place.

» Fear among potential customers of losing a federal job, student financial aid, the right to own a firearm, or eligibility for federally subsidized housing can put downward pressure on cannabis sales.

» If marijuana is legalized at the federal level, the entire business environment will change, allowing large, well-established companies in other industries, such as alcohol, tobacco, and pharmaceuticals, to compete for market share.

So, what does this mean for investors? Regulations generally move in a direction that favors growth and investment opportunity. At this time, more than two-thirds of Americans live in a jurisdiction that has some form of legal cannabis. The country is trending toward a repeal of prohibition, but that will likely be a slow and clumsy process from a regulatory standpoint.

If you're looking to invest in licenses and permits, consider states with a more limited number of granted permits. States that limit the number of permits make those permits more valuable by doing so. You also want to consider states that have constitutions providing for voter referendums. As you do, you'll notice that most states that allow for referendums are west of the Mississippi and business friendly. There's a historical reason for that. Those states joined the union in the 19th century, and their state constitutions are based on the Spanish and French democratic models that allow voters to pass laws by referendum. As a result, and generally speaking, states with voter referendum and business-friendly regulatory environments tend to have legislation providing for some degree of legalized cannabis.

WARNING

Be careful when you're considering investing in any company whose licenses are based on narrow zoning laws. I (coauthor Steve) have invested in real estate that was once coveted because it was zoned for cannabis only to have the city loosen its zoning restrictions six months later. I paid a premium for the property, only to see its value drop when zoning laws made more real estate available for cannabis businesses. I could have avoided that mistake by researching more thoroughly what was on the ballot or what was being discussed by the zoning committee.

Brushing up on state cannabis laws

Although cannabis is federally illegal, each state has the right to legalize it within its borders and set the rules and regulations for personal and commercial growth, production, transportation, sale, possession, and use. States fall into one of the following five categories:

>> **Fully legal:** Both medicinal and adult use are allowed.

>> **Fully illegal:** No medicinal or adult use is allowed or decriminalized (see the final item in this list for more about decriminalization).

>> **Medical and decriminalized:** Medical use is legal, and possession and use is decriminalized.

>> **Medical only:** Marijuana is legalized only for medical use, which in some states allows only cannabidiol (CBD) oil use (CBD doesn't contain the psycho-active ingredient THC).

>> **Decriminalized:** Possessing or using small amounts of marijuana will not lead to arrest, prosecution, prison time, or a criminal record (decriminalization details vary by state).

TIP

The easiest way to find out where each state in the U.S. stands on legalization is to search the web for "marijuana legal states." You'll see a color-coded map like the one shown in Figure 2-1. State marijuana laws change frequently, so access a map from a reliable source that has current information, such as weedmaps.com/learn/laws-and-regulations.

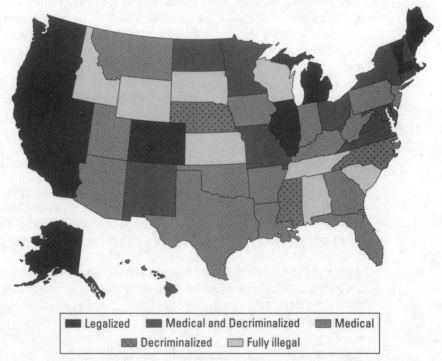

FIGURE 2-1:
Check out an online map to determine overall legal status.

Legend: ■ Legalized ■ Medical and Decriminalized ▨ Medical ▦ Decriminalized ▢ Fully illegal

© John Wiley & Sons, Inc.

State laws and enforcement of those laws can negatively impact cannabis businesses and investors in several ways, including the following:

>> Every state in which marijuana is legal has numerous rules and regulations that apply to marijuana growers, producers, sellers, and distributors. These rules and regulations govern everything from verifying the identities of buyers to packing, labeling, and tracking products, and all of them add to the cost and complexity of doing business.

>> Marijuana taxes vary by state, with adult-use marijuana typically taxed at a much higher rate than medical marijuana. Higher taxes add to the product cost and can drive sales to illegal sellers, negatively impacting sales for legal businesses.

>> States vary in the number of legal cannabis businesses they allow, how much they charge for licenses, and how quickly they implement legalization, which can all impact how successful cannabis businesses are in each state.

>> Some states require marijuana businesses to reserve large amounts of cash before applying for a license. This practice encourages *rolling up* marijuana businesses — a method that involves acquiring and merging small businesses to increase their collective value. In these states, large marijuana businesses have a distinct advantage over smaller operations.

>> State laws may stipulate residency requirements for investors in cannabis businesses.

>> Some states in which marijuana is legal are less stringent in enforcing laws against illegal sales, which can negatively impact sales for legal businesses.

Considering local laws, too

In states where cannabis is legal, local municipalities can separately regulate its growth, production, and sale within their borders. They are also allowed to add taxes and fees to commercial efforts above and beyond those of the state. In some cases, municipalities can completely ban commercial endeavors. For example, Colorado Springs permits medical sales but has continued to ban adult-use dispensaries. Penalties can vary significantly from one municipality to another.

These variations and costs can negatively impact the sales and profits of cannabis businesses, even in states in which cannabis is legal.

Examining cannabis laws in other countries

As an investor, you want to know about a cannabis company's range of operations — specifically, the countries it serves around the world. A company that operates in several countries may be less susceptible to changes in laws and regulations than a company operating in only one country. In addition, a company's global reach reflects its ambitions for growth. Here's a list of countries in which cannabis is legal or decriminalized to some degree:

>> Australia

>> Canada

>> Germany

>> Italy

- » Mexico
- » The Netherlands
- » New Zealand
- » South Korea
- » Spain
- » Switzerland
- » Uruguay
- » U.S. Virgin Islands

REMEMBER

Carefully research each market before investing in companies that operate in it. Examine the laws and enforcement of those laws, cannabis demand, the costs of doing business, competition from illegal sellers, and other factors to gain a better understanding of the potential for sales, profits, and growth, as well as the risks involved.

Riding the Waves of Politics and Culture

Cannabis has a long history of use in many areas, including medicine, textiles, religion, and even magic (in the ancient world). Perspectives about the plant, its uses, and its users have changed frequently around the world, especially over the last 100 years. In the United States, cannabis has been a lightning rod for debate among politicians, scientists, and citizens over whether it has medicinal benefits and whether those potential benefits outweigh the potential risks, especially with respect to adult use.

As an investor, you want to stay tuned to the news and the opinions of the day, because attitudes toward cannabis can change overnight and significantly impact the value of any investments you have in the industry, especially in the short term. A single study concluding that marijuana poses a significant danger to a user's health or to society overall could derail any positive momentum in the industry.

The following sections highlight the areas of focus, so you know what to look for, and bring you up to speed on the political and cultural climate surrounding cannabis as of the time of writing.

Checking the nation's pulse

Legalization of cannabis for both medical and adult use in the United States began as a movement with early activists coming from the more traditionally recognized user demographics of artists, musicians, and the so-called stoner culture. However, growing acceptance, along with expanding numbers of states legalizing use, has begun to show that cannabis acceptance is a very big tent, encompassing people from every demographic of age, race, income, gender, location, and political party.

This section explores the factors that are driving people to change their attitudes about cannabis, examines the prevailing attitudes and perspectives, and encourages you to stay abreast of the ever-evolving social and political climate.

Acknowledging the drivers of change

Acceptance and use among the middle-American, middle-income, middle-aged white constituency has come mostly from three drivers.

>> **Monetary impact to the community:** With Amendment 64 in Colorado, voters approved adult-use cannabis with an extremely high tax burden (on consumers and the industry) that directs funds to the state's rural education efforts through a grant program for school construction projects. Colorado was the first state to implement voter-approved adult-use cannabis sales, and the resulting state income from sales tax, excise tax, and fees has provoked revenue-envy among other states across the country, forcing both politicians and voters to sit up and take notice. In any state where adult (recreational) cannabis use is legal, the taxes and fees are fairly steep and show some promise of easing state budgetary constraints.

>> **Reduction in stigma due to medical marijuana:** After a few states legalized medicinal marijuana, more people started to accept its value as a health management tool. Increasingly, people are hearing from friends, relatives, and acquaintances who have had success using marijuana in many forms to help mitigate symptoms related to severe and chronic illness, as well as more mundane aches and pains. Specifically, the use of marijuana to alleviate nausea and stimulate appetite in cancer patients, along with the support of physicians, has helped drive the narrative that marijuana can be used as medicine.

REMEMBER

In addition, statistics showing the drop in fatal opioid overdoses in states where marijuana is legal have helped drive the awareness of its benefits to society. One study estimated that "legalization and access to adult-use marijuana reduced annual opioid mortality in the range of 20 to 35 percent, with particularly pronounced effects for synthetic opioids."

>> **The rising tide of positive media coverage:** Traditional media outlets have begun to join bloggers in their efforts to expose more people to the well-researched and substantiated facts about marijuana. As marijuana messaging becomes more positive in the press, it's beginning to alleviate fears and break down resistance to legalization.

Recognizing differences in attitudes about medical and adult-use cannabis

The difference in public perception regarding medical versus adult marijuana use is reflected in how it's taxed — medical marijuana is taxed at a significantly lower rate. Medical use is gaining acceptance quickly, as witnessed by the growing number of states legalizing it. Adult use is still mired in stigma but working to break through.

Growing numbers of scientific research studies demonstrating the value of cannabis for treating symptoms associated with many diseases, illnesses, and ailments are helping people recognize marijuana's medicinal value. Add to this the thousands of media articles, publications, blog posts, and positive word of mouth about medical usage, and the world is beginning to turn toward a positive perspective on at least one segment of the industry.

Keeping pace with evolving attitudes

As perspectives related to medical cannabis change, sometimes at lightning speed, limited numbers of early adopters are turning into an avalanche of support. This has been translating to additional support for adult use as people share their success stories through the press, social media, and word of mouth.

The dire warnings of societal destruction have failed to materialize, and even some ardent opponents have acknowledged the value of the industry and the benefits to individuals. Some dramatic pivots have occurred, even with constituencies that had virulently opposed cannabis, as they've hopped on the bandwagon. For example, former Speaker of the House John Boehner went from staunch opposition to joining the board of directors of a cannabis company!

As attitudes evolve, turn to social media and the internet to follow the discussion. With half the customer base under 35 years old, online and mobile interactions are leading the charge, and bloggers, along with cannabis websites, are a primary source of information.

Debunking misconceptions of cannabis and users

Many of the anti-cannabis voices have harped on the myths of unintended consequences and unfounded allegations to drive fear of legalization. The largest misconception is rooted in the negative stereotype of the "stoner" culture. The reality is a much broader and more inclusive demographic.

Many of today's cannabis dispensaries break with the stereotypical image of the old "head shop." The background music isn't exclusively reggae or heavy metal, and you're now much less likely to see the walls adorned with Jamaican flags and pictures of Bob Marley. The only black lights you're likely to see are those used by receptionists along with sophisticated ID scanners as they check for ID authenticity, age, or medical card compliance before allowing customers to enter secured "budrooms" for purchase. (A *budroom* is an area inside a dispensary where products are displayed and sold; it's often set up like a jewelry store, with products stored under glass.) Online sales also have high hurdles to protect against underage use.

Cannabis is becoming big business, and companies are building sophisticated marketing and branding designed to be welcoming and to appeal to all legal-aged demographics. Market share based on price and exclusivity is creating brands that cater to upscale clientele with store space that can look like a high-end jewelry store or a tasteful, yet hip, hangout.

Clientele are breaking old molds, too. In 2017, BDSA's profiles of cannabis dispensary shoppers showed that about half of them were aged 21 to 35, and the other half were older. Six in ten had college degrees or higher education. Nearly half lived in the suburbs. About half were married with children. Sixty-two percent were employed with an average annual income of $74,900.

Many misconceptions about cannabis and its users fall into the category of myths of "unintended consequences" — the idea that legalization will result in vast increases in homelessness, crime, black market activity, overdose, impaired driving, addiction, and teen use. Science and research have debunked these myths:

» Homelessness and crime have not increased due specifically to legalization of cannabis. After controlling for increased populations and traditional movement of people, the increases in homelessness are in line with those locations that have not legalized, and the levels are what are expected in those locations, regardless of cannabis use.

» Statistics show that black market activity has actually decreased in areas with legal adult use.

>> Due to a lack of receptors in specific areas of the brain, people have no biological means to overdose on THC alone or to become biologically addicted (though emotional addiction or habitual use is as likely as with other substances and habits such as chocolate or exercise). No reported and confirmed deaths have been linked specifically to cannabis overconsumption.

>> Teen use has not increased in states with legalization. U.S. numbers show that teen marijuana use is currently holding at its lowest level in 20 years.

>> Impaired driving from marijuana alone is a small fraction of the rate of impaired driving reported by law enforcement. In Colorado, statistics show that number to be close to 6 percent of all reports.

Examining activism

The original effort to legalize marijuana was started at the grassroots level by individuals with a great deal of passion and an understanding of the long odds necessary to overcome years of fear and prejudice against cannabis. The focus was on marijuana as medicine and its value in alleviating symptoms, such as seizures and nausea, associated with certain illnesses, such as epilepsy and cancer.

Generations of Americans growing up since the Nixon era's War on Drugs and the "Just Say No" campaign of First Lady Nancy Reagan in the 1980s had developed the perspective that equated marijuana with other Schedule 1 substances.

Yet these early activists were able to overcome steep hurdles, going directly to state constituencies with amendments on statewide ballots that succeeded in demonstrating the will of the people and the power of well-researched facts. As early-adopter states demonstrated success with regulation, state revenue generation, economic drivers, and resident acceptance, more formalized groups began to organize.

In response, groups opposing the legalization of marijuana became more active, as well. They were often heavily funded by industries that have seen marijuana as a threat to market share for their own products (such as pharmaceutical medications), and bolstered by equally passionate individuals who believe that marijuana is a dangerous drug.

However, as the tide has turned, the grassroots constituencies promoting cannabis have successfully recruited professional trade organizations to join their cause, such as Colorado Leads and the Cannabis Trade Federation. These organizations are working to secure the industry as a whole and to further the march toward legitimacy through professionalism and promotion of industry-standard practices as seen in many other established industries.

WHAT'S A SCHEDULE 1 SUBSTANCE?

The legal foundation of the U.S. government's war against drug abuse is the Controlled Substances Act, which is part of the Comprehensive Drug Abuse and Control Act of 1970. As a result of these acts, the U.S. Drug Enforcement Agency (DEA) divides controlled substances into five categories called "schedules," based on each drug's safety, potential for addiction and abuse, and whether it has any legitimate medical use:

- Schedule 1 substances are deemed to have no accepted medical use and a high potential for abuse. They include heroin, LSD, marijuana (cannabis), ecstasy, methaqualone (commonly referred to by the brand name Quaalude), and peyote ("magic mushrooms").

- Schedule 2 substances are also considered dangerous and are deemed to have a high potential for psychological or physical dependence. They include cocaine, methamphetamine, methadone, hydromorphone, meperidine, oxycodone, fentanyl, Dexedrine, Adderall, and Ritalin.

- Schedule 3 substances carry a low to moderate potential for physical or psychological dependence. They include ketamine, anabolic steroids, testosterone, and products containing less than 15 milligrams of hydrocodone per dose or less than 90 milligrams of codeine per dose.

- Schedule 4 substances are deemed to have a low potential for abuse and a low risk of dependence. They include Xanax, Soma, Darvon, Darvocet, Valium, Ativan, Talwin, and Ambien.

- Schedule 5 substances consist of products that contain limited concentrations of narcotics — typically cough suppressants, antidiarrheal medications, and analgesics.

Tuning into cannabis culture

Until recently, the perception of the cannabis culture has been aligned closely with the stoner culture as portrayed in popular movies such as Cheech and Chong's *Up in Smoke* and *Fast Times At Ridgemont High*, in which Sean Penn plays Jeff Spicoli, a failing high-school student who routinely gets high before class, emerging from a VW van surrounded by clouds of smoke.

While these and other Hollywood comedies always portray a stereotype of the cannabis culture, the parody is mixed with the realities of Jamaican reggae culture and generations of real users consuming the illegal substance. An era of tacit acceptance began when military personnel used cannabis during deployment in Vietnam and returned to the United States with a newfound appreciation of its calming effects and, in some cases, the counterculture that had formed around it.

Cannabis has been grown, sold, transported, and consumed around the world, developing its own subcultures along the way and helping to shape the identity and perceptions of those locations. Amsterdam is a prime example. As the character Vincent, played by John Travolta in the cult classic *Pulp Fiction*, puts it:

> It breaks down like this: It's legal to buy it, it's legal to own it, and if you're the proprietor of a hash bar, it's legal to sell it. It's legal to carry it, but that doesn't really matter 'cause get a load of this, all right? If you get stopped by the cops in Amsterdam, it's illegal for them to search you. I mean, that's a right the cops in Amsterdam don't have.

Along the way to legalization, many high-profile cultural icons, including Willie Nelson, Bill Maher, and Snoop Dogg, began to acknowledge their own consumption publicly, making it more acceptable to talk about. The consumption question was even raised during the 1996 U.S. presidential race, when then-candidate Bill Clinton remarked that while a student in England in the 1960s, he had experimented with marijuana but had "not inhaled."

Today's cannabis culture is as individualized as the people who consume it in one way or another for their own personal reasons, whether as medicine for symptom relief, enhancement of athletic performance, adult use for social activities, exploration of artistic appreciation, or relaxation. The culture is no longer defined by the Tetrahydrocannabinol (THC) for the "high," but includes other cannabinoids, such as CBD, and other benefits from the plant.

The culture has evolved to unapologetic and unabashed use by soccer moms and a growing number of professional athletes. Recent news stories showcase the increasing acceptance of cannabis use among high-profile athletes, with articles following NFL player Josh Gordon and his conflicts over consumption with the Cleveland Browns; New England Patriots coach Bill Belichick's perspectives on consumption by his players; ultrarunner Jenn Shelton, who was featured in the *New York Times* bestseller *Born to Run;* and ultrarunners Avery Collins and Jeff Sperber, who have sung the praises of adding cannabis to their workouts or recovery regimen; as well as admissions from multiple retired athletes, including NBA player Matt Barnes, who has remarked that he consumed prior to each game.

But not everyone in the traditional cannabis culture is happy about the transition to mainstream that has come with legalization and the professionalization of the industry. A segment of the consumer population continues to lament the decline of the counterculture. However, even as cannabis becomes more mainstream, the industry is likely to continue to cater to the counterculture as well, as evidenced by the industry's support of massive events such as the unofficial cannabis celebration holiday 4/20 on April 20th of each year, which is focused on the mass civil disobedience of public consumption.

REMEMBER

Regardless, one thing is clear: The cannabis industry, use, and culture are growing around the world with no signs of stopping, and this growth is driving a huge shift in cultural diversity among cannabis users.

Accounting for the High Costs of Doing Business

The cannabis industry is brutal. Businesses are pressured from all directions. They can't get loans from federally insured banks or accept credit or debit card payments; they're not allowed to claim standard business deductions; they can't conduct business across state lines; and they struggle daily to comply with a long, growing, and ever-changing list of rules and requirements. You really have to wonder how any cannabis businesses survive — most don't. The profit margins are slim, and the room for error even slimmer.

The following sections open your eyes to the high costs of doing business in the cannabis industry so you're well aware of what any cannabis business you're thinking of investing in is up against.

Regulatory and compliance costs

When people read about the amount of money cannabis generates for governments, they generally think that's tax revenue collected from retail sales, but that's just a portion of their proceeds. Governments also claim revenue in the form of licensing fees and compliance fees and penalties. These fees, costs, and penalties vary considerably based on the type of business (for example, cultivation, manufacturing, or dispensary), and the state and location within the state.

License application fees and related costs alone can cost tens or even hundreds of thousands of dollars. Most groups and individuals who purchase licenses are very well funded. You generally need a lobbyist, an application consultant, and a lawyer who specializes in cannabis license applications to guide you through the process, which is highly political and frequently subjective. Laypeople generally don't score licenses.

In addition to the cost and hassle of getting licensed, there are compliance costs, including the cost of training personnel, buying or leasing software to help with compliance, and the costs of generating and submitting regular reports. To add to the costs and complexities of doing business in the cannabis industry, any compliance violations can result in hefty fines and the possibility of the business losing its license.

Federal, state, and local taxes

Even though the United States has declared marijuana federally illegal, it still demands its share of any revenue a cannabis business generates. So, too, do state and local governments. Here's a list of taxes that most legal cannabis businesses are required to pay:

>> **Federal income tax, which is calculated on total revenue instead of net profit, because cannabis businesses are prohibited from deducting business expenses.** Also, cannabis businesses that don't use banks have to pay their taxes in cash and pay an extra 10 percent for the privilege.

>> **Federal Insurance Contributions Act (FICA) taxes on wages paid to employees.** FICA taxes cover Social Security retirement and disability, along with Medicaid costs.

>> **State taxes.** All states where marijuana is legal charge sales tax, which customers end up paying, but some states also include an excise tax that can be charged to customers or to businesses. For example, Alaska charges an excise tax on the transfer or sale of marijuana from a grow operation to a retail store or manufacturing facility.

>> **Business and occupation taxes.** In some states, such as Washington, anyone who holds a producer, processor, or retailer marijuana business license is required to pay a business and occupation tax.

>> **Cultivation tax.** California charges a cultivation tax on harvested cannabis that enters the commercial market.

>> **Municipal sales tax.** Some municipalities also charge a sales tax, although this is paid by the customer, not by the cannabis business.

Security costs

Cannabis businesses have two things that attract thieves: money and drugs. You've probably heard plenty of stories in the news about thieves driving cars or trucks through doors or walls in attempts to steal cash and product from retail locations and grow operations. Some locations have even been robbed during operating hours.

To remain viable, cannabis businesses must protect themselves, their staff, and their customers, and that protection comes at a price. Security costs typically cover the following:

>> Security expertise to evaluate the business location, install equipment, and train the staff on security protocols and all security requirements for the cannabis industry

>> Cameras coupled with enough secure storage for retaining video for the required number of days or weeks

>> External lights on motion sensors or timers

>> Locks, safes, secured cabinets, and lockable refrigerators (for items that must be kept cold)

>> Security staff (in some situations)

>> Internal and external door-locking mechanisms with badged or passcode access

>> Barriers, such as opaque exterior windows, to obscure the view of products in retail locations

>> Security alarms

>> Separate and secured storage areas

>> Controlled delivery areas

Businesses also need to account for a higher cost of business insurance and the costs associated with failed or successful break-ins and thefts. For example, even if a plan to rob a business is foiled, one or more employees may be harmed or the building may be damaged.

Chapter 3

What Is a Cryptocurrency?

S o you've come to this chapter, and your first question is probably this: "What the heck is a cryptocurrency, anyway?" Simply stated, a *cryptocurrency* is a new form of digital money. You can transfer your traditional, non-cryptocurrency money like the U.S. dollar digitally, but that's not quite the same as how cryptocurrencies work. When cryptocurrencies become mainstream, you may be able to use them to pay for stuff electronically, just like you do with traditional currencies.

However, what sets cryptocurrencies apart is the technology behind them. You may say, "Who cares about the technology behind my money? I only care about how much of it there is in my wallet!" The issue is that the world's current money systems have a bunch of problems. Here are some examples:

» Payment systems such as credit cards and wire transfers are outdated.

» In most cases, a bunch of middlemen like banks and brokers take a cut in the process, making transactions expensive and slow.

» Financial inequality is growing around the globe.

» Around 3 billion unbanked or underbanked people can't access financial services. That's approximately half the population on the planet!

Cryptocurrencies aim to solve some of these problems, if not more. This chapter introduces you to crypto fundamentals.

Beginning with the Basics of Cryptocurrencies

You know how your everyday, government-based currency is reserved in banks? And that you need an ATM or a connection to a bank to get more of it or transfer it to other people? Well, with cryptocurrencies, you may be able to get rid of banks and other centralized middlemen altogether. That's because cryptocurrencies rely on a technology called *blockchain*, which is *decentralized* (meaning no single entity is in charge of it). Instead, every computer in the network confirms the transactions.

The following sections go over the basics of cryptocurrencies: their background, benefits, and more.

The definition of money

Before getting into the nitty-gritty of cryptocurrencies, you need to understand the definition of money itself. The philosophy behind money is a bit like the whole "which came first: the chicken or the egg?" thing. In order for money to be valuable, it must have a number of characteristics, such as the following:

>> Enough people must have it.

>> Merchants must accept it as a form of payment.

>> Society must trust that it's valuable and that it will remain valuable in the future.

Of course, in the old days, when you traded your chicken for shoes, the values of the exchanged materials were inherent to their nature. But when coins, cash, and credit cards came into play, the definition of money and, more importantly, the trust model of money changed.

Another key change in money has been its ease of transaction. The hassle of carrying a ton of gold bars from one country to another was one of the main reasons cash was invented. Then, when people got even lazier, credit cards were invented. But credit cards carry the money that your government controls. As the world becomes more interconnected and more concerned about authorities who may or may not have people's best interests in mind, cryptocurrencies may offer a valuable alternative.

TECHNICAL STUFF

Here's a fun fact: Your normal, government-backed currency, such as the U.S. dollar, must go by its fancy name, *fiat currency*, now that cryptocurrencies are around. Fiat is described as a legal tender like coins and banknotes that have value only because the government says so.

Some cryptocurrency history

The first ever cryptocurrency was (drumroll please) Bitcoin! You probably have heard of Bitcoin more than anything else in the crypto industry. Bitcoin was the first product of the first blockchain developed by some anonymous entity who went by the name Satoshi Nakamoto. Satoshi released the idea of Bitcoin in 2008 and described it as a "purely peer-to-peer version" of electronic money.

TECHNICAL STUFF

Bitcoin was the first established cryptocurrency, but many attempts at creating digital currencies occurred years before Bitcoin was formally introduced.

Cryptocurrencies like Bitcoin are created through a process called *mining*. Very different than mining ore, mining cryptocurrencies involves powerful computers solving complicated problems.

Bitcoin remained the only cryptocurrency until 2011. Then Bitcoin enthusiasts started noticing flaws in it, so they decided to create alternative coins, also known as *altcoins*, to improve Bitcoin's design for things like speed, security, anonymity, and more. Among the first altcoins was Litecoin, which aimed to become the silver to Bitcoin's gold. But as of the time of writing, thousands of cryptocurrencies are available, and the number is expected to increase in the future.

Key crypto benefits

Still not convinced that cryptocurrencies (or any other sort of decentralized money) are a better solution than traditional government-based money? Here are a number of solutions that cryptocurrencies may be able to provide through their decentralized nature:

>> **Reducing corruption:** With great power comes great responsibility. But when you give a ton of power to only one person or entity, the chances of their abusing that power increase. The 19th-century British politician Lord Acton said it best: "Power tends to corrupt, and absolute power corrupts absolutely." Cryptocurrencies aim to resolve the issue of absolute power by distributing

power among many people or, better yet, among all the members of the network. That's the key idea behind blockchain technology anyway.

» **Eliminating extreme money printing:** Governments have central banks, and central banks have the ability to simply print money when they're faced with a serious economic problem. This process is also called *quantitative easing*. By printing more money, a government may be able to bail out debt or devalue its currency. However, this approach is like putting a bandage on a broken leg. Not only does it rarely solve the problem, but the negative side effects also can sometimes surpass the original issue.

For example, when a country like Iran or Venezuela prints too much money, the value of its currency drops so much that inflation skyrockets and people can't even afford to buy everyday goods and services. Their cash becomes barely as valuable as rolls of toilet paper. Most cryptocurrencies have a limited, set amount of coins available. When all those coins are in circulation, a central entity or the company behind the blockchain has no easy way to simply create more coins or add on to its supply.

» **Giving people charge of their own money:** With traditional cash, you're basically giving away all your control to central banks and the government. If you trust your government, that's great, but keep in mind that at any point, your government is able to simply freeze your bank account and deny your access to your funds. For example, in the United States, if you don't have a legal will and own a business, the government has the right to all your assets if you pass away. Some governments can even simply abolish bank notes the way India did in 2016. With cryptocurrencies, you and only you can access your funds. (Unless someone steals them from you, that is.)

» **Cutting out the middleman:** With traditional money, every time you make a transfer, a middleman like your bank or a digital payment service takes a cut. With cryptocurrencies, all the network members in the blockchain are that middleman; their compensation is formulated differently from that of fiat money middlemen's and therefore is minimal in comparison. Flip to Chapter 4 in Book 9 for more on how cryptocurrencies work.

» **Serving the unbanked:** A vast portion of the world's citizens has no access or limited access to payment systems like banks. Cryptocurrencies aim to resolve this issue by spreading digital commerce around the globe so that anyone with a mobile phone can start making payments. And yes, more people have access to mobile phones than to banks. In fact, more people have mobile phones than have toilets, but at this point the blockchain technology may not be able to resolve the latter issue.

Common crypto and blockchain myths

During the 2017 Bitcoin hype, a lot of misconceptions about the whole industry started to circulate. These myths may have played a role in the cryptocurrency crash that followed the surge. The important thing to remember is that both the blockchain technology and its byproduct, the cryptocurrency market, are still in their infancy, and things are rapidly changing. The following list gets some of the most common misunderstandings out of the way:

» **Cryptocurrencies are good only for criminals.** Some cryptocurrencies boast anonymity as one of their key features. That means your identity isn't revealed when you're making transactions. Other cryptocurrencies are based on a decentralized blockchain, meaning a central government isn't the sole power behind them. These features do make such cryptocurrencies attractive for criminals; however, law-abiding citizens in corrupt countries can also benefit from them. For example, if you don't trust your local bank or country because of corruption and political instability, the best way to store your money may be through the blockchain and cryptocurrency assets.

» **You can make anonymous transactions using all cryptocurrencies.** For some reason, many people equate Bitcoin with anonymity. But Bitcoin, along with many other cryptocurrencies, doesn't incorporate anonymity at all. All transactions made using such cryptocurrencies are made on public block-chain. Some cryptocurrencies, such as Monero, do prioritize privacy, meaning no outsider can find the source, amount, or destination of transactions. However, most other cryptocurrencies, including Bitcoin, don't operate that way.

» **The only application of blockchain is Bitcoin.** This idea couldn't be further from the truth. Bitcoin and other cryptocurrencies are a tiny byproduct of the blockchain revolution. Many believe Satoshi created Bitcoin simply to provide an example of how the blockchain technology can work. Almost every industry and business in the world can use the blockchain technology in its specific field.

» **All blockchain activity is private.** Many people falsely believe that the blockchain technology isn't open to the public and is accessible only to its network of common users. Although some companies create their own private blockchains to be used only among employees and business partners, the majority of the blockchains behind famous cryptocurrencies such as Bitcoin are accessible by the public. Literally anyone with a computer can access the transactions in real time. For example, you can view the real-time Bitcoin transactions at www.blockchain.com.

Risks

Just like anything else in life, cryptocurrencies come with their own baggage of risk. Whether you trade cryptos, invest in them, or simply hold on to them for the future, you must assess and understand the risks beforehand.

Some of the most talked-about cryptocurrency risks include their volatility and lack of regulation. Volatility got especially out of hand in 2017, when the price of most major cryptocurrencies, including Bitcoin, skyrocketed above 1,000 percent and then came crashing down. However, as the cryptocurrency hype has calmed down, the price fluctuations have become more predictable and followed similar patterns of stocks and other financial assets.

Regulations are another major topic in the industry. The funny thing is that both lack of regulation and exposure to regulations can turn into risk events for cryptocurrency investors.

Gearing Up to Make Transactions

Cryptocurrencies are here to make transactions easier and faster. But before you take advantage of these benefits, you must gear up with crypto gadgets, discover where you can get your hands on different cryptocurrencies, and get to know the cryptocurrency community. Some of the essentials include cryptocurrency wallets and exchanges.

Wallets

Some *cryptocurrency wallets,* which hold your purchased cryptos, are similar to digital payment services like Apple Pay and PayPal. But generally, they're different from traditional wallets and come in different formats and levels of security.

REMEMBER

You can't get involved in the cryptocurrency market without a crypto wallet. Be sure to get the most secure type of wallet, such as hardware or paper wallets, instead of using the convenient online ones.

Exchanges

After you get yourself a crypto wallet (see the preceding section), you're ready to go crypto shopping, and one of the best destinations is a cryptocurrency exchange. These online web services are where you can transfer your traditional money to buy cryptocurrencies, exchange different types of cryptocurrencies, or even store your cryptocurrencies.

WARNING

Storing your cryptocurrencies on an exchange is considered high risk because many such exchanges have been exposed to hacking attacks and scams in the past. When you're done with your transactions, your best bet is to move your new digital assets to your personal, secure wallet.

Exchanges come in different shapes and forms. Some are like traditional stock exchanges and act as a middleman — something crypto enthusiasts believe is a slap in the face of the cryptocurrency market, which is trying to remove a centralized middleman. Others are decentralized and provide a service where buyers and sellers come together and transact in a peer-to-peer manner, but they come with their own sets of problems, like the risk of locking yourself out. A third type of crypto exchange is called *hybrid,* and it merges the benefits of the other two types to create a better, more secure experience for users.

Communities

TIP

Getting to know the crypto community can be the next step as you're finding your way in the market. The web has plenty of chat rooms and support groups to give you a sense of the market and what people are talking about. Here are some ways to get involved:

>> **Crypto-specific Telegram groups:** Many cryptocurrencies have their very own channels on the Telegram app. To join them, you first need to download the Telegram messenger app on your smartphone or computer; it's available for iOS and Android.

>> **Crypto chat rooms on Reddit or BitcoinTalk:** BitcoinTalk (bitcointalk. org/) and Reddit (www.reddit.com/) have some of the oldest crypto chat rooms around. You can view some topics without signing up, but if you want to get involved, you need to log in. (Of course, Reddit isn't exclusive to cryptos, but you can search for a variety of cryptocurrency topics.)

>> **TradingView chat room:** One of the best trading platforms out there, TradingView (www.tradingview.com/) also has a social service where traders and investors of all sorts come together and share their thoughts, questions, and ideas.

>> **Invest Diva's Premium Investing Group:** If you're looking for a less crowded and more investment/trading-focused place to get support, you can join the investment group at learn.investdiva.com/join-group.

REMEMBER

On the flip side, many scammers also target these kinds of platforms to advertise and lure members into trouble. Keep your wits about you.

Making a Plan Before You Jump In

You may just want to buy some cryptocurrencies and save them for their potential growth in the future. Or you may want to become more of an active investor and buy or sell cryptocurrencies more regularly to maximize profit and revenue. Regardless, you must have a plan and a strategy. Even if your transaction is a one-time thing and you don't want to hear anything about your crypto assets for the next ten years, you still must gain the knowledge necessary to determine things like the following:

>> What to buy

>> When to buy

>> How much to buy

>> When to sell

The following sections give you a quick overview of the steps you must take before buying your first cryptocurrency.

Select your cryptos

Thousands of cryptocurrencies are out there at the time of writing, and the number is growing. Some of these cryptos may vanish in five years. Others may explode over 1,000 percent and may even replace traditional cash. The most famous cryptocurrencies right now include Ethereum, Ripple, Litecoin, Bitcoin Cash, and Stellar Lumens.

You can select cryptocurrencies based on things like category, popularity, ideology, the management behind the blockchain, and its economic model.

TIP

Because the crypto industry is pretty new, it's still very hard to identify the best-performing cryptos for long-term investments. That's why you may benefit from diversifying among various types and categories of cryptocurrencies in order to manage your risk. By diversifying across 15 or more cryptos, you can stack up the odds of having winners in your portfolio. On the flip side, overdiversification can become problematic as well, so you need to take calculated measures.

Analyze, invest, and profit

When you've narrowed down the cryptocurrencies you like, you must then iden-tify the best time to buy them. For example, in 2017 many people started to believe in the idea of Bitcoin and wanted to get involved. Unfortunately, many of those people mismanaged the timing and bought when the price had peaked. Therefore, they not only were able to buy fewer bits of Bitcoin (pun intended), but they also had to sit on their losses and wait for the next price surge. By analyzing the price action and conducting proper risk management, you may be able to stack the odds in your favor and make a ton of profit in the future.

Chapter 4

How Cryptocurrencies Work

Cryptocurrencies, and more specifically Bitcoin, have been one of the first use cases for blockchain technology. That's why most people may have heard about Bitcoin more than they have about the underlying blockchain technology.

This chapter gets into detail about how cryptocurrencies use blockchain technology, how they operate, and how they're generated, as well as some crypto geek terms you can impress your date with.

Explaining Basic Terms in the Cryptocurrency Process

Cryptocurrencies are also known as digital coins, but they're quite different from the coins in your piggy bank. For one thing, they aren't attached to a central bank, a country, or a regulatory body.

Here's an example. Say you want to buy the latest version of *Cryptocurrency Investing For Dummies* from your local bookstore. Using your normal debit card, this is what happens:

1. **You give your card details to the cashier or the store's point-of-sale system.**

2. **The store runs the info through, essentially asking your bank whether you have enough money in your bank account to buy the book.**

3. **The bank checks its records to confirm whether you do.**

4. **If you do have enough, the bank gives a thumbs-up to the bookstore.**

5. **The bank then updates its records to show the movement of the money from your account to the bookstore's account.**

6. **The bank gets a little cut for the trouble of being the middleman.**

Now if you wanted to remove the bank from this entire process, who else would you trust to keep all these records without altering them or cheating in any way? Your best friend? Your dog walker? (Here's hoping you didn't say the crown prince of Nigeria.) In fact, you may not trust any single person. But how about trusting *everyone* in the network?

REMEMBER

Blockchain technology works to remove the middleman. When applied to cryptocurrencies, blockchain eliminates a central record of transactions. Instead, you distribute many copies of your transaction ledger around the world. Each owner of each copy records your transaction of buying the book.

Here's what happens if you want to buy *Cryptocurrency Investing For Dummies* using a cryptocurrency:

1. **You give your crypto details to the cashier.**

2. **The shop asks everyone in the network to see whether you have enough coins to buy the book.**

3. **All the record holders in the network check their records to see whether you do. (These record holders are called nodes, which are covered in more detail later in this chapter.)**

4. **If you do have enough, each node gives the thumbs-up to the cashier.**

5. **The nodes all update their records to show the transfer.**

6. **At random, a node gets a reward for the work.**

That means no organization is keeping track of where your coins are or investigating fraud. In fact, cryptocurrencies such as Bitcoin wouldn't exist without a whole network of bookkeepers (nodes) and a little thing known as *cryptography*. The following sections explain that and some other important terms related to the workings of cryptocurrencies.

Cryptography

Shhh. Don't tell anyone. That's the *crypto* in *cryptography* and *cryptocurrency*. It means "secret." In the cryptocurrency world, it mainly refers to being "anonymous."

Historically, cryptography is an ancient art for sending hidden messages. (The term comes from the Greek word *krypto logos*, which means *secret writing*.) The sender *encrypts* the message by using some sort of key. The receiver then has to *decrypt* it. For example, 19th-century scholars decrypted ancient Egyptian hiero-glyphics when Napoleon's soldiers found the Rosetta Stone in 1799 near Rosetta, Egypt. In the 21st-century era of information networks, the sender can digitally encrypt messages, and the receiver can use cryptographic services and algorithms to decrypt them.

What does Napoleon have to do with cryptocurrencies? Cryptocurrencies use cryptography to maintain security and anonymity. That's how digital coins, even though they're not monetized by any central authority or regulatory body, can help with security and protection from double-spending, which is the risk of your digital cash being used more than once.

Cryptography uses three main encryption methods:

>> **Hashing:** Hashing is something like a fingerprint or signature. A *hash function* first takes your input data (which can be of any size). The function then performs an operation on the original data and returns an output that represents the original data but has a fixed (and generally smaller) size. In cryptocurrencies such as Bitcoin, it's used to guess the combination of the lock of a block. Hashing maintains the structure of blockchain data, encodes people's account addresses, and makes block mining possible. You can find more on mining later in this chapter.

>> **Symmetric encryption cryptography:** *Symmetric encryption* is the simplest method used in cryptography. It involves only one secret key for both the sender and the receiver. The main disadvantage of symmetric encryption is that all parties involved have to exchange the key used to encrypt the data before they can decrypt it.

>> **Asymmetric encryption cryptography:** *Asymmetric encryption* uses two keys: a public key and a private key. You can encrypt a message by using the receiver's public key, but the receiver can decrypt it only with their private key.

Nodes

A *node* is an electronic device doing the bookkeeping job in the blockchain network, making the whole decentralized thing possible. The device can be a computer, a cellphone, or even a printer, as long as it's connected to the internet and has access to the blockchain network.

Mining

As the owners of nodes (see the preceding section) willingly contribute their computing resources to store and validate transactions, they have the chance to collect the transaction fees and earn a reward in the underlying cryptocurrency for doing so. This process is known as *mining*, and the owners who do it are *miners*.

REMEMBER

Not all cryptocurrencies can be mined. Bitcoin and some other famous ones can. Some others, such as Ripple (XRP), avoid mining altogether because they want a platform that doesn't consume a huge amount of electricity in the process of mining; power usage is one of the issues with blockchain, actually. Regardless, for the most part, mining remains a huge part of many cryptocurrencies to date.

Here's how mining works: Cryptocurrency miners solve cryptographic puzzles (via software) to add transactions to the ledger (the blockchain) in the hope of getting coins as a reward. It's called mining because of the fact that this process helps extract new cryptocurrencies from the system. Anyone, including you, can join this group. Your computer needs to "guess" a random number that solves an equation that the blockchain system generates. In fact, your computer has to calculate many 64-character strings or 256-bit hashes and check with the challenge equation to see whether the answer is right. That's why it's so important that you have a powerful computer. The more powerful your computer is, the more guesses it can make in a second, increasing your chances of winning this game. If you manage to guess right, you earn Bitcoins and get to write the "next page" of Bitcoin transactions on the blockchain.

Because mining is based on a form of guessing, for each block a different miner guesses the number and is granted the right to update the blockchain. Whoever has the biggest computing power combined, controlling 51 percent of the votes, controls the chain and wins every time. Thanks to the law of statistical probability, the same miner is unlikely to succeed every time. On the other hand, this game can sometimes be unfair because the biggest computer power will be the first to solve the challenge equation and "win" more often.

Proof-of-work

If you're a miner and want to actually enter your block and transactions into the blockchain, you have to provide an answer (proof) to a specific challenge. This proof is difficult to produce (hence all the gigantic computers, time, and money needed for it), but others can very easily verify it. This process is known as *proof-of-work,* or PoW.

For example, guessing a combination to a lock is a proof to a challenge. Going through all the different possible combinations to come up with the right answer may be pretty hard, but after you get it, it's easy to validate — just enter the combination and see whether the lock opens! The first miner who solves the problem for each block on the blockchain gets a reward. The reward is basically the incentive to keep on mining and gets the miners competing to be the first one to find a solution for mathematical problems. Bitcoin and some other minable cryptocurrencies mainly use the PoW concept to make sure that the network isn't easily manipulated.

REMEMBER

But this whole proof-of-work thing has some downsides for blockchain technology. One of the main challenges is that it wastes a lot of computing power and electricity just for the sake of producing random guesses. That's why new cryptocurrencies have jumped on an alternative wagon called proof-of-stake (PoS), covered in the next section.

Proof-of-stake

Unlike PoW, a *proof-of-stake* (PoS) system requires you to show ownership of a certain amount of money (or *stake*). That means the more crypto you own, the more mining power you have. This approach eliminates the need for the expensive mining extravaganza. And because the calculations are pretty simple to prove, you own a certain percentage of the total amount of the cryptos available.

Another difference is that the PoS system offers no block rewards, so the miners get transaction fees. That's how PoS cryptos can be several thousand times more cost-effective than PoW ones. (Don't let the PoS abbreviation give you the wrong idea.)

REMEMBER

But of course, PoS also can have its own problems. For starters, you can argue that PoS rewards coin hoarders. Under the proof-of-stake model, nodes can mine only a percentage of transactions that corresponds to their stake in a cryptocurrency. For example, a proof-of-stake miner who owns 10 percent of a cryptocurrency would be able to mine 10 percent of blocks on the network. The limitation with this consensus model is that it gives nodes on the network a reason to save their coins instead of spending them. It also produces a scenario in which the rich get richer because large coin holders are able to mine a larger percentage of blocks on the network.

Proof-of-importance

Proof-of-importance (PoI) was first introduced by a blockchain platform called NEM to support its XEM cryptocurrency. In some ways PoI is similar to PoS because participants (nodes) are marked as "eligible" if they have a certain amount of crypto "vested." Then the network gives a "score" to the eligible nodes, and they can create a block that is roughly the same proportion to that "score." But the difference is that the nodes won't get a higher score only by holding onto more cryptocurrencies. Other variables are considered in the score, too, in order to resolve the primary problem with PoS, which is hoarding. The NEM community in particular uses a method called "harvesting" to solve the PoS "hoarding" problem.

Here's how Investopedia defines harvesting: "Instead of each miner contributing its mining power in a cumulative manner to a computing node, a harvesting participant simply links his account to an existing supernode and uses that account's computing power to complete blocks on his behalf." (Find out more about harvesting later in this chapter.)

Transactions: Putting it all together

REMEMBER

Here's a summary of how cryptocurrencies work (check out the preceding sections for details on some of the terminology):

1. **When you want to use cryptos to purchase something, first your crypto network and your crypto wallet automatically check your previous transactions to make sure you have enough cryptocurrencies to make that transaction.**

   For this, you need your private and public keys.

2. **The transaction is then encrypted, broadcast to the cryptocurrency's network, and queued up to be added to the public ledger.**

3. **Transactions are then recorded on the public ledger through mining.**

   The sending and receiving addresses are wallet IDs or hash values that aren't tied to the user identification, so they are anonymous.

4. **For PoW cryptos, the miners have to solve a math puzzle to verify the transaction. PoS cryptos attribute the mining power to the proportion of the coins held by the miners, instead of utilizing energy to solve math**

problems, in order to resolve the "wasted energy" problem of PoW. The PoI cryptos add a number of variables when attributing the mining power to nodes in order to resolve the "hoarding" problem that's associated with PoS.

Cruising through Other Important Crypto Concepts

Earlier in this chapter, you find out about basics of cryptocurrencies and how they're related to blockchain technology. The following sections get a few more concepts out of the way, just in case someone starts talking to you about them. Other factors make cryptocurrencies so special and different from your government-backed legal tender, also known as *fiat currency,* such as the U.S. dollar.

Adaptive scaling

Adaptive scaling is one of the advantages of investing in cryptocurrencies. It means that it gets harder to mine a specific cryptocurrency over time. It allows cryptocurrencies to work well on both small and large scales. That's why cryptocurrencies take measures such as limiting the supply over time (to create scarcity) and reducing the reward for mining as more total coins are mined. Thanks to adaptive scaling, mining difficulty goes up and down depending on the popularity of the coin and the blockchain. This can give cryptocurrencies a real longevity within the market.

Decentralization

The whole idea behind blockchain technology is that it's *decentralized.* This concept means no single entity can affect the cryptocurrencies.

TECHNICAL STUFF

Some people claim cryptocurrencies such as Ripple aren't truly decentralized because they don't follow Bitcoin's mining protocol exactly. Ripple has no miners. Instead, transactions are powered through a "centralized" blockchain to make it more reliable and faster. Ripple in particular has gone this route because it wants to work with big banks and therefore wants to combine the best elements of fiat money and blockchain cryptocurrency. Whether non-minable currencies such as Ripple can be considered true cryptocurrencies is up for discussion, but that fact doesn't mean you can't invest in them.

Harvesting

Harvesting is an alternative to the traditional mining used to maintain the integrity of a blockchain network. It was designed by a blockchain platform called NEM to generate its own currency called XEM. According to finder.com, this is how harvesting works: "Every time someone carries out a transaction, the first computer to see and verify the transaction will notify nearby users of that transaction, creating a cascade of information. This process is called 'generating a block.' Whenever someone with more than 10,000 vested XEM generates a block in NEM, they receive the transaction fees on that block as payment." Also, as explained earlier in this chapter, harvesting uses a PoI system rather than PoS and PoW.

Open source

Cryptocurrencies are typically *open source.* That means that miners, nodes, and harvesters alike can join and use the network without paying a fee.

Public ledger

A ledger is the age-old record-keeping system for recording information and data. Cryptocurrencies use a *public ledger* to record all transactional data. Everyone in the world can access public blockchains and see entire transactions happening with cryptocurrencies.

Note that not all blockchains use a public ledger. Some businesses and financial institutions use private ledgers so that the transactions aren't visible to the world. However, by doing so, they may contradict the original idea behind blockchain technology.

Smart contracts

Smart contracts are also called *self-executing contracts, blockchain contracts,* or *digital contracts.* They're just like traditional contracts except that they're completely digital. Smart contracts remove the middleman between the buyer and the seller so you can implement things like automatic payments and investment products without the need of a central authority like a bank.

A smart contract is actually a tiny computer program that's stored and runs on a blockchain platform. Because of that, all the transactions are completely distributed, and no centralized authority is in control of the money. Also, because it's stored on a blockchain, a smart contract is *immutable.* Being immutable means that after a smart contract is created, it can never be changed again; it can't be tampered with, which is an inherited feature from blockchain technology.

WARNING

However, being immutable comes with its own disadvantages. Because you can't change anything in the smart contract, that means that if the code has any bugs, you can't fix them either. This makes smart contract security more difficult. Some companies aim to combat this problem by auditing their smart contracts, which can be very costly.

As time goes by, you can expect better coding practices and development life cycles to combat smart contract security problems. After all, smart contracts are still a pretty young practice with their whole life of trial and error ahead of them.

Stick a Fork in It: Digging into Cryptocurrency Forks

What you get from a cryptocurrency fork won't fill your tummy, but it may fill your crypto wallet with some money! Many popular cryptocurrencies were born as a result of a split (fork) in another cryptocurrency like Bitcoin. The following sections explain the basics of these cryptocurrency splits and how you may be able to profit from them.

What is a fork, and why do forks happen?

Sometimes when a group of developers disagrees with the direction a specific cryptocurrency is going, the members decide to go their own way and initiate a *fork*. Imagine an actual physical fork. It has one long handle, and then it divides into a bunch of branches. That's exactly what happens in a cryptocurrency fork.

As explained earlier in this chapter, some cryptocurrencies are implemented within open source software. Each of these cryptocurrencies has its own protocol that everyone in the network should follow. Examples of such rule topics include the following:

>> Block size

>> Rewards that miners, harvesters, or other network participants get

>> How fees are calculated

REMEMBER

But because cryptocurrencies are essentially software projects, their development will never be fully finished. There's always room for improvement. Crypto developers regularly push out updates to fix issues or to increase performance. Some of these improvements are small, but others fundamentally change the way the original cryptocurrency (which the developers fell in love with) works. Just as in any type of relationship, you either grow together or grow apart. When the disagreements among a group of developers or network participants intensify, they can choose to break up, create their own version of the protocol, and cause a potential heartbreak that requires years of therapy to get over. Okay, the last part doesn't really happen.

Hard forks and soft forks

Two types of forks can happen in a cryptocurrency: a hard fork and a soft fork.

Most cryptocurrencies consist of two big pieces: the protocol (set of rules) and the blockchain (which stores all the transactions that have ever happened). If a segment of the crypto community decides to create its own new rules, it starts by copying the original protocol code and then goes about making changes to it (assuming the cryptocurrency is completely open source). After the developers have implemented their desired changes, they define a point at which their fork will become active. More specifically, they choose a block number to start the forking. For example, as you can see in Figure 4-1, the community can say that the new protocol will go live when block 999 is published to the cryptocurrency blockchain.

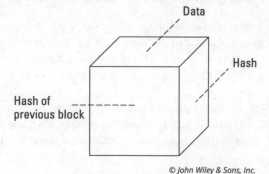

FIGURE 4-1:
An example of a hard fork.

© John Wiley & Sons, Inc.

When the currency reaches that block number, the community splits in two. Some people decide to support the original set of rules, while others support the new fork. Each group then starts adding new blocks to the fork it supports. At this point, both blockchains are incompatible with each other, and a *hard fork* has occurred. In a hard fork, the nodes essentially go through a contentious divorce and don't ever interact with each other again. They don't even acknowledge the nodes or transactions on the old blockchain.

On the other hand, a soft fork is the type of breakup where you remain friends with your ex. If the developers decide to fork the cryptocurrency and make the changes compatible with the old one, then the situation is called a *soft fork*. You can see the subtle difference in the example shown in Figure 4-2.

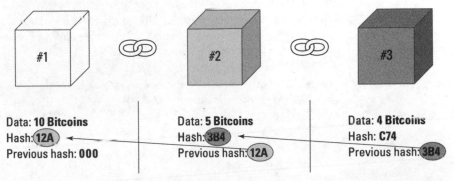

FIGURE 4-2:
An example of a soft fork.

Data: **10 Bitcoins**
Hash: **12A**
Previous hash: **000**

Data: **5 Bitcoins**
Hash: **3B4**
Previous hash: **12A**

Data: **4 Bitcoins**
Hash: **C74**
Previous hash: **3B4**

© John Wiley & Sons, Inc.

Say the soft fork is set to happen at block 700. The majority of the community may support the stronger chain of blocks following both the new and old rules. If the two sides reach a consensus after a while, the new rules are upgraded across the network. Any non-upgraded nodes (that is, stubborn geeks) who are still mining are essentially wasting their time. The community comes back together softly, and everyone lives happily ever after — until the next major argument, of course.

Free money on forks

Because a new fork is based on the original blockchain, all transactions that previously happened on the blockchain also happen on the fork. The developers of the new chain take a "snapshot" of the ledger at a specific block number the fork happened (like 999 in Figure 4-1) and therefore create a duplicate copy of the chain. That means if you had a certain amount of cryptocurrencies before the fork, you also get the same amount of the new coin.

REMEMBER

To get free coins from a fork, you need to have the cryptocurrency on a platform that supports the fork before the block number at which the fork occurs. You can call this free money. But how valuable the coins are all depends on how well the new fork performs and how popular it gets within the community.

A FORKING EXAMPLE: BITCOIN VERSUS BITCOIN CASH

Even the celebrity of cryptocurrencies, Bitcoin (BTC), has seen forks. One of the well-known Bitcoin forks happened on August 1, 2017. That's the birthday of Bitcoin Cash. In this case, the developers couldn't agree on what the size for a block should be. Some wanted the block size to go from 1MB to 2MB, but others wanted to increase it even more, to 32MB. Some people in the community loved the new big idea, while others thought the other group was crazy. So both groups decided to go their own ways. Bitcoin Cash adapted a brand-new symbol (BCH), too. People who already had BTC got the same amount of BCH added to their crypto wallets.

Only time will tell whether BCH ever surpasses the original protocol's value. But hey, at least the forkers got some value out of it!

Chapter **5**

Entering the World of ESG Investing

The acronym ESG has undoubtedly become one of the hottest topics in investment management in recent years. Google searches for the term "ESG investing" have grown exponentially in the last few years, so it's certainly caught people's attention! As a result, executive management has a range of new stewardship topics to contend with, now that global warming issues have created "E"nvironmental concerns, and the COVID-19 pandemic has further highlighted "S"ocial issues. (Corporate "G"overnance issues have always been closely monitored by the investment community.)

But what's all the fuss about? Is ESG investing a passing fad or a long-term trend that will dominate investment management for the foreseeable future? This chapter looks at the fundamentals behind ESG investing, highlights some of the key drivers behind it, and identifies some of the goals and standards that have been established.

Surveying the Current ESG Landscape

Broadly defined as the analysis of a company's environmental, social, and governance practices, ESG first grabbed the financial world's attention following a 2005 United Nations Global Compact report, which claimed that incorporating ESG factors into capital markets would make it possible to "do well by doing good." Since then, the significance of ESG issues has experienced a meteoric rise. The Principles for Responsible Investment (PRI) network of investors, which was introduced in 2006, has grown from 63 asset manager and owner signatories with US$6.5 trillion in assets under management to more than 3,000 signatories with over US$103 trillion in assets under management. Driven by increased stakeholder attention to corporate environmental impacts and investors realizing that strong ESG performance can safeguard a company's success, ESG is no longer a niche investment concept.

REMEMBER

As the world is changing, there is a greater requirement to understand what risks or opportunities a company faces from ESG issues that may determine its long-term prospects. The COVID-19 pandemic has highlighted the need to consider these factors even further, hence the recent surge in investments in this space. Even within this century, the context in which businesses operate has changed radically. Businesses have generally profited from economic growth, globalization, increased consumption, and fossil fuels, and have strengthened and developed their role as the major providers of goods, jobs, and infrastructure worldwide. Consequently, their contribution to essential sustainability issues, such as climate change, biodiversity, social diversity, and inclusion, has also grown. In addition, the rise of technology has allowed stakeholders, as well as shareholders, to challenge businesses on how they behave.

Consequently, transparent measurement and disclosure of sustainability performance is now deemed to be an essential part of effective business practices and a necessity for maintaining trust in business as a force for good. Corporate reporting is a means by which stakeholders, including investors, can identify and measure companies' performance, just as companies themselves use reporting internally to inform decision-making. Financial reporting has developed as a result of internationally recognized accounting standards that bring transparency, accountability, and competence to financial markets around the world. Therefore, while sustainability disclosure is inevitably more complex than financial reporting, internationally recognized sustainability standards will be the basis for calculating relevant ESG ratings.

Exploring What ESG Is (and Isn't)

In recent years, the term "ESG" has generally become synonymous with socially responsible investment. However, ESG should be seen as more of a risk management framework for evaluating companies and not as a stand-alone investment strategy. ESG measures the sustainability and societal impact of an investment in a company. These criteria help better determine the future financial performance of companies. Likewise, impact investing is more about the type of investments a manager is targeting, while ESG factors are part of an assessment process to apply nonfinancial factors to a manager's analysis in identifying material risks and growth opportunities. Also, impact investing seeks to make a measurable, positive, environmental, or social effect with the investments that a fund manager purchases, whereas ESG is a "means to an end," serving to identify nonfinancial risks that may have a material impact on an asset's value.

Moreover, ESG is often incorrectly commingled with terms such as *corporate sustainability* and *corporate social responsibility* (CSR). While some overlap exists, these terms aren't interchangeable:

>> **Corporate sustainability** is an umbrella term used to describe the long-term creation of stakeholder value by encompassing opportunities and managing risks resulting from economic, environmental, and social developments. To many companies, corporate sustainability is about "doing good" and doesn't require any set conditions.

>> **Corporate social responsibility** is an embedded management concept where companies incorporate the concerns of key stakeholders into their operations and activities. In comparison, ESG assesses a company's ESG practices, together with more traditional financial measures.

Finally, ESG is also commonly intermingled with ethical investing. However, taking an ESG approach is effectively a precursor to the point of investing. It provides a framework that allows you to consider "E" "S," and "G" issues facing a company and to score them either individually or collectively to identify where they sit relative to each other. This leads investors to consider stocks that may be "best-in-class" from an ESG score perspective or exclude them entirely because, for example, their environmental score doesn't reflect their values. Ethical investing involves selecting investments based on ethical or moral principles. Such investors typically avoid "sin stocks," such as those related to gambling, alcohol, or firearms, which can be implemented via an ESG exclusions strategy (where sin stocks are explicitly excluded from a portfolio).

TIP

You may be used to gauging financial ratios when investing in stocks, from the relative price-to-earnings (P/E) ratio to EBITDA margins. (Yes, earnings before interest, taxes, depreciation, and amortization — good thing there's an acronym to use.) All of those ratios are still relevant, but now you can view the same stocks through an additional lens. The sustainability evaluation of ratings firms is normally blended into a single ESG score, similar to the stock recommendations offered by investment banks and brokers. Just as mainstream research analysts calculate different recommendation valuations for the same companies, using largely the same information, so ESG analysts also differ on their recommended scores.

The following sections look at the different components of ESG, including financially material indicators, how those indicators can differ according to industry sector, and how various ESG strategies can be applied across these factors. These elements can be analyzed in the *ESG Cube,* which represents the intersections between these factors.

Defining the breadth of ESG

Unlike common financial ratios, there aren't a common set of ratios that neatly define what a good "E," "S," or "G" score looks like. And whether you should aggregate the three siblings together or you should consider each one individually depends on your determination of what issues you believe are most relevant from an ESG perspective. Indeed, some of the factors may be more material to some stocks than others. For example, the environmental risks associated with a bank will be less material than those facing a mining company, while such risks may be counterbalanced by more concerns over governance with a bank. Also, to what degree should you be concerned, and what data or methodology will you use to gauge that concern? As you can see, ESG analysis brings an entirely new set of indicators that you need to consider, which can result in a complex analysis that isn't reasonable for a layperson to calculate.

Of course, investment managers are offering to take all of that hassle away from you and present you with products that incorporate the myriad of factors in different ways. And as the investment world has moved toward passive investment, a number of these products will be index driven. To ensure that you're familiar with these new products and that they closely track the performance of established benchmarks, many of the new products will be ESG variations of traditional indexes, such as the S&P 500 or FTSE 100 indexes. So, they represent what you "know and love" with just a few exclusions here, some different weightings there, or a bias or tilt toward or away from given stocks. This should be easy for most investors to comprehend.

Then there is the version for sophisticated investors, including large asset owners such as pension funds and family offices, where that approach won't pass the "smell test" given the level of fees they are paying for investment management. They expect a much more active management approach, with full consideration of the complex interdependencies that can be analyzed in this process. One way to visualize the approach that an asset manager could take is to consider a matrix, or a three-dimensional cube. An asset owner considers at least three dimensions to be important:

>> What are the key industry sectors that exhibit the greatest ESG risks or opportunities?

>> Which ESG execution strategy approach should you employ to benefit from this data?

>> What are the material ESG components that affect a company's financial performance?

Welcome to the concept of the *ESG Cube*, which represents the intersections between these factors. Figure 5-1 illustrates the cube, using three axes: Industry Sectors on the X-axis, ESG Strategies on the Y-axis, and Material Indicators on the Z-axis.

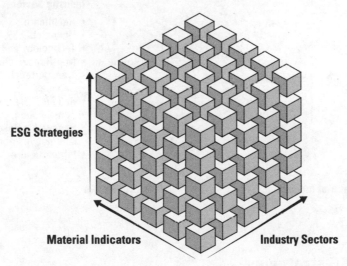

FIGURE 5-1:
ESG Cube with intersections between factors.

Each of these dimensions can be further categorized, as you find out in the following sections.

Industry sectors

Figure 5-2 expands on the concept by adding the industry sectors utilized in the Sustainability Accounting Standards Board (SASB) Materiality Map:

>> Healthcare

>> Financials

>> Technology and communications

>> Non-renewable resources

>> Transportation

>> Services

>> Resource transformation

>> Consumption

>> Renewable resources and alternative energy

>> Infrastructure

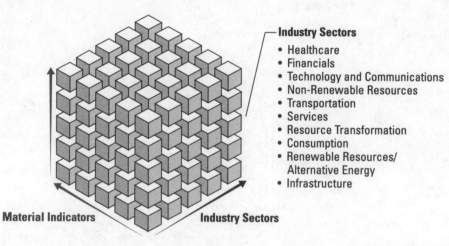

FIGURE 5-2:
Industry sectors per the SASB's Materiality Map.

© John Wiley & Sons, Inc.

ESG strategies

The most common ESG integration strategies that asset managers tend to employ on behalf of their clients are outlined in Figure 5-3:

>> **Screening:** Excluding or including stocks based on exposure to certain factors

>> **Best-in-class:** Selecting stocks based on high ESG scores

>> **Stock rating:** Using an ESG performance rating system

>> **Value integration:** Integrating ESG issues into stock valuations

>> **Thematic:** Focusing portfolios on certain themes

>> **Engagement:** Maintaining an ongoing dialogue on ESG issues

>> **Alignment:** Affiliating with social or environmental goals

>> **Activism:** Using voting capacity to engage companies

>> **Systematic:** Employing quantitative or data-driven factors

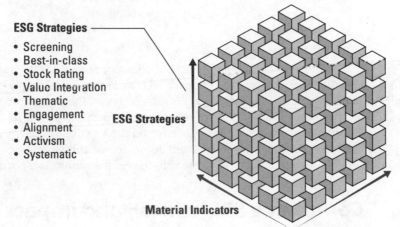

ESG Strategies
- Screening
- Best-in-class
- Stock Rating
- Value Integration
- Thematic
- Engagement
- Alignment
- Activism
- Systematic

ESG Strategies

Material Indicators

© John Wiley & Sons, Inc.

FIGURE 5-3:
Popular ESG
investment
strategies.

Material indicators

Figure 5-4 shows the details of the cube's third dimension, where the SASB has identified, per industry sector, the likely financially material ESG issues. These are just indicators, and investors can choose their own material issues that are relevant to their values. They are as follows:

>> **Environment:** Greenhouse gas emissions and biodiversity impacts

>> **Social capital:** Human rights/community relations and data security and privacy

>> **Human capital:** Diversity/inclusion and fair labor practices

>> **Business model and innovation:** Life cycle impacts of products and product packaging

>> **Leadership and governance:** Supply chain management and accident/safety management

Material Indicators

- GHG Emissions
- Biodiversity Impacts
- Human Rights/
  Community Relations
- Data Security/Privacy
- Diversity/Inclusion
- Fair Labor Practices
- Life cycle Impacts of Products
- Product Packaging
- Supply Chain Management
- Accident/Safety Management

ESG Strategies

Material Indicators

© John Wiley & Sons, Inc.

FIGURE 5-4:
Material
indicators per
the SASB's
Materiality Map.

REMEMBER

ESG strategies, applicable by type of client or sustainability preference, can be visualized relative to given industry sectors. For example, you might have a client seeking an alignment strategy (ESG Strategies on the Y-axis), focused on a social or environmental goals solution (Material Indicators on the Z-axis) within the transportation sector (Industry Sectors on the X-axis). If specific companies from the transportation sector are overlaid on top of this approach, a Best-in-Class filter could also be applied to identify the right addition to a portfolio.

Comparing SRI, ethical, and impact investing to ESG

Having identified that strictly speaking, ESG isn't actually an investing style, but a consideration of relevant ESG issues to manage risk, it's worth considering how ESG ratings can be used in various sectors of the social investment arena. This starts with social investing as an umbrella term that assumes the provision of finance to achieve a combination of economic, social, and environmental goals. Some of the more specialized approaches are described here, with each one increasingly representing a more tangible approach to investment:

>> *Sustainable and Responsible Investing* (SRI) uses relevant ESG criteria to choose companies for investment, typically based on a negative screening approach to exclude companies that produce or sell harmful substances, like tobacco, and those that engage in harmful activities, such as polluting or violating human rights. SRI doesn't necessarily include positive screening to include companies that engage in beneficial activities, such as using sustainable practices or producing clean technologies. There are attempts to establish standards and indexes in areas like climate change and human rights to further facilitate such investments.

>> In *ethical investing*, investments are selected or excluded according to the individual investors' personal beliefs and values. Similar to SRI, ethical investing may exclude investments in certain industries (such as firearms) and is connected with the movement to divest from fossil fuel companies. The key difference with SRI is that ethical investing tends to be more issue-based and produces a more personalized result, whereas SRI normally uses one all-encompassing set of parameters to select investments.

>> *Impact investing* goes a step further by intentionally looking to produce both financial return and positive social or environmental impacts that are actively measured, so it's much harder to apply ESG factors. Impact investors attempt to generate specific, positive impacts using financial instruments, and then require the companies to report evidence that the impacts have really been produced. It's distinct from SRI in that it seeks positive impacts associated with areas such as renewable energy, sustainable agriculture, water management, and clean technology. Many of the independent companies or funds in such areas may not have specific ESG ratings. Moreover, measuring the actual social and environmental impact is difficult, and a standardized measurement system (the Impact Reporting and Investment Standards, or IRIS) has been developed to facilitate measurement and produce comparable impact performance data, rather than using ESG criteria. IRIS (iris.thegiin.org/about/) is a free, publicly available resource that is managed by the Global Impact Investing Network (GIIN) for measuring, managing, and optimizing impact.

REMEMBER

Socially responsible investments can be used to represent the political and social environment of the day. Therefore, it's important for investors to recognize that if a given social value falls out of favor, their investment may also suffer. Considering such investments through an ESG lens may guard against some of these issues. Similarly, investors should carefully read any fund prospectuses to ensure that the philosophies being employed are in line with their values.

REMEMBER

COVID-19 has helped illustrate the growing importance of social issues, many of which have been further exacerbated by the COVID-19 pandemic, while others that weren't already a priority have appeared on the radar. Some of these include occupational health and safety, responsible purchasing practices, supply chain issues, and digital rights, including privacy. Looking beyond the pandemic, further social issues that have been highlighted include human rights, mental health, and access to healthcare.

Determining whether ESG delivers good investment performance

ESG integration is consistent with a manager's fiduciary duty to take into account all relevant information and material risks. It should be remembered that ESG integration isn't just a negative screen in the investment process that limits one's investment universe. Therefore, because it includes a more thorough application of traditional financial analysis, it isn't constrained by reduced diversification and can include companies with poor ESG ratings if they are believed to be "mending their ways."

Along these lines, nearly all large institutional investors are using ESG data in some capacity. More specifically, the PRI members have pledged to incorporate ESG issues into investment decision-making processes. For example, BlackRock, the world's largest asset manager, has announced that sustainability, including a company's ESG performance, will be BlackRock's new standard for investing. In addition, one of the key reasons that firms undertake ESG analysis is to assess risk. However, such ESG analysis is also a way of uncovering investing opportunities by spotting companies that are improving their "E," "S," or "G" profiles before the broader market does.

REMEMBER

So, although the ESG trend was well underway before the COVID-19 crisis in 2020, it has served as the first main confirmation that ESG-informed investing doesn't come at a cost to performance and can be a guide to future-proof investments while boosting returns. This has proven the resilience of ESG investing and provided a significant boost to sustainability while the world is establishing how to "build back better." Nevertheless, some investors rightly highlight the concept of "ESG momentum," produced by the sheer weight of money that has flown into "good" companies that are expected to become the champions of the future. Performance data can be inconsistent and period-dependent, but there is also evidence that over the long term, ESG has outperformed relative to the broader market.

WARNING

On the other hand, some investors question whether ESG stocks exhibit true alpha and contend that the stock market returns from technology stocks in recent times have fueled ESG performance, given that the typical ESG mutual fund has at least 20 percent of its assets in technology stocks. If the technology bubble bursts (perhaps due to anti-trust enforcement), and as investors move toward value stocks (which should be ESG-friendly as well!) and away from growth stocks, where will the alpha or additional performance for ESG strategies come from? Just be aware of the potential for a speculative bubble in ESG investing.

Understanding ESG's Impact on the Environment, Society, and Governance

Having left 2020 behind us, with most of us feeling bruised and battered, the poster child continues to be climate change in the environmental corner, but COVID-19 will stay front and center in the social corner for longer than some people think.

Meanwhile, supply chain management is holding its own in the middle of the ring for governance (or rather, stewardship). The requirement to make sense of ESG has never been greater; the following sections can help.

Meeting environmental and global warming targets

Many challenges face the environment, but the clear focus is on climate change and the move toward net-zero emissions by 2050. This means that all man-made greenhouse gas (GHG) emissions must decline dramatically (need for decarbonization), and what we can't stop emitting needs to be removed from the atmosphere through reduction measures. Thus, reducing the Earth's net climate balance to zero and stabilizing global temperatures is a key goal. While there is an increasing focus on issues such as biodiversity and water management, from an investment point of view, the performance of the energy sector has been relatively poor in recent years, and the COVID-19 pandemic has exacerbated that trend due to lower gross domestic product–related demand and investors continuing to exclude fossil fuel stocks from their portfolios.

While there was an expectation that the pandemic might divert focus away from climate change targets, it seems to have accelerated structural changes in the energy sector, which will present opportunities for policy reform and renewable energy. Meanwhile, new players will participate in the transition to the low-carbon economy because there is now a greater awareness of the risks and opportunities linked to proactively addressing climate issues. Starting in January 2021, with a supportive Democratic government in place in the United States continuing to back a major green deal in Europe to help fund the energy transition and the COP26 (United Nations Climate Change Conference) having taken place in Britain in 2021, the fight against global warming seems to be heating up!

Therefore, on one hand, you have the largest asset manager in the world, BlackRock's CEO Larry Fink, releasing a statement to other CEOs emphasizing that climate risk is investment risk, and there is a need for consistent and comparable data. On the other hand, there is expectation for a surge in clean energy policies and investment, putting the energy system on track to achieve the sustainable energy objectives in full, including those established in the Paris Agreement. However, the global energy companies' transition to renewable energy will require a major investment of time and money, so monitoring their ESG credentials in the interim period is necessary.

Providing solutions to social challenges

The global COVID-19 pandemic has shone a spotlight on the social aspects of ESG, with social issues rising from third place to first in the list of investors' ESG priorities in 2020. While the pandemic has obliged some companies to temporarily deprioritize ESG efforts, investors still believe a strong ESG strategy has a positive impact on share price and flexibility. The additional impact of social movements, such as Black Lives Matter and Me Too, has compelled executive boards to incorporate social risks front and center within new standards for corporate governance structures. Human rights; community relations; customer welfare; and employee health, safety, and well-being have all been moved up the prioritization line.

Furthermore, in addition to boardroom diversity, the attention of companies and investors will move toward diversity across companies, from executive management to the overall workforce. Policies on equal pay, equal opportunity, and corporate culture will also come under closer inspection as the idea of corporate social responsibility morphs into the new concept of corporate purpose, with greater emphasis on all stakeholders as well as shareholders.

WARNING

However, while disclosures on ESG factors are becoming more standardized and widespread in general, social aspects are still seen as the most difficult element to analyze and integrate from an ESG perspective.

Meeting corporate governance requirements

While corporate governance practices have always been a key valuation factor for companies, for fixed income as much as equities, governance has also received a lot of attention during the COVID-19 pandemic — not only for how corporate boards are ensuring the health and safety of their employees and business partners, but also their wider reach into their supply chain management and how they are coping. At a time when their employees may be on government-supported job retention schemes, attention is also being paid to how management is playing its part in executive compensation plans.

The old days of shareholder resolutions serving as an appliance to identify and inspect governance issues — leading to reform in company practices and the acceptance of standards (for example, annual director elections, board gender diversity, and so on) — have changed to a more proactive stance, where asset managers are more engaged and lead policy initiatives and change within some organizations. This greater engagement has led to joint approaches on corporate access, from analysts on the ESG team to traditional financial analysts. Proposals for enhanced ESG disclosures from companies in their sustainability reports will also allow asset managers and owners to further incorporate ESG risk assessments into their investment decisions.

Investors are also pushing for executive pay to be tied to ESG initiatives so that boards will be compelled to achieve social and other key targets, rather than paying "lip service" to ESG integration. Already, it's clear that governance is much more about stewardship, assuming a given level of accountability as well as responsibility to generate sustainable benefits, rather than hiding behind the preordained rules that have been handed down through the organization. Some would argue that ESG could be transformed into ESS (Environment, Social, and Stewardship) to recognize the role of stewardship in this process. Regardless, there should be a seamless link between stewardship and wider ESG integration, with investors systematically assessing companies based on ESG risks.

Using International Standards to Determine ESG Objectives

The global regulatory ecosystem is moving fast, with many countries upholding ESG requirements in regulations. A recent study suggests that in the last decade, governments have enacted over 500 new measures globally to advocate ESG issues. Numerous market participants feel that regulatory developments are a key driver in the uptake of ESG investing. While many voluntary disclosure bodies have contributed to an increase in the availability of ESG data by pushing for greater disclosure and creating frameworks and standards, and therefore the success of the ESG explosion in recent years, the sense is that we're at the point where we need further mandatory disclosure requirements.

However, a group of five sustainability standard-setters has declared their own intent to collaborate better, appearing to accept the complaints of "reporting overload" with the "competing initiatives" concerns. It was felt that the plethora of entities was holding up progress and encouraging jurisdictional fragmentation. However, this statement of intent comes at a time when the European Union (EU) has set in motion a large-scale legislative program to make ESG concerns a central piece of regulation in the financial services industry, which will further increase disclosure requirements. Ultimately, the market should put a common, standardized disclosure mechanism in place, whereby material reporting will be unearthed that provides more informed input to the ESG rating models, which should lead to greater consistency on ESG scores.

WARNING

Although companies report a lot more sustainability information than in the past, much of the disclosure is aimed at a broader set of stakeholders, which limits its usefulness to investors. They are more interested in a subset of sustainability issues representing key business drivers for value creation, such as the industry-specific factors identified by the Sustainability Accounting Standards

Board (SASB). Corporate sustainability reporting has generally lacked an investor focus, encouraging companies to primarily report information on broader ESG factors, which affects the ratings that data providers have been able to produce. The majority of ESG risks that investors want to see are more industry-specific factors.

The following sections emphasize the increasing shift to regulatory oversight on sustainability as well as the roles played and foresight shown by the United Nations and the disclosure reporting standard-setters in building the agenda that has contributed to the success of ESG.

Leading the charge: European legislation on ESG

In Europe, the EU Commission has introduced new disclosure requirements related to sustainable investments. The Sustainable Finance Disclosure Regulation (SFDR) requires all financial market participants in the EU to disclose on ESG issues, with additional requirements for products that promote ESG characteristics or that have sustainable investment objectives. This regulation aims to limit the risk of greenwashing by financial market participants while increasing transparency, which allows investors to better understand how ESG and sustainability influence their investments.

Parallel to this, the EU Commission has also introduced the Taxonomy Regulation, which establishes an EU-wide taxonomy (akin to a dictionary) of economic activities that can be viewed as environmentally sustainable, using reference to six environmental objectives. This will enable investors and clients to identify environmentally sustainable investments, while bringing greater clarity for asset managers.

The regulation was implemented around three pillars: the elimination of greenwashing, regulatory neutrality, and a level playing field for all investors. Added to this, the EU Commission has agreed to introduce new standards on climate change through the launch of two climate benchmarks: the EU Climate Transition benchmark and the EU Paris-aligned benchmark. The regulatory environment is clearly driving institutional investors toward a substantial change in ESG practices, but that may help them get ahead of regulation or mandatory reporting in other jurisdictions.

Ahead of its time: The United Nations

Going back to much earlier days, one has to applaud the foresight of the United Nations (UN) and their influence on the development of sustainable investing in this century. In all, the United Nations have provided a significant contribution to supporting investors' drive to sustainable impact:

» Starting early in the century, the UN formed the Global Compact, a non-binding pact to encourage businesses worldwide to adopt sustainable and socially responsible policies and report on their implementation. See www.unglobalcompact.org/.

» The Principles for Responsible Investment (PRI) initiative then corralled together a network of international investors to work to put the six principles into practice. The principles were developed by the investment community and signaled the view that ESG issues affect the performance of investment portfolios and therefore should be given suitable consideration by investors in order to fulfill their fiduciary duty. This allows investors to incorporate ESG issues into their decision-making and ownership practices and so better align their objectives with those of society at large. See www.unpri.org/.

» The Sustainable Development Goals (SDGs) came next, in 2015. The SDGs have enabled institutional investors to transition from a "cause no harm" investment approach to one that focuses on driving long-term value through investments that support long-term development impact. Some investors feel that the ESG framework offers less direction for investors than the SDGs, given the standardization and language for areas of impact, which offer more opportunity for investors to track and compare progress. See sdgs.un.org/goals.

Staying focused: The Sustainability Accounting Standards Board

The main standard-setter that has focused on helping businesses identify, manage, and report on the sustainability topics that are financially material to their investors is the Sustainability Accounting Standards Board (SASB). Their reporting standards also differ by industry, which enables investors and companies to compare company performance within an industry. Moreover, they are discussing with the International Financial Reporting Standards (IFRS) Foundation and merging with the International Integrated Reporting Council (IIRC) to form the Value Reporting Foundation (VRF) to focus on the global alignment of a corporate reporting system.

Given the IFRS Foundation's credibility related to financial reporting, that can only add weight to establishing further validity around sustainability disclosure standards for capital markets. The IFRS, in conjunction with the SASB, the CDP, the Climate Disclosure Standards Board (CDSB), the Global Reporting Initiative (GRI; see the next section), and the IIRC, should be able to provide a disclosure standard/framework that enables companies to disclose information that is useful to investors and other stakeholders. In turn this will further enhance the core data that the rating agencies need to develop their ESG scores.

TIP

Visit www.sasb.org/ for more information.

Building a framework: The Global Reporting Initiative

The Global Reporting Initiative (GRI) is one of the predominant independent standards organizations helping businesses and other organizations communicate their impacts on issues such as climate change, human rights, and corruption. As one of the first entities involved, they provide a framework that addresses broad social, environmental, and economic performance on how an organization is reporting to stakeholders, providing a guide to their approach to "proving" impact.

A key element for investors is their set of tools for integrating SDGs into sustainability reporting. Moreover, they are a key player in the collaboration between five sustainability, ESG, reporting framework, and standard-setting organizations that are attempting to create a more comprehensive corporate reporting platform. Given the IFRS Foundation's proposal to also work with these entities, this could level the playing field to help investors and businesses deliver long-term value that benefits not only capital market participants but also the world in general. Again, this should provide more clarity to the information that ESG rating agencies require to provide material scores.

TIP

Check out www.globalreporting.org/ for more information.

Index

Numbers

8-K form, 342
10-K form, 342
10-K wraps, 439
10-Q form, 342
30-day SEC yield, 189–190
60 Minutes (TV show), 210–211
401(k) plan, 58–59

A

absorption, 506–507
accountants, 399
accounting
  accrual, 410
  essential principles, 101–102
  scandals, 429
Accounting for Dummies (Tracy and Tracy), 440
accounting value, 143–144
accounts receivable, 151
accrual accounting, 410
accrual interest, 199
ACH (automated clearing house), 365
Acorns, 361
activation price, 379
active investors, 318, 322–324
activism
  cannabis investing, 556
  ESG investing, 591
adaptive scaling, 579
advisor funds, 269
advisors
  credentials, 16
  fee-based, 16
  finding, 16
  millionaires' use of, 11

after-tax returns, 29
agency bonds
  about, 205
  default risk, 207
  government's actual commitment, 206
  issuers, 205
  taxes, 207
  yield, 207
Airbnb, 474
Alcoa, 434
alignment, ESG investing, 591
Ally Invest, 352
altcoins, 565. *See also* cryptocurrencies
American Association of Individual Investors, 345–346
American Express, 423
American Stock Exchange, 100
analysts, 124–125
ancillary businesses, 532–533, 534–535. *See also* cannabis investing
angel investors, 537
annual reports, 438–439
annuities, 60
antispy software, 344
antivirus software, 344
apartments, 482–483
Apple, 423
Apple Pay, 568
Apples Podcasts, 340
appreciation, 28–29
apprenticeships, 55
Argentina, 172
Arithmetic of Active Management, 322
Artisan Wealth Management, 208
ask price, 428
asset allocation, 467–468

K

KB Home, 426–427

Krantz, Matt, 343

Kroc, Ray, 535

L

laddering, 221–224

Lambert, David, 208–209, 220

laptop, mobile trading with, 363

large cap, 156

large purchases, saving for, 53

last-mile boot camps, 55

LastPass, 345

leadership, 591

leading economic indicators (LEI), 107

lease options, 494

Legg Mason Capital Management Value Trust fund, 323

lenders, use of fundamental analysis, 400

lending investments, 12

  long-term risks, 12

leverage

  defined, 10–11

  negative, 464

  positive, 464

  real estate, 464

liabilities

  on balance sheet, 148, 392

  mutual funds, 245

liability claims, 429–430

liability insurance, 83

life insurance, 84, 466

limit orders, 285, 379, 542

limited liability company (LLC), 460

Lindbergh, Charles, 169

liquidation, 442

liquidity

  corporate bonds, 201

  defined, 457

  real estate investments, 457

liquidity ratios, 411

Litecoin, 565, 570

litigation, 429–430

living expenses, 52–53, 72–73

LLC (limited liability company), 460

load funds, 253–255

loads (sales charge)

  hidden, 255–256

  mutual funds, 252–257

  myths about, 253–254

  statistics, 252

local law enforcement, 519

local newspapers, 519

location of real estate investments

  business-friendly environment, 518

  commercial property considerations, 521

  community's reputation, 517–518

  deciding on, 498

  economic development incentives, 517

  evaluating a region, 500–504

  finding properties to add value, 498–500

  government's effect, 516–517

  job growth and income levels, 503

  local market

    barriers to entry, 511–516

    building permits and absorption, 506–507

    occupancy levels, 508–509

    overview, 504–505

    path of progress, 510–511

    rental levels, 509–510

    renting versus buying, 507–508

    supply and demand for real estate, 505–510

  neighborhoods

    crime rates, 518–519

    local law enforcement, 519

    local newspapers, 519

    pride of ownership, 519–520

    schools, 518

    sexual offender databases, 519

  overview, 497

  population growth, 502

  property knowledge sheets, 520–522

  tax considerations, 517

  timing the real estate market, 524–525

long-term bonds, 162

long-term capital gain taxes, 62, 496

long-term disability insurance, 83

operating expenses, 257–260

overview, 251

performance and risks, 260–265

short-term stars becoming also-rans, 260–263

investors, use of fundamental analysis, 400

money market funds, 13–14

online investing, 367

open-end, 139, 226–227, 238–240

overview, 236

scandals, 249

shareholders, 237

taxable distributions, 250

volatility, 249–259

N

Nakamoto, Satoshi, 565

NAPFA (National Association of Personal Financial Advisors), 218

Nasdaq, 100

Nasdaq Composite Index, 331

NASDAQ-100 Trust Series 1, 280

National Association of Personal Financial Advisors (NAPFA), 218

National Credit Union Administration (NCUA), 94

national munis, 212

National Taxpayers Union, 107

Navistar, 24–25

NCUA (National Credit Union Administration), 94

negative absorption, 485, 507

negative interest rates, 45

negative leverage, 464

negative returns, 184

neighborhoods

crime rates, 518–519

local law enforcement, 519

local newspapers, 519

pride of ownership, 519–520

schools, 518

sexual offender databases, 519

Nelson, Willie, 558

NEM blockchain platform, 578, 580

net asset value, 239

net earnings, 102

net equity, 148

net income, 102

net operating income (NOI), 498–499

net price calculator, 81

net profit, 102

net stockholders' equity, 148

net worth, 101, 148

Netflix, 12

Netherlands, 552

new money, investing, 24

New York Stock Exchange, 363

New York Stock Exchange (NYSE), 100

New Zealand, 552

newsletters, 125

Nixon, Richard, 556

No Transaction Fee (NTF) funds, 275–277

nodes, 576

NOI (net operating income), 498–499

no-load funds

myths about, 253–255

No Transaction Fee funds versus, 276

no-money-down properties, 490

nonrecurring items, 153

nonsystemic risk, 304–305

North American Securities Administrators Association, 16, 362

novice investors, 129

NTF (No Transaction Fee) funds, 276

number of shares outstanding, 426

O

Oakmark, 271

Obamacare (Patient Protection and Affordable Care Act), 62

occupancy levels, 508–509

old buildings, tax credits for, 459–460

on close order, 543

on open order, 543

online banking, 91–93

U

UBS, 358
UITs (unit investment trusts), 228–229
unbanked, 566
underperformers, 230–231, 265
undervalued companies, 144, 424, 540
undeveloped land
  buying, 485–486
  care and feeding, 485
  carrying costs, 486
  drawbacks and risks of, 485–486
  improvements needed, 486–487
  lack of depreciation, 486
  mortgages, 486
  opportunity costs, 485
  zoning and environmental issues, 487
unemployment rate, 504
Uniform Application for Investment Adviser
    Registration (Form ADV), 16
unit investment trusts (UITs), 228–229
United Nations (UN), 599
United Parcel Service, 121
Up in Smoke (movie), 557
Upton, Kate, 282
Uruguay, 546, 552
U.S. Virgin Islands, 552
USAA, 272
utility stocks, 130, 136

V

vacancy rates, 509
vacation homes
  downsides to, 474
  purchasing, 473–475
  tax tips, 474–475
valuation, 390
valuation ratios, 411
value
  about, 141
  accounting, 143–144
  accounting for, 145–157
  book, 143–144
  earnings, 144

  intrinsic, 143–144
  market, 142–143
  sales, 144
value integration, ESG investing, 591
value investing, 423–424, 540
value investors, 141, 414, 415–416
Value Reporting Foundation (VRF), 599
value stocks, 118, 415
valued-added properties, 498–500
Van Wagoner Capital Management, 262
Van Wagoner Emerging Growth fund, 262–263
Van Wagoner, Garrett, 262
Vanguard Group, 94, 217, 255, 268–269, 277,
    322, 355, 356
Vanguard's Investor Questionnaire, 320
Venezuela, 566
Verizon, 423
vertically integrated companies, 532. *See also*
    cannabis investing
Vinik, Jeffrey, 292
virtual private network (VPN), 345, 364
viruses, computer, 344
Visa, 426
vocational schools, 55
volatility, 34
  bonds, 192–194
  mutual funds, 249–250
  short-term, 419–420
volume (stock table), 110–112

W

wages, 504
Wall Street Journal, 105, 113, 337
Wall Street Survivor (online trading simulator), 346
wallets, cryptocurrency, 568
Walsh, Gerri, 231
Walt Disney Company, 41
The Warren Buffett Way (Hagstrom), 421–423
websites
  Acorns, 361
  Ally Invest, 352
  American Association of Individual Investors,
    345–346
  Apple, 340

About the Authors

Brendan Bradley is the author of *ESG Investing For Dummies* and the coauthor of *FinTech For Dummies.* He is associated with a number of FinTech firms, acting as non-executive chairman for Fregnan and iPushPull while being on the advisory board of FinTech Circle, Limeglass, RISE Financial Technologies, and Waymark Tech. He is also a co-founder of Seismic Foundry, a seed-stage venture capital group. With all of these firms, he is focused on developing new ideas around changing market structure, regulation, and technology as an investor, entrepreneur, and consultant. He has worked in the financial services industry for more than 30 years, leading the product/business development for most of the current high volume/revenue contracts traded on Eurex and the London International Financial Futures and Options (LIFFE) (now operating under the Intercontinental Exchange, or ICE), and playing a major role in the development of the European futures and options industry.

Kiana Danial is the author of *Cryptocurrency Investing For Dummies* and an award-winning, internationally recognized personal investing and wealth management expert. She's a highly sought-after professional speaker, author, and executive coach who delivers workshops and seminars to corporations, universities, and investment groups. She frequently appears as an expert on many TV and radio stations and has reported on the financial markets directly from the floor of the New York Stock Exchange and Nasdaq. Kiana has been featured in the *Wall Street Journal, TIME* magazine, *Forbes, TheStreet.com,* and many other publications as well as on CNN. She has won numerous awards, including Best Financial Education Provider at Shanghai Forex Expo in 2014, New York Business Women of Influence Honoree in 2016, and the Personal Investment Expert of the Year award from Wealth & Finance International in 2018.

Steve Gormley is a renowned expert in the legal marijuana sector, with nearly 30 years experience developing, branding, marketing, launching, managing, and operating businesses in the U.S. and international markets. Steve currently serves as CEO and director for Radiko Holdings (CES: RDKO), a publicly traded Canadian cannabis and CBD company, domiciled in Calgary with operations in California and Nevada. Steve also serves as COO of Silverback Investments, Inc., a management services company providing business solutions to licensed, lawfully operating medical marijuana cultivation and distribution businesses. Silverback is focused on the Michigan market. He has worked in cannabis retail, cultivation, manufacturing, distribution, lobbying, and finance. He is the author of *Investing in Cannabis For Dummies.*

Robert S. Griswold, MBA, MSBA, is a successful real estate investor and active, hands-on property manager with a large portfolio of residential and commercial rental properties who uses print and broadcast journalism to bring his many years of experience to his readers, listeners, and viewers. He is the author of *Property Management For Dummies* and *Property Management Kit For Dummies,* and coauthor of *Real Estate Investing For Dummies* and *Landlord's Legal Kit For Dummies.* He has been the real estate expert for NBC San Diego, with a regular on-air live-caller segment since 1995. Robert has been recognized twice as the No. 1 real estate broadcast journalist in the nation by the National Association of Real Estate Editors. He's the president of Griswold Real Estate Management, Inc., managing residential, commercial, retail, and industrial properties throughout Southern California and Nevada.

Matt Krantz is a nationally known financial journalist who specializes in investing topics. He has been a writer for *USA TODAY* since 1999, where he covers financial markets and Wall Street, concentrating on developments affecting individual investors and their portfolios. His stories routinely signal trends that investors can profit from and sound warnings about potential scams and issues investors should be aware of. Krantz has written or co-written *Online Investing For Dummies, Fundamental Analysis For Dummies, Investment Banking For Dummies,* and *Mint.com For Dummies.* Matt also writes a daily online investing column called "Ask Matt," which appears every trading day at USATODAY.com and in *USA TODAY.* He answers questions posed by the website's audience in an easy-to-understand manner.

Paul Mladjenovic is a certified financial planner (CFP), national seminar leader, author, and consultant. Since 1981, he has specialized in investing, financial planning, and home business issues. During those 30-plus years, he helped thousands of students and readers build wealth through his nationwide seminars, workshops, conferences, and coaching program. Paul has written *Stock Investing For Dummies, High-Level Investing For Dummies, Micro-Entrepreneurship For Dummies, Zero-Cost Marketing, Precious Metals Investing For Dummies,* and *The Job Hunter's Encyclopedia.* His national (and online) seminars include "The $50 Wealth-Builder," "Ultra-Investing with Options," and the "Home Business Goldmine," among others. The full details on his (downloadable) financial and business startup audio seminars can be found at www.RavingCapitalist.com.

Eric Tyson is an internationally acclaimed and best-selling personal finance author, lecturer, and advisor. Through his work, he is dedicated to teaching people to manage their money better and to successfully direct their own investments. He has been involved in the investing markets for more than three decades. In addition to investing in securities, Eric has also successfully invested in real estate and started and managed his own business. He has counseled thousands of clients on a variety of investment quandaries and questions. An accomplished personal finance writer, Eric is the author of numerous best-selling books, including *For Dummies* books on personal finance, mutual funds, taxes (coauthor), and home buying (coauthor). His work has been featured and quoted in hundreds of national and local publications, including *Kiplinger's Personal Finance Magazine, Los Angeles*

Times, Chicago Tribune, and the *Wall Street Journal,* and on NBC's *Today Show,* ABC, CNBC, PBS's *Nightly Business Report,* FOX, CNN, CBS national radio, Bloomberg Business Radio, and National Public Radio. You can visit him on the web at www.erictyson.com.

Russell Wild is a NAPFA-certified financial advisor and principal of Global Portfolios, an investment advisory firm based in Allentown, Pennsylvania. He is one of only a handful of wealth managers in the nation who is both fee-only (takes no commissions) and who welcomes clients of both substantial and modest means. The author or coauthor of two dozen nonfiction books, Wild has written *Investing in Bonds For Dummies, Exchange-Traded Funds For Dummies,* and *Index Investing For Dummies.* No stranger to the mass media, Wild has shared his wit and wisdom on such shows as *Oprah, The View, CBS Morning News,* and *Good Day New York* and in hundreds of radio interviews. A member of the National Association of Personal Financial Advisors (NAPFA) since 2002, Wild is also a longtime member and past president of the American Society of Journalists and Authors (ASJA). His website is www.globalportfolios.net.

Publisher's Acknowledgments

Senior Acquisitions Editor: Tracy Boggier

Compilation Editor: Georgette Beatty

Project Manager: Linda Brandon

Copy Editor: Christine Pingleton

Technical Editor: James Taibleson

Production Editor: Mohammed Zafar Ali

Cover Image: © Explode/Shutterstock